www.wadsworth.com

wadsworth.com is the World Wide Web site for Wadsworth and is your direct source to dozens of online resources.

At *wadsworth.com* you can find out about supplements, demonstration software, and student resources. You can also send e-mail to many of our authors and preview new publications and exciting new technologies.

wadsworth.com
Changing the way the world learns®

FROM THE WADSWORTH SERIES IN SPEECH COMMUNICATION

Intercultural Communication

A Reader

Tenth Edition

Larry A. Samovar
San Diego State University

Richard E. Porter
California State University, Long Beach, Emeritus

THOMSON
™
WADSWORTH

Australia • Canada • Mexico • Singapore • Spain
United Kingdom • United States

THOMSON

★ ™

WADSWORTH

Executive Editor: Deirdre Anderson
Publisher: Holly J. Allen
Assistant Editor: Nicole George
Editorial Assistant: Mele Alusa
Technology Project Manager: Jeanette Wiseman
Marketing Manager: Kimberly Russell
Marketing Assistant: Neena Chandra
Project Manager, Editorial Production: Cathy Linberg

Print/Media Buyer: Judy Inouye
Permissions Editor: Stephanie Keough-Hedges
Production Service and Compositor: Graphic World
Text Designer: Ellen Pettengell
Copyeditor: Graphic World Publishing Services
Cover Designer: Roy Neuhaus
Cover Image: © José Ortega/SIS
Printer: Banta, Harrisonburg

Printed in the United States of America
1 2 3 4 5 6 7 0 05 04 03 02

For more information about our products, contact us at:
Thomson Learning Academic Resource Center
1-800-423-0563
For permission to use material from this text,
contact us by: **Phone:** 1-800-730-2214
Fax: 1-800-730-2215
Web: http://www.thomsonrights.com

Library of Congress Control Number: 2002101498
ISBN 0-534-56495-X

Wadsworth/Thomson Learning
10 Davis Drive
Belmont, CA 94002-3098
USA

Asia
Thomson Learning
60 Albert Street, #15-01
Albert Complex
Singapore 189969

Australia
Nelson Thomson Learning
102 Dodds Street
South Melbourne, Victoria 3205
Australia

Canada
Nelson Thomson Learning
1120 Birchmount Road
Toronto, Ontario M1K 5G4
Canada

Europe/Middle East/Africa
Thomson Learning
Berkshire House
168-173 High Holborn
London WC1V 7AA
United Kingdom

Latin America
Thomson Learning
Seneca, 53
Colonia Polanco
11560 Mexico D.F.
Mexico

Spain
Paraninfo Thomson Learning
Calle/Magallanes, 25
28015 Madrid, Spain

Contents

Preface

We do not believe it is an overstatement to assert that facility as an intercultural communicator may be one of the most important skills you will ever develop. You need only look around your world to see a challenging future in which you will interact with people who represent a wide range of cultural backgrounds. You must prepare yourself to meet this challenge, and this will not be easy because you must be willing to change in order to become an effective intercultural communicator. You must be willing to communicate; have empathy toward foreign and alien cultures; develop a universalistic, realistic approach to the universe; and be tolerant of views that differ from your own. Intercultural communication offers the arena for this interpersonal contact. It is your ability to change, to make adjustments in your communication habits and behaviors that supplies you with the potential to make that contact successful.

Intercultural communicative behavior not only must be void of racism and ethnocentrism, but also must reflect an attitude of mutual respect, trust, and worth. We emphasize that intercultural communication will not be successful if, by actions or words, communicators act in a condescending manner. Every individual and every culture wants to believe it is as worthy as any other. Actions that demonstrate a feeling of one's own superiority will stifle meaningful interaction. To be racist or ethnocentric is to condemn intercultural communication to failure. The reward for adopting the behaviors and attitudes necessary to overcome racism and ethnocentrism is the exhilaration that comes when you have connected successfully with someone far removed from your own sphere of experience.

The occasion of this tenth edition of our book is one of excitement. The fact that we have been received with the popularity to warrant another new edition is exciting and obviously pleasing. Yet, as we proceeded, we wanted to be cautious enough to preserve the basic framework and philosophy that has sustained us through the previous nine editions. It would have been improvident of us to abandon an orientation to intercultural communication that has found wide acceptance for over three decades. The field, as well as the authors, however, have continued to evolve. We knew, therefore, that some reshaping would be necessary.

This new edition grants us the opportunity to combine two complementary positions. First, it reflects our continued belief that the basic core of the field should not be changed for the sake of simply being novel; such change would deprive the book of those concepts that have been infused in all of the previous editions. Second, it reflects our belief that as our intercultural contacts change in number and intensity, there is a need to present essays that mirror that change. We have perceived each new edition as an opportunity to examine that change and to stake out new territory for the field—territory that takes into account the complexities of communicating in the 21st century.

As the field of intercultural communication has grown, we have attempted to grow with it and to fuse the old with the new. In 1972, the first edition contained 34 articles and essays. The ninth edition contained 45, and in this tenth edition we include 44 articles in our collection of readings. In this tenth edition, we have 28 new essays, 15 of them prepared especially for this volume.

APPROACH

The basic energizing motive for this book has remained the same since both of us became interested in the topic of intercultural communication more than 30 years ago. We sincerely believe that the ability to communicate effectively with people from diverse cultures and co-cultures benefits each of us as individuals and has potential to benefit the more than 6 billion people with whom we share this planet. We have intentionally selected materials that will assist you in understanding those intercultural communication principles that are instrumental to your success when you interact with people from diverse cultures.

Fundamental to our approach is the conviction that communication is a social activity; it is something people do to and with one another. The activity might begin in our heads, but it is manifested in our behaviors, be they verbal or nonverbal. In both explicit and implicit ways, the information and the advice contained in this book is usable; the ideas presented can be translated into action.

USE

As in the past, we intend this anthology to be for the general reader, so we have selected materials that are broadly based, comprehensive, and suitable for both undergraduate and graduate students. Although the level of difficulty varies from essay to essay, we have not gone beyond the level found in most textbooks directed toward college and university students.

Intercultural Communication: A Reader is designed to meet three specific needs. The first comes from a canon that maintains that successful intercultural communication is a matter of highest importance if humankind and society are to survive. Events during the last thirty years have created a world that sees us linked together in a multitude of ways. From pollution to economics to health care, what happens to one culture potentially happens to all other cultures. This book, then, is designed to serve as a basic anthology for courses concerned with the issues associated with human interaction. Our intention is to make this book theoretical and practical so that the issues associated with intercultural communication can be first understood and then acted upon.

Second, the book may be used as a supplemental text to existing service and basic communication skill courses and interpersonal communication courses. The rationale is a simple one: Understanding other cultures is indispensable in this age of cross-cultural contact. It matters very little if that contact is face-to-face or on the public platform.

Third, the book provides resource material for courses in communication theory, small group communication, organizational and business communication, and mass communication, as well as for courses in anthropology, sociology, social psychology, social welfare, social policy, business, and international relations. The long list of possible uses only underscores the increased level of intercultural interaction that is characteristic of what is often now called the "global village."

ORGANIZATION

The book is organized into four closely related parts. In Part 1, "Intercultural Communication: An Introduction," our purpose is twofold: We hope to acquaint you with the basic concepts of intercultural communication while at the same time arousing your interest in the topic. Hence, the essays in this part are both theoretical and philosophical. The selections explain what intercultural communication is and why it is important.

Part 2, "Sociocultural Backgrounds: What We Bring to Intercultural Communication," has two chapters that both work toward the same goal: They seek to examine the influence of sociocultural forces on human interaction. Chapter 2 deals with how these forces direct the communication patterns of people from international cultures. To make this point, we have selected cultures from East Asia, India, Africa, Egypt, and Germany. Although many cultures have been omitted from our analysis, you will still be able to gain an appreciation of the link between culture and behavior.

Chapter 3 moves us from the international arena to co-cultures that operate within the United States. Here again space constraints have limited the total number of co-cultures we could include. Yet we believe that through the selection of groups such as Latinos, African Americans, Asian Americans, the disabled, homosexuals, women, and the elderly, you will get an idea of the cultural diversity found in those groups with whom most of you have regular contact. Many of these co-cultures, as well as others, are so important to the study of intercultural communication that we return to them in later chapters.

In Part 3, "Intercultural Interaction: Taking Part in Intercultural Communication," our analysis focuses on the verbal and nonverbal symbols used in intercultural communication, as well as their contexts. In Chapter 4, we offer readings that will introduce you to some of the difficulties you might encounter when your intercultural partner uses a different language system. We will look at how these verbal idiosyncrasies and distinctions influence problem solving, speaking, perception, translation, interpreting, and understanding.

Chapter 5 is also concerned with symbols and explains some of the ways in which cultural diversity in nonverbal messages can influence the entire transaction. Differences in movement, facial expressions, eye contact, silence, space, time, and the like are detailed so that you might have a better appreciation of how culture and communication work in tandem.

Chapter 6 continues with the theme of how culture modifies interaction. This time, however, the interaction is examined in a specific context. The assumption is that culturally diverse rules influence how members of a culture behave in certain settings. To clarify this important issue, we have selected "places" where cultures often follow rules that differ from those found in North America. More specifically, we look at settings related to business, groups, negotiations, counseling, health care, and education.

Part 4, "Intercultural Communication: Seeking Improvement," contains two chapters that are concerned with improving intercultural communication. The readings offered in Chapter 7 are intended to provide you with knowledge about and suggestions for improving intercultural communication. Each essay presents practical recommendations.

The eighth and final chapter probes the ethical and future dimensions of intercultural communication. Essays that deal with moral issues and the future directions and challenges of intercultural communication are at the center of this chapter. The intent of this chapter is to ask you not to conclude your study of intercultural communication with the reading of a single book or the completion of one course. We believe that the study of intercultural communication is a lifetime endeavor. Each time we want to share an idea or feeling with someone from another culture, we face a new and exhilarating learning experience. We urge everyone to seek out as many of these experiences as possible. A philosopher once wrote, "Tomorrow, when I know more, I'll recall that piece of knowledge and use it better."

ASSISTANCE

As in the past, many people have helped us rethink and reshape this project. We express appreciation to our editor Deirdre Anderson, and, of course, to Rebecca Hayden, who had enough courage and insight 30 years ago to decide that intercultural communication should and would become a viable discipline. All of these editors were stern enough to keep us in check while at the same time allowing us the flexibility to move in new directions.

In a culture that values change, this collection would not have survived for more than 30 years if we had not been fortunate enough to have so many scholars willing to contribute original essays to each edition. Here, in the tenth edition, we acknowledge the work of Polly A. Begley, Dawn O. Braithwaite, Charles A. Braithwaite, Julia T. Wood, Valerie C. McKay, Mary Fong, Edwin R. McDaniel, Wenshan Jia, Peter Andersen, Young Yun Kim, David W. Kale, Mary Jane Collier, Aaron C. Cargile, Guo-Ming Chen, Steve Quasha, Stella Ting-Toomey, Sidney Ribeau, Sheryl Lindsley, William J. Starosta, Robert Shuter, John Baldwin, Michael Hecht, Shirley van der Veur, Ronald L. Jackson, II, Celnisha L. Dangerfield, Mei Zhong, Nina M. Reich, Donald G. Ellis, Ifat Moaz Carolyn Roy, James Manseau Sauceda, and Nagesh Rao. We thank all of you for letting us expose your work to thousands of other people who share your commitment to intercultural matters.

For their helpful comments and suggestions on the revision of this edition of the text, a sincere thanks goes to Joel Franks, San Jose State University; Laura Hahn, Humboldt State University; Joseph Hemmers, Carroll College; Nemi Jain, Arizona State University; Charlota Krolokke, Humboldt State University; Jessup Lee, University of Houston; Ronald Long, Central Missouri State University; George Musambira, Western Kentucky University; Deleasa Randall, Ashland University; Bob Schuessler, North Seattle Community College; and Jawed Zouari, Seattle Central College.

Finally, we express our gratitude to the countless users of previous editions who have allowed us to "talk to them" about intercultural communication. Although it may have been a rather intangible connection, we have greatly appreciated it all the same.

Larry A. Samovar
Richard E. Porter

part 1

Intercultural Interaction: An Introduction

Every tale can be told in a different way.

GREEK PROVERB

Intercultural communication is not new. It has existed as long as people from different cultures have been encountering one another. As intercultural contacts have increased both here and abroad, people have accepted that cultural diversity has become a fact of life. Only during the last 30 years, however, have people begun a serious and systematic study of exactly what happens during intercultural contacts. They now want to know how cultural diversity is reflected when people come together, when the communication process involves people from different cultures.

Perhaps the initial impetus for the study of intercultural communication was the recognition that technology has produced the means for humankind's self-destruction. Historically, intercultural communication, more often than not, has employed a rhetoric of force rather than reason. But with agents of change sweeping the world, perhaps people are now seeking interaction through communication rather than traditional force. The reason for this new study is also pragmatic. Our mobility, increased contact among cultures, a global marketplace, and the emergence of multicultural organizations and workforces require the development of communication skills and abilities that are appropriate to a multicultural society and to life in a global village.

Traditionally, intercultural communication took place only among an extremely small portion of the world's populace. Ministers of state and government, certain merchants, missionaries, explorers, and a few tourists were the primary travelers and visitors to foreign lands. Until rather recently, as Americans you had little contact with other cultures, even within your own country. Members of nonwhite races were segregated. Only in recent years have laws changed to foster integrated schools, workforces, and, to some extent, neighborhoods. In addition, those who made up the vast, white, middle Euro-America remained at home, rarely leaving their own county. This situation, of course, has changed markedly; America is now a mobile society among other increasingly mobile societies.

This increased contact with other cultures and domestic co-cultures makes it imperative that you make a concerted effort to understand and get along with people who may be significantly different from you. Your ability, through increased awareness and understanding, to coexist peacefully with people who do not necessarily share your backgrounds, views, beliefs, values, customs, habits, or lifestyles can benefit you in your own neighborhoods and can be a decisive factor in forestalling international conflict.

Before we begin our inquiry, we must specify the nature of intercultural communication and recognize that people who hold various viewpoints see it somewhat differently. From what we have already said, you should suspect that the topic of intercultural communication can be explored in a variety of ways. Scholars who look at it from a mass-media perspective are concerned with such issues as international broadcasting, worldwide freedom of expression, the Western domination of information, and the use of modern electronic technologies for instantaneous worldwide transmission of information. Other groups investigate international communication with an emphasis on communication among nations and governments; this is the communication of diplomacy and propaganda. Still others are interested in the communication inherent in international business, which includes such diverse concerns as negotiations and communication within multicultural organizations.

Our concern is with the more personal aspects of communication: What happens when people from different cultures interact face-to-face? Hence, our approach examines the interpersonal dimensions of intercultural communication as it occurs in various contexts. The articles we have selected for this collection focus on those variables of both culture and communication that come into play during the communication encounter—that time when participants from different cultures are trying to share ideas, information, and feelings.

Inquiry into the nature of intercultural communication has raised many questions, but it has produced few theories and far fewer answers. Most of the inquiry has been associated with fields other than communication, primarily anthropology, international relations, social psychology, and socio- and psycholinguistics. Although the range of research topics has been wide, the knowledge gained has not been coordinated. Much that has emerged has been more a reaction to current sociological, racial, and ethnic concerns than an attempt to define and explain intercultural communication, but it is clear that knowledge of intercultural communication can help solve communication problems before they arise. Schoolteachers who understand cultural differences in motivation and learning styles are better able to deal with their multicultural classrooms. Even something as simple as cultural differences in the use of eye contact might greatly improve the communication process. And perhaps those who realize that some people treat illness as a curse may be better able to deliver necessary health care. In essence, we believe many problems can be avoided by understanding the components of intercultural communication. This book, by applying those components to numerous cultures, seeks to contribute to that understanding.

Go online

to the ***Intercultural Communication: A Reader*** Web site
at the Wadsworth Communication Café,
www.wadsworth.com/communication_d/.

From the home page, select "Course Materials," then "Speech Communication," and then "Intercultural Communication." From the textbook menu, select Intercultural Communication: A Reader to access the book's Web site. Click on "…For Students" and use the drop-down menus at the top of the page to select a chapter and select a study aid resource. A practice quiz and an InfoTrac College Edition activity are included for each chapter.

You can complete the InfoTrac College Edition Activities by using the passcode that comes free with each new copy of this text. InfoTrac College Edition is an easy-to-use database of reliable, full-length articles from hundreds of top academic journals and popular sources. You can expand your learning about the concepts illustrated in each reading by completing the InfoTrac College Edition activities.

chapter 1

Approaches to Understanding Intercultural Communication

This exploration of intercultural communication begins with a series of diverse articles that will (1) introduce the philosophy underlying our concept of intercultural communication; (2) provide a general orientation to, and overview of, intercultural communication; (3) theorize about the analysis of intercultural transactions; (4) provide insight into cultural diversity; and (5) demonstrate the relationships between culture and perception. Our purpose at this point is to give you a sufficient introduction to the many diverse dimensions of intercultural communication so that you will be able to approach the remainder of this volume with an appropriate frame of reference that will make further inquiry interesting, informative, and useful.

We begin with an essay by the two editors of this book titled "Understanding Intercultural Communication: An Introduction and Overview." This piece will introduce you to some of the specific subjects and issues associated with the study of intercultural communication. As a preface to the essay, we begin by reminding you of the importance of intercultural communication both at home and aboard. Next we discuss the purpose of culture, attempt to define it, and offer a review of the characteristics of culture. We then turn our attention to the specific dimensions of culture that are most germane to human communication—aspects of culture that form the field of intercultural communication. By examining these major variables (cultural values, worldview, social organizations, verbal and nonverbal language), you will better understand what happens when people of diverse cultural backgrounds attempt to share feelings and ideas. By knowing at the outset of the book what the study of intercultural communication entails, you should have a greater appreciation for all the essays that follow.

Our second essay, by Harry C. Triandis, introduces you to another way of approaching intercultural communication. Triandis begins by underscoring one of the propositions of this book—that culture and communication are linked. You will see this connection when he speaks of culture including "the knowledge that people need to have in order to function effectively in their social environment." To help you identify what "knowledge" is most useful when interacting with another culture, Triandis examines what he calls *cultural syndromes*. A cultural syndrome "is a shared pattern of beliefs, attitudes, self-definitions, norms, and values organized around a theme." To help understand other cultures Triandis discusses the following syndromes: *complexity, tightness, individualism and collectivism, vertical and horizontal cultures, active-passive cultures, universalism-particularism, diffuse-specific, instrumental-expressive, emotional expression or suppression,* and the *weights given to different attributes in social perception.* Triandis believes that when people come into contact with members of other cultures, miscommunications occur because they are not aware of these syndromes. Hence, we ask you to learn about these syndromes as part of your training in intercultural communication.

The next selection is written by Satoshi Ishii, Donald Klopf, and Peggy Cooke, and employs the concept of *worldview* as a means of looking at culture. As you will see, a culture's worldview represents a collective description of how the cosmos and universe function and how each individual fits into that religious and philosophical scheme. More specifically, worldview helps each person find answers to questions about pain, suffering, death, and the meaning of life. The basic premise the authors express is that worldview shapes a culture's **psyche** and helps the members of that culture make sense of the world. Worldview also, as the author's note, distinguishes one culture from another.

Although worldviews can take a variety of forms (scientific, metaphysical, and religious), most scholars agree with the assertion of Ishii, Klopf, and Cooke: that religion is the most "pervasive determinant of worldview." Even a secular person is touched by the writings, attitudes, beliefs, and ethics advanced by the great religious traditions. To help you appreciate the sway of religion on culture, the authors highlight the major dimensions of Eastern and Western religions. As a means of connecting religion to culture and communication, the authors end their essay with a discussion of some of the problems that might occur when Eastern and Western worldviews collide.

In the last article about identity, Rod Janzen provides you with a viewpoint that suggests how you might conceptualize ethnic relations and ethnic identity in the United States. In "Five Paradigms of Ethnic Relations," he traces the history of ethnic identity in the United States and provides you with a set of five possible ways of conceptualizing ethnicity as society engages in the 21st century. His development of the five paradigms, or categories, of ethnicity is based on the elements of language, religion, culture, race, and political tradition.

Understanding Intercultural Communication: An Introduction and Overview

LARRY A. SAMOVAR
RICHARD E. PORTER

Human beings draw close to one another by their common nature, but habits and customs keep them apart.
CONFUCIUS

THE IMPORTANCE OF INTERCULTURAL COMMUNICATION

The need for intercultural communication, as you might suspect, is as old as humankind. From wandering tribes to traveling traders and religious missionaries, people have encountered others different from themselves. These earlier meetings, like those of today, were often confusing and hostile. The recognition of alien differences, and the human propensity to respond malevolently to them, were expressed more than 2,000 years ago by the Greek playwright Aeschylus, who wrote: "Everyone's quick to blame the alien." This sentiment is still a powerful element in today's social and political rhetoric. For instance, it is not uncommon in today's society to hear people say that most, if not all, of the social and economic problems of the United States are caused by minorities and immigrants.

Although intercultural contact has a long history, today's intercultural encounters are far more numerous and of greater importance than in any previous time in the past. So that you might appreciate the significance of the study of intercultural communication, we will pause for a moment and briefly highlight the widespread nature of cultural interaction.

New technology, in the form of transportation and communication systems, has accelerated intercultural contact. Trips once taking days, weeks, or even months are now measured in hours. Supersonic transports now make it possible for tourists, business executives, or government officials to enjoy breakfast in San Francisco and dinner in Paris—all on the same day.

Innovative communication systems have also encouraged and facilitated cultural interaction. Communication satellites, sophisticated television transmission equipment, and digital switching networks now allow people throughout the world to share information and ideas instantaneously. Whether via the Internet, the World Wide Web, or a CNN news broadcast, electronic devices have increased cultural contact. For example, the world now has 1.2 billion television sets, which allows people, regardless of their location, to perceive the same image and message (Higgins, 1995, p. 6). As noted in *U.S. News & World Report*: "Television's impact on the world community cannot be overstated" (1996, p. 48).

Globalization of the economy has further brought people together. At the conclusion of World War II, the United States emerged as the only military and economic superpower. Most of the rest of the world's economy was in disarray. Because industry in the United States was not damaged during World War II, it was the dominant economic force in the world; however, this preeminence in business is not the case as we enter the 21st century. For example, according to Harris and Moran (1996), there are now "more than 37,000 transnational corporations with 207,000 foreign affiliates" (p. 18). This expansion in globalization has resulted in multinational corporations participating in various international business arrangements such as joint ventures and licensing agreements. These and countless other economic ties mean that it would not be unusual for someone to work for an organization that does business in many countries.

Changes in immigration patterns have also contributed to the development of expanded intercultural contact. Within the boundaries of the United

States, people are now redefining and rethinking the meaning of the word *American*. Neither the word nor the reality can any longer be used to describe a somewhat homogeneous group of people sharing a European heritage. We have now become, as author Ben J. Wattenberg (1989) tells us, "the first universal nation, a truly multi-cultural society marked by unparalleled diversity" (p. 31).

The last few paragraphs have told you that, with or without your desire or consent, you are now thrust into contact with countless people who often appear alien, exotic, and perhaps even wondrous. Whether negotiating a major contract with the Chinese, discussing a joint venture with a German company, being supervised by someone from Mexico, counseling a young student from Cambodia, or working alongside someone who speaks no English, you encounter people with cultural backgrounds that are often strikingly different from your own. Understanding these backgrounds is essential if you are to be successful in both your social and professional lives.

COMMUNICATION AND CULTURE

Concern about cultural diversity has resulted in the marriage of culture and communication and the recognition of intercultural communication as a unique field of study. Inherent in this fusion is the idea that intercultural communication entails the investigation of those elements of culture that most influence interaction when members of two or more cultures come together in an interpersonal setting. To better understand that influence, we first examine the essential elements of culture and then explain how these elements modify the communication process.

UNDERSTANDING CULTURE

People in Paris eat snails, but people in San Diego put poison on them. Why? People in Iran sit on the floor and pray five times each day, but people in Las Vegas stand up all night in front of slot machines. Why? Some people speak Tagalog, whereas others speak English. Why? Some people paint and deco-

rate their entire bodies, but others spend millions of dollars painting and decorating only their faces. Why? Some people talk to God, but others have God talk to them. Why?

The general answer to all these questions is the same. Your culture supplies you with the answers to these and countless other questions about what the world looks like and how you live and communicate within that world. From the instant of birth, a child is formally and informally taught how to behave. This omnipresent and commanding power of culture leads Hall (1977) to conclude that "there is not one aspect of human life that is not touched and altered by culture" (p. 14). In many ways Hall is correct: Culture is everything and everywhere. More important, at least for the purposes of this book, culture and communication work in tandem—they are inseparable. In fact, it is often difficult to decide which is the voice and which is the echo.

Culture helps govern and define the conditions and circumstances under which various messages may or may not be sent, noticed, or interpreted. Your entire repertoire of communicative behaviors depends largely on the culture in which you have been raised. Remember, you are not born knowing how to dress, what toys to play with, what to eat, which gods to worship, or how to spend your money and your time. Culture is both teacher and textbook. From how much eye contact you make to explanations of why you get sick, culture plays a dominant role in your lives. It is the foundation of communication, and when cultures are diverse, communication practices may be different. This important point is clearly illustrated by Smith (1966), who wrote:

> In modern society different people communicate in different ways, as do people in different societies around the world; and the way people communicate is the way they live. It is their culture. Who talks with whom? How? And about what? [T]hese are questions of communication and culture. A Japanese geisha and a New England librarian send and receive different messages on different channels and in different networks. When the elements of communication differ or change, the elements of culture differ or change. Communication and culture are inseparable. (p. 1)

The Basic Function of Culture

The anthropologist Haviland (1993) suggests that "[p]eople maintain cultures to deal with problems or matters that concern them" (p. 29). It is believed that your ancestors created cultures for the same reasons. Both then and now, culture serves the basic need of laying out a predictable world in which an individual is firmly oriented. Culture enables you to understand your surroundings. As the English writer Thomas Fuller wrote 200 years ago, "Culture makes all things easy." Although this view might be slightly overstated, culture does ease the transition from the womb to this new life by giving meaning to events, objects, and people in the environment. In this way culture makes the world a less frightening and mysterious place.

A Definition of Culture

It should be clear to this point that culture is ubiquitous, multidimensional, complex, and pervasive. Because culture is so broad, there is no single definition or central theory of what it is. Definitions range from the all-encompassing ("it is everything") to the narrow ("it is opera, art, and ballet"). For our purposes we define *culture* as the deposit of knowledge, experience, beliefs, values, attitudes, meanings, social hierarchies, religion, notions of time, roles, spatial relationships, concepts of the universe, and material objects and possessions acquired by a group of people in the course of generations through individual and group striving.

Characteristics of Culture

Regardless of the definition employed, most people agree about the major characteristics of culture. Examining these universal characteristics will help you understand this nebulous concept called *culture* and enable you to see how these characteristics influence communication.

Culture Is Not Innate; It Is Learned. We begin with the single most important characteristic of culture and the one that is hardest to explain. It is the most important because it goes to the heart of what is called *culture*.

Without the advantages of learning from those who lived before, you would not have culture. Therefore, you can appreciate why we said that learning was the most important of all the characteristics of culture. Babies cut off from all adult care, training, and supervision would instinctively eat, drink, defecate, urinate, gurgle, and cry. But what they would eat, when they would eat, where they would defecate, and the like would be random. All of you are born with basic needs—needs that create behavior—but how you go about meeting those needs and developing other coping behaviors are a matter of learning. As Bates and Plog (1990) note:

> Whether we feed ourselves by growing yams or hunting wild game or by herding camels and raising wheat, whether we explain a thunderstorm by attributing it to meteorological conditions or to a fight among the gods—such things are determined by what we learn as part of our enculturation. (p. 19)

Enculturation usually takes place through *interaction* (your parents kiss you and you learn about kissing—whom to kiss, when to kiss, and so on), *observation* (you watch your father do most of the driving of the family car and you learn about sex roles—what a man does, what a woman does), and *imitation* (you laugh at the same jokes your parents laugh at and you learn about humor—it is funny if someone slips and falls but doesn't get hurt).

Most of you would have a difficult time pointing to a specific event or experience that taught you about such things as direct eye contact, your use of silence and space, the concept and importance of attractiveness, your view of aging and the elderly, your ability to speak one language over another, your preference for activity over meditation, or why you prefer one mode of dealing with conflict over another. All of our examples show that learning the perceptions, rules, and behaviors of cultural membership usually go on without your being aware of it.

One thing that should be clear is the idea that you learn your culture in a host of ways. As many of our examples have noted, most of what you learn is communicated through your interactions with other people. Early in life you receive normative instructions from family and friends; however, numerous other "teachers" also pass on the messages of culture.

We will pause a moment and look at just a few of these "instructors" and the "instructions" they offer.

A powerful set of instructions comes from **proverbs.** Proverbs are found in nearly every culture. Often called *maxims* or *adages*, these sayings create vivid images that are easy to learn and difficult to forget. They are repeated with such regularity as you grow up that they soon become part of your belief system. We will look at a few proverbs from various cultures and note for you how the specific proverbs are linked to a cultural value or belief.

"One does not make the wind blow but is blown by it." This Asian view implies that people are guided by fate rather than by their own devices.

"Order is half of life." This German view stresses the value of organization, conformity, and structure.

"The mouth maintains silence in order to hear the heart talk." This Belgian saying implies the value of intuition and feelings in interaction.

"He who speaks has no knowledge and he who has knowledge does not speak." This saying from Japan demonstrates the value of silence.

"How blessed is a man who finds wisdom." This Jewish expression states the importance of learning and education.

"A zebra does not despise its stripes." From the Maasai of Africa, this saying expresses the value of accepting things as they are, of accepting oneself as one is, and of avoiding the envy of others.

"Loud thunder brings little rain." This Chinese proverb teaches the importance of being reserved instead of being boisterous.

"A man's tongue is his sword." Arabs are taught to enjoy words and use them in a powerful and forceful manner.

"A single arrow is easily broken, but not in a bunch." This proverb is found in many Asian cultures as a means of stressing the group over the individual.

"He who stirs another's porridge often burns his own." The Swedish are a very private people and attempt to teach this value through this proverb.

"The duck that quacks is the first to get shot." This Japanese proverb stresses the importance of silence.

You also learn your culture from **folk tales** and **folklore.** Whether it be ancient myths of your culture or current popular culture, folklore is value-laden and teaches and reinforces what a culture deems important. The story might be about the tough, independent, fast-shooting cowboy of the Old West or how Pinocchio's nose grew larger when he lied. Whether it be glorifying Columbus because he was daring, Abraham Lincoln learning to read by drawing letters on a shovel by the fireside, or the Saturday morning cartoon characters defending democracy and fighting for what is "right," folklore constantly reinforces your fundamental values.

Yours is not the only culture that "teaches" important values through folk tales. The English have their *Canterbury Tales,* which stress proper manners, courtly behavior, and dignity. The Japanese know the ancient story called *The Tale of the Forty-Seven Ronin,* which teaches them the importance of duty, obligation, and loyalty. And for the Sioux Indians, the legend of "Pushing Up the Sky" teaches what people can accomplish if they work together.

People learn about their culture even from sources as subtle as **art.** The anthropologist Nanda (1994) points out the link between art and culture when she writes: "One of the most important functions of art is to communicate, display, and reinforce important cultural themes and values" (p. 403). In Asian cultures most art depicts objects, animals, and landscapes. It seldom focuses on people. American and European art, however, emphasizes people. These differences reflect the Asian view that nature is more powerful and important than a single individual and the American and European views that people are the center of the world.

As we conclude this section on learning, remember that large numbers of people, usually living in the same geographic area, share the experience and behaviors we have been discussing. This sharing makes a culture unique. Polish poet Stanislaw Lec said it far more eloquently when he reminded you that because of culture, "All of our separate fictions add up to a joint reality."

Culture Is Transmitted from Generation to Generation. The American philosopher Thoreau once wrote: "All the past is here." He could have been talking about culture. For cultures to exist, endure, and perpetuate, they must make sure that their crucial "messages" and elements get passed on.

According to Brislin (1993), "[i]f there are values considered central to a society that have existed for many years, these must be transmitted from one generation to another" (p. 6). This characteristic supports the idea that culture and communication are linked. Communication makes culture a continuous process. Once cultural habits, principles, values, dispositions, and the like are "invented," they are communicated to each individual within that culture. The strong need for a culture to tie each generation to past and future generations is demonstrated by Keesing (1965), who tells us, "[a]ny break in the learning chain would lead to a culture's disappearance" (p. 28).

Culture Is Based on Symbols. The first two characteristics—that culture is learned and passed from generation to generation—lead directly to the next idea: that your symbol-making ability enables you to both learn and pass on your culture from individual to individual, group to group, and generation to generation. Through language—be it verbal, nonverbal, images, or icons—it is "possible to learn from cumulative, shared experience" (Smith, 1986, pp. 1–2). An excellent summary of the importance of language to culture is offered by Bates and Plog (1990):

> Language thus enables people to communicate what they would do if such-and-such happened, to organize their experiences into abstract categories ("a happy occasion," for instance, or an "evil omen"), and to express thoughts never spoken before. Morality, religion, philosophy, literature, science, economics, technology, and numerous other areas of human knowledge and belief—along with the ability to learn about and manipulate them—all depend on this type of higher-level communication. (p. 20)

The portability of symbols allows you to package and store them as well as transmit them. The mind, books, pictures, films, videos, computer disks, and the like enable a culture to preserve what it deems to be important and worthy of transmission. Hence, each individual, regardless of his or her generation, is heir to a massive "library" of information that has been collected in anticipation of his or her entry into the culture. In this sense, culture is historical as well as preservable. Each new generation might "write" more, but the notes from the past represent what we call culture. As the French novelist Proust wrote: "The past remains the present."

Culture Is Subject to Change. Cultures are dynamic systems that do not exist in a vacuum and therefore are subject to change. From the wandering nomad thousands of years ago, to CNN's news in the 2000s, cultures are constantly being confronted with ideas and information for "outside" sources. This contact has the potential to bring change to any culture. This characteristic of change through contact is yet another example of how communication and culture are alike—both are constantly changing.

We must make two points about cultural change. First, cultures are highly adaptive. History abounds with examples of how cultures have been forced to alter their course because of natural disasters, wars, or other calamities. Events in the last few hundred years have scattered Jews throughout the world, yet the Jewish culture has adapted and survived. And think for a moment about the adjustments made by the Japanese since the end of World War II. Their government and economy were nearly destroyed during the war, yet because they could adapt, their culture endured. They are now a major economic force in the world.

Second, we would be remiss if we did not remind you that although many aspects of culture are subject to change, the deep structure of a culture resists major alterations. That is, changes in dress, food, transportation, housing, and the like, though appearing to be important, are simply attached to the existing value system; however, values associated with such things as ethics and morals, work and leisure, definitions of freedom, the importance of the past, religious practices, the pace of life, and attitudes toward gender and age are entrenched so deeply in a culture that they persist generation after generation. Barnlund (1989) clearly makes this point when he writes: "The spread of Buddhism, Islam, Christianity, and Confucianism did not homogenize the societies they enveloped. It was usually the other way around: Societies insisted on adapting the religions to their own cultural traditions" (p. 192).

Culture Is Ethnocentric. The disposition toward ethnocentrism might well be the characteristic that most directly relates to intercultural communication. The important tie between ethnocentrism and communication can be seen in the definition of the term itself. Sumner (1940) is generally credited with the introduction of the term to the study of group relations and culture. He defined *ethnocentrism* as "the technical name for the view of things in which one's own group is the center of everything, and all others are scaled and rated with reference to it" (p. 13). In other words, ethnocentrism becomes the perceptual prism through which cultures interpret and judge all other groups. The power and impact of ethnocentrism is clearly noted by Keesing (1965): "Nearly always the folklore of a people includes myths of origin which give priority to themselves, and place the stamp of supernatural approval upon their particular customs" (p. 45). These priorities and judgments include everything from what the "out-groups" value to how they communicate. Feelings that "we are right" and "they are wrong" cover every aspect of a culture's existence. Examples range from the insignificant ("People should paint their bodies, not only their faces") to the significant ("We must fight and die for what is right").

Our discussion thus far should not lead to the conclusion that ethnocentrism is always intentional because it usually is not. Like culture itself, ethnocentrism is mostly learned at the unconscious level. If, for example, our schools are teaching U.S. history, geography, literature, and government, they are also, without realizing it, teaching ethnocentrism. The student, by being exposed only to this single orientation, is therefore developing the view that the United States is the center of the world, as well as learning to judge that world by North American standards—the standards he or she has been taught. If most of the authors, philosophers, scientists, composers, and political leaders you have studied are white males, then you will use the values of white males to judge other cultures. The historic omission of African Americans, Latinos, Asians, Native Americans, and women from most textbooks is, in a very real sense, teaching ethnocentrism.

THE ELEMENTS OF INTERCULTURAL COMMUNICATION

Culture, as we have presented the concept, is a complete pattern for living. It is elaborate, abstract, and pervasive. Countless aspects of culture help determine and guide communication behavior. Three cultural elements have the potential to affect situations in which people from different backgrounds come together: (1) perception, (2) verbal processes, and (3) nonverbal processes.

Perceptual Elements

The German novelist Hermann Hesse wrote: "There is no reality except the one contained with[in] us." This essay has been about the manner in which our cultures help create and shape our realities. In its simplest sense, *perception* "is the process by which an individual selects, evaluates, and organizes stimuli from the external world" (Singer, 1987, p. 9). Perception, in other words, is an internal process whereby you convert the physical energies of the world outside of you into meaningful internal experiences. Because that world embraces everything, you can never completely know it. As Singer (1987) notes: "We experience everything in the world not as it is—but only as the world comes to us through our sensory receptors" (p. 9).

Much of what is called perception has its roots in biology: The act of bringing the outside world to your consciousness involves a great deal of your nervous system and its complex chemistry and anatomy. Although these aspects of perception are important, for our purposes the evaluation and action dimensions of perception are more pertinent. That is, the world looks, sounds, tastes, and feels the way it does because our culture has given you the criterion of perception.

Most communication scholars, while granting that perceptions are part of every communication event, have evolved a fairly consistent taxonomy for isolating those perceptual variables that have the potential to seriously impede the intercultural encounter. The three major sociocultural elements that directly influence perception and communication are (1) cultural values, (2) worldview (religion), and (3) social organizations (family and state).

Values. Formally, a value may be defined as an enduring belief that a specific mode of conduct or end-state of existence is personally or socially preferable to another (Rokeach, 1968, p. 5). Values "represent a learned organization of rules for making choices and for resolving conflicts" (Rokeach, 1968, p. 161). Although each of us has a unique set of values, some values tend to permeate a culture. These are called *cultural values*.

Cultural values are usually derived from the larger philosophical issues that are part of a culture's milieu. Hence, they tend to be broad-based, enduring, and relatively stable. Values generally are normative in that they inform a member of a culture about what is good and bad, right and wrong, true and false, positive and negative, and the like. Cultural values define what is worth dying for, what is worth protecting, what frightens people, what are proper subjects for study and for ridicule, and what types of events lead individuals to group solidarity. Most important, cultural values guide both perception and behavior.

As we have already indicated, values are learned; they are not universal. In many Native American cultures, where there is no written history, age is highly valued. Older people are sought out and asked to take part in many important decisions. Younger people admire them and include them in social gatherings.

Cultural values, as you would suspect, go well beyond the perception and treatment of the elderly. There are literally thousands of values found in every culture. Most scholars agree, however, that the cultural values that most directly influence intercultural communication relate to *individualism, family, religion, materialism, human nature, science and technology, progress and change, competition, work and leisure, equality, gender roles, nature and the environment, time, formality and informality, talk, silence, assertiveness,* and *interpersonal harmony.*

Before we move from values to worldview and social organization, it might be helpful if we pause and indicate why the institutions associated with these two elements hold such a powerful sway over the members of a particular culture.

First, the institutions of church, family, and state *carry the messages that matter most to people.* They explain to you the things for which you should strive (material possessions or a spiritual life), where you fit into the grand scheme of things (a belief in fate or the power of free choice), and what to expect from life (life will be easy or life will be difficult).

Second, these institutions are important because they *endure.* From the early Cro-Magnon cave drawings in southern France to the present, religion, family, and community exert a strong pull. Generation after generation is told about Moses, the Buddha, Allah, and the like. Whether it be the Eight-Fold Path, the Ten Commandments, or the Five Pillars of Islam, the messages in these writings survive. And just as Americans know about the values contained in the story of the Revolutionary War, so Mexicans are aware of the consequences of the Treaty of Guadalupe Hidalgo.

Third, *the content generated by these institutions is deeply and emotionally felt.* Think for a moment about the violent reactions that can be produced by "taking God's name in vain," calling someone's mother a "dirty name," or by setting a match to the American flag. Countries have been able to send young men to war and politicians have attempted to win elections by arousing people to the importance of "God, country, and family."

Finally, the deep structure of a culture is important because the institutions of family, church, and state *give each individual his or her unique identity.* When you think about who you are, you most likely conclude that you are a member of a family (my name is Jane Smith or Yuko Minami), that you have a religious orientation (I am a Mormon or Buddhist), and that you live in a special place (I live in the United States or I live in Japan). Regardless of their culture, all individuals perceive themselves as members of these organizations.

Worldview. Each group of people from the earliest origins of civilization has evolved a worldview. A *worldview* is a culture's orientation toward such things as God, nature, life, death, the universe, and other philosophical issues that are concerned with the meaning of life and with "being." The link between worldview, culture, and communication is clearly stated by Pennington (1985) when she noted: "If one understands a culture's world view and cosmology, reasonable accuracy can be attained in predicting behaviors and motivations in other dimensions" (p. 32). In short, your worldview helps you locate your place and rank in the universe. Perhaps more than any other factor, worldview influences issues ranging from how you view other people to how you spend your time. Olayiwola (1989) argues that worldview even influences the social, economic, and political life of a nation (pp. 19–26). Reflect for just a moment on how your concepts of death, illness, and the environment often direct the choices you make and the goals you seek. The point with regard to intercultural communication should be clear: Diverse concepts produce different choices and behaviors.

The issues associated with worldview are timeless and represent the most fundamental basis of a culture. A Hindu, with a strong belief in reincarnation, will not only perceive time differently than a Christian, but also will have different answers to the major questions of life than will a Catholic, a Muslim, a Jew, a Taoist, or an atheist.

Worldview influences a culture at a deep and profound level. Its effects often are subtle and do not reveal themselves in obvious ways. It might be helpful to think of a culture's worldview as analogous to a pebble being tossed into a pond. Just as the pebble causes ripples to spread and reverberate over the entire surface of the pond, worldview spreads itself over a culture and permeates every facet of it.

Social Organizations. The manner in which a culture organizes itself is directly related to the institutions within that culture. These institutions take a variety of configurations and can be formal or informal. The families who raise you and the governments with which you associate and hold allegiance to all help determine how you perceive the world and how you behave within that world. We will briefly look at the institutions of family and state in order to see their place in the study of intercultural communication.

American author William Thayer once wrote: "As are families, so is society." His words clearly express the importance of family to both culture and each individual. The family is among the oldest and most fundamental of all human institutions. As Galvin and Brommel (1991) point out: "We are born into a family, mature in a family, form new families, and leave them at death" (p. 1). The family

helps the culture "teach" the child what the world looks like and his or her place in that world. Remember, the family greets you in this new world once you leave the comfort of the womb. The family is charged with transforming a biological organism into a human being who must spend the rest of his or her life around other human beings—human beings who expect the individual to act much like all of the other people in that culture.

The family is also important because by the time the other major cultural institutions can influence the child, the family has already exposed the individual to countless experiences. From your introduction to language to your ways of expressing love, the family is the first teacher. Just think for a moment of some of the crucial attitudes, values, and behaviors that the family first initiates. Any list would have to include self-reliance, responsibility, obedience, dominance, social skills, aggression, loyalty, sex roles, age roles, and the like. Keep in mind that at the moment of birth, a human being's development can take any number of paths. A child born in India perceives many people living together in one house and is learning about extended families. By being in the same house with older people, the child is also learning to value the aged. In most of Africa the entire village raises a child, and the child thus learns about the extended family.

A simple Swedish proverb and a well-known one from the United States offer us an excellent summary of the link between family and how we communicate with other people: "Children act in the village as they have learned at home," and "The apple does not fall far from the tree."

When we speak of formal and informal government as a social organization, we are talking about much more than a culture's political system. The Cuban brand of communism or the autocratic governments in some Arab countries produces a different individual than does North American or Norwegian democracy. And China's long continuous history as a country and culture will have a profound influence on the character of people raised in this country. Hence, the term *government,* as it is used in this context, also refers to one's community as well as the history of that community. The importance of government, state, or community is clearly marked by the words of historian Theodore Gochenour, who wrote: "The cultural traits of people are rooted in the history which has molded them." This observation could also serve as a definition of culture.

The history of any culture serves as the origin of the cultural values, ideals, and behaviors. History can help answer such questions as why one type of activity evolved over another. The value Mexicans place on "talk," for example, goes back in part to the socializing that was part of the marketplace during the Aztec period.

We can find countless instances of how the history of a culture determines its view of the world. For example, to comprehend the modern-day Jew, and his or her way of perceiving events and people, you would have to realize what the historian Van Doren (1991) attempted to point out when he wrote: "The history of Judaism and the Jews is a long and complicated story, full of blood and tears" (p. 16). Because of this long history of discrimination and persecution, when Jews make fundamental choices about education, freedom, war, civil rights, and the like, they rely on their history.

Japan is yet another country that vividly reflects the links between history, culture, and behavior. Because it is a series of islands, Japan has a history and character not only molded by isolation but also strongly influenced by almost constant seismic activity and its consequences. According to Reischauer (1988), this isolation and separation "has produced in the Japanese a strong sense of self-identity and also an almost painful self-consciousness in the presence of others" (p. 32). Reischauer (1991) continues: "[I]solation has caused the Japanese to be acutely aware of anything that comes from outside" (p. 32).

As we conclude this section on the impact of history, we remind you that thousands of examples can be found of the tandem relationships among history, worldview, and family. We have offered a handful of those as a means of demonstrating that by knowing the deep structure of culture you can better understand how that structure influences perception and communication. And we submit that the most compelling problem associated with intercultural communication is cultural diversity in perceptual processes.

Verbal Language

The importance of language to the study of intercultural communication is clearly captured in Ralph Waldo Emerson's simple sentence: "Language is the archives of history." Emerson is telling you that it is impossible to separate your use of language from your culture because language is not only a form of preserving culture but also a means of sharing culture. In its most basic sense, language is an organized, generally agreed-upon, learned symbol system that is used to represent the experiences within a geographic or cultural community.

Culture teaches you both the symbol (dog) and what the symbol stands for (a furry, domesticated pet). Objects, events, experiences, and feelings have particular labels or names solely because a community of people (a culture) has arbitrarily decided to so name them.

If we extend this notion to the intercultural setting, we can observe how different cultures can have both different symbols and different responses. Culture even influences the unadorned word *dog* we used in the last paragraph. In some areas of the world, such as Hong Kong and Korea, dogs are considered a culinary delight and often are eaten. In the United States, dogs sit on the family couch and are not cooked; hence, the word *dog* conveys a quite different meaning in the United States than it does in Hong Kong. If you take our superficial example and then apply it to every word and meaning you know, then you can begin to visualize the influence of culture on how you send and receive messages. Think for just a moment about the variety of meanings various cultures have for words such as *freedom, sexuality, trespassing, birth control, social security, leadership, assertiveness, affirmative action,* and *AIDS.*

Even the way people use language shifts from culture to culture. In the Arab tradition, "verbal language patterns that emphasize creative artistry by using rhetorical devices such as repetition, metaphor, and simile are highly valued" (Lustig, 1988, p. 102). Yet Japanese culture encourages minimum verbal communication. A Japanese proverb gives credence to this outlook by offering this advice: "By your mouth you shall perish." By multiplying this example across the countless cultures you may come into contact with, you can see how differences in language reflect differences in culture.

People living within the same geographic boundaries can also use language in ways that differ from the dominant culture. You should be aware of the rich examples that can be drawn from African-American communication. And most women, because they are raised to be polite and to focus on the other person, use language in a unique manner. They ask more questions than men and consciously or unconsciously let men control the flow of conversation.

Nonverbal Language

As we have indicated, the ability to use words to represent feelings and ideas is universal. All human beings also use nonverbal symbols to share internal states. Although the process of using your actions to communicate is universal, the meanings for those actions often shift from culture to culture. Hence, nonverbal communication becomes yet another element that one must understand to interact effectively with people from different cultures.

We will briefly introduce you to three important nonverbal categories (bodily behavior, time, and space) that are reflected during intercultural interaction. We remind you before we begin, however, that we do not intend to expose you to the literally thousands of nonverbal behaviors found in nearly every culture, but rather, with just a few simple examples, we will try to make you aware of the role of nonverbal message in the study of intercultural communication.

Bodily Behavior. Most scholars agree that other people can attach meaning to our movement (kinesics), facial expressions, eye contact and gaze, touch, concepts of time, and space. Let us briefly offer one or two examples for each element.

Body Movements. When we speak of "body movements," we are talking about both posture and specific gestures. A culture's use of both of these forms of movement can offer considerable insight into its deep structure and value system. For example, in many Asian cultures the bow is much more

than a greeting. It signifies a culture's concern with status and rank. In Japan, for example, low posture during the bow indicates respect (Ishii, 1973, pp. 163–180).

The manner in which we sit can also communicate a message. In Ghana and Turkey, sitting with one's legs crossed is extremely offensive (Rich, 1989, p. 279). People from Thailand believe that because the bottoms of the feet are the lowest part of the body, they should never be pointed at a person (Cooper & Cooper, 1994, pp. 22–23). In fact, for the Thai people, the feet take on so much significance that people avoid stomping with them.

Some of your most elementary gestures are culture-bound. You make a zero with your index finger and thumb as a way of "saying" everything is perfect. Yet this same gesture means money in Japan, is an insult in Malta and Greece, and is perceived as an obscene gesture in Brazil.

Even the taken-for-granted sign that you make for beckoning is culturally based. In the United States, a person who wants to signal a friend to come makes a gesture with one hand, holding the palm up and with the fingers more or less together and moving toward his or her own body. Koreans and Vietnamese express this same idea by cupping the hand with the palm down and drawing the fingers toward the palm.

Facial Expressions. Although most people agree that universal facial expressions do exist, cultural norms often dictate how, when, and to whom facial expressions are displayed (Porter & Samovar, 1998). In many Mediterranean cultures, people exaggerate signs of grief or sadness. It is not uncommon in this region of the world to see men crying in public. Yet in the United States, white males often suppress the desire to show these emotions. Japanese men even go so far as to hide expressions of anger, sorrow, or disgust by laughing or smiling.

There even are differences in how co-cultures employ facial expressions as a form of communication. Summarizing the research on gender differences, Pearson, West, and Turner (1995) report that, compared to men, women generally use more facial expressions and are more expressive, smile more, are more apt to return smiles, and are more attracted to others who smile (p. 123).

Touch. Instances of touch as a form of communication demonstrate how nonverbal communication is a product of culture. In Germany, both women and men shake hands at the outset of every social encounter; in the United States, women seldom shake hands. In the Arab culture, men often greet each other by kissing and hugging. In Thailand, people do not touch in public, and to touch someone on the head is a major social transgression. Even co-cultures differ in their use of touch. In the United States, women give and receive more touch than do men, yet men tend to initiate the touch.

Concept of Time. Concepts and uses of time are also important when people of different cultures come together. Most Western cultures think of time in lineal–spatial terms. You are timebound. Your schedules and your lists dominate your lives. The Germans and the Swiss are even more aware of time than Americans. Trains, planes, and meals must always be on time. This is not true for many cultures. Activity, not a clock, determines action. Most Native American languages, for example, have no words for seconds, minutes, or hours. Hence, for American Indians, and for many other cultures, being tardy is quite different than it is for members of the dominant culture.

The pace at which a culture carries out its life also reflects its use of time. In Mexico a slower pace is valued, whether when conducting a business meeting or visiting with friends. And in Africa, where a slow pace is also valued, "people who rush are suspected of trying to cheat" (Rich, 1989, p. 278).

Use of Space. It is well known that Arabs and Latins tend to interact more closely than do North Americans, and you also know how uncomfortable you can feel when people from these cultures get too close. This shows how use of space is yet another behavior that is directly related to past experience.

Distance, however, is just one aspect of the use of space as a form of communication; physical orientation is also influenced by culture. North Americans prefer to sit facing or at right angles to one another, whereas Chinese generally prefer side-by-side seating. The English and Germans are conditioned to waiting in a straight line when seeking service in public, but Arabs see nothing wrong with propelling and jostling themselves into the best possible position to secure service. This is a clear example of how the use of space can send different messages.

CONCLUSION

As American society continues to accept immigrants and refugees at a rate far greater than any other country in the world, you will see a rapid increase in cultural diversity. If you assert the value of cultural diversity and claim to espouse and accept a multicultural global village orientation, then you must be prepared to accept and tolerate the potential conflicts embedded in cultural differences. A free, culturally diverse society can exist only if diversity is permitted to flourish without prejudice and discrimination, both of which harm all members of the village. Remember the words of Thomas Jefferson as you begin your study of intercultural communication. In just a single written sentence he was able to capture the need for all of us to be tolerant of divergent views: "It does me no injury for my neighbor to say there are twenty gods, or no God."

References

Barnlund, D. C. (1989). *Communicative styles of Japanese and Americans: Images and realities.* Belmont, CA: Wadsworth.

Bates, D. G., & Plog, F. (1990). *Cultural anthropology,* 3rd ed. New York: McGraw-Hill.

Brislin, R. (1993). *Understanding culture's influence on behavior.* Fort Worth, TX: Harcourt Brace.

Cooper, R., & Cooper, N. (1994). *Culture shock: Thailand.* Portland, OR: Graphic Arts Center.

Galvin, K. M., & Brommel, B. J. (1991). *Family communication: Cohesion and change,* 3rd ed. New York: Harper Collins.

Hall, E. T. (1977). *Beyond culture.* Garden City, NY: Anchor.

Harris, P. R., & Moran, R. T. (1996). *Managing cultural differences: Leadership strategies for a new world of business,* 4th ed. Houston, TX: Gulf Publishing.

Haviland, W. A. (1993). *Cultural anthropology,* 7th ed. Fort Worth, TX: Harcourt Brace.

Higgins, A. G. (1995, October 19). Multimedia readiness of U.S. ranked No. 1. *San Diego Union Tribune,* A-6.

Ishii, S. (1973). Characteristics of Japanese nonverbal communication. *Communication, 2,* 163–180.

Keesing, F. M. (1965). *Cultural anthropology: The science of custom*. New York: Holt, Rinehart, & Winston.

Lustig, M. W. (1988). Cultural and communications patterns of Saudi Arabians. In L. A. Samovar & R. E. Porter (Eds.), *Intercultural communication: A reader*, 5th ed. Belmont, CA: Wadsworth.

Nanda, S. (1994). *Cultural anthropology*, 5th ed. Belmont, CA: Wadsworth.

Olayiwola, R. O. (1989). The impact of Islam on the conduct of Nigerian foreign relations. *The Islamic Quarterly, 33*, 19–26.

Pearson, J. C., West, R. L., & Turner, L. H. (1995). *Gender and communication*, 3rd ed. Dubuque, IA: Wm. C. Brown.

Pennington, D. L. (1985). Intercultural communication. In L. A. Samovar & R. E. Porter (Eds.), *Intercultural communication: A reader*, 4th ed. Belmont, CA: Wadsworth.

Porter, R. E., & Samovar, L. A. (1998). Cultural influences on emotional expression: Implications for intercultural communication. In P. A. Andersen & L. K. Guerrero (Eds.), *Handbook of communication and emotion: Research, theory, applications and context*. San Diego: Academic Press.

Reischauer, E. D. (1988). *The Japanese today: Change and continuity*. Cambridge, MA: Harvard University Press.

Rich, W. V. (1989). *International handbook of corporate communication*. Jefferson, NC: McFarland.

Rokeach, M. (1968). *Beliefs, values, and attitudes*. San Francisco: Jossey-Bass.

Singer, M. R. (1987). *Intercultural communication: A perceptual approach*. Englewood Cliffs, NJ: Prentice-Hall.

Smith, A. G. (Ed.). (1966). *Communication and culture: Readings in the codes of human interaction*. New York: Holt, Rinehart, & Winston.

Smith, H. (1986). *The religion of man*. New York: Harper & Row.

Sumner, W. G. (1940). *Folkways*. Boston: Ginn & Co.

Time. (Fall 1993). p. 3.

U.S. News & World Report. (1996). p. 48.

Van Doren, C. (1991). *A history of knowledge: The pivotal event, people, and achievements of world history*. New York: Ballantine Books.

Wattenberg, B. J. (1989, February 13). Tomorrow. *U.S. News & World Report*, p. 31.

Concepts and Questions

1. Samovar and Porter maintain that intercultural communication is more prevalent than ever before in recorded history. Do you believe that most people are prepared for this increase in intercultural contact? If not, why?

2. How has this increase in cultural contact touched your life?

3. Why is culture an important consideration in human interaction?

4. What is meant by the statement "culture is learned"? Can you think of examples that demonstrate this "learning" process?

5. What is the relationship between culture and perception?

6. Why is worldview important to the study of intercultural communication? How does one's worldview contribute to how one perceives the world?

7. What is meant by the phrase "cultural values"? How might these values influence intercultural communication?

8. What is meant by the statement "culture teaches both the symbol and what the symbol stands for"?

9. What aspects of nonverbal communication must we consider during intercultural communication?

Culture and Conflict

Harry C. Triandis

A report that appeared in the *New York Times* claimed that on January 9, 1991, at a meeting where the Foreign Minister of Iraq, Tariq Aziz, met the Secretary of State of the United States, James Baker, they miscommunicated. According to the report Baker was very clear that the United States would attack, if Iraq did not leave Kuwait. But he said it calmly. The miscommunication occurred because next to Aziz was seated Saddam Hussein's brother, who paid attention only to *how* Baker talked, rather than to *what* he said. He reported back to Baghdad "the Americans will not attack. They are weak. They are calm. They are not angry. They are only talking."

We do know that Western individualist cultures sample mostly the *content* of communications, whereas Eastern, collectivist cultures sample mostly the *context* of communication (Gudykunst, 1993; Triandis, 1994). Thus, it is plausible that Hussein's brother, who had little exposure to the West, did not sample the conversation correctly. Also, Baker did not throw anything at Aziz, to show that he was angry. He acted calmly. It is doubtful that Baker could have thrown anything. People cannot change their behavior that drastically, just because they are interacting with members of other cultures. We do not know what report Aziz gave to Hussein, but it is plausible that Hussein paid special attention to his brother's assessment, since trust in collectivist cultures is much greater within the intimate in-group than within the outer in-group. In any case, we do know that a war took place after that meeting. Cultural differences often cause miscommunications and conflict.

Conflict is greater when the two cultures are very different than when they are similar. Technically this difference is called "cultural distance" (Triandis, 1994).

From the *International Journal of Psychology*, 2000, 35 (2), 145–152. Copyright © 2000. Reprinted by permission of Taylor and Francis, Inc., http://www.routledge-ny.com. Harry C. Triandis is in the Department of Psychology at the University of Illinois at Urbana-Champaign.

CULTURAL DISTANCE

Cultural distance is greater when people speak different languages. Even speaking languages that are related can be a problem. For example the ancient Greek root of *sympathetic* is "to feel together." That is fairly close to the English meaning. But modern Greek, Italian, Spanish, and French use terms that are derived from that root yet mean "a nice, pleasant person." So, "I am sympathetic" does not translate correctly into "Je suis sympatique!"

Triandis (1994) listed many funny examples of mis-translations. For instance, at the office of an Italian physician: "Specialist in women and other diseases." Of course, what happens when languages are members of the same language family (say, Indo-European) can be even more of a problem when the languages have very different structures (e.g., tonal or click languages).

Cultural distance is also larger when people have different social structures, such as family structures. Todd (1983) has identified eight types of family structure, and simple terms like "aunt" may convey different meanings when the family structure is different.

Religions, of course, can be a great source of differences in points of view. Even when one knows that the other person believes something different, there is the problem that humans use themselves as the anchors for such judgments. The diplomat may not believe that it is possible for the other diplomat to have such "outlandish" beliefs. A well-established social psychological phenomenon is called the "false consensus" effect (Mullen et al., 1985). Even when people know about this bias they cannot wipe it out (Krueger & Clement, 1994). The phenomenon is that if we agree with a particular position we believe that most other people also agree with it; if we disagree with a particular position we believe that most people disagree with it. The phenomenon is even stronger when we interact with people who are similar to us in dress, profession, etc.

Differences in standards of living can create cultural distance. When the cost of sending a letter is a substantial fraction of one's budget, it may not be as likely that one will send the letter as when the cost of the letter is trivial in relation to one's budget.

Values differ substantially between cultures (Schwartz, 1992, 1994). These values are related to the cultural syndromes that we will discuss here.

MEANING OF CULTURE

Culture is a shared meaning system, found among those who speak a particular language dialect, during a specific historic period, and in a definable geographic region (Triandis, 1994). It functions to improve the adaptation of members of the culture to a particular ecology, and it includes the knowledge that people need to have in order to function effectively in their social environment.

Cultures differ drastically in the amount of aggression that is found both within and between them. For example, the Lepcha of the Indian Himalayas had one murder two centuries ago (Segall, Ember, & Ember, 1997). Homicide rates in some segments of U.S. society are extremely high. There is evidence that the absence of fathers during socialization is a factor in high rates (Segall et al.). There is some evidence that high between-cultures aggression is related to high within-culture aggression (Segall et al.). Warfare is associated with the unpredictability of resources, conflicts over territory, and is found most usually in societies that permit aggression within the family, where the media of communication portray aggression, where there are warlike sports, and where there is severe punishment for wrongdoing (Segall et al.). There is evidence that democracies do not fight with each other (Ember, Ember, & Russett, 1992) so much so that some analysts have argued that it is "counterproductive to support any undemocratic regimes, even if they happen to be enemies of our enemies" (Ember & Ember, 1994).

Shared patterns of elements of subjective culture constitute subjective cultural syndromes (Triandis, 1996). A cultural syndrome is a shared pattern of beliefs, attitudes, self-definitions, norms, roles, and values organized around a theme.

Cultural differences are best conceptualized as different patterns of sampling information found in the environment (Triandis, 1989). In collectivist cultures (most traditional cultures, most Asian and Latin American cultures) people are more likely: (a) to sample the collective self (reflecting inter-

dependence with others) and to think of themselves as interdependent with their groups (family, co-workers, tribe, co-religionists, country, etc.) rather than to sample the individual self (reflecting an independent self) and to see themselves as autonomous individuals who are independent of their groups (Markus & Kitayama, 1991); (b) to give more priority to the goals of their in-group than to their personal goals (Triandis, 1995); (c) to use in-group norms to shape their behaviour more than personal attitudes (Abrams, Ando, & Hinkle, 1998; Suh, Diener, Oishi, & Triandis, 1998); and (d) to conceive of social relationships as communal (Mills & Clark, 1982) rather than in exchange theory terms (Triandis, 1995). That is, they pay attention to the needs of others and stay in relationships even when that is not maximally beneficial to them. There is evidence that these four aspects are interrelated (Triandis & Gelfand, 1998).

The sampling of collectivists focuses on groups, and people are seen as appendages of groups; the sampling of individualists focuses on individuals. A recent example is the coverage of the Kosovo war: CNN and BBC cover the refugees (individuals) in great detail. The Russian and the Serbs present nothing about the refugees on their television. The *Times* of London (April 7, 1999) had a story about a member of the Russian Duma who was so upset that the Russian TV did not mention the refugees at all that he went on a hunger strike. Finally, 12 days into the war an independent Russian station mentioned the refugees. We called a friend in Belgrade and asked her if she knew why NATO was bombing her city. She did not! Of course, such control of information is part of the war effort, but when it is consistent with the culture it is a natural bias. Culture shapes us, so we pay more attention to individuals and to the internal processes of individuals (attitudes, beliefs) if we are raised in individualist cultures, and more attention to groups, roles, norms, duties, and intergroup relationships if we are raised in a collectivist culture.

Collectivist cultures have languages that do not require the use of "I" and "you" (Kashima & Kashima, 1997, 1998). They also have many culture-specific relational terms that are not found in individualist cultures, such as *philolimo* in Greek (Triandis, 1972), which is a positive attribute of an individual who does what the in-group expects; *amae* in Japanese, which reflects tolerance of deviation from norms by a dependent person (Yamaguchi, 1998); *simpatia* among Latin Americans (Triandis, Marin, Lisansky, & Betancourt, 1984), which reflects the expectation that social relationships will include mostly positive and very few negative behaviours, and so on.

Collectivists use action verbs (e.g., he offered to help) rather than state verbs (e.g., he is helpful). This is because they prefer to use context in their communications. Zwier (1997), in four studies, obtained support for this cultural difference. Specifically, she found that the accounts of events given by Turkish and Dutch students show this difference. She content analyzed the radio commentaries of Turkish and Dutch radio personalities and found the same difference. She asked Turkish and Dutch students to write a letter requesting a favour, and content analyzed the letters. She examined the writing of Turkish/Dutch bilinguals when writing in the two languages, and found the same pattern.

The contrasting cultural pattern is individualism. Here people tend to (a) sample the individual self; this pattern is very common in North and Western Europe, North America (except in Mexico), Australia, and New Zealand, where the self is conceived as independent of in-groups; (b) give priority to personal goals; (c) use attitudes much more than norms as determinants of their social behaviour; and (d) pay attention to their own needs only and abandon interpersonal relationships that are not optimally beneficial to them. Individualist cultures have languages that require the use of "I" and "you" (Kashima & Kashima, 1997, 1998). English is a good example. It would be difficult to write a letter in English without the use of these words. Individualists are very positive about "me" and "we," whereas collectivists are sometimes ambivalent about "me" but very positive about "we."

CULTURAL SYNDROMES

Complexity

Some cultures (e.g., hunters and gatherers) are relatively simple, and other cultures (e.g., information

societies) are relatively complex. The organizing theme of the syndrome is complexity. For example, in complex societies one finds subgroups with different beliefs, attitudes, etc., whereas in simple societies individuals are in considerable agreement about their beliefs and attitudes. In fact, cultural uniformity and conformity are higher in simple than in complex societies. Simple cultures have few jobs; if we take into account specialties such as urologist and general practitioner, complex cultures have a quarter of a million different jobs (see *Dictionary of Occupational Titles*). The size of settlements is one of the best ways to index cultural complexity (Chick, 1997).

Tightness

Tight cultures have many rules, norms, and ideas about what is correct behaviour in each situation; loose cultures have fewer rules and norms. In tight cultures, people become quite upset when others do not follow the norms of the society, and may even kill those who do not behave as is expected, whereas in loose cultures people are tolerant of many deviations from normative behaviours.

Thus, conformity is high in tight cultures. In Thailand, which is a loose culture, the expression "*mai bin rai*" (never mind) is used frequently. In Japan, which is a tight culture, people are sometimes criticized for minor deviations from norms, such as having too much suntan, or having curly hair (Kidder, 1992). Most Japanese live in fear that they will not act properly (Iwao, 1993).

Tightness is more likely when the culture is relatively isolated from other cultures, so that consensus about what is proper behaviour can develop. It is also more likely that tightness will occur in situations where people are highly interdependent (when the other deviates from norms it hurts the relationship) and where there is a high population density (high density requires norms so that people will not hurt each other; also when the other deviates one notices it).

When cultures are at the intersections of great cultures (e.g., Thailand is at the intersection of China and India), contradictory norms may be found, and people cannot be too strict in imposing norms. Also, when the population density is low, it may not even be known that a person who is miles away has behaved improperly. Cosmopolitan cities are loose, except when they have ethnic enclaves, which can be very tight, whereas small communities are relatively tight.

Individualism and Collectivism

Triandis (1994) has suggested that individualism emerges in societies that are both complex and loose; collectivism in societies that are both simple and tight. For example, theocracies or monasteries are both tight and relatively poor; Hollywood stars live in a culture that is both complex and loose. This speculation has not been tested rigorously, but the data seem to hang together reasonably well so that it may be the case that, for instance, contemporary Japan, which is now quite complex, is less collectivist than the Japan of the 19th century. In fact, reports of 19th-century travelers to Japan (see Edgerton, 1985) mentioned hundreds of rules for how to laugh, sit, etc., which apparently no longer operate in modern Japan.

Bond and Smith (1996) did a meta-analysis of studies of conformity that used the Asch paradigm, and found that collectivist cultures were higher in conformity than individualist cultures. This is what we would expect if tightness and collectivism were closely linked.

Kim and Markus (1998) showed that in the West people see "uniqueness" as desirable, whereas in East Asia it is often seen as "deviance"; in the West "conformity" is sometimes seen as undesirable, but in East Asia it is seen as "harmony." For example, content analyses of advertisements from the United States and Korea show different frequencies of uniqueness and conformity themes. Conformity themes were used by 95% of the Korean and 65% of the American advertisements; uniqueness themes were used by 89% of the American and 49% of the Korean advertisements.

Vertical and Horizontal Cultures

Vertical cultures accept hierarchy as a given. People are different from each other. Hierarchy is a natural state. Those at the top "naturally" have more power and privileges than those at the bottom of the hierarchy. Horizontal cultures accept equality as a given. People are basically similar, and if one is to divide any resource it should be done equally (Triandis, 1995).

Active–Passive Cultures

In active cultures individuals try to change the environment to fit them; in passive cultures people change themselves to fit into the environment (Diaz-Guerrero, 1979). The active cultures are more competitive, action-oriented, and emphasize self-fulfillment; the passive ones are more cooperative, emphasize the experience of living, and are especially concerned with getting along with others. In general, individualist cultures are more active than collectivist cultures, though the relationship between the two cultural syndromes is not strong.

Universalism–Particularism

In universalist cultures people try to treat others on the basis of universal criteria (e.g., all competent persons regardless of who they are in sex, age, race, etc. are acceptable employees); in particularist cultures people treat others on the basis of who the other person is (e.g., I know Joe Blow and he is a good person, so he will be a good employee; Parsons, 1968). In general individualists are universalists and collectivists are particularists.

Diffuse–Specific

Diffuse cultures respond to the environment in a holistic manner (e.g., I do not like your report means I do not like you). Specific cultures discriminate different aspects of the stimulus complex (e.g., I do not like your report says nothing about liking you; Foa & Chemers, 1967).

Instrumental–Expressive

People may sample more heavily attributes that are instrumental (e.g., get the job done) or expressive (e.g., enjoy the social relationship). In general, individualists are more instrumental and collectivists are more expressive. When Latin Americans meet a friend in the street, they are likely to stop and chat, even when they are late for an appointment. The importance of the social relationship eclipses the importance of the instrumental relationship (Levine & Norenzayan, 1999).

Emotional Expression or Suppression

People may express their emotions freely, no matter what the consequences, or they may control the expression of emotion. The free expression of negative emotions can disrupt relationships, so collectivists tend to control such emotions. Individualists are often high in emotional expression. For example, Stephan, Stephan, and de Vargas (1996) tested the hypothesis that people in collectivist cultures would feel less comfortable expressing negative emotions than people in individualist cultures, and found strong support for that hypothesis.

In addition, the instigation of emotion is often culture specific. Stipek, Weiner, and Li (1989) found that when Americans were asked to recall what made them angry they remembered mostly events that happened to them personally; when Chinese were given that task they remembered mostly events that occurred to other people. This self-focus versus other focus is an important contrast between individualism and collectivism (Kagiteibasi, 1997).

The Weights Given to Different Attributes in Social Perception

In addition to sampling different attributes, members of different cultures give different weights to the attributes that they sample. For example, in a conflict situation an individual might sample the ethnicity of the other person, his profession, and his competence. Members of some cultures will give most of the weight to ethnicity and react to the other person on the basis of ethnicity; members of other cultures will give most of the weight to competence and profession, and disregard ethnicity. Triandis (1967) reviewed many cross-cultural studies showing differences in the weights used in social perception. In general members of collectivist cultures tend to sample and weigh ascribed attributes more heavily, whereas members of individualist cultures sample and weigh achieved attributes more heavily.

One can identify many more syndromes, such as those reflected in the Kluckhohn and Strodtbeck (1961) value orientations, the culture of honour (Nisbett & Cohen, 1996), and others. This introduction is sufficient for our purposes.

CULTURAL SYNDROMES AND THE SITUATION

Humans have a predisposition to respond that can be traced to culture, but their behaviour depends very much more on the situation. For example, all humans have both collectivist and individualist cognitions, but they sample them with different probabilities depending on the situation. For instance, when the in-group is being attacked, most humans become collectivists.

The larger the in-group, the less effective it is likely to be in calling for individuals to do what the in-group authorities want done. A call to arms by a clan leader is more likely to be effective than a call to arms by a state, though penalties may make the latter effective in many countries.

Certain factors increase the probability that the collectivist cognitive system will be activated. This is most likely to happen when (a) the individual knows that most other people in the particular situation are collectivists, which makes the norm that one must act as a collectivist more salient; (b) the individual's membership in a collective is especially salient, for instance, the individual represents a country; (c) within an in-group the situation emphasizes what people have in common, for instance, common goals; (d) within an in-group the situation emphasizes that people are in the same collective, for instance, people use the same uniforms; and (e) within an in-group the task is cooperative.

Certain factors increase the probability that the individualistic cognitive system will be activated. This is most likely to happen when (a) others in the situation are and behave like individualists, which makes individualist norms more salient; (b) the situation makes the person focus on what makes him or her different from others (Trafimow, Triandis, & Goto, 1991), for instance, the person is dressed very differently from the rest of the group; and (c) the task is competitive.

Culture is relevant for understanding conflict in at least two domains: How conflict starts and how conflict evolves. Problems of poor communication are the major causes of the first, and problems of the way members of different cultures treat out-groups are relevant for understanding the second of these domains.

CULTURAL SYNDROMES AND COMMUNICATION

When people come into contact with members of other cultures, they are often not aware of their miscommunications, because they think that the others are more or less like they are. This is the stage of *unconscious incompetence*. After some interpersonal difficulties people realize that they are miscommunicating, but they do not know exactly what is wrong. That is the stage of *conscious incompetence*. As they get to know more and more about the culture of the other, they begin communicating correctly, but they have to make an effort to communicate in a different way. That is the stage of *conscious competence*. Finally, after they develop habits of correct communication with members of the other culture, they reach the stage of *unconscious competence*, where the communication is effortless, and correct.

A very serious problem in communication is that people do not perceive the same "causes" of behaviour (Miller, 1984; Morris & Peng, 1994). We call these *attributions*. When the actor thinks that a behaviour is due to one cause and the observer thinks that the behaviour is due to a different cause, they each give a different meaning to the behaviour. For instance, a diplomat may invite another diplomat to dinner. The inviter may do so because he likes the other diplomat. The invitee, however, may use the cause "his boss told him to invite me." Obviously, the meaning of the invitation is different for the two diplomats.

There are training procedures called "culture assimilators" (Fiedler, Mitchell, & Triandis, 1971), which consist of 100 or so episodes involving interactions between members of the two relevant cultures, and each episode is followed by four attributions. Usually three attributions are "incorrect" from the point of view of the culture the trainee is learning about, and one is "correct." The trainee selects one attribution, and gets feedback as to whether it is the correct one from the point of view of the culture she is trying to learn about. Trainees who go through this training gradually learn to make the correct attributions from the point of view of the other culture. This reduces miscommunications (Bhawuk, 1998).

There is a well-researched phenomenon. When two groups, A and B, are in conflict, if a member of group B does something "nice," members of group A attribute the behaviour to external factors (e.g., he was forced to do it by the circumstances); when a member of group B does something "nasty," members of group A attribute it to internal factors (e.g., they are nasty "by nature"). The attributions that group B makes about the behaviour of group A are exact mirror images; that is, when A does something nice it is due to external factors, and when A does something nasty it is due to internal factors. When a member of group A makes attributions about the actions of members of group A, if the action is positive it is attributed to internal factors and if it is negative it is attributed to external factors.

In all cultures, when we ask actors why they did something they report external causes, but observers of these actions tend to use causes internal to the actor. This is called the "fundamental attribution error." In short, people all over the world have a tendency to make attributions incorrectly. However, those from individualistic cultures are even worse in this bias than those from collectivist cultures.

Another factor in miscommunications is the tendency of collectivists to sample the context of communications more than individualists, which results in their paying more attention to gestures, eye contact, level of voice, the direction of the two bodies, touching, the distance between the bodies, and the like. There is a large opportunity for errors and misinterpretations in the way people interpret paralinguistic cues. Also, the way people use time can result in misunderstandings, because people from monochronic time cultures are used to carrying out one conversation at a time, whereas people who use polychronic time carry several conversations simultaneously, which confuses and frustrates the users of monochronic time.

The structure of messages can be another source of difficulties. Western people tend to organize their thoughts and messages in a linear fashion: fact 1, fact 2, etc., generalization, conclusion. In many other cultures people start with the conclusion, and then find facts that fit the conclusion, and permit deviations from a straight line. In some cases the argument is like a spiral, starting from general ideological or mystical considerations, and gradually zeroing to a conclusion (Triandis, 1994). The extent to which ideology versus pragmatic matters are sampled also varies with culture. Glenn (1981) gave an interesting example. At a UN conference, the Russians advocated the use of reinforced concrete structures (ideal for all), whereas the American delegates said that "it depends on what works best" (pragmatic). Delegates from the Third World interpreted the exchange in favour of the Russians. They thought that the Americans were saying that "we are not good enough to use what they are using."

When a universalist meets a particularist there can be interpersonal difficulties. For example, when presenting a position, the universalist may expect that all the facts will "fit in" with the position, whereas the particularist may not feel that this is necessary. When such expectations are present, the particularist might need to start the presentation with a universalist position (e.g., "we are all in favour of peace") and then present the particularist view.

Another source of miscommunication is that in some cultures communication is "associative" and in others "abstractive." In the West it is typically abstractive. That is, one abstracts the most important elements of the argument and organizes them for the presentation. An associative presentation can present anything that is vaguely related to the point, which can frustrate the Westerner (Szalay, 1993). For example, in 1932 the finance minister of Japan was assassinated after agreeing to a 17% revaluation of the yen. In 1971, the American Treasury Secretary Connaly, oblivious to Japanese history, demanded a 17% revaluation of the yen. His Japanese counterpart rejected it without explanation. When Connaly suggested a 16.9% upward revaluation, the Japanese minister accepted it (Cohen, 1991).

Examples of associative communications abound. The *Los Angeles Times*, on February 12, 1977, published a conversation between two Egyptians. One was Westernized and the other was traditional. The communication of the traditional was not understood by the Westernized. Another example was the presentation of the Egyptian ambassador to the UN in 1967, in which he accused the Americans of actively helping the Israelis. The American ambassador asked for proof, but the Egyptian answered that no proof was needed because it was "obvious that the Americans had intervened. How else could one explain that three quarters of the Egyptian air force was destroyed in a few hours? Only a large, powerful country could do this."

In sum, cultural distance can result in miscommunications, which may lead to international conflict. We now turn to the way the conflict is carried out, and look at the role of cultural syndromes in this area.

CULTRAL SYNDROMES AND CONFLICT

We need to distinguish conflict within the in-group from conflict between groups. Individualism is associated with conflict inside a culture, such as crime or divorce. Collectivism is associated with conflict between groups, such as ethnic cleansing or war.

Factors that have been found to increase aggression (see Triandis, 1994) include biological factors (e.g., high levels of testosterone), social structural factors (such as low family cohesion, few intimate relationships, low father involvement in the upbringing of sons, isolation from kin, anonymity, all of which are associated with individualism), high levels of arousal (because of frustration, competition), hot weather, modeling (aggressive models, aggressive people receive more status in the society), gender marking (men and women are seen as very different), retaliation, economic inequality, few resources (associated with collectivism), social stress (e.g., high levels of inflation), ease of being aggressive (e.g., availability of weapons), and low costs (aggression does not lead to punishment). Clearly there are many factors, many of which do not have much to do with cultural patterns. Yet culture is important for many of these factors (Segall et al., 1997).

Some of the factors, such as weak families, are associated with individualism, and lead to within-group aggression, and others are associated with collectivism.

When interacting with in-group members, people from collectivist cultures tend to be unusually sensitive to the needs of the others, supportive, helpful, and even self-sacrificing. However, when interacting with out-group members they are usually indifferent and, if the two groups have incompatible goals, they are even hostile.

Once the in-group has been called to action against an out-group by in-group authorities, vertical collectivists are especially likely to become aggressive. This pattern leads to especially high levels of hostility when a "culture of honour" is present. Such cultures are found in situations where there are no police (or other authorities that can resolve conflict), so that people have to protect themselves against intruders by means of their personal efforts (Nisbett & Cohen, 1996). To extrapolate to the international scene, conflict would be higher if international bodies such as the United Nations did not exist.

Certain combinations of cultural syndromes can lead to treating the out-group inhumanely. In simple cultures the distinction between different kinds of "others" is unlikely to occur. In vertical cultures, there is likely to be a perception that "others" are very different, just as it is ordinary that people at the top and bottom of a hierarchy are seen as very different. In active cultures the elimination of out-groups (e.g., ethnic cleansing) is likely to be seen as an especially good way to change the sociopolitical environment. In universalist cultures, treating all out-group members the same fits the cultural pattern. If one enemy is to be killed, all should be killed. In diffuse cultures, making distinctions between different kinds of enemies is not likely, so that all out-group members are likely to be treated badly. Instrumental cultures may be particularly effective in eliminating their enemies.

Thus, when a particular combination of cultural syndromes is found, namely active, universalistic, diffuse, instrumental, vertical collectivism, inhumane treatment of out-groups is likely to occur.

All humans are ethnocentric (Triandis, 1994). That means that they think of their in-group as the standard of what is good and proper, and of other groups as good only to the extent that they are sim-

ilar to the in-group. Ethnocentrism also results in members of a culture seeing their own norms and behaviour as "natural" and correct and those of members of other cultures as "unnatural" and "incorrect." Ethnocentrism leads people to see their norms as universally valid; to avoid questioning norms, role definitions, and values; and to help in-group members, feel proud of the in-group, and simultaneously to reject out-groups (Triandis, 1994).

The rejection of out-groups is especially likely to occur in collectivist cultures. In extreme collectivist cultures out-groups are often seen as "not quite human" and "not deserving any rights." Although individualists are capable of dealing with out-groups in an inhuman way (e.g., the Mai Lai incident during the Vietnam war), collectivists are even more extreme in dealing with out-groups (e.g., the rape of Nanking; Chang, 1997, where an estimated 300,000 civilians were killed; the Holocaust). Fortunately, the particular combination of active, universalistic, diffuse, instrumental vertical collectivism is rare, so that such incidents do not occur frequently.

Furthermore, as indicated earlier, typical collectivism is usually incompatible with the active, universalistic, and instrumental syndromes so that the above-mentioned combination is really rare. Nevertheless, in the 20th century we have witnessed many cases of genocide and ethnic cleansing, so we cannot ignore the data.

One way to avoid these inhuman actions would be to monitor cultures that tend toward this undesirable combination of syndromes and to change them to reduce the probability of occurrence of the particular combination of syndromes. There is very little research about the factors that result in the various syndromes mentioned earlier, but we do know something about the occurrence of collectivism.

PREVALENCE OF COLLECTIVISM

Collectivism is found in societies that are not affluent (Hofstede, 1980), especially where there is only one normative system, that is a single culture that is not cosmopolitan. There is a fair amount of evidence about the attributes of collectivism and the causes of the development of this cultural pattern (Triandis, 1990).

Collectivism is also high among the lower social classes of any society (Kohn, 1969; Marshall, 1997), among those who have not traveled (Gerganov, Dilova, Petkova, & Paspalanova, 1996) or were socially mobile, and have not been exposed to the modern mass media (McBride, 1998). When the major economic activity is based on agriculture, rather than on hunting, fishing, industry, or service, collectivism is often high.

Collectivism, thus, is found in societies that are relatively homogeneous (so that in-group norms can be widely accepted), where population density and job inter-dependence are high (because they require the development and adherence to many rules of behaviour), among members of the society who are relatively old (Noricks et al., 1987) and who are members of large families (because it is not possible for every member to do his or her own thing), and in groups that are quite religious (Triandis & Singelis, 1998). When the in-group is under pressure from the outside, collectivism increases. Thus, one consideration in international relations is whether the advantages of putting pressure on a country out-balance the disadvantages of increasing the collectivism of the country.

CONCLUSION

We examined two major ways in which culture is related to conflict. One is that cultural distance increases the probability of miscommunication. There are training programmes that can overcome this problem. The second is the way a combination of cultural syndromes results in the inhuman treatment of out-groups.

References

Abrams, D., Ando, K., & Hinkle, S. (1998). Psychological attachment to groups: Cross-cultural differences in organizational identification and subjective norms as predictors of workers' turnover intentions. *Personality and Social Psychology Bulletin, 24*, 1027–1039.

Bhawuk, D. P. S. (1998). The role of culture theory in cross-cultural training. A multimethod study of culture specific, culture general, and culture theory-based assimilators. *Journal of Cross-Cultural Psychology, 29*, 630–655.

Bond, R., & Smith, P. B. (1996). Culture and conformity: A meta-analysis of studies using Asch's (1952b,

1956) line judgement task. *Psychological Bulletin, 119*, 111–137.

Chang, I. (1997). *The rape of Nanking: The forgotten holocaust of World War II*. New York: Basic Books.

Chick, G. (1997). Cultural complexity: The concept and its measurement. *Cross-Cultural Research, 31*, 275–307.

Cohen, R. (1991). *Negotiating across cultures*. Washington, DC: United States Institute of Peace.

Diaz-Guerrero, R. (1979). The development of coping style. *Human Development, 22*, 320–331.

Dictionary of Occupational Titles, 4th ed. (1977). [Supplements in 1986.] Washington, DC: Superintendent of Documents, U.S. Government Publications Office.

Edgerton, R. B. (1985). *Rules, exceptions. and social order*. Berkeley, CA: University of California Press.

Ember, M., & Ember, C. R. (1994). Prescriptions for peace: Policy implications of crosscultural research on war and interpersonal violence. *Cross-Cultural Research, 28*, 343–350.

Ember, C. R., Ember, M., & Russett, B. (1992). Peace between participatory polities: A cross-cultural test of the "Democracies rarely fight each other" hypothesis. *World Politics, 44*, 573–599.

Fiedler, F. E., Mitchell, T., & Triandis, H. C. (1971). The culture assimilator: An approach to cross-cultural training. *Journal of Applied Psychology, 55*, 95–102.

Foa, U., & Chemers, M. M. (1967). The significance of role behaviour differentiation for crosscultural interaction training. *International Journal of Psychology, 2*, 45–57.

Gerganov, E. N., Dilova, M. L., Petkova, K. G., & Paspalanova, E. P. (1996). Culture-specific approach to the study of individualism/collectivism. *European Journal of Social Psychology, 26*, 277–297.

Glenn, E. (1981). *Man and mankind: Conflicts and communication between cultures*. Norwood, NJ: Ablex.

Gudykunst, W. (Ed.). (1993). *Communication in Japan and the United States*. Albany, NY: State University of New York Press.

Hofstede, G. (1980). *Culture's consequences*. Beverly Hills, CA: Sage.

Iwao, S. (1993). *The Japanese woman: Traditional image and changing reality*. New York: Free Press.

Kagiteibasi, C. (1997). Individualism and collectivism. In J. W. Berry, M. H. Segall, & C. Kagiteibasi (Eds.), *Handbook of cross-cultural psychology* (2nd ed., pp.1–50). Boston, MA: Allyn & Bacon.

Kashima, E. S., & Kashima, Y. (1997). Practice of the self in conversations: Pronoun drop, sentence co-production and contextualization of the self. In K. Leung, U. Kim, S. Yamaguchi, & Y. Kashima (Eds.), *Progress in Asian social psychology, Vol. 1* (pp. 165–180). Singapore: Wiley.

Kashima, E. S., & Kashima, Y. (1998). Culture and language: The case of cultural dimensions and personal pronoun use. *Journal of Cross-Cultural Psychology, 29,* 461–486.

Kidder, L. (1992). Requirements for being "Japanese": Stories of returnees. *International Journal of Intercultural Relations, 16,* 383–394.

Kim, H., & Markus, H. R. (1998). *Deviance or uniqueness, harmony or conformity? A cultural analysis.* Unpublished manuscript.

Kluckhohn, F., & Strodtbeck, F. (1961). *Variations in value orientation.* Evanston, IL: Row, Peterson.

Kohn, M. K. (1969). *Class and conformity.* Homewood, IL: Dorsey Press.

Krueger, I., & Clement, R. W. (1994). The truly false consensus effect: An ineradicable egocentric bias in social perception. *Journal of Personality and Social Psychology, 67,* 596–610.

Levine, R. V., & Norenzayan, A. (1999). The pace of life in 31 countries. *Journal of Cross-Cultural Psychology, 30,* 178–205.

Markus, H., & Kitayama, S. (1991). Culture and self: Implications for cognition, emotion and motivation. *Psychological Review, 98,* 224–253.

Marshall, R. (1997). Variances in levels of individualism across two cultures and three social classes. *Journal of Cross-Cultural Psychology, 28,* 490–495.

McBride, A. (1998). Television, individualism, and social capital. *Political Science and Politics, 31,* 542–555.

Miller, J. G. (1984). Culture and the development of everyday social explanation. *Journal of Personality and Social Psychology, 46,* 961–978.

Mills, J., & Clark, M. S. (1982). Exchange and communal relationships. In L. Wheeler (Ed.), *Review of personality and social psychology, Vol. 3* (pp. 121–144). Beverly Hills, CA: Sage.

Morris, M. W., & Peng, K. (1994). Culture and cause: American and Chinese attributions for social and physical events. *Journal of Personality and Social Psychology, 67,* 949–971.

Mullen, B., Atkins, J. L., Champion, D. S., Edwards, C., Handy, D., Story, J. E., & Venderklok, M. (1985). The false consensus effect: A meta-analysis of 115 hypothesis tests. *Journal of Experimental Social Psychology, 21,* 262–283.

Nisbett, R. E., & Cohen, D. (1996). *Culture of honor.* Boulder, CO: Westview.

Noricks, J. S., Agler, L. H., Bartholomew, M., Howard-Smith, S., Martin, D., Pyles, S., & Shapiro, W. (1987). Age, abstract things and the American concept of person. *American Anthropologist, 89,* 667–675.

Parsons, T. (1968). *The structure of social action.* New York: Free Press.

Schwartz, S. H. (1992). Universals in the content and structure of values: Theoretical advances and empirical tests in 20 countries. In M. Zanna (Ed.), *Advances in experimental social psychology, Vol. 25* (pp. 1–166). New York: Academic Press.

Schwartz, S. H. (1994). Beyond individualism and collectivism: New cultural dimensions of value. In U. Kim, H. C. Triandis, C. Kagiteibasi, S. C. Choi, & O. Yoon (Eds.), *Individualism and collectivism: Theory, method and applications* (pp. 85–122). Newbury Park, CA: Sage.

Segall, M. H., Ember, C. R., & Ember, M. (1977). Aggression, crime, and warfare. In J. W. Berry, M. H. Segall, & C. Kagiteibasi (Eds.), *Handbook of cross-cultural psychology, Vol. 3,* 2nd ed., (pp. 213–254). Boston, MA: Allyn & Bacon.

Stephan, W. G., Stephan, C. W., & de Vargas, M. C. (1996). Emotional expression in Costa Rica and United States. *Journal of Cross-Cultural Psychology, 27,* 147–160.

Stipek, D., Weiner, B., & Li, K. (1989). Testing some attribution-emotion relations in the People's Republic of China. *Journal of Personality and Social Psychology, 56,* 109–116.

Suh, E., Diener, E., Oishi, S., & Triandis, H. C. (1998). The shifting basis of life satisfaction judgements across cultures: Emotions versus norms. *Journal of Personality and Social Psychology, 74,* 482–493.

Szalay, L. B. (1993). *The subjective worlds of Russians and Americans: A guide for mutual understanding.* Chevy Chase, MD: Institute of Comparative Social and Cultural Studies.

Todd, E. (1983). *La troisieme planete.* Paris: Editions du Scuil.

Trafimow, D., Triandis, H. C., & Goto, S. (1991). Some tests of the distinction between private and collective self. *Journal of Personality and Social Psychology, 60,* 649–655.

Triandis, H. C. (1967). Toward an analysis of the components of interpersonal attitudes. In C. Sherif & M. Sherif (Eds.), *Attitudes, ego-involvement, and change* (pp. 227–270). New York: Wiley.

Triandis, H. C. (1972). *The analysis of subjective culture.* New York: Wiley.

Triandis, H. C. (1989). The self and social behaviour in differing cultural contexts. *Psychological Review, 96,* 506–520.

Triandis, H. C. (1990). Crosscultural studies of individualism and collectivism. In I. Berman (Ed.), *Nebraska Symposium on Motivation* (pp. 41–133). Lincoln, NE: University of Nebraska Press.

Triandis, H. C. (1994). *Culture and social behaviour.* New York: McGraw-Hill.

Triandis, H. C. (1995). *Individualism and collectivism.* Boulder, CO: Westview Press.

Triandis, H. C. (1996). The psychological measurement of cultural syndromes. *American Psychologist, 51*, 407–415.

Triandis, H. C., & Gelfand, M. (1998). Converging measurement of horizontal and vertical individualism and collectivism. *Journal of Personality and Social Psychology, 74*, 118–128.

Triandis, H. C., & Singelis, T. M. (1998). Training to recognize individual differences in collectivism and individualism within culture. *International Journal of Intercultural Relations, 22*, 35–48.

Triandis, H. C., Marin, G., Lisansky, J., & Betancourt, (1984). *Simpatia* as a cultural script of Hispanics. *Journal of Personality and Social Psychology, 47*, 1363–1374.

Yamaguchi, S. (1998, August). *The meaning of* amae. Paper presented at the Congress of the International Association of Cross-Cultural Psychology, Bellingham, WA.

Zwier, S. (1997). Patterns of language use in individualistic and collectivist cultures. Unpublished doctoral dissertation, Free University of Amsterdam, The Netherlands.

Concepts and Questions

1. Differentiate between message *content* and message *context*. How do different cultures react to content and context? How might cultural diversity in attending to content and context affect intercultural communication?
2. What does Triandis mean by cultural distance? How does language affect cultural distance?
3. What is Triandis referring to when he discusses different patterns of sampling information found in the environment? How might these differences affect intercultural communication between an individual from a collectivist culture and someone from an individualistic culture?
4. What differences may be found in the use of "I" and "you" in collectivistic and individualistic cultures?
5. What is cultural tightness? How might cultural diversity in tightness affect intercultural communication?
6. Differentiate between vertical and horizontal cultures.
7. How is culture relevant for understanding conflict?
8. Triandis holds that a very serious problem in communication is that people do not perceive the same "causes" of behavior. How does culture diversity affect the perception of causes?
9. How does culture affect interpersonal aggression? What cultures do you believe would be least prone to violence?
10. What are the characteristics of a collectivistic culture?

Our Locus in the Universe: Worldview and Intercultural Communication

SATOSHI ISHII

DONALD KLOPF

PEGGY COOKE

Worldview shapes cultures and serves to distinguish one culture from another. Its importance stems from the role it plays in defining reality or explaining the purpose of human life. Worldview, thus, represents one of the most fundamental qualities of culture impacting all aspects of how a culture perceives the environment. Nurius (1994) reflects that the propensity for individuals to establish and sustain an image of a comprehensive, orderly, and predictable world fulfills one of the most fundamental human needs. Pennington (1985) proclaims that worldview must be given high, if not first, priority in the study of culture because it permeates all other components of culture. She further suggests that by understanding a culture's worldview, it is possible to attain reasonable accuracy in predicting behaviors and motivations in other dimensions. As such, worldview becomes a critical element of successful intercultural communication.

The worldview concept deserves the comprehension of communication scholars, and in this paper we delineate its qualities, types, and religious perspectives.

WORLDVIEW DEFINED

Although the term "worldview" probably originated in German philosophy as *Weltanschauung*, literally

From the *Dokkyo International Review*, No. 12, (1999), 302–317. Reprinted by permission of the publisher. Satoshi Ishii teaches at Dokkyo University, Japan. Donald Klopf teaches at the University of Hawaii and West Virginia University. Peggy Cooke teaches at the University of Washington.

worldview, it has come to represent a variety of approaches to help understand the underpinnings of cultural diversity. It consists of the most general and comprehensive concepts and unstated assumptions about life.

Anthropologists Spradley and McCurdy (1980) define worldview as the way people characteristically look out on the universe. To communication educationalists Paige and Martin (1996), worldview is one of the lenses through which people view reality and the rest of the world. Sociologists Cosner, Nock, Steffan, and Rhea (1987) define it as a definition of reality. The psychologist Harriman (1947) relates worldview's association with *Weltanschauung* and considers it to be a total frame of reference.

Reflecting a religious perspective, Helve (1991) characterizes worldview as a systemized totality of beliefs about the world. In the same vein, Emerson (1996) conceives it as a set of assumptions about how the world is and ought to be organized. Nurius (1994), operating from a social work orientation, assumes a tack at odds with other worldview advocates. She uses the term *assumptive worlds* to describe clusters of fundamental assumptions that individuals hold about themselves and the world around them. And, in the simplest of terms, psychologist Furnham (1993) describes worldview as *Just World Beliefs*.

Samovar, Porter and Stefani (1998) offer a more inclusive view in their definition: "Worldview is culture's orientation toward God, humanity, nature, questions of existence, the universe and cosmos, life, death, sickness, and other philosophical issues that influence how its members see the world."

Klopf (1998) also offers an inclusive perspective that relates to many fields of study. He perceives worldview as providing a frame of reference for understanding a culture's ways of perceiving, thinking, and speaking, it being a system of beliefs about the nature of the universe and its effects on the environment. Worldview deals with a culture's orientation toward ontological matters such as God, humankind, lower forms of life, inanimate objects, supernatural beings, nature, and matters concerning the relations of humans to one another. Worldview thus serves to explain how and why things got to be the way they are and why they continue that way. It assists people during crises and helps them adjust to environmental conditions.

ELEMENTS OF WORLDVIEW

What constitutes worldview? The definitions given above included some of the elements. We add others beginning with an anthropological analysis extended by Redfield (1953). He argues that the framework is the same for every culture's interpretation of worldview. His system includes twelve general conceptions of these elements:

1. The self or principal actor on humankind's stage
2. The others, those within the purview of the self
3. Other people—the unidentifiable mass
4. Differences between men and women
5. Distinctions between "we" our own people and "they" other people
6. Distinctions between what is human and what is not
7. Invisible beings, forces, principles
8. Animals
9. Concepts of human nature
10. A spatial orientation
11. A temporal orientation
12. Ideas about birth and death

Pennington's (1985) conception of worldview elements appear in the form of ten questions. The salient characteristics of her list are:

1. The culture's dominant beliefs and attitudes about a human's place in nature and society
2. The general pattern of relationships between humans and nature
3. The relationship between humans and the culture's supreme being
4. The supreme being's power over life and events
5. Humans' competitive or cooperative nature
6. Humans' expressions of their beliefs
7. Humans' myths about the origins of people
8. Humans' beliefs in the supernatural
9. The living patterns as group practices
10. The ways a group uses rituals, prayers, and other ceremonies.

Psychologists Gilgen and Cho (1979) perceive worldview in an East-West dichotomy, the East based on religions associated with the Eastern world and the West with European and American thought. These are compared as follows:

EAST	WEST
Humans are one with nature and perceive the spiritual and physical as one.	Humans are separate from nature and overshadowed by a personal God.
Mind and body are one.	Humans consist of mind, body, and soul.
Humans should accept their basic oneness with nature rather than try to control it.	Humans have to manipulate and control nature to survive.
Humans are one with nature; they should feel comfortable with anyone.	Humans should reward actions competitive in spirit.
Science and technology creates an illusion of progress.	Science and technology provide the good life.
Enlightenment causes differences to disappear and brings oneness with the universe, coming about through meditation.	No such belief.

Dodd (1987) categorizes worldview elements into nine groupings—some of which tend to contrast the East and West.

Shame/Guilt. An Easterner bringing shame to a group is likely to be cast out of it. Westerners consider the individual more important than the group. Saving face is essential in the East; not so in the West.

Task/People. The East accentuates people relationships. The West stresses task accomplishment.

Secular/Spiritual. Eastern spiritual cultures rely on intuition and introspection. Secular Western cultures are analytical and logical.

Dead/Living. The East believes the dead can influence the living, bringing them luck or harm. The West is less prone to think that way.

Humans/Nature. Humans are either subject to nature, in harmony with nature, or should control nature. The East favors harmony; the West control.

Doing/Being. The East prefers harmonious relations, being rather than doing. The West wants to do things.

Linear/Cyclical. In the East life is birth, life, death, rebirth. In the West, birth, life, death.

Good/Evil. Humans are either good or evil, or a mix of good and evil.

Fatalism/Control. To the fatalist what happens is beyond a person's control, tending to be an Eastern view. In the control view, people are masters of their own destiny, tending to be a Western view.

FORMATION OF WORLDVIEWS

Worldview is implicit, implied but not verbally expressed. Helve (1991) believes it is improbable that people would be aware of their worldview. How it is formed, therefore, is a matter of speculation.

Worldview evidently develops in early childhood. Helve determined through empirical research that its actual growth can be comprehended by applying one or all of the theories identified as *cognitive development*, *social learning*, or *socialization*. She concluded each extended a sensible explanation.

Rubin and Peplau (1975) credit the child's parents, religious instruction, and instruction in the schools attended as contributors. Each child's maturation, their experiences in the physical environment, and their activities in the social environment contribute to worldview's formation. Then, too, children draw conclusions from their own experiences about what the world is like. Each child is a product of a social community, and the child's way of seeing the world is shaped by shared images and constructions of the child's social group or class.

Children and young people conceptualize the world in various ways at different stages in their growth according to their own mental development. Infancy, childhood, and adolescence involve distinct stages in thinking and learning. The shaping of their needs, values, beliefs, and attitudes vary from stage to stage and so too will their worldview undergo change as they mature.

Emerson (1996) places stress on religion in developing worldview. By outlining what ought to be and by creating and reinforcing group norms through interaction, religion has a substantial influence on a person's worldview. Religion shapes reasoning. It also provides the meaning, importance, and properness of different social arrangements and institutions. Religion infuses all of these with universal if not transcendent significance.

Religious beliefs and practices differ, of course, and that is why, Emerson contends, people possess different worldviews. Those with conservative worldviews base their moral authority in the transcendent. Those holding more liberal views participate in the religious and secular cultures that root moral authority in humans. They stress reason and revelation.

Even though Emerson emphasizes religion's role in worldview development, he recognizes a person's position in the social structure as significant even though he perceives it as only secondary. Reasonable people who live in dissimilar parts of the world are exposed to unlike realities. This dissimilar exposure leads each to arrive at separate worldviews.

Emerson's point is substantiated by Cooke (1992) who measured worldview among university students in Japan, Korea, Puerto Rico, and the United States. Her findings reveal significant differences between the four groups. Each group arrived at different conceptions of the worldview.

Chamberlain and Zika (1992) attribute the meaning of worldview to numerous sources, religion being just one. They feel worldview stems from a variety of sources and that it is inappropriate to constrain it to a purely religious dimension.

TYPES OF WORLDVIEW

Helve (1991) classifies worldview into three types. In doing so, she appears to endorse the Chamberlain and Zika position. Helve's types are *scientific*, *metaphysical*, and *religious*.

The *scientific* worldview is based on the rules laid down by the exact sciences. It is open and self-correcting in accordance with new systematic and methodical findings. Helve found it to appear most clearly among scientific scholars. A quasi-scientific worldview results from television, magazine, and newspaper influences, she notes, and it is more "information based" as a worldview than scientific. Those with a scientific bent do not harbor this quasi-scientific worldview.

A *metaphysical* worldview tends to be based on abstract general reasoning without an empirical base. For example, the metaphysical worldview of young children may contain beliefs in imaginary beings like Santa Claus, ghosts, witches, fairies, and elves. Older children may include elements of magic and superstition. Teenagers might construct their worldviews around horoscopes and act in accordance with the advice they give. The metaphysical worldview is apt to consist of certain types of unnatural beings, their characteristics, and their relationships. These beings originate partly in the traditions of religion and partially in folklore, some of which is created by the mass media.

The third type of worldview is *religious*. For most people, religion serves as the foundation of their worldview. The content of their beliefs will vary from person to person depending upon their religious perspective. A Catholic's worldview undoubtedly will differ from that of a Jew, a Protestant's from a Buddhist, a Muslim's from a Taoist, and a Shintoist's from a Confucianist.

THE RELIGIOUS PERSPECTIVE

Religion, as we have related, is a deep and pervasive determinant of worldview. Even the most secular of people feel religion's influence. Those who reject religious faith still follow much of the religious heritage that influences their culture. Most people, theists and atheists alike, adhere to the commandment, "Thou shalt not kill"—a tenet virtually all cultures respect.

Dimensions of Religion

Religion, Emerson (1996) attests, is multidimensional. He conceptualizes it along two dimensions, religiosity and orthodoxy, each with two subdivisions, public and private. Religiosity refers to the intensity and consistency of religious practices. Orthodoxy is the degree to which one's beliefs center on a guiding authority, for example, the Scriptures of the Church.

Private religiosity is one's own personal, undisclosed religious practice. Examples include the frequency of prayer and holy script reading as well as a doubt-free faith. Public religiosity describes the religious activities practiced with other people. It is manifest in frequent church attendance and participation in membership functions.

Private orthodoxy refers to held beliefs that rely on a transcendent authority, a god, or a supernatural being. Heavy reliance on holy scripture while verbalizing and making decisions is an example. Public orthodoxy is the sharing of beliefs in the company of others.

EASTERN AND WESTERN RELIGIONS

As a more manageable way of thinking about the world's diverse faiths, Smart (1988) groups them into two major divisions: Eastern and Western. Each can help increase an understanding of the impact religion has on the content and development of one's worldview. Eastern and Western religious traditions account for about ninety percent of the world's population. The remaining ten percent consists of Shamanists, Animists, Atheists, and the like.

Religious Similarities

Although the two divisions have few common teachings, they do possess similarities typical of all religions. Samovar, Porter, and Stefani (1998) identify five such similarities: the most important being *sacred writings*. All of the world's major religions have writings revered by believers. These writings are the vehicles for dissemination of the religion's knowledge and wisdom. Included are the Bible, the written centerpiece for the Christian religion; the Hebrew Bible or Old Testament, the sacred book of the Jews; the Koran, the Muslim writings; the Vedas, the sacred writings of the Hindus; and the Pali Canon, where the teachings of the Buddha are inscribed.

A similarity is an *authority figure*. God, Allah, Jesus the Son of God, or the Buddha is an authority figure who is someone greater than the religion's members, one they turn to for guidance.

Rituals are the third similarity. They are practices required of the membership or acts that are forbidden to the members. For example, believers must be baptized or circumcised. They must fast on certain days or pray at special times. They may not eat pork or perhaps beef. These acts embody humility, restraint, and awareness, behaviors of great significance.

Speculation typifies all religions. Humans seek answers to life's mysteries—what is life, death, suffering, origins of the universe—and religions supply answers, speculative at best.

Religion also includes an *ethic*, a set of moral principles for the membership to observe. For most religions, the set contains items such as marital fidelity, paying honor to mother and father, prohibiting killing, stealing, lying.

Eastern

The countries of Eastern and Southern Asia (Korea, China, Japan, India, and others) embrace religious traditions that feature harmony as the ultimate good (Smart, 1988). Harmony is the major tenet found in Hinduism, Shintoism, Buddhism, Confucianism, and Taoism.

Although these religions differ considerably, their foundations are similar. Deity is in every place in every form, rather than a single place or form. Harmony impacts behavior because everything is benign, nothing is worth worrying about. True believers respond to crucial issues with a smile. Being pleasant helps keep things in perspective because nothing is going to mean much in the long run anyway.

Ethically, Eastern religions do not hold with an absolute right. Everything is relative to the situation. Then, too, life is circular. One's essence takes another form at death, termed *reincarnation*. This goes on and on without end. What is desirable is in every thing in the world, not just in special places or acts called sacred. What is important is the here and now.

In Figure 1, Ishii (1990) characterizes Eastern and Western worldviews. The polytheistic represents the East and the monotheistic the West. In the polytheistic view, the gods/goddesses/deities, human beings, and natural beings are all relative to each other. They are changeable, not absolute or rigid. Deities can reside anywhere, in rocks, animals, and humans. In the figure the triangular relationship of the three entities symbolizes this relative relationship. No hierarchy is present between the three. Their domains are relative and flexible as implied by the broken ovals connected by lines within the world/universe circle.

Figure 1 *Contrastive Worldviews (Ishii, 1990).*

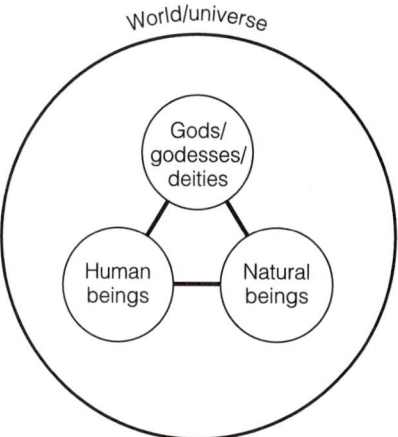

Model of polytheistic worldview

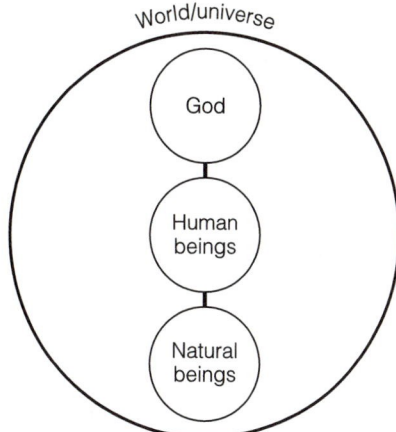

Model of monotheistic worldview

Western

The West's capsulation of religion and hence worldview is in sharp contrast to the Eastern. The Western religions perceive the ultimate good as transformation. Members of the Jewish, Islamic, and Christian faiths believe that divine grace is the desired end, whether in this life or the next.

Differences among these religions are obvious, yet they have a common foundation. They are monotheistic, believing in one God who is "out there" and everything else is here, with a great gulf in between. The world is split in two—the way it was intended to be versus the way it is. There is the good and desirable and there is sin.

In the Western religions, Smart (1988) informs us, everything is headed somewhere, to the Kingdom of God or to heaven, to an end. At the end of an individual's life will be an accounting or payoff, either life or death or resurrection of the body. At the end of all human life will be an apocalypse, a disclosure.

The things that belong to God and religion are sacred. They are special, to be treated with awe and reverence. What is important is felicity—happiness or bliss—beyond this earthly life.

In Figure 1, the monotheistic worldview depicts the existence of one almighty God who ranks first above all else. Human beings rank next in the hier-archy and natural beings last. These rankings are absolute and unchangeable as shown by the solid ovals vertically aligned within the world/universe circle. The domains of the three are not related one to the other.

COLLIDING WORLDVIEWS

Figure 1 also reveals two distinct worldviews, ones clearly at odds with each other. The separation is immortalized in the words of Rudyard Kipling: "Oh, East is East, and West is West, and never the twain shall meet." The two are so unlike they will never be capable of sharing their ideas and feelings about anything. Nevertheless, Kipling's next lines in his *Ballad of East and West* extend hope. He thinks that strong men and women when standing face to face regardless of their breed, birth, or border can in-teract successfully. Whether one's view is Eastern or Western, Kipling holds out hope for satisfying verbalizing.

Unfortunately, fruitful intercultural relations are not always the norm even when strong men and women meet together. Too often imbroglios like Captain Cook's Hawaiian adventure bring out the worst in people. Misunderstandings and occasional serious consequences result.

No less contentious are the frequent encounters between developers and environmentalists, those who want to conquer and direct the forces of nature and those who maintain humans are subject to nature. Those conflicts are being fought at every level, local, national, and international.

Clark (1998) warns us that environmental destruction is accelerating, not decelerating. At the local level the loss of forests, soil erosion, and overdrafts of ground water are common occurrences. Increased yields of timber and food crops are unsustainable. People worldwide are mining nature's resource base. Human-induced global warming, overgrazing, and deforestation are compounding droughts. Pollution problems are multiplying as waters are poisoned or salinated, as forests and lakes are decimated by acid rain, and as cities worldwide suffer from foul air.

Recall that Dodd (1987) reminded us about our relationship with nature. Either we are subject to nature, in harmony with it, or should control it. Today's state suggests harmony is absent, control is not working, and soon we will be subject to total natural disaster. Worldviews are colliding as we communicate closer and closer with our fellow humans throughout the world.

Clark (1989) points a finger at the Western worldview, placing blame for environmental conditions directly on the West. Although major polluters, soil eroders, and deforesters are prevalent in the East as well, Clark believes it is the Western worldview that is destroying the environment. She suggests that the Western worldview lacks proper values and goals and has grown obsolete. All worldviews, she claims, require adjustment if humans are to survive. But the most in need of redoing is that of the West whose enormous military, technological, and economic power impinges upon the entire globe.

UNTYING THE GORDIAN KNOT

In her book, *Ariadne's Thread: The Search for New Modes of Thinking* (1989), Clark gives us a thread with which we might find our way out of the labyrinth created by colliding worldviews. Her way may help untie the Gordian knot in which disparate worldviews are enmeshed as they attempt to exist together in the 21st century.

In ages past, she argues, worldviews evolved gradually, often imperceptibly. With today's enormous powers unleashed by science and technology from the Western worldview creating excessive environmental change, humankind can no longer rely on the old, indiscernible thinking. Human goals need to be reordered.

All worldviews require some degree of adjustment if the species is to survive. Tracing the beliefs and assumptions underlying them is the first step in making social change possible. This first step is one students of communication can undertake learning to understand the differences in worldview globally, and to comprehend the beliefs and assumptions on which they are based.

Clark cautions that imposing a new worldview certainly will fail unless it comes from within the cultural context. A culture's people must actively participate in the change making. For a new worldview to evolve everyone must participate in the change process.

In her 1998 *Zygon* article, Clark expounds on her new worldview in detail. Her plan may be far too esoteric for students in intercultural courses to consider. They can exit their courses with the rudiments of the worldview concept. If they do, as Pennington (1985) believes, reasonable preciseness can be reached in predicting behaviors and motivations in the social, economic, and political lives of the globe's cultures. As Smart (1988) prompts us, we ignore at our peril the worldview dimensions of our interactions with other cultures.

References

Calhoun, L. G., & Cann, A. (1994). Differences in assumptions about a just world: Ethnicity and point of view. *The Journal of Social Psychology, 131,* 765–770.

Chamberlain, K., & Zika, S. (1992). Religiosity, meaning in life, and psychological well being. In J. F. Schumacher (Ed.). *Religion and mental health.* New York: Oxford University Press.

Clark, M. E. (1989). *Ariadne's thread: The search for new modes of thinking.* New York: St. Martin's Press.

Clark, M. E. (1998). Human nature: What we need to know about ourselves in the twenty first century. *Zygon, 333,* 645–659.

Cooke, P. (1992). *The relationship between culture and worldview: A cross cultural comparison of Japan, Korea, Puerto Rico, and the United States.* Unpublished master's thesis, West Virginia University, Morgantown, VA.

Cosner, L., Nock, S., Steffan, P., & Rhea, B. (1987). *Introduction to sociology,* 2d ed. San Diego, CA: Harcourt Brace.

Dodd, C. H. (1987). *Dynamics of intercultural communication,* 2d ed., Dubuque, IA: W. C. Brown.

Dunbar, E. (1996). Sociocultural and contextual challenges of organizational life in Eastern Europe: Implications for cross cultural training and development. In D. Landis & R. S. Bhagat (Eds.), *Handbook of intercultural training,* 2d ed. Thousand Oaks, CA: Sage.

Emerson, M. O. (1996). Through tinted glasses: Religion, worldviews, and abortion attitudes. *Journal for the Scientific Study of Religion, 35,* 41–55.

Furnham, A. (1993). Just world beliefs in twelve societies. *The Journal of Social Psychology, 133,* 317–329.

Gilgen, A., & Cho, J. (1979). Questionnaire to measure Eastern and Western thought. *Psychological Reports, 44.*

Harriman, P. L. (1947). *The new dictionary of Psychology.* New York: Philosophical Library.

Helve, H. (1991). The formation of religious attitudes and worldviews: A longitudinal study of young Finns. *Social Compass, 38,* 373–392.

Ishii, S., Okabe, R., Kume, T., & Hirai, K. (1990). *Ibunks komyunikeshon kiwado.* Tokyo: Yuhikaku.

Jandt, F. E. (1995). *Intercultural communication: An Introduction.* Thousand Oaks, CA: Sage.

Klopf, D. W . (1998). *Intercultural encounters: The fundamentals of intercultural communication.* Englewood, NJ: Morton.

Nurius, P. S. (1994). Assumptive worlds, self-definition, and striving among women. *Basic and Applied Social Psychology, 15,* 311–327.

Paige, R. M., & Martin, J. N. (1996). Ethics in intercultural training. In D. Landis & R. S. Bhagat (Eds.), *Handbook of intercultural training,* 2d ed. Thousand Oaks, CA: Sage.

Pennington, U. L. (1985). Intercultural communication. In L. Samovar & R. E. Porter (Eds.), *Intercultural communication: A Reader,* 4th ed. Belmont, CA: Wadsworth.

Redfield, R. (1953). *The primitive world and its transformation.* Ithaca, NY: Cornell University Press.

Rubin, Z., & Peplau, L. A. (1975). Who believes in a just world? *Journal of Social Issues, 31,* 65–89.

Samovar, L., Porter, R. E., & Stefani, L. A. (1998). *Communication between cultures.* Belmont, CA: Wadsworth.

Smart, R. (1988). Religion-caused complications in intercultural communication. In L. Samovar & R. E. Porter (Eds.), *Intercultural communication: A reader,* 5th ed. Belmont, CA: Wadsworth.

Spradley, J. P., & McCurdy, U. W. (1980). *Anthropology: The cultural perspective,* 2d ed. Prospect Heights, IL: Waveland.

Concepts and Questions

1. Ishii, Klopf, and Cooke assert that worldview shapes culture. How does your worldview contribute to your culture?

2. What is the most significant aspect of worldview? How does cultural diversity in this dynamic lead to differing worldviews?

3. Specify in general terms how worldview differs between Eastern and Western cultures.

4. How does Shame/Guilt affect worldview? In which cultures might this factor be most prevalent?

5. How is worldview formed? Are there cultural differences in the mechanisms by which worldview is formed?

6. What is a scientific worldview? What various cultures are most likely to have a scientific-based worldview?

7. What does a metaphysical view tend to contribute to a worldview?

8. What is religiosity? How does it contribute to shaping a worldview?

9. Differentiate between Eastern and Western religious perspectives regarding ethics.

Five Paradigms of Ethnic Relations

ROD JANZEN

A major focus of contemporary American education is the nature and character of interethnic relationships. This is evident whether the analysis and debate is about global issues, the domestic multicultural agenda, or social issues in general. The views expressed in the debate reflect a diverse set of ideological assumptions, though these are often concealed rather than explicit.

The present study is based on an intensive review of the literature pertaining to interethnic relationships, as well as the author's attendance at numerous interpretive presentations on diverse forms of "multiculturalism." From this review, I have identified five different perspectives, or paradigms, on the basis of which Americans in general define ethnic relations.

Our view of different ethnic and cultural groups is conditioned by the paradigms that guide our understanding of and vision for interethnic relationships. This is the case whether one is an administrator, teacher, student, or member of the community. Educators, in particular, need to come to terms with the diversity of interethnic paradigmatic understanding. While this paper does not offer specific solutions to our national multicultural dilemma, it will hopefully help clarify some of the reasons why solutions to our problems do not come easily in this complicated time.

The first paradigm is *Traditional Eurocentric Racism*. In this vision, America is defined as predominantly northern and western European in its culture and institutions, with a dominant Anglo-Saxon and Protestant foundation. In this vision, which reflects the actual development of American history, other "white" Europeans are always at some point (usually within the second generation) pulled into the northern European center (Novak 1971, 114).

From *Social Education*, 1994, Volume 58, Number 6, pp. 349–353. Reprinted by permission of the National Council for the Social Sciences. Rod Janzen teaches at Fresno Pacific College, Fresno, California.

Irish immigrants, for example, initially experienced extensive discrimination due to their ethnic uniqueness and their adherence to Catholicism. Immigrants from southern Europe experienced similar bias. Because of their later date of mass immigration, they also had to deal with discrimination related to job competition with "real" Americans. The fact that many eastern Europeans were adherents of Orthodox Christianity (a tradition with which most Americans were not familiar) further complicated matters. Still, American citizens in general wanted Irish and southern and eastern European immigrants, now that they were here, to become "like" them, i.e., to become northern and western European in customs and beliefs. If one could assist in "Protestantizing" Catholic ecclesiastical and theological traditions along the way, so much the better.

Paradigm I thus describes a way of thinking and acting which brought all "white" Americans into the national fold, with one exception. Traditional Eurocentric racism never fully accepted the Jewish people because of their non-Christian religious commitment, even though Jews tended to adhere, for the most part, to northern and western European cultural traditions (Takaki 1993, 298). Jews thus found themselves occupying a quasi-purgatorial niche in American society.

According to the Paradigm I way of thinking and acting, non-Europeans were never fully accepted as "Americans." Blacks, American Indians, Asians, and Mexicans, for example, were all considered inferior peoples, culturally and intellectually. The Irish, southern Europeans, and (to a lesser extent) Jews could at some point be recognized as "real" Americans as they were assimilated (with certain stereotypical perceptions still held and acted upon), but persons in the non-European groups were never fully accepted, due to an ethnocentric bias against the cultures from which they claimed descent. Citizens of the United States wanted members of inferior ethnic groups to become "like" them with regard to customs practiced, dress, religion, and attitude toward work (though the work of the inferior peoples might be supervised by European-Americans); but they were not regarded as equals.

Paradigm I thus describes the historical American approach to latter-day non-Anglo-Saxon immigrants. This was also the approach applied to America's indigenous peoples. It established a vision still held, in different forms, by many American citizens today who fear and do not want an America which might become darker physically, less Christian religiously, and less European with regard to its understanding of the best way to design social-political institutions. Even in the field of education, there are many who hold certain Paradigm I principles, even though they do not put their thoughts in print.

Paradigm II, *Melting Pot Assimilations*, offers a different point of view, and an alternative interpretation of American history. In the melting pot vision, various cultural groups from all over the world, whether they originate in Europe, Asia, the United States itself, the Middle East, Africa, or South America, are treated with essential equality in the United States. In their constant interaction—one culture crossing over into another—they begin at some point to join together to create one large heterogeneous mixture (Zangwill 1909, 37, 199).

Like the tiger who runs around a tree and turns into a stack of pancakes in the well-known folk tale, the various immigrant groups rotate ever more rapidly around whatever the central but constantly fluctuating definition of America has become. In the end, the United States itself is explained as a complete mixing together of various cultural traditions with regard to language, customs, religion, economic system, and political system.

With regard to language, for example, all immigrant groups eventually accept an Americanized form of English as a common tongue. Simultaneously, capitalism is accepted as the best economic system. Even though not all Americans belong to the same religious denomination, there is general acceptance of comparable moral principles and values. The Old Testament's Ten Commandments, for example, are valued in the Christian, Jewish, and Muslim traditions.

Through the relationship with other melting pot citizens, one ceases at some point to perceive oneself in any terms other than "American." Individual ties to ethnic groups culturally rooted in other parts of the world are not considered important or relevant. These connections in fact are seen as representing potentially disruptive forces which can give the melting pot too many distinctive and distracting ingredients, leaving citizens the sense that there is no melted-together foundational understanding of what it means to be an American. Individual immigrants are expected to discard connections to ancestral homes. Further, by marrying across ethnic boundaries in the North American "new world," they assist in the creation of a new world people, the "American people."

Paradigm II suggests that most immigrants in the past jumped into the pot voluntarily and with great enthusiasm (Fitzgerald 1980, 82), ridding themselves of many remnants of past existence. As the newly arrived cultures of the world melted into the pot, they did, of course, bring cultural traditions along with them. These customs, in various manifestations, continued to inform the debate with regard to what made someone an "American." Since everybody was equal before the law, the new immigrants could feel that they had as much ethnically based influence on what defined America as anyone who had melted into the pot at some earlier time.

Paradigm II is a description and vision for America still held by many. Indeed, a number of educators lament the fact that this model is no longer as widely accepted in the late 20th century. The melting pot paradigm does not, however, provide an accurate account of what actually transpired in American history. That story is perhaps more adequately portrayed in Paradigm I, particularly into the 1940s.

Paradigm II suggests, in a visionary sense, the melting away of all original ethnic cultures and traditions. The best part of each theoretically becomes part of what makes America a unique and great interethnic experiment. Constant interaction theoretically stirs the multicultural stew together, and a gloriously harmonious unification is the end result of such mixing.

In fact, however, most new immigrants to America found themselves pressured by the power of the institutionalized public school system and generally accepted American cultural principles to give up most ethnic traditions, unless these happened to be Anglo-Saxon Protestant in nature, and to melt into an essentially northern and western European cultural pot. Instead of melting equitably into the American soup, immigrants had first to shed essential aspects of traditional cultural belief and practice (Alba 1981, 91).

In the end, most non-Anglo-Saxon ethnic traditions were lost, with the exception of such customs as the placing of Christmas trees in American homes during the month of December and (more recently, in California) the production of tamales during that same time of year. The fact that America's large population of ethnic Germans has had so little impact on the predominant culture in the United States is perhaps the best example of the way in which the melting pot process has actually functioned. During World War I, many states even outlawed the use of German in church services (Teichroeb 1979, 96).

Paradigm II thus denotes a melting pot which in actual fact "melted away" non-Anglo-Saxon traditions. Yet this paradigm has become an integral part of mainstream American thought. It is a worldview which has been taught and promoted in American public schools both as ideal and fact, and one which has been accepted by the media in general through much of the 20th century. A large number of Americans thus still believe strongly that this is the most accurate description of historical American interethnic relationships.

Both Paradigms I and II promote philosophies which are essentially assimilationist in nature. Each paradigmatic understanding assumes a common set of cultural standards which new immigrants must accept either voluntarily or by compulsion.

Many melting pot theorists today, however, call themselves "multiculturalists." They believe in the vision of a melting pot which encourages new immigrants to add to the ever-changing, melted-together, contents of the pot significant (not superficial) aspects of their traditional ethnic cultures, even as those persons are themselves transformed into ethnic "Americans" (Glazer 1991, 18).

Generally speaking, Paradigms III, IV, and V are most often used to define the multicultural way of thinking. With these paradigms we move directly into the waters of pluralism, with its emphasis on the retention and maintenance of traditional cultural beliefs and practices. There is a significant difference of opinion, however, even among advocates of pluralism, with regard to how it should be interpreted.

Paradigm III, *Ethnic Nationalism*, for example, suggests that each ethnic group, regardless of origin, should preserve its unique character, customs, languages, and ways of knowing without being assimilated. In this vision, the ethnic community is the principal source of one's personal and group identity.

America itself is held together, in this model, by a collective commitment to democratic institutions and practices and by the English language, which each cultural group teaches alongside other ethnic languages. Ethnic nationalism assumes the establishment of certain relationships across cultural boundaries. It expects, however, that most immigrants and Americans who have retained strong ethnic identities will focus their attention on their own cultural groups, the source of the ethnic nationalist's primary identity (Barrera 1988, 42).

Exponents of the ethnic nationalist vision often identify their ideas with the cultural mosaic concept promoted by the Canadian government. That vision was founded historically on the basis of a bicultural, French/English confrontation. Rather than being purely "multi-cultural" in nature, primary institutional support was traditionally given to two identifiable language groups (Lipset 1990, 179). Since 1971, however, the Canadian Government through its Cabinet-level Ministry of Multiculturalism and Citizenship, has encouraged every ethnic group living in Canada to retain ideological and behavioral uniqueness via substantial government-funded programs (McConaghy 1993, 190).

Pluralists who support ethnic nationalism seek to preserve special cultural and linguistic understandings and customs which have generally diminished in cosmopolitan settings. Ethnic nationalists thus emphasize the importance of retaining, in some measure, closed ethnic enclaves within American society at large. They remind us that it is not possible to express certain beliefs and feelings outside the boundaries of specific psycho-cultural-linguistic traditions. The center, in the ethnic nationalist vision is, therefore, a weak one.

Much of the Afrocentric curriculum movement fits this particular paradigm, though when it places additional emphasis on viewing the world through the lens of a myriad of cultural perspectives it might also find itself positioned within the parameters of Paradigm IV and V definitions (Hilliard 1992, 13). Persons who suggest the viability of creating semi-independent ethnic republics within the United States follow this model most closely (Barrera 1988, 160).

It is important to note that the Paradigm III model assumes that each national grouping contains within itself a multiplicity of ethnicities. Within the Laotian group, for example, the Hmong represent a unique group of people (traditionally semi-nomadic and illiterate). Ethnic nationalism thus has major implications for schooling if educators seek to meet the psychological needs, ways of knowing, and cultural expectancies of different native groups.

Paradigm IV, *Globalism*, provides a different pluralist twist by suggesting that the increasing economic, ecological, and political interconnectedness of modern life demands that we reach consensus on an international ideological and behavioral center which then forms the foundation for all world cultures, rather than thinking only in terms of what might hold Americans together (Paradigms I, II, and V) or with regard to those customs which provide communally separated cultural uniqueness (Paradigm III).

In this *Star Trek* vision, a Planet Earth melting pot is formed on the basis of continuous discussion concerning that which is common in the experience of all ethnic cultures, including common elements in the beliefs and practices of the various global religions (Fersh 1989, 17). In this model, one's own cultural identity is not of primary importance, except insofar as it provides input into the establishment of the new world order's central principles.

There is a continuous search for the center in the globalist vision, via unending discussion with regard to commonly accepted principles. The center itself draws upon the experiential and intellectual traditions of all world cultures. Global awareness, in this vision, may be promoted for social, economic, religious, or other reasons, but a central raison d'être is the importance of working together peaceably as world citizens.

While the global ideological center is being sought, that which separates and distinguishes each nationality is not simply overlooked. Through the process of constant interethnic discussion, each ethnic group is given influential power with regard to the creation of the new earth culture. In order for this culture to be equitably based, in view of the world's political, economic, and demographic contexts, a tremendous amount of negotiation and discussion is demanded. One global model sometimes referred to is the United Nations, which is organized and functions in such a way that the rights of those nations which are not as strong militarily, economically, or demographically are still theoretically protected.

Paradigm IV appeals to those pluralists who fear the possibility of the interethnic conflict which has sometimes accompanied ethnic nationalist emphases—in Yugoslavia or the former Soviet Union, for example—though supporters of Paradigm III counter that the underlying reason for conflict in those regions is indeed the historical attempt by some ethnic groups to destroy the cultural vitality of neighboring ethnic groups.

Ironically, if the global vision were actuated in the way its proponents seem to desire, it might ultimately establish a culture very similar to what some melting pot enthusiasts, in a more specifically nationalistic way, appear to envision for their ideological and interpretive position based on Paradigm II. The entire world, however, would now find itself melted together.

If there were, for example, nearly complete global interethnic fusion, brought about in part by increased personal relationships, leading to cross-ethnic marriage en masse worldwide, it might be difficult eventually to distinguish one ethnic tradition from another. People might then rather define themselves in terms of highly idiosyncratic interests, behaviors, and beliefs. (This is what the melting pot model envisions on a national scale.) For this to happen, however, global citizens would have to begin thinking transformatively in terms of internationally recognized principles and be open to almost continuous change, over a long period of time, with regard to the agreed-upon nature of those axioms.

Paradigm V, *Centered Pluralism*, is a more conservative and pragmatic approach to pluralistic multiculturalism than that suggested by either ethnic nationalist or global paradigms. An underlying assumption of centered pluralism, for example, is that America needs to continue to hold itself together as a vital national system, and that this will not happen, politically or socially, unless certain established central traditions are adhered to by most citizens (Banks 1992, 32).

Centered pluralists, like ethnic nationalists, therefore insist that all Americans speak a common language (English) though they simultaneously encourage both the retention of first languages (where this is relevant) and the learning of additional official languages. Centered pluralists are also committed to democratic institutions though these are not defined from an exclusively Anglo-Saxon constitutional perspective.

In both of these emphases, centered pluralism is much more prescriptive in nature than globalism. Paradigm V also goes much further than ethnic nationalism in its general support for a commonly accepted and centrally established knowledge base. It suggests, for example, that all Americans have a common literacy foundation. This literacy base is expected to be a multicultural one, so that not all books read and studied are those written by Europeans and European-Americans, with those particular ethnic interpretations (as different as they might be). Still there are common intellectual threads, primary readings, and conventional subjects which hold Americans to similar standards of interpretation.

This paradigm also supports a national commitment to communal as well as individual socioeconomic traditions, a mixture of capitalism and socialism. Centered pluralism even allows for the possibility that democracy itself might be understood differently—and perhaps in more helpful ways—in other cultural traditions. The two-party political system and representative republicanism might therefore be reviewed with regard to operational effectiveness in the modern American context. Centered pluralism assumes, however, an underlying commitment to the kind of general principles enunciated in the United States Constitution's Bill of Rights (Haynes and Kniker 1990, 306).

Centered pluralism thus establishes a commitment to many traditional "American" beliefs and practices. At the same time, this paradigm assumes the integrity of indigenous cultural identities. A central set of beliefs and practices, previously established, undergoes continuous gradual metamorphosis through constant, desired reflective interaction between various ethnic groups and their respective traditions. In this process all ethnic communities have some impact on the slowly changing character of the American "center." Centered pluralism assumes nearly complete ethnic equality and cultural acceptance. It represents a practical response to assimilationist critics of Paradigm III who attack

ethnic nationalist multiculturalism for perceived divisive tendencies.

Interestingly enough, centered pluralism, in many ways, correlates to a paradigm hinted at by Milton Gordon in the mid-1960s (in his book, *Assimilation in American Society*). It is a vision, which, if Gordon was correct in his analysis, ultimately and paradoxically establishes a melting pot. Unlike that actuated historically, this melting pot provides full cultural equality (Gordon 1964, 158).

In this way the eventual outcome of a commitment to centered pluralism appears to be similar in nature to that predicted by melting pot multiculturalists, even as the latter do not place much emphasis on retention and maintenance of ethnic uniqueness. If, for example, all cultures are treated equally, one would expect that through direct association and intermarriage most ethnic groups would eventually melt away into one new American culture, still predominantly Anglo-Saxon in its foundation but with Arab-American, African-American, Asian-American, Pacific Islander–American, and Latin-American nuances.

Centered pluralism differs from melting pot assimilationism, however, in its willingness to support affirmative action to assist in leveling out the playing field for those ethnic groups which have experienced substantial discrimination and prejudice based on their association with certain ethnic traditions in the past. In theory, most of these are people other than non-northern, non-western Europeans; in practice, most of them are non-Europeans. Centered pluralists recognize a need to eradicate ethnocentric concepts already embedded in the American psyche and social order. Paradigm V thus envisions a melting pot which incorporates much greater ethnic diversity than that anticipated by melting pot multiculturalists.

Unlike the vision presented in the globalist Paradigm IV, centered pluralism is not international in character. Though centered pluralists speak in terms of internationalization of the curriculum, for example, their primary focus is on the United States of America.

The fact that Americans tend to view interethnic relationships from the perspective of these paradigms, and that there are divergences even among those who call themselves "pluralists," makes for a

Table 1 *Interethnic Relationships*

Categories	Paradigm 1	Paradigm 2	Paradigm 3	Paradigm 4	Paradigm 5
Language	English	English	English/multi-lingualism	English/multi-lingualism	English/multi-lingualism
Religion	Christian (Protestant)	Christian	Multireligious	Beliefs common to world religions	Multireligious
Culture	European (NW European Anglo-Saxon dominant)	European	Multicultural	World culture	Multicultural American
Race	Caucasian	Caucasian	Mixed/separate ethnic groups	Mixed	Mixed
Political	European constitutional democracy (NW European Anglo-Saxon dominant)	Constitutional democracy	Democracy responsive to ethnic needs	World democracy	Constitutional democracy

very confusing situation for educators. Educators are not only asked to "multiculturalize" the curriculum but to decide, in effect, which of at least four paradigmatic understandings best describes their personal perception of multiculturalism, which then may differ from that proposed by other educators and academia. All of the paradigms discussed in this article, for example, have supporters in the public school system. Teachers are required to attend inservice workshops and often volunteer to enroll in classes which certainly expose them to some form of "multiculturalism," but which may be suggesting any one of four very different versions of that concept.

It is important to note that this article's thesis that there are five general ethnic relations paradigms does not suggest that all multiculturalists abide by these theoretical paradigms in any pure sense. They may, in fact, operate out of the perspective of one or more of these models, some rationally and with purpose, others chaotically and illogically.

In addition, teachers and educators must deal with a general public whose opinions, according to polls, are much more weighted toward assimilationist models (Paradigms I and II). It is perhaps most confusing that supporters of four of the paradigms (II through V) have representative leaders who all refer to themselves as "multiculturalists," and who all employ the same term, from Nathan Glazer to James Banks to Mario Barrera. So the following

question continually arises, "Who are the real multiculturalists?" and we see constant struggle, attack, and counterattack between advocates of the various paradigmatic approaches.

It is the hope of this writer that a paradigmatic understanding of why we have reached this point of multicultural confusion will be useful in helping us to comprehend why we are doing what we are doing. Further, it will push members of the educational audience, as they listen to presentations on multiculturalism, as they read articles and curriculum documents which describe the multiculturalist vision, to be more demanding with regard to what particular philosophical position is being encouraged by presenters and writers. It is always important to know the assumptions, values, and goals of one's mentors. With this knowledge, the debate will continue with the reflective educator much more knowledgeable of the deep complexity of this issue.

References

Alba, R. D. (1981). The twilight of ethnicity among American Catholics of European ancestry. *Annals, 45,* 86–97.

Banks, J. (1992). Multicultural education: For freedom's sake. *Educational Leadership, 49,* 32–36.

Barrera, M. (1988). *Beyond Aztlan.* Notre Dame: University of Notre Dame Press.

Fersh, S. (Ed.). (1989). *Learning About Peoples and Cultures*. Evanston, IL: McDougal, Littel.

Fitzgerald, F. (1980). *America Revised*. New York: Vintage Press.

Glazer, N. (1991). In defense of multiculturalism. *New Republic, 205*, 18–22.

Gordon, M. (1964). *Assimilation in American Life*. New York: Oxford University Press.

Haynes, C. C., & Kniker, C. R. (1990). Religion in the classroom. *Social Education, 54*, 305, 306.

Hilliard, A. G. (1992). Why we must pluralize the curriculum. *Educational Leadership, 49*, 12–15.

Lipset, S. (1990). *Continental Divide*. New York: Routledge.

McConaghy, T. (1993). Ontario to implement antiracist policies. *Phi Delta Kappan, 75*, 190, 191.

Novak, M. (1971). *The Rise of Unmeltable Ethnics*. New York: Macmillan.

Takaki, R. (1993). *A Different Mirror*. Boston: Little, Brown.

Teichroeb, A. (Ed.). (1979). Military surveillance of Mennonites in World War I. *Mennonite Quarterly Review, 53*, 95–127.

Zangwill, I. (1909). *The Melting Pot*. New York: Macmillan.

Concepts and Questions

1. Explain what Janzen means when he writes, "Our view of different ethnic and cultural groups is conditioned by the paradigms that guide our understanding and vision for interethnic relationships"? Can you offer some examples?

2. Which of Janzen's paradigms do you believe has most shaped American culture?

3. Which of Janzen's paradigms do you believe contributes to racism? Why?

4. Can you think of categories besides the five suggested by Janzen (language, religion, culture, race, and political tradition) that are reflected in the five paradigms?

5. What are the significant differences between the five paradigms advanced by Janzen?

6. Which of the five paradigms do you believe would be the most useful model for our society in the twenty-first century? Why?

7. How would someone from a culture very different from your own respond on his or her first visit to your city? To your home?

8. If the United States emerges into a pluralistic, multicultural society, what contributions can we make as a way of preparing for this society? What problems might appear in this new society?

42   Chapter 1 Approaches to Understanding Intercultural Communication

part 2

Sociocultural Back[...]
What We Bring to [...]
Communication

All persons are puzzles until at last we find in some word o[...]

straightway all their past works and actions lie in light befo[...]

RALPH WALDO EMERSON

One of the most important aspects of human communication is that the past experiences you bring to a communication event will affect your behavior during an encounter. It is common knowledge that each of you acts according to the personal uniqueness you bring to the communication event. Think for a moment about those countless situations when you and some friends shared what you believed to be the same experience, yet when you started to discuss the event you soon discovered there were differences in your perceptions. What you deemed dull your companions found exciting; what you considered pointless they found meaningful. The messages you received were the same for each of you; yet because each of you has a unique personality and background, each person experienced a variety of feelings, sensations, and responses. Each of you brought different backgrounds to the event and, as a result, each attributed different meanings to the shared experience. In short, the event meant what it did to you because of your unique past history.

We contend that for you to understand any communication encounter you must appreciate the idea that communication consists of much more than the mere analysis of messages. The messages you receive, and the responses you make to them, are products of your unique personal history. And those histories often produce major differences among people.

Individual past personal histories take on added significance when the dimension of culture is introduced because each of you is a product of both your individual experiences and your culture—a culture you share with other people. As defined in Part 1, *culture* refers to those cumulative deposits of knowledge, beliefs, views, values, and behaviors that are acquired by a large group of people and passed on from one generation to the next. In this sense, culture affects you both consciously and unconsciously; it not only teaches you how and what to think about but also dictates such values as what is attractive and what is ugly, what is good and what is evil, and what is appropriate and what is not. In short, your culture tells you how to pret your world. Furthermore, culture teaches you such things as how and to strangers, how to greet friends, when to speak and when to remain and even how to display your anger properly. When you are interacting with others and become disturbed by their actions, you can, for instance, cry, become physically violent, shout, or remain silent. Your behaviors are a manifestation of what you have learned, and they are largely influenced by your culture.

These cultural influences affect your ways of perceiving and acting; they contain the societal experiences and values that are passed from generation to generation. Because these behaviors are so much a part of your persona, there is a danger that you might forget that behaviors are culturally engendered and vary among cultures. This is why a person from Japan, for example, might remain silent if disturbed by someone's actions whereas an Israeli or an Italian person would more likely verbalize the displeasure.

Whatever the culture, you can better understand your behavior and the reactions of others if you realize that what you are hearing and seeing is a reflection of that culture. As you might predict, this understanding is greatly facilitated when your cultural experiences are similar to those of the people with whom you are interacting. Conversely, when different and diverse backgrounds are brought to a communication encounter, it is often difficult to share internal states and feelings. In this section, we focus on those difficulties by examining some of the experiences and perceptual backgrounds found in a variety of international cultures (Chapter 2) as well as those found in several American co-cultures (Chapter 3).

GO ONLINE

to the *Intercultural Communication: A Reader* Web site

at the Wadsworth Communication Café,
www.wadsworth.com/communication_d.

From the home page, select "Course Materials," then "Speech Communication," and then "Intercultural Communication." From the textbook menu, select *Intercultural Communication: A Reader* to access the book's website. Click on "…For Students" and use the drop-down menus at the top of the page to select a chapter and select a study aid resource. A practice quiz and an InfoTrac College Edition activity are included for each chapter.

You can complete the InfoTrac College Edition Activities by using the passcode that came free with each new copy of this text. InfoTrac College Edition is an easy-to-use database of reliable, full-length articles from hundreds of top academic journals and popular sources. You can expand your learning about the concepts illustrated in each reading by completing the InfoTrac College Edition activities.

chapter 2

International Cultures: Understanding Diversity

We begin with this question: How do you learn to interact with and understand people who come from very different parts of the global village? This answer is not simple, yet it is at the core of this book. The need for such understanding is obvious. If you look around the world at any particular moment, you will find diverse cultures in constant interaction with one another. The nightly news makes it abundantly clear that all cultures, including those that are very different, are linked together in the global community. Events that happen in one part of the world can influence events all over the world. Be it the global economy; concerns about food, water, or energy; or other disagreements that could even precipitate nuclear war, no culture can remain isolated from the rest of the world.

Two things are important if you are to understand people from international cultures: (1) you need to have a fund of knowledge about the people of other cultures; and (2) you must learn to appreciate their diversity. This chapter offers essays that are intended to assist you with both of those assignments. You will be exposed to six essays that explore the rich diversity among cultures. Although six cultures are only a small sampling of the countless cultures found throughout the world, these six will enable you to see how people in other cultures view their world. Worldview establishes how people perceive themselves, each other, and their places in the universe, and it serves as an underlying pattern for interaction within a culture. We begin with China.

The importance of China as a major player on the world stage cannot be overstated. China is currently the world's most populace nation, with a population exceeding 1.2 billion. China's increasing participation in the world's economic arena and recently granted "most favored nation" trading status by the United States will increase dramatically the level of interpersonal contact between the United States and China. This contact will occur at all levels of interaction, ranging from simple tourism to the negotiation of complex contracts and agreements covering trade and investment. Your ability to interact successfully with others from China will require that you understand much of the deep underlying value structure of the Chinese culture.

One dynamic of the Chinese culture is "face," which is intimately tied to how the Chinese feel and communicate with one another. In his article "The Chinese Conceptualizations of Face: Emotions, Communication, and Personhood," Wenshan Jia discusses the Chinese concept of face. He demonstrates how face extends far beyond the idea of mere personal embarrassment and incorporates emotional, communicative, and personhood dimensions that govern interaction within the Chinese culture. From the emotive perspective, affect and human feelings are fundamental aspects of face. From a communicative view, face is a dynamic and fluid aspect that requires management throughout interaction. When viewed from a personhood perspective, face is a sacred object to be seen by the community. As Jia suggests, understanding Chinese face concepts and practices can generate important discoveries about the Chinese people and Chinese culture.

Staying in the region of Asia, we turn to an examination of the Korean culture through an essay by James H. Robinson, "Communication in Korea: Playing Things by Eye." Robinson maintains that to engage in effective communication with Koreans you must understand the crucial Korean element of *nunch'i*. In Western terms, *nunch'i* is a keen social sense that allows Koreans to "read" other people and even grasp many of the unstated nuances often overlooked in many communication situations. According to Robinson, this acute visual perception allows Koreans to "read the eyes of others and to evaluate quickly and accurately another's emotions, attitudes, and reactions or likely reactions to a given proposal or situation." Robinson offers examples of how *nunch'i* can influence verbal messages, decision making, silence, pauses, and rhetorical questions.

Although countless dimensions define each culture, one particular characteristic usually identifies one culture over another. For example, in the United States a heightened sense of individualism distinguishes it from most other cultures. In India, as Gannon points out in the next essay, religion (Hinduism) forms the central theme of that culture. So strong is the pull of religion in India that it leads Gannon to believe that "Indian culture and society cannot be understood without reference to that tradition." Hence, our next selection, titled "India: The Dance of Shiva," offers us that reference. Because for the Hindu people life is seen as a series of cycles, Gannon believes that the best way to understand this Indian culture is by looking at the five most important cycles of Hinduism. These are the cycles of philosophy, life, family, social interaction, and work and recreation (rejuvenation). Gannon links each of these cycles directly to the cultural life of India. An awareness of these cycles, and the perceptions they produce, can help facilitate communication with the people from Indian culture.

Our next exploration is not of a country but of a continent: Africa. Specifically, Shirley van der Veur explores "communication and cultural patterns evident in Africa South of the Sahara." She notes that it is important to recognize that there is not one monolithic African culture but that 56 countries in Africa comprise approximately 2,000 ethnic or cultural groups. In her article, "Africa: Communication and Cultural Patterns," van der Veur shows how stereotypes and limited perceptions of Africa and Africans lead to misunderstanding. To help you gain a better perspective of this area of the world, van der Veur discusses the dominant worldviews and religious orientations found in African cultures. She concludes with an examination of the dominant values found among various African cultures. Through the use of proverbs, van der Veur examines such value dimensions as collectivism, being, high context, and respect for age. Her vital message for you is that in order to understand African cultures, you must leave behind your stereotypes and preconceptions of a *National Geographic* view of Africa and realize the vastness and complexity of the continent.

We now move from Africa to the Middle East as we explore the ancient and fascinating culture of Egypt. In an essay titled "Communication With Egyptians," Polly Begley isolates those cultural elements that are most crucial when interacting with Egyptians. She believes that the following elements most be considered: (1) Islamic history, religious beliefs, and politics; (2) the Egyptian values of tradition, social relationships, and hierarchical structure; and (3) language and worldview. Begley offers numerous examples of how these three elements are manifested when Egyptians and non-Egyptians come together.

Finally, we turn our attention to Europe to examine some communicative aspects common to northern European cultures. Northern European cultures, while not as diverse as Asian, are still quite different from the culture of the United States. As the European community continues with its economic consolidation and adopts a single European currency—the Euro—international competition for a share of European markets is going to increase.

Simultaneously, the mergers and acquisitions of American and European companies, which may possess quite different corporate cultures, are adding to the cultural diversity of the business world—and not necessarily smoothly. For instance, on May 7, 1998, the *Seattle Times* reported, "Chrysler is being acquired by Germany's Daimler-Benz ...in a deal that weds two companies whose image and corporate cultures are vastly different" (p. D3). In the four years since that merger, some of the major problems affecting the operation of the company have become evident. In some instances, top American managers were forced to resign primarily because cultural differences in business practices made the integration of the companies quite difficult.

Understanding how communication can operate successfully in these environments is a major concern of intercultural communication. To help us gain insight into the differences in culture and communication practices between American and northern European cultures, we turn to Robert A. Friday's article, "Contrasts in Discussion Behaviors of German and American Managers." Here Friday traces cultural expectations of both German and American managers across several dimensions, pointing out the differences and how they may lead to misunderstandings and ineffective communication. Specifically, he is concerned with cultural differences as they relate to (1) the perception of business, (2) interpersonal credibility, (3) assertiveness and fair play, (4) problem solving, and (5) education and training. Friday ends his essay by attempting to increase cultural understanding between German and American managers who share a common environment.

The Chinese Conceptualizations of Face: Emotions, Communication, and Personhood

WENSHAN JIA

Upon seeing a face, we immediately produce a symbolic framework that confronts us with a complex and ancient cultural experience. We would probably not be able to perceive, nor to recognize, those similar to us were we not able to grasp and separate that which is essential from that which is accidental.

PATRIZIA MAGLI, 1989

H: So he slapped you in the face?

L: Yes, he did.

H: Have your parents slapped your face?

L: No, they never.

H: Do you know that someone slaps others' faces in China?

L: No, I don't.

H: When Ning Li slapped your face, what was your feeling?

L: I was mad, because this is the biggest insult in China.

H: How mad were you?

L: I was very, very mad. How could he slap my face, even my father didn't. I was so angry. I didn't remember what I did. . . . I pulled the knife from my pocket. . . .

This paper was first presented at the annual convention of the National Communication Association, November 1997, in Chicago, Illinois. All rights reserved. Permission to reprint must be obtained from the author and publisher. Wenshan Jia teaches at the State University of New York at New Paltz.

According to *The China News Digest ad hoc* news reporter Yuan-Zhang Li (1996), the dialogue above is from the direct examination of defendant Wenkai Li (L) by his attorney Michael Henegen (H) in the Idaho double murder trial that ended on March 1, 1996. The defendant argued that the killings should be ruled manslaughter. Wenkai Li claimed that he had stabbed Ning Li and his wife to death because Ning Li had used profanity in commenting on his girlfriend and slapped his face. According to the reporter, the judge and the prosecutors did not know how to interpret a slap in the face in a Chinese context. They solicited answers to the following questions online so that people who are knowledgeable on this subject might provide some explanation. The questions are as follows: In China, (1) what kind of insult is a slap in the face? (2) Is it common or rare? (3) What is the general response to a slap in the face? (4) Do you know anyone who has been slapped in the face? How did he or she respond to it? (5) Could a slap in the face result in a killing?

A similar story is heard about the 1989 Chinese pro-democracy movement. According to Yizi Chen (1990), a former key figure in the right-wing faction of the Chinese Communist Party who has been in exile in the United States, the demonstrating students in Tiananmen Square circulated the rumor on a poster that the National Education Minister of China at the time was the illegitimate son of Deng Xiaoping. After he was told about this poster, Deng became too angry to control himself. He branded the movement "counter-revolutionary" and decided to use tanks to take revenge against the students.

Typical western responses to such stories would be that they are both stories of disproportionally violent reactions to insults, and that a slap in the face would mean the same thing anywhere. However, in the Chinese view, what happens in both cases constitutes a grave loss of face or "*diou lian*" for Wenkai Li, an average Chinese youth, and Deng Xiaoping, a seasoned Chinese politician. Although many studies have been conducted to help us understand the concept of face in general (Goffman, 1967; Brown & Levinson, 1987) and in the Chinese context (Smith, 1894; Hu, 1944; Ho, 1976), very few of them, in my opinion, have generated a detailed account of the Chinese concepts and practices of face that can help Western people understand cases like these of Wenkai Li and Deng Xiaoping. Perhaps the reason is that the studies largely fall within the rationalist paradigm—a culturally biased modern Western perspective (Jia, 1997/98), which excludes many cultural dimensions of the Chinese concept of face salient in Chinese culture, such as emotions, communication, and being.

This article attempts to provide an intricate account of Chinese face practices within an interpretive framework beyond the rationalist one. The framework used here integrates emotions, communication, and identity as interrelated components of the Chinese face concepts, and is complemented by a historical perspective. This interpretative framework is derived from Carbaugh's interpretive framework of cultural communication that encompasses personhood, communication, and emotions (1994).

A SYNCHRONIC INTERPRETATION: THE INTERPRETIVE FRAMEWORK OF CULTURAL COMMUNICATION

Carbaugh's cultural communication model of personhood, communication, and emotions (1994) seems capable of capturing the complexity and multiplicity of the Chinese concepts of face. Carbaugh first grounds this model in a larger theoretical perspective—the cultural communication perspective that has come out of ethnographic studies of communication in indigenous cultures. He then argues that personhood, communication, and emotions are culturally constructed and enacted *in situ*. A given culture implies a given system of feeling, acting, and being, which is patternable from a cultural, systematic, and comparative perspective. Carbaugh makes three assumptions about communication: (1) communication is the primary social process; (2) communication involves structures and processes of meaning making; and (3) communication is situated action, involving particular forms and functions.

He makes four assumptions of culture: (1) culture is a system of symbols, symbolic forms, and meanings; (2) culture systems have integrative and transformative potential; (3) the culture system is mutually in-

telligible, commonly accessible, and deeply felt; and (4) culture is also historically grounded. As he states: "the cultural system is created with highly distinctive meanings that are being projected from a very particular past" (1994, p. 25). Of tradition in relation to communication, he writes: "But tradition is not merely an impersonal voice from a past; it is continually reactivated, and potentially transformed, in situated performances" (1994, p. 30). Comparatively speaking, this model seems to have the following commendable aspects:

1. It goes beyond both the rationalist and the ethnocentric biases. The model is multi-dimensional and dialectical. It embraces process as well as structure; transformation as well as integration; feeling as well as being; history as well as the present; emotions as well as strategic thinking and action.
2. It comes from ethnographic studies grounded in indigenous cultures, transcends them, and finally attends to "local standards of coherence as they are used communally" (Carbaugh, 1994, p. 39).
3. The model itself is the product of the creative synthesis of the modern and postmodern Western scholarships with the etic bent and the indigenous cultures with the emic tendency.

In other words, Carbaugh treats all cultures as conceptually equal and makes selective use of both the emic and etic elements of the Western scholarship and both the etic and emic elements of other cultures in his development of the model. As he points out about the model, cultural studies of communication, emotion, and personhood "provide initial starting points for inquiry, raising certain points of communication to the foreground so as to understand better not simply what persons are saying, but also what they are saying about themselves, the kinds of persons they speak to, the way they enact communicative acts and sequences, and what they feel. Responding to these probes will enable us to tell cultural stories about communication, thereby throwing a cultural conversation into some light, making otherwise inscrutable ways more available for scrutiny" (1994, pp. 39–40).

In the following, I shall first identify the emotional, communicative, and personhood dimensions of Chinese face practices, respectively. Next I will identify the five historical phases of the Chinese concept of face and discuss five transformative moments of the concept in light of the three dimensions of Chinese face practices.

Emotions and Face

First of all, there flows a forceful torrent of human feelings in this reservoir of the Chinese face. The Chinese character *mianzi* is often used in parallel to *renqing*, meaning "human feelings." For example, according to *Zhongguo de renching he mianzi (The Chinese feelings and face)* (Editorial of *Teacher Zhang Monthly*, 1990), a book published in Taiwan, in daily conversations among Chinese, one often hears the frequent use of *qing mian*, an idiomatic phrase, meaning "feeler-face" or "affective face." In the Chinese Communist Revolution, people were urged to be *tiemian wuqing*, meaning "to become iron-faced and get rid of good feelings" toward anyone, including their most intimate relations, who had made any mistakes according to the judgment of the Chinese Communist Party. These examples suggest that in Chinese culture, affect or human feelings is a fundamental part of face.

A primary way to judge how much (if any) of *lian* or *mianzi* is given (*ge mianzi*), added (*zen mianzi*), earned (*zeng mianzi*), rewarded (*shang lian/mianzi*), saved (*liu mianzi*), and so on, is through socially shaped and activated feelings. A primary way to measure the magnitude of *mianzi* is also through such feelings. One has to cultivate a culturally meaningful way to feel in order to find out what has happened to face so that one will be able to function in a given culture. Feelings associated with the Chinese *lian* and *mianzi* tend to be shared by culturally competent members of the Chinese society. To feel is not only personal, but also cultural. According to *Li-Chi, Book of Rites*, a Chinese classic, there are seven human feelings: "enjoyment, anger, sorrowfulness, happiness, love, disgust and desire" (Legge, 1967, p. 50). Several authors have highlighted the significance of "feelings" in the Chinese concept of face. Cheng (1986) argues that the Confucian ideal of society is social and political harmony. Harmonious human relationships can be ensured through the appeal to human feelings. Human feelings are a primary motive for the management of face. Hui-ching Chang and G. Richard Holt argue that "the central character of Chinese relationship lies in its emphasis upon human emotion (*ren-ching*), the standard against which the quality of *mien-tze* is measured" (1994, p. 103) and on which *mientze* is built (1994, p. 107). Various feelings are not only "deeply felt" in the heart, but also intensely felt and expressed in the face.

The editorial board of *Teacher Zhang Monthly* in Taiwan (1990) has made a study of human feelings and *mianzi* in Taiwan and has identified five kinds of apprehension generated from concern over human feelings and *mianzi*. They are: fear of expressing love; fear of talking about sex; fear of talking with authority figures; fear of revealing one's own shortcomings; and fear of speaking and performance in general. To conclude, in the Chinese view, emotions overflow from the face. In order to crack the core of the face, one has to tap into the emotions shown on or felt in the face. This is why Chinese face practices can be most effectively understood in light of emotions and feelings.

Communication and Face

Communication is also a fundamental part of face. From a communication perspective, face is not a static concept but a dynamic and fluid one. When we talk about face, we should talk about the co-enactment, co-construction, and the coordinated management of face. Whatever happens to face and however it happens, whether it is lost, regained, hurt, and torn apart, it happens in communication; it is an inseparable part of communication, a product of communication, and a motive and means for communication. Communication also helps perpetuate and transform the concept of face with both the possible tendencies to reinforce and dilute it. The concept of face is deeply interactive. For example, Ho says: "Reciprocity is inherent in face behavior" (1976, p. 867). Face is an emotional response to any expected critical system enlivened by the culture or to the real and the imagined audiences nurtured by the culture. Face is a dynamic system expressive of a given type of humanity, sociality, and community. To be human in a given way means to interact in a given set of ways. To unavoidably act into each other's activities makes the face as a relational concept possible.

The fewer written legal codes that people create for regulating a people's interaction, the more significant the unwritten concept of face becomes in such a community. It is understandable why Stella Ting-Toomey, based on the nine studies on face work in her book and her previous research on the same topic, concludes: "face appears to represent the civilized, balanced point of situated interaction in a given culture" (1994, p. 335). To present and manage the Chinese face is like playing the Chinese shadow puppet show (*piyinxi*), a constant management or negotiation of social balance. Well-enacted "facework, in essence, is viewed as an artful process of diffusing and managing self-focused emotions and other-focused emotions" (Ting-Toomey, 1994, p.4) through communication—interpersonal, group, or intrapersonal. Physically, face is the most expressive vehicle of "the seven feelings and six drives," which language is hardly capable of expressing. If someone violates the communal codes through theft, impiety, betrayal, divorce, or in some other way, he or she tends to stay at home; if obligated, he or she would find an excuse not to leave the house, or take a less-trodden road with the face lowered downward to avoid eye contact with neighbors. Community members, on sight, would look at him or her with various kinds of facial expressions that display either chill, disdain, or displeasure without voicing them. Face, in this sense, functions as the barometer of the communal check.

To the Chinese, who value the nonconfrontational style of interaction, verbal language is too direct to express disapproval and disdain, especially in the face-to-face context. It would not only induce conflicts, but also make the verbal critic lose face because he or she has used an inappropriate means of indicating disapproval (words in the face-to-face context), which has caused the wrongdoer to lose face again. The most acceptable means of expressing disapproval of the socially and morally unacceptable behavior of the persons so that they are punished for their wrongdoing is therefore the indirect, nonverbal, but highly expressive cold faces of the community members. That is why the phenomenologist Emmanuel Levinas says: "Face and discourse are tied. The face speaks. It speaks, it is in this that it renders possible and begins all discourse" (Levinas, 1985, p. 87). To the Chinese, face is a primary form of social interaction. To be sensitive to other people's face and to be able to interpret the constantly changing facial expressions of the people with whom you interact are very important skills of social survival and acceptance, but also effective skills of social and professional promotion in the Chinese society.

Personhood and Face

Part of the force of a given culture is not only teaching the appropriate ways to feel and act, but also teaching the appropriate ways to be. Perhaps to be is eventually made possible by long-standing ways of feeling and acting. To Hamlet, "to be or not to be" is a question. It is a question raised not only by and for Hamlet himself, but also for all humankind. However, the occasionally blurring boundary between to be and not to be in Chinese culture is drawn by face more than by the codified law. The two Chinese idiomatic phrases *diou lian*, meaning "to lose face," and *diou ren*, meaning "to lose personhood or humanity," are used interchangeably in everyday Chinese life. In this sense, face is but another name for "the Chinese personhood." Chinese tend to be obsessed with face as a sacred object to be seen by the community and tend to under-nurture the sense of self so much that they have difficulty achieving a clear awareness of self.

An extreme case in traditional China is that a wronged person would hang himself or herself in front of the house of the wrongdoer to cause the wrongdoer to lose face. Through suicide, one could also regain his or her own face. In modern China, such a story may still be heard. Face concern still seems to overcome self. Contemporary Chinese tend to have a feeble self that always hides itself, with a strong but painful desire to come out. When it does come out, it is damaging to others and damaging to itself as well. This happens when the unarticulated (it is not to be articulated because it violates the face concern), hidden, or taken-forgranted assumption is not understood, and when the perceived violations of this assumption by other parties go so far as to threaten the sense of survival.

This sacred object (face) is for the community, of the community, by the community, and in the community. It is a communal object nurtured and protected by all through community-oriented feelings, action, and being. Physically, everyone has a distinct face, but the face as the sacred object should be shared and guarded by all. Every physical face is but a constituent of this sacred dynamic. If one is not capable of protecting one's own face, one is violating this communal code. This represents a special kind of personhood—the ideal Chinese personhood with each person preferably enmeshed with other persons and each family as an inseparable member of the empire/nation. The rationale for treating the face as the sacred object seems to be like this:

- Face holds the uppermost and frontal position in the body. Self, to the Chinese, resides in the chest, below the face, something of a lower level and primarily remains "asleep," to borrow from John Fitzgerald's description of the Chinese self (1993, p. 40); hips are treated as if they were not part of the body. A story goes that in the military coup called the Xi'an Incident in 1937, The Chinese Nationalist Government Leader Chiang Kai-shek hid himself in a small and shallow cave in the Li Hill near Xi'an City, China, with his hands covering his face inside the cave and with his hips and legs protruding outside it. This act suggests that he, like an average Chinese, was more concerned with saving his own face (here by covering it) than saving his own life. As a result, he was still caught by one of his rebellious inferiors. If you were to pat or even slap a Chinese person on the hips, he or she would feel that you are being playful with him or her. The feet occupy the lowest part of the body. To ask a Chinese person to walk on the head with the feet upwards or to ask him or her to cross between someone else's legs are some of the traditional Chinese interpersonal strategies to cause him or her to lose face. For example, someone who is not able to pay a debt may be forced by the lender to do so while calling the lender "grandpa" or "grandma." Then, the lender would release the person from the debt because he had gained a lot of face by having had the other person crawling across his legs and call him "ancestor." By walking on the victim's own head and by crossing between the victimizer's legs, the victim's face is

positioned at the same height as the victimizer's hips. Natural hierarchies inspire the Chinese notion of social hierarchy. Therefore, it is the Chinese logic that the human body is a structure of physical hierarchy in which the face is positioned at the highest level and thus treated as a sacred object and symbol instead of any other parts of the body below the face that are closer to the ground.

- Traditionally, Chinese tend to have few indigenous gods, and the few gods they have play only a marginal role in organizing social activities. Instead, the Chinese have a strong tradition of ancestor worship. This ancestor worship is carried out through daily observance of the face. It is a typical Chinese belief that either dead ancestors wish that their offspring will glorify them (earn them face) or that the living members of the clan or community will see to it that their descendants live up to the dead ancestors' expectations. Someone who fails is said to have besmeared his or her dead ancestors' faces, or to have caused them to lose face in heaven. In this sense, one's own identity is intimately linked to one's dead ancestors' identity. Internal or ritualistic communication with one's dead ancestors functions to motivate one to fulfill communal expectations.

- Finally but perhaps most importantly, face practices are the enactment of the real Chinese personhood—*junz*, meaning "gentleman." Confucius classifies people into two kinds— *junzi* and *xiao ren* (meaning persons). A *junzi* is said to have *mianzi*, which is maintained by a higher social status or position and commands a higher level of respect from the community, along with wider access to both symbolic and material resources. A *xiao ren* is one without any status or position, thus with neither *mianzi* nor *lian*—the lowest level of humanity as determined by social conduct demonstrating low moral character. Confucius uses the same words for "gentleman" and "emperor," suggesting that all people should emulate their Emperor as the moral model. Those who have done so successfully are called *junzi*. According to the ideal, a *junzi* should be like an Emperor who is able to maintain harmony throughout society as well as in his social and family relations through appealing to human feelings and cultivating virtues such as *ren* (benevolence), *yi* (righteousness), *li* (rites), *zhi* (aspiration), and *xeng* (trust). This *junzi*hood is achieved through expanding *mianzi* until it embraces the whole community and ideally all of humanity (Cheng, 1986, p. 341).

To conclude, the Chinese concept of face reflects a unique Chinese view of what a person should be and how this type of personhood can be constructed through the hierarchically structured, communally oriented, relationally and morally defined, emotionally anchored, and harmony-driven face negotiations. One's life may be over with the death of the body, but his or her face remains a part of the community.

A DIACHRONIC INTERPRETATION OF THE CHINESE CONCEPT OF FACE

Carbaugh's interpretive framework also recognizes that a cultural system is historically grounded. It seems to suggest that the history of each cultural system contains its own integral and transformative potential. Carbaugh also seems to suggest that each cultural system has its own logic of meaning and forces of change. I argue more here explicitly than Carbaugh that culture is always in interaction with history and communication. That interaction itself creates space for cultural change that is reflected through the changing concepts of personhood, changing patterns of communication, and changing ways to feel and emote. Informed by this perspective, I am delineating an interpretation of the Chinese concept of face from a historical perspective that complements a synchronic interpretation as elaborated previously.

Historically, the Chinese concept of face has experienced five stages of transformation that are observable from the vantage points of Chinese personhood, communication, and emotion. The five stages are: (1) The Formative Stage before Confucius (before 551 B.C.); (2) The Mature Stage (551 B.C. to the late 1800s); (3) The Anti-Tradition Stage (late 1800s–1949); (4) The Communist Revolution Stage (1949–1978); (5) The Free Market Economy Stage (1978–now).

The Formative Stage

Little recorded literature from this stage is available except *The Shi Ching*, a collection of folk poetry written in a dialogue form before Confucius. *The Shi Ching* is from the Early Slavery Period, when the family institution was yet to be developed. However, recorded experience was a primary intellectual source from which Confucian ideas drew. Two pieces of evidence are found in relation to the formation of the Chinese concept of face. In the folk poem "Ode to People in the Sung State" (Shang, 1979, pp. 23–24), a dialogue in a singsong form is carried on between workers and a general who is supervising them after he has been released by the Zheng State as a captive. The general was defeated in a war between the two states. The workers sing: "With big eyes wide open, big belly and big beard, the general is coming back after surrendering his weapons." The general's aide on behalf of the general responds in singing: "We still have so many raw materials to make such weapons. What's the big deal abandoning his big weapons?" The workers: "Although we still have basic materials, we have so little red paint available to paint the weapons."

Such a dialogue would never have been possible after Confucius for two reasons: First, it would have been regarded as a challenge to the authority, thus threatening the face of the defeated general who was the workers' current boss. Second, it would have been more of an argument related to the loss of dignity, moral integrity, and credibility than to the loss of material objects such as weapons. The loss of face is only slightly implied in the dialogue because the general should not have thrown away the rare and valuable weapons and caused a heavy loss of ammunition for the state he was defending. One glimpses in the dialogue the personhood of simplicity and authenticity that is tied to the ability or inability to secure materials necessary for survival.

In the other document "Wise Words, Xiaoya" from *Shi Ching* (The Education Bureau of Changzhou City, 1981, p. 310), the following value statement is found: "The silver-tongued people are thick-faced" (*hou yan*; *yan*, another term for *lian*). Being thick-faced is after all much less serious than loss of face. The former term suggests that face at that time was still immobile and remained an integral part of the human body and could have varying degrees of social sensitivity. Conceptually, it was not yet regarded as a social object figuratively independent from the human body and as a social object that could be lost, earned, and given. However, after Confucius, the Chinese concept of face acquired a life of its own, almost conceptually separate from the human body. Anything could be done to face that could be done to an inanimate object such as a mask or a ball.

The Mature Stage

All of the discussions of face in the latter four stages deal with the full-fledged concept and practices of face elaborated at this stage. Because of Confucius's central emphasis on human feelings, human relations in a hierarchy, and social harmony, the Chinese concept of face has been used to influence people to strive toward Confucian ideal, but the resulting social and moral burdens have also had negative consequences. With the Confucian ideal of cultivating gentlemanhood as a central goal, much less attention would be given to the quest for Truth and to the quest for ways to accumulate material possessions in this period, compared with the West.

In this stage, conceptually, face became separable from the human body and was treated as an object of central value or "symbolic capital" (Yang, 1994, p. 200), which could be destroyed and protected; which could be accumulated and earned; which could be torn apart so as to sever the relationship between face and body; and could be removed from one's own human body and given to someone as a most valuable gift in order to salvage the relationship or establish the relationship. This is the stage when face had become "a key to the combination lock of many of the most important characteristics of the Chinese" (Smith, 1894, p. 17). It experienced Confucianization of some sort (Cheng, 1986).

The Anti-Tradition Stage

This stage is the first most conscious moment for the transformation of the Chinese concept of face. With the impending threat to the yellow race from the Western powers, many Chinese intellectuals began to reflect critically upon their own culture while studying and introducing modern Western ideas.

The most representative call in this period is "Down with the Confucian temple!" There was a lot of fiction critical of the Confucian ideal of personhood. In this fiction can be found some tragic-comic Chinese characters that are depicted as hypocritical, weak, and obsessed with the concern for their face practices, the spirit of the traditional Chinese culture. In Lu Xun's "Kong Yiji," Kong is a poor scholar in the countryside. While carrying a wine jug he meets someone who asks him what's in the jug. Kong answers that it is wine. In truth, it is rice. But Kong is afraid of losing face, for he is afraid of revealing that he is too poor to buy more than a jug of rice. In addition, as a scholar, he is afraid of being laughed at if it becomes known that he tills the land to make a living.

In Lu Xun's story "The Story of A.Q.," A.Q. is a poor peasant wandering in the city. A soldier beats him, but he does not fight back physically. Instead, he mutters to the person and later to himself and others: "My son has just beaten me." Underlying this muttering is the Confucian belief that if someone beats his father, he has committed a heinous moral crime. A.Q.'s rationalization elevates him morally and portrays his attacker as immoral. As a result, A.Q. still feels good despite having been beaten black and blue. Lu Xun calls this "the strategy of spiritual victory." Indeed, such a critical response by Lu Xun to the traditional Chinese face practices toward China in Lu Xun's era (1930s) is driven by the Chinese desire to maintain its national face despite Western threats to China.

First of all, the iconoclastic attitude expressed by modern Chinese scholars like Lu Xun toward Chinese tradition is more emotional than rational. It was a group feeling of face loss resulting from the humiliations of the Chinese by the Western powers. Generally speaking, the transformation of the Chinese face practices was minimal and superficial. Although the Confucian personhood was virtually killed symbolically, no clear alternative personhood was created. Besides, the Confucian personhood as a cultural practice still remained intact. The critical Chinese intellectuals came to realize that they were playing an intellectual game too seriously with life and blood. The mirror was broken, but not reframed. Communication was desperate and emotion was more out of self-control. The post face loss in-fight, with pain exemplified by the war between the Chinese Communist Party and the Chinese Nationalist Party, characterizes this stage of a shattered consciousness of identity.

The Communist Revolution Stage

The Chinese Communists were one of the most radical groups emerging out of the past one hundred years in modern history. They replaced Confucianism with Marxism, human feelings and social harmony with class struggle. They offered revolutionary personhood in place of the Confucian personhood (Vogel, 1965). The following quotation from Mao suggests two types of personhood—one abandoned and the other preferred by the Communists: "A revolution is not a dinner party, or writing an essay, or painting a picture, or doing embroidery; it cannot be so refined, so leisurely and gentle, so temperate, kind, courteous, restrained and magnanimous. A revolution is an insurrection, an act of violence by which one class overthrows another" (Bantam Books, 1967, pp. 6–7).

Mao held that "revolutionaries" should be united, lively, modest, hardworking, and responsible for the Party and the people (Bantam Books, 1967) and should be cruel and heartless to "the class enemies," including one's most intimate relations who did not follow Mao's party line. One landmark idiomatic phrase from this period is "*tie mien wu qing*," meaning "to be iron-faced and free of good feelings" toward people who disagree with Mao and his party. Face is originally made of flesh and blood, and humans cannot go without feelings. However, this Maoist slogan is in sharp contrast with the Confucian ideal.

Confucius built his ideas on the basis of recognition and respect for general humanity with the goal of enhancing it. Mao built his ideas on the assumption that humanity is relative and humanity and human feelings can be done away with to achieve the "revolutionary" goal. Basically, he asked people to change themselves into military/revolutionary instruments. Humanity is more powerful than Mao's ideas; the Confucian ideal that respects and aims to enhance humanity and social harmony is more powerful than Mao's ideas and power. Such a Maoist revolutionary personhood is already deceased, but of course its corpse is still stinking.

The Free Market Economy Stage

Face is undergoing another transformation. The watershed slogan in this stage is "If you keep your face, you lose rice" (*gu le mianzi mei fan chi*). It suggests that face is viewed as something that should be devalued, because it may hinder survival in a more and more competitive market economy. In a social satire play performed in China in 1995, a factory manager overhears that Little Wang has privileged access to first-class train tickets through some important relation in the ticketing office of the train station. He asks Little Wang for help. In fact, Little Wang gets the tickets by sleeping all night in the open square of the train station so that he can get up the earliest and stand at the head of the line in front of the train ticketing office.

Little Wang, instead of admitting that he does not have a special relation, lies to his boss that he can secure the train tickets. As a result, he sleeps on the floor for more nights in the open square and buys the tickets for his boss. In return, Wang is respected by his superiors and fellow workers alike as a person who "proves" he has great social relations. He gains face but loses many nights of sheltered sleep, but no one except Wang himself knows how he got the tickets. In their laughter at Little Wang, the Chinese audience are perhaps laughing about themselves and laughing off their face concerns. The audience's laughter at Little Wang already signals an initial change in their attitude toward Chinese face practices. The play seems to warn the Chinese audience that the more face one wants to have, the more one suffers and the more pretentious one becomes; one should protect one's self and self-interest by not wanting to maintain face.

To divide the development of the Chinese face concepts and practices into stages is unavoidably linear. However, it shows that the Chinese concept of face has historical variations that must have been shaped in the continuous interactions among many kinds of contingent social forces within the society. These variations have important implications for a historical understanding of what developmental stages the Chinese personhood has undergone, how Chinese communicated in different historical stages, and what different emotional contours they have constructed.

In other words, the Chinese concept of face may imply three distinct and interrelated histories of Chinese culture: the history of the development of Chinese personhood, the historical development of Chinese communication patterns, and the historical development of Chinese emotions, which are interacting with, constituting, and defining one another. However, due to diversity within and among the contemporary Chinese communities in the world, each of these five different variations of face concepts and practices may be observed in different Chinese communities respectively. This makes it much more challenging to study Chinese face concepts and practices. But of course, generally speaking, the Confucian concept of face is much deeper, more latent, and more powerful than the others.

CONCLUSION

Face, especially in the context of Chinese face concepts and practices, is intimately tied to how a Chinese person feels and emotes, how he or she communicates with others, and what or who he or she actually is. In other words, the Chinese face is but a holistic concept that implicates given emotions, communication, and identity. Chinese face concepts and practices are also historically and situationally variable. How you feel, how you communicate, and who you are change as your face concepts and practices change. Face is not fake or superficial; on the contrary, it is substantial or crucial, for it may be the very stuff that makes us act socially and psychologically.

In this sense, to understand face concepts and practices may be an effective entry point in scrutinizing a culture. This chapter suggests that to understand Chinese face concepts and practices from a cultural communication perspective can generate startling discoveries about Chinese culture and Chinese people, from typical Chinese such as Wenkai Li to high-ranking officials such as Deng Xiaoping.

References

Bantam Books (Ed.). (1967). *Quotations from Chairman Mao Tse-tung*. New York: Bantam Books.

Brown, P., & Levinson, S. (1987). *Politeness*. Cambridge, MA: Cambridge University Press.

Carbaugh, D. (1994). Cultural communication and intercultural encounters: Personhood, strategic and emotions. *Theoria Sociologica, II* (3), 17–45.

Chang, H., & Holt, R. (1994). A Chinese perspective on face as inter-relational concern. In S. Ting-Toomey (Ed.), *The challenges of facework*. Albany: State University of New York.

Chen, Y. (1990). *Zhong Guo: Shinan de gaige yu huigu (China: Retrospect and prospect for a decade's reform)*. Taiwan: Lienjing Publishing.

Cheng, C. (1986). The concept of face and its Confucian roots. *Journal of Chinese Philosophy, 13*, 329–348.

Editorial. *Teacher Zhang Monthly*. (1990). *Zhongguo de renching he mientze (Chinese feelings and face)*. Beijing, P. R. China: Friendship Publishing.

Education Bureau of Changzhou City. (Ed.). (1981). *Dictionary of Chinese idioms*. Jiangsu Province, P. R. China: Jiangsu Province People's Press.

Fitzgerald, J. (1993). The invention of the modern Chinese self. In M. Lee & A. D. Syrokomla-Stefanowska (Eds.), *Modernizing the Chinese past* (pp. 25–41). Sydney, Australia: Wild Peony.

Goffman, E. (1967). On facework. In E. Goffman (Ed.), *Interaction ritual* (pp. 5–45). New York, Pantheon.

Ho, D. Y. (1976). On the concept of face. *American Journal of Sociology, 81* (4).

Hu, H. C. (1944). The Chinese concepts of "face." *The American Anthropologist, 46*.

Hwang, K. (1987). Face and favor: The Chinese power game. *American Journal of Sociology, 92* (4), 944–974.

Jia, W. (1997/98). The Chinese concept of face, a cultural/discourse analysis. In G. M. Chen (Ed.), *Conflict management in Chinese, a special issue of Intercultural Communication Studies, VII: 1*.

Legge, J. (Trans.). (1967). *Li chi, book of rites*, Vol. 1. New Hyde Park, NY: University Books.

Levinas, E. (1985). *Ethics and infinity*. Pittsburgh, PA: Duquesne University Press.

Li, Y. (1996). "Slap in the face" said crucial in Idaho Double Murder Case. *China News Digest US Regional, US 96-014*.

Magli, P. (1989). The face and soul. In M. Feher, R. Naddaff, & N. Tazi (Eds.), *Fragments of the history of the human body, part two*. New York: ZONE.

Shang, L. (1979). *One hundred ancient Chinese folk poems*. Shanghai, P. R. China: Shanghai Classics Publishing House.

Smith, A. H. (1894). *Chinese characteristics*. New York: Fleming H. Revell Company.

Ting-Toomey, S. (Ed.). (1994). *The Challenges of facework*. Albany: State University of New York Press.

Vogel, E. (1965). From friendship to comradeship: The change in personal relations in communist China. *China Quarterly, 21*, 46–60.

Yang, M. M. (1994). *Gifts, favors and banquets: The art of social relationships in China.* Ithaca, NY: Cornell University Press.

Concepts and Questions

1. Describe the concept of face as a dynamic of Chinese culture.
2. What is the relationship between feelings and the concept of face in Chinese culture?
3. What does Jia imply by the statement: "We should talk about the co-enactment, co-construction, and the coordinated management of face?"
4. In what manner does face serve to manage self-focused emotions?
5. What type of connection is there between self-concept and face in Chinese culture?
6. In interpersonal communication situations, how does face help mediate the interaction between people?
7. How might the Chinese concept of face be used to mete out punishment during interaction?
8. It appears that for the Chinese, face is somewhat akin to a commodity in that it can be accumulated or lost. This being the case, how might the desire to accrue face affect interaction?
9. How would an understanding of face facilitate communication between you and a Chinese citizen?
10. If you failed to understand the concept of face, what kinds of problems might arise during interaction with a Chinese citizen?

Communication in Korea: Playing Things by Eye

JAMES H. ROBINSON

Intercultural communication is a process full of excitement and frustration. These extremes may be especially heightened in business and professional communication, where the financial success of an enterprise is at stake. In such intercultural communication between Koreans and Westerners, the Korean concept of *nunch'i*[1] may play an important role. In Korea, *nunch'i* is a critical variable in the maintenance of social relationships. Literally, a Korean could not survive in Korea without this perceptive skill. Miscommunication between Western and Korean professionals occurs because Koreans have *nunch'i* and expect Westerners to have it too, or because Westerners do not have *nunch'i*, do not know what it is, and do not even know that anyone else expects them to have it. The following definition will outline the importance of *nunch'i* in Korean society, relate it to two other cultural concepts that predominate in East Asia, and provide concrete examples of how *nunch'i* contributes both to successful communication among Koreans and to miscommunication between Westerners and all East Asians.

NUNCH'I

In Korean, *nunch'i* means "eye measured" (Kang, 1972; Park, 1979). Martin and his colleagues define *nunch'i*'s nominative usage as "tact, savoir faire, sense, social sense, perceptiveness, an eye for social situations" and its predicate function as the attempt

From *IEEE Transactions on Professional Communication* (September 1996), 129–137. Copyright by the Institute of Electrical & Electronics Engineers, Inc. Reproduced by Permission of the Publisher. Jame H. Robinson teaches at St. Cloud State University, St. Cloud, Minnesota.

"to read one's mind, probe one's motives, [study] one's face, [grasp] a situation, [see] how the wind blows" (Martin et al., 1967). More figuratively, it could be translated as eye sense of playing things by eye (Kim, 1977). As a Korean proverb proclaimed, "If you have a quick sense of nunch'i, you can even eat pickled shrimp in a Buddhist temple" (Lee, 1967). As Buddhists are vegetarians, the pickling process and the eating of flesh would both be regarded as barbaric, and especially so in a Buddhist temple. Consequently, the social skills required to behave in this fashion would be an example of having the quickest sense of *nunch'i*.

Scholars have referred to *nunch'i* as a non-logical process variable that uses visual perception to discover the hidden agenda behind all forms of expression in social interaction. According to Lee (1967), this *nunch'i* goes "beyond good sense or common sense." *Nunch'i* is more intuitive and sensitive than logical or rational. It does not lead to fixed decisions as one might find with good sense or common sense. As it depends on interpersonal rapport, *nunch'i* is instead a situational ethic used to solve interpersonal problems (Lee, 1967). In addition, the *nun* in *nunch'i* means "eye," and so *nunch'i* is both related to using the eyes to perceive the world and to reading the eyes of others. Yum (1987) refers to *nunch'i* as "perceptiveness or sensitivity with eyes." According to Kalton (1990), *nunch'i* is used also to read the eyes and to assess "quickly and accurately . . . another's emotions, attitudes, and reaction or likely reaction to a given proposal or situations." K. Kim (1975) states that Koreans use *nunch'i* to interpret facial expressions, words, and "a mysterious 'alpha' hidden in . . . inner hearts."

Because of *nunch'i*, Koreans are also very concerned about what others see and think about them: about what another's *nunch'i* tells about oneself. This concern is related to an emphasis in Confucian-influenced societies on self-control. Maturity within such a society means "controlling," "hiding," or "masking" one's emotions (Cho, 1988). A negative reaction may be manifest in a face that becomes as expressionless as stone rather than in some verbal explosion. Expressions of affect are found in the eyes rather than on the face or from the whole body. Because of this emphasis on self-control, Yum (1987, p. 80) says that *nunch'i* becomes crucial in under-

standing "minute nonverbal cues, on reading between the lines, and on hearing between the sounds" to penetrate the mask that hides one's desires. The height of the art of *nunch'i* would be to give someone something before he or she asked for it. Such behavior manifests pure genius, as it avoids the speaker's having to give a "yes" or "no" answer to a request. According to Song (1971, p. 32), "*nunch'i* can distinguish between sincerity and falsehood, detect the good will hidden behind a grimace, uncover the villain that keeps smiling, and unmask the wolf in sheep's clothing."

In their analysis of *nunch'i*, S. H. Choi and S. C. Choi (1991) have identified two *nunch'i* processes in face-to-face communication: *nunch'i* execution and *nunch'i* figuring-out. The first is an initiating action where an indirect message, which is often nonverbal, is communicated: for example, when a wife comes up and stands next to a husband who is standing by a counter, this *nunch'i* move means that the husband needs to move so that the wife can open a cabinet. (In U.S. culture, a more verbal move, such as "excuse me," might be expected.) A *nunch'i* figuring-out behavior is a response to a *nunch'i* execution: for example, the husband perceives the wife's proximity and moves out of the way.

In order for a *nunch'i* interaction to be successful, both execution and figuring-out moves are required. As in the previous example, the wife has to send the correct message, and the husband has to receive it. But if the wife had executed the act without the corresponding figuring-out process by the husband, the communication act fails. The result could be (and indeed was) an argument. At the same time, if the husband initiates a figuring-out process when no *nunch'i* execution has been sent from the wife, the communication will also fail. Specifically, if the wife just wanted to be close to the husband and had no interest in opening the cabinet, then moving away to make room for the wife would not be a good response. In other words, proximity can have more than one meaning, and can be a *nunch'i*-executed move or not; it all depends on the context or the situation.

Dualism

One cultural concept related to *nunch'i* is dualism. According to Song (1971) and Kang (1972), *nunch'i* can have both positive and negative sides. From the positive side, *nunch'i* is foreseeing. When a mother predicts misbehavior by a child and praises the child for good behavior before the child has a chance to misbehave, the mother uses *nunch'i* as foreseeing (Choi, 1980). When a foreign visitor to Korea notices that often what he or she requires is provided before even asking, this is the positive manifestation of *nunch'i*. This foreseeing would be the height of good behavior.

Korean scholars also describe *nunch'i* as having a negative side. In interactions with Korean students, this foreseeing can frustrate American educators. For example, American college administrators may encounter situations where students make an appointment, but when they arrive for what was supposed to be an important decision, the student talks of trivialities and leaves before coming to the point. Administrators may wonder what happened: with *nunch'i*, the student foresaw that it was not a good time to raise an important issue (Kalton, 1990). According to Kang (1972), this negative side also encourages deception for a higher goal of harmony. Koreans would be reluctant to hurt anyone's feelings with the truth when a watering down of the truth would preserve harmony as well as face. For example, a Korean shop owner gives the customer an unrealistic time of completion for repairs because the owner's *nunch'i* perceives that it will make the customer feel better at least for the moment (Crane, 1967).

This deception that Kang describes can also result in a self-denial stance in dyadic communication. For example, Koreans will often decline the first and even a second offer of food, drink, or favors, even if they are hungry, thirsty, or in great need. In this situation, *nunch'i* is a strategy to negotiate the difference between a polite offer and a real offer (Kim, 1979). With *nunch'i*, the first offer is interpreted to have two potential meanings: (1) a politeness strategy used before one eats something in public, or (2) an offer of food. For example, on a train, before eating a boiled egg as a snack, a person may actually offer it to others in the vicinity, but this offer is politeness if only given once, and to accept it would be unthinkable. With a second offer, the latter of these two hypotheses is reinforced, although not conclusively so. With the third offer, the second hypothesis is accepted as well as the offer itself. If our train traveler made a second and then a third offer, then it

would be obvious that the offer was sincere and not out of politeness and so should be accepted.

From both of these two sides, *nunch'i* is used to avoid unpleasantness for oneself by foreseeing the behavior of others and to avoid unpleasantness for others by using deception. While this first strategy could be very helpful in cross-cultural interactions with Americans, the second one could be misunderstood as dishonesty and result in negative stereotypes if not lead to social conflict.

Hierarchy

A second cultural concept related to *nunch'i* is hierarchy. *Nunch'i* might not exist in Korea without a hierarchical social system. Hierarchical social relations, expressed through senior–junior dyads, are manifestations of the yin-yang concept and of the five Confucian relationships. For Confucian-oriented societies, social interaction relies on balancing yin and yang. According to Cheng (1987, p. 34), yin and yang have hierarchical characteristics: yang means the "creative, forwarding-pushing, dominating and manifest, systemic force," and yin the "receptive, recessive, dominated, hidden, informed and background force." The yin-yang dyad in social relations is also expressed through the responsibilities of each participant in the five Confucian relationships: "king-justice, subject-loyalty," "father-love, son-filiality," "husband-initiative, wife-obedience," "elder brother-brotherly love, younger brother-reverence," and "friends-mutual faith" (Yum, 1987, p. 77). In Confucian societies, these relationships are dominated by the hierarchical father-son dyad, but in Western cultures, the egalitarian husband-wife dyad is the more dominant model (Kang, 1972; Park, 1979).

Within these hierarchical relationships, interaction is highly ritualized, with great importance placed on the proper behavior and the proper language for both juniors and seniors. For example, juniors would very seldom drink alcohol or smoke in front of seniors. Juniors would also need to use polite-formal language to seniors, whereas seniors would use informal-impolite language forms with juniors for most daily interactions. At times, juniors prefer silence or a simple "yes" in attempting a verbal response to a senior within this complex hierarchical system of interaction.

In this hierarchical system, *nunch'i* can function as a social equalizer. Without it, juniors would be absolutely helpless. With it, juniors have a chance to achieve their individual needs from a disadvantaged position. R. H. Kim (1979, p. 6) said that *nunch'i* "is an inevitable by-product of a rigidly stratified class society where force rather than reason, class status rather than individual ability, political power rather than hard work, have been used as methods of accumulating wealth by the social elite." In this class society, juniors must use their "quick sense" of *nunch'i* in their interactions with seniors to gain their individual needs. Argumentation, logic, and objectivity would only elicit disdain by seniors and society. When a child resorts to rational means, adults would characterize the child as "impudent" (Kim, 1979, p. 6).

According to C. S. Choi (1980), juniors use *nunch'i* to offset the authoritarian pressures of seniors within this hierarchical social system. The end result is a *"nunch'i* culture" that operates in a "cold war" of interpersonal relations and relies heavily on covert expression or what is not said and not done more than on overt verbal or nonverbal communication. Always full of tension, the juniors or equals have to use *nunch'i* to read the mind of the senior or the equal, to manipulate the situation, and to escape any negative repercussions. Because of the infringement of seniors, one's behavior is more often than not expressed through a "silent mind." Rather than expressing oneself, this *nunch'i* culture creates a *"nunch'i* personality" that does not express individual needs. Koreans use *nunch'i* as a tactic for gathering data, as a means to analyze that data, and as a means of keeping one's own secrets. This *nunch'i* personality is similar to that of a secret agent or a private detective (Choi, 1980, pp. 120–121).

For example, I was once fired from a part-time job in Korea but did not realize it until I was halfway down the hallway. The firing was marked by a really polite goodbye with an unusually deep bow. If I had used my *nunch'i*, I could have foreseen this event from the just prior conversation and work and either respectfully resigned or politely made an appropriate apology, which would have saved some face, if not my job. In other words, my employment status was at risk, and I did not even know it until it was too late because my *nunch'i* was too slow. If it had been

faster, I would have at least had a shot at changing the outcome. As it was, I was helpless.

C. S. Choi (1980, p. 122) also claims that *nunch'i* is a cultural reaction to a life of pain and oppression from seniors and invasion by outsiders. As a survival strategy or a social release valve, *nunch'i* is similar to a traditional Korean song of the blues, a story of grief and tears. Thus a smile may mean pain, a nonplussed look happiness, a polite word anger, and an impolite expression friendliness—or the other way around, depending on the situation. For international businesspeople, they should realize that *nunch'i* was developed and perfected in Korea to manipulate foreigners, especially invaders. Although the invaders of the past were mostly military personnel, the present-day invader is the international businessperson.

PROFESSIONAL COMMUNICATION

The second part of this essay provides examples of how *nunch'i* influences professional communication. The first set of examples will explicate this communication process between Koreans. The second set will describe the miscommunication that results when Koreans expect *nunch'i*-related behaviors from Americans or other Westerns in communication, or put another way, when Western businessmen enter into communication with Koreans without any cultural understanding of Korean culture.

Korean Interactions

S. H. Choi and S. C. Choi (1991) give an example of how hidden messages that rely on *nunch'i* are communicated in office situations. In this situation someone from within your office drops by, but you do not have time to talk with him or her because of a pressing deadline. In this Korean situation, the *nunch'i*-emitted verbal message would be, "What time is it now?" The visitor should then realize that the co-worker knows very well what time it is and is simply providing an indirect means of communicating the fact that the visitor should leave so that the co-worker can continue with the work at hand. The visitor would then announce the intent of leaving and leave. S. H. Choi and S. C. Choi have indicated that one appropriate response would be, "Oh, it's already 4 o'clock, I'd better leave now. I've an appointment at 4:15." As S. H. Choi and S. C Choi (1991, p. 57) comment:

> In such a case, two parties could communicate their "real" intentions without either party indicating knowledge of the internally transmitted message. The faces of both parties are saved by virtue of the neutrality of the Noon-Chi exchange in an otherwise "no win" situation.

If, on the other hand, the visitor had responded by referring to the surface message, the communication would have been destroyed.

The second example concerns how *nunch'i* can even affect the decision of when to leave the office at the end of the day. In Korea, office work does not follow the clock as much as it does the dictates of the immediate supervisor or boss. Most Korean offices are organized within a large number of desks in a large room. The supervisor or boss has a desk at the head of several rows of desks but in the same room. In short, the boss always knows who is at his or her desk. Typically, when anyone leaves, he or she announces this departure with one of several polite phrases.

In most situations, the juniors in the office cannot leave work until the boss has left. In Janelli's interview data (1993, p. 207), when he asked about coerced overtime and how one knew when one could leave work, one response was, "We have to use our *nunch'i*" to "appraise the mood of our superior" before leaving work. If the employee perceived that the boss was not in a good mood, the employee would stay until after the boss left. But if the boss had had a good day, then the employee could announce his departure before the boss has actually left. In this daily interaction, the mood or *kibum* of the boss was more important than the time clock in determining when the juniors in the office could leave the office for home, and the only means of determining the boss's *kibum* was through *nunch'i*. Without *nunch'i*, a junior would never be able to leave the office before the boss did.

S. H. Choi and S. C. Choi (1991, p. 10) document the role of pauses and silences in *nunch'i* through a videotape study of the interactions between a shop owner, who is also an uncle, and the shop manager, who is a nephew, in a resort complex. In the first situation, the uncle is supervising the nephew in regard to the placement of some mats in front of the store the day after some of these mats had been stolen. The nephew is placing mats on the sidewalk in the very place where they were stolen the day before. The interaction begins:

UNCLE: Why did you put this mat in here?

NEPHEW: (two-second pause) This one? (glancing sidewise at the uncle, in a fainting voice)

UNCLE: Yeah.

NEPHEW: (We're) going to use tomorrow (in fainting voice). . .

In essence, the two-second pause by the nephew is a *nunch'i* response that expresses politeness and deference to the uncle. A direct response to the question would have been impolite. The problem of theft is communicated only through *nunch'i* in this communication and never mentioned directly. The reference to tomorrow is perhaps an indirect indication that the nephew will make sure that the mats are not stolen, in the near future at least.

In a second situation (Choi & Choi, 1991, p. 14), silence as well as a pause acts as a *nunch'i*-emitted message that might be characterized as a nonplused response by the nephew:

NEPHEW: (putting up a fake Christmas tree).

UNCLE: Look, that branch seems to be longer than that one at the bottom.

NEPHEW: (no response)

UNCLE: Oh maybe not?

NEPHEW: (one-second pause) No, it's not.

In this case, the silence by the nephew did not mean that he did not hear the uncle but that the uncle was wrong. This *nunch'i*-emitted silence was received by the uncle, who then corrected himself in a hedging manner. After a short pause, a *nunch'i*-emitted expression of politeness and deference, the nephew is then able to agree with the restatement of the uncle. As S. H. Choi and S. C. Choi relate (1991, p. 14), if the nephew's final response had followed directly after the uncle's initial statement, both the uncle and the nephew would have lost face and the interaction would have ended disastrously.

In a third situation, ellipsis is used as a *nunch'i* strategy of communication. Ellipsis is a common communication strategy in which the speaker omits an element because it is understood. For example, "Been busy today?" is interpreted as a question that means, "Have you been busy today?" The first two words are simply omitted. At the sentence level in Korea, subject ellipsis is very common in formal writing as well as oral communication. As a *nunch'i* strategy, the participant in an interaction can actually be omitted from the context (Choi & Choi, 1991, p. 20). For example:

UNCLE: We haven't finished that "Doruko" painting yet have we?

NEPHEW: What is Doruko painting? (as if in monologue} Which one?

UNCLE: That . . . that one which looks like a mud . . . mud . . .

NEPHEW: Oh we did, didn't we?

In this interaction, the nephew does not know what Doroko painting is and so he behaves as if the participants in the interaction were not there; he omits both his uncle and himself from the interaction by posing a rhetorical question to himself. This rhetorical response is followed by an indirect response to the uncle. If the nephew had simply confessed that he did not know what the doruko painting was, he would have lost face as an incompetent assistant to the uncle, and the uncle would have lost some degree of face, as his choice of assistant would be revealed to be less than brilliant. By omitting both interlocutors from this conversation for this brief instant to ask a rhetorical question to himself, in which he then made the indirect reference to the paintings in front of them, the nephew uses a *nunch'i* strategy to cover up his ignorance and to save his face. The uncle participates in this *nunch'i* communication by defining doruko painting as a mud painting.

In these three interactions, the nephew used the three *nunch'i* strategies of pauses, silence, and ellipsis to preserve harmony in the relationship with the uncle and to maintain his face as well as that of the uncle. These strategies sent messages to the uncle that were figured out by the uncle and then responded to in kind within

two channels of communication: one at the literal level and one at the meta-message level.

Intercultural Interactions

As one might imagine, *nunch'i*-related behaviors can also cause miscommunication between Americans or other Westerners and Koreans. As an Australian manager in Korea once commented, "I initially found that it was difficult to elicit the 'real' views of my staff when it came to debating various sales and merchandising strategies." This Western manager continued that in "my experience . . . initially you may get either 'silence' or, be told 'That won't work in Korea'." This manager stressed, "The trick is to break that invisible barrier so that you can mix in your staff's invaluable field experience and obvious cultural knowledge and gain an understanding of how your objective can still be achieved with some 'Koreanizing' of its implementation" (Bardey, 1994).

From the Korean perspective, Janelli, in his ethnography of a South Korean conglomerate, wrote: "The greatest consensus in their South Korean mid-level managers' critique of the United States appeared in their views of American interpersonal relations in business dealings" (1993, p. 57). Essentially, this criticism focused on how Americans lack sensitivity to others in business matters. In other words, Americans are more concerned with the letter of the law or contract and less concerned with human beings. Koreans, on the other hand, tend to be more sensitive to others in both social and business interactions. *Nunch'i* is one of the causes of the invisible barrier referred to by the Australian manager, and it also creates a sensitivity gap between Koreans and Westerners. The following three examples will show how the lack of *nunch'i* on the part of Westerners in Korea can result in disastrous miscommunication.

De Mente, in his book on cross-cultural communication for Western businessmen in Korea, provides the first example. He states that "one of the extraordinary skills the foreign businessman should have to succeed in Korea is the ability to read faces—or to read *nunch'i* (noon-chee), in Korean terms" (1988, p. 83). He comments that Americans often are confronted with the statement "Things are done differently in Korea," and that these "businessmen need *nunch'i* in order to understand the rationale behind 'things are done differently in Korea' and to learn a different set of 'management and negotiating skills'" (1988, p. 85). In support of this point, De Mente describes an incident involving the foreign manager of a joint-venture company in Seoul.

> The firm's office was located in a very expensive but inconvenient location in Yoido, near the National Assembly Building. The foreign manager found a nice suite of offices in the downtown area of Seoul, less expensive and far more convenient for both employees and visitors. At the last moment, the Korean president refused to allow the move to take place, and would not explain his reasons to the foreign manager. The situation developed into a sticky impasse that created a great deal of ill will on both sides. (De Mente, 1988, pp. 83–84)

The office manager had explained his reasons for wanting to move the office, and believed his rationale had been understood and accepted by his joint-venture partner. He had therefore proceeded in good faith. The Korean president had opposed the move from the beginning, however, and had relied on the foreigner's ability to read *nunch'i* to understand that he was firmly against the move, although he had not said so directly.

> The Korean president preferred the Yoido location because it was one of the most prestigious districts in the city. It gave the company "face" on the highest government and business levels, and . . . the Yoido location had nothing to do with rent and everything to do with where the company president wanted his car to pull up in the morning. (De Mente, 1988, pp. 83–84)

The president and other Korean personnel did not simply come out and tell the foreigner that there was no way they were going to move the offices because they did not want to confront him directly with their objections and cause him to lose face in a contest he could not win. They felt it was up to him to ask the right questions and to "read" the right answers. In the end, both sides lost face in a classic cause of failure in cross-cultural communications.

The second example comes from interview data collected by the author. In this situation, a Western businessman visits a Korean firm. During this visit, the Korean counterpart takes off from his office—with permission, of course—and spends as much

time as necessary with his Western guest. In the course of their discussions, when the Western guest needs to send a fax back to the home office, the Korean counterpart provides this service. Entertainment is funded completely by the Korean counterpart, either through his expense account or with personal funds. But, when the Korean businessman visits his new friend in his office in England, what had been a great relationship falls apart completely. After providing great hospitality in Korea, the Korean businessman expected the same when he became the guest. But the Western businessman did not have the *nunch'i* to realize that all the hospitality in Korea had a cost.

So, when the Korean businessman visits, his Western counterpart delays any interaction until after he has finished his work. After emitting several nonverbal signals of impatience, the Korean businessman emits a verbal *nunch'i* cue by asking to send a fax—thinking that this would remind the Western counterpart of one favor provided in Korea. After the Korean businessman sends his fax, he has to wait some more. In absolute frustration, he gives up and makes an excuse to leave. On his way out, insult is added to injury, as the Western counterpart finally interrupts his work to say, "But you can't go; you haven't paid for the fax."

CONCLUSION

In short, *nunch'i* is a cultural concept that Western professionals need to understand before doing business or working in Korea or with Koreans in the United States. In particular, Western professionals need to pay great attention to pauses, silences, and rhetorical questions that may appear in their interactions with Korean businessmen. These responses are examples of *nunch'i*-executed communication acts that signal disagreement or a lack of understanding.

Most important, Western professionals should understand that when their Korean counterparts say something such as, "We do not do it that way in Korea," this direct verbal message indicates that a series of *nunch'i*-executed messages have been previously emitted without the proper *nunch'i* figuring-out process on the part of the Western businessperson. When a Korean uses this phrase, he or she is providing the contents of the message that you should have said or at least thought in response to the series of *nunch'i*-executed moves. In other words, you should have said, "Oh, this won't work in Korea?" At the least, you probably should have kept your mouth shut when encountering a seemingly non-logical statement or response. If you learn to perceive these *nunch'i*-executed messages and to respond properly, you have made the first step in identifying which Western business practices will and will not work in a country such as Korea.

Notes

1. Throughout the text, the McCune-Reischauer system of romanization is used, with the exception of direct quotes. See "Tables of the McCune-Reischauer system for the romanization of Korean," Trans. Korean Branch Roy, Asiatic Society, vol. 38, p. 121, Oct. 1961; or E. F. Klein, "Romanization of Korean: Problems, experiments, suggestions." (1979). In D. R. McCann, et al. (Eds.), *Studies on Korea in transition*. Honolulu, HI: University of Hawaii Press, pp. 174–199.

References

Bardey, T. (1994, June 25). "Changes . . . ? What changes!" *Korea Herald*.

Cheng, C. Y. (1987). Chinese philosophy and contemporary human communication theory. In D. L. Kincaid (Ed.), *Communication theory: Eastern and Western perspectives*. San Diego, CA: Academic Press, pp. 23–43.

Cho, Y. D. (1988). "Speaker's *nunch'i*: Koreans' gazing behavior in face-to-face interaction," unpublished manuscript, p. 13.

Choi, C. S. (1980). *Han-kuk-in-oi Sa-hui-joek seong-kyok* [The Social Character of Korea], 2d ed. Seoul, Korea: Gai Mun Sa.

Choi, S. H., & Choi, S. C. (1991). "Noon-chi: An indigenous form of Koreans' politeness communication," presented at the Department of Psychology, University of Hawaii, unpublished.

Crane, P. S. (1967). *Korean patterns*. Seoul, Korea: Roy, Asiatic Society.

De Mente, B. (1988). *Korean etiquette and ethics in business*. Lincolnwood, IL: National Textbook.

Janelli, R., & Yim, D. (1993). *Making capitalism: The social and cultural construction of a South Korean conglomerate*. Stanford, CA: Stanford University Press.

Kalton, M. (1990). Korean ideas and values. In I. Davies (Ed.), *The Korea papers: Profile in educational exchange*. Washington, DC: National Association for Foreign Student Affairs, vol. 23, p. 14.

Kang, S. P. (1972). *The East Asian culture and its transformation in the West*. Seoul, Korea: American Studies Institute.

Kim, H. C. (R. H.) (1977). Education and the Korean immigrant child. *Integrated Education, 15*, 15–18.

Kim, H. C. (R. H.) (1979). "Understanding Korean people, language, and culture," paper prepared for the Superintendent of Public Instruction, Bellington, WA.

Kim, K. (1975). Cross-cultural differences between Americans and Koreans in nonverbal behavior. In H. Sohn (Ed.), *The Korean language: Its structure and social projection*. Honolulu, HI: Center for Korean Studies, University of Hawaii, pp. 5–18.

Lee, O. Y. (1967). *In this earth and in that wind*. D. I. Steinberg, trans. Seoul, Korea: Roy, Asiatic Society, Korea Branch.

Martin, E. M., Lee, Y. H., & Chang, S. U. (1967). *A Korean, English Dictionary*. New Haven, CT: Yale University Press.

Park, M.S. (1979). *Communication styles in two different cultures: Korean and American*. Seoul, Korea: Han Shin Publications.

Song, Y. I. (1971). Nunch'i. *Korea Journal, 11*, 32, 43.

Yum, J. O. (1987). Korean philosophy and communication. In D. L. Kincaid (Ed.), *Communication theory: Eastern and Western perspectives*. San Diego, CA: Academic Press, pp. 71–86.

Concepts and Questions

1. What does Robinson mean when he writes, "In order for a *nunch'i* interaction to be successful, both execution and figuring-out moves are required"?
2. Do members of the dominant culture in the United States have a concept similar to *nunch'i*? What is it?
3. How would you relate hierarchical relationships to *nunch'i*?
4. How can *nunch'i* function as a social equalizer?
5. What is the link between *nunch'i* and silence?
6. Why does Robinson suggest that *nunch'i* is a historical reaction to pain?
7. How does *nunch'i* influence the decision-making process?
8. Can you think of some ways, not mentioned by Robinson, where our lack of knowledge regarding *nunch'i* could impede intercultural communication?

India: The Dance of Shiva

MARTIN J. GANNON

Sex may drive the soap operas in America. But in India, what really moves the dishwashing liquids are serials based on ancient myths of Indian gods.

KARP AND WILLIAMS (1998), P. A1

India is a country bursting with diversity—virtually every writer describes it as one of the most culturally and geographically diverse nations in existence. It is the second largest country in the world, with a population of 950 million, and it is about one third the size of the United States.

Religious diversity is a major feature of India, and it is fitting that our image of, and cultural metaphor for, this country should be based on religion. As Swami Vivekananda so succinctly stated: "Each nation has a theme in life. In India religious life forms the central theme, the keynote of the whole music of the nation."

For 2,000 years of its history, India was almost completely Hindu. But for the past millennium or more, Indian culture has been a synthesis of different racial, religious, and linguistic influences; Hinduism itself has undergone many changes owing to the impact of other faiths. Therefore, it is incorrect to contend that Indian culture is solely a Hindu culture. However, to begin to understand India, we must start with Hindu traditions. The overwhelming majority of Indians are still tradition oriented, and changes in their culture and society cannot be understood without reference to that tradition.

There are numerous deities or gods in the Hindu religion, each being different manifestations of one Supreme Being. The most important gods are Brahma (the Creator), Vishnu (the Preserver), and Shiva (the Destroyer). Among the greatest names and appearances of Shiva is Nataraja, Lord of the Dancers. The Dance of Shiva has been described as the "clearest image of the activity of God which any art or religion can boast of" (Coomaraswamy,

From Martin J. Gannon, *Global Cultures*, 2d ed. Thousand Oaks, CA: Sage Publications, 2001, pp. 57–80. Reprinted by permission of Sage Publications.

1924/1969, p. 56), and it also reflects the cyclical nature of Hindu philosophy. Through this metaphor, we will begin to explore Indian culture and society.

Among Hindus, dancing is regarded as the most ancient and important of the arts. Legend attributes to it even the creation of the world: Brahma's three steps created earth, space, and sky. Every aspect of nature—man, bird, beast, insect, trees, wind, waves, stars—displays a dance pattern, collectively called the Daily Dance (*dainic nrtya*). But nature is inert and cannot dance until Shiva wills it; he holds the sacred drum, the *damaru*, whose soundings set the rhythms that beat throughout the universe. Shiva is like a master conductor, and the Daily Dance is the response of all creation to his rhythmic force.

Shiva is seen as the first dancer, a deity who dances simply as an expression of his exuberant personality (Banerji, 1983, p. 43). His dance cannot be performed by anyone else, because Shiva dances out the creation and existence of the world. But just as the mortal dancer gets tired, so, too, does Shiva lapse periodically into inactivity. The cosmos becomes chaos, and destruction follows the period of creation. This concept of the Dance of Shiva is innate in the Eastern ideas of movement and history—it is continuous and both constructive and destructive at the same time (Gopal & Dadachanji, 1951).

The Dance of Shiva represents both the conception of the world processes as a supreme being's pastime or amusement (*lila*), and the very nature of that blessed one, which is beyond the realm of purpose or understanding (Coomaraswamy, 1924/1969). The dance symbolizes the five main activities of the supreme being: creation and development (*srishti*); preservation and support (*sthiti*); change and destruction (*samhara*); shrouding, symbolism, illusion, and giving rest (*tirobhava*); and release, salvation, and grace (*anugraha*).

India's history reflects the cycles of chaos and harmony epitomized by the Dance of Shiva. Time after time, India has recovered from episodes that would have ended the existence of any other nation. In fact, Shiva's son, Ganesh, is the symbol of good arising from adversity. According to the legend, Parvati, the consort of Shiva, would spend hours bathing, dressing, and adorning herself. This often meant that Shiva was kept waiting, so Parvati set their son Ganesh on guard to prevent Shiva bursting in on her unannounced and catching her in a state of unreadiness. One day, Shiva was so frustrated by Ganesh's actions that he cut off the child's head. Distraught, Parvati completely withdrew from her lord, and Shiva realized he would have to restore the child to her if he was to win her back. He resolved to use the first available head he could find, which happened to be that of a baby elephant. The boy regained his life and now had the added advantage of the elephant's wisdom. Similarly, India's past and present contributions to art, science, and the spiritual world of the unknown are immense, despite periods of turmoil and apparent anarchy.

CYCLICAL HINDU PHILOSOPHY

The Indian perspective on life tends to differ most sharply from that of Europe and the United States in the value that it accords to the discipline of philosophy (Coomaraswamy, 1924/1969, p. 2). In Europe and America, the study of philosophy tends to be regarded as an end in itself—some kind of mental gymnastic—and as such, it seems of little importance to the ordinary man or woman. In India, philosophy tends to overlap with religion, and it is regarded as the key to life itself, clarifying its essential meaning and the way to attain spiritual goals. Elsewhere, philosophy and religion pursued distinct and different paths that may have crossed but never merged (Munshi, 1965, p. 133). In India, it is not always possible to differentiate between the two.

In Hindu philosophy, the world is considered illusory, like a ream, the result of God's *lila*. According to one interpretation, *Bharata Varsha*, the ancient name of India, literally means "land of the actors" (Lannoy, 1971, p. 286). In an illusionary world, people cannot achieve true happiness through the mere physical enjoyment of wealth or material possessions. The only happiness worth seeking is permanent spiritual happiness as distinguished from these fleeting pleasures. Absolute happiness can result only from liberation from worldly involvement through spiritual enlightenment. Life is a journey in search of salvation (*mukti*), and the seeker, if he or she withstands all of the perils of the road, is rewarded by exultation beyond human experience or perception

(*moksha*). In the same way that the Dance of Shiva leads the cosmos through a journey, Hindu philosophy directs each individual along a path.

There are basically four paths or ways that lead to the ideal state: intense devotion or love of God (*bhakti yoga*), selfless work or service (*karma yoga*), philosophy or knowledge of self (*nana yoga*), and meditation or psychological exercise (*raja yoga*). The four ways are not exclusive, and an individual may choose or combine them according to the dictates of temperament and circumstance. Whatever path is followed, every Hindu is aware of the difficulty of reaching the ideal state in a single lifetime. This is the point at which the concept of reincarnation, or the cycle of lives, becomes important.

Individual souls (*jivas*) enter the world mysteriously; by God's power, certainly, but how and for what purpose is not fully explainable (Smith, 1958, p. 100). They begin as the souls of the simplest forms of life, but they do not vanish with the death of their original bodies. Rather, they simply move to a new body or form. The transmigration of souls takes an individual *jiva* through a series of complex bodies until a human one is achieved. At this point, the ascent of physical forms ends, and the soul begins its path to *mukti*. This gives an abiding sense of purpose to the Hindu life—a God to be sought actively and awaited patiently through the cycles of many lives.

The doctrine of reincarnation corresponds to a fact that everyone should have noticed: The varying age of the souls of people, irrespective of the age of the body ("an old head on young shoulders"). Some people remain irresponsible, self-assertive, uncontrolled, and inept to their last days; others are serious, friendly, self-controlled, and talented from their youth onward. According to Hindu philosophy, each person comes equipped with a highly personalized unconsciousness, characterized by a particular mix of three fundamental qualities: *sattva* (clarity, light); *rajas* (passion, desire); and *rajas* (dullness, darkness). Their relative strength differs from one person to another, but in the Hindu idea of destiny, the unconscious has an innate tendency to strive toward clarity and light (Kakar, 1978).

The birth of a person into a particular niche in life and the relative mix of the three fundamental qualities in an individual are determined by the balance of the right and wrong actions of his or her soul through its previous cycles. The rate of progress of the soul through this endless cycle of birth, life, and death—the soul's karma—depends on the deeds and decisions made in each lifetime. One way of mapping the probable karma of an individual is to consult astrological charts at the time of his or her birth, and this is an important tradition in Indian society.

The Dance of Shiva portrays the world's endless cycle of creation, existence, destruction, and re-creation, and Hindu philosophy depicts the endless cycle of the soul through birth, life, death, and reincarnation. We will now turn to examining the cycle of individual life within that greater series of lifetimes.

THE CYCLE OF LIFE

According to Hindu philosophy, a person passes through four stages of life, the first of which is that of a student. The prime responsibility in life during this stage is to learn. Besides knowledge, the student is supposed to develop a strong character and good habits, and emerge equipped to produce a good and effective life.

The second stage, beginning with marriage, is that of a householder. Here, human energy turns outward and is expressed on three fronts: family, vocation, and community. The wants of pleasure are satisfied through the family, wants of duty through exercising the social responsibilities of citizenship, and the wants of success through employment.

The third stage of life is retirement, signifying withdrawal from social obligations. This is the time for a person to begin his or her true education—to discover who one is, and what life is all about. It is a time to read, think, ponder over life's meaning, and to discover and live by a philosophy. At this stage, a person needs to transcend the senses and dwell in harmony with the timeless reality that underlies the dream of life in this natural world.

The Hindu concept of retirement is exemplified in a story told by a traveler in India (Arden, 1990, p. 132). The traveler saw a white-bearded man seated on a blanket, writing in a notebook. The man looked up and smiled as the traveler walked past. "Are you a Buddhist?" the traveler asked, to which the man shook his head. "A Hindu? A Muslim?"

Again, he shook his head, and replied, "Does it matter? I am a man." The traveler asked what the man was writing. "The truth," he said, "only the truth."

The final stage is one of *sannyasin*, defined by the *Bhagavad-Gita* as "one who neither hates nor loves anything." In this stage, the person achieves *mukti* and is living only because the time to make the final ascent has not come. When he or she finally departs from this world, freedom from the cycle of life and death is attained.

A person can pass through the four stages of life in a single lifetime or stay at each stage for many lifetimes. Even Buddha is reputed to have passed through several hundred lives. Progress is determined in light of the activities and inclination of the person at each stage of life. For example, Indian religion is replete with rituals, the primary purpose of which is to receive the blessings of God. Each ceremony involves the singing of religious songs (*bhajans*) and discourses by priests and other religious people (*satsang*). The sincerity with which people indulge in these activities and apply the tenets of the philosophy in their practical life determines their progress through the cycle of life and death. A person may expound philosophy at great length, go to the temple every day, and offer alms to saints and the poor, yet indulge in all sorts of vices. These contradictions in life are resolved on death by karma, which dictates that upon reincarnation, each person will receive rewards or punishment for his or her accumulated good and bad deeds.

The Hindu desire for positive outcomes of daily activities, resulting in positive karma, leads us to a brief discussion of the importance of astrology. With so much at stake, almost everyone in India consults the stars, if not on a daily basis, then at least on important occasions. Matching the horoscopes of a bride and groom is as much a part of planning a marriage as choosing the flower arrangements. It is routine for Indians to consult the stars about the best day to close on a house or sign an important contract. When it was revealed that an astrologer helped former President Ronald Reagan's wife, Nancy, set her schedule, Americans hooted with derision. In contrast, no one in India batted an eye when India's former prime minister, Narasimha Rao, delayed naming his cabinet because an astrologer warned that the intended day was not auspicious enough.

Like Hindu philosophy, the Indian concept of time is cyclical, characterized by origination, duration, and disappearance ad infinitum. This is reflected in the dramatic structure of a traditional Sanskrit play. These plays are typically based on the themes of separation and reunion, and they tend to end as they begin. Various devices are used—the dream, the trance, the premonition, and the flashback—to disrupt the linearity of time and make the action recoil upon itself (Lannoy, 1971, p. 54). Similarly, the Dance of Shiva is a repetitive cycle of creation, existence, and destruction; constant change within a period of time, but ultimately, time itself is irrelevant.

In an attempt to neutralize the anguish of impermanence and change, the carved religious images that every village home possesses are made of permanent materials, such as clay or metal. This also reveals the functional role of the image in a materially restricted environment. The practice of religion at home is one of the main reasons Hinduism was able to survive the invasion of foreign powers over the centuries. And just as religion is important to the family, so, too, the family plays a dominant factor in Indian society.

THE FAMILY CYCLE

Most Indians grow up in an extended family, a form of family organization in which brothers remain together after marriage and bring their wives into their parental household or compound of homes. Recent migration to cities and towns in search of economic opportunities has contributed to the weakening of many traditions, including that of extended families. In this section, we describe family traditions that exist most strongly in the India of about 400 million people that continues to be affected marginally by industrialization. While weakened in some parts of society, many aspects of the family cycle are still important to all.

The preference for a son when a child is born is as old as Indian society. A son guarantees the continuation of the generations, and he will perform the last rites after his parents' death. This ensures a peaceful departure of the soul to its next existence in the ongoing cycle of life. The word *putra*, or son,

literally means "he who protects from going to hell." In contrast, a daughter has negligible ritual significance. She is normally an unmitigated expense—someone who will never contribute to the family income and who, upon marriage, will take away a considerable part of her family's fortune as her dowry. Although formally abolished, the institution of dowry is still widespread in India, but it is becoming increasingly fashionable among educated Indians not to indulge in the practice.

A striking reflection of this gender preference is the continued masculinization of the Indian population, particularly in the north. There are 108 males to 100 females. The main reasons for this outcome are the higher mortality rate of female children and the tendency to limit family size once there is a sufficient number of sons. Also, the recent availability of sex determination tests has allowed women to ensure that their firstborn is a boy, because they can abort unwanted female children.

Just as the Dance of Shiva represents preservation, overlooking, and support, parents tend to nurture their children with great care. A Hindu child grows up in the security of the extended family and has few contacts with other groups until it is time for school. Although the mother is chiefly responsible for the care of the child, there is also close contact with other females and mother-surrogates, and this continues for much longer than in many other cultures. A child is usually breastfed for at least two years (although significantly less in the case of a female child) and will be fed any time that it cries. Consequently, most infants are virtually never left alone.

The strong ties of home life do not conflict with the Hindu belief in the liberty of the soul removed from worldly concerns. Love of family is not merely a purpose in itself but a way to the final goal of life. Love will not yield the rewards of *mukti* when it remains self-centered; that is why Hindus try to diffuse their love over sons, daughters, guests, and neighbors (Munshi, 1965, p. 115).

Children in India are considered sacred, a manifestation of God, but if the Hindu ideal is a very high degree of infant indulgence, reality is somewhat different in the poorer areas of India. Here, there are typically many young children under one roof, and 1 in 10 will die in infancy, so babies are not regarded as extraordinary creatures. Except for the firstborn son, they tend to be taken for granted. This is reinforced by the belief in rebirth; because an individual is not born once and once only, he or she cannot be regarded as a unique event. The mother has probably witnessed the birth of several babies and may have seen them die, too. When her child cries, falls sick, or is accidentally hurt, she is not beset with feelings of intense guilt. A mother's work may be long and hard, both in the home and in the fields, so she is unable to give her child undivided attention.

Even as the Dance of Shiva leads the world through the joys of existence, an element of chaos is inherent in the world's Daily Dance. Similarly, nature in India has been full of threats to a child's safety—famine, disease, and chronic civil disorder. As a rule, until modern times, more than half of all deaths befell children in their first year of life. But as the nation got a grip on its affairs, and as campaigns against diseases such as malaria and smallpox took hold, mortality rates fell. By 1981, nearly three out of four newborns could expect to survive to age 20 (Narayana & Kantner, 1992, p. 26). The cultural importance of children is derived from the need to carry on the cycle of life. This continued importance is reflected in statistics that show that although death rates since 1921 have fallen, birth rates have declined much more slowly.

Government attempts to regulate the birth rate have become synonymous with its sterilization programs. Resentment against coerced sterilization in India helped defeat Indira Gandhi's government in 1977. As a result of the political fallout, birth control was set back as a popular cause. Middle-class Indians, influenced by education and the desire for an improved standard of living, are increasingly adopting family planning methods. But when the formidable psychic barrier of traditional Hindu beliefs in the life cycle is considered, it seems clear that rapid population growth will continue in the poorer, rural areas.

An Indian father is frequently remote, aloof, and a much-feared disciplinary figure, just as Shiva is distant from the world he nurtures. But there are also special bonds between father and son, and the relationship is one of mutual dependence. A son must obey his father unquestioningly, pay him respect, and offer complete support in every need both in life and after death. The father owes his son support, a good education, the best possible marital arrangement, and inheritance of property. One Indian proverb reads: "A son should be treated as a prince for five years; as a slave for ten years; but from his sixteenth birthday, as a friend."

The son learns that women are lower in status than men very early in life. The position of any woman in this hierarchical society means that she must constantly be making demands and pleading with superiors for one thing or another. The son soon develops an attitude of superiority. A female's authority can seldom be absolute, except for the unchallengeable position that the senior grandmother may inherit. A son finds out that anger may be productive; violent outbursts of anger are often effective if directed against someone of uncertain status. Similarly, the destructive powers of the Dance of Shiva are effective in creating new opportunities and patterns.

The relative position of men and women is clear in Indian society, and the question of competitive equality is not customarily considered. The Hindu marriage emphasizes identity, not equality. Generally, women are thought to have younger souls, and therefore, they are nearer to the world than men and inferior to them. Girls are trained to be submissive and docile, and to fulfill culturally designated feminine roles. The ideal of womanhood in Indian tradition is one of chastity, purity, gentle tenderness, self-effacement, self-sacrifice, and singular faithfulness. Throughout history, Indian women have had dual status—as a wife, she seduces her husband away from his work and spiritual duties, but as a mother, she is revered.

Among the crosses women have had to bear in Indian society are female infanticide, child marriage, *purdah* (feminine modesty and seclusion), marital mistreatment, and the low status of widows. Until the mid-19th century, the voluntary immolation of the widow on her husband's funeral pyre (*sati*) was not uncommon; the widow believed her act would cleanse her family of the sins of the three generations. Poor families are more likely to be fearful of not being able to scrape together enough money to find their daughters husbands and may resort to killing infant girls. Generally speaking, however, the lower down the economic hierarchy, the more equal are the relations between the sexes. Of course, many factors can bring about or alleviate hostile feelings toward women, but they often view the various forms of mistreatment suffered by women as part of their destiny as a woman. The Dance of Shiva is not destined to lead to joy throughout the world, and if the corresponding experience of humankind includes some unhappiness for women in society, that is simply the way things are.

A man's worth and recognition of his identity are bound up intimately in the reputation of his family. Lifestyle and actions are rarely seen as the product of individual effort, but are interpreted in the light of family circumstance and reputation in the wider society. Individual identity and merit are enhanced if the person has the good fortune to belong to a large, harmonious, and closely knit family, which helps safeguard a child's upbringing and advance a person in life. The family contributes to decisions that affect an individual's future, maximizes the number of connections necessary to secure a job or other favors, comes to aid in times of crisis, and generally mediates an individual's experience with the outside world. For these reasons, the character of the respective families weighs heavily in the consideration of marriage proposals.

Arranged marriage is still the norm in India. Advertisements regularly appear in European and American newspapers to identify potential candidates. The Western concept of romantic love arises from the Western concept of personality and, ultimately, from the un-Indian concept of equality of the sexes. Still, the concept of life as an illusion makes the idea of loveless marriage easier to understand.

Marriages are usually for a lifetime, because divorce is considered socially disgraceful. The average age for Indian women to marry is 18 to 19, whereas only about 13% of U.S. women of this age are married. The percentage of Indian women aged 15 to 19 who are married ranges from 14% in states where a high value is put on female education, to more than 60% in less developed states (Narayana & Kantner, 1992, p. 31). In the case of child marriage, the girl lives at her parents' home until she is about 15 or 16 years of age, after which she moves to the home of her husband's family. A newly arrived daughter-in-law is sometimes subject to varying forms of humiliation until she becomes pregnant. This treatment originated historically from the urgent need to ensure the early birth of a son in times of low life expectancy. Also, the size of the dowry that a girl brings with her can also determine how she is treated or mistreated in her husband's home. The husband's family may keep making demands on her for additional support from her family and, if it is not forthcoming, she may be tortured or even burned alive, although the outcry against such treatment seemingly has diminished such illegal practices.

The restricted life of women in the conservative atmosphere of India does not prevent them from developing a strong sense of self-respect. Their ultimate role is to preserve unity and continuity in the chain of life, and there is pride and dignity in their sense of identity with the family and their role as wife and mother. Indian society seems to have given women, rather than men, resilience and vitality under the difficult circumstances of life in that country. But ultimately, all respond to the Dance of Shiva, and whether that brings great joy or unhappiness to the current life is irrelevant compared to the ongoing search for salvation, or *mukti*.

Since the beginning of time, dancing has been a rite performed by both men and women; Shiva and his wife, Parvati, are often depicted in ancient sculptures as one composite figure, half male and half female. Typical figurines of Shiva are four-armed, with broad masculine shoulders and curving womanly hips. Similarly, there is a place for both genders to contribute to Indian society today. In this century, Indian women have undergone a social revolution more far-reaching and radical than that of men. While this process has been going on, women have attained positions of distinction in public and professional life. The political dominance of Indira Gandhi is one example of how women can be held in high esteem by all Indians.

In summary, it can be seen that the extended family unit is still a strong feature of Indian society. Just as the Dance of Shiva wills all nature to respond to its rhythm, so, too, each member of the family fulfills a role dictated by family tradition.

THE CYCLE OF SOCIAL INTERACTION

A sense of duty (*dharma*) is the social cement in India; it holds the individal and society together. Dharma is a concept that is wider than the Western idea of duty, because it includes the totality of social, ethical, and spiritual harmony (Lannoy, 1971, p. 217). Dharma consists of three categories: universal principles of harmony (*sanatana dharma*), relative ethical systems varying by social class (*varnashrama dharma*), and personal moral conduct (*svadharma*). Among the prime traditional virtues are leading a generous and selfless life, truthfulness, restraint from greed, and respect for one's elders. These principles are consistent with a virtual global idea of righteousness. Hinduism has progressed through India's moments of crisis by lifting repeatedly the banner of the highest ideals. The image of the Dance of Shiva is strongly evoked by the following passage from the *Bhagavad-Gita*:

> Whenever the dharma decays, and when that which is not dharma prevails, then I manifest myself. For the protection of the good, for the destruction of the evil, for the firm establishment of the national righteousness, I am born again and again. (Deutsch, 1968, p. 31)

The oldest source of ethical ideas is the *Mahabharata*, or Great Epic (of Bharata), the first version of which appeared between the seventh and sixth centuries B.C. It is a huge composite poem of 90,000 couplets, in 18 books, that traces the rivalry between two families involved in an unrelenting war. The story is interrupted by numerous episodes, fables, moral tales, and long political and ethical discourses, all of which illustrate the illusory nature of the world and encourage the reader to strive for God. This sacred book, a repository of Hindu beliefs and customs, is based on the assumption that dharma is paramount in the affairs of society. The epics took at least 1,000 years to compose and are still the most widely read and respected religious books of the Hindus. The most popular and influential part of the epics is the *Bhagavad-Gita* ("Song of the Blessed One"), a book Gandhi once said "described the duel that perpetually went on in the hearts of mankind."

A recent European traveler in India gave this illustration of the power of dharma. Sitting precariously among local people on top of a bus during a long journey, the traveler was astounded when a sudden shower of money fell into the dusty road behind them. An Indian alongside the traveler began shouting and pounding on the roof of the bus for the driver to stop. At some distance down the road, the bus pulled over and the man rushed away. All of the passengers disembarked and waited for the Indian to return, laughing at his comic misfortune and manic disappearance. Eventually the man reappeared, clutching a big handful of notes, including Western money. It was then that the traveler realized his own wallet was gone from his back pocket; it had come loose and blown away from the top of the bus, scattering the equivalent of a year's income for the average native (about $350). The Indian, a total stranger, had run back and convinced the poverty-stricken locals to hand over the money they were gathering ecstatically from their fields. The traveler began to thank his new friend for his troubles, but with the comment "It was my duty," the Indian declined to take any reward.

It is generally believed that social conflict, oppression, and unrest do not stem from social organizations, but originate in the nonadherence to dharma by those in positions of power. Their actions have created the cycle of disharmony. Hindus see a quarrel as a drama with three actors—two contestants and a peacemaker—and not one of the protagonists but the peacemaker is seen as the victor in the dispute, because he or she has restored harmony (Lannoy, 1971, p. 198).

Individuals who head institutions are believed to be the sole repositories of the virtues and vices of the institution. Traditionally, social reform movements focused not so much on abolishing the hierarchical organizations or rejecting the values on which they are based, but on removing or changing the individuals holding positions of authority in them (Kakar, 1978). For example, during the declining years of both the Mughal and British Indian Empires, the ruling classes enjoyed lives of luxury and extravagance in India. Conspicuous consumption by the aristocratic elites at the expense of the productive classes still exists in the India of the early 21st century. The identity may have changed, but the attitude remains.

The issues behind the social and political ferment in India today are not rooted primarily in economic deprivation and frustration, although these make the mix more volatile (Narayana & Kantner, 1992, p. 2). Rather, it is the widespread feeling that the institutions on which the society was founded no longer work. In a reflective piece written shortly after the assassination of Rajiv Gandhi, the New Delhi correspondent of *The Economist* ("Death Among the Blossoms," 1991) wrote that:

> The state is seen as corrupt and callous, incapable of delivering justice or prosperity to the people. . . . The police and civil servants are seen as oppressors and terrorists. The law courts are venal and can take decades to decide a case. The rule of law does not seem to be working in settling people's grievances. What seems to work is violence and money, and all political parties are engaged in a mad race to maximize the use of both. . . . Amid this moral decay, religious, ethnic and caste crusades have a growing appeal. People find a purity in them which they do not find in secular, national parties. And an increasing number of people are willing to kill in the name of causes that they find holier than the discredited law of the land. (p. 40)

The tragic recourse to mob violence by religious followers at different times in the country's history is a contradiction that astounds casual observers of India. How can such terrible things happen in a country where everyone believes in harmony and awaits the ultimate consequences of good and bad deeds in reincarnation? Hindus believe that *sila*, character or behavior, has its roots in the depths of the mind rather than in the heat of the action (Lannoy, 1971, p. 295). Because all worldly acts are transient, part of the illusion of life, they can have no decisive moral significance. Within the Dance of Shiva, destruction exists as strongly as creation and preservation; so it is with India.

This is not to say that violence is condoned by the Hindu faith; just the opposite applies. However, Hindus avoid the theological use of the terms "good" and "evil," and they prefer to speak of "knowledge" and "ignorance"—*vidya* and *avidya*. Destructive acts done by people who are ignorant are not regarded as sins, but those acts committed by people aware of their responsibilities are counted against them in their seeking of *mukti*.

Bathing in the holy water of the Ganges is believed to wash away all the sins of the person, and it is required of every Hindu at least once in his or her life. Indians tend to synthesize or integrate with nature because they assume that this is the natural relationship of human beings with the world, unlike Westerners, who tend to exploit the physical environment for their own purposes. But the belief in the spiritual purity of the Ganges is so strong that government attempts to clean up the badly polluted waters have little chance of being effective. Many people simply do not accept that anything can spoil the Ganges's perfection. As a consequence, rotting carcasses of both animals and partly cremated people are a common sight along the riverbanks. The image of death among life, decomposition next to creation, and pollution mixed with purity is evocative of the Dance of Shiva.

Another pervasive social dimension in India is the caste system (*verna*), which is now officially outlawed but is still a source of constant tension. Following the assumed natural law that an individual soul is born into its own befitting environment, Hindus assume that an individual belongs to a caste by birth. There are four main castes, each of which contributes to society in specific ways: (1) Brahmans, seers or religious people; (2) administrators; (3) producers such as skilled craftspeople and farmers; and (4) followers or unskilled laborers. Each of these natural classes has its appropriate honor and duties, but as privilege has entered the scale, with top castes profiting at the expense of those lower down, the whole system has begun to disintegrate. Below the system is a fifth group, the untouchables, who lie outside of the major activities of society. Its members are engaged in work that is considered socially undesirable and unclean. Untouchability, as it exists today, is often described as a perversion of the original caste system.

Within each caste or group, there are numerous subcastes, or *jati*, that influence the immediacy of all daily social relations, including work. About 3,000 *jati* exist, and they are further divisible into about 30,000 sub-*jati*, with unwritten codes governing the relationships between *jatis*. Friendships with members of the same *jati* tend to be closer and more informal than do those with members of other *jatis*. As a general rule, a person's name provides information not only about his or her *jati* but also about the region of the country from which the person's family originated. For example, Gupta is a family name from the trading class, although many have gone into the professions, especially teaching. Most Guptas come from the North Indian states of Haryana, Uttar Pradesh, and West Bengal.

The *jati's* values, beliefs, and prejudices become part of each individual's psyche or conscience. The internalized *jati* norms define the right actions, or dharma, for an individual—he or she feels good or loved when living up to these rules, and guilty when transgressing them.

When society was divided strictly by caste, there was no attempt to realize a competitive equality, and within each caste, all interests were regarded as identical. But that also meant that equality of opportunity existed for all within the caste—every individual was allowed to develop the experience and skills that he or she needed to succeed at the caste's defined role. The castes were self-governing, which ensured that each person was tried and judged by his peers. Central authorities viewed crimes committed by upper-caste members more severely than those of the lower caste. Because it was simply not possible to move outside of the caste, all possibility of social ambition, with its accompanying tension, was avoided. This suits the Hindu belief in harmony. The comprehensiveness of the caste system, together with holistic dharma, contributed to the stability that prevailed among the vast mass of people for much of India's history. Preservation of order, interspaced with disorder, is a characteristic of the Dance of Shiva.

The worst facet of the caste system falls on the untouchables. This caste has come to be the symbol of India's own brand of human injustice, victims of a system that kept people alive in squalor. Of course, social hierarchy is universal, found not only among the Hindus but also among the Muslims, Christians, Sikhs, Jains, and Jews (Srinivas, 1980). There is also a prevalence of pollution taboos in all civilizations, including the most advanced and modern; eliminating dirt is an attempt to introduce order into the environment (Lannoy, 1971, p. 146). But Hindu society pays exceptional attention to the idea of purity and pollution, and historically, this has resulted in the virtual ostracism of the untouchables from the rest of society.

By way of historical explanation, Hindus believed that proximity to the contaminating factor constitutes a permanent pollution that is both collective and hereditary. Therefore, they had a dread of being polluted by members of society who were specialists in the elimination of impurity. Hindu society was more conscious of grading social groups according to their degree of purity than of a precise division of castes into occupations. The untouchables—traditionally, society's cleaners, butchers, and the like—were at the bottom of the Hindu hierarchy because they were considered irrevocably unclean. A similar caste system was developed in Japan, and it, too, has been outlawed, although its effects are still being felt.

Although India's traditional social structure was based on institutionalized inequality, today the government, and supposedly the nation, too, is committed to social equality. Beginning with Mahatma Gandhi, public figures have tried to reform the attitudes of Indian society toward the untouchables. Gandhi named them *Harijan*, literally, "Children of God." The entire caste system was declared illegal by the Constitution, and today, untouchables are guaranteed 22.5% of government jobs as compensation for traditional disfavor. These policies have met with some success, but such a deep-rooted prejudice cannot be eliminated by a mere stroke of the pen.

The ambiguity of caste in occupational terms is another wedge by which the lower castes push their way upward on the scale. However, ambiguity is not so great as to render the system inoperative. Violations of caste norms, such as inter-caste marriage, still evoke responses of barbaric ferocity. Educated Indians look upon such incidents as throwbacks to the inhumanity of feudal times that must be dealt with sternly by the authorities. But efforts to create greater equality of opportunity for members of the traditionally disadvantaged castes meet stiff resistance from these same ranks (Narayana & Kantner, 1992, p. 5).

Additional reforms remain problematical, as recent history suggests. In 1990, the government introduced policies reserving 27% of central and state jobs for these castes and Christian and Muslim groups that were socially backward. In protest, dozens of upper-caste students burned themselves to death. The upper-caste Brahmans, a mere 5.5% of the population, have traditionally run government departments, but the struggle for jobs in India is so intense that the students saw themselves as victims of injustice, not historical oppressors. The prime minister at the time, V. P. Singh, was forced to resign when the government's coalition partner withdrew its support of the government, mainly over caste reform issues.

The Harijan quickly realized their ability to assert their democratic rights as equal citizens through organized political activity. The effect of politicization of caste in modern times has made it clear that power is becoming ascendant over status. Modern education also acts as a solvent of caste barriers. These factors hold out the best hope for the disappearance of caste over the longer term.

The hierarchical principle of social organization has been central to the conservatism of Indian tradition. Among the criteria for ordering are age and gender. Elders have more formal authority than younger people, and, as we have already related, men have greater authority than women. Many times, women are not involved in social functions or conversations and are required to cover their heads in front of elders or mature guests. Most relationships are hierarchical in structure, characterized by almost maternal nurturing on the part of the superior, and by filial respect and compliance on the part of the subordinate. The ordering of social behavior extends to every institution in Indian life, including the workplace, which we will examine shortly.

It is clear that the traditional social structure of India is undergoing change and reform. This is consistent with the evolutionary aspects of the Dance of Shiva. But any change requires the destruction of old ways, and pressure is beginning to build within the old system. It may be that before those changes are complete, Shiva will rest, and chaos will rule for a time. Or, perhaps a new rhythm is beginning for the dance of the 21st century, and the Daily Dance of Indian society will quietly adjust in response.

THE WORK AND RECREATION (REJUVENATION) CYCLE

There are several different perspectives on the importance of work: to earn a living; to satisfy the worldly interests of accomplishments, power, and status; and to fulfill the desire to create and care for the family. An aspect considered more important in India is that work enables, prepares, and progresses the individual through the cycle of life toward the ultimate aim of achieving *mukti*. The Indian approach to work is best defined by the *Bhagavad-Gita*: "Both renunciation and practice of work lead to the highest bliss. Of these two, the practice of work is better than its renunciation" (Deutsch, 1968, p. 60).

Work was prescribed originally as duty (dharma) without any concern for material outcomes. Castes were occupational clusters, each discharging their roles and, in turn, being maintained by the overall system. But meeting the obligations to one's relatives, friends, and even strangers, as well as maintaining relationships, constituted the ethos of the system. Even with the rapid expansion of industrial activity in the 20th century, requiring large-scale importation of Western technology and work forms, Indians have internalized Western work values only partially. Today, with government-mandated affirmative action, it is not unlikely that someone from a higher caste may work for someone from a lower caste. Many Indians have developed a state of mind that allows them to put aside caste prejudice in the workplace but, on returning home, to conduct all of their social activities strictly according to caste norms.

We have already seen how family life develops an acute sense of dependence in the individual that serves to fortify the participative and collective nature of society. Similarly, most Indian organizations have numerous overlapping in-groups, with highly personalized relationships between the members of each group. They cooperate, make sacrifices for the common good, and generally protect each other's interests. But in-groups often interfere with the functioning of formally designated sections, departments, and divisions, and they can lead to factionalism and intense power plays within an organization. Just as disorder within order is a characteristic of the Dance of Shiva, so, too, is incompetence often overlooked because work performance is more relationship oriented than contractual in nature. A competent person may be respected but not included in a group unless he or she possesses the group characteristics.

Family, relatives, caste members, and people speaking the same language or belonging to the same religion may form in-groups. Typically, there are regionally oriented subgroups, formed on the basis of states, districts, towns, and villages from which people's families originated. Within the group, Indians are informal and friendly.

Geert Hofstede's (1980) attitudinal survey of the cultural differences among some 53 countries is especially helpful in the case of India, which tends to cluster with those countries where there is a high degree of uncertainty avoidance. Indians tend to work with lifelong friends and colleagues and minimize risk-taking behavior. This orientation is consistent with the Hindu philosophy of life as an illusion, Indians' preoccupation with astrology, and their resignation to karma. India also falls with those countries characterized by large power distances. However, India ranks 21st of the 53 nations on individualism. Although we might expect a more collectivistic orientation, this ranking may reflect the influence of British rule. Finally, India has a high score on masculinity, which is consistent with the emphasis on male domination in Hinduism. Generally, the values described by Hofstede reflect a historical continuity and resilience of the Indian social system, despite the onslaught of foreign invasions, colonial rulers, and economic dislocations.

The hierarchical principle continues to be a source of stagnation in modern Indian institutions. Younger people have a limited, or no, say in decision making. Persistent critical questioning or confrontations on issues necessary to effect change simply do not occur. Any conflict between intellectual conviction and developmental fate manifests itself in a vague sense of helplessness and impotent rage. Gradually, the younger workers resign themselves to waiting until they become seniors in their own right, free to enjoy the delayed gratification that age brings with it in Indian society. The apparent lack of control and ambition displayed by the participants at work is similar to the resignation of the world to the will of Shiva. The world responds to Shiva's rhythm, captive of its pace, and is unable to influence it.

The importance of honoring family and *jati* bonds leads to nepotism, dishonesty, and corruption in the commercial world. These are irrelevant abstract concepts; guilt and anxiety are aroused only when individual actions go against the principle of primacy of relationships, not when foreign standards

of ethics and efficiency are breached. This creates legendary tales of corrupt officials that are shared widely among travelers and businesspeople who have spent time in India.

Indian organizations have been shaped by colonial experiences that have bureaucratized them and polarized the positions of the rulers (managers) and the ruled (workers). As a consequence, the role of the manager tends to be viewed as that of an order-giver or autocrat. In "Going International" (1983), a popular management training videotape, there is a telling vignette involving an American manager and one of his Indian subordinate managers. As a general rule, American managers perceive their role to be that of a problem solver or facilitator and attempt to involve subordinates in routine decisions (Adler, 1997). The American manager in this videotape attempted to use this style with his Indian subordinate, who wondered about his superior's competence and held him in some contempt for not being autocratic. The clear implication is that American managers must act more authoritatively in India than in the United States.

In the areas of rejuvenation and recreation, one of their sources for the Indian people is participation in the many religious festivals held throughout the year. These festivals are usually associated with agricultural cycles or the rich mythology of India's past. In some regions, community festivals involve the active participation of not only Hindus, but also members of other religions. Family bonds are emphasized and strengthened repeatedly through the joint celebration of religious festivals. The Indian sense of fun and play is given free rein during the festivities, which often include riddles, contests of strength, role reversals, and rebellious acts. Just as the Dance of Shiva is an expression of his joy and exuberance, festivals give Hindus an opportunity to express their feelings of devotion and happiness.

Religious raptures, possessions, and trances are common during Indian seasonal festivals. This is a structured and, in some cases, highly formalized phenomenon that enriches the consciousness of the individual and the group. There are also the attendant dangers of degeneration into hysterical mob psychology, which Indian history has witnessed many times. Festivals allow the discharge of intense emotion that is otherwise submerged in a network of reciprocity and caste relations, but they also can be used to reestablish order. In this sense, festivals mirror the activity, relapse, and reordering of the cosmos that is the result of the Dance of Shiva. But just as the dancer cannot help dancing, the celebrant is not always capable of restraining his or her religious fervor.

Memorials to the grand line of India's "modern gods"—Mahatma Gandhi, Jawaharlal Nehru, and now Indira Gandhi—are as much the objects of pilgrimages as any temple or festival. Indira Gandhi was killed by her own trusted Sikh bodyguards just five months after she ordered the storming of the Golden Temple at Amritsar by the Indian army to dislodge Sikh rebels. Her home in New Delhi is now a museum and shrine visited by thousands daily. The spot in her garden where she was gunned down is bracketed by two soldiers; her bullet-ridden *sari* (dress) is on display inside. Crowds gather before these, many weeping.

Another Indian example is that of N. T. Rama Rao, a former movie star and chief minister of the state of Andhra Pradesh from 1983 to 1989. Rama Rao acted in leading roles in more than 320 films with mythical, historical, and folklore themes. Among the masses, Rama Rao was associated with the qualities of the gods he played, and when he gave up his movie career to establish a new political party, he was voted into office immediately. The fact that his party's radical Hindu fundamentalist policies sometimes caused strife within society is not inconsistent with the concurrently constructive and destructive nature of the Dance of Shiva.

The favorite pastime of Indians is watching movies, either at movie theaters or through renting videos from the shops that have sprung up all over the country, and today, India's "Hollywood" is the second largest producer of films in the world. Movies that draw on images and symbols from traditional themes are dominant in popular Indian culture. They incorporate but go beyond the familiar repertoire of plots from traditional theater. Films appeal to an audience so diverse that they transcend social and spatial categories. The language and values from popular movies have begun to influence Indian ideas of the good life and the ideology of social, family, and romantic relationships. Robert Stoller's definition of fantasy, "[the] protector from reality, concealer of truth, restorer of tranquility, enemy of fear

and sadness, and cleanser of the soul" (1975, p. 55), includes terms that are equally attributable to the illusory nature of the Dance of Shiva, and it is easy to understand why films play such a major role in Indian recreation and rejuvenation.

CONCLUSION

India is the heart of Asia, and Hinduism is a convenient name for the nexus of Indian thought. It has taken 1,000 to 1,500 years to describe a single rhythm of its great pulsation, as described by the *Mahabharata*, or Great Epic. By invoking the image and meaning of the Dance of Shiva, and drawing parallels between this legendary act of a Hindu deity and many of the main influences of traditional Indian life, we have attempted to communicate the essence of India's society in this chapter.

It is not always possible to identify a nicely logical or easily understandable basis for many of the contradictions that exist in Indian society, just as it is difficult to explain the existence of racism, sexism, and other forms of intolerance and injustice in Western countries. In India, the philosophy of life and the mental structure of its people come not from a study of books but from tradition (Munshi, 1965, p. 148). However much foreign civilization and new aspirations might have affected the people of India, the spiritual nutrient of Hindu philosophy has not dried up or decayed (Munshi, 1965, p. 148); within this tradition, the role of the Dance of Shiva, described as follows, is accepted by all Hindus (Coomaraswamy, 1924/1969):

Shiva rises from his rapture and, dancing, sends through inert matter pulsing waves of awakening sound. Suddenly, matter also dances, appearing as a brilliance around him. Dancing, Shiva sustains the world's diverse phenomena, its creation and existence. And, in the fullness of time, still dancing, he destroys all forms—everything disintegrates, apparently into nothingness, and is given new rest. Then, out of the thin vapor, matter and life are created again. Shiva's dance scatters the darkness of illusion (*lila*), burns the thread of causality (*karma*), stamps out evil (*avidya*), showers grace, and lovingly plunges the soul into the ocean of bliss (*ananda*). (p. 66)

India will continue to experience the range of good and bad, happiness and despair, creation and destruction. Through it all, its people will continue their journey toward *moksha*, salvation from the worldly concerns of humankind. Hindu philosophy is the key to understanding India and how a nation of such diversity manages to bear its immense burdens while its people seem undeterred and filled with inner peace and religious devotion.

And through it all, Shiva dances on.

References

Adler, N. (1997). *International dimensions of organizational behavior* (3d ed.). Cincinnati, OH: South-Western College Publishing.

Arden, N. (1990, May). Searching for India among the great trunk road. *National Geographic*, 186, 177–185.

Banerji, P. (1983). *Erotica in Indian dance*. Atlantic Highlands, NJ: Humanities Press.

Coomaraswamy, A. (1969). *The dance of Shiva*. New York: Sunwise Turn. (Original work published 1924.)

Death among the blossoms. (1991, May 25). *The Economist*, 322, 39–41.

Deutsch, E. (1968). *Bhagavad gita*. New York: Holt, Rinehart & Winston.

Going international: Part 2, Managing the overseas assignment. (1983). [Videotape]. (Available from Copeland Griggs Productions, San Francisco, 415/668-4200).

Gopal, R., & Dadachanji, S. (1951). *Indian dancing*. London: Phoenix House.

Hofstede, G. (1980). *Culture's consequences*. Beverly Hills, CA: Sage Publications.

Kakar, S. (1978). *The inner world*. New York: Oxford University Press.

Karp, J., & Williams, M. (1998, April 22). Leave it to Vishnu: Gods of Indian TV are Hindu deities. *Wall Street Journal*, A1, A6.

Lannoy, R. (1971). *The speaking tree: A Study of Indian culture and society*. New York: Oxford University Press.

Munshi, K. (1965). *Indian inheritance* (Vol. 1). Bombay, India: Bharatiya Vidya Bhavan.

Narayana, G., & Kantner, J. (1992). *Doing the needful*. Boulder, CO: Westview University Press.

Smith, H. (1958). *The religions of man*. San Francisco: Harper Collins.

Srinivas, M. (1980). *India: Social structure*. Delhi: Hindustan.

Stoller, R. (1975). *Perversion: The erotic form of hatred*. New York: Pantheon.

Concepts and Questions

1. Why is dance an appropriate metaphor to help you understand Indian culture?

2. How does the "dance of Shiva" help define the deep structure of Indian culture?

3. How do European and American cultural perspectives of life in relation to the study of philosophy differ from that of Indian culture?

4. Gannon suggests that for the Hindu, life is a journey in search of salvation. How does the "dance of Shiva" facilitate this journey?

5. What is the structure of the Indian family? What roles and relationships exist between men and women? How do children fit into the structure of the Indian family?

6. Describe the Indian caste system and how it functions within Indian culture.

7. How does "institutionalized inequity" relate to the caste system?

8. How do the Hindu concepts of purity and pollution affect interpersonal relationships?

9. How does the hierarchical principle of Indian culture cause stagnation in the modern society?

10. How do Indian cultural values toward words differ from those found in the U.S.?

Africa: Communication and Cultural Patterns

SHIRLEY VAN DER VEUR

When I was in Naples [Italy] in February 1955, on my way to the United States, I startled six of my white missionary friends when I suddenly ordered our taxi-driver to stop.

"What is the matter, Ndaba?" the Reverend John Marsh asked me.

"There is a friend of mine over there," I replied, and no sooner had I said that than I banged the door of the taxi behind me and hurried across the street to see my friend who also had seen me. We just fell into each other's arms. I was so happy to see him, he was so happy to see me.

The only sound I could understand from him was "Somalia," and when I reciprocated this with "Rhodesia," he apparently understood me, and cried, "Africa."

I repeated, "Yes, Africa." We shook hands again and indicated by gestures the taxi which I had unceremoniously stopped and which was impatiently waiting for my return.

"What was that, Ndaba?" the Reverend John Marsh asked.

"I don't know except that he's an African like me," I said.

"But we thought he was a friend of yours!" the Reverend John Marsh cried with surprise.

"Oh, yes, he is, although I have never met him before."[1]

This essay is about communication and cultural patterns evident in Africa South of the Sahara. One note of caution before we begin: it is important to realize that great cultural diversity exists among the approximately 2,000 ethnic groups in Africa. Africa is composed of 56 countries, and it is so vast that the continental United States could fit within it three and one-half times! When studying intercultural communication in this enormous region, it is imperative to be conscious of the dynamic nature of

This original essay appears here in print for the first time. All rights reserved. Permission to reprint must be obtained from the author and the publisher. Shirley van der Veur is a Returned Peace Corps Volunteer who served in Lesotho and a former Fulbright fellow who studied in Botswana, South Africa, and the United Kingdom. She currently teaches at the University of Montana.

African cultures, realizing that they are not "timeless," but ever changing. There is not one monolithic African culture just as there is not one Native American culture or one European culture.

In this essay, I have chosen to discuss Africa South of the Sahara, where cultural patterns are quite a bit different from North Africa. Even in Africa South of the Sahara, societies vary in organization of kinship and economic structure. For example, Africa has both matrilineal and patrilineal peoples; a few remaining gathering and hunting societies, such as the San in Botswana and Namibia or the Mbuti in the Democratic Republic of Congo; herding cultures like the well-known Maasai people of East Africa or the Fulani of West Africa; and traditional cultures based primarily on fishing and farming. Moreover, African cultures have been directly impacted by colonialism, Western education, and advancing urbanization.

THE IMPORTANCE OF AFRICA

As we enter the 21st century, it's wise for us to reflect on past affiliations between the West and Africa and to reconceptualize future relationships. During the 19th century, after exporting more than 10 million West and Central Africans to the Americas, the international slave trade became defunct. Colonial rule, which began in approximately 1900 and lasted through the 1960s and beyond, in some cases profoundly and irreversibly changed Africa. The Cold War between the superpowers of the United States and the Soviet Union began in the post–World War II era and symbolically ended with the fall of the Berlin Wall. The Cold War significantly impacted Africa in that both superpowers attempted to influence African countries politically by providing economic development and, sometimes, military aid. Now that the Cold War has ended, Africans are speculating about their position in the New World Order. What will the effects be on African countries that receive less economic assistance? Will decreased attention from the West and the East improve the future situation in Africa, or will it create more suffering? These questions are but a few of the many that explore future relationships between Africa and the rest of the world.

Americans need to improve their understanding of the unequal power relationships between the United States and African governments, and to promote more egalitarian affiliations. Communication technologies are increasingly reaching the African continent. African universities and other institutions now have capabilities to communicate globally via e-mail. The University of Zambia and Eduardo Mondlane University in Mozambique are taking innovative steps to make the Internet accessible to its university population and to put African expertise on the Internet. As Mondlane's Deputy Vice-Chancellor, Venancio Massingue, puts it: "You cannot be part of the global village by just sitting and waiting to be 'globalized.' We want to be the globalizers" ("How Two African Universities Have Moved Ahead," 1999, p. A52).

The development of mutually beneficial trade relationships will also entail that Americans communicate effectively with African cultures. The new South Africa, in particular, promises to be a lucrative market for those who know how to conduct themselves appropriately in various cultural situations. Moreover, as the African-American population develops greater intimacy with the African continent through religious, economic, and social ties, more Americans will become aware of contemporary Africa. Evidence of this trend can be seen in the growing popularity of Kwanzaa (Swahili for "fresh fruits"), an African-American holiday that celebrates the reaffirmation of African culture by highlighting the seven basic principles of unity, self-determination, collective work and responsibility, cooperative economics, purpose, creativity, and faith.

STEREOTYPES AND LIMITED PERCEPTIONS OF AFRICA AND AFRICANS

The fact that Africa is one of the least understood areas of the globe becomes clear to me every time I teach my introductory African Studies class at Montana Tech of the University of Montana. On the first day of class, I ask students what images come to mind when I say "Africa." Invariably, responses include elephants, giraffes, Nelson Mandela, poverty, ethnic conflict, jungles, tropical heat, villages, and corruption. Although it's true that all these people, places, and issues exist in Africa, the full picture is much more varied and complex.[2] For example, would it surprise you to know that women in Africa produce 70% of the staple food crops? Or that tropical rainforest occupies less than one tenth of the continent? Or that it snows in the mountainous, southern African country of Lesotho?

Sadly, many Americans think of Africa as one enormous, but monolithic "country." I remember overhearing an embarrassing conversation in the United States among three women: an American, a Nigerian, and a Swazi. The Swazi woman sang her national anthem for the other two women. The American woman remarked on the beauty of the song, but she could not understand why Nigeria did not have the same national anthem as Swaziland. The African women were stunned that the American did not know that each African country had its own anthem. The American thought that Nigeria and Swaziland were states of "the country of Africa," not separate countries.

The American public has gleaned limited, often erroneous, information about Africa through popular culture. Some Africanists theorize that Americans have two main stereotypes of African people: savages and innocents. In old *Tarzan* films, Africans are shown as violent heathens wearing body paint, feathers, and bones in their noses, or, conversely, as passive servants dominated by whites. In such popular films as *The Gods Must Be Crazy*, Africans are seen as being completely unaware of 20th-century technologies. And while *National Geographic* films and publications provide the general public with fantastic photographs of African wildlife, human complexities in Africa often seem to be highlighted only as an afterthought to environmental topics, suggesting that wildlife population is of greater importance than human population in Africa.

In *Dark Continent: Africa as Seen by Americans* (1983), Michael McCarthy, an African American and African Studies scholar, connects negative images of Africans to contemporary racial problems in the United States and cites the theory of evolution as the basis for our racist ideas about African people. Using "objective" scientific methods, scientists of the late 1800s placed Africans on the lowest rung of the human hierarchy, declaring that the African "race" was biologically determined to be inferior to all other races. Ethnocentric reports written by foreign missionaries who sought to convert culturally and religiously "inferior" people provide another example of the way negative messages of Africans emerged in the West. McCarthy also points out that the international slave trade had a tremendously negative impact on the images of Africans, who were classified as beastly barbarians in order to justify the heinous buying and selling of African peoples. African Americans, he writes, absorbed some of these malicious messages, culminating in their "psychological scarring" (p. 147).

Although images and beliefs from the late 19th and early 20th centuries may be thought of as irrelevant today, many disagree. As Basil Davidson, a British scholar of Africa, writes: "Though vanished from serious discussion, they still retain a kind of underground existence. [This misguided opinion of Africa] has settled like a layer of dust and ashes on the minds of large numbers of otherwise thoughtful people, and is constantly being swirled about" (1969, p. 25). In other words, although most Americans know that traditional stereotypes of Africans are antiquated and rooted in bigotry, the malignant residue of these beliefs still remains, buried in the minds of many Americans. Further supporting the idea that the Western world continues to perceive Africans and their value systems from an ethnocentric, superior stance, Jan Janheinz, author of *Muntu: African Culture and the Western World* (1990), writes: "Simply by applying a certain vocabulary, one can easily turn Gods into idols, faces into grimaces, votive images into fetishes, discussion into palavers and distort real objects and matters of fact through bigotry and prejudice" (p. 20).

On a lighter note, it is interesting to remember that all people are capable of creating stereotypes based on limited information. For instance, a young man from Cameroon once laughingly told me about his well-educated mother's reaction upon learning that he was going to attend school in Montana. At that time, the world media was devoting ample coverage to the infamous "Unabomber," Ted Kaczynski, who had been plotting terrorist activities out of Lincoln, Montana. His mother, who had been keeping up with the international news on CNN in Cote d'Ivoire, tried to convince her son to study elsewhere, for fear he would open up an explosive letter!

HISTORICAL CONTEXT OF AFRICA

The 1884 partitioning of Africa by the colonial powers of England, France, Germany, Portugal, Spain, Belgium, and Italy created the map of Africa as we know it today. The European powers subdivided the continent along geographic boundaries, for the convenience of colonists, and without regard for indigenous cultures. As a result, ethnic groups were often either split among several countries or grouped together with other Africans of different cultural heritage. Throughout the colonial period, individualistic Western cultures dominated Africa's collectivist cultures, which led to a disintegration of many African cultural practices on the continent.

When South African Archbishop Desmond Tutu said, "One of the ways of helping to destroy a people is to tell them they don't have a history, they have no roots" (Stewart, 1997, p. 15), he was referring to colonialism, which promoted the idea that Africa had no history before European occupation. Ali Mazrui, a well-known Kenyan scholar, believes that the Western world holds the deeply ingrained idea that Africans are a people without a history. He tells of an Oxford history professor who proclaimed to a mass audience: "Maybe in the future there will be African history, but at the moment there is none. There is only the history of Europeans in Africa. The rest is darkness and darkness is not a subject of history" (Dugan, 1995). Yet, other contemporary historians of Africa have documented many large-scale ancient, medieval, and early-modern societies in present-day Egypt, Sudan, Chad, Mali, Burkina Faso, Nigeria, Zimbabwe, South Africa, Ghana, Uganda, and so on, as well as smaller, less hierarchical societies that existed across the continent (Khapoya, 1998, pp. 68–110).

DOMINANT WORLDVIEW IN AFRICAN CULTURES

A culture's "worldview" pertains to its relationship to nature, humanity, God, and the universe. Because there are approximately 2,000 cultures in Africa, it is impossible to identify one worldview that encompasses the continent. For example, the following historical description of a cultural practice of the

Mbuti people who live in Central Congo reveals that the rainforest was pivotal to their lives:

> When a child is born, . . . it is bathed in water mixed with the juice of a forest vine, it is clothed with a circlet around the waist, decorated with one or two small pieces of pierced wood and with similar circlets around the wrists, and it is an object of pride and interest and concern to every member of the band. The vine circlets, the juice, and the wooden ornaments are not only for decoration, but place the child in this way always in physical contact with the physical forest, which as well as being the protector is the life giver. (Turnbull, 1965, p. 305)

Similarly, cattle has traditionally been a central component of the worldview of herding cultures, just as water permeated the worldview in cultures that live along the coastline, rivers, or lakes. And as many African cultures become urbanized, their worldviews are transformed to reflect their new cultural realities. Nevertheless, throughout Africa, certain cultural motifs recur. For one thing, human lives are not so compartmentalized as they are in the industrialized world, an issue that I will explore later in this essay. In addition, Africans perceive themselves primarily as members of a larger group and secondly as individuals. As one African scholar puts it, "in terms of African thought, life can be meaningful only in community, not in isolation" (Moyo, 1996, p. 273).

It has been said that Africans *live* their religious faith, whether it be Christianity, Islam, or a traditional African religion. An ideal written into the Constitution of the United States is the separation of power, especially of church and state, based on the teachings of the French philosopher, Montesquieu. The "separation of church and state" that we Americans consider so vital doesn't exist in Africa. John Mbiti, an African theologian, explains:

> Because traditional religions permeate all the departments of life, there is no formal distinction between the sacred and the secular, between the religious and the non-religious, between the spiritual and the material areas of life. Wherever the African is, there is his religion: he carries it to the fields where he is sowing seeds or harvesting a new crop; he takes it with him to the beer party or to attend a funeral ceremony. (Mbiti, 1970, pp. 36–37)

While the American public wrestles with the issue of school prayer, people from African cultures routinely mesh religion and education in schools. In the predominantly Christian region of Southern Africa, Bible scripture, prayers, and hymns are an essential part of the school curriculum. In rural Islamic Sudan, religion also permeates the school lives of teachers and students (Howard, 2001). American members of the Baha'i faith have also remarked on the ability of African Baha'is to merge their faith into all aspects of their lives.

African worldviews also differ in the African concept of group membership. This idea is eloquently encapsulated in a Nigerian child's remark: "Everyone has a friend; no one is born alone" (Onyefulu, 1996, p. 3). In contrast, the highly individualistic society of the United States pervasively conveys the idea that people are born alone and die alone, and that it is up to the individual to do something worthwhile with his or her life.

RELIGIONS OF AFRICA

The principal religions practiced across the continent are African Traditional Religions, Christianity, and Islam; only small minorities practice Hinduism, Buddhism, Judaism, and Baha'i faiths. Islam dominates North Africa as far south as Senegal, Gambia, Nigeria, Chad, and Sudan, and as far to the east as Somalia and Ethiopia. Significant pockets of Islam exist as far south as Mozambique, Malawi, and South Africa. The West Coast and Central and Southern Africa are predominantly composed of people practicing African Traditional Beliefs, Christianity, or a combination of both. African Traditional Religions still influence many African people today, including those who are Christians and Muslims. In other words, Africans have blended elements of African Traditional Religions into Christianity and Islam to create religious perspectives that are uniquely African.

Although African Traditional Religions vary, they do tend to have some characteristics in common: belief in a supreme being, belief in spirits/ divinities, belief in life after death, religious leaders and sacred places, and witchcraft and magic practices (Moyo, 1996, p. 275). God, or a supreme being, is seen as the source of all life and the creator of the universe. African societies have words for the concept of God within their own languages. In Lesotho, Botswana, and parts of South Africa, the word for God is *Modimo,* while in Zimbabwe the term is *Mwari.* Among the Yoruba of Nigeria the word for God is *Olorun,* and the Kalenjin people of Kenya call God *Asis* or *Asista.*

Divinities, common in West Africa but not in East or Southern Africa, exist as servants or messengers of the Supreme Being. Divinities are referred to as *orisha* by the Yoruba of Nigeria and as *bosom* by the Akan of Ghana. Some divinities are associated with natural elements such as the sky, earth, stars, moon, trees, mountains, rivers, and so on. This relationship between divinities and nature was once commonly classified as *animism,* a term that Africanists often consider pejorative.

Ancestral spirits are more universal than divinities in African Traditional Religions. God is worshipped through ancestor spirits seen as intermediaries between living descendants and the Supreme Being. Ancestor spirits have been compared to guardian angels and patron saints in the Catholic doctrine.

In African Traditional Religions there is a common belief in life after death in the form of ancestors. The dead may be reincarnated in the form of animals that protect the living descendants. Or the dead can come back to "haunt" those who did them wrong. In a broad sense, when Africans speak of the importance of community, they may extend the concept to both living and dead members of a society.

Spirit mediums, people who communicate with the ancestor spirits, are just some of the religious leaders in African Traditional Religions. African leaders may be female or male, and among certain groups, heads of families also play leading religious roles in matters that relate to their families. Some cultures may or may not have regular shrines where religious rituals are conducted. Among the Zulu in South Africa, certain household rooms may be designated for contact with the ancestors. Among other ethnic groups, mountains and caves may also serve as special places associated with the Supreme Being.

Belief in witchcraft and magical powers is widespread across the continent. Witches (women) and sorcerers (men) represent evil elements that use power to destroy life. Magic practices can be used either to harm or to protect people. The Southern African term *Mhuti* refers to the practice of ritual murder for the purpose of witchcraft. *Juju* refers to West African witchcraft and magic.

PROVERBS AND AFRICAN VALUES

One way of examining common African values that transcend specific cultures is to analyze proverbs from across the continent. Because most African cultures used to communicate orally rather than through the written word, succinct verbal messages in the form of proverbs became an important way to transmit culture to the next generation. As Zormeier and Samovar note, "discover the meaning of the proverb and you will understand something of what is important to its user" (2000, p. 225). In the following section, I will examine the concepts of collectivism and respect for age, as well as the intercultural concepts of "being versus doing cultures" and "high-context versus low-context cultures," as reflected in African proverbs.

Collectivism in African Societies

"When spider webs unite, they can tie up a lion." (Leslau and Wolf, 1962, p. 23) —Ethiopia

"A brother is like one's shoulder." (Leslau and Wolf, 1962, p. 56) —Somalia

"A single bracelet does not jingle." (Leslau and Wolf, 1962, p. 19) —Congo

"If relatives help each other, what evil can hurt them?" (Leslau and Wolf, 1962, p. 24) —Ethiopia

"When the ants unite their mouths, they can carry an elephant." (Pradervand, 1989, p. 131) —Burkina Faso

"Go the way that many people go; if you go alone you will have reason to lament." (Stewart, 1997, p. 121) —Zambia

"When the bee comes to your house, let her have beer; you may want to visit the bee's house some day." (Leslau and Wolf, 1962, p. 19) —Congo

"The elephant never gets tired of carrying his tusks." (Stewart, 1997, p. 31) —Liberia

One of the outstanding qualities of most cultures in Africa is that they are based on collectivism. The needs of the group take precedence over the individual. The continent's prevalent collectivist ethos is thought to have arisen out of a need for group survival in harsh environments where people depended on living together. For instance, gathering plants for consumption, hunting by spear, planting, weeding, and harvesting agricultural products by hand required a group effort to complete these labor-intensive tasks. In addition, the communal good led to strict societal rules that served as a powerful deterrent to social transgressions (Khapoya, 1998, pp. 44–45).

In Africa, collectivism is built on the extended family, which is important to all individual family members. Grandparents routinely live with their adult children and often look after their grandchildren while the parents are at work. Family members also feel a responsibility to share their resources with each other. For example, the eldest child in a family might feel obligated to pay the school fees for his or her younger siblings. Another fairly common example of the strength of the extended family in Africa is the "fostering" of children. In some parts of Africa, children often spend extended periods in the homes of aunts, uncles, and so on when necessary. In Botswana and Lesotho, there are also instances when childless couples will be given a child or children by members of their extended family who already have many children.

Traditionally, important nonkinship groups called "age grades" existed throughout much of Africa; in parts of West Africa they continue to function nominally, but in most African societies, they disappeared entirely. Age grades consisted of segregated groups of males or females who were born within a few years of each other. These groups passed through distinct stages together, performing socially prescribed functions. In a delightful children's book entitled *Ogbo: Sharing Life in an African Village* (1996), African author Ifeoma Onyefulu, describes the roles and duties of various age grades in a Nigerian village. One age grade, composed of young boys, kept the village clean for festivals; another age grade of village mothers swept dead leaves and grasses from the main water supply, and took turns watching that stray cows did not destroy people's vegetable crops. An age grade of middle-aged men built a nursery school for the village and made judicial decisions important to the entire village. A group of young men built houses for the poor, and age grades composed of village elders offered "wise words" to younger people.

Influenced by Western individualism and capitalism through Christian ideology and colonialism, African cultures have experienced an erosion of their indigenous, collectivist roots. Urban migration and the cash economy now make it possible for many Africans to become self-sufficient without depending on the extended family and larger community. The group now exercises less influence and control over its youth than in previous times. An interesting example of the way that the collectivist ethos has changed in Africa is seen in the indigenous concept of marriage. Historically, marriage was a bond between two families, not individuals. Marriages were arranged by family elders not only to find trustworthy mates for their children, but also to form strategic political and economic alliances among extended families and/or ethnic groups. But today, marriages are seldom arranged, and young people regularly choose their partners.

In recent years, there has been a revival of collectivism across Africa, whereby people have come together in self-help groups to improve their standard of living. Discussing this trend, the vice-president of the National Farmers' Association of Zimbabwe comments: "We want to re-create traditional African solidarity, but on a new basis. We want to get people together so that they can find their own solutions to their own problems. If we get together, we can find solutions to all our problems. But we have to get together first. That is the starting point" (Pradervand, 1989, p. 81). Members of a women's club in central Kenya explain how they started to work together: "We started in 1980. Three of us got together to discuss how we could help each other. At the time of our grandmothers, helping each other was the rule: plowing, weeding, grinding flour for a celebration—all of that was done collectively" (Pradervand, 1989, p. 97). Remembering the strength of their grandmothers prompted these women to reorganize as a group in order to empower themselves against oppressive socioeconomic, cultural, and political conditions.

Being Cultures

"Events follow one another like the days of a week." (Leslau and Wolf, 1962, p. 58) —Tanzania

"Don't be in a hurry to swallow when chewing is pleasant." (Stewart, 1997, p. 57) —Malawi

"Do not hurry the night, the sun will always rise for its own sake." (Stewart, 1997, p. 63) —Eritrea

"While it shines, bask! Tomorrow there may be clouds." (Stewart, 1997, p. 67) —Malawi

Being cultures have been described as polychronic in their time orientation. The terms *polychronic time* (P-time) and *monochronic time* (M-time), coined by Edward T. Hall, refer to the way time is incorporated into a culture. People from P-time cultures place involvement with people above preset time schedules; appointments are handled in a flexible manner. In P-time cultures, life tends to be less compartmentalized into distinct units, merging economic and family activities together. When African women tend the crops in their fields, they bring their babies with them; they do not separate food production and child care.

Many years ago, an American colleague and I organized a gardening workshop in Lesotho. As people from an M-time culture, we developed a timetable defining the time allotted for the workshop into a series of distinct units. As the workshop continued, it became obvious that our preconceived notions of how a workshop should proceed did not agree with the way the Basotho (the people of Lesotho) participants envisaged it. The workshop participants were inclined to ignore the schedule, continuing with their discussion until they thought they had completely exhausted the subject rather than adhere to a previously made plan.

In rural Lesotho and other African countries, there is an indigenous sense of time. It is more flexible than in monochronic cultures and tends to relate to the position of the sun and to the animals that appear at certain times of the day. In Botswana various times of the day are described as *mahube a naka sa kgomo*, which translates to "the time that the cows awaken," and *phirimana*, which means "the time in the evening when the hyenas come out" (Matumo, 1993, pp. 515–516). Other words exist that specify mid-morning, midday, or mid-afternoon; communication about time goes smoothly when people specify the time as designated by nature.

High-Context Cultures

"Seeing is better than hearing." (Leslau and Wolf, 1962, p. 43) —Nigeria

"When a man is coming near you, you need not say: 'Come here.' (Leslau and Wolf, 1962, p. 9) —Ghana

"When a fool is told a proverb, its meaning has to be explained to him." (Leslau and Wolf, 1962, p. 10) —Ghana

"Do not say the first thing that comes to your mind." (Leslau and Wolf, 1962, p. 34) —Kenya

"Sorrow is like a precious treasure, shown only to friends." (Leslau and Wolf, 1962, p. 38) —Kenya

"Silence is also a form of speech." (Stewart, 1997, p. 95) —Fulani of West Africa

Edward T. Hall explains, "high-context (HC) communication is one in which most of the information is either in the physical context or internalized in the person, while very little is in the coded, explicit, transmitted part of the message. Low-context (LC) communication is just the opposite; i.e., the mass of the information is vested in the explicit code" (Hall, 1983, p. 47). It is fair to claim that most African cultures tend to be in the realm of high-context communication rather than low-context communication when placed on a continuum.

An interesting observation made by a Kenyan scholar living in the United States highlights the difference in context between the United States and Kenya (Khapoya, 1998, pp. 29–30). He explained that when he dined in American homes without remarking before or during the meal on the beauty and taste of the food, Americans would often worry that he was displeased by the food. Even if he ate voraciously, not leaving a morsel on his plate, the American host would not be convinced that he liked the food. He discovered the importance of verbally conveying his appreciation of the food to his American friends. In Kenya, if his hosts saw him appreciatively eating his meal, they would know that he was enjoying it without necessarily needing him to express his pleasure verbally.

Another aspect of HC cultures is that "people in places of authority are personally and truly (not just in theory) responsible for the actions of subordinates, down to the lowest man" (Hall, 1976, p. 98). In a wonderful book entitled *In the Shadow of the Sacred Grove*, an American woman describes her one-year sojourn with her fiancée in a village in Cote d'Ivoire in West Africa. In her book, she describes the responsible role of her landlord, Donnisongui: "[H]e was not only to see that we were comfortable, but he was responsible for our actions while we were in the village, and had we done anything to anger the villagers, they would have to come to Donnisongui" (Spindel, 1989, p. 8). This account provides an example of the way that responsibility rests with a powerful person in HC cultures.

Respect for Age

"You do not teach the paths of the forest to an old gorilla." (Leslau and Wolf, 1962, p. 17) —Congo

"It is the duty of children to wait on elders, and not the elders on children." (Leslau and Wolf, 1962, p. 36) —Kenya

"We start as fools and become wise through experience." (Leslau and Wolf, 1962, p. 58) —Tanzania

"It's a bad child who does not take advice." (Leslau and Wolf, 1962, p. 8) —Ghana

Within African societies, there is a strong sense of respect for the elderly. Grandparents and great-grandparents are not taken care of in nursing homes; they live with their extended family. Because extended families are still large, some young people are always available to meet the needs of the elderly. African societies also tend to be formal, especially regarding the relationship between young and old. After staying with an American family, a Cameroonian man wrote home incredulously with stories about how the children in his host family "rudely" addressed their elders simply as John or Mary. Grandparents, aunts, and uncles are addressed with titles as a sign of respect in his culture.

Other examples abound about African ways of treating the elder members of families and societies at large. A mid-western American university has an ongoing educational exchange with a teacher-training college in Southern Africa. While the American university sent vibrant, young students from their teacher education program, the African teacher-training college sent its senior educators to the United States. The attitude of the decision makers was markedly different. The Africans were honoring their elderly, retired teachers by sending them abroad, whereas the American administrators made sure that they sent the best and the brightest young or middle-aged teachers who would be able to use the information they gleaned abroad to internationalize American education.

CONCLUSION

The purpose of this essay has been to offer some brief, introductory information about communication and cultural patterns on the African continent. Because the American public knows little of Africa and its peoples other than the limited images portrayed in the Western media, it is of great importance that Africanists and Africans in America educate the general population about the vast, complex continent known as Africa. In 1991, while conducting research on the life of a young, Kenyan woman who was a graduate student in the United States, I was told by an American student how much she had learned from her Kenyan friend about Africa: "I thought Kenya was totally what you see on *National Geographic*—people running around half dressed, hitting bongo drums, killing animals, and that's all there was to Kenya" (van der Veur, 1992, p. 17). Her African friend was able to tell her about city life in Nairobi, an urban center of more than 1 million people in 1989, as well as her childhood in the agricultural highlands of Western Kenya.

Clearly, the message of this essay is that despite the vastness and complexity of the continent comprising more than 50 independent nations, one may safely claim that some common cultural patterns exist in Africa. Collectivist, polychronic, high-context cultures dominate this world region. Another important lesson to be gleaned is that African cultures, just like all other cultures, are dynamic and ever-changing. A fallacy often held about Africa is that people live as their ancestors did hundreds of years ago. The people of Africa have experienced a long history of organized civilizations and smaller stateless societies. There have been cultural clashes with, and an integration of, European cultures, Christianity, and Islamic religions. We can be sure that in the future, the global economy and information technologies will bring about ever-larger changes in African cultures.

Notes

1. Ndabaningi Sithole, *African Nationalism*, 2nd Edition (New York: Oxford University Press, 1968), pp. 67–68. Ndabaningi Sithole of the independent country of Zimbabwe (formally called Rhodesia) describes this moment of cultural affinity between himself and another African man from Somalia, a country with distinctly different African languages and ethnic groups from Zimbabwe.
2. See Lyons, Robert, and Chinua Achebe. *Another Africa* (New York: Anchor Books, 1997).

References

Davidson, B. (1969). *The African genius*. Boston: Little, Brown and Co.

Dugan, D. (Producer). (1995). *Africa: A history denied* [Video]. Alexandria, VA: Time-Life Video and Television.

Hall, E. (1976). *Beyond culture*. Garden City, NY: Anchor.

Hall, E. (1983). *The dance of life: The other dimension of time*. Garden City, NY: Anchor.

How Two African Universities Have Moved Ahead in Information Technology. (1999, April 2). *The Chronicle of Higher Education, 134*, A52.

Howard, S. (2001). Chalk and dust: Teachers' lives in rural Sudan. In D. L. Bowen & E. Early (Eds.), *Everyday Life in the Muslim Middle East* (2nd ed.). Indianapolis: Indiana University Press.

Janheinz, J. (1990). *Muntu: African culture and the Western world* (rev. ed.). New York: Grove Weidenfeld.

Khapoya, V. (1998). *The African experience: An introduction* (2nd ed.). Upper Saddle River, NJ: Prentice Hall.

Leslau, C., & Wolf, L. (Eds.). (1962). *African proverbs*. White Plains, NY: Peter Pauper Press.

Lyons, R., & Achebe, C. (1997). *Another Africa*. New York: Anchor Books.

Matumo, Z. I. (Ed.). (1993). *Setswana-English-Setswana Dictionary*. Gaborone, Botswana: Macmillan.

Mbiti, J. S. (1970). *Concepts of God in Africa*. London: SPCK.

McCarthy, M. (1983). Dark continent: Africa as seen by Americans. Vol. 75. In *Contributions in Afro-American and African Studies*. Westport, CT: Greenwood Press.

Moyo, A. (1996). Religion in Africa. In A. A. Gordon & D. L. Gordon (Eds.), *Understanding Contemporary Africa* (pp. 273–301). Boulder, CO: Lynne Reinner Publishers.

Onyefulu, I. (1996). *Ogbo: Sharing life in an African village*. New York: Harcourt Brace and Company.

Pradervand, P. (1989). *Listening to Africa: Developing Africa from the grassroots*. New York: Praeger.

Sithole, N. S. (1968). *African nationalism* (2nd ed.). New York: Oxford University Press.

Spindel, C. (1989). *In the shadow of the sacred grove*. New York: Vintage Books.

Stewart, J. (Ed.). (1997). *African proverbs and wisdom: A collection for every day of the year from more than forty African nations*. Secaucus, NJ: Carol Publishers.

Turnbull, C. (1965). *The forest people*. New York: Doubleday Books.

van der Veur, S. M. (1992). *Intercultural education: A story of an African woman*. Unpublished manuscript.

Zormeier, S. M., & Samovar, L. A. (2000). Language as a mirror of reality: Mexican American proverbs. In L. A. Samovar & R. E. Porter (Eds.), *Intercultural communication: A reader* (9th ed.). (pp. 225–229). San Francisco: Wadsworth.

Concepts and Questions

1. Why does van der Veur believe it is important for you to know about and understand Africa?
2. Why does van der Veur suggest that Africa is one of the least understood places in the world?
3. How do images of and beliefs about Africa prevalent during the 19th and early 20th centuries affect American perceptions of Africa today?
4. How has the 1884 partitioning of Africa by European colonial powers affected the ethnic distribution among African countries?
5. What are some of the central components of the worldviews found among African ethnic groups?
6. How do church–state relationships in Africa tend to differ from those found in the United States?
7. Describe some of the common characteristics of African Traditional Religions.
8. How does the African propensity toward collectivism affect family structures and relationships?
9. How might the African tendency toward "being" cultures affect your interaction with tribal Africans?
10. Considering traditional African cultures as being "high-context," what adjustments would you have to make in your interaction patterns when working with tribal Africans?

Communication with Egyptians

POLLY A. BEGLEY

Cairo made my eyeballs ache. It is a city of coloured splendour, alive and moving, with a hundred gay pigments astir in the sunshine, and every thoroughfare stuffed full, as it seems, of processioning and pageantry.

ARTHUR EDWARD COPPING, 1910

As the sun rises above the ancient land of Pharaohs, the *Muezzin* calls faithful Muslims to prayer over the city's loudspeakers. Egypt, claiming more than 4,000 years of history, is a country of extremes: An ancient center of learning and mystery, overwhelming poverty next to grand architectural wonders, sandstorms and sunshine mingling with smog, and the fertile Nile Valley surrounded by desert. The 6,671 kilometers of the Nile River is life-blood for Egyptian civilization. The Nile is known as a "precious gift yet a perilous master" (Crawford, 1996, p. 39). The unpredictable river gives life through its waters while periodically destroying canals, houses, or entire towns.

People have long been intrigued by Egyptian culture—mysterious pyramids, sacred temples hewn from rocky cliffs, enigmatic hieroglyphs, and centuries-old traditions. The Greek historian Herodotus, born around 484 B.C., was one of the first scholar-tourists to extol the wonders of Egypt to the rest of the world. Modern architecture, philosophy, mathematics, literature, and science have all been influenced by Egyptian wisdom. Specifically, Socrates, Aristotle, and Pythagoras all learned from the Egyptians. Even our alphabet may have evolved from ancient hieroglyphs (Crawford, 1996). Modern Egyptologists still wonder at the near-perfect preservation of writings on 3,000- to 4,000-year-old stones and temples. In villages along the Nile today, the *Fellahin*, or peasants,

employ the same tools and agricultural methods from Pharaonic periods. Government experts sent to these communities are told that modern irrigation ideas are unnecessary because "we have done it this way for thousands of years." Clearly, one must know a great deal about Egypt's history, customs, and traditions before she or he is prepared to appreciate the rich tapestry of its culture.

We cannot presume that this brief essay can comprehensively cover thousands of years of history and tradition. Scholars who focus on cultural studies know that learning is a continual process. Even a lifetime of study and experience, however, would not be enough to unravel the secrets of Egyptian civilization. The purpose of the review, then, is to seek an understanding of interactions among Egyptians and non-Egyptians by examining relevant cultural characteristics. Specifically, the primary emphasis will be on aspects of culture that influence intercultural communication. To this end, we will discuss the three important aspects of culture: (1) worldview and religion, (2) values, and (3) language.

EGYPTIAN WORLDVIEW AND RELIGION

Worldview represents common perception among the members of a cultural group. Samovar and Porter (2000) define *worldview* as "a culture's orientation toward such things as God, nature, life, death, the universe, and other philosophical issues that are concerned with the meaning of life and with 'being'" (p. 11). A religion or philosophy essentially attempts to explain the unexplainable for the people of a particular community.

The Egyptian worldview began as a culmination of various African civilizations and beliefs. The name *Egypt* came from the Greek name *Aegyptos*, but before that it was *Kemet*, Blackland, to the native peoples (Crawford, 1996). When the Sahara dried up and became a desert, several African groups migrated to the Nile Valley. The harsh famine and flood cycles of life near the Nile forced the people to become organized and ever vigilant. Religion was an important part of this orderly existence, and as many as 2,000 deities were part of Kemetic beliefs. The lack of distinction between science, art, and religious philosophy is reflected in the belief that each action in everyday life was the earthly symbol of a divine activity.

Kemet developed into a great civilization because of divine leadership and geography. The Pharaohs were incarnations of the Universal God, Horus, and they ruled with absolute and divine power in early Kemet. The first monarch, Menes, established his dynasty around 3150 B.C. when he united upper and lower Kemet. The nation had an advantage geographically during the early dynastic period because vast scorching deserts protected the population from invaders on most sides (Brega, 1998). Herodotus wrote of a mighty army of 50,000 soldiers that was literally swallowed by the sands about 2,500 years ago. Archaeologists recently discovered remains deep in the desert that may prove the tale of this lost army (Stowe, 2000). Essentially, ancient Kemet people could focus on nation building, art, science, and philosophy because they were spared from the threat of external attack.

Today, Pharaonic-era beliefs are confined to museums and tourist sites, but traces of Kemet could never be completely erased from the Nile, sands, and people of this ancient land. In 619 A.D., nomadic Arabs invaded Egypt, and eventually Islam replaced other religious beliefs to become the prevailing worldview in modern Egypt. Ancient Egyptian history is considered to be anti-Islamic and has been replaced with Islamic history in Egyptian schools (Gershoni & Jankowski, 1995). Christianity is the only other religious minority and has dwindled to less than 13% of the population. A small enclave of Christians lives in central Egypt, but violence plagues their relations with their Muslim neighbors. Egyptian Muslims find solace in the religious beliefs of Islam and answer questions of existence through the sacred words of the Islamic holy book (Koran). An examination of Islamic history, principles, contemporary practices, and the role of religious beliefs within politics can provide insight into the behavioral and communicative patterns of its adherents.

Islamic History

The historical roots of Islamic beliefs are important to intercultural communication because religion influences every part of everyday life in Egyptian Muslim communities. Islam began with Mohammed, who was the last of God's prophets. God spoke to Mohammed through the angel Gabriel about 610 A.D., and the messages were recorded in the Koran. The Koran, the book of Islam, is the only miracle claimed by Mohammed and considered to be the exact words of God. This holy book contains 114 chapters (or *suras*) and outlines the will of God for the loyal followers of Islam (Waines, 1993).

Although descriptions of Mohammed range from praising to condemning, no one can argue that he did not have a vast influence on all of Arabia, including Egypt. Historically, the Middle East was turbulent. Vast areas, harsh deserts, warring tribes, and a precarious value placed on human life contributed to turmoil in the region. Although numerous leaders had previously attempted to create a consolidated empire, Mohammed and his followers were able to unite all of Arabia under their control. When Islam was first introduced to Egyptians, an established set of ancient beliefs dated back thousands of years. These beliefs included countless deities and complicated rituals for Egyptians. In contrast, Islamic beliefs were easy to understand and to follow for the common people.

Islamic beliefs dominate every moment from birth to death and beyond. Almost 85% to 90% of Egypt's population, and more than 1 billion people worldwide, are followers of Islam. Muslims seek Islam to find "the peace that comes when one's life is surrendered to God" (Smith, 1991, p. 222). This worldview reflects one of the youngest and fastest growing major religions in the world. Some of the reasons why this religion is appealing to a large number of people can be understood by examining the principles of Islam such as tenets, pillars, and universal allure.

Islamic Principles

Four tenets are central to understanding Islam: (1) it is a monotheistic religion; (2) God created the world; (3) humans are fundamentally good from birth because they are God's creations and without "original sin." Muslims believe in the innate goodness of humanity, but contemporary societies "forget" their divine origins; and (4) for each Muslim there will be a day of judgment when God decides whether each person will go to heaven or be condemned to hell (Smith, 1991).

Islam outlines five pillars for Muslims. First, *shahada* (creed) is the confession of faith: *"La ilaha illa 'llah"* and is translated as "There is no God but God, and Muhammad is his prophet" (Smith, 1991, p. 244). Second, *salat* (prayer) is an important part of everyday life. Muslims are required to stop for prayer five times a day facing in the direction of the holy city of Mecca. Murphy (1993) described the call to prayer in Cairo, Egypt: "'God is great', the muezzins proclaim, their words furiously amplified to rock concert proportions through the city's narrow and winding streets, a celebration of holiness at 70 decibels" (p. 1). Third, *zakat* (giving alms) to the poor is expected of each person. Fourth, *sawm* (fasting) during the month of Ramadan is required. This fast prompts Muslims to be disciplined and reminds them to be more charitable to the hungry and the poor within their societies. Finally, the *hajj* (pilgrimage) to Mecca is a requisite trip for those who are able to make the journey (Nigosian, 1987).

Islam possesses a universal allure, which appeals to Egyptians. This allure comes about, first, because Islam is a religion of action, not of contemplation. Second, Muslims from all cultural and ethnic groups are recognized as equal members within the religion. Believers are thus united in an international fraternity of Islam. Mohammed's words are clear on this issue: "A Muslim is the brother of a Muslim; he neither oppresses him nor does he fail him, he neither lies to him nor does he hold him in contempt" (Lippman, 1995, p. 185). Third, Islam does not require complicated rituals or sacrifices. If one repeats the shahada creed, then he or she is a Muslim. Good Muslims follow the five pillars. The accepting simplicity of Islam unites and strengthens the people of Egypt.

Islam and Politics

Egyptian government has long recognized the power of Islam within the general populace. Each political group publicly supports the *Shari-a* (religious laws), advocates that religious principles should be taught in schools, and allows family concerns to be decided by Islamic ideologies. The constitution also declares Islam the state religion. Government support of Shari-a, however, has not prevented a rising number of secular laws. An ongoing Egyptian dilemma stems from trying to balance Islamic religious laws with attempts to bring modernization to industry and business. The introduction of new technology, as well as Western influences, have promoted lenient secular laws that are often contrary to traditional religious standards.

An increasing number of secular laws, technological advance, outside influence, a population explosion, and rising unemployment have created factions of religious fundamentalism. Some Egyptians believe that problems in their country are the result of society, especially the government, ignoring the principles of Islam. Religious beliefs offer the hopes of stability and orderliness during times of agitation and change. This Islamic fundamentalism has caused increased demands for a return to Shari-a (Sisk, 1992), which has resulted in increasing numbers of Egyptians following the Islamic pillars and practicing segregation by gender; more women in recent years have adopted full or partial veils in public places, and sporadic protests of foreign intrusion have occurred in Egyptian cities.

Sojourners should be aware of Islamic religious beliefs while conducting business or traveling in Egypt. The Koran exhorts everyone, especially women, to cover themselves modestly. Egyptians wear less revealing clothing and feel more comfortable communicating with others who adopt conservative attire. Egyptians also feel that it is their responsibility to help others in need. There is a long tradition of Egyptians taking anyone into their tent for sustenance or shelter from the harsh desert. Sojourners who receive help while in Egypt are told that "God wills it," as explanation for Egyptian hospitality. Travelers or business executives who display knowledge of and respect for Islamic beliefs are more likely to establish friendships and profitable business relations in Egypt. Although religious beliefs are an important part of Egyptian culture, they are only one part of understanding communication with Egyptians. In the next section, we will consider Egyptian cultural values that are relevant to intercultural communication.

EGYPTIAN VALUES

Cultural values are vital areas of study for intercultural communication scholars. Samovar and Porter (2000) state that:

> Cultural values define what is worth dying for, what is worth protecting, what frightens people, what are proper subjects for study and for ridicule, and what types of events create group solidarity. Most important, cultural values guide both perception and behavior. (p. 11)

If we can discover why people act a certain way, their fears, and their passions, then we can begin to understand how to improve communication among people of diverse cultures. Three fundamental values in Egyptian culture are tradition, relationships, and hierarchical devotion.

Tradition

World histories reveal that the groups of people who have had the richest traditions have also had long-lived societies. Weick (1995) points out that cultures characterized by a "tradition of conduct" or that have a "well-developed folklore of action should survive longer than those that do not" (p. 126). These traditions of conduct serve to pass expertise and experience to the next generations. An Egyptian proverb points out the worth of past knowledge: *Lost is the person who forgets his or her past.* Because Egyptian culture is 4,000 to 5,000 years old, it is not surprising that tradition is an important value.

This importance within the Egyptian population is reflected in several different ways. Egypt has a tradition of being a rural nation. The peasant farmers along the Nile are proud of their farming heritage and are often resistant to change. Ancient paintings depict types of donkey-powered water wheels that are still in use today. Egyptians have survived countless epidemics, floods, droughts, and conquerors. The population has "a centuries-old capacity for letting life flow by, a little like the Nile, . . . and it is as though the present generations had inherited a seen-it-all-before attitude from their forbears" (Wayne & Simonis, 1994, p. 33). Their unity in pleasure and suffering, while holding onto their tra-

ditions, contributes to the endurance of Egyptian culture for thousands of years.

Religious traditions, as previously mentioned, are an important part of life in Egypt. Ancient Egyptians thought that "every action, no matter how mundane, was in some sense a religious act: plowing, sowing, reaping, brewing, building ships, waging wars, playing games—all were viewed as earthly symbols for divine activities" (West, 1995, pp. 46). Contemporary Egyptians also maintain that their religious beliefs play a pivotal role in family, politics, business, and education.

Egyptians may express polite interest in the traditions and ancestors of guests in their country. Higher regard is attributed to the person who can recite details about his or her family members from the past four to five hundred years. This strong value placed on tradition serves to pass on knowledge, but can also inhibit rapid changes. Visitors to Egypt should never underestimate the amount of time that it will take to establish relationships, new contacts, or introduce technological innovations.

Relationships

Egyptians have the capability to endure, but there is still something that frightens them. The people of Egypt fear loneliness, and they wish to always be surrounded by a network of relatives and friends (Hopwood, 1982). They combat loneliness by placing great value on relationships. The importance of relational harmony developed from the time Menes united upper and lower Kemet in 3150 B.C. Nile Valley inhabitants found that collectivism was the most effective way for a diverse group of people with limited resources to live in peace.

In Egyptian collectivism, family, social, and business are all relationships that are taken seriously and give Egyptians great pleasure. The crucial events of a person's lifetime are birth, marriage, and death. These principle daily concerns of everyday life emphasize the interconnectedness of the individual with the family. Each person represents a social collective and sacrifices his or her needs for the greater good of that group.

Reassurance and warmth from familial relations are feelings replicated in other relationships. Kinship terms are used in various situations to reinforce positive connections among people. For example, "Egyptian politicians, from the President on down, emphasize their position as 'father figures' to the masses" (Inhorn, 1996, p. 159). The family is the basic building block of society and is a model for interactions throughout society.

The first questions that Egyptians ask guests in a conversation concern group affiliations. "Where is your family?" "Where is your father?" "Where are your classmates or co-workers?" Egyptians assume that people prefer group travel or activities. Tourists commonly report that locals never give oral directions, but always insist on accompanying them directly to their destination—no matter how far away.

A relational focus is also reflected in the blurred boundary lines between social and business interactions. Officials constantly maintain open-door policies and engage in friendly discussions with several people at one time. Building and maintaining good relations take priority over other activities in society. Egyptians often conduct lengthy business meetings without ever touching on business matters. A sojourner in Egypt realizes the power of relations after waiting at an Egyptian Embassy for five hours to get a visa. Even then, there is no guarantee the paperwork will be processed before closing time. On the other hand, if good relations have been established with the family who runs the hotel, then its members may realize that one of their son's classmates works in the embassy. The visa would be delivered within half an hour to the door of the hotel after a single phone call. Relationships are a source of pleasure and are also a way to get things done in a rigidly structured society.

Hierarchical Structure

Hierarchies according to age, gender, and experience are crucial in Egyptian society. Ancient traditions outline the proper place and behavior of each person in society. Interpersonal relationships are characterized by "a worldview professing the existence of a cosmic hierarchical order: The sound order of things is a descending scale of superiors and subordinates" (Yadlin, 1995, p. 157). The cosmic order begins with the major religions of Egypt. Pharaohs were considered to be god-rulers who were divine mediators for the people. The Nile civiliza-

tion may have been one of the first matriarchal civilizations because ancient Pharaohs inherited the throne through the female bloodline (Crawford, 1996). In this agrarian society, male and female deities ruled from the heavens, and both men and women were responsible for the collective security of the family.

In Islam as well, humans submit to God's will in all matters. God is the ultimate creator, authority, and judge for all people. The first words that sojourners will learn upon arrival in Egypt are *Insha'allah*. The translation of this word is, "If God wills it." Explanations such as, "God decides," or "It's when God wants it," reflect the accepted order of life. Muslims do not question their fate because God alone knows their destiny. A part of that destiny for Egyptians is fulfilling their roles in the overall social structure of society.

In Muslim families, the oldest male in the family wields authority and power. This patriarch is responsible for the safety and well-being of his family members. Sons and daughters consider carefully how their public behavior influences their family. The oldest son may conduct business or interactions with international contacts, but the father makes final decisions. Muslims regard these roles and practices as a natural part of life, and women and men are staunch advocates and devotees of the traditional hierarchical order. Hierarchies are produced and reinforced through the language of family and societal communication.

EGYPTIAN LANGUAGE AND CULTURE

Language is a powerful tool. Our manner of speech can have a significant influence on another's behavior. The words that we choose can reflect the way that we look at the world and perceive others. For centuries, Arabs have recognized the power of language and have used Arabic to convey unity, worldview, and artistic impressions. Arabic is one of the oldest living languages in the world. It is the beautiful and flamboyant language spoken by Egyptians and other people of the Middle East.

If you venture into an Egyptian city, you will hear the rhythmic Arabic verses of the Koran chanted aloud during daily prayers. Walls of Egyptian mosques are not painted with pictures or scenes—they are covered with decorative Arabic calligraphy. A sojourner who learns a few words of Arabic will quickly gain friends in this region. Egyptians are also willing to share their knowledge of Arabic with others. On many occasions, a well-timed response of *Mish muskmlla* (no problem) or *Insha'allah* (if God wills it) will elicit approval and improve relations with Egyptians.

Arabic and Unity

What we say, how we say it, and why we say it are all related to our culture. Egyptians use their language to construct appropriate national identities and unity within the population. For example, Egyptians did not consider themselves Arabs until the 7th century when Arabic became the predominant way to communicate in the region (Lippman, 1995). Today, Egyptian children learn only in Arabic and are taught to memorize and proudly recite lengthy verses of the Koran. The Middle East consists of various countries, cultural, and ethnic groups, but Egyptians will readily proclaim, "But we are all Arabs!"

Arabic helps promote unity within a region just as different linguistic styles can cause disunity. For example, bargaining in Egypt is considered to be an enjoyable way to pass time and build relationships. Historically, Egyptians expect and love haggling, but for Israelis, "trading was not a pleasurable pastime, but part of a struggle for survival in a hostile environment. Thus, where bargaining has positive connotations for the Arab, for the Israeli it is reminiscent of a rejected and despised way of life" (Cohen, 1990, p. 139). Negotiations between Israel and Egypt have been taking place since 1948, and their different linguistic styles have caused more than one impasse during talks.

Arabic and Worldview

Arabic is used to convey the Islamic worldview. "Classical Arabic (which is also the written language) is sacred" because it is the dialect of the Koran (Hall, 1977, p. 31). The importance of the Koran within Islamic societies actually preserved the integrity of the classical tongue. Other major languages branched out into various dialects, or became obsolete, but classical Arabic is still widely spoken among Muslims of every region. Public prayers and ceremonies worldwide are conducted in Arabic even if the Muslim adherents are not Middle Eastern Arabs.

Second, *jihad* is an Arabic word from the Koran that has often been incorrectly translated as "holy war." The mere mention of an Islamic *jihad* has been depicted within Western literature as religious fanatics on a killing rampage, and terrorist attacks are automatically attributed to Islamic fundamentalists (Hopfe, 1976). "Literally the word [*jihad*] means 'utmost effort' in promotion and defense of Islam, which might or might not include armed conflict with unbelievers" (Lippman, 1995, p. 113). Although there are some violent fundamentalist groups, these factions cannot realistically represent the whole of Islamic followers.

Finally, Western readers of Koranic translations have reported that the holy book is repetitive, confusing, and lacks compelling features (Nigosian, 1987). Muslims maintain that these translations do not reflect the astounding beauty and rhythmic qualities of the original Arabic verses. The linguistic style of Koranic writings serves as a model for literature and speech throughout Islamic societies.

Writing as Art

Ancient hieroglyphs used the same word to signify both writing and art. Ancient Kemetic texts focused on "medicine, science, religion, social and cosmic organization, and the life cycle" (Crawford, 1996, p. 9). Arabic is now used as an art form in Egypt. One of the foremost sights in every Egyptian city is the Mosque decorated inside from top to bottom with Arabic calligraphy. Egyptian homes commonly have a scroll depicting the 99 names of God in exquisite script. The mastery of spoken and written classical Arabic is indicative of education and rank in Egypt. Arabic is a language that pleases the eyes, ears, and spirits of the people. Sojourners who learn Arabic or adopt a descriptive and elegant style of speaking in another language will attain a higher level of credibility while in Egypt.

CONCLUSION

This article reviews aspects of the Islamic worldview, cultural values, and language that influence communication with Egyptians. Visitors to Egypt find that travel or business ventures are more rewarding experiences if they take the time to learn about specific cultural characteristics. If its 5,000 years of history and tradition can provide a rich cultural heritage and wisdom for Egyptians, then other cultures can also learn from one of the oldest civilizations in the world.

References

Brega, I. (1998). *Egypt: Past and present*. New York: Barnes & Noble.

Cohen, R. (1990). Deadlock: Israel and Egypt negotiate. In F. Korzenny & S. Ting-Toomey (Eds.), *Communicating for peace: Diplomacy and negotiation, 14* (p. 136–153). Newbury Park, CA: Sage Publications.

Crawford, C. (1996). *Recasting ancient Egypt in the African context: Toward a model curriculum using art and language*. Trenton, NJ: Africa World.

Gershoni, I., & Jankowski, J. P. (1995). *Redefining the Egyptian nation, 1930–1945*. New York: Cambridge University.

Hall, E. T. (1977). *Beyond culture*. Garden City, NY: Anchor Books.

Hopfe, L. M. (1976). *Religions of the world*. Beverly Hills, CA: Glencoe.

Hopwood, D. (1982). *Egypt: Politics and society 1945–1981*. London: Allen and Unwin.

Inhorn, M. C. (1996). *Infertility and patriarchy: The cultural politics of gender and family life in Egypt*. Philadelphia: University of Pennsylvania.

Lippman, T. W. (1995). *Understanding Islam: An introduction to the Muslim world* (2nd ed.). New York: Meridian.

Murphy, K. (1993, April 6). World report special edition: A new vision for Mohammed's faith. *Los Angeles Times*, p. 1.

Nigosian, S. (1987). *Islam: The way of submission*. Great Britain: Crucible.

Samovar, L. A., & Porter, R. E. (2000). Understanding intercultural communication: An introduction and overview. In L. A. Samovar & R. E. Porter (Eds.), *Intercultural communication: A reader*, 9th ed., pp. 5–16. Belmont, CA: Wadsworth.

Sisk, T. D. (1992). *Islam and democracy: Religion, politics, and power in the Middle East*. Washington, DC: United States Institute of Peace Press.

Smith, H. (1991). *The world's religions: Our great wisdom traditions*. San Francisco, CA: Harper Collins.

Stowe, M. A. (2000, August 28). Swallowed by the sands: Archaeologists hope to solve the mystery of Persia's lost army of Egypt. Discovering Archaeology: Scientific American. [Internet] www.discoveringarchaeology.com/articles.082800-sands.shtml.

Waines, D. (1995). *An introduction to Islam*. Great Britain: Cambridge University.

Wayne, S., & Simonis, D. (1994). *Egypt and the Sudan*, 3rd ed. Hawthorn, Australia: Lonely Planet.

Weick, K. (1995). *Sensemaking in organizations*. Thousand Oaks, CA: Sage Publications.

West, J. A. (1995). *The traveler's key to ancient Egypt: A guide to the sacred places of ancient Egypt*. Wheaton, IL: Quest Books.

Yadlin, R. (1995). The seeming duality: Patterns of interpersonal relations in a changing environment. In S. Shamir (Ed.), *Egypt from monarchy to republic: A reassessment of revolution and change* (p. 151).

Concepts and Questions

1. Why does Begley say it is hard to "think like an Egyptian"?

2. What aspects of Islamic history offer insights into the Egyptian culture? What aspects of your own culture would offer valuable insights for someone wanting to study your culture?

3. Why does Begley assert that "Islamic beliefs dominate every moment from birth to death and beyond"?

4. Begley offers four tenants central to understanding Islam. What are they? Does your worldview have similar or dissimilar tenants?

5. What does Begley mean when she writes "Islam is a relation of action, not contempation"? Is your religion one of action or contemplation?

6. Why is Arabic language so very important to the Egyptians? What aspects of their language make it unique?

7. What does Begley imply when she talks about Arabic as art?

8. What communication patterns within your culture might present problems when communicating with someone from Egyptian culture?

Contrasts in Discussion Behaviors of German and American Managers

ROBERT A. FRIDAY

AMERICAN MANAGERS' EXPECTATIONS

Business Is Impersonal

In any business environment, discussion between colleagues must accomplish the vital function of exchanging information that is needed for the solution of problems. In American business, such discussions are usually impersonal.[1] Traditionally the facts have spoken for themselves in America. "When facts are disputed, the argument must be suspended until the facts are settled. Not until then may it be resumed, for all true argument is about the meaning of established or admitted facts" (Weaver, 1953) in the rationalistic view. Much of post–WWII American business decision making has been based on the quantitative MBA approach which focuses on factual data and its relationship to the ultimate fact of profit or loss, writing strategy plans, and top-down direction. After all of the facts are in, the CEO is often responsible for making the intuitive leap and providing leadership. The power and authority of the CEO has prevailed in the past 40 years, with no predicted change in view (Bleicher & Paul, 1986, pp. 10–11). Through competition and contact with West Germany and Japan, the more personal approach is beginning to enter some lower level decision-making practices (Peters & Waterman, 1982, pp. 35–118).

Another reason for the impersonal nature of American business is that many American managers do not identify themselves with their corporations. When the goals and interests of the corporation match up with those of the American manager, he

or she will stay and prosper. However, when the personal agenda of the American manager is not compatible with that of the corporation, he or she is likely to move on to attain his or her objective in a more conducive environment. Most American managers can disassociate themselves from their business identity, at least to the extent that their personal investment in a decision has more to do with their share of the profit rather than their sense of personal worth.

In contrast, "the German salesman's personal credibility is on the line when he sells his product. He spends years cultivating his clients, building long-term relationships based on reliability" (Hall, 1983, p. 67). This tendency on the part of Germans is much like American business in the early part of this century.

The cohesiveness of the employees of most German businesses is evidenced in the narrow salary spread. Whereas in the United States the ratio of lowest paid to highest paid is approximately 1 to 80, in Germany this ratio is 1 to 25 (Hall, 1983, p. 74).

GERMAN MANAGERS' EXPECTATION

Business Is Not as Impersonal

The corporation for most Germans is closely related to his or her own identity. German managers at Mobay are likely to refer to "Papa Bayer" because they perceive themselves as members of a corporate family that meets most of their needs. In turn, most German managers there, as elsewhere, have made a lifelong commitment to the larger group in both a social and economic sense (Friday & Biro, 1986–87). In contrast to the American post–WWII trend is "the German postwar tradition of seeking consensus among a closely knit group of colleagues who have worked together for decades [which] provides a collegial harmony among top managers that is rare in U.S. corporations" (Bleicher & Paul, 1986, p. 12). Our interviews suggested that many German managers may enter a three-year-plus training program with the idea of moving on later to another corporation. This move rarely occurs.

While a three-year training program appears to be excessively long by American standards, one must understand that the longer training program works

From *International Journal of Intercultural Relations*, Vol. 13, 1989, pp. 429–455. Reprinted by permission of Pergamon Press, Inc., and the author.

on several levels that are logical within the German culture. The three or more years of entry level training is a predictable correlation to the German and USA relative values on the Uncertainty Avoidance Index[2] (Hofstede, 1984, p. 122). The longer training period is required to induct the German manager into the more formal decision-making rules, plans, operating procedures, and industry tradition (Cyert & March, 1963, p. 119), all of which focus on the short-run known entities (engineering/reliability of product) rather than the long-run unknown problems (future market demand).

On another level the "strong sense of self as a striving, controlling entity is offset by an equally strong sense of obligation to a code of decency" (McClelland, Sturr, Knapp, & Wendt, 1958, p. 252). Induction into a German company with an idealistic system of obligation requires a longer training period than induction into an American company in which the corporate strategy for productivity is acquired in small group and interpersonal interaction.[3] The German manager who moves from one corporation to another for the purpose of advancement is regarded with suspicion partly because of his lack of participation in the corporate tradition, which could prove to be an unstabilizing factor.

Our preliminary interview results suggested uncertainty avoidance (Hofstede, 1984, p. 130) in everyday business relationships, especially the German concern for security. For example, most of the transfer preparation from the German home office to the [United States] consists of highly detailed explanations of an extensive benefits package. Since the German manager sees a direct relationship between his or her personal security and the prosperity of his or her company, business becomes more personal for him or her. Similarly, Americans who work in employee-owned companies are also seeing a clear relationship between personal security and the prosperity of their company.

AMERICAN MANAGERS' EXPECTATIONS

Need to Be Liked

The American's need to be liked is a primary aspect of his or her motivation to cooperate or not to cooperate with colleagues. The arousal of this motivation occurs naturally in discussion situations when direct feedback gives the American the desired response, which indicates a sense of belongingness or acceptance. The American "envisions the desired responses and is likely to gear his actions accordingly. The characteristic of seeing others as responses is reflected in the emphasis on communication in interaction and in the great value placed on being liked. . . . [The] American's esteem of others is based on their liking him. This requirement makes it difficult for Americans to implement projects which require an 'unpopular' phase" (Stewart, 1972, p. 58).

For Americans, the almost immediate and informal use of a colleague's first name is a recognition that each likes the other. While such informality is common among American business personnel, this custom should probably be avoided with Germans. "It takes a long time to get on a first-name basis with a German; if you rush the process, you may be perceived as overly familiar and rude. . . . Germans are very conscious of their status and insist on proper forms of address. Germans are bewildered by the American custom of addressing a new acquaintance by his first name and are even more startled by our custom of addressing a superior by first name" (Hall, 1983, pp. 57–58). When such matters of decorum are overlooked during critical discussions, an "unpopular phase" may develop.

> The need to be liked is culturally induced at an early age and continued throughout life through regular participation in group activities. They [Americans] are not brought up on sentiments of obligation to others as the Germans are, but from kindergarten on they regularly participate in many more extracurricular functions of a group nature. In fact, by far the most impressive result . . . is the low number of group activities listed by the Germans (about 1, on the average) as compared with the Americans (about 5, on the average). In these activities the American student must learn a good deal more about getting along with other people and doing things cooperatively, if these clubs are to function at all. (McClelland et al., 1958, p. 250)

This cultural orientation in relation to group participation will be revisited later in the closing discussion on "learning styles, training, instruction, and problem solving."

GERMAN MANAGERS' EXPECTATIONS

Need to Be Credible

The German counterpart to the American need to be liked is the need to establish one's credibility and position in the hierarchy. The contrast between American informality and mobility and German formality and class structure is a reflection of the difference between these two needs. In the absence of a long historical tradition, Americans have developed a society in which friendships and residence change often, family histories (reputations) are unknown, and, therefore, acceptance of what one is doing in the present and plans to do in the future is a great part of one's identity. In order to maintain this mobility of place and relationships, Americans rely on reducing barriers to acceptance through informality.

Germans, with their strong sense of history, tradition, family, and life-long friendships, tend to move much less often, make friendships slowly, and keep them longer than Americans. Because one's family may be known for generations in Germany, the family reputation becomes part of one's own identity, which in turn places the individual in a stable social position.[4]

The stability of the social class structure and, thus, the credibility of the upper class in Germany are largely maintained through the elitist system of higher education.

> Educational achievement has been a major factor in determining occupational attainment and socioeconomic status in the post–World War II era. University education has been virtually essential in gaining access to the most prestigious and remunerative positions. Some of the most enduring social divisions have focused on level of education. (Nyrop, 1982, p. 113)

A German's education most often places him or her at a certain level which, in turn, determines what they can and can't do. In Germany, one must present credentials as evidence of one's qualification to perform *any* task (K. Hagemann, personal communication, May–September, 1987). Thus, the German societal arrangement guarantees stability and order by adherence to known barriers (credentials) that confirm one's credibility. In Germany, loss of credibility would be known in the manager's corporate and social group and would probably result in truncated advancement (not dismissal since security is a high value).

The rigid social barriers established by education and credentials stand in direct contrast to the concepts of social mobility in American society. "Our social orientation is toward the importance of the individual and the equality of all individuals. Friendly, informal, outgoing, and extroverted, the American scorns rank and authority even when [he or she] is the one with the rank. American bosses are the only bosses in the world who insist on being called by their first names by their subordinates" (Kohls, 1987, p. 8). When Germans and Americans come together in discussion, the German's drive is to establish hierarchy, the American's is to dissolve it.

AMERICAN MANAGERS' EXPECTATIONS

Assertiveness, Direct Confrontation, and Fair Play

In comparing Americans with Japanese, Edward Stewart relates the American idea of confrontation as "putting the cards on the table and getting the information 'straight from the horse's mouth.' It is also desirable to face people directly, to confront them intentionally" (Stewart, 1972, p. 52). This is done so that the decision makers can have all of the facts. Stewart contrasts this intentional confrontation of Americans to the indirection of the Japanese, which often requires the inclusion of an intermediary or emissary in order to avoid face to face confrontation and thus, the loss of face. However, this view may leave the American manager unprepared for what he or she is likely to find in his or her initial discussion with a German manager.

The American manager is likely to approach his or her first discussion with German managers in an assertive fashion from the assumption that competition in business occurs within the context of cooperation (Stewart, 1972, p. 56). This balance is attained by invoking the unspoken rule of fair play.

Our games traditions, although altered and transformed, are Anglo-Saxon in form; and fair play does mean for us, as for the English, a standard of behavior between weak and the strong—a standard which is curiously incomprehensible to the Germans. During the last war, articles used to appear in German papers exploring this curious Anglo-Saxon notion called "fair play," reproduced without translation—for there was no translation.

Now the element which is so difficult to translate in the idea of "fair play" is not the fact that there are rules. Rules are an integral part of German life, rules for behavior of inferior to superior, for persons of every status, for every formal situation. . . . The point that was incomprehensible was the inclusion of the other person's weakness inside the rules so that "fair play" included in it a statement of relative strength of the opponents and it ceased to be fair to beat a weak opponent.

. . . Our notion of fair play, like theirs [British], includes the opponent, but it includes him far more personally. . . . (Mead, 1975, pp. 143–145)

I am not implying that the American is in need of a handicap when negotiating with Germans. It is important to note however, that the styles of assertiveness under the assumption of American equality (fair play) and assertiveness under the assumption of German hierarchy may be very different. The general approach of the German toward the weaker opponent may tend to inspire a negative reaction in the American, thus reducing cooperation and motivation.

GERMAN MANAGERS' EXPECTATIONS

Assertiveness, Sophistication, and Direct Confrontation

The current wisdom either leaves the impression or forthrightly states that Americans and Germans share certain verbal behaviors which would cause one to predict that discussion is approached in a mutually understood fashion.

If North Americans discover that someone spoke dubiously or evasively with respect to important matters, they are inclined to regard the person thereafter

as unreliable, if not dishonest. Most of the European low-context cultures such as the French, the Germans, and the English show a similar cultural tradition. These cultures give a high degree of social approval to individuals whose verbal behaviors in expressing ideas and feelings are precise, explicit, straightforward, and direct. (Gudykunst & Kim, 1984, p. 144)

Such generalizations do not take into account the difference between *Gespräch* (just talking about—casually) and *Besprechung* (discussion in the more formal sense of having a discussion about an issue). *Besprechung* in German culture is a common form of social intercourse in which one has high level discussions about books, political issues, and other weighty topics. This reflects the traditional German values, which revere education. Americans would best translate *Besprechung* as a high level, well-evidenced, philosophically and logically rigorous debate in which one's credibility is clearly at stake—an activity less familiar to most Americans.

The typical language of most Americans is not the language many Germans use in a high level debate on philosophical and political issues.

In areas where English immigrants brought with them the speech of 16th and 17th century England, we find a language more archaic in syntax and usage than [sic] present-day English. Cut off from the main stream, these pockets of English have survived. But the American language, as written in the newspapers, as spoken over the radio (and television), . . . is instead the language of those who learned it late in life and learned it publicly, in large schools, in the factory, in the ditches, at the polling booth. . . . It is a language of public, external relationships. While the American-born generation was learning this public language, the private talk which expressed the overtones of personal relationships was still cast in a foreign tongue. When they in turn taught their children to speak only American, they taught them a one-dimensional public language, a language oriented to the description of external aspects of behavior, weak in overtones. To recognize this difference one has only to compare the vocabulary with which Hemingway's heroes and heroines attempt to discuss their deepest emotions with the analogous vocabulary of an English novel. All the shades of passion, laughter close to tears, joy tremulous on the edge of revelation, have to be summed up in such phrases as: "They had a fine time." Richness in American writing comes from the invocation of objects which themselves have overtones rather than from the use of words which carry with them a linguistic aura. This tendency to a flat dimension of speech has not been reduced by the maintenance of a classical tradition. (Mead, 1975, pp. 81–82)

Since many Americans tend not to discuss subjects such as world politics, philosophical, and ethical issues with a large degree of academic sophistication, a cultural barrier may be present even if the Germans speak American style English. In a study of a German student exchange program, Hagemann observed that "it was crucial for the Germans, that they could discuss world-politics with their American counterparts, found them interested in environmental protection and disarmament issues and that they could talk with them about private matters of personal importance. . . . If they met Americans who did not meet these demands the relationships remained on the surface" (Hagemann, 1986, p. 8).

This tendency not to enter into sophisticated discussions and develop deeper relationships may be a disadvantage for many Americans who are working with Germans (see Figure 1). In addition, in a society in which one's intellectual credibility[5] establishes one's position in the group and thus determines what one can and can't do, Besprechung can become quite heated—as is the case in Germany.

FOCUS: WHEN BESPRECHUNG AND DISCUSSION MEET

The management style of German and American managers within the same multinational corporation is more likely to be influenced by their nationality than by the corporate culture. In a study of carefully matched national groups of managers working in the affiliated companies of a large U.S. multinational firm, "cultural differences in management assumptions were not reduced as a result of working for the same multinational firm. If anything, there was slightly more divergence between the national groups within this multinational company than originally found in the INSEAD multinational study" (Laurent, 1986, p. 95).

On the surface we can see two culturally distinct agendas coming together when German and American managers "discuss" matters of importance. The American character with its need to remain impersonal and to be liked avoids argumentum ad hominem. Any attack on the person will indicate disrespect and promote a feeling of dislike for the other, thus promoting the "unpopular phase," which, as Stewart indicates, may destroy cooperation for Americans.

In contrast, the German manager, with his personal investment in his position and a need to be credible to maintain his or her position, may strike with vigor and enthusiasm at the other's error. The American manager with his lack of practice in German-style debate and often less formal language, education, and training, may quickly be outmaneuvered, cornered, embarrassed, and frustrated. In short, he or she may feel attacked. This possible reaction may be ultimately important because it can be a guiding force for an American.

Beyond the question of character is the more fundamental question of the guidance system of the individual within his or her culture and what effect changing cultural milieu has on the individual guidance system. I define guidance system as that which guides the individual's actions. In discussing some of the expectations of German and American managers, I alluded several times to what could be construed as peer pressure within small groups. How this pressure works to guide the individual's actions, I will argue in the next section, has great implications for developing programs for American success in Germany.

Viewed as systems of argumentation, discussion and Besprechung both begin a social phase even though Americans may at first view the forcefulness of the Germans as anti-social (Copeland & Griggs, 1985, p. 105). However, a dissimilarity lends an insight into the difference in the guidance systems and how Germans and Americans perceive each other.

American discussion, with the focus on arriving at consensus, is based on the acceptance of value relativism (which supports the American value of equality and striving for consensus). The guidance system for Americans is partly in the peer group

Figure 1 *Development of Discussion Behavior at a Glance*

American	Focus	German
Impersonal—act as own agent—will move on when business does not serve his/her needs or when better opportunity arises	Relationship to business	Not as impersonal—corporation is more cohesive unit—identity more closely associated with position, and security needs met by corporation
Need to be liked—expressed through informal address and gestures	Personal need	Need for order and establishment of place in hierarchy—expressed through formal address and gestures
Short-term—largely informal—many procedures picked up in progress	Orientation to corporation	Long-term training—formal—specific rules of procedure learned
Based on accomplishment and image— underlying drive toward equality	Status	Based on education and credentials—underlying drive toward hierarchy
Assertive, tempered with fair play—give benefit of doubt or handicap	Confrontation	Assertive—put other in his/her place
Discussion about sports, weather, occupation: what you do, what you feel about someone. Logical, historical analysis rarely ventured. Native language sophistication usually low.	Common social intercourse	Besprechung—rigorous logical examination of the history and elements of an issue. Politics favorite topic. Forceful debate expected. Native language sophistication high.

pressure, which the individual reacts to but may not be able to predict or define in advance of a situation. Therefore, some Americans have difficulty articulating, consciously conceiving, or debating concepts in their guidance system but rather prefer to consider feedback and adjust their position to accommodate the building of consensus without compromising their personal integrity.

German *Besprechung*, with the focus on arriving at truth or purer concepts, rejects value relativism in support of German values of fixed hierarchy and social order. The German *Besprechung* is argumentation based on the assumption that there is some logically and philosophically attainable truth. The guidance system for Germans is composed of concepts that are consciously taken on by the individual over years of formal learning (à lá Hall) and debate. While a German makes the concepts [his or her] own through *Besprechung*, [his or her] position is not likely to shift far from a larger group pressure to conform to one hierarchical code.

The peer pressure of the immediate group can often become a driving force for Americans. The irony is that many Germans initially perceive Americans as conformists and themselves as individualists, stating that Americans can't act alone while Germans with their clearly articulated concepts do act alone. Amer-

icans, on the other hand, often initially perceive Germans as conformists and themselves as individualists stating that Germans conform to one larger set of rules while Americans do their own thing.

LEARNING STYLES, TRAINING, INSTRUCTION, AND PROBLEM SOLVING

Education and Training

The ultimate function of group process in American corporations is problem solving and individual motivation (being liked). For Germans motivation is more of a long-term consideration such as an annual bonus or career advancement. Problem solving for Germans is more compartmentalized and individualized.

The contrasting elements discussed earlier and outlined in both "At a Glance" summaries (Figures 1 and 2) indicate that considerable cultural distance may have to be traveled by Germans and Americans before they can be assured that cooperation and motivation are the by-products of their combined efforts. The contrasting elements are, of course, a result of the organization and education—the acculturation— of the minds of Germans and Americans. In this section I will examine the different cultural tendencies

Figure 2 *Manager Background at a Glance*

American	Focus	German
Peer pressure of immediate group—reluctant to go beyond the bounds of fair play in social interaction—backdrop is social relativism	Guidance system	Peer pressure from generalized or larger social group—forceful drive to conform to the standard—backdrop is consistent and clearly known
Generally weaker higher education—weak historical perspective and integrated thought—focus is on the future results—get educational requirements out of the way to get to major to get to career success	Education	Higher education standards generally superior, speak several languages, strong in history, philosophy, politics, literature, music, geography, and art
More group oriented—social phase develops into team spirit—individual strengths are pulled together to act as one	Problem solving	More individualized and compartmentalized—rely on credentialed and trained professional
Informal awareness—get the hand of variations—often unconscious until pointed out	Learning	Formal awareness—specific instruction given to direct behavior—one known way to act—highly conscious

from the perspective of Hall's definitions of formal and informal culture and discuss some implications for intercultural training and education.

The first level of concern is general preparation for the managerial position. As an educator I must take a hard look at the graduates of our colleges and universities as they compare to their German counterparts. I am not attempting to imply that Germans are better than Americans. All cultural groups excel in some area more than other cultural groups.

> Germans are better trained and better educated than Americans. A German university degree means more than its U.S. equivalent because German educational standards are higher and a smaller percentage of the population wins college entrance. Their undergraduate degree is said to be on par with our master's degree. It is taken for granted that men and women who work in business offices are well educated, able to speak a foreign language, and capable of producing coherent, intelligible, thoughtful communications. German business managers are well versed in history, literature, geography, music and art. (Hall, 1983, p. 58)

Americans tend to focus on the present as the beginning of the future, whereas Germans tend to "begin every talk, every book, or article with background information giving historical perspective" (Hall, 1983, p. 20). While Hall makes a strong generalization, a contrary incident is rare. American college graduates are not known for having a firm or detailed idea of what happened before they were born. While some pockets of integrated, sophisticated thinking exist, it is by no means the standard. Indeed, many American college students are unable to place significant (newsworthy) events within an over-all political/philosophical framework two months after the occurrence.

In contrast, college educated Germans tend to express a need to know why they should do something—a reasoning grounded in a logical understanding of the past. Compared to the rigorous German theoretical and concrete analysis of past events, Americans often appear to be arguing from unverifiable aspirations of a future imagined. While such vision is often a valuable driving force and the basis for American innovation and inventiveness, it may not answer the German need to explicitly know why and, thus, may fall short (from a German perspective) in group problem solving when these two cultures are represented. From the educational perspective, one must conclude that more than a few days of awareness training is needed before successful discussions can result between German and American managers, primarily because of what is not required by the American education system. The contrary may also be true in the preparation of Germans to work with Americans. Tolerance for intuitive thinking may well be a proper focus in part of the German manager's training prior to working with American managers.

Formal and Informal Culture

The unannounced and largely unconscious agenda of small group process among Americans is usually more subtle than the German formal awareness but equally as important. American individuals come together in the initial and critical social phase, "size up" each other, and formally or informally recognize a leader. In a gathering of hierarchical equals the first to speak often emerges as the leader. At this point the embers of team spirit warm once again. As the group moves through purpose and task definition, members define and redefine their roles according to the requirements of the evolving team strategy. Fired with team spirit, inculcated through years of group activity and school sports, the group produces more than the sum of their individual promises.

"In the United States a high spontaneous interest in achievement is counterbalanced by much experience in group activities in which the individual learns to channel achievement needs according to the opinions of others. . . . Interestingly enough, the American 'value formula' appears to be largely unconscious or informally understood, as compared to the German one, at any rate" (McClelland et al., 1958, 252). Though this observation is 30 years old, it still appears to be quite accurate. The use of modeling (imitation) as a way of acquiring social and political problem-solving strategies is also a way of adjusting to regionalisms. In taking on different roles, Americans become adept at unconsciously adjusting their character to meet the requirements of different situations. In short, says Hall, "Compared to many other societies, ours does not invest tradition with an enormous weight. Even our most powerful traditions do not generate the binding force which is common in some other cultures. . . . We Americans have emphasized the informal at the expense of the formal" (Hall, 1973, p. 72).

The German learning style is often characterized by formal learning as defined by Hall (Hall, 1973, p. 68). The characteristics of German frankness and directness are echoed in Hall's example of formal learning: "He will correct the child saying, 'Boys don't do that,' or 'You can't do that,' using a tone of voice indicating that what you are doing is unthinkable. There is no question in the mind of the speaker about where he stands and where every other adult stands" (Hall, 1973, p. 68). German formal awareness is the conscious apprehension of the detailed reality of history which forms an idealistic code of conduct that guides the individual to act in the national interest as if there was no other way.[6]

American informal awareness and learning is an outgrowth of the blending of many cultural traditions, in an environment in which people were compelled to come together to perform group tasks such as clearing land, building shelter, farming, and so on. The reduction of language to the basic nouns and functions was a requirement of communication for the multilingual population under primitive conditions. Cultural variations will always be a part of the vast American society. Americans have had to "get the hang of it" precisely because whatever *it* is, *it* is done with several variations in America.

In a sense, the informal rules such as "fair play" are just as prescriptive of American behavior as the system of German etiquette is prescriptive of much of German social interaction, including forms of address (familiar *Du* and the formal *Sie*). Even the rules for paying local taxes, entering children in schools, or locating a reputable repair person vary by local custom in America and can only be known by asking.[7] The clear difference is that the rules are not overtly shared in America.

The American expectations or informal rules for group discussion are general enough to include the etiquette of American managers from different ethnic backgrounds. As long as notions of equality, being liked, respect, fair play, and so on guide behaviors things run smoothly. "Anxiety, however, follows quickly when this tacit etiquette is breached. . . . What happens next depends upon the alternatives provided by the culture for handling anxiety. Ours include withdrawal and anger" (Hall, 1973, p. 76). In the intercultural situation, the American who participates informally in group behavior may feel that something is wrong but may not be able to consciously determine the problem. Without the ability of bringing the informal into conscious awareness, which is a function of awareness and education, many Americans may flounder in a state of confusion, withdrawal, and anger.

CONCLUSION

What should become apparent to intercultural trainers working with companies that are bringing German and American personnel together is that they are working with two populations with distinct learning and problem-solving styles. The American is more likely to learn from an interactive simulation. Within the situation the American can "get the hang of" working with someone who has a German style. Trainers and educators of American managers know that the debriefing of the role play, which brings the operative informal rules into conscious awareness, is the focus of the learning activity. The short-term immersion training so often used today can only supply some basic knowledge and limited role-play experience.

What must never be forgotten in the zeal to train American managers is that their basic guidance system in America is a motivation to accommodate the relative values of the immediate group. While the general cultural awareness exercises that begin most intercultural training may make Americans conscious of their internal workings, much more attention must be given to inculcate an understanding of German social order and the interaction permitted within it.

Knowledge of the language and an in-depth orientation to the culture for the overseas manager and spouse should be mandatory for American success in Germany and German success in the United States. "The high rate of marital difficulties, alcoholism and divorce among American families abroad is well known and reflects a lack of understanding and intelligent planning on the part of American business" (Hall, 1983, p. 88). In our pilot program we became quite aware of the fact that German spouses require much more preparation for a sojourn to America. American short-term planning is in conflict with the long-term preparation needed for most Americans who are going to work with Germans. In Germany the role of the spouse (usually the female) in business includes much less involvement than in the United States. We suspect this has much to do with the lack of attention to spouse preparation that we have observed thus far.

RECOMMENDATION

Long-term programs should be established that provide cultural orientation for overseas families at least three or four years before they start their sojourn with beginning and increasing knowledge of the language as a prerequisite for entry. Such programs should attend to the general instructional deficiencies of Americans in the areas of history, philosophy, and politics as studied by Germans, prepare Germans to expect and participate in an informal culture guided by value relativism in a spirit of equality, incorporate cultural sharing of German and American managers and their families in social settings so the sojourners can come together before, during, and after their individual experiences to establish a formal support network. Segments of such programs could be carried on outside the corporate setting to allow for a more open exchange of ideas. In America, colleges and universities could easily establish such programs. Many American colleges and universities that have served as research and development sites for business and industry are also developing alternative evening programs to meet the educational needs in the community. Also, corporate colleges are an ideal setting for extended in-house preparation. In such learning environments, professors can come together with adjunct faculty (private consultants and trainers) to produce a series of seminars that combine lecture instruction, small group intercultural interaction, networking, media presentations, contact with multiple experts over time, and even a well planned group vacation tour to the sojourner's future assignment site.

Part of the programs should be offered in the evening to avoid extensive interference with the employee's regular assignments and to take advantage of the availability of other family members who should be included in intercultural transfer preparation. Cost to the corporation would be greatly reduced in that start-up funds could be partly supplied through federal grants, travel costs would be lessened, and program costs would be covered under regular tuition and materials fees. As a final note, I strongly recommend that such programs for American managers be viewed as graduate level education since they will be entering a society in which education is a mark of status.

Notes

1. Future references to America and Americans should be understood as referring to the North Eastern United States and the citizens thereof, while references to Germany and Germans should be understood as West Germany and the citizens thereof.
2. Actual German values were 65, with a value of 53 when controlled for age of sample, while the actual USA values were 46, with a value of 36 when controlled for age of sample.
3. For a quick overview of how small group and interpersonal communication is related to corporate success in America see Peters and Austin, 1985, pp. 233–248.
4. These comparative descriptions correspond to the German social orientation and the American personal orientation discussed by Beatrice Reynolds (1984, p. 276) in her study of German and American values.
5. "In Germany, power can be financial, political, entrepreneurial, managerial or intellectual; of the five, intellectual power seems to rank highest. Many of the heads of German firms have doctoral degrees and are always addressed as 'Herr Doktor.'" (Copeland & Griggs, 1985, p. 120). While there may be exceptions to this rule, exceptions are few and hard to find.
6. "Yet this rigidity has its advantages. People who live and die in formal cultures tend to take a more relaxed view of life than the rest of us because the boundaries of behavior are so clearly marked, even to the permissible deviations. There is never any doubt in anybody's mind that, as long as he does what is expected, he knows what to expect from others" (Hall, 1973, p. 75). "In Germany everything is forbidden unless it is permitted" (Dubos, 1972, p. 100).
7. The perplexing problem for German executives who are new in the United States is that in Germany everything is known thus, you should not have to ask to find your way around. But in the USA where change is the watch word, one has to ask to survive.

References

Bleicher, K., & Paul, H. (1986). Corporate governance systems in a multinational environment: Who knows what's best? *Management International Review*, 26 (3), 4–15.

Copeland, L., & Griggs, L. (1985). *Going international: How to make friends and deal effectively in the global marketplace*. New York: Random House.

Cyert, R. M., & March, J. G. (1963). *A behavioral theory of the firm*. Englewood Cliffs, N.J.: Prentice-Hall.

Dubos, R. (1972). *A god within*. New York: Charles Scribner's Sons.

Friday, R. A., & Biro, R. (1986–87). Pilot interviews with German and American personnel at Mobay Corporation (subsidiary of Bayer), Pittsburgh, PA. Unpublished raw data.

Gudykunst, W. B., & Kim, Y. (1984). *Communicating with strangers: An approach to intercultural communication*. Reading, Mass.: Addison-Wesley.

Hagemann, K. (1986). *Social relationships of foreign students and their psychological significance in different stages of the sojourn*. Summary of unpublished diploma thesis, University of Regensburg, Regensburg, Federal Republic of Germany.

Hall, E. T. (1973). *The silent language*. New York: Doubleday.

——. (1983). *Hidden differences: Studies in international communication—How to communicate with the Germans*. Hamburg, West Germany: Stern Magazine Gruner + Jahr AG & Co.

Hofstede, G. (1984). *Culture's consequences: International differences in work-related values*. Beverly Hills, CA: Sage Publications.

Kohls, L. R. (1987). *Models for comparing and contrasting cultures*, a juried paper, invited for submission to National Association of Foreign Student Advisors, June, 1987.

Laurent, A. (1986). The cross-cultural puzzle of international human resource management. *Human Resource Management*, 25, 91–103.

McClelland, D. C., Sturr, J. F., Knapp, R. N., & Wendt, H. W. (1958). Obligations of self and society in the United States and Germany. *Journal of Abnormal and Social Psychology*, 56, 245–255.

Mead, M. (1975). *And keep your powder dry*. New York: William Morrow.

Nyrop, R. F. (Ed.) (1982). *Federal republic of Germany, a country study*. Washington, D.C.: U.S. Government Printing Office.

Peters, T., & Austin, N. (1985). *A passion for excellence*. New York: Warner Communication.

Peters, T., & Waterman, R. (1982). *In search of excellence*. New York: Warner Communication.

Reynolds, B. (1984). A cross-cultural study of values of Germans and Americans. *International Journal of Intercultural Relations*, 8, 269–278.

Stewart, E. C. (1972). *American cultural patterns: A cross-cultural perspective*. Chicago: Intercultural Press.

Weaver, R. M. (1953). *The ethics of rhetoric*. South Bend, Ind.: Regnery/Gateway.

Concepts and Questions

1. How does the American expectation that business is impersonal differ from the corresponding German expectation? How might these differing expectations affect discussion behavior during American–German business discussions?
2. How does the German concept of corporate identity differ from the American? How does this affect entry-level training and career goals?
3. Compare and contrast an American manager's need to be liked with the German manager's need to be credible.
4. How might American and German styles of assertiveness differ? What cultural dynamics might account for these differences?
5. What is the German concept of *Besprechung*? How might Americans perceive its practice by Germans during business discussions? Do you believe the typical American businessperson is adequately prepared to engage in *Besprechung*?
6. How do American and German managers differ in terms of the focus of their fundamental educational backgrounds? How does this influence their approaches to business discussions?
7. Compare and contrast the formal and informal aspects of the German and American cultures as they relate to the conduct of business.
8. Differentiate between German "formal learning" and American "informal awareness and learning." How do these cultural dynamics affect each other's approaches to business discussions?
9. What kind of training program do you believe would be most effective in training American businesspeople to interact effectively with German counterparts?

chapter 3

Co-Cultures: Living in Two Cultures

I n Chapter 2, we focused on international cultures—cultures that exist outside the immediate borders of the United States. In this chapter, we turn our attention to the multicultural aspects of diverse cultural groups living within the United States. In most instances, members of these groups hold dual or multiple cultural memberships, hence the term *co-cultures*. The groups that constitute these co-cultures may share a common religion, economic status, ethnic background, age, gender, sexual preference, or race. In every respect, these co-cultures share many of the same characteristics found in any culture. They often have a specialized language system, shared values, a collective worldview, and common communication patterns. These diverse co-cultures have the potential to bring new experiences and ways of interacting to a communication encounter. Their communicative behaviors can often be confusing and baffling to members of the dominant culture. Anyone who is not aware of and does not understand the unique experiences of these co-cultures may experience serious communication problems.

As the United States continues to develop into a pluralistic and multicultural society, the need and opportunity for effective communication between the dominant culture and the co-cultures as well as among the co-cultures themselves will increase. You cannot be an effective communicator with members of co-cultures unless you reduce your prejudices and stereotypes and develop an understanding of what each co-culture is really like. Prejudices and stereotypes will often lead you to make assumptions about members of co-cultures that are incorrect, hurtful, and even insulting.

Admittedly, many more co-cultures exist than we have been able to include here. Our selection was based on three considerations: (1) limited space and the necessity for efficiency prohibited a long list of co-cultures; (2) we wanted to include some social communities that are often in conflict with the dominant culture; and (3) we wanted to emphasize the co-cultures with which you are most likely to interact. To this end, we selected a representation of the major co-cultures resident within the United States. We should add, however, that additional co-cultures will be examined in subsequent chapters as we explore the verbal and nonverbal dimensions of intercultural communication.

We begin this chapter with an essay that provides an ideological position from which intercultural communication among co-cultures may proceed. Young Yun Kim, in her essay "*Unum* and *Pluribus*: Ideological Underpinnings of Interethnic

Communication in the United States," examines the historical development of American social institutions that were based on such liberal themes as equal rights and equal opportunity and enshrined in the Declaration of Independence, the Constitution, and the Bill of Rights. But, Kim is quick to point out that "Americans today are far from being of a same mind about various social issues" such as interethnic or interracial relations. As she notes, "interethnic relations have become a perpetual sore spot in the American consciousness in which many Americans are galvanized into an "us-against-them" posture leading to a "politics-of-difference" and a "politics-of-recognition."

Having established the current social dilemma, Kim goes on to analyze the issues of race, ethnicity, and interethnic relations. Her analysis reveals four types of interethnic communication messages: *assimilation, pluralism, reconciliation,* and *extremism,* all of which she describes in detail.

The African-American co-culture in the United States is unique because of the history of slavery and the treatment of Blacks as property rather than people. In the next article, "Defining Black Masculinity as Cultural Property: Toward an Identity Negotiation Paradigm," authors Ronald L. Jackson, II and Celnisha L. Dangerfield give us an insightful analysis of culture and a description of the difficulty faced by many Black males in defining their masculine role. Jackson and Dangerfield perceive Black masculinity as cultural, ontological, historical, communicative, and gendered.

Worldview is without doubt the greatest contributor to the deep structure of a culture. And, diversity in worldview makes a significant contribution to perceived differences between people during intercultural communication. Among American co-cultures, the greatest diversity in worldview can easily be found between Native Americans and the traditional European American culture. In order for you to obtain some understanding of Native American worldview, we present the next essay, "Does the Worm Live in the Ground? Reflections on Native American Spirituality," by Michael Tlanusta Garrett and Michael P. Wilbur. They will introduce you to Native American spirituality through four basics elements of Native American culture: medicine, harmony, religion, and vision. From these cultural elements, the authors reveal practical implications for effective intercultural communication.

In the last two decades, the gay co-culture has clearly emerged as one of the most vocal and visible groups on the American scene. Because of perceived impropriety in their sexual preferences and the consequent prejudice and discrimination, the gay co-culture has evolved over time, by the coalescing of disparate groups and individuals who often have only one factor in common: homosexuality. In his article, "Gay Culture," Michael Bronski traces the historical development of the gay culture. He shows how "gay sexuality, like race, was seen by the dominant culture as an insurmountable barrier to an authentic 'American' identity," which cannot assimilate along the same lines as certain European immigrants. He then describes many of the characteristics of the gay culture and provides you with an understanding of the crucial elements of the co-culture to enhance attempts at intercultural communication.

In the last decade, much attention has been focused on a social community previously taken for granted by many segments of American society—women. Because women are so much a part of everyone's perceptual field and daily life, very few scholars, until recently, studied this group as a co-culture. Yet the experiences of females, regardless of the culture, often produce unique ways of perceiving the world and interacting in that world. Events such as the Paula Jones sexual harassment allegations against former President Clinton; successful campaigns for local, state, and national political office by women in unprecedented numbers; and the advancement of women in the business setting have produced a situation that now confirms that the co-culture of women does indeed exist, and that society must give serious consideration to this feminine culture and how it differs from the masculine culture.

One major difference between the feminine and masculine communities is their communicative behaviors. Julia T. Wood and Nina M. Reich believe that these behaviors "can complicate interactions and relationships." The authors begin by making the important distinction between sex (determined by genetic codes that program biological features) and gender (often thought of as the cultural meaning of sex). Their position is that "sex is an individual property, whereas gender is a social construction." Wood and Reich believe that social expectations for males and females and interaction in sex-segregated children's play in groups are major contributors to gender development. These interactions, according to the authors, produce two very different sets of rules regarding communication. Girls learn to be cooperative, not to criticize, and to pay attention. Boys, on the other hand, are taught to be assertive, to focus on outcomes, and to be competitive. As you would suspect, these behaviors produce different styles of communication. Wood and Reich explore those styles in great detail. They conclude their essay by suggesting six ways communication between males and females might be improved.

During recent congressional debates, the well-being and security of the elderly were the focus of much attention. The vocal opposition raised to proposed changes in Social Security and Medicare by this group and its advocates (such as the American Association of Retired People, AARP) has focused national attention on the co-culture of the senior citizen. In the next essay, "Understanding the Co-Culture of the Elderly," Valerie C. McKay describes the cultural dimensions and dynamics of the elderly in the United States. She introduces us to both the positive and negative stereotypes associated with the elderly and the consequences those stereotypes have on understanding the co-culture of the elderly. She then discusses the communication aspects of grandparent–grandchild relationships and the communication dynamics prevalent in this unique intergenerational relationship.

In recent years, it has become apparent that disabled persons are a co-culture in our society. Although there are approximately 14 million disabled Americans between the ages of 16 and 64, they often find themselves either cut off from or misunderstood by the dominant nondisabled culture. Dawn O. Braithwaite and Charles A. Braithwaite look at some of the reasons for this isolation in "'Which is My Good Leg?': Cultural Communication of Persons with Disabilities." They specifically examine how disabled persons view their communication relationships with nondisabled persons. Reviewing research consisting of more than 100 in-depth interviews with physically disabled adults, the Braithwaites have discovered that these disabled people go through a process of redefinition that involves three steps: (1) redefining the self as part of a "new" culture, (2) redefining disability, and (3) redefining disability for the dominant culture. By becoming familiar with these steps, you can learn to improve your communication with members of the disabled co-culture.

Unum and *Pluribus*: Ideological Underpinnings of Interethnic Communication in the United States

YOUNG YUN KIM

The United States was founded as a construction organized by the ideology of "classical liberalism" in the Enlightenment tradition—a tradition rooted in the theories of European and Anglo-American philosophers such as John Locke, Adam Smith, and John Dewey. Central to this ideology is the theme of *individualism*, "the social priority of the individual vis-a-vis the State, the established Church, social classes . . . or other social groups" (Abercrombie, 1980, p. 56). While recognizing the existence of infinite individual differences, classical liberalism also stresses *universalism* that sees human nature presupposing and transcending social group categories such as ethnicity and race. As Michael Billig and associates (1988) have noted: "The assertions 'We are all human' and 'We are all individuals' are both equally and self-evidently 'true'" (p. 124). The liberal themes of individualism and universalism are further linked to the theme of *procedural equality*, that is, "equal rights" and "equal opportunities" afforded to all individuals in the form of "human rights"—the basic requisite of a free and democratic society. Enshrined in the Declaration of Independence, the Constitution, the Bill of Rights, and democratic and capitalistic institutions, these and related liberal principles constitute the core of the American cultural ethos, projecting a vision of American society

that seeks to transcend a monolithic tribal ancestral and territorial condition. Essayist Henry Grunwald captured this liberal tradition in a bicentennial essay (*Time*, July 5, 1976):

> The U.S. was not born in a tribal conflict, like so many other nations, but in a conflict over principles. Those principles were thought to be universal, which was part of the reason for the unprecedented policy of throwing the new country open to all comers. (p. 35)

Given these traditional ideals, however, Americans today are far from being of a same mind about various social issues. In fact, the opposite is true when it comes to "interethnic" (or "interracial") relations. Ever since the Reconstruction era of the late 19th century when "civil rights" debates began (cf. Wilson, 1998), American society has experienced an extraordinary degree of unease, conflict, self-criticism, and mutual-criticism as it struggled to reconcile the ideals of individualism, universalism, and procedural equality with the reality of inequality, real or perceived, along particular ethnic/racial group lines. In recent decades, the traditional primacy of the individual has been increasingly challenged by the claims of the primacy of ethnic group identity over individual identity, particularistic group grievances that are historically and institutionally rooted, and the necessity to redress such grievances so as to achieve equal group status.

This American dilemma continues to stir heated public debates. Indeed, interethnic relations have become a perpetual sore spot in the American consciousness. It galvanizes Americans into "us-against-them" posturing in the form of "identity politics"—also described as "politics of difference" and "politics of recognition." Essayist Russell Baker (*The New York Times*, May 5, 1994) laments this situation in an essay entitled "Gone with the Unum":

> I have always been an "*E Pluribus Unum*" person myself, but the future does not look bright for an "*E Pluribus Unum*" America. The melting pot in which the Pluribus were to be combined into the Unum was not the success its advertisers had promised. . . . What is new these days is the passion with which we now pursue our tribal identities. . . . O, Unum, what misery we courted when we forsook thee for Pluribus. (p. A15)

This original essay appears here in print for the first time. This essay is a modified version of an article of the same title that was published in *International Journal of Intercultural Relations* (Kim, 1999). All rights reserved. Permission to reprint must be obtained from the author and publisher. Young Yun Kim teaches at the University of Oklahoma.

ANALYSIS

This author has sought to better understand and appreciate the often-contentious political landscape of the contemporary United States with respect to issues of race, ethnicity, and interethnic relations. To this end, differing views and opinions of American people have been scrutinized against the backdrop of the classical-liberal ideological tradition.

Guiding this analysis is a systemic, interactive theoretical conception of interethnic communication (Kim, 1997). In this model, an individual's communication behavior influences, and is influenced by, multiple layers of contextual factors including the ideological milieu of the society at large. On the one hand, societal ideology serves as a "common sense" for everyday thinking of ordinary individuals—an intellectual "frame" that they do not themselves invent but that has a history (Billig, 1991, p. 1). What individual Americans think, say, or do about ethnicity, race, and interethnic relations are at least partly reflections of, or responses to, the liberal ideological tradition of the society at large. In turn, the contents of everyday opinions communicated are themselves potential seeds for continuing evolution of the societal ideological tradition. The reciprocal nature of the ideology and communication behavior is a "stimulus-and-response" rather than a one-directional causal relationship. In turn, communication messages are not merely expressions of speakers' passive thoughts; to say something is very often to "fight"—in the sense that messages serve as strategy and tactics for advocating one's own version of the ideology in the broader society so as to affect the ideological milieu itself.

Ideology, in this sense, refers to "lived ideology"— "a latent consciousness or philosophy," "a society's way of life," or "what passes for common sense within a society" (Billig, 1991, pp. 27–29). Ideology is seen as a set of social forces that stimulates, substantiates, and constrains the intellectual beliefs and expressions of thinking individuals. Individuals do not blindly follow the dictates of the mental schema within the ideology, but formulate and express their opinions by invoking socially shared beliefs *as their own*. Even in making remarks that are self-serving or internally contradictory, communicators are assumed to consider their argument "reason-able" or even "persuasive" in the eyes of a "rational" audience. In Billig's (1991) words:

> To maximize their chances of being persuasive, speakers should make appeal to the *sensus comunis*, which they share with their audience. Particularly useful were commonplaces, or the sort of moral maxims, which are laden with clichéd appeals to values. Thus, orators' discourse, which seeks to create new movements of opinion towards a position not commonly shared, will rehearse old commonly shared stereotypes. (p. 21)

Based on the fundamental linkage between an individual's communication behavior and the societal ideology, a variety of data have been analyzed to identify multiple ways the traditional ideology of classical liberalism plays out in the contemporary American interethnic communication messages. Among the data examined in the present analysis are messages of political and civic leaders, activists, academicians, and ordinary citizens. All of the data have been found in public sources such as published books and journals, articles in newspapers and news magazines, and interviews broadcast on radio and television. Some of them are captured in naturally occurring events, whereas others were expressed in the form of personal reflections and testimonials. The data have been analyzed through a qualitative-interpretive exercise to surface the ideological themes underlying the publicly communicated messages.

The analysis has revealed four types of interethnic communication messages: (a) assimilationism; (2) pluralism; (3) reconciliation; and (4) extremism. Each of these message types is described in the following discussion. Commonly rooted in the ideology of classical liberalism, these message types nonetheless illuminate the differing sets of beliefs and moral visions being voiced by Americans today. Together, they constitute a full spectrum of ongoing debates and arguments about what American society is, should be, and should be doing, with respect to issues of ethnicity, race, and interethnic relations.

MESSAGES OF ASSIMILATIONISM

Three core principles of classical liberalism—individualism, universalism, and procedural equality—continue to directly and powerfully underpin the mainstream thinking of Americans about inter-ethnic relations. These liberal ideals shape the arguments commonly referred to as *assimilationism*. Employing such metaphors as "melting pot" and "color-blind society," assimilationist messages project a societal vision in which immigrants and indigenous ethnic minorities are mainstreamed into the normative culture and institutions. In this vision, the government is responsible for universally applying societal rules to all its citizens irrespective of skin color and religious creed. Immigrants and ethnic minorities, in turn, are expected to assimilate themselves socially and culturally, so as to become fully functional in the American society.

Assimilationist messages celebrate personal achievement and self-reliance. These messages place individual identity over and above group identity and question the validity and morality of categorical thought. Although each person is unique, all humans are also endowed with the same set of universal human needs, rights, and responsibilities. Prejudice directed for or against individuals simply based on group membership is morally wrong, not only because it is irrational but also because its focus on social categories contravenes the intellectual or moral prescription to value the unique qualities of every individual. The primacy of the individual over the group hinges on the value of equality as it pertains to the premise of common human nature and basic human rights that call for equal applications of laws and rules to all people regardless of their group categories. A fair society is one in which all individuals, regardless of their backgrounds, are granted equal rights and equal opportunity.

Equality in this view means "fair play"—rooted in a "biopsychological" (or "naturalistic") worldview and the notion of "equity." This view accepts and appreciates differential individual merits in the allocation of resources and status based on the presumption that "there is a natural distribution of human talent, ranging from the few individuals of genius and talent to the defective and delinquent" (Rossides, 1976, p. 9). Each person, and each person alone, is seen as ultimately responsible for his or her own achievement of status. Everyone is expected to "play by the rules." Insistence on group-based policies such as affirmative action in

college admissions and employment practices is "un-American"—one that endangers the larger fraternity of all Americans and obscures differential individual merits that must be *earned* individually. Emphasis on group identity over individual identity is deemed wrong because it renders itself to what essayist Pico Iyer (1990) calls "state-sponsored favoritism" that mandates racial or ethnic "preferences" or "quotas" and "reverse discrimination." Iyer (1990), himself an Indian-born immigrant and world traveler, expresses his objection to such practices as follows:

> As an alien from India, I choose to live in America precisely because it is a place where aliens from India are, in principle, treated no better (and no worse) than anyone else. . . . The problem with people who keep raising the cry of "racism" is that they would have us see everything in terms of race. They treat minorities as emblems, and everyone as typecast. . . . As an Asian minority myself, I know of nothing more demeaning than being chosen for a job, or even a role, on the basis of my race. Nor is the accompanying assumption—that I need a helping hand because my ancestors were born outside Europe—very comforting. . . . Are we, in fact, to cling to a state of childlike dependency? (p. 86)

The assimilationist emphasis on individualism, universalism, and procedural equality has been repeatedly promoted in Presidential inauguration addresses. Presidents, regardless of their party affiliations, have exalted the assimilationist values as the very heart of the American identity—a common identity constituted by individual identities and one that transcends category-based distinctions. President Clinton, for example, spoke of American citizens' "primary allegiance to the values America stands for and values we really live by" and stated: "Long before we were so diverse, our nation's motto was E Pluribus Unum—out of many, we are one. We must be one—as neighbors; as fellow citizens; not separate camps, but family" (*Weekly Compilation of Presidential Documents, 31,* October 23, 1996, p. 1851). The universal principles of individual identity and procedural equality are amply echoed in remarks of many other Americans. A newspaper reader wrote to the editor of *The New York Times Magazine* (April 29, 1992), objecting to an earlier article "Cultural Baggage" on the significance of ethnic group identity:

> I've been fighting ethnic labels since I was 12 or 13, and decided that only I had a right to define myself. . . . I am not almost WASP. I am African-American. I'm also part Cherokee from both sides of my family. But so what? . . . I've taken risks with my life that only I am responsible for, and I have reaped substantial rewards for daring to be myself and not just different. (p. 10)

Stanley Crouch, an African-American essayist, speaks to the common humanity of all races in arguing against racial politics in his book, *Always in Pursuit* (1998): "We . . . observe ourselves functioning in almost every capacity and exhibiting every inclination from the grand to the gaudy, from the idealistic to the shallow ethnic con" (p. 268). Likewise, Richard Lacayo, in an essay entitled "Whose peers?" in a special issue of *Time* magazine (Fall 1993), objects to those who have argued for a guarantee of minority representation in jury composition in courtroom trials:

> [Some] advocates argue that just such a guarantee of minority representation should be part of the law. . . . If that is so, is the only solution an outright racial-quota system? And how finely would the jury need to be divided? Could Latinos in general judge other Latinos? Or would Cuban Americans be needed for the trial of Cuban Americans, Mexican Americans for other Mexican Americans and so on? If the goal is better justice and greater legitimacy, American juries certainly need to be more representative. But in a just society, the process of creating a true assembly of peers need not be reduced to a systematic gathering of the tribes. (p. 61)

Perhaps one of the most compelling articulations of the traditional liberal ideals and of disapproval of identity politics is offered by Glenn C. Loury (1993), a professor of economics at Boston University, as he reflects on his own social identity as an African-American and his individual identity as a human being:

> The most important challenges and opportunities that confront me derive not from my racial condition, but rather from my human condition. I am a husband,

a father, a son, a teacher, an intellectual, a Christian, a citizen. In none of these roles is my race irrelevant, but neither can racial identity alone provide much guidance for my quest to adequately discharge these responsibilities. . . . The expression of my individual personality is to be found in the blueprint that I employ to guide this project of construction. The problem of devising such a plan for one's life is a universal problem, which confronts all people, whatever their race, class, or ethnicity. (pp. 7–10)

MESSAGES OF PLURALISM

Directly challenging the aforementioned assimilationist messages are the messages of *pluralism* or "multiculturalism." Prominent in pluralist messages is the idea of the sanctity of the group. This notion is locally rooted in the experiences of unequal treatment, perceived or real, of certain individuals along ethnic lines. To varying degrees, pluralist messages replace the old "melting pot" metaphor with newer ones such as "mosaic," "quilt," and "salad bowl" that emphasize the distinctiveness of ethnic groups. As such, pluralist messages uphold *group identity* as a vital, if not primary, construct of a personhood, highlighting a fact of life that we are different "types" of persons defined by social categories such as race, ethnicity, language, culture, and national origin. Rooted in the world view of *relativism* that classifies humanity into categories of distinct qualities, pluralist messages emphasize in-group sameness and point to the existence of a "natural attitude" (cf. Garfinkel, 1967) for their moral and intellectual claims for group distinctiveness.

Pluralist messages are predicated on the persistent reality of racial and ethnic prejudice—a reality in which the old liberal ideal of procedural equality is seen as not working well when it comes to serving the needs of certain minority groups. The sense of systematic mistreatment along ethnic and racial lines has given way to a new demand for a new politics of resentment and victimization. Instead of defining equality procedurally in terms of fairness of rules, pluralist messages advocate the contrary belief in *status equality* (in place of procedural equality)— a demand for equal results in the interest of "emancipation" of specific groups that are historically "oppressed" or presently in need of institutional support through remedial laws and public policies. This outcome-based conception of equality is opposed to the procedure-based, universalistic view of equality, in that it allows for differential procedural treatments relative to different groups. Along this line, arguments have been made for a redistribution of power and resources to overcome racial inequalities (Hacker, 1992). Some pluralists advocate such an action as a remedy for status inequalities between and among ethnic and racial groups.

This pluralist position rejects the biopsychological explanation of inequality and replaces it with a "sociocultural" (or "structural") explanation. That is, human beings are inherently equal in their original states, but their original natures become distorted and corrupted in the process of interaction with others in society and through the development of institutions such as language, culture, property, law, and "social stratification" among people (Tsuda, 1986, pp. 62–63). The traditional liberal notions of individual identity, universalistic application of laws, rules, rights, and responsibilities to everyone, and procedural equality without respect to equal outcomes are deemed a false ideology in that it serves only the end of legitimizing the capitalist system of "winners" and "losers" in society. In seeking group identity, relativism, and status equality, pluralist messages present race and ethnicity not merely as a basis for claiming cultural and social distinctiveness, but also as a central rallying point, a focal means to combat unjust practices such as "institutional racism." Prominent in these messages, accordingly, are terms such as ethnic "empowerment," "pride," "dignity," and "justice." Debunking the important liberal value of American life such as "intellectual freedom" and "free speech," pluralist messages demand suppression of "hate speech," loosely defined as words that a minority group finds offensive.

Specifically, schools and universities have sought to bring about a greater diversity of the university curriculum by replacing it with one "that would focus on the achievements of marginalized peoples and on the sins of the nation's founders" (Traub, 1998, p. 25). In San Francisco, for instance, the school board is reported to be developing a plan to require every high school student in the district to read works by authors of color (*The New York Times*, March 11, 1998, p. A21). Many university campuses have rejected the idea of an immutable "canon" of indispensable Western classics in favor of recognizing the reality of ethnic diversity in the United States. Curriculum changes like these have become commonplace, reflecting the emergence of pluralism in national consciousness at the end of the 1980s advocating the normative rights of minority groups. Some advocates of pluralism even have attempted to extend the pluralist messages to arguing for a guarantee of minority representation as part of the law. Believing that race influences not only prominent cases such as the Rodney King trial but also most cases involving minority defendants, Sheri Lynn Johnson, a law professor, believes defendants should be guaranteed three members of their own racial group of a 12-member jury (cited in Lacayo, 1993, p. 61).

The pluralist themes underlie a remark made by a Native American civilian worker at a military station:

> I don't feel too good about White people. They seem like they treat Indians as lower. I dislike the treatment . . . they kind of look down on me because I am an Indian. . . . I fit in the Indian world more than the White world. There is a lot of difference between the Indian [world] and the White world. (cited in Kim, Lujan, & Dixon, 1998, p. 295)

Also expressing the pluralist themes is the following reaction to the recent court decision finding the practice of race-based affirmative action programs in admission decisions at the University of Michigan (*The New York Times*, Editorials/Letters, March 30, 2001):

> Even with affirmative action in place, law school classes here at the University of Michigan are overwhelmingly dominated by white men. The compelling interest in maintaining such programs applies not just to minority students, but to all students who will now see even fewer nonwhite faces and even fewer nonwhite faces as law school classes become even more homogeneous. Our legal system has produced yet another significantly disappointing decision, and many of us here fear that America is on the verge of taking one giant leap backward. (p. A22)

Molefi Keith Asante, an author and the chairman of the Department of African-American studies at Temple University, offers an eloquent argument against the "old" assimilationist ideals. In its place, Asante advocates the pluralist counter-ideals of group identity and status equality based on a particularistic view of human nature. In an essay entitled "Racism, Consciousness, and Afrocentricity," Asante (1993) reflects on his experience of growing up in a racist society and explains how he came to reject W. E. B. Du Bois' notion of "double consciousness" as a tragic outcome inescapable in the "Eurocentric" society. Asante, thus, proposes "Afrocentricity" as an alternative intellectual model based on which African Americans can claim an equal identity and status as a distinct people:

> The feeling that you are in quicksand is inescapable in the quagmire of a racist society. You think that you can make progress in the interpretation of what's happening now only to discover that every step you take sinks the possibility of escaping. You are a victim despite your best efforts to educate those around you to the obvious intellectual mud stuck in their minds. . . . Even from my young adult years I thought a precondition of my fullness, a necessary and natural part of my maturity, was the commitment to be who I am, to be Afrocentric. . . . Afrocentricity is the active centering of the African in subject place in our historical landscape. This has always been my search; it has been a quest for sanity. (pp. 142–143)

MESSAGES OF RECONCILIATION

Straddled between the aforementioned ideological poles of assimilationism and pluralism are the voices of ideological reconciliation. These voices are what sociologist Alan Wolfe in *One Nation, After All* (1998) asserts as occupying "the vital center"—the "middle" America. Based on 200 in-depth interviews conducted in Boston, Atlanta, Tulsa, and San Diego metropolitan areas, Wolfe (1998) found "little support for the notion that middle-class Americans are engaged in bitter cultural conflict with one another" (p. 278). Instead, according to Wolfe, they are "struggling to find ways in which their core beliefs can be reconciled with experiences that seem to contradict them" (p. 281), while insisting on a set of

values "capacious enough to be inclusive but demanding enough to uphold standards of personal responsibility" (p. 322).

The messages of reconciliation reflect the struggle of Americans seeking moderation, tolerance, accommodation, integration, and balance. At the same time, reconciliation messages indicate a great deal of ambivalence and even contradiction in the way many Americans think about the issues of race, ethnicity, and interethnic relations. They may, for example, support bilingual programs, but only if they are short-lived and not used as a political goal or instrument of power demanded by every group for its own separate slice of the political pie. They may support multiculturalism, but only to the extent that ethnic identity is subsumed under the common "American identity" that emphasizes individualism. Or, they may support affirmative action programs based on group identity, but consider "quota" systems as unfair, divisive, and ultimately counterproductive.

Messages of reconciliation such as these can be traced to the mainstream, integrationist civil rights movement led by Martin Luther King, Jr. In this movement, the traditional liberal ideals of individualism and procedural equality have been largely upheld in the struggle to eliminate systematic discrimination against African Americans as a group. Such a position of integration and reconciliation is eloquently expressed in the widely quoted "I Have a Dream" speech King delivered before the Lincoln Memorial on August 28, 1963:

> So I say to you, my friends, that even though we must face the difficulties of today and tomorrow, I still have a dream. It is a dream deeply rooted in the American dream that one day this nation will rise up and live out the true meaning of its creed—we hold these truths to be self-evident, that all men are created equal. . . . I have a dream my four little children will one day live in a nation where they will not be judged by the color of their skin but by the content of their character. I have a dream today. (in C. S. King, 1993, p. 101)

More recently, an attempt at ideological reconciliation was voiced in a remark President Clinton made during a roundtable discussion on race televised on PBS (Public Broadcasting System) on July 9, 1998: "I believe there is an independent value to having young people learn in an environment where they're with people of many different racial and ethnic backgrounds. And the question is, How can you balance that with our devotion to merit?" (*The New York Times*, July 9, 1998, p. A21). A similar stance of reconciliation has been recently voiced by Hugh Price, President of the National Urban League. In his keynote address at the League's 1998 annual conference, Price shared his belief that the current conditions in the United States offer blacks the "best shot we have ever had to shove ourselves the rest of the way into the American mainstream" (*The New York Times*, August 13, 1998). Racial discrimination still exists, Hughes pointed out, but African-American parents must take greater responsibility for the education of their children:

> With unemployment so low, employers are gobbling up almost every willing and able worker with a pulse. Shame on us if we don't seize this historic opening in the economy. . . . I think we are moving rapidly toward the day when if you've got something to put on the table, employers aren't going to care what color you are. (p. A23)

Likewise, on Columbus Day in 1992, Niles Bird Runningwater, then president of the Indian student association at the University of Oklahoma, communicates a message of reconciliation:

> We don't choose to protest this fallacy of American history, but rather to celebrate the survival and continuance of Indian peoples . . . By doing this we can fully acknowledge 500 years of coexistence of Indian and non-Indian peoples in America. . . . We're trying to do our part in togetherness and participation by eliciting communication and excitement concerning the respect of others' cultures. (*The Oklahoma Daily*, March 24, 1992, p. 3)

Moderate voices such as these often escape media attention or get lost in the midst of loud and conspicuous voices of committed ideologues from the left and the right. Yet messages of reconciliation are all around us when we look for them. In his autobiography *Walking with the Wind* (1998), John Lewis, a leader of the civil rights movement since the 1960s and currently a Democratic Congressman from Georgia, articulates his abiding faith in the "Beloved Community," a vision of what society could become were people of all class and ethnic backgrounds to reach across the barriers that divide them. Richard Rorty, in his book *Achieving Our Country* (1998), argues for ideological moderation and objects to intransigent "leftists" and "conservatives." In *Someone Else's House* (1998), Tamar Jacoby professes her faith in interethnic integration and calls for realism that appreciates the real progress between blacks and whites that has taken place in American society and of insisting on the need for both blacks and whites to stay on the long and slow course of integration. An ideological reconciliation is also sought by Gerald Graff in *Beyond the Culture Wars* (1992) and by Alan Ryan in *Liberal Anxieties and Liberal Education* (1998). Both authors support the principles of multiculturalism and other pluralistic theories, while insisting that category-based ideas of cultural diversity in the academe must be moderated and put in dialogue with traditional courses to avoid continuation of a disconnected curriculum and mutual resentment.

MESSAGES OF EXTREMISM

The full spectrum of American public discourse on interethnic relations further includes the marginal voices of separatism, often characterized as "extremist" views. Whereas the aforementioned messages of assimilationism, pluralism, and reconciliation commonly adhere to the societal goal of interethnic *integration* (while disagreeing on specific visions as to how to achieve this goal), extremist messages often express a preference for a maximum in-group–out-group *separation*. Some of the most unambiguous separatist messages come from those identified with "extreme right" groups including the Ku Klux Klan, Neo-Nazi, Skinheads, and those of the so-called Patriot movements. Members of such groups are known for their commitment to racial purism, the supremacy of the white race, and, in some cases, even arms training and preparation for a race war (The Southern Poverty Law Center, 1998). George Burdi, who is reported to be working to revitalize the Neo-Nazi movement through a newly powerful network, the Internet, states his separatist view toward blacks:

> To put black men and women in American society, which is traditionally and essentially established on

European traditions, and to say, "Here you go, you're an equal, now compete," is just as ridiculous as assuming that you could move white people to the Congo and have them effectively compete. . . . the progeny of slaves cannot live in harmony with the progeny of slavemasters. (*The New York Times Magazine*, February 25, 1996, pp. 40–41)

Of course, separatist messages come from the "extreme left" as well, including such contemporary ethnic nationalist groups as the New Black Panthers and the Nation of Islam. Among such messages are Leonard Jefferies' description of white Americans as "ice people" and Louis Farrakhan's call for black nationalism and economic reparations, his assertion of black racial superiority, and his condemnation of Jews as "bloodsuckers," which have been widely reported (e.g., *Time*, February 28, 1994, pp. 21–25). Farrakhan is also reported to have called the United States "the Great Satan" during a visit in 1996 to Iran and proclaimed: "You can quote me: God will destroy America at the hands of the Muslims (*Time*, February 26, 1996, p. 12; *The Washington Post*, February 26, 1996, pp. A1, A6). Farrakhan explains his separatist view in an interview featured in *Time* (February 28, 1994, pp. 21–25) as follows:

My ultimate aim is the liberation of our people. So if we are to be liberated, it's good to see the hands that are holding us. And we need to sever those hands from holding us that we may be a free people, that we may enter into a better relationship with them than what we presently have. (p. 25)

Extreme separatist messages are heard even from those who are unaffiliated with a recognized extremist group. Although not always explicit, separatist views can be easily inferred from the inflammatory rhetorical devices employed to condemn or scapegoat an out-group or position the in-group as "victims." Among such messages is the phrase "culture war" Patrick Buchanan used in a speech he delivered during the 1992 Republican convention, connoting an unmistakable line drawn to "defend" what is believed to be *the* authentic American culture. Indeed, separatist messages appear to be becoming increasingly louder: Robert Kimball (1990) characterizes black studies in universities as "this war

against Western culture" (p. xi); minority student protesters at Stanford University chant "Down with racism, Western culture's got to go" (*The New York Times*, October 25, 1995, pp. A1, B8); a black student leader at Northwestern University insists that no black people can be racists "because racism is a function of power" (*The New York Times*, October 25, 1995, p. B8); a group of Hispanic students at Cornell University occupy a building to demand separate Hispanic housing (*The New York Times*, April 20, 1994, p. B8).

Thus, the extremes meet. As much as the separatist messages of the extreme right and the extreme left differ dramatically in respective claims, they converge in rigid in-group–out-group distinction, characterization of the in-group as "victims," full-blown confrontational rhetorical posturing, and fortification of mutually intransigent moral claims. Separatist messages of both kinds violate the rationality and civility normally expected by most Americans in public discourse. As such, extremist messages are deemed to be beyond the realms most Americans consider "reasonable." As Billig et al. (1988) observe, "the extreme bigot is free to play consistently and unambiguously in an area which is beyond reality but which taunts reality. There is no need to hedge and qualify statements in order not to pass a seemingly unreasonable judgment" (p. 118). It is not surprising, then, that separatist arguments do not resonate with the American public at large and, instead, are usually met with messages of rejection of one kind or another.

Even though mainstream Americans diverge in their views on the locus of American life (individual vs. group identity); the nature, rights, and responsibilities of humans (universalism vs. relativism); and the meaning of equality (procedural equality vs. status equality), they are largely united in their objection to the separatist vision of the United States and in their shared condemnation of "hate" messages as fundamentally "un-American."

Exemplifying such common reactions to separatist messages are the responses of several readers to a *Time* magazine cover story featuring Farrakhan, entitled "Price and Prejudice" (February 28, 1994, pp. 21–34). Their letters to the editor characterize Farrakhan in such unflattering terms as a "wild, hate-mongering preacher," "the Minister of Rage," "streetwise hipster who shrewdly plays to the motions of the most miserable and hopeless of his own people." One reader admonishes the editor for even featuring the story in the magazine:

> As an African American, I find it very upsetting that every time Farrakhan speaks the media give him a microphone and an amplifier. . . . We should stop pointing fingers and making excuses that seem to confuse and anger more than unite our community. We can't continue at this level. We just can't.

Others have responded to Farrakhan's separatist messages by warning against putting group identity over individual identity. Shelby Steel, an African American professor at San Jose State University, points to the danger of excessive claims of group identity in an opinion column in *The New York Times* (March 13, 1994, p. E17):

> Louis Farrakhan personifies a specific territory in the collective imagination of black America. (Only this place in the imagination explains the vast disparity between his prominence and his rather small following.) It is the territory where the group ceases to be a mere identity or culture and becomes a value in itself. Here the group becomes synonymous with truth, and no longer needs approval from others. . . . It is precisely their break from universal truths—tolerance, brotherhood, fair-mindedness—that enables them to assert the supremacy of their group.

A more reconciliatory response to Farrakhan is seen in the American Jewish Committee's one-page political advertisement placed in *The New York Times* (February 24, 1994, p. B12). This advertisement message is offered as a message countering "verbal attacks by leaders of the Nation of Islam on whites, women, Jews, Catholics, Arabs, gays, and African Americans who criticize their persistently divisive message" (p. B12):

> We, the undersigned, believe the best response we can give to those who teach hate is to join our voices, as we have so often joined forces, in a better message—of faith in each other, of shared devotion to America's highest ideals of freedom and equality. "We must all learn to live together as brothers," the Reverend Dr. Martin Luther King, Jr., said, "or we will all perish together as fools. That is the challenge of the hour." Together, we strive to meet that

challenge. For with all our differences, we are indeed united, as Americans. (p. B12)

SYNTHESIS

The present analysis has revealed varied renditions of the liberal ideological tradition. Classical liberalism is reproduced by individual Americans not so much in terms of a set of universally commonsensical values, as in the form of often dilemmatic and sometimes embattled conflicting values. Communication messages addressing issues of race, ethnicity, and interethnic relations do not automatically mirror the traditional liberal themes of individualism, universalism, and procedural equality. Rather, they are dynamically challenged by the contrary themes of group identity, particularism, and equal group status. This ideological dialectic undergirds messages of assimilationism and pluralism, along with messages of reconciliation and separatism. These themes and counter-themes of classical liberalism broadly help us understand the full spectrum of messages we hear today. The traditional individualistic and universalistic ideals and the principle of procedural equality are most closely aligned with messages of *assimilationism*, generally identified as the position of the mainstream political right. On the other hand, messages of *pluralism*, often associated with the mainstream political left, advocate the primacy of group identity, application of laws and public policies relative to historical and institutional conditions particular to a group, so as to close the existing unequal status between groups. Struggling between these two ideological views are the moderating, balancing, integrating, and often-conflicted messages of *reconciliation* representing Middle America. In contrast, messages of *extremism* are commonly identified with the views of the extreme right and the extreme left—messages that emphasize in-group victimhood and moral superiority and maximum in-group–out-group separation.

Together, these four ideological positions constitute an *ideological circle* described in Figure 1. In this circle, the four positions are differentiated based on two bipolar dimensions: (1) the horizontal dimension of classical liberal and contrary themes, and (2) the vertical dimension of integrationist and separatist visions for the American society. The op-

Figure 1 *Ideological Circle*

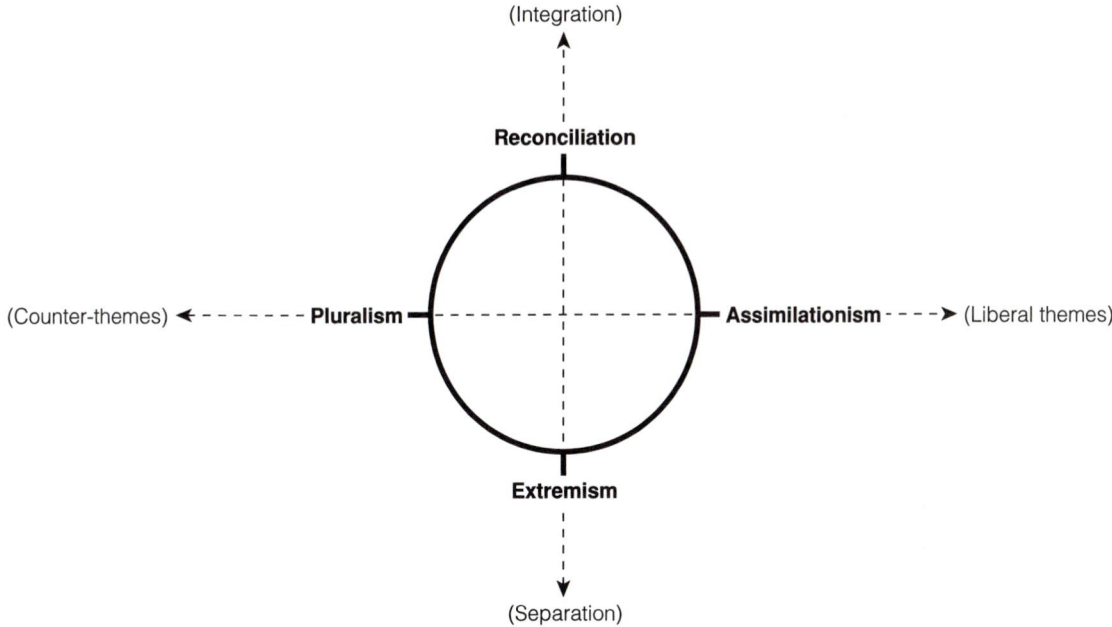

positional relationship between the assimilationist messages of liberal themes and pluralist messages of counter-themes is indicated by their respective positions of three o'clock and nine o'clock. Linking these two message types are the integrationist messages of reconciliation placed at the twelve o'clock position. The separatist messages of extremism (from both the extreme political right and the extreme political left) are merged into the six o'clock position, opposite from the position of the integrationist messages of reconciliation.

Even while being rigorously challenged by the voices advocating pluralism and extremism, the classical liberal ideals continue to occupy the mainstay of American consciousness on interethnic relations in the form of assimilationism and reconciliation. The liberal tradition contains its own contrary themes, unresolved tensions, a dialectic—an ideological push-and-pull that often gives rise to heated debates. These debates are not confined to the level of intellectual analysis; both themes and counter-themes have arisen from, and passed into, everyday consciousness of Americans who reflect on, and speak to, various issues of ethnicity and race. Indeed, we do not blindly follow the dictates of classical liberalism. Rather, we

exercise a degree of freedom in making our own individual interpretations and judgments *within the constraints of the liberal ideological tradition.*

This conclusion is largely supported by findings from public opinion polls. In a 1997 Time/CNN poll of more than 1,100 Americans, 96% of the respondents agreed with the assimilationist statement, "It should be the duty of all immigrants to learn English if they plan to stay in this country." In response to the question, "Which comes closest to your view on bilingual education in public schools?" only 11% agreed with the pluralist view that that "children of immigrants should be taught in their native language indefinitely." This is in sharp contrast with the 48% of the respondents who indicated "children of immigrants should be taught in their native language only until they know enough English to join regular classes," and with the remaining 40% who said "all children should be taught in English" (Gray, 1998, p. 70).

Similar sentiments underlie the decisive passage of "Proposition 227" in 1998 by California voters, thereby eliminating all bilingual education programs and replacing them with intensive English language instructions. Likewise, when "Ebonics" ("Black English") was endorsed by the Oakland Unified School

District Board of Education at the end of 1996 as a legitimate language program, many public leaders who often diverge ideologically with respect to interethnic relations converged in denouncing and rejecting it as an "extremist," "dangerous," and "divisive" idea. From the camp commonly known as the "political right," Republican Senator Lauch Faircloth of North Carolina persisted in stating what had become the common view: "But I think Ebonics is absurd. This is a political correctness that has simply gone out of control." Similar voices were heard from the "political left" as well. Jesse Jackson stated: "I understand the attempt to reach out to these children, but this is an unacceptable surrender, bordering on disgrace" (cited in Lewis, 1998).

Senior *Wall Street Journal* editor Joseph N. Boyce was even more indignant: "As a black person and father of four, I find such notions insulting and, yes, racist" (cited in Palmeri, 1997). Poet Maya Angelou was also quoted to have been "incensed" by the plan, while Oakland writer Ishmael Reed labeled it a "travesty" (cited in Palmeri, 1997). Relatedly, the results of Gallop polls taken over the recent decades (1972 through 1997) show a dramatic increase in the percentage of white Americans who are willing to vote for a black candidate for president (from 35% to 93%) and who approve of marriage between blacks and whites (25% to 61%) (*USA Today*, August 8, 1995, p. A11).

The continuing efficacy of liberal ideology transcending ethnic categories is also reflected in the fact that, roughly from the 1960s to the 1990s, the number of interracial marriages in the United States has escalated from 310,000 to more than 1.1 million and that the incidence of births of mixed-race babies has multiplied 26 times as fast as that of any other group. As of the early 1990s, 52% of Jewish Americans, 65% of Japanese Americans, and 70% of Native Americans are reported to have married out of their faith, race, or ethnic heritage (Smolowe, 1993, pp. 64–65). Increasingly, individuals of mixed racial and ethnic backgrounds add complexity to the ideological dialectic. Arvil Ward (1993), half Asian and half Black, describes his identity experience as follows:

> I found myself in an argument on a flight from Washington D.C. to Memphis. . . . This time it was with a member of the Black Freedom Fighters Coalition, or so his jacket, which was covered in epigrams and names

from black history, said. A few minutes into our flight, he noticed that I was reading Shelby Steele's *The Content of our Character*. Since he asked, I started to tell him what I thought I understood of the conservative Steele's ideas. . . . "Why do you clutter up your mind with all that stuff?" he asked, his voice dripping with drama like a preacher. . . . He asked me what right I had to say I was Black. Yeah, I had black skin, he agreed, but I didn't sound Black. . . . "You Filipino, right?. . . . It is people like you that will sell us out when the revolution comes," he said. . . . Could he have known that all my life, I struggled for black acceptance, many times at the expense of my Asian side? (pp. 111–112)

Exactly how the nature of American interethnic relations and the underlying forces of ideological beliefs will unfold in the future remains to be seen. Meanwhile, debates will doubtlessly continue as Americans struggle with competing visions of *Unum* and *Pluribus*—visions of what it means to be Americans. Free and public debates, indeed, are essential for American society to guard itself against stagnation, disintegration, and entropy. The very fact that interethnic issues continue to engage American passion is itself an affirmation, and a hallmark, of the American liberal tradition. This tradition contributes to the stability of the American democracy, one that most Americans recognize, cherish, and celebrate. In the essayist Grunwald's (1976) words:

> So one must love America, most of all and most deeply for its constant, difficult, confused, gallant and never finished struggle to make freedom possible. One loves America for its accomplishments as well as for its unfinished business—and especially for its knowledge that its business is indeed unfinished. . . . One ultimately loves America for not what it is, or what it does, but for what it promises. . . . we must deeply believe, and we must prove, that after 200 years the American promise is still only in its beginning. (p. 36)

References

Abercrombie, N. (1980). *Class, structure and knowledge.* Oxford: Basil Blackwell.

Asante, M. (1993). Racism, consciousness, and Afrocentricity. In G. Early (Ed.), *Lure and loathing: Essays on race, identity, and the ambivalence of assimilation* (pp. 127–148). New York: Penguin.

Baker, R. (1994, May 5). Gone with the Unum. *The New York Times*, p. A15.

Billig, M. (1991). *Ideology and opinions: Studies in rhetorical psychology*. London: Sage.

Billig, M., Condor, S., Edwards, D., Gane, M., Middleton, D., & Radley, A. (1988). *Ideological dilemmas: A social psychology of everyday thinking*. London: Sage.

Crouch, S. (1998). *Always in pursuit: Fresh American perspective, 1995–1997*. New York: Pantheon Books.

Garfinkel, H. (1967). *Studies in ethnomethodology*. Englewood Cliffs, NJ: Prentice-Hall.

Graff, G. (1992). *Beyond the culture wars: How teaching the conflicts can revitalize American education*. New York: Norton.

Gray, P. (1998). Teach your children well. *Time*, 69–71.

Grunwald, H. (1976, July 5). Loving America. *Time*, 35–36.

Hacker, A. (1992). *Two nations: Black and White, separate, hostile, unequal*. New York: Charles Scribner's Sons.

Iyer, P. (1990, September 3). The masks of minority terrorism. *Time*, 86.

Jacoby, T. (1998). *Someone else's house: America's unfinished struggle for integration*. New York: The Free Press.

Kim, Y. Y. (1997). The behavior-context interface in interethnic communication. In J. Owen (Ed.), *Context and communication behavior* (pp. 261–291). Reno, NV: Context Press.

Kim, Y. Y. (1999). Unum and Pluribus: Ideological underpinnings of interethnic communication in the United States. *International Journal of Intercultural Relations, 23*(4), 591–611.

Kim, Y. Y., Lujan, P., & Dixon, L. (1998). "I can walk both ways": Identity integration of American Indians in Oklahoma. *Human Communication Research, 25*(2), 252–274.

Kimball, R. (1990). *Tenured radicals: How politics has corrupted higher education*. New York: Harper & Row.

King, C. S. (1993). *The Martin Luther King, Jr. companion: Quotations from the speeches, essays, and books of Martin Luther King, Jr.* (selected by Coretta Scott King). New York: St. Martin.

Lacayo, R. (1993, Fall). Whose peers? *Time* (Special Issue, The New Faces of America), 60–61.

Lewis, J. (1998). *Walking with the wind: A memoir of the movement*. New York: Simon & Shuster.

Loury, G. (1993). Free at last? A personal perspective on race and identity in America. In G. Early (Ed.), *Lure and loathing: Essays on race, identity, and the ambivalence of assimilation* (pp. 1–12). New York: Allen Lane/Penguin.

Palmeri, A. (1997, October). *Ebonics and politics: A Burkian analysis*. Paper presented at the annual meeting of the National Communication Association, Chicago.

Rorty, R. (1998). *Achieving our country: Leftist thought in twentieth-century America*. Cambridge, MA: Harvard University Press.

Rossides, D. (1976). *The American class system: An introduction to social stratification*. Washington, DC: University Press of America.

Ryan, A. (1998). *Liberal anxieties and liberal education*. New York: Hill & Wang.

Smolowe, J. (1993, Fall). Intermarried . . . with children. *Time* (Special issue: The New Faces of America), 64–65.

Southern Poverty Law Center (1998, Spring). *Intelligence Report*, 90.

Traub, J. (1998, June 28). Nathan Glazer changes his mind, again. *The New York Times Magazine*, 22–25.

Tsuda, Y. (1986). *Language inequality and distortion*. Philadelphia: John Benjamin.

Ward, Arvil (1993). Which side are you on? *Amerasia Journal, 19*(2), 109–112.

Wilson, K. (1998, May). The contested space of prudence in the 1874–1875 civil rights debate. *Quarterly Journal of Speech, 84*(2), 131–149.

Wolfe, A. (1998). *One nation, after all*. New York: Viking.

Concepts and Questions

1. Why has the *E Pluribus Unum* concept of a "melting pot" society failed to materialize in contemporary American society?

2. How do "tribal identities" contribute to interethnic conflict?

3. What characterizes messages of assimilation? From whom are messages of assimilation most likely to emerge?

4. Can or do messages of assimilation lend themselves to improved interethnic communication?

5. Give an example of a message of pluralism. How do messages of pluralism differ from messages of assimilation?

6. What are messages of reconciliation? How do they relate to messages of assimilation and messages of pluralism?

7. From whom are messages of reconcilation most likely to emanate?

8. What are messages of extremism? Which groups of American society are most likely to promulgate messages of extremism?

9. How can an understanding of the philosophical underpinings of the messages of assimilation, plurality, reconcilation, and extremism lead to better interethnic communication?

10. How can the Amercian struggle between *Unum* and *Pluribus* be resolved?

Defining Black Masculinity as Cultural Property: Toward an Identity Negotiation Paradigm

Ronald L. Jackson, II

Celnisha L. Dangerfield

Black masculinist scholarship cannot afford to accept, approve, and adopt the same cultural, social, and political agendas as traditional White masculinist scholarship. The two areas of gender theory share some commonalities, however there is a distinction that emerges at the intersection where gender meets culture.

Jackson, 1997, p. 731

Theory, by its very nature, is something that can be proven wrong. It has voids because no one theory can possibly characterize all aspects of a given phenomenon. Communicologist Stanley Deetz (1992) explains: "A theory is a way of seeing and thinking about the world. As such, it is better seen as the 'lens' one uses in observation rather than as the 'mirror' of nature" (p. 66). The existing lenses used to explore Black masculinity, as a communicative aspect of gendered lives, require correction. Any time a body of theory, set of discoveries, or range of conceptualizations are no longer effective in explaining the phenomena or behaviors they purport to describe, a paradigm shift is needed.

After having reviewed the existing interdisciplinary literature and conceptualizations of Black masculinity, we feel we have read a set of foreign autobiographies, few of which pertain to the first author of this essay, a Black male. Married, middle-class, educated spiritual Black men, who are goal-driven, employed, competent, and non-criminal are missing from both the vast amount of literature and the constellation of media representations of Black males. The indisputable and tragic reality is that Black males have been pathologized and labeled as violent/criminal, sexual, and incompetent/uneducated individuals. This prevalent set of stereotypical depictions of Black masculinity as a stigmatized condition or of Black males as an "endangered species" makes it extremely difficult to theorize Black masculinities in the same ways as White or other marginalized group masculinities. Black masculinities are first and foremost cultural property communicated in everyday interaction as manifestations of Black identities.[1]

Traditionally, the impulse among gender theorists in many disciplines including communication has been to interpret the incendiary nature of masculinity studies in the specter of the European American experience. The assumption made is that all masculine persons function in homogeneous ways.[2] However, a growing contingent of Black writers, including bell hooks, Clyde Franklin III, Patricia Hill Collins, Richard Majors, Michelle Wallace, Philip Brian Harper, Naim Akbar, Haki Madhubuti, Earl Ofari Hutchinson, and others, have proposed that Black masculinities are cultural property, and that they are ritualistically, explicitly, and implicitly validated by communities within everyday interactions. We agree with bell hooks' (1992) assertion about scholarship pertaining to Black masculinities. She writes:

> [The literature on black masculinity] does not interrogate the conventional construction of patriarchal masculinity or question the extent to which Black men have internalized this norm. It never assumes the existence of black men whose creative agency has enabled them to subvert norms and develop ways of thinking about masculinity that challenge patriarchy. (p. 89)

Essentially, the literature presupposes complicity with hegemony and never questions whether Black men have been affected by their own exclusion from the mainstream to the extent that they have constructed their masculinities differently. In assuming that all masculinities are the same, one presupposes that all men should completely share the burden of U.S. White male patriarchal allegations without sharing the licenses to White male privilege, Black men to be the "endangered species" and still function in a position of privilege, hence with the same sensibilities as White men. So, we are persuaded by hooks' argument that social depictions of Black masculinities as dominate are "fantastical" and "narrow" (p. 89). While introducing a Black masculine paradigm, this article issues a challenge to rethink how cultural particularity influences the existing range of Black masculinities, which significantly diverge from culture-generic characterizations of what it means to be masculine.

Feminist thinkers, who encapsulate and hold liable negative masculine tendencies for the American fixation on power, competition, greed, control, and institutionalized exclusion, have inspired a large segment of critical masculinity scholarship. Consequently, the versions of masculinity that are described are often culturally generic, fragmented, and aloof. Very few gender studies depict masculinities as positive, healthy, mature, productive, and balanced identities, but these masculinities do exist. The gender descriptors "masculinity" or "masculinist" usually refer to antagonistic, puerile, insecure, very unaware, and chaotic male identities. It is true that masculine, like feminine, persons enact a wide range of behaviors on a daily basis, from dysfunctional to quite functional. So, theorizing masculinities, in terms of a gendered continuum ranging from healthy to unhealthy and positive to negative self-definitions, is both necessary and revolutionary.

As mentioned previously, the everyday existence of healthy and productive human beings is not so new, which means that some gender theories have slipped with respect to how they account for healthy masculinities. This near absence of critical gender commentary on cultural masculinities only accents the inseparable link between power, ideology, and the politics of representation. It is the intent of this essay to address this void in gender thinking and offer a paradigm that may serve as some basis for explaining productive and counter-productive masculine behaviors, while accenting culture as a means of understanding masculine realities.

This article is organized into four parts. First, the article begins by defining the terms *masculinity* and *femininity* and then discussing male and female sex and gender role stereotypes. Second, we provide a brief overview of three prominent social and racial stereotypes of Black masculinities. Third, a theoretic paradigm of Black masculine identities is introduced. Finally, the essay concludes with implications of the Black masculinity studies and suggestions for future research.

DEFINING MASCULINITY AND FEMINITY

Clearly, masculine and feminine mystiques socially dominate how we see the world. It only takes a quick survey of child-rearing practices among parents and mass-mediated reinforcements of sex and gender role stereotypes to see that these images are sharply divided. When writers speak of masculinities and femininities, we often assume we know what the terms mean, and we also presume that these universal categories are reasonable ways to conceptualize lived realities. Rather than totally discard the terms, we recommend that the terms be redefined as perceptual categories in flux. In order to discuss definitions of masculinity and femininity, it is appropriate to return to the distinctions between sex and gender. The contemporary conversation concerning sex and gender is similar to that of race and ethnicity. The first term in each pair refers to biologically conceived characteristics of an individual, whereas the latter pertains to social ascriptions and prescriptions.

Sex Roles

Just as one may be able to determine another's sex and/or race by observing optic markers, such as the hair, skin, lips, eyes, musculature, and so on, he or she may also be able to determine one's sex by the same means. This is what we call "preverbal communication," the communication that occurs via physiognomic markers before the talk begins. When we speak of sex roles rather than sex, expectations emerge. Sex roles are the biological prescriptions about what males and females should do with their bodies. For example, one female role is to procreate. Males are expected to talk with a deep voice. Although it is generally easier to visually identify a male or a female, gender identities are more intricate.

Gender Roles

Gender roles refer to ways women and men are socially and culturally assigned feminine and masculine behaviors. For instance, men are socially expected to actively pursue women for a dating and mating relationship. Women are socially expected to be more nurturing and affectionate than men. These gender roles are socializations that begin at birth. Family and friends purchase products that are blue for newborn boys. Purchased newborn gifts are typically pink if for girls, and if you don't know the sex of the baby, green is appropriate. A family would probably find it insulting to receive a baby boy's gift that is pink. Another gender role is seen with boys, who are normally socialized to play with trucks, whereas girls are typically encouraged to play with Barbies. This supposedly keeps the presumptions of what constitutes masculinity and femininity intact.

This social logic inspired both Toys 'Я Us and FAO Schwarz to come up with Boys' World and Girls' World in 1999. It must have sounded like a great idea at the time, until Toys 'Я Us received negative feedback about their discriminatory and sexist toy lines in the Girls' World section. Toys like Barbies, cookware, cleaning supplies, phones, and so on were placed in Girls' World, and trucks, cars, tools, monsters, race tracks, and video games were placed in Boys' World. This arrangement lasted for all of about two days as consumers complained that Toys 'Я' Us was promoting stereotypes by suggesting that boys should have all of the fun while girls stay in the house, cook, clean, and talk on the phone. This short-lived fiasco with Toys 'Я' Us escaped much of the national media's attention.

FAO Schwarz was a bit more strategic in its placement of toys. They divided toys by color. So, both sections had almost the same exact toys, except that the Ggirls' section had pink, orange, yellow, and green toys and the boys' section had blue, black, purple, and green toys. They have somehow managed to reduce the negative feedback level significantly. The description of "FAO Girl," however, is still stereotypical. It reads:

> Introducing FAO Girl. Because girls just wanna have fun. And fun stuff. This great new line will take your FAO Girl from homeroom to her room in style with a huge selection of hair accessories and jewelry, plush toys and pillows and cool gadgets—everything every girl can't do without. FAO Girls are filled with glamour, giggles and guts! (www.fao.com)

Body politics theorist Moira Gatens (1996) provides a valuable commentary concerning this problem of social stereotyping. She states:

> Masculinity and femininity as forms of sex-appropriate behaviors are manifestations of a historically based, culturally shared phantasy [sic] about male and female biologies, and as such sex and gender are not arbitrarily connected. The connection between the female body and femininity is not arbitrary in the same way that the symptom is not arbitrarily related to its etiology. Hence, to treat gender, the symptom, as the problem is to misread its genesis (p. 13)

Gatens conceptualization is insightful with regards to the dual functions of gender—body and role. Majors & Billson (1992) contend that gendered beings are not merely socially characterized however, but in the case of males, are also forced to "attain masculinity" by "being responsible and being a good provider for the self and family" (p. 30). In other words, masculinity is earned and achieved, rather than socially prescribed. We concur with Majors & Billson that masculinity is not necessarily natural or innate as is implied by Gatens' references to biologies; rather, it is learned.

Clearly, the intellectual analysis of the link between sex roles and gender stereotypes is non-unique. Sigmund Freud explored this issue in the early 1900s, and countless gender theoreticians comment on this phenomenon on a daily basis. But, are these academic assessments parochial? Have we redefined masculinities in such a way that they are no longer recognizable to the general population? It seems that socially understood conventions about masculinity include the medieval image of the "man as protector of his woman and family" to the more commonplace "man as the head of the household" and "primary breadwinner" motifs. Gender scholars' discussions of sex role orientations and gender stereotypes are often antiquated conceptualizations that have outlived their epistemological utility. This is not to say that social discourse has completely discarded these notions, but that we must move forward because the analyses are stale. In an effort to do so, we recommend analyses of gendered relationships as behavioral institutions confined by context-based realities. With this in mind, masculinities are not to be understood as a singular or unitary reality, but as multiple masculinities, pluralized to accent an anti-essentialist perspective, which accounts for variegations resulting from culture, class, sexual preference, religion, and other axes of difference.

For the purposes of this chapter, *masculinity* is defined as a perceptual and cosmological category in flux. It is composed and validated by culturally particular behavioral tendencies that are consonant with personal, social, and communal expectations. Although women may have masculine tendencies, we will discuss masculinity as a perceptual category that is male-centered.

Thus far, we have discussed the voids and inconsistencies in masculinity research and provided some insights about sex and gender role stereotyping. Stereotypes are important information as indicators of problems within a given social context. Moreover, stereotypes inhibit social relationships and often offer inaccurate and damaging perspectives about others. Because stereotypes of all kinds are dangerous yet instructive, we would be remiss in discussing Black masculine identities without some discussion of the social stereotypes that make them problematic and inhibit them.

Stereotyping Black Masculine Bodies

Ribeau, Baldwin & Hecht (1997), in their studies of satisfying Black-White communication, indicated that the primary issue of concern to the Black participants they studied was *negative* stereotyping. They defined *negative* stereotyping as "the use of rigid racial categories that distort an African American's individuality" (p. 149). Negative stereotypes can be both racial and social. Racial stereotypes coupled with sex role stereotypes produce a rather interesting pastiche because discussions of the dual function of role and body are elicited. The public narratives pertaining to Black men's lives comply with several racialized social projections about the Black masculine body as (1) violent, (2) sexual, and (3) incompetent. These descriptors have been used to degrade and stigmatize black males and are considered projections be-cause of what they imply about the insecurities, fears, and anxieties *society* has about Black males.

Black Masculine Body as Violent/Criminal. The media have helped to portray the black man as a violent person who often becomes ensconced in a life of crime. Nightly newscasts parade criminal offenders, the likes of which appear to represent a disproportionate number of non-white offenders. According to Entman and Rojecki (2000):

> The FBI estimated that 41% of those arrested for violent crimes in 1997 were Black (and 57% were White); 32% of those arrested for property crimes were Black. . . . Public [mass-mediated] perceptions exaggerate the actual racial disproportion. . . . By a 1.5:1 (241 to 160) ratio, White victims outnumber Blacks in news reports. . . . The average story featuring Black victims was 106 seconds long; those featuring white victims, 185 seconds long. (pp. 79–81)

These authors have illustrated that the public portrayals of Blacks as violent are often misguided and unjustly framed. Several recent studies have confirmed that the media tend to reinforce racial stereotypes, social deviancy, and delinquency of black males (Dixon & Linz, 2000; Entman, 1992; Entman and Rojecki, 2000; Gray, 1997; Heider, 2000). For example, Dixon & Linz (2000) analyzed local television news programming in Los Angeles to uncover whether Blacks, Latinos, and Whites were equally represented as lawbreakers. Their results indicated that televised crime stories presented on Los Angeles news stations were biased in their coverage. Blacks were found to be almost 2.5 times more likely to be portrayed as felons than Whites. Also, with an actual arrest rate of 21% in Orange County, California, the televised coverage showed Blacks as perpetrators of crime 37% of the time. Dixon & Linz argue that biased coverage of this sort solidifies the perception that Black males are habitual lawbreakers, much more so than Whites or any other cultural group. The reality, in Los Angeles and Orange County, was that Blacks were arrested less frequently than Whites and Latinos. This stereotypical portrayal of Blacks as criminals is political. The politics of race and black masculine identity have produced a peculiar anxiety in the United States. This is also evidenced in the perception of the black masculine body as a sexual object.

Black Masculine Body as Sexual. Notwithstanding the myths of Black sexual prowess and phallus size, there is historical significance to the "Black Masculine Body as Sexual" stereotype. Historically, when white slave owners wanted to penalize the black male for acts of aggression or disobedience, they would perform one of two activities: emasculation or a picnic. Emasculation refers to cutting off the penis. This removal of the phallus symbolized the denial of black masculinity. Essentially, this would prevent the black male's body from performing its normal sexual reproductive function and eliminate the threat of miscegenation. This was only one form of lynching. Another form was the picnic. The social etymology of the term *picnic* is "pick a nigger." Picnics were festivals and family gatherings in which white slave owners would bring their children, wives, and friends to witness the hanging of a black slave who was deemed disobedient. For example, Cunningham (1996) recounts that Emmett Till, a 14-year old black boy, was lynched in Mississippi for whistling at a white girl. This was done at a picnic. Till's death became the signpost of Black racial misery throughout the South.

These acts of aggression against blacks signified prohibition and assimilation. The slave master's narrative suggested that Black male bodies were lynched when they did not comply. The truth is that the slave's body was at once an object of disgust and admiration; hence, his body was seen as a threat (Best, 1996). His body was used as an object of labor, and in the process, his body became very muscular. This was especially threatening because it attracted white women, who were forbidden from contact with Blacks.

Black Masculine Body as Incompetent/Uneducated. Several deficit/deficiency models of black masculinity have proposed a pathologized version of these identities. Oliver (1989) contends that: "Blacks are disproportionately represented among Americans experiencing academic failure, teenage pregnancy, female-headed families, chronic unemployment, poverty, alcoholism, drug addiction, and criminal victimization" (p. 15). These social problems, presumably caused primarily by Black males, have led to perceptions of black masculine incompetence as a result of a process of inferiorization. It is not that some black males intrinsically sense they cannot achieve, but rather that the social conditions and mass media reinforcement of stereotypes remind and convince the Black male population that they will experience struggle. It is inevitable. For example, Entman & Rojecki (2000) assert:

> More generally, television's visuals construct poverty as nearly synonymous with "Black," and surveys show Whites typically accept this picture, even though poverty is not the lot of most Black people and more Whites are poor than Black. . . . In this sense news images encourage the sense of the prototypical Black as poor and the prototypical poor person as Black. (p. 102)

The media links Black poverty with Black crime, incompetence, and poor education. These false media images seem almost insurmountable. Eventually, images of this sort will affect anyone's worldview. This is not to suggest that black male delinquency or deviancy is excusable, but that not all Blacks or Black males are delinquent. Sociologist Manning Marable (2001) asks:

> What is a Black man in an institutionally racist society, in the social system of modern capitalist America? The essential tragedy of being Black and male is our inability, as men and as people of African descent, to define ourselves without the stereotypes the larger society imposes upon us, and through various institutional means perpetuates and permeates within our entire culture. (p. 17)

These social conditions and stereotypes coupled with cultural expectations for black males can be overwhelming. Besides the social idea of black macho rigidity (or the tough guy image), cultural mandates on Black masculinity have historically been centered on being a good provider. As a result, a Black male who cannot take care of his family almost immediately loses his "rights to manhood" or is viewed as not being a man. If the stereotypes of Black male incompetency and/or uneducability were true, Black manhood would be easily surrendered. Adaptative and protective behaviors are often employed to counter these stereotypes and have created a dual sensibility with respect to how Black masculinity is defined in Black versus White communities.

The three stereotypes just discussed are powerful statements that tremendously influence how Blacks define this perceptual category of masculinity and negotiate their masculinities in light of how they are socially and communicatively perceived. That negotiation of identity within varying contexts produces the "in flux" nature of Black masculine identities. This vacillated or dual consciousness is characteristic of the communicative process of negotiating identities. Identity negotiation refers to the win, loss, or exchange of one's ability to maintain one's own cultural worldview. It is, by nature, an act of resilience to outside pressures to constrict self-definitions and consequently self-efficacy. As Marable (2001) suggests, Black masculine identity development is impossible without acknowledging and countering the stereotypes that threaten the survival of Black masculinity.

BLACK MASCULINE IDENTIES PARADIGM

Precepts to the Paradigm: Negotiating Black Masculine Identities

We choose to theorize Black masculinities rather than culturally generic or universal masculinities because the latter are foreign to me. One's behaviors are potent enactments of one's worldview coupled with cultural sensibilities. Additionally, the cosmological trivium of communication, history, and identity is culturally inscribed on the canvas we call the Self. Human beings are informed and transformed by the intricate *labyrinth* of agony, desire, pleasure, power, and difference. This labyrinth is literally the means by which we gauge self-efficacy and attachment to our personal and relational histories. As masculine persons, however, we establish positions that grant agency to the self and limit access to "Others." *Agency* is a power-laden term that presupposes that people are defensive about how they will control their lives. It is about authority, permission, boundaries, and rules, and by establishing these things, it enables the Self to make choices and explore the world without inhibitions. But, because identities are co-defined in everyday interactions with others, agency is sometimes negotiated and

ends up resting externally with the "Other." This is the juncture at which the *labyrinth* becomes heightened, and therefore most visible. As Audre Lorde (1984) cautions: "For Black women as well as Black men, it is axiomatic that if we do not define ourselves for ourselves, we will be defined by others— for their use and to our detriment" (p. 45). The frustration of a displaced agency causes the "I" (i.e., masculine person) to struggle to reacquire stability and control over his choices, worldview, and life possibilities. The "Other," in the previously described scenario, can be anyone from another Black masculine person to another Cultural feminine person. Incidentally, both may be males.

Can Manhood Be Revoked?

The entire process of removing the agency of masculine persons is often referred to as *emasculation* or "revoking one's manhood." Three obvious assumptions are being made with this reference. The first is that men are the only ones who qualify as masculine, which of course is false. The second is that all men are masculine and all masculine persons are *men*; yet, some may be males or boys.[3] Masculinity is a perceptual category that attends each stage of self-development—boyhood, maleness, and manhood. Third, another assumption is that manhood can be revoked. Manhood is a category of being. Rationally, it does not seem possible to revoke a person's sense of being, but because being a man is highly significant among masculine persons, boys and males must define it so that it is achievable. Boys and males define *manhood* as a subconscious extension of the self that is externally presented and licensed. Being on the exterior, manhood is more likely to be seized.

When it is defined this way, it is worn like paraphernalia; consequently it can be undressed relatively easily. Manhood, in its purest manifestation as defined by men, cannot be revoked, partly because it is internalized. It is not a standpoint or position that is defined solely or even primarily by a "way of knowing," but rather a way of being. It is a life-force that is achieved after reaching a level of spiritual, emotional, mental, and ontological maturity, consciousness, and balance and having one's manhood coextensively and relationally validated by one's community. One who has achieved manhood is aware of the ontological spatial boundaries and functions along the borders between himself and others to achieve desired ends, but is conscious of not "losing himself" in the identity negotiation process. "Losing himself" is always a threat because of the exhaustive code switching mandate as he attempts to coordinate his actions with others, as well as the possibility that his masculine identity may become anonymous, silenced, suppressed, and accessorized. So, he must always be cognizant of the effects of identity negotiation; this is accomplished through policing and maintaining surveillance over his identity. Keeping oneself in balance is the goal of masculine behaviors. It also defines struggle, the centerpiece of Black masculine identities (see Figure 1).

Explaining the Black Masculine Identities Paradigm

Masculinities in general are perceptual categories in flux; therefore, defining black masculine identities requires that black masculine perceptions are taken into account. Stuart Hall (1997) asserts that identities are the labels given to the different ways interactants are positioned by and position themselves in past and present social narratives. Essentially, all definitions of *masculinity* are a matter of positionality.

Black masculine social positionings are primarily communication phenomena. Positioning is the axis of ontological difference among separate, but often overlapping, masculine identities. That is, positions facilitate how masculinity is understood and enacted at any given moment. If any of the following factors is threatened, the perceptual position can shift from positive to negative as an instinctive protective response; hence masculinities are not stable, predictable forces. They are as fluid as one's perceptions.

Five factors affect Black masculine positionality: *struggle*, *community*, *achievement*, *independence*, and *recognition*. These factors offer some explanation for how masculinities are selected and enacted. It is important to remember that masculinities vary with respect to conditions, maturity, and positionality. Masculinity, as with all behavioral manifestations, can be conceptualized along the twin registers of self-efficacy and symbiosis. *Self-efficacy* refers to the degree to which an individual feels he or she has control over his or her life. *Symbiosis* refers to the attachment one has to a certain life-space and/or relational history that is partly defined by a different, foreign, or asymmetrical cultural experience, such as the case with *African Americans*. So, a person who has a strong Black cultural identification and is militant may hate Whites because of what he has learned about slavery, yet he is forced to interact with Whites if he wants to be employed. He becomes unavoidably attached to an American culture that has become synonymous with whiteness, while attempting to maintain a commitment to an African ancestral heritage.

This historical symbiosis may cause him to behave negatively toward anyone who looks White. On the other hand, a Black person who has a strong Black identification may feel self-efficacious, and therefore have little problem initiating and maintaining relationships with Whites despite what he knows about slavery. Both persons function this way for a variety of reasons. The factors of positionality offer some explanation for how masculinities are selected and enacted. As stated previously, it is important to remember that masculinities vary with respect to ontological condition, maturity, and positionality.

Figure 1 *Black Masculine Identity Model*

Struggle and the Mandala

Psychoanalyst Carl Jung contended that the self, as an archetype, is naturally motivated to move toward growth, perfection, and completion. The ultimate symbol of the self, he argues, is the mandala, a diagram that contains a circle inside of a square or vice versa. The dialectic between the shapes is consistent with the conscious, subconscious, and unconscious elements of the self; hence, the combination of the three represents the total self, which is in constant pursuit of balance and wholeness. It is particularly interesting that Jung applies the second law of thermodynamics, the principle of entropy, to explain his interpretations of dreams. This law is also an important component of chaos theory. The actual principle states that when hot and cold objects merge, the hotter flows into the colder to create a sense of equilibrium. No matter what conceptual label is used to describe entropic behavior, it refers to the degree to which disorder in a human or object-centered system may be managed. Because we, as human beings, are naturally incomplete, we often strive toward perfection and balance, and sometimes this is done on a most subconscious level.

So, it may appear on the surface that one may be stagnated or polarized in a certain life-stage; we often behave in ways that are meant to evoke recognition, approval, and validation. Black masculine persons do this by taking agency in defining the "spaces" where they live. Place, space, home, and territory are metaphors often used in postmodern research to describe positions of the self in society. Home is a particularly useful metaphor because of its implicit property of privacy, self-protection, shelter, and comfort. Place, space, and territory are much more public terms that fuse the constitutive features of adjacency, interconnectedness, isolation, possession, yet fragmentation. In both cases, something clearly accents a void that needs to be filled. The motivation to do so characterizes struggle, but the behavioral quest is about human possibility and growth. This is why struggle is at the center of the mandala. To speak of achievement and independence, for instance, one must at some point address the issue of potentiality and ask: "What are the possibilities of my achievement, or of my being independent?"

On a psychic level, struggle can be understood as the effort to seek out portions to fulfill our (self-observed) conscious needs and desires. The peculiar operation of conscious behavior in the social domain is that it nourishes and reproduces subconscious motivations, but the social domain initially constitutes these self-understandings. Consciousness, by nature, is fragmentary and an enactment of self-recognition. The fascinating dimension of consciousness is how it gets perpetuated on a daily basis via communicated identities.

Recognition. Human beings clearly coexist, and consequently we coordinate our behaviors so that human activity is somewhat synthesized and rule-governed. Michael Walzer (1997) offers an interesting approach to managing social diversity by rethinking coordination as toleration. His central thesis is that difference can be tolerated if humans can recognize how we are basically alike and dissolve commitments to group localities. He supports this thesis by expounding on what he names "regimes of toleration," which are multinational instances of submerged difference for the sake of human totality. Although intriguing, Walzer's analysis oversimplifies human difference and proposes an alternative that mimics "the melting pot" concept; however, Walzer is correct in suggesting that human difference makes social coordination problematic for those who find the activity of recognition to be a hassle. The discourse humans use to capture the thoughts we have about the Other is significant.

As Chandra Mohanty (1994) points out: "The central issue, then, is not one of merely acknowledging difference; rather, the more difficult question concerns the kind of difference that is acknowledged and engaged" (p. 146). Personhood is founded on what the Canadian philosopher Charles Taylor coins the "politics of recognition." The entire concept of masculinity is predicated on recognition. Therefore, the natural progression of gender relationships depends on this social process. Taylor asserts that a politics of recognition requires that "Others" recognize and identify the authentic "I," and offer it permission to proceed with a given behavior.

So, self-authenticity is discovered within the dynamics of human interaction; meanwhile the "Other" serves the function of recognizing and validating that construction. In cases where the "Other" fails to recognize or refuses to validate masculine behavior, then either the masculine person discontinues the behavior or suffers social penalty, which is sometimes more punitive than any other kind. Certainly, people can and often do present themselves differently to different people. This is but another facet of recognition politics. This perceptual factor, which affects positionality, is explained by Ribeau, Baldwin & Hecht (1997) as understanding "the feeling that there was a genuine exchange of thinking, feeling and caring" (p. 150).

Independence. Independence is about self-authorization, autonomy, and freedom of self-expression. All human beings seek it at some point in their lives, often as teenagers. As one matures, the manner and mode of self-expression often becomes more sophisticated. It is then more about transformation of the self. When scholars merge Black masculinities and independence in their conversations, they often evoke notions of resistance to dependence, control of situations, and ultimately deviancy. Independence does begin with self-assertion but does not need to end with abnormality or delinquency. Perhaps the best method of pursuing this phenomenon is to theorize *male* masculinities as spaces that are attached to behavioral modes of existence, so that a male's (based on Akbar's distinctions) masculinity will be perceived differently than a boy's or a man's. For example, a male's masculine quest for independence may be read as an unwillingness to commit himself to a relational partner, whereas a man's masculine assertion of independence may be related to self-development. That is, he may find it necessary to separate himself in order to understand himself better, as a separate entity rather than a dependent pair. The healthiest relationships are interdependent; in these exchanges, there is some balance between autonomy and dependence.

Achievement. At first glance, achievement may appear to reflect only acquisition, but its real concern is with accomplishment of personal and collective goals. Personal goals may range from materialistic items such as owning a BMW to the spiritual goal of being at peace and one with God. The personal impinges directly on the collective. The content of and progress toward one's aspirations of achievement automatically affect the success and survival of the collective. This is reflected in the African-American affirmation "I am because we are, and because we are; therefore I am." This is much different than the quote representing the individualist, competitive, survival-of-the-fittest nature of Cartesian thought— "I think therefore I am." Masculine behavior cannot be substantiated as an intricate identity matrix if the only achievement concerns are with an individual's materialistic bread-winning capabilities. The cultural community to which he belongs is also critical. The commitment to the immediate and extended family, the church, and to the preservation of African-American culture is critical.

The discussion of achievement cannot ignore the reality of cultural identity *negotiation* among Black males. Roberts (1994) maintains:

> African American men must negotiate two cultural models of human relationships. . . . The Euro-American model emphasizes values such as competition, individualism, and domination as central to the human condition. The African model for human relationships, conversely, stresses the importance of group and community needs over individual aspirations, cooperation over competitive relationships, as well as interconnectedness among people. (p. 384)

In seeking to achieve one's goals, both cultural modes of behavior may be enacted in rapid succession such that they appear to be simultaneously engaged. The real danger is when Black masculine persons cease from embracing indigenous African-centered values, hence negotiating African cultural aspects of their identities. Staying grounded in one's cultural worldview, while functioning within a "Euro-American model," is difficult when switching back and forth between two modes of consciousness; however, this activity is important. This is what is meant by the popular phrases in the Black community— "stay Black" and "keep it real." They are admonitions to remain aligned with one's culture as one pursues his aspirations rather than relinquishing or negotiating aspects of the cultural self in the process.

Community. It is impossible to define one's self alone while living in a community of persons who must validate one's presence. Here, Black manhood is achieved ritualistically and behaviorally, while

Black masculinity is perceptually reaffirmed. So, Black manhood is the behavioral category and Black masculinity is the perceptual category. Essentially, by this definition, *manhood* is relationally discovered via one's actions. The community not only affirms but also contractualizes the behaviors of Black men via interaction. The value of Black manhood is what it gives to the rest of the community. If one is unproductive, then the community must question his value. Manhood is both an agreement and social, political, and/or cultural assignment contractually arranged. As a result of the contract, Black men are figuratively bound to the community, which is the co-author of normative masculine behavior.

Black manhood is a behavioral category in flux developing with age, experience, stability, cultural consciousness, self-comfort, and spiritual awareness, and affirmed by the community. The "community" can be defined broadly as in a global or diasporic "family" and/or locally as in the neighborhood in which one lives. Therefore, it is increasingly difficult to agree on universal criteria for Black manhood because communities change and are often diverse. Nonetheless, the community affirms one's masculinity, no matter whether one is homosexual or heterosexual, fatherless or not, employed or unemployed, male or female. The composite cultural community may not be the adjudicates of masculinity or manhood; sometimes, those that affirm are persons who function similarly to the adjudicated individual. Nonetheless, the community plays a viable role in how masculinities are constituted and positioned.

These five factors that affect Black masculine positionality—struggle, community, achievement, independence, and recognition—are important aspects of repositioning Black masculinities to counter pathological depictions of Black masculinity. These factors offer some explanation for how masculinities are selected and enacted but also facilitate the redefinition of Black masculinity as cultural property.

IMPLICATIONS OF BLACK MASCULINIST RESEARCH

Black masculine identities are deployed and negotiated with struggle at the center of the exchange. Recognition, independence, achievement, and com-

munity are four factors that affect masculine positioning. So, you might ask: What are the implications for females or homosexuals? In conceptualizing masculinities, it is my attempt to be critical, yet inclusive. Based on the definition of *masculinity* given in this essay, both sets of persons can be masculine, although we have diverged at times from a unitary gender framework to a male conception of masculinity in order to accent unique concerns of that group of masculine persons. We are aware that class is a dominant and interceding factor of masculine realities as well. It is not discussed here because of the scope and nature of this essay. Clearly, many scholars have combined race, class, and gender, rationalizing that these terms are inseparable, especially as we write about the intersection of power and social formations. Likewise, it could be argued that sexual preference, physical ability, and a host of other ontological facets cannot be disjoined. Difference as a pillar of identity must be constituted, grounded in critical examinations of everyday experiences. These experiences and personal histories are numerous and must be deconstructed in order to better understand the formation and maturation of self-definitions.

The study of Black masculinities is an effort to recombine the African-American gender community. That should remain the goal. Theorizing masculinity as cultural, ontological, historical, communicative, and gendered is one progressive formula to achieve this goal. Extant gender research purviews the communicative, sociological, and psychological dimensions of male behavior. That should continue, and it should be culturally specific. If Black masculine theory is described as a set of explanations that stipulates a defining relationship between Black males and their environment, then certainly communication scholars should continue to create, develop, and sustain this circuit of inquiry. Empirical studies should explore this barren terrain. If Black masculine theory's primary function is to illustrate its opposition to feminine ways of knowing, however, then the venture is counterproductive. There are truly unique concerns that Black men share about their masculinities. This article begins that dialogue in the discipline of communication.

References

Best, S. M. (1996). "Stand by your man": Richard Wright, lynch pedagogy, and rethinking black male agency. In M. Blount & G. P. Cunningham (Eds.), *Representing black men* (pp. 131–154). New York: Routledge.

Collins, P. (1991). *Black feminist thought: Knowledge, consciousness, and the politics of empowerment*. New York: Routledge.

Cunningham, G. P. (1996). Body politics: Race, gender, and the captive body. In M. Blount & G. P. Cunningham (Eds.), *Representing black men* (pp. 131–154). New York: Routledge.

Deetz, S. (1992). *Democracy in an age of corporate colonialization: Developments in communication and the politics of everyday life*. Albany: SUNY Press.

Dixon, T., & Linz, D. (2000). Overrepresentation and underrepresentation of African Americans and Latinos as lawbreakers on television news. *Journal of Communication, 50(2)*, 131–154.

Entman, R. M. (1992). Blacks in the news: Television, modern racism and cultural change. *Journalism Quarterly, 69(2)*, 341–361.

Entman, R. M., & Rojecki, A. (2000). *The Black image in the White mind: Media and race in America*. Chicago: University of Chicago.

FAO Girl. (2000). Available: www.fao.com.

Gatens, M. (1996). *Imaginary bodies: Ethics, power, and corporeality*. New York: Routledge.

Gray, H. (1997). *Watching race: Television and the struggle for the sign of blackness*. Minneapolis: University of Minnesota Press.

Hall, S. (1997). *Representation: Cultural representatives and signifying practices (culture, media, and identifiers)*. Thousand Oaks, CA: Sage.

Heider, B. (2000). *White news: Why local news programs don't cover people of color*. Mahway, NJ: Lawrence Earlbaum Associates.

hooks, b. (1992). *Black looks: Race and representation*. Boston: South End.

Jackson, R. L. (1997, July). Black "manhood" as xenophobe: An ontological exploration of the Hegelian dialectic. *Journal of Black Studies 27(6)*, 731–750.

Lorde, A. (1984). *Sister outsider*. Freedom, CA: Crossing Press.

Madhubuti, H. (1990). *Black men: Obsolete, single, dangerous?* Chicago: Third World Press.

Majors, R., & Billson, J. (1992). *Cool pose: The dilemmas of Black manhood in America*. New York: Lexington Books.

Marable, M. (2001). The Black male: Searching beyond stereotypes. In M. Kimmel & M. Messner (Eds.), *Men's lives* (6th ed.). Boston: Allyn & Bacon.

Mohanty, C. (1994). On race and violence: Challenges for liberal education in the 1990s. In H. Giroux & P. McLaren (Eds.), *Between borders: Pedagogy and the politics of cultural studies*. New York: Routledge.

Oliver, W. (1989). Black males and social problems: Prevention through Afrocentric socialization. *Journal of Black Studies, 20(1)*, 15–39.

Ribeau, S., Baldwin, J., & Hecht, M. (1997). An African American communication perspective. In L. Samovar & R. Porter (Eds.), *Intercultural communication: A reader* (8th ed., pp. 147–153). Belmont, CA: Wadsworth.

Roberts, G. (1994). Brother to brother: African American modes of relating among men. *Journal of Black Studies, 24(1)*, 379–390.

Walzer, M. (1997). *On toleration*. New Haven, CT: Yale University Press.

Endnotes

1. We purposefully use the term "Black" instead of African American for two reasons: (1) to accent the body politic inherent in seeing the color black during interracial interaction and (2) to make the point that "Black" refers to peoples throughout the Diaspora who are Black, from Brazil to Trinidad to the United States and beyond. These Black masculinities share the common positionalities and overall struggle discussed in the Black masculine identity theory.

2. Incidentally, these are often the same people who believe that all humans share the same desires, interests, needs, and motivations.

3. According to Nakim Akbar (1991): "A male is a biological entity.... One need not look beyond the observable anatomical characteristics to determine that he is a male. Maleness is also a mentality that operates with the same principles as biology. It is a mentality dictated by appetite and physical determinants. This mentality is one guided by instincts, urges, desires, and feelings. He is in this mentality a whining, crying, hungry, and dependent little leech. The next stage in the transformation from the biologically bound definition of 'male' is the development of the 'boy.' The movement is determined by the development of discipline. Once the mind has become disciplined, the boy is in a position to grow into reasoning. ... When the primary use of your reason is for the purpose of scheming or lying then you are fixated in the boyish mentality. ... The thing that transforms a boy into becoming a man is knowledge." (pp. 3–12).

Questions and Concepts

1. What do Jackson and Dangerfield imply when they assert that masculinity is negotiated?
2. How do media stereotypes of Black males affect Black masculine identity?
3. Discuss the link between sex roles and gender stereotypes.
4. How do Jackson and Dangerfield define masculinity?
5. What are the stereotypes of Black masculine bodies described by Jackson and Dangerfield? How do these stereotypes correspond to actual social reality?
6. How does the Jackson and Dangerfield identity paradigm lead to the development of Black masculine identity?
7. What are Jackson and Dangerfield inferring when they ask the question "Can manhood be revoked?"
8. What factors affect Black male positionality?
9. How does the notion of struggle influence Black male identity?
10. What roles do recognition, independence, achievement, and community play in establishing Black male identity?

Does the Worm Live in the Ground? Reflections on Native American Spirituality

MICHAEL TLANUSTA GARRETT

MICHAEL P. WILBUR

Everyone knows that grandparents and grandchildren often have a very special bond that goes beyond words. Still, from time to time, the way grandchildren act can get on the nerves of grandparents (and, of course, the way grandparents act can get on children's nerves, too). Tsayoga was a good little boy—sensitive, quiet, inquisitive, but also very stubborn. He was a good boy, but he had to do things his own way, and he couldn't always understand why things weren't the way he thought they should be. "But why?" he might ask his grandfather—over and over and over. Sometimes, Grandfather would get a little frustrated with the boy who might be busy listening but not hearing. "Tsayoga," the old man would say abruptly sometimes, "does the worm live in the ground, or does the worm fly in the sky?" "Grandfather," the little boy would answer, "the worm lives in the ground." "Well, OK then," Grandfather would reply.

OVERVIEW

There seems to be a great deal of misunderstanding these days about what Native American spirituality actually means and what it involves (Matheson, 1996). This misunderstanding in mainstream American culture has developed for several reasons, in-

Reprinted from *Journal of Multicultural Counseling and Development*, 27, October 1999, pp. 193–201. © ACA. Reprinted with permission. No further reproduction authorized without written permission of the American Counseling Association. Michael Tlanusta Garrett teaches at Western Carolina University, Cullowhee, North Carolina. Michael P. Wilbur teaches at the University of Connecticut, Storrs.

cluding the historical exploitation of *Native* (term used interchangeably with *Native American* and *Indian*) culture and the often stereotyped portrayal of Native Americans in the media as noble savages or hostile Indians bent on destruction. In addition, more recently, misunderstanding has developed as a result of non-Native Americans attempting to interpret or conduct Indian ceremonies or spiritual practices without always having a true understanding of the meaning or power of those ceremonies or practices for the Indian nation from which it comes, or without being "qualified" to do so (i.e., being trained as a Medicine person).

For this and other historical reasons, many Native American traditionalists often share very little of the "true knowledge" of certain beliefs or ceremonies for fear that this knowledge will be misunderstood or misused as it has been historically (Deloria, 1994). Bear in mind, it has only been since 1978, with the passage of the American Indian Religious Freedom Act, that Native Americans have been able to legally practice their spirituality and traditional ways in this country. That is only 20 years . . . not a long time. For Native American traditionalists, protecting the sacred ways was and is a matter of survival, but it is also a matter of respect for the power that is involved in such ways. This power goes beyond anyone individual and, according to the traditions, must be respected and treated with great care so as to do no harm.

So who are Native Americans, and what is this power to which we refer? Across the United States, there are more than 558 federally recognized and several hundred state-recognized Native American nations (Russell, 1998). Given the wide-ranging diversity of this population consisting of 2.3 million people, it is important to understand that the term *Native American spirituality* encompasses the vastness and essence of more than 500 different tribal traditions represented by these hundreds of Indian nations. Navajo, Catawba, Shoshone, Lumbee, Cheyenne, Cherokee, Apache, Lakota, Seminole, Comanche, Pequot, Cree, Tuscarora, Paiute, Creek, Pueblo, Shawnee, Hopi, Osage, Mohawk, Nez Perce, Seneca—these are but a handful of the hundreds of tribal nations that exist across the United States. Is it possible to grasp the essence of so many rich and diverse spiritual traditions? One wonders how Grandfather might respond.

To better understand some of the basic concepts relating to Native American spirituality, it is necessary to consider some of the underlying values that permeate a Native worldview and existence. Several authors have described common core values that characterize "traditionalism" across tribal nations (Heinrich, Corbine, & Thomas, 1990; Herring, 1990; Little Soldier, 1992; Peregoy, 1993; Thomason, 1991). Some of these values include the importance of community contribution, sharing, acceptance, cooperation, harmony and balance, noninterference, extended family, attention to nature, immediacy of time, awareness of the relationship, and a deep respect for elders (Dudley, 1992; Dufrene, 1990; J. T. Garrett & M. T. Garrett, 1994, 1996; M. T. Garrett, 1996, 1998; Heinrich et al., 1990; Herring, 1990, 1997; Lake, 1991; Plank, 1994; Red Horse, 1997). All in all, these traditional values show the importance of honoring through harmony and balance what is believed to be a very sacred connection with the energy of life; this is the basis for Native spirituality across tribal nations.

Different tribal languages have different words or ways of referring to this idea of honoring one's sense of connection, but the meaning is similar across nations in referring to the belief that human beings exist on Mother Earth to be helpers and protectors of life. In Native communities, it is not uncommon, as an example, to hear people use the term *caretaker*. Therefore, from the perspective of a traditionalist, to see one's purpose as that of caretaker is to accept responsibility for the gift of life by taking good care of that gift—the gift of life that others have received and the surrounding beauty of the world in which we live. The purpose of this article is to share some of the basic cultural elements contributing to what is known as Native American spirituality and to offer implications for counseling. Four concepts central to Native American spirituality will be discussed, including Medicine, Relation, Harmony, and Vision. To begin with, however, it is important to consider what it means from a traditional Native American perspective to "walk in step."

WALKING IN STEP

As you hear the sound of the drum rumbling low to the sharp, impassioned cries of the singers, the vibration moves through you like a storm that rises in the distance, building slowly in the azure sky, then unloading in a rhythmic yet gentle pounding of the soil. Anyone, Native or non-Native, who has ever had the opportunity to experience the colors, movement, sounds, tastes, and smells of the powwow (a pan-traditional, ceremonial giving of thanks) understands the feeling that passes through you. It is different for every person, but if you really experience the feeling, you know that it is connection. For some, it is a matter of seeing old friends or making new ones. For some, it is the image of the dancers moving in seemingly infinite poses of unity and airy smoothness to every flowing pound of the drum. For some, it is the laughter and exchange of words and gestures. For some, it is silent inner prayer giving thanks for another day of life. For some, it is the delicious taste of your second and third helping of that piping hot fry bread. Whatever it is, in the end, it is coming together on one level or another, and walking in step with the Greater Circle.

As one reads the aforementioned description of what it is like to experience a powwow, it becomes easier to relate to the experience of someone who might actually be there by paying attention to the senses and to the resulting emotional experience of the event. This is an important lesson in coming to understand how a Native person might experience the world from a traditional point of view. More or less, the essence of Native American spirituality is about "feeling." The feeling of connection is something that is available to all of us, although experienced in differing ways. It is important to note that the spiritual beliefs of Native Americans depend on several factors, including level of acculturation (traditional, marginal, bicultural, assimilated, pan-traditional); geographic region; family structure; religious influences; and tribally specific traditions. (For further discussion of levels of acculturation, see J.T. Garrett & M. T. Garrett, 1994; M.T. Garrett, in press.) It is possible, however, to generalize to some extent about

several basic beliefs characterizing Native American traditionalism and spirituality across tribal nations. Adapted from Locust (1988), the following elaborates on some basic Native American spiritual and traditional beliefs:

1. There is a single higher power known as Creator, Great Creator, Great Spirit, or Great One, among other names (this being is sometimes referred to in gender form, but does not necessarily exist as one particular gender or another). There are also lesser beings known as spirit beings or spirit helpers.
2. Plants and animals, like humans, are part of the spirit world. The spirit world exists side by side with and intermingles with the physical world. Moreover, the spirit existed in the spirit world before it came into a physical body and will exist after the body dies.
3. Human beings are made up of a spirit, mind, and body. The mind, body, and spirit are all interconnected: therefore, illness affects the mind and spirit as well as the body.
4. Wellness is harmony in body, mind, and spirit: unwellness is disharmony in mind, body, and spirit.
5. Natural unwellness is caused by the violation of a sacred social or natural law of creation (e.g., participating in a sacred ceremony while under the influence of alcohol, drugs, or having had sex within four days of a ceremony).
6. Unnatural unwellness is caused by conjuring (witchcraft) from those with destructive intentions.
7. Each of us is responsible for our own wellness by keeping ourselves attuned to self, relations, environment, and universe. (pp. 317–318)

This list of beliefs in Native American spirituality crosses tribal boundaries but is by no means comprehensive. It does, however, provide a great deal of insight into some of the assumptions that may be held by a "traditional" native person. To better understand more generally what it means to "walk in step" according to Native American spirituality, it is important to discuss four basic cultural elements: Medicine, Harmony, Relation, and Vision.

MEDICINE: EVERYTHING IS ALIVE

Walk into any classroom of children these days and ask them playfully, "Have you had your Medicine today?" and many of them will tell you yes. If you ask them what kind of medicine, sadly, they will tell you Ritalin, or a painkiller, or some type of cold medicine, among other things. In native tradition, the concept of "Medicine" is starkly different from what medicine has become in mainstream American society. So what is Medicine? Crowfoot, a Blackfoot leader, spoke the following words in 1890 as he lay dying:

> What is life? It is the flash of a firefly in the night. It is the breath of a buffalo in the wintertime. It is the little shadow which runs across the grass and loses itself in the sunset.

In the preceding quote, once again, the importance of experiencing life through the senses and through one's emotional experience becomes apparent as a way of understanding Medicine. In the traditional way, Medicine can consist of physical remedies such as herbs, teas, and poultices, for physical ailments, but Medicine is simultaneously something much more than a pill you take to cure illness, get rid of pain, or correct a physiological malfunction. Medicine is everywhere. It is the very essence of our inner being; it is that which gives us inner power. Medicine is in every tree, plant, rock, animal, and person. It is in the light, the soil, the water, and the wind. Medicine is something that happened 10 years ago that still makes you smile when you think about it. Medicine is that old friend who calls you up out of the blue just because he or she was thinking about you. There is Medicine in watching a small child play. Medicine is in the reassuring smile of an elder. There is Medicine in every event, memory, place, person, and movement. There is even Medicine in "empty space" if you know how to use it.

In many Native American traditions, every living being possesses this inner power called Medicine that connects us to all other living beings through the heart; however, if we fail to respect our relations (with all living beings, the Creator, Mother Earth, ourselves, and the Four Directions) and to keep ourselves in step with the universe, we invite illness by falling out of harmony and balance, much like a dancer failing to move in step with the rhythm of the drum. A person's Medicine is his or her power, and it can be used for creative purposes or destructive purposes—either contributing to or taking away from the Greater Circle of Life. Being in harmony means being "in step with the universe"; being in disharmony means being "out of step with the universe."

HARMONY: EVERYTHING HAS PURPOSE

Every living being has a reason for being. Traditional Native Americans look on life as a gift from the Creator. As a gift, it is to be treated with the utmost care out of respect for the giver. This means living in a humble way and giving thanks for all of the gifts that one receives every day, no matter how big or small. The importance of humility is illustrated in the following words spoken by Tecumseh, Shawnee leader, more than a century ago:

> When you arise in the morning, give thanks for the morning light, for your life and strength. Give thanks for your food and the joy of living. If you see no reason for giving thanks, the fault lies in yourself.

One of the reasons it is so important in the traditional way to maintain a humble stance is not for fear of punishment by the Creator, but rather to maintain a keen awareness of all the gifts that surround us and to keep our spirit open and receptive. In this way, we are able to be of service to others and much more able to walk the path of peace. The person who walks with their peace is very difficult to get off balance.

Acceptance is a very important part of living in harmony and balance in a worldview that emphasizes that everyone and everything has a reason for being. There is no such thing as a good experience or a bad experience because everything that happens is of value in offering us the opportunity to learn and "see more clearly" how to live in harmony (M. T. Garrett & J. E. Myers, 1996; Herring, 1994; Tafoya, 1997). Therefore, in the traditional way, trying to control things or people is considered a waste of energy because it is believed that everything is as it should be at any given point in time.

Native American spirituality often places great emphasis on the numbers four and seven. The number four represents the spirit of each of the directions—east, south, west, and north—usually depicted in a circle. The number seven represents the same four directions as well as the upper world (Sky), lower world (Earth), and center (often referring to the heart, or sacred fire) to symbolize universal harmony and balance (visualized as a sphere). In the traditional way, you seek to understand what lessons are offered to you by giving thanks to each of the four directions for the wisdom, guidance, strength, and clarity that you receive. Not every tribe practices the directions in this way, but almost all tribes have some representation of the four directions as a circular symbol of the harmony and balance of mind, body, and spirit with the natural environment (and spirit world).

It is interesting to note, however, that, unlike in other religious traditions, in Native American spirituality it is considered disrespectful—even arrogant—for a person to "ask" anything of the Creator. Rather, people give thanks for what they do have. It is assumed with the Creator as with people that if something is to be revealed to you, it will be revealed when it is time. This view emphasizes once again the values of respect and humility. Traditionalists seek help and guidance more directly from spirit helpers or spirit guides. The Creator is one to be honored and revered by walking the path of harmony and balance, respecting all one's relations.

RELATION: ALL THINGS ARE CONNECTED

Central to Native American spiritual traditions is the importance of "relation" as a total way of existing in the world. The concept of family extends to brothers and sisters in the animal world, the plant world, the mineral world, Mother Earth, Father Sky, and so on. The power of relation is symbolized by the Circle of Life (sometimes referred to as the Web of Life), so commonly represented throughout the customs, traditions, and art forms of Native people (Dufrene, 1990). This Circle of Life is believed, in many tribal traditions, to consist of the basic elements of life: fire/sunlight, earth, water, and wind. These four points

also denote, in Cherokee tradition for instance, spirit, nature, body, and mind referred to as the Four Winds (or the Four Directions). The concept of relation is further illustrated by Black Elk, Oglala Lakota Medicine Man, in the following excerpt:

> You have noticed that everything an Indian does is in a circle, and that is because the Power of the World always works in circles, and everything tries to be round. . . . The sky is round, and I have heard that Earth is round like a ball, and so are all the stars. The wind, in its greatest power, whirls. Birds make their nests in circles, for theirs is the same religion as ours. . . . Even the seasons form a great circle in their changing, and always come back again to where they were. The life of a person is a circle from childhood to childhood, and so it is in everything where power moves. (as cited in M. T. Garrett, 1998, p. 75)

The circle thus reflects not only the interrelationship of all living beings but the natural progression or growth of life itself. Harmony and balance are necessary for the survival of all life. Thus, living in "proper relations" and giving thanks to "all our relations" are common phrases in Indian country.

Respect for Medicine also means practicing respect for the interconnection that we share. Across tribal nations, certain natural or social laws must be observed out of respect for relation. These often point to restrictions on personal conduct regarding such things as death, incest, the female menstrual cycle, witchcraft, certain animals, certain natural phenomena, certain foods, and marrying into one's own clan and in strict observance of ceremonial protocol (Locust, 1988). In general, a rule of thumb in Native tradition is that you (1) never take more than you need, (2) give thanks for what you have or what you receive, (3) take great care to use all of what you do have, and (4) "give away" what you do not need (or what someone else may need more than you).

VISION: EMBRACE THE MEDICINE OF EVERY LIVING BEING AND YOUR VISION

Across tribal nations, many different ceremonies are used for healing, giving thanks, celebrating, clearing the way, and blessing (Lake, 1991). Among the various traditions, a few examples of ceremonies include sweat lodge, vision quest, clearing-way ceremony, blessing-way ceremony, pipe ceremony, sunrise ceremony, sun dance, and many, many others (Heinrich et al., 1990; Lake, 1991). One of the functions of ceremonial practice is to reaffirm one's connection with that which is sacred. In American mainstream ideology, the purpose of life consists of "life, liberty, and the pursuit of happiness." From a traditional Native perspective, a corollary would be "life, love, and learning." Once you understand and respect the Medicine, learn to live in harmony, and honor your relations, the final important step in the traditional way of knowing what to do with the gift of life with which you have been blessed:

> In a conversation with his aging grandfather, a young Indian man asked, "Grandfather, what is the purpose of life?" After a long time in thought, the old man looked up and said, "Grandson, children are the purpose of life. We were once children and someone cared for us and now it is our time to care." (Brendtro, Brokenleg, & Van Bockern, 1990, p. 45).

Now, that is not to say that Native Americans believe that the purpose of everyone's life is to go and have children, but the deeper value of the relationship as an integral part of seeking purpose is evident. In the traditional way, one moves through the "life circle" from *being cared for to caring for* (Red Horse, 1980, 1997).

It is important throughout life to either seek your vision or continue honoring your vision. In Native tradition, vision is an inner knowledge of your own Medicine and purpose in the Greater Circle revealed to you through your spirit helpers. This means connecting with your inner power and opening yourself to the guidance of the spirits. This may happen in ceremony, or it may happen in other ways such as through dreams, particular signs, animal messengers, or certain experiences/events that come your way for a reason. Understanding one's vision is understanding the direction of one's path as a caretaker moving to the rhythm of the sacred heartbeat. As Black Elk, an Oglala Lakota Medicine man, put it: "The good road and the road of difficulties, you have made me cross: and where they cross, the place is holy."

CONCLUSION

One wonders, as we reflect on Native American spirituality, about the question that my great-grandfather posed to my father so many times when he was being a stubborn, inquisitive little boy: "Does the worm live in the ground, or does the worm fly in the sky?" This is a question we should ask ourselves when we interact with Native Americans. This is a question we should ask ourselves the next time a delicate, colorful butterfly wanders past us. Things are not always as they seem.

References

Brendtro, L. K., Brokenleg, M., & Van Bockern, S. (1990). *Reclaiming youth at risk: Our hope for the future.* Bloomington, IN: National Education Service.

Deloria, V. Jr. (1994). *God is red: A Native view of religion.* Golden, CO: Fulcrum.

Dudley, J. I. E. (1992). *Choteau Creek: A Sioux reminiscence.* Lincoln: University of Nebraska Press.

Dufrene, P. M. (1990). Exploring Native American symbolism. *Journal of Multicultural and Cross-Cultural Research in Art Education, 8,* 38–50.

Garrett, J. T., & Garrett, M. T. (1994). The path of good medicine: Understanding and counseling Native Americans. *Journal of Multicultural Counseling and Crosscultural Development, 22,* 134–144.

Garrett. J. T., & Garrett, M. T. (1996). *Medicine of the Cherokee: The way of right relationship.* Santa Fe, NM: Bear & Company.

Garrett, M. T. (1996). Reflection by the riverside: The traditional education of Native American children. *Journal of Humanistic Education and Development, 35,* 12–28.

Garrett, M. T. (1998). *Walking on the wind: Cherokee teachings for harmony and balance.* Santa Fe, NM: Bear & Company.

Garrett, M. T. (in press). Red as an apple: Native American acculturation and counseling with or without reservation. *Journal of Counseling & Development.*

Garrett, M. T., & Myers, J. E. (1996). The rule of opposites: A paradigm for counseling Native Americans. *Journal of Multicultural Counseling and Development, 24,* 89–104.

Heinrich, R. K., Corbine, J. L., & Thomas, K. R. (1990). Counseling Native Americans. *Journal of Counseling & Development, 69,* 128–133.

Herring, R. D. (1990). Understanding Native American values: Process and content concerns for counselors. *Counseling and Values, 34,* 134–137.

Herring, R. D. (1994). The clown or contrary figure as a counseling intervention strategy with Native American Indian clients. *Journal of Multicultural Counseling and Development, 22,* 153–164.

Herring, R. D. (1997). Counseling Native American youth. In C. C. Lee & B. L. Richardson (Eds.), *Multicultural issues in counseling: New approaches to diversity* (2nd ed., pp. 37–47). Alexandria, VA: American Counseling Association.

Lake, M. G. (1991). *Native healer: Initiation into an ancient art.* Wheaton, IL: Guest.

Little Soldier, L. (1992). Building optimum learning environments for Navajo students. *Childhood Education, 68,* 145–148.

Locust, C. (1988). Wounding the spirit: Discrimination and traditional American Indian belief systems. *Harvard Educational Review, 58,* 315–330.

Matheson, L. (1996). Valuing spirituality among Native American populations. *Counseling and Values, 41,* 51–58.

Peregoy, J. J. (1993). Transcultural counseling with American Indians and Alaska Natives: Contemporary issues for consideration. In J. McFadden (Ed.), *Transcultural counseling: Bilateral and international perspectives* (pp. 163–191). Alexandria, VA: American Counseling Association.

Plank, G. A. (1994). What silence means for educators of American Indian children. *Journal of American Indian Education, 34,* 3–19.

Red Horse, J. G. (1980). Indian elders: Unifiers of families. *Social Casework, 61,* 490–493.

Red Horse, J. G. (1997). Traditional American Indian family systems. *Families, Systems, & Health, 15,* 243–250.

Russell, G. (1998). *American Indian facts of life: A profile of today's tribes and reservations.* Phoenix, AZ: Russell.

Tafoya, T. (1997). Native gay and lesbian issues: The two-spirited. In B. Greene (Ed.), *Ethnic and cultural diversity among lesbians and gay men* (pp. 1–10). Thousand Oaks, CA: Sage.

Thomason, T. C. (1991). Counseling Native Americans: An introduction for non-Native American counselors. *Journal of Counseling & Development, 69,* 321–327.

Concepts and Questions

1. How do the authors define the concept of Native American spirituality?

2. Why do some Native Americans tend not to reveal the true knowledge of their spiritual ceremonies with non-Native Americans?

3. What is meant by a "sense of connection"? How does that sense direct Native American behavior?

4. What do Garrett and Wilbur refer to when they write about "walking in step"? What feelings would generally be associated with walking in step?

5. What seven generalizations do the authors draw regarding Native American spiritual and traditional beliefs? How might these beliefs affect intercultural communication?

6. What is the role of Native American Medicine in experiencing life? How does the concept of medicine apply to the individual?

7. How does the concept of harmony relate to purpose? How do the numbers four and seven relate to harmony?

8. Garrett and Wilbur assert that for Native Americans all things are connected. How does this sense of connectedness affect the concept of family?

9. What is the Circle of Life? How does it relate to the concept of relation?

10. What do the authors imply when they speak of "seeking your own vision"?

Gay Culture

MICHAEL BRONSKI

ay culture, in its widest definition, is simply how gay people live their lives: how they have sex, where they socialize, how they dress, how they create extended-family and social networks, how they regard themselves in relation to heterosexual society, how they express themselves artistically. Since the gay community is composed of women and men with a wide range of other identities—racial, national, class, ethnic, religious—its boundaries are open-ended. Because gay and lesbian identity is defined by sexual attraction to members of the same gender, sexuality is, necessarily, at the heart of gay culture.

It is unclear which same-gender sexual behavior began to constitute an "identity." Historian John Boswell, in *Christianity, Social Tolerance, and Homosexuality*, argues that this coalescing began to happen in 13th-century Europe; Michel Foucault contends that the emergence of distinct sexual identities is a product of a 19th-century urge to classify and contain sexual experience. The presence of molly-houses (taverns where homosexual men could meet), as well as commonly known public cruising places, in early-18th-century London indicates that the beginnings of a solid social identity of male "homosexuality" was forming. This identity entailed self-definition as someone whose sexual attraction to the same gender placed him outside of the accepted norm, and the acknowledgment that others—a community—shared these desires.[1]

Homosexual populations congregated in urban areas because cities offered anonymity and the critical mass of people needed to form a community. Historically, in the United Kingdom and Europe, rural and agricultural life was centered on the biological family. Individuals who decided, for whatever reason, not to fit into that mold could find a new life in the city. This was easier for men, who had more economic and social freedom, but was possible for women as well.

The evolution of a contemporary gay identity and community is complicated. Its manifestations reflect the cultural differences of individual members. Like African slave culture, gay culture was, and is, formed by the coalescing of disparate groups and individuals who often have only one factor in common. Homosexual desire cuts across race, nationality, class, ethnicity, and religion. The coming together that occurs is instigated by a shared sexual desire and a rebellion against oppression. An individual's sexual identity may evolve over time, and it is only one aspect of a conglomerate of personal identities. As a result there is no single "gay identity"—just as there is no single African-American, Jewish-American, or Italian-American identity. What those identities do have in common, however, is a connection to visible, public communities.

Because gay communities do not have the kinship patterns that sustain other communities, structure must be easily discernible to those who need to know about it. At the same time it must be secretive enough to protect itself: it must be simultaneously visible and invisible. Over the years special codes developed—language, dress, mannerisms, and specific interests—by which gay people could recognize one another. The gay male practice of referring to other, absent, gay men with female names or as "she" and "her" began in 18th-century London. This was, in part, a protective device that allowed men to appear heterosexual in their public lives. Dress was also a way for gay men and lesbians to recognize one another. In Victorian London, some gay men wore green-tinted carnations to indicate they were homosexual, and in early-20th-century New York wearing a red scarf was an indication of male homosexuality. For lesbians in the 1930s wearing slacks or "sensible" clothes might have been a sign of more than simple nonconformity in dress. In the 1950s, wearing chinos, crewneck sweaters, or loafers were all ways for gay men to recognize one another publicly. Lesbians with DA haircuts, or wearing men's shirts, might be recognized as nonheterosexual.[2]

Gay codes existed on a thin line: obvious enough to be read by gay people, but sufficiently obscure to remain invisible to straights. As it became safer to be more open about being gay, coded clothing or styles would often cross the line and become "gay fashion." The line between perceived tolerance and incipient violence was always shifting, and the need to be mindful of the code was important. To overstep or misperceive the line could lead to harassment or physical attack.

The need to create codes and alternative realities is a major component of a gay culture and sensibility. The image of the male homosexual as "creative"—a stereotype ranging from serious novelist to interior decorator, from filmmaker to dress designer, from renowned stage performer to drag queen—is well established. Indeed, a great deal of gay male culture has been centered on the creation, cultivation, and appreciation of the arts. One explanation of gay male culture's impulse to creativity is that it is predicated on imagining and acting out alternatives to the restrictions of the closet. Although this still occurs now, it is, historically, part of a complex legacy of invention and subversion that both formed and continues to inform gay culture today. Gay people have had to learn, by necessity, how to perform—to be who they were not and invent personae and scenarios acceptable to the straight world.

Gay culture was formed largely in reaction to mainstream society's repression. Its evolution and creativity were shaped by resistance, as were those of African slave culture. Although the hidden nature of gay culture allowed a degree of safety for gay people who were able to "pass" as heterosexual, it also permitted gay culture to be more subversive. Unlike African slave culture, which was always clearly identifiable, gay culture often coexisted, invisibly, within the larger culture. The power of gay culture is the power to critique mainstream culture, particularly in areas of sexuality and gender, to be able to speak the "truth" or offer an alternative model.

The character of the West African trickster in slave culture has a gay corollary. In Western culture, the roots of the trickster were in the European tradition of the fool and the court jester. Like the fool in *King Lear* and the medieval jester, the trickster challenges and debates prevailing authority and culture. The Mattachine Society, one of the first gay movement organizations in the United States, derived its name both from the société Mattachine—a secret medieval French society of unmarried men

who wore masks to perform masques and rituals, often as a form of social protest—and from the Italian *mattaccino*, the court jester who was able to speak the truth while wearing a mask.[3]

The idea of the mask that protects the wearer while allowing him to speak truthfully is resonant in much of gay culture. The most obvious contemporary incarnation of the trickster is the quick-witted, sharp-tongued drag queen. Never without a retort and frequently exposing hypocrisy, the drag queen critiques with wit and the perceptiveness of an outsider. The act of "drag" itself is a comment on prevailing gender roles. The gay trickster is embodied in the high-profile visibility of RuPaul, the performers in Jennie Livingston's documentary film *Paris Is Burning*, Mae West's jokes at the expense of male vanity, and working drag performers in gay clubs.[4]

Using verbal wit and wordplay, the trickster is able to take the ordinary and expose hidden meaning, as in this classic drag monologue from the 1950s:

> I was walking down the street the other day with my friend Flora. We were all gussied up and ready for a night on the town, and maybe a little business. Suddenly on the corner of Seventh and Christopher a cute cop comes up and stops us. "What are you ladies doing here?" he asked. "Why, officer," I replied, "we're just two girls out on the town." "Well," he replied, "you better be careful. There are a lot of prostitutes around here. But I guess it's fine, as long as you know what you're doing. You don't want anyone mistaking you for what you're not." "Don't worry, officer," I said. "I've never been mistaken in my life."[5]

While the secretiveness of gay culture protected homosexuals, it also helped create paranoia about them in mainstream culture. If homosexual identity was detectable only through public self-disclosure or being caught in homosexual activity, it was possible that *anyone* might be a homosexual.

If the idea of overt homosexuality was threatening, the notion of the "hidden homosexual"—and a hidden culture—was more so. A secret subcultural world organized around an antisocial sexuality was seen as a grave threat to the heterosexual status quo. The threat was even more dangerous because, culturally, homosexuality had come to represent sexual pleasure without the burden of reproduction—a forbidden, but attractive, alternative. On a personal level, the idea of the hidden homosexual was threatening because it implied the possibility of a hidden homosexual in everyone. Both popular and psychoanalytic literature of the 1950s were rife with the notion of the "latent homosexual."

The threat of gay culture is not simply that it celebrates sexual nonconformity and pleasure, but that, by its very existence—particularly since gay liberation—it offers critiques of the more repressive strictures of organized heterosexuality. The dominant culture, while strongly drawn to gay culture, is terrified of it precisely because it represents, on some level, such a compelling alternative. If it weren't so seductive, it wouldn't be such a threat.

The closet amplifies the discomfort mainstream culture feels with gay culture. The "hidden" homosexual becomes the "secret" homosexual: the fugitive becomes the schemer. This is the same as the long-lived fantasy that there is a secret Jewish conspiracy running the world's economic system. A palpable social fear of gay cultural control began to surface as homosexuals were becoming more visible in the late 1950s and early 1960s. Conservatives saw homosexuals and Communists, often one and the same, infiltrating the U.S. government and even the army. (This fear fuels the overheated rhetoric of the current gays-in-the-military debate. The federal government's "don't ask, don't tell" policy is a tacit admission that not homosexuality but homosexual visibility is the problem.)

Because gay sexuality, like race, was seen by the dominant culture as an insurmountable barrier to an authentic "American" identity, gay culture could not "assimilate" along the same lines as certain European immigrant models. Its impact on the mainstream culture occurred through "influence" rather than assimilation. This influence, when detected, was seen as culturally corrosive and destructive. Psychoanalysts blamed a gay-run fashion industry for publicly humiliating women. Heterosexual theater critics worried that Broadway was in the grip of gay playwrights and directors who were promoting a homosexual agenda. Conservative morality campaigns of the 1970s and 1980s followed this lead and accused gay men of having too much influence in cultural endeavors: in music, publishing, design, fashion, and the art world. In the mid-1990s, the

"velvet mafia"—a gay network of influential men in the entertainment industry—has been exposed. Yet like the Jewish executives who closeted Jewish performers and avoided specifically Jewish content in films, most of these homosexual power brokers— some of whom, like Barry Diller or David Geffen, are openly gay—actively avoid promoting gay themes in their projects.[6]

The discomfort with gay culture grew as the gay movement brought about legal and social reform. The concept of inappropriate gay cultural power appears in right-wing propaganda videos like *Gay Rights, Special Rights,* and *The Gay Agenda.* It has even surfaced in Judge Anthony Scalia's dissent in *Romer v. Evans,* a 1996 Supreme Court decision that upheld the right of the state to prohibit antigay discrimination. Scalia describes homosexuals as a group that "enjoys enormous influence in American media and politics."

Although there are similarities between gay culture and other subcultures, there are also important differences. One of the reasons gay culture could maintain its protective, camouflaged status within mainstream culture was that it did not conform to traditional definitions of a subculture. Shared identity, experiences, styles, and customs are the traditional hallmarks of a subculture, as is the ability to pass these down through biological family networks and community institutions. Members of a religious denomination may not share the religion's exact beliefs, and a national identity may be fractured by sharply defined subgroups within it, yet there are acknowledged parameters by which these subcultures are delineated and acknowledged. Gay culture is far less defined in its structure.

Gay men and lesbians do not discover their sexuality or their identity through the biological family. Much of the time, biological families resist accepting or even tolerating this identity. Gay culture is thus placed distinctly outside the family networks that nurture most other subcultures. Gay folk wisdom has it that gay men and lesbians are the only minority born into the enemy camp. In fact, much of the gay subculture is shaped in direct resistance to the institutionalized heterosexuality of the biological family. This situation, in conjunction with its hidden status, allows the gay subculture to evolve more quickly and with more dexterity than other subcultures.

Many distinct ethnic communities decrease in size during the process of assimilation. Second or third generations often identify themselves as "Americans," not as Italian Americans or Polish Americans. Marriage outside of the group also tends to weaken identification with the subculture. The gay community, on the other hand, is always expanding as more and more people discover their homosexual identities and come out. This resembles not the assimilation model of European Americans but rather the African-American model, in which racial identity is reinforced as the differences between subculture and mainstream culture are reinforced.[7]

The protean nature of gay culture comes, in part, from its being defined by sexuality. Human eroticism is fluid. It encompasses not only the heterosexual and homosexual but also a wide range of desire from the most banal to the most transgressive sexual actions. Desires may exist as nascent "feelings," often not even admitted, or may manifest as full-fledged fantasies. If desires are strong enough, and social attitudes permit, acting on them is possible.

The fluidity of sexuality is both real and theoretical to most people. They may acknowledge a range of sexual desires or fantasies but decide to limit themselves to one identity. Gay self-identification—"I am a homosexual"—is an act of determined willfulness in a culture that promulgates heterosexuality as the only normal, healthy sexual identity. The threat of gay culture is that it destabilizes the presumption of a heterosexual norm.

One of the ways that gay culture in its broadest sense—how gay people live their lives—clearly manifests itself to mainstream culture is through the production of art, both high and popular. This art can realistically depict the lives of gay people—Radclyffe Hall's *The Well of Loneliness*, John Rechy's *City of Night*—or it can reflect the realities of gay experience in terms not explicitly gay. Critics often describe the paintings and sculpture of Michelangelo, the plays of Oscar Wilde, the writings of Gertrude Stein, and the work of Tennessee Williams as coded representations of gay experience. In both cases, art that is produced about, from, or within gay culture destabilizes the heterosexual norm. This is particularly true when the art is identified as the work of an openly gay artist.

Such an identification mandates that homosexuality, simply by being discussed, becomes visible.

The emergence of a once-hidden heterosexuality as a material reality generates a cultural crisis for mainstream culture: if homosexual desire can "inspire" a great piece of art, it must have some intrinsic worth. Yet if we view art and culture, either high or low, as an expression of the creator's inner life/emotions/thoughts/imagination, logic insists that homosexual desire is going to manifest itself in the creative process. If some, or all, of the artist's erotic imagination is homosexual, that is going to be an influence.[8]

The literary and political ramifications of the connections between sexuality and creativity are complex. Although art can and may be judged on its own merits, its creation is inseparable from the experience of its creator. Most critics have no trouble discussing a distinct heterosexual artistic process: how male artists were "inspired" by great love or, in a misogynistic reversal, how women artists created art because they had lost, or were denied, a great love.

Many subcultures have supplied mainstream culture with venues of pleasure, but the relationship of gay culture to various culture industries makes it unique. Susan Sontag has noted that "homosexuals have pinned their integration into society on promoting the aesthetic sense," and this is largely true. By creating and promoting popular culture—style, design, and fashion as well as theater, film, and the visual arts—gay influence (as opposed to "assimilation") has had an enormous role in shaping mainstream culture. Other subcultures have made influential contributions to mainstream culture, but they have not had gay culture's wide-scale, concrete involvement in the production of popular culture. What happens when gay culture—the lives and artistic work of gay people—is labeled as such?

The first reaction is often to dismiss it. The overwhelming amount of "great art" and popular culture created by artists known to have experienced homosexual desire or behavior prohibits the wholesale dismissal of the work of gay and lesbian artists. Yet the impulse to dismiss or diminish the work of homosexual artists persists. In the popular imagination, homoeroticism, by its nonreproductive nature, cannot lead to creativity. Traditional psychoanalytic literature also reinforced the idea of the "noncreative" homosexual as it proclaimed homosexuality a stage of stunted emotional development.[9]

When an artist's homosexuality is known, mainstream culture will often dismiss the work as inauthentic. In the early 1960s, critics, blatantly misinterpreting the works of Tennessee Williams, William Inge, and Edward Albee, attacked these playwrights for "negative" portrayals of heterosexuality, marriage, and women, claiming that they were "likely to have an infective and corrosive influence on our theater." The attack was less on the plays than on the writers for their relatively open homosexuality: they were "gay playwrights."[10]

The marginalization by categorization of the art and culture of those outside the mainstream does not apply exclusively to works by homosexuals. Women, along with African Americans and ethnic minorities, have had their artistic creations deemed inferior—the strategies range from "She didn't write it" or "She wrote it but she only wrote one" to "He wrote it but it's only about life in the ghetto; it's not universal" or "It's pretty good for a novel by a . . ."[11]

Acknowledgment that homosexual desire can inform significant artistic achievement causes a panic reaction: appreciation of "homosexual art" carries the implication that the viewers/readers may be homosexual themselves. No man reads Emily Bronte and worries that he may be a woman, and no white person reads Richard Wright or Toni Morrison and worries that she or he may turn into an African American. The perceived boundaries of "the other" in gender and race are firm. This is not always the case with sexual orientation. It is the innate understanding that human sexuality has homosexual potential—no matter what someone's stated sexual identity might be—that lies at the heart of the great discomfort mainstream culture feels toward art and popular culture created by gay people.

Openly gay artists and their work continually provoke backlash. After Oscar Wilde was convicted of sodomy in 1895, his books were removed from bookstores, the up-until-then successful productions of his plays were closed, and his work was virtually unproducible for almost 20 years; legal proof of his homosexuality destroyed his career. Sir Thomas Inskip, the British Attorney-General, wrote of Radclyffe Hall's 1928 groundbreaking lesbian novel, *The Well of Loneliness*: "it is a mission-ary work, appealing for recognition of the status of people who engage in these practices, and there is not a word to suggest that people who do this are a pest to society and to their own sex." The outcry against the book was caused by Hall's unapologetic refusal to downplay her mannishness, a public display of her lesbianism, as well as by the book's content. In recent times, right-wing attacks on Robert Mapplethorpe's photography were fueled as much by his refusal to hide his homosexuality, sadomasochistic activities, attraction to African-American men, and HIV status as they were a response to the sexually explicit nature of the photographs.

All unmodified subcultures pose a threat to the perceived cohesion of the dominant culture. This threat is usually decreased through the process of assimilation, but when subcultures exert influence rather than undergo assimilation, the threat they pose may remain intact. Thus, subculture and dominant culture coexist in an uneasy truce, haunted by the possibility that underlying tensions will erupt: culture wars. Even when subcultural influence is acknowledged, it is usually in pejorative terms (i.e., as a bad influence).

Although aspects of white European subcultures can be assimilated into U.S. mainstream culture, this is not true for gay culture, or even works of high or popular art that are labeled as gay or produced by openly gay people. Historically, openly gay culture has fallen outside the parameters of what has been construed as authentically American. This has also been true of African-American and Asian-American cultures. Yet these cultures have had tremendous influence on mainstream culture. The impact of African-American music and language, for example, on mainstream U.S. culture has been incalculable. But this cultural influence does not carry with it the implicit social acceptance that accompanies traditional models of assimilation.

This paradigm is complicated by the dominant culture's schizophrenic relationship to the pleasure-producing elements of subcultures. Although the dominant culture is attracted to and wants the pleasure-based alternatives of subcultures, it also realizes that they are a threat to the tightly controlled, repressive systems that define it. Yet the impulse to obtain pleasure is so strong that the dominant culture, no matter how repressive, seeks new venues of pleasure and freedom.

The ever-present threat posed by "influencing" subcultures can be titillation under duress and allows the dominant culture to enjoy the pleasure-generating aspects of subcultures without acknowledging their origins. While African-American culture is always identifiable as such, its influence on rock, for instance, can be ignored or misrepresented. In this sense, appropriation is a form of enforced "closeting."

The position of gay culture is more complex because, although it can be appropriated by the dominant culture, it can also self-closet, hide itself, to gain a degree of safety as well as to be more palatable to the mainstream. The self-closeting of gay culture complicates the paradigm of influence. Because much gay culture is not labeled as such, its influence is less overtly detectable. This makes it both more likely to infiltrate mainstream culture and, at the same time, more threatening.

Gay culture, because it is predicated on nonreproductive sexuality—pleasure for its own sake—strikes at the heart of how mainstream culture is organized. The burden of representing pleasure in a repressive culture has made homosexuality and gay culture a lightning rod for all of mainstream culture's ambivalence and anxiety about sexuality and pleasure. Although gay culture remained hidden, it was possible for the mainstream to ignore it while still enjoying its benefits. When homosexuals insisted that they and gay culture be more visible, this was no longer possible.

The growth of a gay movement that not only encouraged visibility but also politicized sexuality forced the relationship between gay culture and mainstream culture to a new level of conflict. As gay men and lesbians demanded legal rights and acknowledgment of their lives, mainstream culture found it increasingly problematic to deal with the once-hidden gay culture. As the tensions between gay culture and mainstream culture rose, they erupted into the culture wars. As gay men and lesbians come out in larger numbers than ever before, manifesting their political and cultural presence, they raise the vital question of who can be an American. For the problem for mainstream culture is not gay culture, but openly gay culture; not gay artists, but openly gay artists; not gay people, but openly gay people.

Notes

1. Material on the early formation of community, particularly the molly-houses, can be found in Alan Bary's *Homosexuality in Renaissance England* and David E. Greenberg's *The Construction of Homosexuality*. Documentation of lesbian life is more difficult to obtain; Greenberg has passing references to lesbian clubs, but Emma Donoghue's *Passions Between Women* is the best source.

2. Visibility of lesbian culture is more difficult to chart than that of gay male culture. Donoghue's *Passions Between Women* charts visible lesbian identity, partly through cross-dressing, whereas Lillian Faderman's *Surpassing the Love of Men* uses "intimate friendships" as a signifier of lesbianism (which may not necessarily have a sexual component). Blanche Wiesen Cook's *Women and Support Networks* examines lesbian visibility in circles of political activism.

3. Discussions of the root "Mattachine" can be found in Harry Hay's interview in Jonathan Ned Katz's *Gay American History*, Stuart Timmons's *The Trouble with Harry Hay*, Urvashi Vaid's *Virtual Equality*, and Harry Hay's *Radically Gay*, edited by Will Roscoe. The cultural roles of jester and fool are discussed in Bakhtin's *Rabelais and His World*.

4. Feminist responses to drag have varied. Robin Morgan, in *Going Too Far*, condemns drag as antiwoman "black face." Pamela Robertson's *Guilty Pleasures* views it as highly subversive, and in *Transgender Warriors*, Leslie Feinberg describes a history of cross-dressing and drag in revolutionary political movements.

5. Variants of this monologue have been performed by professional and amateur drag performers since the mid-1940s. Although the piece could be read in Mae West's voice, there is no evidence connecting it to her. Charles Pierce renders an updated version of it on *Charles Pierce: Recorded Live at Bimbo's San Francisco*, an undated recording probably from the late 1960s.

6. The specter of a gay male cultural conspiracy preoccupies much antihomosexual writing; see Edmund Bergler's *Fashion and the Unconscious* and William Boldman's *The Season*. Interestingly, although paranoia about the hidden homosexual is rampant in 1950s McCarthyism, psychoanalysts such as Irving Biever and Charles Socarides named paranoia as a defining characteristic of the gay male personality.

7. John D'Emilio's *Sexual Politics, Sexual Communities* notes that the gay community is always growing. Whereas ethnic communities tend to become small, Margaret Mead notes, in *The Third Generation*, that as

assimilation continues, younger generations will often reclaim some aspects of earlier ethnic culture.

8. This argument relies on a notion of idealized cultural production because most low and even high art is a product of consumer culture. See Patrick Brantlinger's *Bread and Circuses* and Debora Silverman's *Selling Culture*.

9. Edmund Bergler's *Homosexuality: Disease or Way of Life?*, using a complicated but ludicrous argument, attacks Proust, Melville, and Maugham as inauthentic artists because of their homosexuality.

10. These arguments about gay playwrights can be found in Goldman's *The Season*, Kaier Curtin's *"We Can Always Call Them Bulgarians,"* and Michael Bronski's *Culture Clash*. See also Benjamin DeMotte's essay "But He's a Homosexual . . ." in *New American Review, 1* (1967).

11. Methods of suppressing and negating minority writings are discussed in Joanna Russ's *How to Suppress Women's Writing* and Toni Morrison's *Playing in the Dark*.

Concepts and Questions

1. How does Bronski define gay culture? How does his definition of culture correspond to other traditional definitions of culture?

2. What differences in identity are found between homosexuals and heterosexuals? How has this difference affected the development of gay culture?

3. What similarities does Bronski draw between African slave culture and gay culture?

4. How has the secretiveness of gay cultures affected their perception by the mainstream culture?

5. In what ways has mainstream culture's discomfort with gay culture affected the manner in which traditional society has reacted to gay culture? How has this reaction been transformed into legal and social reforms?

6. Although there are similarities between the gay co-culture and other co-cultures, there are also important differences. What are some of these differences?

7. What prospects do you see for assimilation of the gay co-culture into the mainstream culture?

8. How does the production of art (i.e., paintings, books, plays, movies) manifest how gay people live their lives to the mainstream culture?

9. How does mainstream culture tend to react to the discovery that an accomplished, highly regarded artist is gay?

Gendered Speech Communities

JULIA T. WOOD

NINA M. REICH

Men are from Mars, Women are from Venus.

This is the outrageous claim—and book title—that has made John Gray both very famous and very rich. His series of Mars and Venus books (*On a Date, In the Bedroom, Together Forever*, etc.) portray women and men as radically different because of innate and unchangeable factors. Years of research, however, indicate that most differences between the sexes are neither as unalterable nor as substantial as Gray claims. Rigorous study of gender differences shows that John Gray's claims are highly exaggerated and fuel stereotypes about both women and men (see Wood, in press, for a more detailed critique of Gray's work). Yet Gray's books have captured millions of readers because they emphasize something that we know from our own experiences—there are some differences between how most women and men communicate, and those differences can complicate interaction and relationships.

In this article we'll discuss what those differences are and how they do—or don't—support a Mars and Venus view of the sexes. Despite John Gray's book title, women and men are really from the same planet—Earth. Yet planet Earth includes many different social communities—ones defined by ethnicity, religion, sexual orientation, (dis)abilities, gender, sex, and so forth. People have a lot in common because they belong to the same species and live on the same planet. At the same time, differences reflect people's participation in different social communities.

After reading this article, you should understand how we learn gendered ways of communicating and

This essay was revised for the current edition of this book. All rights reserved. Permission to reprint must be obtained from the authors and the publisher. Julia T. Wood teaches at the University of North Carolina at Chapel Hill. Nina Reich is a doctoral student at the University of North Carolina at Chapel Hill.

why misunderstandings sometimes arise when masculine and feminine communication styles interact. Insight into gendered communication styles will allow you to interact effectively with people who communicate in both masculine and feminine ways. In addition, you will be empowered to choose the style of communication you want to use in various situations. This will make you an effective communicator in a range of contexts, and you won't have to engage in interplanetary explanations to do so!

THE SOCIAL-SYMBOLIC CONSTRUCTION OF GENDER

Perhaps you have noticed that we use the terms *feminine* and *masculine* as well as the terms *women* and *men*. The former refer to gender and the latter to sex, which are distinct phenomena. *Women, men, male,* and *female* are words that specify sex, which biology determines. In contrast, *feminine* and *masculine* designate genders, which are meanings for each sex that society constructs and sustains. Before we can understand gendered communication patterns, we need to clarify what gender is and how it differs from sex.

Sex

Sex is determined by genetic codes that program biological features. Of the 49 pairs of human chromosomes, one pair controls sex. Usually this unit has two chromosomes, one of which is always an X chromosome. If the second chromosome is a Y, the fetus is male; if it is an X, the fetus is female. (Other combinations have occurred: XYY, XXY, XO, and XXX.) During gestation, genetic codes direct the production of hormones so that fetuses develop genitalia and secondary sex characteristics consistent with their genetic makeup. (Again, there are exceptions, usually caused by medical interventions. See Wood, 2001, for a more thorough discussion.)

We rely on biological features to classify people as male and female: external genitalia (the clitoris and vagina for a female, the penis and testes for a male) and internal sex organs (the uterus and ovaries in females, the prostate in males). Hormones also control secondary sex characteristics such as percentage of body fat (females have more fat to protect the womb when a fetus is present), how much muscle exists, and amount of body hair. There are also differences in male and female brains. Females generally have greater specialization in the right hemisphere, which controls integrative and creative thinking, whereas males typically have more developed left lobes, which govern analytic and abstract thought. Usually, females also have better developed corpus callosa, which are the bundles of nerves connecting the two brain lobes. This suggests that women may be more able to cross to the left hemisphere than men are to cross to the right (Hines, 1992). All of these are sex differences controlled by biology.

Gender

Gender is considerably more complex than sex. For starters, you might think of gender as the cultural meaning of sex. A culture constructs gender by arbitrarily assigning certain qualities, activities, and roles to each sex and by then inscribing these assignments into the fabric of social life. This means that we are not born with a gender, but we become gendered as we internalize and then embody society's views of femininity and masculinity. Thus, gender is a social creation—not an innate, individual characteristic.

Gender refers to social beliefs and values that specify what sex *means* and what it allows and precludes in a particular society at a specific time. Because there is diversity among societies and each one changes over time, the meaning of gender is neither universal nor stable. Instead, femininity and masculinity reflect the beliefs and values of particular cultures in certain eras.

It should now be clear to you that gender and sex are not synonymous. Sex is biological, whereas gender is socially constructed. Sex is innate, whereas gender is learned and, therefore, changeable. Sex is established by genetics and biology, whereas gender is produced and reproduced by particular societies at particular times. Barring surgery, sex is permanent, whereas gender varies over time and across cultures. Whereas our sex stays the same across situations, we may choose to embody different genders in different situations. For instance, both women and men tend to be more nurturing with children and pets than in work situations. Sex is an individual property, whereas gender is a social construction.

BECOMING GENDERED

Let's now look more closely at how people become gendered. Many factors influence our gender development. Two of the most imporant are (1) the continuous communication of social expectations for males and females, and (2) interaction in sex-segregated children's play groups.

Communication of Social Expectations and Development of Gender

Cultural constructions of gender are communicated to individuals through a range of structures and practices that make up our everyday world. From birth on, individuals are besieged with communication that presents cultural prescriptions for gender as natural and right. Beginning with the pink and blue blankets wrapped around newborns, gender socialization continues in interactions with parents, teachers, peers, and media. In magazines and on television, we are more likely to see women in the home and men in the boardroom; girls in soft colors and frilly fashions and boys in stronger, darker colors and rugged clothes; women needing help and men performing daring rescues; men driving cars and women riding in them. In cartoons and prime-time programming we see male characters being more active (bold, dominant, aggressive) than female characters (more subdued, subordinate, and gentle). In kindergarten and elementary school, children are more likely to see women as teachers and men as principals, a difference that sends a clear message about the status society prescribes to each sex. In offices, virtually all secretaries and receptionists are female, sending the message that assisting others is part of feminine identity. When children visit toy stores, they see pink bicycles with delicate baskets for girls and blue or black bicycles with sturdy baskets for boys. As children participate in the many spheres of society, they receive continuous messages that reinforce social views of gender.

The pervasive messages about how boys and girls are "supposed to be" make gender roles seem natural, normal, and right. Because cultures systematically normalize arbitrary definitions of gender, we seldom reflect on how *unnatural* it is that half of humans are assumed to be deferential, emotional, and interested in building relationships whereas the other half are assumed to be ambitious, assertive, and self-sufficient (Janeway, 1971; Miller, 1986). If we do reflect on social definitions of masculinity and femininity, they don't make a great deal of sense!

The intensity and pervasiveness of social prescriptions for gender ensure that most females will become predominantly feminine (nurturing, cooperative, sensitive to others) and most males will become predominantly masculine (assertive, competitive, independent). Notice that we stated *most* females and males will become *predominantly* feminine or masculine. Very few, if any, people are exclusively one gender. You can be masculine, feminine, or—like most of us—a combination of genders that allows you to be effective in diverse situations.

Peer Interaction's Impact on Development of Gender

A second significant influence on the development of gender is peer interaction among children. As children play together, they teach each other how to be boys and girls. Insight into the significance of play was pioneered by Daniel Maltz and Ruth Borker (1982), who studied children at play. The researchers noticed recreation was usually sex-segregated, and boys and girls tended to favor discrete kinds of games—the ones that are socially prescribed for each sex through media, advertising, toy manufacturers, parents, and so forth. Whereas girls were more likely to play house, school, or jump rope, boys tended to play competitive team sports like football and baseball. Because different goals, strategies, and relationships characterize some girls' and boys' games, the children learned divergent rules for interaction. Engaging in play, Maltz and Borker concluded, contributes to socializing children into predominantly masculine and feminine identities (again, notice the word, *predominantly*).

Maltz and Borker's classic study has been replicated by other researchers, who have shown that their findings continue to hold up in the present time. Psychologist Campbell Leaper (1994, 1998) reports that children still tend to prefer sex-segregated play groups, a finding that is reinforced by other researchers (Clark, 1998; Harris, 1998; Moller & Serbin, 1998). Leaper and the other researchers also report that the sex-segregated play groups engage in different kinds of games that, in turn, socialize them into different ways of communicating.

Girls' Games. Many games that girls typically play, such as house and school, require just two or three people so they promote personal relationships. Further, these games don't have preset or fixed rules, roles, and objectives. Whereas touchdowns and home runs are goals in boys' games and roles such as pitcher, forward, and blocker are clearly defined, how to play house is open to negotiation. To make their games work, girls talk with each other and agree on rules, roles, and goals: "You be the mommy and I'll be the daddy, and we'll clean house." From unstructured, cooperative play, girls learn three basic rules for how to communicate:

1. Be cooperative, collaborative, inclusive. It's important that everyone feels involved and has a chance to play.
2. Don't criticize or outdo others. Cultivate egalitarian relationships so the group is cohesive and gratifying to all.
3. Pay attention to others' feelings and needs and be sensitive in interpreting and responding to them.

In sum, games that are more likely to be played by girls emphasize relationships more than outcomes, sensitivity to others, and cooperative, inclusive interpersonal orientations.

Boys' Games. Unlike girls' games, some of the games that boys are more likely to play involve fairly large groups (for instance, baseball requires nine players plus extras to fill in) and proceed by rules and goals that are externally established and constant (there are nine innings, three strikes and you're out). Also, boys' games allow for individual stars—MVP, for instance—and, in fact, a boy's status depends on his rank relative to others. The more

structured, large, and individualized character of boys' games teaches them three rules of interaction:

1. Assert yourself. Use talk and action to highlight your ideas and to establish both your status and leadership.
2. Focus on outcomes. Use your talk and actions to make things happen, to solve problems, and to achieve goals.
3. Be competitive. Vie for the talk stage. Keep attention focused on you, outdo others, and make yourself stand out.

Some of the games more likely to be played by boys emphasize achievement—both for the team and the individual members. The goals are to win for the team and to be the top player on it. Interaction is more an arena for negotiating power and status than for building relationships with others, and competitiveness is customary in masculine communities.

The nature of interaction in the games that society encourages girls and boys to play teaches children society's prescriptions for males and females. It's not surprising, then, that most girls and boys learn some different ways of communicating. We use the qualifying word, "most," to remind you that we are discussing general differences, not absolute ones. Some women sometimes act in ways that are considered masculine and some women have a primarily masculine style. Some men sometimes act in ways that are considered feminine and some men have a primarily feminine style. In most situations, however, most females adopt a primarily feminine style of communicating and most males adopt a predominantly masculine one.

In combination, messages woven into the fabric of society and peer interaction among children clarify how people become gendered.

FEMININE AND MASCULINE COMMUNICATION COMMUNITIES

Beginning in the 1970s, scholars noticed that some groups of people share communication practices not common to, or understood by, people outside of the groups. This led to the realization that there are distinctive speech communities, or communication communities. William Labov (1972) defined a speech community as existing when a set of norms regarding how to communicate is shared by a group of people. Within a communication community, members embrace similar understandings of how to use talk and what purposes it serves.

Once scholars realized that distinctive speech communities exist, they identified many, some of which are discussed in this book: African Americans, Native Americans, gay men, lesbians, and people with disabilities. Members in each of these groups share perspectives that outsiders seldom have. By extension, the values, viewpoints, and experiences that are distinct to a particular group influence how members of that group communicate. That's why there are some gender differences in why, when, and how we communicate.

Feminine and masculine speech communities have been explored by many scholars (Aries, 1987; Beck, 1988; Coates & Cameron, 1989; Johnson, 1989; Kramarae, 1981; Spender, 1984; Tannen, 1990a, b; Treichler & Kramarae, 1983; Wood, 1993a, b, c, 2001; Wood & Inman, 1993). Their research reveals that most girls and women operate from assumptions about communication and use rules for communicating that differ in some ways from those endorsed by most boys and men.

At the heart of the process by which we become gendered is human communication. It is through interaction with others that we learn what masculine and feminine mean in our society and how we are expected to think, talk, feel, and act. Communication is also the primary means by which we embody gender personally. When we conform to social prescriptions for gender, we reinforce prevailing social views of masculinity and femininity. Table 1 summarizes how these differences in gender communities may affect communication.

MEN AND WOMEN IN CONVERSATION: GENDERED PATTERNS AND MISUNDERSTANDINGS

Differences learned in childhood may be carried into adult interaction. Individuals who are exclusively feminine or masculine limit their effective-

Table 1 *Differences Between Feminine and Masculine Communication Culture*

Feminine Talk	Masculine Talk
1. Use talk to build and sustain rapport with others.	1. Use talk to assert yourself and your ideas.
2. Share yourself and disclose to others.	2. Personal disclosures can make you vulnerable.
3. Use talk to create symmetry or equality between people.	3. Use talk to establish your status and power.
4. Matching experiences with others shows understanding and empathy ("I know how you feel").	4. Matching experiences is a competitive strategy to command attention. ("I can top that.")
5. To support others, express understanding of their feelings.	5. To support others, do something helpful—give advice or tell them how to solve a problem.
6. Include others in conversation by asking their opinions and encouraging them to elaborate. Wait your turn to speak so others can participate.	6. Don't share the talk stage with others; wrest it from them with communication. Interrupt others to make your own points.
7. Keep the conversation going by asking questions and showing interest in others' ideas.	7. Each person is on her or his own; it's not your job to help others join in.
8. Be responsive. Let others know you hear and care about what they say.	8. Use responses to make your own points and to outshine others.
9. Be tentative so that others feel free to add their ideas.	9. Be assertive so others perceive you as confident and in command.
10. Talking is a human relationship in which details and interesting side comments enhance depth of connection.	10. Talking is a linear sequence that should convey information and accomplish goals. Extraneous details get in the way and achieve nothing.

ness to those situations that call for the gendered style they can enact. On the other hand, individuals who refuse to be restricted to only a feminine or masculine style challenge and sometimes change social views of gender. In addition, they enhance their communication repertoire so they are likely to be competent in a wide range of situations. In the next section, we'll examine some examples of problems that can arise when people don't understand and know how to use both masculine and feminine styles of communication.

Gender Gaps in Communication

To illustrate the practical consequences of limiting yourself to only one gendered style of communication, let's consider some concrete cases of communication. As you read the following examples of common problems in communication between women and men, you'll probably find that several are familiar to you.

- *What counts as support?* Rita is really bummed out when she meets Mike for dinner. She explains that she's worried about a friend who has begun drinking heavily. When Mike advises her to get her friend into counseling, Rita repeats how worried she feels. Next, Mike tells Rita to make sure her friend doesn't drive after drinking. Rita explodes that she doesn't need advice. Irritated at her lack of appreciation for his help, Mike asks, "Then why did you ask for it?" In exasperation Rita responds, "Oh, never mind, I'll talk to Betsy. At least she cares how I feel."

- *Tricky feedback.* Roseann and Drew are colleagues in a marketing firm. One morning he drops into her office to run an advertising plan by her. As Drew discusses his ideas, Roseann nods and says "Um," "Un huh," and "Yes." When he finishes, Roseann says "I really don't think that plan will sell the product." Feeling misled, Drew demands, "Then why were you agreeing the whole time I presented my idea?" Completely confused, Roseann responds, "What makes you think I was agreeing with you?"

- *Expressing care.* Dedrick and Melita have been dating for two years and are very serious. To celebrate their anniversary Melita wants to spend a quiet evening in her apartment where they can talk about the relationship and be with just each other. When Dedrick arrives, he's planned a dinner and concert. Melita feels hurt that he doesn't want to talk and be close.

- *I'd rather do it myself.* Chris is having difficulty writing a paper for a communication class because the professor didn't give clear directions for the assignment. When Chris grumbles about this problem, Pat suggests that Chris ask the professor or a classmate to clarify directions. Chris resists, and says rather sharply, "I can figure it out on my own."

- *Can we talk about us?* Anna asks her fiancé, Ben, "Can we talk about us?" Immediately Ben feels tense—another problem on the horizon. He prepares himself for an unpleasant conversation and reluctantly nods assent. Anna then thanks Ben for being so supportive during the last few months when she was under enormous pressure at her job. She tells him she feels closer than ever. Although Ben feels relieved there isn't any crisis, he's also baffled. If there isn't a problem, he doesn't see why people need to talk about the relationship. He thinks if it's working, you should let it be.

You've probably been involved in conversations like these. And you've probably been confused, frustrated, hurt, or even angry when a member of the other sex didn't give you what you wanted or didn't value your efforts to be supportive. If you're a woman, you may think Mike should be more sensitive to Rita's feelings and Dedrick should cherish time alone with Melita. If you're a man, it's likely that you empathize with Mike's frustration and feel Rita is giving him a hard time when he's trying to help. Likewise, you may think Melita is lucky to have a guy willing to shell out some bucks so they can do something fun together.

Who's right in these cases? Is Rita unreasonable? Is Melita ungrateful? Are Dedrick and Mike insensitive? Is Chris stubborn? Did Roseann mislead Drew? When we focus on questions like these we fall prey to a central problem in gender communication: the tendency to judge. Because Western culture is hierarchical, we're taught to perceive differences as better and worse, not simply as different. Yet, the inclination to judge one person as right and the other wrong whenever there's misunderstanding usually spells trouble for close relationships.

But judging is not the only way we *could* think about these interactions, and it's not the most constructive way if we want to build good relationships. More productive than judging is understanding and respecting different styles of communication. Once we recognize there are many styles of interacting, we can tune into perspectives other than our own and increase our personal communication repertoires.

Understanding Gendered Communication

Drawing on earlier sections of this article, we can analyze the misunderstandings in these five dialogues and see how they grow out of the different interaction styles cultivated in feminine and masculine speech communities. Because there are some differences in how most men and women have learned to communicate, they may have different ways of showing support, interest, and caring. This also implies that they may perceive the same communication in dissimilar ways.

In the first scenario, Rita's purpose in talking with Mike isn't just to tell him about her concern for her friend; she also sees communication as a way to connect with Mike (Aries, 1987; Riessman, 1990; Tannen, 1990b; Wood, 1993b). She wants him to respond to her feelings because that will enhance her sense of closeness to him. Schooled in masculinity, however, Mike views communication as an instrument to do things, so he tries to help by giving advice. Rita feels he entirely disregards her feelings, so she doesn't feel close to Mike, which was her primary purpose in talking with him. Advice would be great, but only after Mike responds to her feelings.

In the second example, the problem arises when Drew translates Roseann's feedback according to masculine rules of interaction. Many women learn to give lots of response cues—verbal and nonverbal behaviors to indicate interest and involvement in conversation—because that's part of using communication to build relationships with others. Masculine communities, however, focus on outcomes more than processes, so many men use feedback to signal specific agreement and disagreement (Beck, 1988;

Fishman, 1978; Tannen, 1990b; Wood, 1993a). When Drew hears Roseann's "ums," "uh huhs," and "yeses," he assumes she is agreeing. According to her community's rules, however, she is only showing interest and being responsive, not signaling agreement.

Dedrick and Melita also experience misunderstanding based on gendered communication styles. In feminine communities, talking is a way—probably the primary way—to express and expand closeness. This is why many women feel close when engaged in dialogue (Aries, 1987; Riessman, 1990; Wood, 1993b). Masculine socialization, in contrast, stresses doing things and shared activities as primary ways to create and express closeness (Cancian, 1987; Swain, 1989; Wood & Inman, 1993). Someone who is predominantly masculine is more likely to express caring for a friend by doing a concrete favor (washing a car, fixing an appliance) or doing something with the friend (skiing, going to a concert) than by talking explicitly about his or her feelings. Notice the pronouns we used in the last sentence. We stated *his or her* to remind you that gender is not the same thing as sex. A woman might have a predominantly masculine communication style, just as a man might have a predominantly feminine style. And both men and women might vary their communication styles to suit different situations.

Those men who are primarily masculine generally experience "closeness in doing" (Swain, 1989). By realizing that doing things is a valid way to be close, feminine individuals can avoid feeling hurt by partners who propose activities. In addition, feminine individuals who want to express care in ways that masculine people prefer might think about what they could do for or with others, rather than what they could say (Riessman, 1990). At the same time, verbal expressions of caring are likely to be preferred by individuals who are predominantly feminine.

Masculinity's emphasis on independence underlies Chris's unwillingness to ask others for help in understanding an assignment. What we've discussed about gender identity helps us understand this difference. Chris's refusal to ask others for help reflects masculine prescriptions that emphasize independence and self-sufficiency. Unless Pat realizes this difference between them, they will continue to frustrate each other.

In the final case, we see a very common misunderstanding in gender communication. Feminine communication communities prioritize the process of communicating, so many women find talking about relationships an ongoing source of interest and pleasure. In contrast, within masculine communication communities, talk tends to be perceived as an instrument for acomplishing things, such as solving problems, rather than a means to enhance closeness (Wood, 1993a, b, c). Given these disparate orientations, "talking about us" sometimes means very different things to most men and women. Anna's wish to discuss the relationship because it's so good makes no sense to Ben, and his lack of interest in a conversation about the relationship hurts Anna. Again, each person errs in relying on inappropriate rules to interpret the other's communication.

Many problems in communication between genders result from faulty translations. This happens when we interpret others according to our rules of communication. Just as we wouldn't assume that Western rules apply to Asian people, so we'd be wise not to assume that one gender's rules pertain to the other. When we understand gender communities and when we respect the logic of each one, we empower ourselves to communicate in ways that enhance our relationships.

COMMUNICATING EFFECTIVELY BETWEEN GENDERS

Whether it's a Northern American thinking that someone who eats with his or her hands is "uncouth" or a woman assuming that a man is "closed" because he doesn't disclose as much as she does, we're inclined to think that what differs from our ways of doing things is wrong. Ethnocentric judgments seldom improve communication or enhance relationships. Instead of debating whether feminine or masculine styles of communication are better, we should learn to see the value of both styles. The information we've covered, combined with this book's emphasis on understanding and appreciating diverse communication styles, can be distilled into six principles for effective communication between members of different social groups.

1. *Suspend judgment.* This is first and foremost. As long as we are judging differences as right or wrong, better or worse, we aren't respecting the distinct integrity of each style. When you find yourself confused in cross-gender conversations, resist the tendency to judge. Instead, explore constructively what is happening and how you and your partner might better understand each other.

2. *Recognize the validity of different communication styles.* We need to remind ourselves that there is a logic and validity to both feminine and masculine communication styles. Feminine emphases on relationships, feelings, and responsiveness don't reflect an inability to adhere to masculine rules for competing any more than masculine stress on instrumental outcomes is a failure to follow feminine rules for sensitivity to others. It is inappropriate to apply a single criterion— either masculine or feminine—to both genders' communication. Instead, we need to realize that different goals, priorities, and standards pertain to each.

3. *Provide translation cues.* Now that you realize men and women tend to learn different rules for interaction, it makes sense to think about helping the other gender translate your communication. For instance, in the first example, Rita might have said to Mike, "I appreciate your advice, but what I need first is for you to talk with me about my feelings." A comment such as this helps Mike interpret Rita's motives and needs. After all, there's no reason why he should automatically understand rules that weren't taught in his communication community.

4. *Seek translation cues.* We can also improve our interactions by seeking translation cues from others. If Rita didn't tell Mike how to translate her communication, he could have asked "What would be helpful to you? I don't know whether you want to talk about how you're feeling or brainstorm ways to help your friend. Which would be better?" This message communicates clearly that Mike cares about Rita and he wants to support her if she'll just tell him how. Similarly, instead of assuming that Rita had deliberately misled him, Drew might have taken a more constructive approach and said, "When you nod-

ded your head while I was talking, I thought you agreed with my ideas. What did it mean?" This kind of response would allow Drew to learn something new.

5. *Enlarge your own communication style*. Studying communication that differs from our own teaches us not only about other cultures and speech communities but also about ourselves and the communities to which we belong. If we're open to learning and growing, we can enlarge our own communication repertoire by incorporating skills that are more emphasized in other groups. Individuals socialized into masculinity could learn a great deal from feminine ways of supporting friends. Likewise, feminine people could expand the ways they experience intimacy by appreciating "closeness in the doing" that is a masculine specialty. There's little to risk and much to gain by incorporating additional skills into our communication repertoires.

As human beings we have the capacity to choose how to present ourselves at different moments and in diverse contexts. Enlarging your personal repertoire empowers you to be effective in a wide range of situations, regardless of whether they call for feminine, masculine, or blended communication styles. For example, a female or a male attorney is likely to be dominant and assertive in a courtroom, yet the same woman or man can be nurturing and supportive when interacting with children. Although you may be primarily feminine or primarily masculine, you do not have to behave consistently in all situations. Instead, you can be an agent who chooses how to present yourself in particular situations.

6. *Suspend judgment*. If you're thinking we already covered this principle, you're right. It's important enough, however, to merit repetition. Judgment is so thoroughly woven into Western culture that it's difficult not to evaluate others and not to defend our own positions. Yet as long as we're judging others and defending ourselves, we're probably making no headway in communicating more effectively. So, suspending judgment is the first and last principle of effective communication between women and men or between members of any communication communities.

SUMMARY

As women and men, most of us have been socialized into primary gender identities that reflect cultural constructions of femininity and masculinity. We become gendered as we interact with our families, childhood peers, and society as a whole—all of whom teach us what gender means and how we are expected to embody it in our attitudes, feelings, and interaction styles. This means communication produces, reflects, and reproduces genders and imbues them with a taken-for-granted status that we seldom notice or question. Through an ongoing, cyclical process, communication, culture, and gender continuously re-create one another.

Because we all live within the overall culture, there is substantial overlap between men and women and between masculine and feminine communication. At the same time, there are some differences between most women's and most men's communication (notice the word "most"). When we fail to recognize that genders sometimes rely on some dissimilar rules for talk, we may misread each other's meanings and motives. To avoid the frustration, hurt, and misunderstandings that occur when we apply one gender's rules to the other gender's communication, we need to recognize and respect the distinctive validity and value of each style. Ideally, we also choose to learn how to use each style effectively.

Mars and Venus and Back to Earth

Let's return to John Gray's claims that differences between women's and men's communication are innate (inborn), absolute, and unchangeable. The research that we've discussed refutes Gray's claims. Our differences are not innate; rather, they are learned in speech communities and from society's communication of prescriptions for gender. The differences we've noted aren't absolute because not all women communicate according to the rules of feminine communities all the time and not all men communicate according to the rules of masculine communities all the time. And clearly our communication styles—because they are learned—are amenable to change. Men do not have to go to their "cave" as Gray suggests. Men can be and at times are expressive and nurturing. Likewise, women can choose to be and are often assertive and outcome oriented.

We can do a lot to minimize the occasional misunderstandings fostered by differences between masculine and feminine communication styles. The first step is to move beyond Gray's simplistic notions that sex determines how we communicate. When we abandon that unfounded idea, we realize that our gendered communication styles are not static. We can choose to adapt our ways of communicating to the demands of various situations. If we decide to enlarge our communication repertoires and choose how to express ourselves from situation to situation, both men and women can be effective in numerous interactions and in our interpersonal relationships.

What we've covered in this article provides a good foundation for the ongoing process of learning not just how to get along with people of both genders, but also how to appreciate and grow from valuing the different perspectives on interaction, identity, and relationships that masculine and feminine communities offer. And we don't have to make an interplanetary flight—or buy a book by John Gray—to learn these things.

References

Aries, E. (1987). Gender and communication. In P. Shaver (Ed.), *Sex and gender* (pp. 149–176). Newbury Park, CA: Sage.

Beck, A. (1988). *Love is never enough.* New York: Harper & Row.

Cancian, F. (1987). *Love in America.* Cambridge, England: Cambridge University Press.

Chodorow, N. J. (1978). *The reproduction of mothering: Psychoanalysis and the sociology of gender.* Berkeley: University of California Press.

Clark, R. (1998). A comparison of topics and objectives in a cross section of young men's and women's everyday conversatoins. In D. Canary & K. Dindia (Eds.), *Sex differences and similarities in communication* (pp. 303–319). Mahwah, NJ: Lawrence Erlbaum.

Coates, J., & Cameron, D. (1989). *Women in their speech communities: New perspectives on language and sex.* London: Longman.

Eichenbaum, L., & Orbach, S. (1983). *Understanding women: A feminist psychoanalytic approach.* New York: Basic Books.

Fishman, P. M. (1978). Interaction: The work women do. *Social Problems, 25,* 397–406.

Gilligan, C. (1982). *In a different voice: Psychological theory and women's development.* Cambridge, MA: Harvard University Press.

Gray, J. (1992). *Men are from Mars, women are from Venus.* New York: HarperCollins.

Harris, J. (1998). *The nurture assumption.* New York: Simon & Schuster/Free Press.

Hines, M. (1992, April 19). *Health Information Communication Network, 5,* 2.

Janeway, E. (1971). *Man's world, woman's place: A study in social mythology.* New York: Dell.

Johnson, F. L. (1989). Women's culture and communication: An analytic perspective. In C. M. Lont & S. A. Friedley (Eds.), *Beyond boundaries: Sex and gender diversity in communication.* Fairfax, VA: George Mason University Press.

Kramarae, C. (1981). *Women and men speaking: Frameworks for analysis.* Rowley, MA: Newbury House.

Labov, W. (1972). *Sociolinguistic patterns.* Philadelphia: University of Pennsylvania Press.

Lakoff, R. (1975). *Language and woman's place.* New York: Harper & Row.

Leaper, C. (1994). *Childhood gender segregation: Causes and consequences.* San Francisco: Jossey-Bass.

Leaper, C. (1998). The relationship of play activity and gender to parent and child sex-typed communication. *International Journal of Behavioral Development, 19,* 689–703.

Maltz, D. N., & Borker, R. (1982). A cultural approach to male-female miscommunication. In J. J. Gumpertz (Ed.), *Language and social identity* (pp. 196–216). Cambridge, England: Cambridge University Press.

Miller, J. B. (1986). *Toward a new psychology of women.* Boston: Beacon Press.

Moller, L., & Serbin, L. (1998). Antecedents of toddler gender segregation: Cognitive consonance, gender-typed toy preferences and behavioral compatibility. *Sex Roles, 35,* 445–460.

Rakow, L. F. (1986). Rethinking gender research in communication. *Journal of Communication, 36,* 11–26.

Riessman, J. M. (1990). *Divorce talk: Women and men make sense of personal relationships.* New Brunswick, NJ: Rutgers University Press.

Spender, D. (1984). *Man made language.* London: Routledge and Kegan Paul.

Surrey, J. L. (1983). The relational self in women: Clinical implications. In J. V. Jordan, J. L. Surrey, & A. G. Kaplan (Speakers), *Women and empathy: Implications for psychological development and psychotherapy* (pp. 6–11). Wellesley, MA: Stone Center for Developmental Services and Studies.

Swain, S. (1989). Covert intimacy: Closeness in men's friendships. In B. J. Risman & P. Schwartz (Eds.), *Gender and intimate realtionships* (pp. 71–86). Belmont, CA: Wadsworth.

Tannen, D. (1986). *That's not what I meant! How conversational style makes or breaks relationships.* New York: Ballantine.

Tannen, D. (1990a). Gender differences in conversational coherence: Physical alignment and topical cohesion. In B. Dorval (Ed.), *Conversational organization and its development: XXXVIII* (pp. 167–206). Norwood, NJ: Ablex.

Tannen, D. (1990b). *You just don't understand: Women and men in conversation.* New York: William Morrow.

Treichler, P. A., & Kramarae, C. (1983). Women's talk in the ivory tower. *Communication Quarterly, 31,* 118–132.

Wood, J. T. (in press). John Gray is from Mars; Women and Men are from Planet Earth. *Southern Communication Journal.*

Wood, J. T. (2001). *Gendered lives: Communication, gender & culture* (4th ed.). Belmont, CA: Wadsworth.

Wood, J. T. (1993a). Engendered relationships: Interaction, caring, power, and responsibility in close relationships. In S. Duck (Ed.), *Processes in close relationships: Contexts of close relationships* (Vol. 3). Beverly Hills, CA: Sage.

Wood, J. T. (1993b). Engendered identities: Shaping voice and mind through gender. In D. Vocate (Ed.), *Intrapersonal communication: Different voices, different minds.* Hillsdale, NJ: Lawrence Erlbaum.

Wood, J. T. (1993c). *Who Cares?: Women, Care, and Culture.* Carbondale: Southern Illinois University Press.

Wood, J. T., & Inman, C. C. (1993). In a different mode: Masculine styles of communicating closeness. *Journal of Applied Communication Research, 21* (279–295).

Zimmerman, D. H., and West, C. (1975). Sex roles, interruptions, and silences in conversation. In B. Thorne & N. Henley (Eds.), *Language and sex: Difference and dominance* (pp. 105–129). Rowley, MA: Newbury House.

Concepts and Questions

1. What does this chapter suggest about girls who are socialized in masculine communities and who play traditionally masculine games and boys who are socialized in feminine communities and who play traditionally feminine games? Which gender's rules of communication would they be likely to learn?

2. What is the difference between a person's sex and his or her gender?

3. Imagine that a friend held up Gray's book *Men are from Mars, Women are from Venus,* and said to you: "This is a great book! It totally explains why men and women communicate differently." What would you say to your friend?

4. Wood and Reich encourage you to learn how to use both masculine and feminine styles of communicating. Why do they advocate this approach? What are positive outcomes they think result from learning multiple ways of communicating?

5. Based on your experiences, what are the most important differences between feminine talk and masculine talk styles of communication?

6. What methods do Wood and Reich suggest to help improve understanding in cross-gender communication? From your personal experiences, can you add to their list?

7. In the examples of miscommunication, one scenario featured Chris unwilling to ask for help with an assignment. Did you assume that Chris was male? Did you assume that Chris's friend, Pat, was a female? How would your views of Chris and Pat's interaction change if they were both male, they were both female, or Chris was female and Pat was male?

Communication Dynamics of the Elderly

VALERIE C. MCKAY

On January 24, 1995, President Clinton, in his State of the Union Address, declared, "Our senior citizens have made us what we are today." Following the vote-counting difficulties of the 2000 presidential election, seniors in Florida were blamed for much of the election fiasco because of their alleged inability to use the newly designed "butterfly ballot" when deciding between candidates ("One Ballot, A lot of Confusion," *L. A. Times*, November 9, 2000). Who are our senior citizens? Why were they mentioned in a keynote address such as a State of the Union message? Was the new election ballot technology as alleged too difficult for them to use? What contributions *have* our senior citizens made toward the progress of our society and culture? Do they truly constitute a co-culture of their own?

The purpose of this article is to illustrate, through research literature and example, the characteristics of the *co-culture of the elderly*. This will be accomplished (1) by discussing the concept of culture and why the population of senior citizens in our society can be conceptualized as a *co-culture*; (2) by analyzing the origin of many negative stereotypes associated with older adulthood, and showing their falsity; (3) by reviewing current research literature describing characteristics of our senior citizens; and (4) by providing some information about our senior citizens that forces us to go beyond the stereotypes and fears inherent in intergenerational communication.

WHAT IS CULTURE?

If we define culture as a *form or pattern for living*, then it logically follows that the lifestyle of our senior citizens has a pattern all its own that is unique

from other forms. As a co-culture, they can certainly be distinguished from the larger culture simply by chronological age. But, if our definition becomes even more specific to include "*language, friendships, eating habits, communication practices, social acts, economic and political activities*" (Porter & Samovar, 1985, p. 19), then we must explore their lifestyle with respect to these activities even further in order to discover the cultural characteristics of this singular group of citizens.

The limitation inherent in conceptualizing a culture or co-culture is the assumption of the homogeneity of the group; in other words, we assume that *most* people within the culture behave *similarly* based on our *generalized* notion of the group. The result of this assumption is, of course, a tendency to stereotype or to form "rigid preconceptions which are applied to all members of a group . . . over a period of time, regardless of individual variations" (Atkinson, Morten, & Sue, 1985, p. 172). Although some may view stereotyping as a means by which we can *generally* understand or become familiar with peoples of other cultures, this process often prevents us from really getting to know individual members of those same cultures. As a result, we fail to get past the uncertainty and unfamiliarity by communicating and engaging in preliminary stages of relationship (friendship) development. In many cases, the diversity (or heterogeneity) *within* a culture is greater than the diversity we find in making comparisons *between* cultures (Catchen, 1989).

WHY SHOULD WE CONSIDER SENIOR CITIZENS A CO-CULTURE?

Although this question will be addressed in further detail later, let's examine some preliminary evidence for the claim. Our first characteristic associated with culture is *language*. Do the elderly speak a different language? Unfortunately, there is little research that has examined singular characteristics of a language used by this particular generation; what have been examined are the patterns of discourse (talk) that occur about and within the lives of older adults (Coupland & Coupland, 1995). So, unlike many cultures that adopt jargon and terms that have meaning only among members of that culture, older adults appear to use language forms that coincide with the dominant culture or their culture of origin—or perhaps other forms have not been explored. What have been frequently examined are the patterns of stereotypical language used to describe older adults—both linguistically and in mediated forms of communication—and most of these patterns are commensurate with the stereotypes we hold of the elderly. This will be discussed in depth later.

Now let's consider friendship and social activities. Friendships among older adults are especially significant in meeting both physical and emotional needs. They provide social support, caregiving, transportation and household help, social-networking, and emotional satisfaction. Many elderly friendships are long term—the result of many years of development and nurturance. Although elderly friendships do not differ significantly in their quality in comparison with other groups, they are especially significant for elderly women who, after the loss of their spouse, are alone, are experiencing a reduction in the quality of life, and are sometimes physically and emotionally isolated from family. In contrast, elderly men, who find themselves alone after the loss of their spouse or with the onset of retirement, are less likely to develop and maintain friendships. For some of these men, the risk of suicide increases with age, accounting for rates three times that of the general population (Perkins & Tice, 1994).

For older adults, friendships revolve around a sense of community, help (such as yard work, housekeeping, and household repairs), transportation, and emotional support. "Friendships provide important psychological and social support for the older adult in the form of companionship, mutual aid, and shared activities" (Roberto & Scott, 1989, p. 29). In rural areas, activities with friends seem to revolve more around outdoor events; in urban areas more activities involve indoor events such as movies, performances, and the like. In fact, one organization called Hospital Audiences, Inc., a nonprofit group, organizes trips and excursions to theater and musical performances for seniors residing in nursing homes in proximity to the New York City area (Schemo, 1994).

Another organization, The Institute of New Dimensions, provides educational opportunities to senior citizens. Volunteers including retired academicians, community leaders, and corporate retirees teach college-level courses. Although degrees are not awarded, the rewards are manifest by increased self-esteem and pride (Prince, 1994). The California State University, Long Beach, College of Health and Human Services also hosts *Senior University*, which offers college-level courses to many seniors from the surrounding Southern California community.

For individuals who are living alone, or who are not ambulatory, senior companion programs provide assistance with household affairs, daily visitation, and friendship. Briggs (1994) reports that the Senior Companion Program (SCP) has been in operation for 20 years and was funded by the Corporation for National Services. He states that the program:

> Matches older volunteers with frail, elderly men and women who might otherwise be forced into nursing homes or hospitals. There are 185 local SCP projects spread throughout all 50 states. Companions shop, prepare meals, some monitor medication and assist with exercise, help manage household affairs—or they just simply drop by and visit. (p. 260)

Another proactive community enterprise, The LIFE (Learning Informally From Elders) project was designed to (1) engage elders in dialogue and problem solving with professionals and policy makers through community forums, and (2) to improve the referral and communication network of professionals who serve elders. The success of this program has been the empowerment of elders in the community of New Haven, Connecticut. For example, whereas health care providers were concerned about the numbers of elders seeking their services, participation in the LIFE forums revealed that elders' primary concerns were for their personal safety in seeking the services in clinics and health centers. One of the first solutions resulting from the LIFE forums was a meeting between project participants and police officials of the New Haven community (Pallett-Hehn & Lucas, 1994).

Organizations such as these are unique to senior citizens, primarily because the needs of the elder community differ from those of younger people. Two issues are particularly noteworthy: (1) elders value their friendships in terms of both satisfying the needs of others and receiving care when needed, and (2) their lives continue to be meaningful and active—contrary to our stereotypical notions of ill health and reclusive lifestyle.

What about culture and communication practices of our older adults? Research has investigated various patterns of inter- and intra-generational talk in the lives of older adults. Some of those patterns include recall and reminiscence (Butler, 1968; Kaminsky, 1984; Lo Gerfo, 1980; Moody, 1984), story telling (Nussbaum & Bettini, 1994), competence and effects of aging on communicative ability (Duran, 1989), accommodation to elders (Ryan, MacLean, & Orange, 1994), intergenerational talk (Giles et al., 1992; Harwood, Giles, & Ryan, 1995; McKay, 1989, 1993), communication and loss (death) (Nussbaum, Thompson, & Robinson, 1989), communication between caregiver and elder parent (Clipp & George, 1990; Eckert & Shulman, 1996), communication between siblings (Cicirelli & Nussbaum, 1989; McKay & Caverly, 1995), and characteristics of communication in long-term marriages (Klinger-Vartabedian & Wispe, 1989; Mare & Fitzpatrick, 1995)—just to name a few. What is unique about the communication patterns of this particular population? To answer this question, let's consider the phenomenon of long-term marriage.

Long-term marriage is a relatively new and rare social phenomenon for two reasons: Before the turn of the 20th century most marriages ended in the death of one spouse, and *now* only one in five marriages is expected to last 20 or more years (Sporakowski & Axelson, 1989); in fact, long-term marriage may be idiosyncratic to the current elderly cohort unless the prevailing high rate of divorce drastically reduces. Consequently, there exists a paucity of research investigating the quality of long-term marriages of our older adult populations. Moreover, upon the death of a spouse, men have more opportunity to remarry than women, primarily because of the lower female mortality rate (there are more available older women than older men); but little research is available that investigates remarriage in late-life.

Some communication researchers have assessed the communicative quality of marriages over the life course. For example, Sillars and Wilmot (1989) explored the intrinsic (implicit, idiosyncratic, and efficient communication forms developed over time), cohort (similar age group), and life-stage (develop-

mental phases) influences on marital communication for young, middle, and older couples. These researchers found that while younger couples' communication patterns were characterized by high levels of disclosure, conflict, and problem solving, older couples appeared to be more passive, less disclosive, and confirmative (the descriptive use of "we" and "us"). Relationships for older couples reflect commitment, shared history, ability to predict others' views, companionship, and dependence; thus, "the relationship is evaluated based on what it has been through, not on what it has the potential to become" (Sillars & Wilmot, 1989, p. 240). Interestingly, communication becomes a significant factor in couple satisfaction and happiness following the husband's retirement. For this age cohort, wives often view their husbands' retirement as an intrusion into their domestic domain, and the need to negotiate roles and responsibilities becomes essential to the satisfactory continuance of the relationship (Treas, 1983).

Whereas high levels of attraction and affection characterize early marriage, later in life attraction may be substituted for affection and the development of a relationship history (Johnson, 1988). This does not mean, however, that sexuality fails to be a significant part of the marital bond or a continuing physical need for any elderly individual. "Contrary to myths accepted by many in Western society, elderly people are highly sexual beings with sexual thoughts and desires that persist into advanced age for most individuals. Unfortunately, the sexual needs of the elderly are often ignored by family members, caregivers, and society in general" (Hodson & Skein, 1994, p. 219). Congruent with our fears of aging and the aged, our tendency is to withdraw touching, affection, and other forms of intimacy in our interaction with the elderly. These authors encourage family and others (e.g., caregivers, nursing home staff) to engage in affectionate behavior with elderly companions to the degree that the relationship allows.

Let's take a moment to go beyond interpersonal communication and relationships to the influence of media and technology in the communicative lives of the elderly. Perhaps we're inclined to believe (stereotype?) that our senior citizens are fearful and apprehensive of technology; that using a computer,

DVD, or cellular phones is beyond their comprehension or need. On the contrary, a growing body of research indicates that technology is both highly used by our seniors *and* significantly and positively influencing their lives.

In fact, recent research has explored many and varied topics linking technology with our elder citizens such as senior networking with friends and family (LeClaire, 1997); online intergenerational communication (Ward & Smith, 1997); online global senior communities (Furlong, 1997); health support networking between nursing home residents and health care facilities (Gustafson, Gustafson, & Wackerbarth, 1997; Lefton, 1997; Purnell & Sullivan-Schroyer, 1997); health care, medical, and prescription/drug resources and information access (Deatrick, 1997; Post, 1997); development of enhanced assistive technology devices for vision, hearing, mobility, and orthopedic impairments made necessary by the increase in use of these devices by seniors (Kaplan, 1997; Mann, 1997; Public Health Reports, 1998); the increased use of cell phones by seniors for emergency purposes (Finn, 1997); specially designed soft and hardware technology for the senior market (Enders, 1995; Francese, 1994; Wylde, 1995); senior use of technology for reference and library resources (Christenson, 1995; Haber, 1986); and of course, studies exploring reasons for acceptance or rejection of technology use among the elderly (Griffin, 1995).

In essence, although seniors' motivation for using technology might differ from that of younger generations, this research suggests that the market is one worth serious consideration. Additionally, the aging of the Baby Boom generation will trigger increased demand and need for technological devices that are adapted to facilitate senior use. Consider, too, that many of our seniors experienced the invention of television, air travel, and telephones, when they were very young. Our contemporary forms of these innovations are simply updated versions of the originals. Even the earliest computers evolved from "super" adding machines called "sequential analyzers" that were developed in the early 1960s. So there is evidence for our claim—the elderly belong to a culture unique to their age cohort.

We must remember, however, that our senior citizens are also as unique and diverse as most members of the younger population in our society perceive themselves to be (Ade-Ridder & Hennon, 1989). Unfortunately, negative stereotypes of older adulthood and our preoccupation with a youth-oriented society combine to prevent many of us from recognizing the value of the wisdom and experience our seniors have to offer. What *are* some of the stereotypical images that we as a society hold of our aging population? What words would you use to describe a senior citizen? What is the origin of your image of a senior citizen? Who is the model for your image of a senior citizen?

STEREOTYPES OF THE ELDERLY

As previously mentioned, stereotypes are rigid generalities that members of society impose on others with whom they are unfamiliar or do not understand. Stereotypes function as a system of categorization; we often fail to recognize those individuals who do not fit the stereotype. Members of the dominant culture (in this case our youth-oriented culture) commonly stereotype the subordinate and minority culture (the aging population) and draw negative stereotypical inferences both preceding and during intergenerational interaction (Giles et al., 1992).

Interestingly, social stereotypes of older adults pre-1980 are in stark contrast to those of post-1980. According to Rosenbaum and Button (1993) this evolution is partly a result of the Reagan era and increased political sensitivity to the needs of our aging population. Before 1980, the aging were seen as frail, in need of assistance, lacking political strength, and generally, a group of deserving poor that had been largely ignored given the prejudices of a youth-oriented society. After 1980 and the years of Reaganomics, the number of Baby-Boomers reaching middle and older adulthood began to rise. The aging were seen as relatively well off, as a potent political force, and as ready and willing to claim their portion of the federal budget with regard to health and social security benefits (Binstock, 1992).

On an interpersonal level, stereotypes of the elderly held by young, middle-aged, and older adults were investigated by Hummert and colleagues (1994). Although both negative and positive stereotypes emerged across all three age groups (young, middle-aged, and elderly), similarities as well as differences in stereotypical characterizations by these age groups were noted. Among the positive stereotypes, The "Golden Ager" is described as active, adventurous, healthy, lively, wealthy, interesting, liberal, and future oriented (to name only a few). "Perfect Grandparents" are wise, kind, trustworthy, loving, understanding, and family oriented. The "John Wayne Conservative" is retired, conservative, old-fashioned, nostalgic, and religious. The "Activist" (a stereotype identified *only* by the elderly adult subjects) is political, sexual, health-conscious, and liberal. Finally, the "Small Town Neighbor" (also identified by the elderly adults *only*) is old-fashioned, quiet, conservative, tough, and nostalgic.

The negative stereotypes include "Shrew/ Curmudgeon," which is described as bored, complaining, ill tempered, bitter, and a hypochondriac. The "Despondent" is depressed, hopeless, sick, neglected, and afraid. Those who are "Severely Impaired" are described as senile, incompetent, incoherent, feeble, sick, slow thinking, and sexless; "Mildly Impaired" are tired, frustrated, worried, and lonely. The "Recluse" is quiet, timid, dependent, forgetful, and naive. A "Self-centered" elder is greedy, miserly, snobbish, emotionless, and humorless. Finally, the "Elitist" (identified by the elderly adults *only*) is demanding, prejudiced, and wary.

Although these stereotypes seem harmless, and in some cases, humorous, we must not fail to realize the consequences of perpetuating these positive and negative images of older adults. "Any minority community that is not well understood generates myths both in its own and the host community. These myths serve functions for both communities—they demystify, they make life more tolerable, they allow subtle discrimination to continue" (Ebrahim, 1992, p. 52). They may prevent members of one culture from getting to know members of another. How many television advertisements can you recall that depict at least one of these elderly stereotypes needing or using their products? Do you find it easy to picture an elderly individual who fits any of these stereotypes? How about one who does not?

Who or what is most responsible for perpetuating stereotypical images of our older adult population? In a study conducted by Robinson and Skill (1995,

p. 386) results indicated that "the elderly continue to be infrequently seen on television and when they do appear, they occupy lead roles at about one half the rate of all other age groups;" and, in attempting to provide a program that appeals to large and diverse audiences, programs are written in a way that "writers believe the target audience views that group." While the success and appeal of these stereotypical images have yet to be determined, the practice continues to be the basis for creating characters both central and peripheral to the story portrayed. As previously noted, the elderly are diverse and heterogeneous and should be represented in accordance with this fact—*just as other age and cultural groups should be*. As suggested by Robinson and Skill (1995, p. 388):

> A starting point in this rather complex process might be through enhancement of elderly images in the mass media. Diverse portrayals of elderly characters may help improve societal attitudes toward the elderly . . . providing positive and negative portrayals of the elderly in all media will afford audience members of all ages the opportunity to increase their knowledge about the elderly and aging, [and] improve their attitudes toward the elderly and aging.

Take a moment to recall the story described at the beginning of this chapter: *One Ballot, A Lot of Confusion* (*L.A. Times*, Nov. 9, 2000) and the representation of our senior voter in Florida. How did you respond? Was it difficult or easy to imagine a confused elderly voter pondering over the voting process and new ballot? Can you easily imagine a younger person such as yourself being just as confused over the new ballot? How many young people actually voted in the last election?

According to Binstock (1992, p. 331), "persons 65 and older do constitute a large block of participating voters. They represent 16.7-21% of those who actually voted in national elections during the 1980's. And this percentage is likely to increase in the next four decades because of projected increases in the proportion of older persons." Although an initial interpretation of this statistic might compel visions of an elderly voting conglomerate with only their self-interests in mind, the statistic itself fails to reveal the heterogeneity of the older adult constituency with regard to opinions and interest in political issues (Hess, 1992). "Diversity among older persons may be at least as great with respect to political attitudes and behavior as it is in relation to economic, social, and other characteristics" (Binstock, 1992, p. 331). Nonetheless, in relation to the total voting population, they constitute a significant proportion of participating voters.

Not surprisingly, our older adult population is well represented by interest groups whose primary goal is to reach both policy makers and the media. Moreover, given the common (mis)representation of the conflict between younger and older political interests (primarily with regard to government spending), an organization by the name of *Generations United* was formed in order to represent "both the young and the old [in] developing policy that benefits all" and is considered a model for building bridges between generations and their respective political interests while promoting a positive image of multi-generational cooperation to the media (Coombs & Holladay, 1995, p. 335). Some of the groups involved in this coalition include AARP (American Association of Retired Persons), NCOA (National Council on the Aging), Gray Panthers, Children's Defense Fund, and the Child Welfare League of America. As noted by Coombs & Holladay (1995, p. 336):

> Aged interest groups are particularly powerful in the public agenda building, policy agenda building, and policy evaluation processes. The new challenge facing the aged interest groups is deciding how best to use their power and to whom they must communicate their political actions.

Now what is your image of the confused elderly voter?

WHAT ARE THE CONSEQUENCES OF STEREOTYPING THE AGING?

Two startling consequences of stereotyping have been revealed in recent research: First, "those who have preconceived notions about minority group members may unwittingly act upon these beliefs" (Atkinson, Morten, & Sue, 1985, p. 172). Stereotyping might function to unknowingly and unintentionally impose limitations or standards on a group

of people (e.g., using elder-speak, viewing the elderly as feeble and infirm). Second, the group may engage in self-fulfilling behavior that reflects the limitations being imposed on them (e.g., the elderly become recluse and isolated, unwilling to interact for fear of negative evaluation or embarrassment).

Overcoming the tendency to stereotype, although difficult, offers us the opportunity to become familiar with and better understand members of another culture, and thus, avoid imposing undeserved views on a group of people. Unfortunately, interaction with older adults has not been found to reduce the negative effects of stereotypical images of older adults in young children; once the stereotypes have been firmly fixed in their minds, they are difficult to eradicate. Not surprisingly, negative stereotypes of the elderly can create fear of aging and the aged that, although unfounded, impedes and inhibits effective and quality communication between generations.

Does stereotyping function to unknowingly and unintentionally impose limitations or standards on a group of people? Does the group being stereotyped engage in self-fulfilling behavior as a consequence of the limitations being imposed upon them? Using Accommodation Theory as the framework for analysis of accommodating behavior found in communication between generations, Ryan, MacLean, and Orange (1994, p. 273) found that "negative nonverbal behaviors were rated as significantly more likely to occur with patronizing style" and that these behaviors were often based on stereotyped expectations of the elderly interactants. The accommodating nonverbal behaviors included simplification and exaggeration of key components of messages, short topics, elderspeak (baby talk directed toward elders), shorter and less complex utterances, and imperatives/interrogatives/repetitions.

Focusing on a comparison of social skills between young and old interactants, Segrin (1994) found that elders may see themselves as impaired or less skilled, especially in interaction with younger people, more as a result of self-comparison than real inability. This misperception, in turn, leads to lower self-esteem and perhaps less self-confidence in such interactions. These results, and those found by Ryan et al. (1994) suggest that (1) young people tend to interact with their elderly counterparts based on stereotypical notions of older adults (often in relation to perceptions of impaired physical and mental abilities), and (2) that acting on these stereotypes results in deleterious effects on the self-esteem and self-confidence of the elderly.

In fact, in a study conducted by Giles et al. (1992), intergenerational talk between young and old was explored in order to identify characteristics and effects of stereotypical images of the elderly. The study focused on the sociolinguistic behavior of both the older adults and young adults functioning in the roles of initiator and respondent in interaction. These researchers concluded that "the message transmitted (i.e., what is attended to, encoded, produced, and responded to) is affected by beliefs, assumptions, and stereotypes"; and specifically, in the case of the aging population, the stereotypes of decrement, incompetence, and inability transcend both the way in which the message is processed and the response that is produced (Giles et al., 1992, p. 290). Furthermore, older adults were viewed as accommodating these stereotypes by engaging in language that depicted themselves as helpless, dependent, immobile, and victims of old age. The authors refer to this behavior as "instant aging" as many of the older individuals participating in the study described themselves as *active and independent* before engaging in interaction with their youthful counterparts.

How can we transcend the barriers between cultures that stereotypes so systematically place in our way? First, we familiarize ourselves with members of the other culture; then, we try communicating with them. Who are our senior citizens? Are they really greedy, lonely, afraid, incompetent, senile, sexless, inarticulate, forgetful, depressed, stubborn, and all of the other characteristics constituting the negative stereotypes previously mentioned? One intergenerational relationship that has the potential to transcend the negative stereotypes of the aging, and perhaps even the fear of aging itself, is that which exists between grandparents and grandchildren.

THE GRANDPARENT–GRANDCHILD RELATIONSHIP

Although the nature of this relationship is as diverse as the individuals who embrace this intergenerational bond, it engenders a unique communicative character all its own. The diversity characterizing the grandparent–grandchild relationship is influenced by factors such as the age(s) of grandparent and grandchild, the sex of relationship participants (as well as maternal or paternal grandparenthood), ethnicity and cultural background, grandparents' work/retirement status, geographical proximity, marital status of both parents and grandparents, and, of course, grandparents' physical health.

Two decades of research exploring the quality, individuality, and character of this distinctive relationship depict a continuum of grandparental involvement. Early research into the nature of this relationship focused primarily on the enjoyable aspects of the relationship for grandparents, especially in relation to recreational activities and presence on holidays. Recent investigations have found some grandparents taking a more participative role in their grandchildren's lives; this is especially evident in situations of divorce, surrogate child care, and grandparents acting as primary child care providers (e.g., grandparents-as-parents or GAP) (McKay, 1989, 1997; McKay & Caverly, 1995).

The intensity and degree of responsibility accepted by the grandparents largely depends on their own life situation, their age, and relations with their own children. Grandparents' concern for the welfare of their grandchild(ren) must often supersede the welfare of, or relations with, their own child (the grandchild's parent), while balancing concerns for their own health or financial status (Jendrek, 1994). Grandparents' full acceptance of responsibility for grandchild-care is often the result of neglect or abuse effected by mothers' emotional problems, drug addiction, and/or alcoholism; partial acceptance from the desire to assist with child day care (due to mothers' employment), personal self-fulfillment, or the need to feel useful (Jendrek, 1994). These circumstances seem to occur across ethnic groups and geographical areas.

Focusing on the communicative nature of the grandparent–grandchild relationship, interviews with numerous grandmothers, grandfathers, grandsons, and granddaughters of various ages and ethnicities, and in several geographical areas, have provided a plethora of knowledge and understanding about this unique bond. Interestingly, the common thread, no matter what the nature of the relationship, is the desire on the part of grandparents to impart, and the desire by grandchildren to listen to, grandparents' stories of their life experiences, family history, and advice. "Inasmuch as life stories function to help people make, shape, and preserve history, the shared stories between grandparent and grandchild provide some common ground in which to negotiate and maintain a relationship" (Nussbaum & Bettini, 1994, p. 78). For example, grandparents provide grandchildren with a source of identity development by sharing stories about their past experiences and other accounts of family history (Baranowski, 1982). Moreover, grandparents achieve a sense of continuity and satisfaction in knowing that the ideas, beliefs, values, and memories shared are carried on into the future (Mead, 1974). Of particular significance, however, is the storyteller, the grandmother or grandfather who plays an integral part in both the characterization and content of the story told (McKay, 1993). These individuals have a lifetime of wisdom and experience to impart; to be unable to do so is a loss not only to the listener but to the teller as well.

CONCLUSIONS AND IMPLICATIONS

Who are our senior citizens? To summarize, they are a co-culture of individuals who engender patterns of friendship, social activities, communication patterns, and political activity that are distinct from other forms. Their attitudes toward work and retirement vary with their needs, their life and social status, and their work history. They are unique in that many can boast long-term marriage in contrast to a younger generation overwhelmed by high divorce rates. They are both politically active *and* politically diverse; their interest in political, economic, and social issues is heterogeneous, even though their political participation as a whole is of significant proportion. The current age cohort has participated in at least one (and possibly two) World Wars, the Depression, and other significant historical events. They have seen dramatic innovations in electronics and technology, television, and computers. They are as varied and diverse as the younger generations perceive themselves to be.

Can we transcend the stereotypes of our aging population and reap the benefits of their wisdom and experience? The answer to this question is beyond the scope of this chapter; however, beginning with the grandparent–grandchild relationship, we can ask the questions and listen to the answers that may penetrate the obstacles that stereotypes of our elderly have so securely placed in our way.

One easy way to understand the culture of the elderly is to accept and perpetuate the predominantly negative stereotypes so easily accepted by our youth-oriented society. A viable alternative, however, is the recognition that, like many other cultures, there exists as much diversity within the elderly population as between it and any other group (Triandis, 1979). The objective of this chapter has been to introduce members of our elderly population; to make the reader aware of the complex and interesting lives they lead; and, at the very least, to dispel some of the negative myths and stereotypes to which our society adheres in order to avoid thinking about aging and the fear that such thoughts provoke. The communication discipline is uniquely qualified to engage in research exploring those aspects of intergenerational relations that will reveal the elderly as a valuable resource of experience and wisdom, and at the same time dispel stereotypes that have prevented the exchange of such resources in the past.

References

Ade-Ridder, L., & Hennon, C. B. (1989). Introduction: Diversity of lifestyles among the elderly. In L. Ade-Ridder & C. B. Hennon (Eds.), *Lifestyles of the elderly: Diversity in relationships, health, and caregiving* (pp. 1–8). New York: Human Sciences Press.

Atkinson, D. R., Morten, G., & Sue, D. W. (1985). Minority group counseling: An overview. In L. A. Samovar & R. E. Porter (Eds.), *Intercultural communication: A reader*. Belmont, CA: Wadsworth.

Baranowski, M. D. (1982). Grandparent-adolescent relations: Beyond the nuclear family. *Adolescence, 17,* 375–384.

Binstock, R. H. (1992). Aging, politics, and public policy. In B. B. Hess & E. W. Markson (Eds.), *Growing old in America* (pp. 325–340). New Brunswick, NJ: Transaction.

Briggs, B. (1994, October). Door-to-door friendship: The senior companion program. *Good Housekeeping,* 260.

Butler, R. N. (1968). The life review: An interpretation of reminiscence in the aged. In B. Neugarten (Ed.), *Middle age and aging* (pp. 486–496). Chicago: University of Chicago Press.

Catchen, H. (1989). Generational equity: Issues of gender and race. In L. Grau (Ed.), *Women in the later years: Health, social, and cultural perspectives* (pp. 21–38). New York: The Haworth Press.

Christenson, M. A. (1995). Assessing an elder's need for assistance: One technological tool. *Generations, 19*, 54–55.

Cicirelli, V. G., & Nussbaum, J. F. (1989). Relationships with siblings in late life. In J. F. Nussbaum (Ed.), *Lifespan communication: Normative processes* (pp. 283–300). Hillsdale, NJ: Lawrence Erlbaum.

Clipp, E. C., & George, L. K. (1990). Caregiver needs and patterns of social support. *Journal of Gerontology, 45(3)*, 102–111.

Coombs, W. T., & Holladay, S. J. (1995). The emerging political power of the elderly. In J. Nussbaum & J. Coupland (Eds.), *Handbook of communication and aging research* (pp. 317–342). Hillsdale, NJ: Lawrence Erlbaum.

Coupland, N., & Coupland, J. (1995). Discourse, identity, and aging. In J. Nussbaum & J. Coupland (Eds.), *Handbook of communication and aging research* (pp. 79–104). Hillsdale, NJ: Lawrence Erlbaum.

Deatrick, D. (1997). Senior-med: Creating a network to help manage medications. *Generations, 21*, 59–60.

Duran, R. L. (1989). Social communicative competence in adulthood. In J. F. Nussbaum (Ed.), *Life-span communication: Normative processes* (pp. 195–224). Hillsdale, NJ: Lawrence Erlbaum.

Ebrahim, S. (1992). Health and ageing within ethnic minorities. In K. Morgan (Ed.), *Gerontology: Responding to an ageing society* (pp. 50–62). London: The British Society of Gerontology.

Eckert, J. W., & Shulman, S. C. (1996). Daughters caring for their aging mothers: A midlife developmental process. *Journal of Gerontological Social Work, 25(3/4)*, 17–32.

Emerman, J. (1997). 'You say you want a revolution?' Toward a virtual community on aging. *Generations, 21*, 63–68.

Enders, A. (1995). The role of technology in the lives of older people. *Generations, 19*, 7–12.

Finn, J. (1997). Aging and information technology: The promise and the challenge. *Generations, 21*, 5–6.

Francese, P. (1994). Cellular consumers. *American Demographics, 16*, 30–35.

Furlong, M. (1997). Creating online community for older adults. *Generations, 21*, 33–35.

Giles, H., Coupland, N., Coupland, J., Williams, A., & Nussbaum, J. (1992). Intergenerational talk and communication with older people. *International Journal of Aging and Human Development, 34(4)*, 271–297.

Griffin, L. N. (1995). Why older people accept or reject assistive technology. *Generations, 19*, 41–46.

Gustafson, D. H., Gustafson, R. C., & Wackerbarth, S. (1997). CHESS (Comprehensive Health Enhancement Support System): Health information and decision support for patients and families. *Generations, 21*, 56–58.

Haber, P. A. (1986). Technology in aging. *The Gerontologist, 26*, 350–357.

Hanson, M. J. (1994). How we treat the elderly. *The Hastings Center Report, 24*, 4–6.

Harwood, J., Giles, H., & Ryan, E. B. (1995). Aging, communication, and Intergroup Theory: Social identity and intergenerational communication. In J. Nussbaum & J. Coupland (Eds.), *Handbook of communication and aging research* (pp. 133–160). Hillsdale, NJ: Lawrence Erlbaum.

Hess, B. B. (1992). Growing old in America in the 1990's. In B. B. Hess & E. W. Markson (Eds.), *Growing old in America* (pp. 5–22). New Brunswick, NJ: Transaction.

Hodson, D. S., & Skein, P. (1994). Sexuality and aging: The Hammerlock of myths. *Journal of Applied Gerontology, 13(3)*, 219–235.

Hummert, M. L., Garstka, T. A., Shaner, J. L., & Strahm, S. (1994). Stereotypes of the elderly held by young, middle-aged, and elderly adults. *Journal of Gerontology, 49(5)*, 240–249.

Jendrek, M. P. (1994). Grandparents who parent their grandchildren: Circumstances and decisions. *The Gerontologist, 34(2)*, 206–216.

Johnson, C. L. (1988). Relationships among family members and friends in later life. In R. M. Milardo (Ed.), *Families and social networks* (pp. 168–169). Newbury Park, CA: Sage.

Kaminsky, M. (1984). The arts and social work: Writing and reminiscing in old age: Voices from within the process. *Journal of Gerontological Social Work, 7*, 3–18.

Kaplan, D. (1997). Access to technology: Unique challenges for people with disabilities. *Generations, 21*, 24–27.

Klinger-Vartabedian, L., & Wispe, L. (1989). The influence of age difference in marriage on longevity. In J. F. Nussbaum (Ed.), *Life-span communication: Normative processes* (pp. 301–318). Hillsdale, NJ: Lawrence Erlbaum.

Leclair, R. B. (1997). How a computer and Seniornet changed my life. *Generations, 21*, 36–37.

Lefton, A. B. (1997). Confidentiality and security in information technology. *Generations, 21*, 50–52.

Lo Gerfo, M. (1980). Three ways of reminiscence in theory and practice. *International Journal of Aging and Human Development, 12,* 39–48.

Mann, W. C. (1997). Common telecommunications technology for promoting safety, independence, and social interaction for older people with disabilities. *Generations, 21,* 28–29.

Mare, M. L., & Fitzpatrick, M. A. (1995). The aging couple. In J. Nussbaum (Ed.), *Handbook of communication and aging* (pp. 185–206). Hillsdale, NJ: Lawrence Erlbaum.

McKay, V. C. (1989). The grandparent-grandchild relationship. In J. F. Nussbaum (Ed.), *Life-span communication: Normative processes* (pp. 257–282). Hillsdale, NJ: Lawrence Erlbaum.

McKay, V. C. (1993). Making connections: Narrative as the expression of continuity between generations of grandparents and grandchildren. In N. Coupland & J. Nussbaum (Eds.), *Discourse and lifespan identity* (pp. 173–185). London: Sage.

McKay, V. C. (1997, November). *The grandparent-grandchild phenomenon: The temporal context as revealed through grandparents' discourse.* Competitively selected paper presented at the annual conference of the National Communication Association, Chicago, IL.

McKay, V. C., & Caverly, R. S. (1995). Relationships in later life: The nature of inter- and intragenerational ties among grandparents, grandchildren, and adult siblings. In J. Nussbaum (Ed.), *Handbook of communication and aging* (pp. 207–225). Hillsdale, NJ: Lawrence Erlbaum.

Mead, M. (1974). Grandparents as educators. *Teacher College Record, 76,* 240–249.

Moody, H. R. (1984). Reminiscence and the recovery of the public world. *Journal of Gerontological Social Work, 7,* 157–166.

Morris, R., and Bass, S. A. (1992). A new class in America: A revisionist view of retirement. In B. B. Hess and E. W. Markson (Eds.), *Growing old in America* (pp. 93–105). New Brunswick, NJ: Transaction.

Nussbaum, J., & Bettini, L. M. (1994). Shared stories of the grandparent-grandchild relationship. *International Journal of Aging and Human Development, 39(1),* 67–80.

Nussbaum, J. F., Thompson, T., & Robinson, J. D. (1989). *Communication and Aging.* New York: Harper & Row.

Pallett-Hehn, P., & Lucas, M. (1994). LIFE: Learning Informally From Elders. *The Gerontologist, 34(2),* 267–270.

Perkins, K., & Tice, C. (1994). Suicide and older adults: The strengths perspective in practice. *Journal of Applied Gerontology, 13(4),* 438–454.

Porter, R. E., & Samovar, L. A. (1985). Approaching intercultural communication. In L. A. Samovar & R. E. Porter (Eds.), *Intercultural communication: A reader* (pp. 15–30). Belmont, CA: Wadsworth.

Post, J. A. (1997). Internet resources on aging. *Generations, 21,* 69–70.

Prince, R. (1994, August 1). Where the elderly find learning brings its joys. *New York Times,* 9.

Purnell, M., & Sullivan-Schroyer, P. (1997). Nursing home residents using computers: The Winchester House. *Generations, 21,* 61–62.

Roberto, K. A., & Scott, J. P. (1989). Friendships in late life: A rural-urban comparison. In L. Ade-Ridder and C. B. Hennon (Eds.), *Lifestyles of the elderly: Diversity in relationships, health, and caregiving* (pp. 129–141). New York: Human Sciences Press.

Robinson, J. D., & Skill, T. (1995). Media usage and portrayals of the elderly. In J. Nussbaum (Ed.), *Handbook of communication and aging* (pp. 359–392). Hillsdale, NJ: Lawrence Erlbaum.

Rosenbaum, W. A., & Button, J. W. (1993). The unquiet future of intergenerational politics. *The Gerontologist, 33(4),* 481–490.

Ryan, E. B., MacLean, M., & Orange, J. B. (1994). Inappropriate accommodation in communication to elders: Inferences about nonverbal correlates. *International Journal of Aging and Human Development, 39(4),* 273–291.

Schemo, D. J. (1994, September 5). Age cannot wither the magic of theatre. *New York Times,* 9.

Segrin, C. (1994). Social skills and psychosocial problems among the elderly. *Research on Aging, 16(3),* 301–321.

Sillars, A. L., & Wilmot, W. W. (1989). Marital communication across the life-span. In J. F. Nussbaum (Ed.), *Life-span communication: Normative processes* (pp. 225–254). Hillsdale, NJ: Lawrence Erlbaum.

Sporakowski, M. J., & Axelson, L. V. (1989). Long-term marriages. In L. Ade-Ridder and C. B. Hennon (Eds.), *Lifestyles of the elderly: Diversity in relationships, health, and caregiving* (pp. 9–28). New York: Human Sciences Press.

Treas, J. (1983). Aging and the family. In D. S. Woodruff & J. E. Birren (Eds.), *Aging: Scientific perspectives and social issues.* Monterey, CA: Brooks/Cole.

Triandis, H. C. (1979). Values, attitudes, and interpersonal behavior. *Nebraska Symposium on Motivation* (pp. 195–259).

Ward, C. R., & Smith, T. (1997). Forging intergenerational communities through information technology. *Generations, 21,* 38–41.

Wylde, M. A. (1995). If you could see it through my eyes: Perspectives on technology for older people. *Generations, 19,* 5–6.

Concepts and Questions

1. How does the co-culture of the elderly differ from the dominant culture in the United States?
2. How do the elderly's personal positive and negative stereotypes differ from the stereotypes held by the younger members of the dominant culture?
3. How do stereotypes of the elderly affect intergenerational communication?
4. What social dynamics affect grandparent–grandchild communication?
5. How would you explain the following sentence: In many cases, the diversity (or heterogeneity) within a culture is greater than the diversity we find in making comparisons between cultures?
6. According to McKay, why are friendships important to older adults?
7. What are some of the major communication patterns existing in "inter- and intragenerational talk"?
8. What does McKay mean when she writes, "The elderly belong to a culture unique to their age cohort"?
9. How would you answer the following question: Who or what is most responsible for perpetuating stereotypical images of our adult population?
10. How well do members of the elderly co-culture seem to adapt to advances and innovations in technology?

"Which is My Good Leg?": Cultural Communication of Persons with Disabilities

DAWN O. BRAITHWAITE

CHARLES A. BRAITHWAITE

Jonathan is an articulate, intelligent, 35-year-old professional man, who has used a wheelchair since he became paraplegic when he was 20 years old. He recalls taking a nondisabled woman out to dinner at a nice restaurant. When the waitress came to take their order, she looked only at his date and asked, in a condescending tone, "and what would *he* like to eat for dinner?" At the end of the meal, the waitress presented Jonathan's date with the check and thanked her for her patronage.[1]

Kim describes her recent experience at the airport: "A lot of people always come up and ask can they push my wheelchair. And, I can do it myself. They were invading my space, concentration, doing what I wanted to do, which I enjoy doing; doing what I was doing *on my own*. . . . And each time I said, 'No, I'm doing fine!' People looked at me like I was strange, you know, crazy or something. One person started pushing my chair anyway. I said [in an angry tone], 'Don't touch the wheelchair.' And then she just looked at me like I'd slapped her in the face."

Jeff, a nondisabled student, was working on a group project for class that included Helen, who uses a wheelchair. He related an incident that really embarrassed him. "I wasn't thinking and I said to the group, 'Let's run over to the student union and get some coffee.' I was mortified when I looked over at Helen and remembered that she can't walk. I felt like a real jerk." Helen later described the incident with Jeff, recalling:

> At yesterday's meeting, Jeff said, "Let's run over to the union" and then he looked over at me and I thought he would die. It didn't bother me at all, in fact, I use that phrase myself. I felt bad that Jeff was so embarrassed, but I didn't know what to say. Later in the group meeting I made it a point to say, "I've got to be running along now." I hope that Jeff noticed and felt OK about what he said."

Erik Weihenmayer, the blind climber who recently scaled Mt. Everest, demonstrated another example of the regular use of nondisabled language by the disabled. During an interview with Matt Lauer on NBC's *Today Show* (June 12, 2001), he remarked that he was glad to get home so that he "could *see* his family."

Although it may seem hard for some of us to believe, these scenarios represent common experiences for people with physical disabilities and are indicative of what often happens when people with disabilities and nondisabled others communicate.

The passage of the Americans with Disabilities Act (ADA), a "bill of rights" for persons with disabilities, highlighted the fact that they are now a large, vocal, and dynamic group within the United States (Braithwaite & Labrecque, 1994; Braithwaite & Thompson, 2000). Disabled people represent one group within American culture that is growing in numbers. One in five people in the United States has some type of disability, which means that people with disabilities constitute a large segment of the American population (Cunningham & Coombs, 1997; Pardeck, 1998).

There are two reasons for increases in the numbers of persons with disabilities. First, as the American population ages and has a longer life expectancy, more people will live long enough to develop age-related disabilities. Second, advances in medical technologies now allow persons with disabilities to survive life-threatening illnesses and injuries, whereas survival was not possible in earlier times. For example, when actor Christopher Reeve became quadriplegic after a horse-riding accident in May 1995, newer advances in medical technology allowed him to survive his injuries and to live with a severe disability.

In the past, most people with disabilities were sheltered and many were institutionalized, but today they are very much a part of the American mainstream. Each of us will have contact with people who have disabilities within our families, among our friends, or within the workplace. Some of us will develop disabilities ourselves. Says Marie, a college student who became paralyzed after diving into a swimming pool:

> I knew there were disabled people around, but I never thought this would happen to me. I never even *knew* a disabled person before *I* became one. If before this happened, I saw a person in a wheelchair, I would have been uncomfortable and not known what to say.

Marie's comment highlights the fact that many nondisabled people feel extremely uncomfortable interacting with disabled people. As people with disabilities continue to live, work, and study in American culture, there is a need for both nondisabled and disabled persons to know how to communicate with one another.

DISABILITY AND CULTURAL COMMUNICATION

The goal of this chapter is to focus on communication between nondisabled persons and persons with disabilities as *intercultural communication* (Carbaugh, 1990). This claim is made because, as will be demonstrated later, persons with disabilities use a distinctive speech code that implicates specific models of personhood, society, and strategic action (see Donal Carbaugh's article in Chapter 1) that are qualitatively different from those models used by nondisabled persons. Because persons with disabilities are treated so differently in American society, distinctive meanings, rules, and speech habits develop that act as a powerful resource for creating and reinforcing perceptions of cultural differences between persons with disabilities and nondisabled persons. The distinctive verbal and nonverbal communication used by persons with disabilities creates a sense of cultural identity that constitutes a unique social reality.

Several researchers have described the communication of disabled and nondisabled persons as cultural communication (Braithwaite, 1990, 1996;

Emry & Wiseman, 1987; Fox et al., 2000; Padden & Humphries, 1988). That is, we recognize that persons with disabilities develop certain unique communicative characteristics that are not shared by the majority of nondisabled individuals in U.S. society. In fact, except for individuals who are born with disabilities, becoming disabled is similar to assimilating from being a member of the nondisabled majority to being a member of a minority culture (Braithwaite, 1990, 1996). That is, the onset of a physical disability requires learning new ways of thinking and talking about oneself and developing new ways of communicating with others.

Adopting a cultural view in this chapter, we start by introducing communication problems that can arise between persons in the nondisabled culture and those in the disabled culture. Second, we discuss some of the weaknesses of the earlier research on communication between nondisabled and disabled persons. Third, we will discuss research findings from interviews with people who have physical disabilities. Results from these interviews show that people with disabilities are engaged in a process of redefinition; that is, they critique the prevailing stereotypes about disability and they communicate in order to redefine what it means to be disabled. Finally, we will talk about important contributions both scholars and students of intercultural communication can make to improve relations between people with and without disabilities.

CHALLENGES FOR COMMUNICATORS WHO ARE DISABLED

When we adopt a cultural view and attempt to understand the communicative challenges faced by people with disabilities, it is useful to distinguish between "disability" and "handicap." Even though people often use these two terms interchangeably in everyday conversation, their meanings are quite different. The two terms implicate different relationships between persons with disabilities and the larger society. The term *disability* describes those limitations that a person can overcome or compensate by some means. Crewe and Athelstan (1985) identified five "key life functions" that may be affected

by disability: (1) mobility, (2) employment, (3) self-care, (4) social relationships, and (5) communication. Some individuals are often able to compensate for physical challenges associated with the first three key life functions through assisting devices (e.g., using a wheelchair or cane), through training (e.g., physical therapy or training on how to take care of one's personal needs), through assistance (e.g., hiring a personal care assistant), or through occupational therapy to find suitable employment.

A disability becomes a *handicap* when the physical or social environment interacts with it to impede a person in some aspect of his or her life (Crewe & Athelstan, 1985). For example, a disabled individual with paraplegia can function well in the physical environment using a wheelchair, ramps, and curb cuts, but he or she is handicapped when buildings and/or public transportation are not accessible to wheelchair users. When a society is willing and/or able to create adaptations, disabled persons have the ability to achieve personal control and lead increasingly independent lives, which is important to their self-esteem and health (Braithwaite & Harter, 2000; Cogswell, 1977; DeLoach & Greer, 1981). For people with disabilities, personal control and independence are vitally important and "maintenance of identity and self-worth are tied to the perceived ability to control the illness, minimize its intrusiveness, and be independent" (Lyons et al., 1995, p. 134). This does not mean that people with disabilities deny their physical condition, but rather that they find ways to deal with it and lead their lives.

In fact, it is important to realize that the practical and technological accommodations that are made to adapt the physical environment for people with disabilities are useful for nondisabled people as well. Most of us are unaware of just how handicapped we would be without these physical adaptations. For example, our offices are located on the upper floors of our respective office buildings. We know that stairs take up a significant amount of space in a building. Space used for the stairwell on each level takes the place of at least one office per floor. So, the most space-efficient way to get people to the second floor would be a climbing rope, which would necessitate only a relatively small opening on each floor; however, very few of us could climb a rope to reach our offices on the second story, so we would be handicapped without stairs or elevators. When a student is walking with a heavy load of library books, automatic door openers, ramps, curb cuts, elevators, and larger doorways become important environmental adaptations that everyone can use and appreciate. Physical limitations become handicaps for all of us when the physical environment cannot be adapted to preempt our shortcomings.

Challenges to Relationships of People with Disabilities

Although it is possible to identify and to cope with physical challenges associated with mobility, self-care, and employment, the two key life functions of social relationships and communication are often much more formidable. It is less difficult to detect and correct physical barriers than it is to deal with the insidious social barriers facing people with disabilities. Coleman and DePaulo (1991) would label these social barriers as "psychological disabling," which is even more common in Western culture where "much value is placed on physical bodies and physical attractiveness" (p. 64).

When people with disabilities begin relationships with nondisabled people, the challenges associated with forming any new relationship are greater. For nondisabled people, this may be caused by a lack of experience interacting with people who are disabled. This leads to high uncertainty about how to talk with a person who is disabled. The nondisabled person feels uncertain about what to say or how to act because he or she is afraid of saying or doing the wrong thing or of hurting the feelings of the person with the disability, much like Jeff did with his group member, Helen, in the example at the beginning of this chapter. As a result, people may feel overly self-conscious and their actions may be constrained, self-controlled, and rigid because they feel uncomfortable and uncertain (Belgrave & Mills, 1981; Braithwaite 1990; Dahnke, 1983; Higgins, 1992). The nondisabled person may try to communicate appropriately, however, "Wishing to act in a way acceptable to those with disabilities, they may unknowingly act offensively, patronizing disabled people with unwanted sympathy" (Higgins, 1992, p. 105).

Interestingly, researchers have found that the type of disability a person possesses does not change the way nondisabled persons react to them (Fichten et al., 1991). So, high levels of uncertainty can negatively affect interaction and relationship development between people. It becomes easier to avoid that person rather than deal with not knowing what to do or say. Although Uncertainty Reduction Theory can be overly simplistic, especially when applied to ongoing relationships, it can help us understand some of the initial discomfort nondisabled people may have when interacting with a stranger or early acquaintance who is disabled.

Even when a nondisabled person tries to "say the right thing," wanting to communicate acceptance to the person with the disability, his or her nonverbal behavior may communicate rejection and avoidance (Thompson, 1982). For example, people with disabilities have observed that many nondisabled persons may keep a greater physical distance, avoid eye contact, avoid mentioning the disability, or cut the conversation short (Braithwaite, 1990, 1991, 1996). In this case, a person's disability becomes a handicap in the social environment because it can block the development of a relationship with a nondisabled person, who finds the interaction too uncomfortable. In all, nondisabled people hold many stereotypes of people from the disabled culture. Coleman and DePaulo (1991) discuss some of these stereotypes concerning disabled people:

> For example they often perceive them as dependent, socially introverted, emotionally unstable, depressed, hypersensitive, and easily offended, especially with regard to their disability. In addition, disabled people are often presumed to differ from nondisabled people in moral character, social skills, and political orientation. (p. 69)

Our long experience talking with nondisabled people about interacting with persons with disabilities has shown us that many nondisabled people find the prospect of these interactions uncomfortable. They tell us they are afraid of saying or doing the wrong thing and embarrassing or hurting the person who is disabled. In addition, nondisabled persons often find themselves with conflicting advice concerning what is expected of them or how to act. On the one hand, they have been taught to "help the handicapped" and, on the other hand, they were told to "treat all people equally." Americans usually conceptualize persons as "individuals" who "have rights" and "make their own choices" (Carbaugh, 1988). When nondisabled persons encounter a person with a disability, however, this model of personhood creates a serious dilemma. For example, should one help a person with a disability open a door or try to help them up if they fall? Nondisabled persons greatly fear saying the wrong thing, such as "See you later!" to a blind person or "Why don't you run by the store on your way home?" to a person using a wheelchair. In the end, it simply seems to be easier to avoid situations where one might have to interact with a disabled person rather than face feelings of discomfort and uncertainty.

It should not be surprising to learn that most people with disabilities are well aware of these feelings and fears many nondisabled persons have. In fact, in research interviews, people with disabilities reveal that they believe they "can just tell" who is uncomfortable around them or not. They are able to describe in great detail both the verbal and nonverbal signals of discomfort and avoidance nondisabled persons portray that we described previously (Braithwaite, 1990, 1996). People with disabilities report that when they meet nondisabled persons, they would hope to get the discomfort "out of the way," and they want the nondisabled person to treat them as a "person like anyone else," rather than focus solely on their disability (Braithwaite, 1991, 1996). Most often they develop ways of communicating that allow them to have their needs met and, if possible, help reduce the uncertainty and discomfort of the nondisabled person (Braithwaite & Eckstein, 2000). For example, two men who are wheelchair users described how they avoid situations where they need to ask strangers for help getting out of their van in a parking lot:

> Well, I have a mobile phone. . . . I will call into the store and let the store manager or whoever know, "Hey, we're in a white minivan and if you look out your window, you can see us! We're two guys in wheelchairs, can you come out and help us get out of the van?"

These men described how they plan ahead to avoid putting nondisabled strangers in potentially uncomfortable communication situations.

Problems with the Research

When we first began looking at the research on communication between nondisabled and disabled persons, three problems came clearly to the forefront. First, very little is known about the communication behavior of disabled people. Although a few researchers have studied disabled persons' communication, most of them have studied nondisabled persons' *reactions* to disabled others. These studies on "attitudes toward disabled persons" are analogous to the many studies that look at majority members' attitudes toward other "minority groups." A look at the intercultural literature as a whole reveals few studies from the perspective of persons representing the minority. Some improvement has been made over the years, but there is still relatively little information on communication from the perspective of people with disabilities. A second, and related, problem was that many researchers talk *about* persons with disabilities, not *with* them. People with disabilities rarely have been represented in survey data; most often these studies consist of nondisabled people reporting their impressions of disabled people. In experimental studies the disabled person is most often "played" by a nondisabled person using a wheelchair. There are still too few studies that give us a sense of how people with and without disabilities interact with one another.

Third, and most significant, the research has been most often conducted from the perspective of the nondisabled person; that is, what *should* people with disabilities *do* to make nondisabled others feel more comfortable? Coming from this perspective, researchers do not give much consideration to the effects on the person with the disability. For example, several studies revealed that nondisabled persons are more comfortable when people with disabilities disclose about their disability, so they suggested that disabled people should self-disclose to make nondisabled others more comfortable. Braithwaite (1991) points out that these researchers have forgotten to look at how self-disclosing might affect persons who are disabled. Therefore, what we see coming from much of the nondisabled-oriented research is an *ethnocentric bias*, which ignores the perspective of people of the disabled culture. Although there has been more research from the perspective of disabled interactants in recent years, there are still few databased studies, and we still have a very incomplete picture of the communication of people who are disabled.

In the remainder of this chapter, we will present selected findings from ongoing studies conducted from the perspectives of disabled people concerning their communication with nondisabled others. To date, more than 100 in-depth interviews have been completed with adults who are physically disabled. All of these people have disabilities that are visible to an observer, and none of them has significant communication-related disabilities (e.g., blindness, deafness, speech impairments). The goal of the research has been to describe communication with nondisabled people from the frame of reference of people who are disabled. Doing research by talking *with* people who are disabled helps elicit information that is important to them, and the researcher strives to describe patterns of responses from the interviews. The interview format allows people with disabilities to describe experiences from their own cultural framework.

PROCESS OF REDEFINITION

A central theme emerging from the interviews is what we call *redefinition*; that is, people who are disabled critique the prevailing stereotypes about being disabled and create new ways of perceiving themselves and their disability. We were able to see three types of redefinition: (1) redefining the self as part of a "new" culture, (2) redefining the concept of disability, and (3) redefining disability for the dominant culture.

Redefining the Self as Part of the Disabled Culture

Most disabled people see themselves as part of a minority group or a co-culture. For some of the interviewees, this definition crosses disability lines; that is, their definition of "disabled" includes all those who have disabilities. For others, the definition is not as broad; when they think of disability they are thinking about others with the same type of disability they have. For example, some of the people with

mobility-related disabilities also talked about blind and deaf people when they discussed disability, whereas others talked only about other wheelchair users. However narrowly or broadly they defined it, however, many do see themselves as part of a minority culture. For example, one of the interviewees described that being disabled "is like *West Side Story*. Tony and Maria; white and Puerto Rican. They were afraid of each other; ignorant of each others' cultures. People are people." Another man explained his view:

> First of all, I belong to a subculture (of disability) because of the way I have to deal with things, being in the medical system, welfare. There is the subculture. . . . I keep one foot in the nondisabled culture and one foot in my own culture. One of the reasons I do that is so that I don't go nuts.

This man's description of the "balancing act" between cultures demonstrates that membership in the disabled culture has several similarities to the experiences of other American cultural groups. Many of the interviewees have likened their own experiences to those of other cultural groups, particularly to the experiences of American people of color. Interviewees described the loss of status and power that comes from being disabled, and they expressed that they believe many people were uncomfortable with them simply because they are different.

When taking a cultural view, it is important to recognize that not everyone comes to the culture the same way. Some people are born with disabilities and others acquire them later. For those people who are not born with a disability, membership in the culture is a process that emerges over time. For some, the process is an incremental one, as in the case of a person with a degenerative disease like multiple sclerosis that develops over many years. For a person who has a sudden-onset disability, such as breaking one's neck in an accident and "waking up as quadriplegic," moving from the majority (a "normal" person) to the minority (a person who is disabled) may happen in a matter of seconds. This sudden transition into the disabled culture presents many significant challenges of redefinition and readjustment in all facets of an individual's life (Braithwaite, 1990; 1996; Goffman, 1963).

If disability is a culture, when does one become part of that culture? Even though a person is physically disabled, how they redefine themselves, from "normal" or nondisabled to disabled, is a process that develops over time. It is important to understand that becoming physically disabled does not mean that one immediately has an awareness of being part of the disabled culture (Braithwaite, 1990, 1996). In fact, for most people, adjusting to disability happens in a series of stages or phases (Braithwaite, 1990; DeLoach & Greer, 1981; Padden & Humphries, 1988). DeLoach and Greer (1981) described three phases of an individual's adjustment to disability: stigma isolation, stigma recognition, and stigma incorporation. Their model helps us understand what is occurring in the process of adjustment to disability as acculturation. During this process, persons with disabilities progress from the onset of their disability to membership in the disabled culture.

The first phase, *stigma isolation*, occurs upon becoming disabled. At this time, individuals focus on rehabilitation and all of the physical changes and challenges they are experiencing. It is likely that they have not yet noticed the changes in their social relationships and communication with nondisabled others.

The second phase, *stigma recognition*, occurs when people who are disabled realize that their life and relationships have changed dramatically and they try to find ways to minimize the effects of their disability. They may try to return to normal routines and old relationships. This can be a frustrating phase because things have often changed more than the disabled people first realize. Especially when trying to reestablish old relationships, newly disabled people may find that their old friends are no longer comfortable with them or that, without shared activities, the friendships may lapse. At this point, people who are disabled start to become aware that they are now interacting as a member of a different culture than they were before, and they begin to assimilate the new culture into their identity and behavior (Braithwaite, 1990; 1996).

This begins the third phase, what DeLoach and Greer (1981) call *stigma incorporation*. At this point, people with a disability begin to integrate being disabled into their identity, their definition of self. They can see both the positive and negative aspects of being disabled and begin to develop ways to overcome and cope with the negative aspects of disability (DeLoach & Greer, 1981). In this stage of adjustment, people with disabilities develop ways of behaving and communicating so they are able to successfully function in the nondisabled culture (Braithwaite, 1990; 1996). This is what Morse and Johnson (1991) call "regaining wellness," when newly disabled individuals begin to take back control of their own lives and relationships, to live as independently as possible, and to adapt to new ways of doing things in their lives. At this point, they are able to develop ways of communicating with nondisabled others that help them live successfully as part of the disabled and nondisabled culture simultaneously (Braithwaite, 1990; 1991; 1996; Braithwaite & Labrecque, 1994; Emry & Wiseman, 1987) or what disability researcher Susan Fox has labeled as interability, intergroup communication (see Fox et al., 2000).

In this phase, then, persons with disabilities incorporate the role of disability into their identity and into their life. One man said: "You're the same person you were. You just don't do the same things you did before." Another put it this way: "If anyone refers to me as an amputee, that is guaranteed to get me madder than hell! I don't deny the leg amputation, but I am ME. I am a whole person. ONE." During this phase, people can come to terms with both the negative and positive changes in their lives. One woman expressed:

> I find myself telling people that this has been the worst thing that has happened to me. It has also been one of the best things. It forced me to examine what I felt about myself. . . . my confidence is grounded in me, not in other people. As a woman, I am not as dependent on clothes, measurements, but what's inside me.

Christopher Reeve demonstrated the concept of stigma incorporation in an interview with Barbara Walters, four months after his devastating accident:

> You also gradually discover, as I'm discovering, that your body is not you. The mind and the spirit must take over. And that's the challenge as you move from obsessing about "Why me?" and "It's not fair" and move into "Well, what is the potential?" And, now, four months down the line I see opportunities and

potential I wasn't capable of seeing back in Virginia in June . . . genuine joy and being alive means more. Every moment is more intense than it ever was.

We can see in this example that stigma incorporation, becoming part of the disabled culture, is a process that develops over time.

REDEFINING DISABILITY

A third type of redefinition discussed by interviewees was redefining the concept of disability. For example, to help others redefine disability, one interviewee will say to them: "People will say, 'Thank God I'm not handicapped.' And I'll say, 'Let's see, how tall are you? Tell me how you get something off that shelf up there!'" His goal in this interchange is to make others see disability as one of many *characteristics* of a person. From this perspective, everyone is helped and handicapped in one way or another—by height, weight, sex, ethnicity, or physical attributes—and people must work to overcome those characteristics of themselves that are handicapping. Short people may need a stool to reach something on a high shelf, and people who are very tall may be stared at and certainly will not be able to drive small, economy-size cars. Most middle-aged professors cannot climb a rope to their office and need the accommodation of stairs. Similarly, people with disabilities must adapt to the physical challenges presented to them. One interviewee, who conducts workshops in disability awareness, talked about how he helps nondisabled people redefine disability:

> I will say to people "How many of you made the clothes that you're wearing?" "How many of you grew the food that you ate yesterday?" "How many of you built the house that you live in?" Nobody raises their hand. Then after maybe five of those, I'll say "And I bet you think you're independent." And I'll say, "I'll bet you, if we could measure how independent you feel in your life versus how independent I feel in mine that I would rate just as high as you do. And yet here I am 'depending' to have people get me dressed, undressed, on and off the john, etc. It's all in our heads, folks. Nobody is really independent." I can see them kind of go "Yeah, I never thought of it that

way." And they begin to understand how it is that somebody living with this situation can feel independent. That independence really is a feeling and an attitude. It's not a physical reality.

It is important to remember that disability is context-specific. For example, a blind person will function better in a dark room than a sighted person, who is handicapped in that environment. Recently, the first author of this chapter spent several days at Gallaudet University in Washington D.C. At Gallaudet, where most students are deaf, the *author* was disabled because she needed interpreters to talk with the students there. At Gallaudet, people talk about being part of Deaf culture, but not about being disabled.

Redefining disability can also be reflected through changing the language we use to talk about disability. One interviewee objected to being called a "handicapped person," preferring the label "persons with a handicapping condition." He explained why: "You emphasize that person's identity and then you do something about the condition." The goal is to speak in ways that emphasize the *person*, rather than the disability. One interviewee, who had polio as a child, rejected the term "polio victim" and preferred to label herself as "a person whose arms and legs do not function very well." One way we have found to accentuate the person is to talk about "*people* with disabilities" rather than "disabled people." The goal is to stress the person first, before introducing the disability, much like using the label "persons of color." These are all forms of strategic action that help create and maintain a sense of unique cultural identity among persons with disabilities (Braithwaite, 1996; Braithwaite & Thompson, 2000).

Redefining disability is also reflected in sensitizing oneself to commonly used labels for being disabled as being a "polio victim," "arthritis sufferer," "being confined to a wheelchair," or "wheelchair bound." When trying to redefine disability as a characteristic of the person, one can change these phrases to "a person with polio," "a person who has arthritis," or a "wheelchair user." At first glance, some readers may think this is no more than an attempt at political correctness, but those who study language and culture know how strongly the words we use affect our perception of others. The way people with disabilities are labeled will affect how they are seen and how they perceive themselves. One of the interviewees discussed her dislike of all the labels that stereotype disabled people negatively. She used a humorous example, talking about what is commonly referred to as "handicapped parking." She explained, "I'd like to call it 'acceptable parking' because there's nothing wrong with the parking—it's not handicapped! The point is, I'd like to stress more positive terms."

There have also been changes in the terms that refer to nondisabled people. In the interviews it was common to use the term "nondisabled" rather than "able bodied" or "normal." Several interviewees used the phrase "TABs" as a humorous reference term for nondisabled people. "TAB" is short for "temporarily able-bodied." One interviewee joked, "Everyone is a TAB. . . . I just got mine earlier than you!" Being called a "TAB" reminds nondisabled persons that no one is immune from disability. Finally, researcher Susan Fox has suggested that we avoid talking about the communication of disabled and nondisabled people and instead use the phrase "interability communication" (see Fox et al., 2000). However we do it, the language we use both creates and reflects the view of people with disabilities and disabled culture.

In addition to redefining disability, the interviewees also redefined "assisting devices" like wheelchairs or canes. For example, one man told the following story about redefining his prosthetic leg:

> Now there were two girls about eight playing and I was in my shorts. And I'll play games with them and say, "which is my good leg?" And that gets them to thinking. Well this one [he pats his artificial leg] is not nearly as old as the other one!

Another interviewee redefined assisting devices this way: "Do you know what a cane is? It's a portable railing! The essence of a wheelchair is a seat and wheels. Now, I don't know that a tricycle is not doing the exact same thing."

In these examples, then, the problem is not the disability or the assisting device, but how one views them. Redefining assisting devices also helps us see how they might mean different things to disabled and nondisabled persons. Several interviewees expressed frustration with people who played with their wheelchairs. One interviewee exclaimed, "This chair is not a toy, it is *part of me*. When you touch my chair, you are touching *me*." Another woman, a business executive, expanded on this by saying, "I don't know why people who push my chair feel compelled to make car sounds as they do it."

REDEFINING DISABILITY WITHIN NONDISABLED CULTURE

Finally, as people with disabilities redefine themselves as members of a culture, and as they redefine what it means to have a disabling condition, they are also concerned with trying to change the view of disability within the larger culture (Braithwaite, 1990, 1996). From the interviews it was clear that most people with disabilities view themselves as public educators on disability issues. People told stories about taking the time to educate children and adults on what it means to be disabled. They are actively working to change the view of themselves as helpless, as victims, or ill and the ensuing treatment such a view brings. One wheelchair user said:

> People do not consider you, they consider the chair first. I was in a store with my purchases on my lap and money on my lap. The clerk looked at my companion and not at me and said, "Cash or charge?"

This incident with the clerk is a story heard from *every* person interviewed in some form or another, just as it happened to Jonathan and his date at the beginning of this chapter. One woman, who had multiple sclerosis and uses a wheelchair, told of shopping for lingerie with her husband accompanying her. When they were in front of the lingerie counter, the clerk repeatedly talked only to her husband saying, "And what size does she want?" The woman told her the size and the clerk looked at the husband and said, "And what color does she want?"

Persons with disabilities recognize that nondisabled persons often see them as disabled first and as a person second (if at all). The most common theme expressed by people with disabilities in all of the interviews is that they want to be *treated as a person first*. One man explained what he thought was important to remember: "A lot of people think that handicapped people are 'less than' and I find that it's not true at all. . . . Abling people, giving them their power back, empowering them." The interviewees rejected those things that would not lead to being seen as persons. A man with muscular dystrophy talked about the popular Labor Day telethon:

> I do not believe in those goddamned telethons . . . they're horrible, absolutely horrible. They get into the self-pity, you know, and disabled folk do not need that. Hit people in terms of their attitudes, then try to deal with and process their feelings. And the telethons just go for the heart and leave it there.

One man suggested what he thought was a more useful approach:

> What I am concerned with is anything that can do away with the "us" versus "them" distinction. Well, you and I are anatomically different, but we're two human beings! And, at the point we can sit down and communicate eyeball to eyeball; the quicker you do that, the better!

Individually and collectively, people with disabilities do identify themselves as part of a culture. They are involved in a process of redefinition of themselves, and of disability. They desire to help nondisabled people internalize a redefinition of people of the disabled culture as "persons first."

CONCLUSION

The research we have discussed highlights the usefulness of viewing disability from a cultural perspective. People with disabilities do recognize themselves as part of a culture, and viewing communication and relationships from this perspective sheds new light on the communication challenges that exist. Some time ago, Emry and Wiseman (1987) first argued for the usefulness of intercultural training about disability issues. They call for unfreezing old attitudes about disability and refreezing new ones. Clearly, the interviews indicate that people who have disabilities would seem to agree.

One question that the interviewees answered concerned how many of them had any sort of training concerning communication, during or after their rehabilitation. We anticipated that they would have been given information that would have prepared them for changes in their communication and relationships as a result of being disabled. We speculated that this education would be especially critical for those who experience sudden-onset disabilities because their self-concepts and all of their relationships would undergo sudden, radical changes. Surprisingly, we found that fewer than 30% of the interviewees received disability-related communication training. Clearly, there are some important gaps in the rehabilitation process, and we would argue that intercultural communication scholars have relevant background and experience for the kind of research and training that could help make the transition from majority to minority an easier one (Braithwaite, 1990; Emry & Wiseman, 1987).

We are encouraged by some advances that are taking place in educational and organizational settings (e.g., Colvert & Smith, 2000; Herold, 2000; Worley, 2000). We also see much work to be done by expanding our studies of people with disabilities, for example for those with nonvisible disabilities (e.g., emphysema, diabetes) and socially stigmatized disabilities like HIV. Overall, we see important contributions for communication scholars to make. Recently, Braithwaite and Thompson published the *Handbook of Communication and People with Disabilities: Research and Application*. They were struck with how many researchers in communication studies are now studying disability communication and how many of these scholars were young and themselves disabled. Clearly, the future does look brighter than when we began our studies in disability and communication some years back; however, we still have a long way to go.

We believe that scholars and students of intercultural communication have an important contribution to make. We also believe that students of intercultural communication should have an advantage in being able to better understand the perspective of people with disabilities, as presented in this chapter. We hope that you will be able to understand and apply intercultural communication concepts and skills and be able to adapt that knowledge to communicating with persons in the disabled culture. Finally, we believe that people with disabilities themselves will better understand their own experience if they study intercultural communication and come to understand the cultural aspects of disability.

For nondisabled persons who communicate with persons who are disabled, we suggest that taking an intercultural perspective leads to the following proscriptions and prescriptions:

DO NOT:
- *Avoid* communication with people who are disabled simply because you are uncomfortable or unsure.
- *Assume* people with disabilities cannot speak for themselves or do things for themselves.
- *Force* your help on people with disabilities.
- *Use terms* like "handicapped," "physically challenged," "crippled," "victim," and so on unless requested to do so by people with disabilities.
- *Assume* that a disability defines who a person is.

DO:
- *Remember* that people with disabilities have experienced others' discomfort before and likely understand how you might be feeling.
- *Assume* people with a disability can do something unless they communicate otherwise.
- *Let people with disabilities tell you* if they want something, what they want, and when they want it. If a person with a disability refuses your help, don't go ahead and help anyway.
- *Use terms* like "people with disabilities" rather than "disabled people." The goal is to stress the *person first*, before the disability.
- *Treat* people with disabilities as *persons first*, recognizing that you are not dealing with a disabled person but with *a person* who *has* a disability. This means actively seeking the humanity of the person you are speaking with and focusing on individual characteristics instead of superficial physical appearance. Without diminishing the significance of a person's physical disability, make a real effort to focus on the many other aspects of that person as you communicate.

Note
1. The quotes and anecdotes in this chapter come from in-depth interviews with people who have visible physical disabilities. The names of the participants in these interviews have been changed to protect their privacy.

References

Belgrave, F. Z., & Mills, J. (1981). Effect upon desire for social interaction with a physically disabled person of mentioning the disability in different contexts. *Journal of Applied Social Psychology, 11*, 44–57.

Braithwaite, D. O. (1990). From majority to minority: An analysis of cultural change from nondisabled to disabled. *International Journal of Intercultural Relations, 14*, 465–483.

Braithwaite, D. O. (1991). "Just how much did that wheelchair cost?": Management of privacy boundaries by persons with disabilities. *Western Journal of Speech Communication, 55*, 254–274.

Braithwaite, D. O. (1996). "Persons first": Expanding communicative choices by persons with disabilities. In E. B. Ray (Ed.), *Communication and disenfranchisement: Social health issues and implications* (pp. 449–464). Mahwah, NJ: Lawrence Erlbaum.

Braithwaite, D. O., & Eckstein, N. (2000, November). Reconceptualizing supportive interactions: How persons with disabilities communicatively manage assistance. Presented to the National Communication Association, Seattle, WA.

Braithwaite, D. O., & Labrecque, D. (1994). Responding to the Americans with Disabilities Act: Contributions of interpersonal communication research and training. *Journal of Applied Communication, 22*, 287–294.

Braithwaite, D. O., & Harter, L. (2000). Communication and the management of dialectical tensions in the personal relationships of people with disabilities. In D. O. Braithwaite & T. L. Thompson (Eds.), *Handbook of communication and people with disabilities: Research and application* (pp. 17–36). Mahwah, NJ: Lawrence Erlbaum.

Braithwaite, D. O., & Thompson, T. L. (Eds). (2000). *Handbook of communication and people with disabilities: Research and application*. Mahwah, NJ: Lawrence Erlbaum.

Carbaugh, D. (1988). *Talking American*. Norwood, NJ: Ablex.

Carbaugh, D. (Ed.). (1990). *Cultural communication and intercultural contact*. Hillsdale, NJ: Lawrence Erlbaum.

Cogswell, Betty E. (1977). Self-socialization: Readjustments of paraplegics in the community. In R.P. Marinelli & A. E. Dell Orto (Eds.), *The psychological and social impact of physical disability* (pp. 151–159). New York: Springer.

Coleman, L. M., & DePaulo, B. M. (1991). Uncovering the human spirit: Moving beyond disability and "missed" communications. In N. Coupland, H. Giles, & J. M. Wiemann, (Eds.), *Miscommunication and problematic talk* (pp. 61–84). Newbury Park, CA: Sage.

Covert, A. L., & Smith, J. W. (2000). What is reasonable: workplace communication and people who are disabled. In D. O. Braithwaite & T. L. Thompson (Eds.), *Handbook of communication and people with disabilities: Research and application* (pp. 141–158). Mahwah, NJ: Lawrence Erlbaum.

Crewe, N., & Athelstan, G. (1985). *Social and psychological aspects of physical disability*. Minneapolis: University of Minnesota, Department of Independent Study and University Resources.

Cunningham, C., & Coombs, N. (1997). *Information access and adaptive technology*. Phoenix: Oryx Press.

Dahnke, G. L. (1983). Communication and handicapped and nonhandicapped persons: Toward a deductive theory. In M. Burgoon (Ed.), *Communication Yearbook 6* (pp. 92–135). Beverly Hills, CA: Sage.

DeLoach, C., & Greer, B. G. (1981). *Adjustment to severe physical disability: A metamorphosis*. New York: McGraw-Hill.

Emry, R., & Wiseman, R. L. (1987). An intercultural understanding of nondisabled and disabled persons' communication. *International Journal of Intercultural Relations, 11*, 7–27.

Fichten, C. S., Robillard, K., Tagalakis, V., & Amsel, R. (1991). Casual interaction between college students with various disabilities and their nondisabled peers: The internal dialogue. *Rehabilitation Psychology, 36*, 3–20.

Fox, S. A., Giles, H., Orbe, M., & Bourhis, R. (2000). Interability communication: Theoretical perspectives. In Braithwaite, D. O., & Thompson, T. L. (Eds). *Handbook of communication and people with disabilities: Research and application* (pp. 193–222). Mahwah, NJ: Lawrence Erlbaum.

Goffman, E. (1963). *Stigma: Notes on the management of spoiled identity*. New York: Simon & Schuster.

Herold, K. P. (2000). Communication strategies in employment interviews for applicants with disabilities. In Braithwaite, D. O., & Thompson, T. L. (Eds). *Handbook of communication and people with disabilities: Research and application* (pp. 159–175). Mahwah, NJ: Lawrence Erlbaum.

Higgins, P. C. (1992). *Making disability: Exploring the social transformation of human variation*. Springfield, IL: Charles C. Thomas.

Lyons, R. F., Sullivan, M. J. L., Ritvo, P. G, & Coyne, J. C. (1995). *Relationships in chronic illness and disability*. Thousand Oaks, CA: Sage.

Morse, J. M., & Johnson, J. L. (1991). *The illness experience: Dimensions of suffering*. Newbury Park, CA: Sage.

Padden, C., & Humphries, T. (1988). *Deaf in America: Voices from a culture*. Cambridge, MA: Harvard University Press.

Pardeck, J. T. (1998). *Social work after the Americans with Disabilities Act: New challenges and opportunities for social service professionals*. Westport, CT: Auburn House.

Thompson, T. L. (1982). Disclosure as a disability-management strategy: A review and conclusions. *Communication Quarterly, 30*, 196–202.

Worley, D. W. (2000). Communication and students with disabilities on college campuses. In Braithwaite, D. O., & Thompson, T. L. (Eds). *Handbook of communication and people with disabilities: Research and application* (pp. 125–139). Mahwah, NJ: Lawrence Erlbaum.

Concepts and Questions

1. In what ways does becoming disabled lead to changes in a person's communication patterns?
2. What are some of the cultural problems inherent in communication between nondisabled and disabled persons?
3. Why do Braithwaite and Braithwaite believe you should learn about the communication patterns of disabled persons? What purpose will be served by your knowing this information?
4. Give examples of what Braithwaite and Braithwaite mean when they say that "the distinctive verbal and nonverbal communication used by persons with disabilities creates a sense of cultural identity that constitutes a unique social reality"?
5. How would you distinguish between *disability* and *handicap*?
6. Why is nonverbal communication a factor when nondisabled persons and persons with disabilities engage in communication?
7. Enumerate the problems Braithwaite and Braithwaite describe relating to the current research being conducted on persons with disabilities?
8. What is meant by the term *redefinition*?
9. How would you answer the following question: If disability is a culture, then when does one become part of that culture?

Intercultural Interaction: Taking Part in Intercultural Communication

If we seek to understand a people we have to put ourselves, as best we can, in that particular historical and cultural background.... One has to recognize that countries and people differ in their approach and their ways, in their approach to life and their ways of living and thinking. In order to understand them we have to understand their way of life and approach. If we wish to convince them, we have to use their language as far as we can, not language in the narrow sense of the word, but the language of the mind.

JAWAHARLAL NEHRU

In Part 3, we are concerned with participation in intercultural communication. We focus, therefore, on verbal communication (Chapter 4), nonverbal forms of symbolic interaction (Chapter 5), and the social and physical context in which interaction takes place (Chapter 6). As we pointed out in introducing Part 2, meanings reside within people, and symbols serve as stimuli to which these meanings are attributed. Meaning-evoking stimuli consist of both verbal and nonverbal behaviors. Although we consider these forms of symbolic interaction separately for convenience, we hasten to point out their interrelatedness. As nonverbal behavior accompanies verbal behavior, it becomes a unique part of the total symbolic interaction. Verbal messages often rely on their nonverbal accompaniment for cues that aid the receiver in decoding the verbal symbols. Nonverbal behaviors not only serve to amplify and clarify verbal messages but can also serve as forms of symbolic interaction without verbal counterparts. In addition, the context in which verbal and nonverbal behaviors occur adds to the evocation of meanings.

When you communicate verbally, you use words with seeming ease because there is a high consensus of agreement about the meanings our words evoke. Your experiential backgrounds are similar enough that you share basically the same meanings for most of the word symbols used in everyday communication. But even within your culture, you sometimes disagree about the meanings of many word symbols. As words move further from the reality of sense data, they become more abstract, and then there is far less agreement about appropriate meanings. What do highly abstract words such as *love*, *freedom*, *equality*, *democracy*, and *good time* mean to you?

Do they mean the same things to everyone? If you are in doubt, ask some friends; take a poll. You will surely find that people have different notions of these concepts and consequently different meanings for these words. Their experiences have been different, and they hold different beliefs, attitudes, values, concepts, and expectations. Yet all, or perhaps most, of these people are from the same culture. Their backgrounds, experiences, and concepts of the universe are quite uniform. When cultural diversity is added to the process of decoding words, however, much larger differences in meanings and usage are found.

Culture exerts no small influence over your use of language. In fact, it strongly determines just what your language is and how you use it. In the narrowest sense, language is a set of symbols (vocabulary) that evoke more or less uniform meanings among a particular population and set of rules (grammar and syntax) for using the symbols. In the broadest sense, language is the symbolic representation of a people, and it includes their historical and cultural backgrounds as well as their approach to life and their ways of living and thinking.

What comes to be symbolized and what the symbols represent are very much functions of culture. Similarly, how you use your verbal symbols is also a function of culture. What you think about or speak with others about must be capable of symbolization, and how you speak or think about things must follow the rules you have for using your language. Because the symbols and rules are culturally determined, how and what you think or talk about are, in effect, a function of your culture. This relation between language and culture is not unidirectional, however. There is an interaction between them—what you think about and how you think about it also affects your culture.

As you can see, language and culture are inseparable. To be an effective intercultural communicator requires that you be aware of the relationship between culture and language. It further requires that you learn and know about the culture of the person with whom you are trying to communicate so that you can better understand how his or her language represents that person.

Another important aspect of verbal symbols or words is that they can evoke two kinds of meanings: denotative and connotative. A *denotative* meaning indicates the referent or the "thing" to which the symbol refers. For example, the denotative meaning of the word *book* is the physical object to which it refers; or, in the case of the set of symbols *Intercultural Communication: A Reader*, the referent is the book you are now reading. Not all denotations have a physical correspondence. As you move to higher levels of abstraction, you often deal with words that represent ideas or concepts, which exist only in the mind and do not necessarily have a physical basis. For example, much communication research has been directed toward changes in attitude. Yet attitude is only a hypothetical construct used to explain behavior; there is no evidence of any physical correspondence between some group of brain cells and a person's attitudes.

The second type of meaning—*connotative*—indicates a valuative dimension. Not only do you identify referents (denotative meaning), but you also place them along a valuative dimension that can be simply described as positive–neutral–negative. Where you place a word on the dimension depends on your prior experiences and how you "feel" about the referent. If you like books, you might place *Intercultural Communication: A Reader* near the positive end of the dimension. When you are dealing with more abstract symbols, you do the same thing. In fact, as the level of abstraction increases, so does your tendency to place more emphasis on connotative meanings. Most people will agree that a book is the object you are holding in your hand, but whether books are good or bad or whether this particular book is good or bad or in-between is an individual judgment based on prior experience.

Culture affects both denotative and connotative meanings. Consequently, a knowledge of how these meanings can differ culturally is essential to effective intercultural communication. For you to make the assumption that everyone uses the same meanings is to invite communication disaster.

Culture affects language and language use in other ways. Many of you tend to believe that your way of using language is both correct and universal and that any deviation is wrong or substandard. This belief can and does elicit many negative responses and judgments when you encounter someone from another culture whose use of language deviates from our own specifications.

What we are trying to point out with these examples should be quite obvious—language and culture are inseparable. In fact, it would be difficult to determine which is the voice and which is the echo. How you learn, employ, and respond to symbols is culturally based. In addition, the sending and the receiving of these culturally grounded symbols are what enable you to interact with people from other cultures. Hence, this part of the book highlights these verbal and nonverbal symbols to help you understand some of the complexities, subtleties, and nuances of language and, at the same time, to acquaint you with how the social and physical contexts influence verbal and nonverbal behavior.

Communication obviously involves much more than the sending and receiving of verbal and nonverbal messages. Human interaction takes place within some social and physical setting that influences how you construct and perceive messages. The sway of context is rooted in the following three interrelated assumptions.

1. *Communication is rule-governed* (i.e., each encounter has implicit and explicit rules that regulate your conduct). These rules tell you everything from what is appropriate attire to what topics can be discussed.
2. *The setting helps you define what "regulations" are in operation.* Reflect for a moment on your own communication behavior as you move to and from the following arenas: classroom, courtroom, church, hospital, and dance hall. Visualize yourself behaving differently as you proceed from place to place.
3. *Most of the communication rules you follow have been learned as part of cultural experiences.* Although cultures might share the same general settings, their specific notion of proper behavior for each context manifests the values and attitudes of that culture. Concepts of turn taking, time, space, language, manners, nonverbal behavior, silence, and control of the communication flow are largely an extension of each culture.

In this part of the book, we offer readings that demonstrate the crucial link that exists between context, culture, and communication. What emerges from these essays is the realization that to understand another culture you must appreciate the rules that govern that culture's behavior in a specific setting. Although intercultural communication occurs in a variety of contexts, we have selected environments related to business, education, and health care to discuss in this part of the book.

GO ONLINE

to the ***Intercultural Communication: A Reader*** website
at the Wadsworth Communication Café,
www.wadsworth.com/communication_d.
From the home page, select "Course Materials," then "Speech Communication," and then "Intercultural Communication." From the textbook menu, select *Intercultural Communication: A Reader* to access the book's website. Click on "...For Students" and use the drop-down menus at the top of the page to select a chapter and select a study aid resource. A practice quiz and an InfoTrac College Edition activity are included for each chapter.

You can complete the InfoTrac College Edition Activities by using the passcode that came free with each new copy of this text. InfoTrac College Edition is an easy-to-use database of reliable, full-length articles from hundreds of top academic journals and popular sources. You can expand your learning about the concepts illustrated in each reading by completing the InfoTrac College Edition activities.

chapter 4

Verbal Processes:
Speaking Across Cultures

As a species, one of your most unique features is your ability to use language (i.e., to receive, store, retrieve, manipulate, and generate linguistic symbols). All 6 billion plus of you acknowledge the past, take part in the present, and prepare for the future. By simply making certain sounds or marks on paper, you can relate to and interact with others. Language is that simple yet complex instrument that gives you the ability to share yourselves with other people. This chapter examines language and its relationship to culture.

This chapter purports that a culture's use of language involves much more than sounds and meanings. It also involves forms of reasoning, how discourse is carried out, specialized linguistic devices such as analogies and idioms, and ways of perceiving the world. Hence, to understand the language of any culture means you must look beyond the vocabulary, grammar, and syntax of that culture. This broad view of culture has guided us in our selection of readings. We urge you to view language from this larger perspective both as you read these articles and as you confront people from different cultures. Our eclectic outlook toward language will help you understand the interaction patterns of cultures and co-cultures that are different from your own. The first two articles will examine this relationship between language and culture.

Fern L. Johnson introduces the idea that "all communication bears cultural origins, conveys cultural meanings, and is interpreted through cultural frameworks" as she introduces you to the relationship between culture and language. In her essay, "Cultural Dimensions of Discourse," she focuses on a language-centered perspective of culture as a way of making sense of the various language patterns that exist daily in the United States. In her analysis, she discusses the distinctions between society and culture, provides you with a discussion of enlightenment and romantic views of culture, and specifies the role of language in culture. In her language-centered perspective, she alludes to systems of cultural abstractions, systems of cultural artifacts, systems of cultural language and communication, and notions of communicative competence and intercultural communicative competence. She concludes her essay by presenting six axioms found in the language-centered perspective on culture that provide a basis both for better understanding the relationship between culture and communication and for becoming a more effective intercultural communicator.

The next essay, titled "The Nexus of Language, Communication, and Culture," by Mary Fong, introduces you to additional fundamental ideas about the relationship between language and culture. Fong begins with a brief review of the Sapir–Whorf hypothesis, which proposed linguistic relativity and was one of the first modern observations of the relationship between language and culture. She then traces later developments in this area that have led to ethnographic research approaches to the study of language and culture. Applying these techniques in two studies of Chinese language use, Fong shows not only the ways in which ethnographic approaches are employed, but also the rich linguistic practices of the Chinese.

The next essay is also concerned with the relationship between culture and language; however, it takes a somewhat different approach, focusing on how changes in the cultural elements can impact language usage. Using the country of China and the Chinese language as a backdrop, Mei Zhong, in her essay "Contemporary Social and Political Movements and their Imprints on the Chinese Language," demonstrates the impact of changes in political structures, social institutions, economic capacities, education systems, artistic expressions, and daily practices as reflected in the Chinese language. To support her contentions that language changes in relationship to social conditions, Mei Zhong traces the history of the Chinese language through the New Culture Era, the New China Era, the Cultural Revolution Era, the Economic Reform Era, and the All-Around Open and Western Influence Era. In each instance she demonstrates how the influences of these eras have been reflected in everyday language usage.

In his essay "Discriminating Attitudes Toward Speech," Aaron Castelan Cargile points out that cultural misunderstandings can occur even if people speak the same language. The reason, of course, is obvious: Language involves much more than simple definitions. As we noted earlier, language is a reflection of our experiences, and as experiences vary so does our use of language. Cargile examines three major differences (i.e., accents, vocabularies, and rates of speech) and how they might impact interactions between people from different cultures. Further, Cargile contends that for some people these variations in language can contribute to negative perceptions. As a means of overcoming these harmful attitudes, Cargile concludes his essay with advice on how to keep our perceptions from impeding intercultural interaction.

Conflict in the Middle East between Israeli-Jews and Palestinians has a long and bloody history. Antecedents of today's conflicts extend over thousands of years. Traditional discord notwithstanding, there might be ways in which the negative stereotypes, mutual delimitization, and severe miscommunication that highlight today's relationships could be managed through an understanding of transformative dialogues. In their essay "Dialogue and Cultural Communication Codes Between Israeli-Jews and Palestinians," Donald G. Ellis and Ifat Maoz analyze cultural communication codes in order to establish dialogue between the opposing sides.

Ellis and Maoz posit that the Israeli-Jewish and Arab cultures have emerged from the special circumstances of their history, resulting in different norms of communication. These different histories are manifest in diverse speech codes that reflect nearly opposite cultural differences. Ellis and Maoz suggest that Arab language employs speech codes that seek "to accommodate" or "go along with," which orients speakers toward harmonious relationships.

On the other hand, they assert that the Israeli-Jewish speech code is direct, pragmatic, assertive, explicit, and clear. These speech code differences are essentially the opposite of one another and, according to Ellis and Maoz, are partially responsible for the failure of dialog to resolve the conflict surrounding the two cultures. The authors believe that by a study of speech codes, you can better understand the linguistic bases of cultural conflict and be better prepared to help mediate that conflict.

Quite possibly one of the most important areas of intercultural communication—both internationally and domestically—is between Americans and Mexicans. The June 11, 2001 issue of *Time* magazine was devoted to a special issue called "Welcome to Amexica," which detailed the unique culture that is developing along both sides of the U.S.–Mexican border. Here a hybrid culture is emerging that is a combination of European American, native-Mexican, and Spanish-influenced Mexican backgrounds. To help you better understand the nature of this culture and the Mexican values that contribute to this culture, our next essay, "Mexican *Dichos*: Lessons Through Language," by Carolyn Roy, explores Mexican values as expressed by *dichos*—popular sayings—that convey values through proverbs, adages, and refrains. In her essay, Roy discusses how the values of the cheerful acceptance of the "will of God," the need to place trust in others with great care, the significance of appearances, the necessity to guard one's privacy and not breach the privacy of others, prescribed gender roles, a communal spirit, and the importance of family are expressed and reinforced through use of Mexican *dichos*.

Cultural Dimensions of Discourse

FERN L. JOHNSON

All communication bears cultural origins, conveys cultural meanings, and is interpreted through cultural frameworks. In this essay, I present a perspective on culture termed the *Language-Centered Perspective on Culture*. This approach features human language as the cornerstone of cultural meaning within an interrelated set of systems for elaborating cultural resources that includes ideational patterns (called *abstractions* in this perspective) and cultural products and events (called *artifacts* in this perspective). The focus on culture developed here provides the perspective for a richer analysis of patterned language use than is conventionally found in sociolinguistics.

The Language-Centered Perspective on Culture offers us a way of making sense holistically of the many systematic patterns of language use that occur everyday in the United States. It also takes us beneath the surface of terms such as *diversity* and *multiculturalism* to see just how important the contrasting worldviews making up the texture of the United States are to personal identities, interpersonal relationships, and basic ideas about the social and political world. This view of culture differs from some others, which will be described as follows.

SOCIETY AND CULTURE DISTINCTIONS

Most communication research operates from a seemingly acultural perspective, meaning that culture does not figure centrally in defining or describing communication processes. When taken for granted, culture

operates as a powerful normative force, creating the illusion that cultural identity is something that belongs only to minorities, immigrants, and other "special" groups. Cultural notions, however, always underlie communication even if they are not made explicit. Most textbooks about communication assume a particular cultural perspective, usually that of the dominant, Anglophile, Eurowhite populace. Regardless of the particular subject—intimate communication, communication between friends, conflict, family communication, managerial communication—a specific cultural foundation underlies most theories of communication and prescriptions for effective communication. For our purposes, let us call this kind of underlying cultural foundation *presumed culture* operating as *default cultural conceptions;* those who write and speak about communication *presume* a substantial degree of cultural commonality among all peoples in the United States. Culture thus becomes an exclusionary mental perspective, equivalent to the default option in a computer program, because it excludes other options unless they are explicitly specified. Increasingly, however, that presumption is invalid, which makes the cultural analysis of communication an imperative for our times.

Depending on the area of study, culture has been more or less emphasized in the analysis of language variation. Most anthropological studies of language either assume or explicitly view language as a cultural practice; this tradition of work embraces culture as the key to understanding how language systems come to be so distinctively different throughout the world and how these systems function to create and sustain different worldviews.

Culture has been less regularly featured in most sociolinguistic studies of language variation. In most sociolinguistic research, social structure predominates as the central organizing concept used to explain language variation. The substantial body of work on language and social class conducted in Great Britain, for example, rests on a model of society in which the different social classes are defined as variables organized vertically within the larger social system: upper class, upper middle class, middle class, lower middle class, lower class. Other labels such as "working class" often substitute as contrasts with middle class to designate a quick reference for occupations requiring manual, unskilled labor.

From *Speaking Culturally: Language Diversity in the United States* (Thousand Oaks, CA: Sage Publications), 2000, pp. 45–68. All rights reserved. Reprinted by permission of the publisher. Fern L. Johnson is Professor of English and Director of the Interdisciplinary Communication and Culture Program at Clark University in Worcester, Massachusetts.

The study of social status and regional dialects in the United States has proceeded similarly by emphasizing those aspects of language use—especially phonological features—that vary depending on the particular class or regional origin of a speaker.

The social structure model looks to *variation within a system* that is organized into social groups with horizontal and vertical (hierarchical) relationships to one another. Social structure is generally associated with "the distribution of rights and duties across status positions in a society" (D'Andrade, 1984, p. 110). Although this model has much to offer by way of documenting systematic differences in language use, the social structure view presupposes that individuals are connected through a larger social system and are—at least theoretically—mobile in their language use just as they are in other aspects of their lives (which fits prevailing U.S. ideology about social mobility). There is, thus, a reifying impact in this tradition, such that differential patterns of language use come to represent the different social strata as functionally complementary categories. Social strata are reified not only on the basis of class and economic power but also according to race and ethnicity.

What is often lost in such analyses is the broader perspective on semantic and pragmatic systems that gives contextual meaning to language. Also missed is the vitality in divergent cultural systems, which accounts for the persistence of disfavored language variations against considerable odds, and the mechanisms through which mainstream institutions function to preserve preferred language varieties and the cultural systems they articulate. Of greatest consequence is the lost opportunity to understand the cultural processes at play when different varieties of language meet face-to-face and ear-to-ear. Sociolinguistics, then, often minimizes complex notions of how culture shapes language use in favor of more standard notions of societal groupings.

From the 1960s through the early 1980s, it was common in the United States to talk about complex societies as containing some set of *sub*cultures, which sometimes equated with minority groups. In the United States, groups such as blacks, Puerto Ricans, criminals, Mexican Americans, urban poor, and Appalachian hill dwellers came to be labeled as subcultures. This perspective positioned the study of "nonstandard" groups and their ways of speaking in a subcultural context to be contrasted with what was understood to be the main culture. Although the concept of culture made its way into the nomenclature of academic study, little emphasis was actually placed on the richness of cultural meanings within the reputed subcultures. Even more problematic, the subcultural orientation powerfully symbolized social worth. All of the meanings of *sub-* carry negative connotations: under, beneath, below, subordinate, secondary, inferior. These connotations tend to imply separate and unequal status for any language variety that happens to be associated with what is labeled a subculture. The only satisfactory way to deal with the problems created by both social structure and subcultural analysis is to reposition the analysis of language variation as a more complex analytical endeavor that begins with the assumption that multiple cultures coexist in complex societies. The move to cultural linguistics requires, then, a much clearer conception of how cultures are constructed, sustained, and changed.

VIEWS OF CULTURE

For all but the most isolated of social groups, culture conveys complexity arising from (1) the communication and intermingling of peoples with different origins, identities, and allegiances and (2) the interplay of the real and imagined past, the perceived present, and the projected future, whether probable or fantasized. Cultures, then, are not "pure" but, rather, are the product and creation of human contact between and across both groups and time. Simply stated, those who share in a culture also display a broad range of individual differences, and contrasting cultures in contact with one another also display the products of their mutual influence.

But what exactly *is* culture? In the many descriptions of culture, common threads can be found. First, cultures comprise symbolic systems that create webs of meaning. Much of what we know and believe to be real has no concrete manifestation at all but is made concrete only through its applications in everyday life: Justice, evil, beauty, and ego are no more than arbitrary abstractions packed with symbolic meanings. Even material cultural products can only be understood based on abstract meanings: The clothes we wear, the food we eat, the pictures we look at in magazines all depend on abstract cultural meanings. Second, cultures—although constantly evolving and changing—endure over long periods. New cultures do emerge, but the level of complexity within cultures is more than a brief blip of human interaction. Third, cultures are learned by humans through both explicit instruction and tacit acquisition that occur in the everyday modeling and practice of meaningful action. We are not naturally of any particular culture, but we develop our skill to function in various cultures over our lifetimes. Once mastered, cultural learning becomes second nature.

In differing degrees, we all participate in multiple cultural systems ranging from our native culture of origin, to the local cultures in which we interact in daily life, to the global culture created through mobility, mass communication, and technology. Each influences the other. In discussing the transnational impact of one culture on another, Ulf Hannerz (1989) talks about how the centers and the peripheries in global affairs intermingle with the effect of "creolized and creolizing cultural forms which grow between center and periphery" (p. 213). Such is also the case nationally where the influences of one culture on another have a creolizing effect; for example, the greater numbers of people in the United States with Mexican origins resulted in changes in food preferences for Anglos but also for Mexican Americans.

The philosophical foundations of the Language-Centered Perspective on Culture contrast with more traditional notions of culture articulated by Western scholars.

Enlightenment and Romantic Views

For purposes of distinguishing theories of culture from one another, Richard Shweder (1984) provides a useful review and synthesis of approaches to explaining culture by contrasting two major streams of thought: the Enlightenment view and the Romantic rebellion against it.

Briefly, Enlightenment theories assume that (1) humans are rational, and (2) significant human practices across cultural settings are ultimately universal (or evolving toward the universal through successive advances of cultural development). The nomenclature of *primitive* and *modern-developed* cultures comes from the Enlightenment perspective. Goodenough (1981) points to the German word *kultur,* which refers to the process of becoming more civilized such that greater or higher *kultur* follows from greater or higher progress in civilization. Contemporary ideas about high culture as distinguished from popular or mass culture derive their meanings from the Enlightenment view.

In contrast, Romantic theories portray human beings as engaging in different modes of rational behavior, sometimes called "nonrational" behavior simply because cultural practices are arbitrary and relative to their systems of meaning. In this view, each culture must be taken as unique, with patterns that represent no natural or universal order but, rather, are relative to one another. Shweder (1984) comments that "the most significant romantic development to emerge . . . is perhaps the definition of culture as arbitrary code" (p. 45).

The Role of Language in Culture

Elaborating on Shweder's analysis, we can compare and contrast culture theories for their perspective on language. The role that language (and communication more broadly) occupies in culture varies considerably across culture theories. One perspective is that language is essentially a vehicle for transporting information and ideas. Like any vehicle, language in this view is a medium for getting from one place to one another. And like any vehicle, language can be improved on, made more efficient and effective, and fueled with higher-quality material. Language, thus, is seen primarily for its role in transmitting the culture, where the metaphor of transmission evokes the notion that getting something from one person to another, one place to another, or one time to another is purely a technical matter—much like engineering and electronics. In the second half of the 20th century, the transmission metaphor for language became especially powerful because it captured the U.S. fascination with science and merging technology.

From a different perspective, the role of language in culture can be seen as formative because language is symbolic action that creates the substance of culture. This view draws on the seminal ideas of George Herbert Mead, whose thinking early in the century provided the foundation for what was to become the symbolic interactionism perspective in social theory. Mead's theories about social life were developed in opposition to the early formulations of radical behaviorism in the United States. Mead's (1934) view was that the external world does not brutally impinge on the individual. Rather, people use language to create situations and indicate those things that become regarded as important, significant, and in the realm of reality:

> Language does not simply symbolize a situation or object that is already there in advance; it makes possible the existence or the appearance of that situation or object, for it is a part of the mechanism whereby the situation or object is created. (p. 78)

Carrying this idea into the realm of culture, language would be said to both symbolize and create culture.

The importance of language for a person's worldview is nowhere more central than in the writings of Benjamin Lee Whorf, whose work builds on that of Edward Sapir, both of whom studied Native-American languages. Concerned primarily with natural languages taken as a whole, and not with the variations within particular languages, Whorf (1940/1956) advanced a "new principle of relativity" related to language and thought; this *linguistic relativity*, said Whorf, "holds that all observers are not led by the same physical evidence to the same picture of the universe, unless their linguistic backgrounds are similar, or can in some way be calibrated" (p. 214). His formulations about the relationship between culture and language (i.e., how one influences the other) are aptly described by Emily Schultz (1990) as a *paradoxical unity* in which culture and language reciprocally influence one another.

The most frequently quoted Whorfian statement addresses how perceived "reality" is affected by the interplay of language and cognition within a culturally specific speech community context:

> We dissect nature along lines laid down by our native language. The categories and types that we isolate from the world of phenomena we do not find there

because they stare every observer in the face; on the contrary, the world is presented in a kaleidoscopic flux of impressions which has to be organized by our minds—and this means *largely by the linguistic systems in our minds* [italics added]. We cut nature up, organize it into concepts, and ascribe significance as we do, *largely because we are parties to an agreement to organize it in this way* [italics added]—an agreement that holds throughout our speech community and is codified in the patterns of our language. The agreement is, of course, an implicit and unstated one, BUT ITS TERMS ARE ABSOLUTELY OBLIGATORY. (Whorf, 1940/1956, pp. 213–214, capitalization in the original)

Notice Whorf's use of the words *largely* and *an agreement* in the first part of the sentence and *absolutely obligatory* in the latter part. It is as though he is likening the relationship between language and thought to that of a contract: In a contract, we agree to certain things even though we may know that other possibilities exist, but once agreed to, the contract is binding. The explicit link to culture is that languages (in all their varieties) are culturally relevant and culturally relative. Cultural frameworks give rise to particular languages, which in turn shape mental processes and the organization of reality, which in turn create cultural frameworks. Cultural frameworks can be renewed, refreshed, and reformulated through ever-changing processes involving language. Hence, thought is relative to language, which is relative to culture.

In current thinking about culture, the work of anthropologist Clifford Geertz (1973, 1983) is prominent for its emphasis on the role of symbols in cultural life. Geertz argues that the sharing of public symbols gives reality to cultural identity; the actual sharing through expression of values, mores, and orientations to the world joins people together through symbolic action in a cultural context. Although Geertz concerns himself with more than language and communication, the relevance of his thinking lies in the claim that to understand a culture, one must be able to understand the "modes of expression" or "symbol systems" used by its participants (1983, p. 70). Rather than seeing culture as interior to the individual, Geertz sees culture as public because meaning is public (1973).

Table 1 *Universal and Situated Culture*

Universal	Situated
Reality is independent of specific cultures	Reality is relative to specific cultures
Humans operate through one system of rationality, which can be perfected to perceive the truth	Humans operate through many different systems of rationality, perceiving different truths
Culture resides in abstract knowledge systems found in people's heads	Culture resides in human action, manifested in human processes and products
Language is a vehicle	Language is symbolic action

Using Shweder's (1984) basic ideas as a foundation, the perspective on culture and role of language in culture can, then, be contrasted. My analysis in this article features a situated viewpoint on culture (aligned with the Romantic view) in contrast with the universal viewpoint (aligned with the Enlightenment view). Table 1 shows the major distinctions in the two viewpoints.

The situated viewpoint shares assumptions with a new stream of social criticism that seeks to document cultural multiplicity. The African-American philosopher Cornel West (1993) boldly stakes out the territory of criticism:

> Distinctive features of the new cultural politics of difference are to trash the monolithic and homogeneous in the name of diversity, multiplicity, and heterogeneity; to reject the abstract, general, and universal in light of the concrete, specific, and particular; and to historicize, contextualize, and pluralize by highlighting the contingent, provisional, variable, tentative, shifting, and changing. (p. 3)

I turn next to the specific perspective that guides my analysis of culture. Working from the premise that U.S. society consists of many cultures, the goal is to understand how meaning is created in these various cultures.

THE LANGUAGE-CENTERED PERSPECTIVE ON CULTURE

The Language-Centered Perspective on Culture emphasizes the special role of language in human interaction. Cultures, as complex systems, are made up of several different symbolic systems that generate meaning. Language, however, binds those systems together in a special way and serves as the major meaning system for contact among peoples.

Humans learn through the cultures in which they are reared, gaining competence as they mature and often possessing passionate loyalty to cultural origins. Even when individuals break off with their cultural roots, linguistic enculturation from within native speech communities provides the foundation from which all other discourse options become elaborated. Speech communities function to center whole cultural systems through discourse. Most people today are entailed in multiple cultures, offering multiple bases for identity.

The locus of cultural identity is sometimes national, sometimes regional, sometimes racially or ethnicity based, always lodged in some dynamic of social class organization, and so forth. "American culture" can be understood, for example, in contrast to the dominant cultural patterns in countries such as England, Italy, Korea, and Iraq. Stewart and Bennett (1991) provide a useful discussion of American cultural patterns, citing dimensions such as individualism and emphasis on selfhood, belief in agency and causality, and separation of social and occupational roles. Other cultural identities arise from region in the sense that "southern culture" varies from "New England culture," and "downeast Mainers" differ from Boston Irish. The locus of still other cultures is local and community based, such as a place labeled "Teamsterville" (Philipsen, 1975), which is a Chicago neighborhood with clear cultural boundaries and rules for speaking. Other loci for culture are race (e.g., African Americans, teenage

African-American males living in urban settings, middle-class African-American women); ethnicity (e.g., Italian, Polish, Swedish); or religious identity (e.g., Hasidic Jews, Sikh Indians, Jehovah's Witnesses). Cultural identity can also reside in lifestyle choices, such as participating in lesbian or gay culture, in pacifism as a way of life, or in gangs. A loosely structured neighborhood, a group that convenes briefly to accomplish some agenda, and a dyadic relationship are not, however, cultures in the sense that I use the term here because they have neither history nor collective identity that transcends their participants.

Adequate description of a culture necessitates a vision of the significant systems that account for action and meaning within that culture. Three such systems—all interrelated—are proposed here as constituting a useful view of cultures (see earlier version in Johnson, 1989):

- system of cultural abstractions
- system of cultural artifacts
- system of cultural language and communication

The three systems are interrelated, with the role of language and communication centrally placed, as seen in Figure 1.

System of Cultural Abstractions

The *system of cultural abstractions* influences and shapes cognitive possibilities and structures the range of choices that are most likely within a culture. Abstractions refer to a particular set of ideational concepts including values, morals, ethics, conceptions of right and wrong, conceptions of good and evil, the logical system, conceptions of justice and laws, rituals, spiritual and religious beliefs, and ideas that in themselves have no concrete or material reality (e.g., honesty, responsibility, kindness).

Several examples clarify the nature of abstractions. In U.S. mainstream culture, the integrity of the individual and the right to privacy are highly valued. This is not the case in Chinese culture, where the language does not even contain words to name and describe the concepts of individuality and privacy. In the realm of religion, predestination is not part of the Judeo-Christian belief system, whereas it plays a central role in Shintoism, the

Figure 1 *Model of Language-Centered Perspective on Culture*

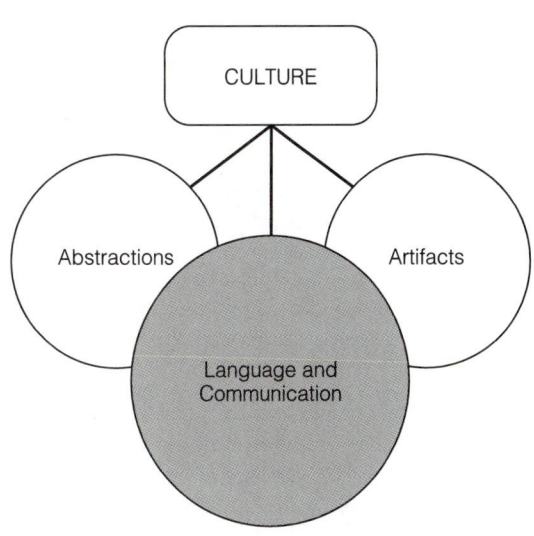

dominant religion in Japan. Those of the Jewish religion have no strong conception of life after death, whereas Christians do.

Looking to legal concepts, democracy in the United States guarantees the right to vote to all citizens who have reached "legal" age (even though women did not win the right to vote until 1920, and even though it took the Voting Rights Act of 1965 to stop such impediments as poll taxes and literacy tests from disenfranchising southern blacks, the primacy of "one man [sic], one vote" to U.S. democracy has never been questioned). Until April 1994, this was not the case in South Africa, where the system of apartheid legally barred blacks, who make up 75% of the population, from voting. Nor does the legal right of a citizen to vote exist in Cuba or North Korea.

The system of abstractions serves as an understructure for much of what is expressed through the system of language and communication. Abstractions lie beneath semantic notions such as *marriage* and *family*, *money* and *savings*, *beauty* and *appearance*, *law* and *justice*. Children must learn these fundamental abstractions and their applications to more specific concepts and notions. A friend told the story of her preschool-age daughter's first close inspection of a Barbie doll. On examining the doll, the child exclaimed: "What's wrong with her? She doesn't have a stomach!" Barbie's almost concave stomach looked quite different from the well-rounded middle sections of both her mother and father. The child's comments reflected her view on what is valued and what is judged normal in the human body. At least for that brief preschool moment, this little girl was untouched by the American social value placed on thin-waisted female bodies.

When we engage in cultural communication within a cultural framework, the abstractions underlying language behavior are usually taken for granted. We become aware of cultural abstractions when circumstances bring together more than one cultural framework in which the differences are conspicuous.

The 1994 case of Michael Fay, a 19-year-old from the United States, demonstrates how an alleged spray-painting spree in Singapore became an international incident because of different cultural conceptions of justice. Most U.S. citizens expressed outrage when Michael was sentenced in Singapore to punishment by caning, a painful and physically injurious beating with a specially prepared bamboo and leather cane, for an offense as minor as graffiti spray painting. Operating with the Western principles of jurisprudence that "the punishment should fit the crime" and that "cruel and unusual punishment" is not appropriate, the sentence of caning struck Americans as excessive and violent. Singapore defended its justice system by displaying its low crime statistics compared to the United States and many other nations. President Bill Clinton intervened with a strong appeal for leniency, and the boy's father vowed to pressure for an embargo and a review of most-favored-nation trade status for Singapore ("Singapore," 1994). The caning took place, but with a reduced number of lashings. This international incident put the clash of notions about justice on center stage.

Looking at another illustration, many misunderstandings occur within U.S. borders because definitions of family and familial responsibility differ across cultural groups. For example, *la familia* as the center of values for most Mexican Americans is never separated from other spheres of activity (Gangotena, 1994). What might be perceived as honorable family responsibility in the Mexican-American cultural tradition would be judged as neurotic family attachment by many other cultural groups. Similarly, the concept of a "mama's boy" with its pejorative connotations in dominant U.S. culture would likely be meaningless within the Mexican-American cultural tradition.

Systems of abstraction, then, make up the ideational foundation for cultures. Abstractions guide behavior and symbolization in language. Discourse across cultures often makes little sense because of conflicting abstractions in the cultures.

System of Cultural Artifacts

The *system of cultural artifacts* includes products of the culture's participants, such as fine and plastic arts, crafts, photography, music, dance, clothing and jewelry, architecture and design, furnishings, material objects such as tools and computers, and so forth. Cultural artifacts express their particular cultural frameworks and sometimes rebel against them.

Artifacts have systematicity through the rules and patterns underlying their production, distribution, and placement. Within a cultural framework, jewelry, for instance, carries gender-related meanings. In Western cultures, women wear more jewelry for adornment than do men, and style varies by gender. African-American men don more jewelry than do Anglo men, which likely expresses continuity with the importance of jewelry in many African cultures. The same is true of men from many Hispanic cultures. Teens and young adults—female and male alike—from various cultural groups now engage in significantly more body piercing than has previously been evident in the United States. It is not uncommon to see piercings all along the ear periphery and through the nose, eyebrow, navel, and tongue (extended occasionally to the nipples and genitalia). In a different cultural tradition, married women among the Surma in southwest Ethiopia customarily make and wear lip plates, which are inserted into pierced holes in the lower lip, sometimes stretching to the size of a saucer. Color in clothing may also carry different symbolic meaning for different cultures. Black has been associated with mourning in the Christian and Judaic traditions, but white symbolizes mourning in China.

Artifacts may be enduring or ephemeral. Products such as books, sculptures, tools, sound recordings, and buildings are relatively (although not absolutely) enduring, whereas musical performances, dance productions, poetry recitations and slams, or chalk drawings on sidewalks are ephemeral. Advances in photography, film, and video make it increasingly possible for cultural groups to preserve artifacts whose inherent nature is ephemeral, thus extending the temporal dimension of their cultural meanings.

Artifacts channel cultural expression in many interesting ways. Artifacts of a more enduring nature often slow or thwart change simply because they exist. The changes in pedagogical style in U.S. schools had to account for the time and money it would take to remove rows of desks that were bolted to the floors of school rooms in neat rows facing the teacher's place at the front of the class. When "Men Only" clubs opened their membership to women, changes were required in such mundane matters as lavatory fixtures, entrances, and decor. In libraries, technology has gradually replaced the many drawers of wooden card catalogs with online computer catalogs, but the physical presence of the catalog drawers and the spaces they occupied slowed change, and explicit planning was required to help library users adapt to the new systems.

Even art or music that is judged heresy finds its basis in rebellion against particular rules and patterns that are culture based; the rebellion, hence, is culturally based. The Impressionist movement among French painters in the late 1800s, the rise of rock-and-roll music in England and the United States in the early 1960s, and the move to "street dress" among Catholic nuns all produced new artifact systems. The changes both departed from prevailing cultural practice and drew on those practices as context for the newer forms.

Cultural artifacts, then, are systematic expressions of arbitrary customs and symbolic meanings within a specific cultural framework. When cultural manifestations such as clothing, art objects, genres of literature, music, and furnishings are stable and well developed, they powerfully symbolize what is significant within a cultural framework. When they change, the change occurs as a kind of dialectic between conventional cultural meanings and oppositional or resistant meanings. Once anchored, the arbitrariness of artifact symbols seems anything but

arbitrary to its users, who come to expect certain artifactual expressions just as they do certain conceptual notions and language practices.

System of Cultural Language and Communication

The system of *language and communication* is the central resource used by human beings to create, maintain, and change culture. Although the languages of the world number 4,000 to 4,500 (Kachru, 1981), it is not natural languages themselves that distinguish one culture from another. Languages encode cultures according to the ways in which they are structured through *rules for use*, which in turn incorporate the system of abstractions of particular cultures. Thus, cultures all have their particular discourse patterns, which convey differing worldviews.

James Gee's (1992) explanation of the term *discourses* shows the complexity of language in its cultural context:

> Each Discourse involves ways of talking, acting, interacting, valuing, and believing, as well as the spaces and material "props" the group uses to carry out its social practices. Discourses integrate words, acts, values, beliefs, attitudes, social identities, as well as gestures, glances, body positions, and clothes. . . . Discourses are always ways of displaying . . . *membership* in a particular social group or social network. (p. 107)

As *pragmatic* systems, discourses express cultural meaning systems.

Communicative Competence. To use a language and to interact with others through a coherent discourse require the acquisition, development, and application of what has been termed *communicative competence*, which is the knowledge system underlying the appropriate use of language in context.

The concept of communicative competence was originally developed by Dell Hymes (1971), who voiced concern about Noam Chomsky's notions of "language performance" as relatively uninteresting. Hymes argued that children must learn not only language rules but also the rules for *use* of language. Their utterances must, among other things, be culturally feasible and appropriate to the situation. Communicative competence is not a simple mastery of how-to rules for language use. Such competence "deals with how we *know* that a given situation requires a given speech variety and communicative approach" (Johnson, 1979, p. 14). In a similar way, Gee (1993) refers to *primary discourse*: that discourse "to which people are apprenticed early in life . . . as members of particular families within their sociocultural settings" (p. 108). As members of groups, people learn other ways to use language throughout their lives, making them users of multiple discourse. Gee calls these *secondary discourses*.

Culture, then, frames communication by directly influencing its form and content. Routine language use, for example, varies from culture to culture. In this regard, Forgas (1988) notes that *communicative episodes* (routine situations in which people interact) are both highly predictable and culturally specific: Culture provides an individual with shared cognitive schemas that shape language use and broader communicative conduct. The most straightforward example is the difference in greeting behaviors from culture to culture.

Communicative competence *within* a cultural system can vary widely from person to person. Some people use language more effectively because their knowledge system is more complex. An individual can also possess different levels of communicative competence *across* cultural systems, such that greater effectiveness and proficiency will be present when that person uses language in one cultural context compared to another.

Intercultural Communicative Competence. The importance of "cultural mindedness," or the ability to understand that cultural systems play a major role in communication, is important for effective functioning in a society of cultural multiplicity. Minimally, cultural mindedness implies cultural empathy. Ideally, it implies *intercultural communication competence*. Young Yun Kim (1991) defines such competence as the "overall *capacity* or *capability* to facilitate the communication process between people from differing cultural backgrounds and to contribute to successful interaction outcomes" (p. 263). Kim emphasizes that intercultural communication competence is not the same as having competence for communication within a specific culture but, rather,

requires "metacompetence," or the ability to explicitly think about and adapt language use and communication to different cultural situations.

In sum, discourse patterns, as the heart of the pragmatics of language, play an especially important role when cultural backgrounds are taken into account. Cultural similarity enhances the prospect that language use will lead to communicative effectiveness. Cultural dissimilarity portends the opposite unless cultural mindedness or intercultural communication competence is developed.

IDEOLOGY AND CULTURAL COMPLEXES

In a multicultural society, there is plenty of room for communicative misunderstanding and conflict based on different language systems, which arise from different cultural systems and their accompanying discourses. Simultaneously with any cultural system that might be designated as mainstream or public, many other cultural systems operate. Such cultural multiplicity can be viewed as represented in Figure 2, which shows cultures coexisting up to any possible number (*n*) that may occur simultaneously in greater or lesser contact with one another.

Societies such as the United States contain many cultural groups and can be said to be *cultural complexes* made up of distinct but interrelated cultures. For reasons elaborated earlier, these different cultures will be designated as *co-cultures* rather than subcultures. In this example, C1 would be the dominant, mainstream culture. C2 through C7 all overlap with C1 and with each other to varying degrees: C3 has the most overlap with C1 and is the cultural group, with C7 close behind but overlapping less with C1; C3, C5, C6, and C9 form an overlapping cluster, but C5 and C9 remain distinct from one another; and so forth. C10 and C11 stand apart from the other cultures as isolates from the cultural complex—a rare situation but certainly possible for small groups.

Using the term *co-cultures* draws attention to the existence of different cultures within the same or contiguous spaces and to the importance of describing each of the coexisting cultures on its own terms.

Figure 2 *Model of Cultural Complex*

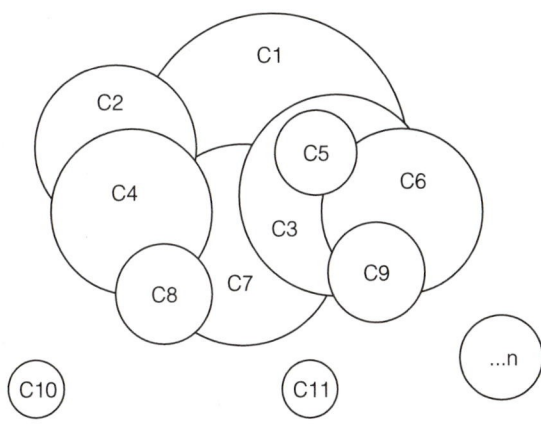

We can think of co-cultures visually as existing on a horizon—a metaphorical space in which cultures exist at the same level of complexity but with different degrees of closeness and separation from one another. Figure 3 represents the co-cultural horizon. Such a visual representation invites inspection of each from the same angle or the same rotation rather than seeing the array laid with some cultures on a higher plane and others on a lower plane. Because the prefix *co-* means to exist together or along with each other, designating multiple cultures as co-cultures gives no particular advantage or status to any one culture in relation to the others in its company. This kind of parity is critical to discovering the principles operating within cultures in a manner free of assumptions transported from the culturally biased gaze of someone in another culture. The co-culture perspective, then, affords the possibility for the unbiased examination of language varieties.

We must keep in mind, however, that whereas cultures coexist in time and reflect complexity through their systems of abstractions, artifacts, and languages, their political relations involve patterns of subordination and privilege such as that represented in Figure 2. To the extent that something like "the American culture" exists, its mainstream manifestations displace, distort, and disregard many other cultural identities coexisting in time space. As one manifestation, notions about Standard English, whether that means a variety of written English or

Figure 3 *Horizon of Co-Cultures*

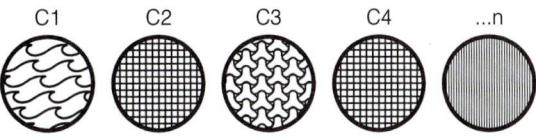

some idea about accent-less spoken English, are purely political in the sense that they exist only because those in privileged positions (e.g., teachers, editors of newspapers and magazines, television network executives, court judges) dictate their terms.

Where one culture's status positions it in a situation of control over the form and content of institutions and social processes, that culture imposes its authority in special ways. The term *dominant ideology* is used to characterize this situation. In multicultural societies, there is often one dominant culture, whose ideology shapes much of public life. Ideology, essentially, is the set of cultural practices and codes of meaning used in a culture. Dominant ideology guides conceptions of reality through repetition of preferred, privileged practices treated as though they were "natural." This control of meaning relegates other cultural systems to the margins by making their systems seem wrong, deviant, unimportant, primitive, or even invisible.

In the U.S. multicultural context, we see cultural ideology at work in the way it constructs and maintains discourse practices in institutional contexts such as work, school, government, and law. Increasingly, ideology gains its force from the media of mass communication (i.e., television, advertising, popular music).

No person—mainstream or marginalized—can command all of the cultures and their corresponding language systems, but varying degrees of cultural mindedness and intercultural communication competence offer promise for bridging communication differences and difficulties that occur in moments of cultural complexity. These abilities are most likely to arise from a good grasp of the relationship between culture and communication and from an understanding of the way in which ideology privileges the discourses of certain cultural systems over others.

AXIOMS IN THE LANGUAGE-CENTERED PERSPECTIVE ON CULTURE

The Language-Centered Perspective on Culture, which frames our consideration of language diversity in the United States, is grounded in six axioms. Together, these axioms form the context for understanding language as a cultural resource.

1. *Cultural inherency of communication: All communication, whether verbal or nonverbal, occurs within cultural frameworks.* Because communication arises within the cultural frameworks of participants, it is neither neutral nor objective but, rather, thickly cultured. Donal Carbaugh's (1990) distinctions between *cultural* and *intercultural* communication convey the two major ways in which cultural frameworks contextualize communication. Cultural communication occurs when the communicative participants share culture. Intercultural communication occurs when the participants do not have full command of one another's cultural patterns or discourses and must somehow communicate across the divide.

2. *Tacit knowledge: Individuals possess tacit knowledge of the cultural systems through which they communicate.* Humans are rule-using and rule-following beings, and they learn their cultures by internalizing the sets of rules that underlie human conduct. The ability to organize behavior through elaborate rule systems allows for cultural communication to occur relatively spontaneously because the rules function out-of-awareness and exist as tacit, unspoken, knowledge. Residing in the cultural mainstream, especially in a country where equality and equal opportunity are constitutional rights, tends to obscure the fact that human action is culturally founded and, thus, culturally variable. As Clifford Geertz (1983) incisively summarizes it: "Given the given, not everything else follows. Common sense is not what the mind cleared of cant spontaneously apprehends; it is what the mind filled with presuppositions . . . concludes" (p. 84). The presuppositions form tacit knowledge. A Norwegian or Swedish Lutheran in Minnesota does not need to remind himself or herself that restraint and reserve are ways of life; demeanor and deportment of this ilk are simply "common sense." Common sense resides deeply in culture.

3. *Ideology and cultural marginalization: In multicultural societies, the ideology of dominant cultural groups produces patterns of cultural abstraction, cultural artifacts, and cultural language practices that displace, silence, or marginalize other cultural groups.* Ideology suppresses marginalized cultures through both tacit and explicit means. Because individuals possess complex tacit knowledge allowing them to function within their cultural communities, they can conduct their daily affairs without a sense that they live cultured lives. In this way, those enculturated into dominant groups take their ideas and interaction patterns for granted. Consider Figure 4, in which C1 as represented in Figure 2 has been imposed over the cultural groups that are clearly shown in the first of the two figures.

An everyday example will demonstrate the process shown in Figure 4. When a television scriptwriter develops the storyline for a soap opera or primetime drama, she or he usually imports dominant ideology into the representation of family organization and gender relations. It may never occur to the scriptwriter that other cultural practices are not only possible but viable within the viewing "public." Similarly, when a teacher defines a good student as one who actively participates in class discussion, she or he discounts the

Figure 4 *Effect of Cultural Ideology*

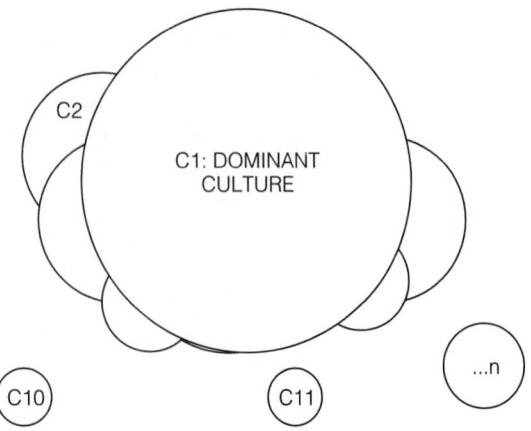

cultural practices of groups where such behavior is seen as disrespectful and inappropriate.

The power of dominant ideology explains why many of the discourse patterns discussed in this book are either unknown to or not well understood by white, non-Hispanic Americans. Those in dominant cultural groups rarely need to know much about the cultural practices of marginalized groups.

4. *Knowledge of the margins: Groups that have been dominated, subjugated, marginalized, made the object of prejudice and bigotry, discriminated against, or otherwise held in relatively powerless positions possess more explicit awareness of the components of their own and other cultural systems.* This axiom is a kind of corollary of the one just discussed. An example shows the implication of this axiom: A Latina with dark hair and complexion who speaks Spanish-accented English and works in a predominantly Anglo environment typically knows that she is different, not only in these ethnic markers, but also in manner of communication, preferences for food and clothing, family values, and so forth. At work, "common sense" must give way to common senses for her, which may or may not lead the individual to deliberately *code-switch* among language varieties and discourses that differ in their cultural foundations. Although this type of code-switching is usually described as *situational* (Hudson, 1980), it is more appropriately an example of *cultural code-switching* and, thus, of intercultural communication where only one side has any genuine knowledge of the cultural differences involved. Cultural code-switching requires at least some degree of explicit knowledge about the cultures from which and to which one is shifting.

This axiom about cultural knowledge at the margins is similar to the premise of what is termed *standpoint epistemologies* in feminism theory. A *standpoint* gives focus to what one knows depending on where one is situated in relation to dominant and subordinated groups. This idea, as expressed by philosopher Sandra Harding (1993), applies well to the United States:

> In societies stratified by race, ethnicity, class, gender, sexuality, . . . the *activities* of those at the top both organize and set limits on what persons who

perform such activities can understand about themselves and the world around them. . . . In contrast, the activities of those at the bottom of such social hierarchies can provide starting points for thought . . . from which humans' relations with each other and the natural world can become visible. (p. 54)

The standpoint of the marginalized, in short, must be cognizant of the cultural practices of the ideologically dominant simply out of necessity.

5. *Historicity and innovation: Culture and its discourses are both passed from one generation to another (i.e., historically founded) and constantly revised and changed (i.e., innovative).* What make cultures so resilient are their historical foundations. Yet, cultures are dynamic rather than static because people are constantly adapting to circumstances, new ideas, and innovations. The creative impulse in people also keeps culture on the move, vitiating static predictability.

Most often, the younger generations bring changes to the culture, which evolves with generational cohorts. Looking back on the recent history of almost any cultural grouping reveals generational contrasts, (e.g., in their values, communication, and expressive forms). Several examples from mainstream U.S. culture demonstrate this cultural dynamic. Values have shifted as environmental exploitation has given way to greater environmental awareness and protection because of the impact of human action on nature. Terms such as *ecology* and *recycling* are now commonplace, even to the point of being used to express ideas metaphorically, as in the phrase *recycling ideas*.

Taking another example, sexual conduct has moved from extensive premarital prohibitions reinforced by all major religious groups, to much greater openness in sexual expression during the 1970s and 1980s because of both a relaxed youth culture and access to birth control, to the present concern about more restricted sexual practices because of the AIDS epidemic. Earlier terms such as *premarital sex* and *open marriage* still exist, but today's prominent semantic notions encode an age of concern about *safe sex* and *sexual preference*.

6. *Cultural interinfluences: In multicultural societies, cultures influence one another, which includes the interinfluence of discourse systems.* Although it is commonplace for people to notice the differences among cultures when they are in close contact with one another, sheer locale, proximity, and intermingling of peoples also create a condition of mutual influence among differing cultures. Cultural groups change in part because of their situatedness within larger cultural complexes. This process was described earlier as cultural creolization. Cultural contact also influences the retention and conscious conservation of certain cultural practices, as might be the case when people refuse to give up their regional dialects and associated meanings even after living in another locale for a long time.

Immigrants provide a compelling case for the simultaneous permanence and change within cultural systems. Once in their new country, immigrant groups often develop *revised cultural patterns* based on the importation of the home culture as it is accommodated to the new environment and cultural situation. Parminder Bhachu's (1985) analysis of Sikhs who migrated from India first to East Africa and then to Britain provides a fascinating illustration of transportation and adaptation of marriage and dowry (*daaj*) patterns through migration. My own suburban locale west of Boston provides a timely example. A substantial number of Brazilians have settled in the area, and as numbers have grown, so have their venues: banks, beauty and barbershops, auto mechanics, restaurants, each of which adapts to the surrounding culture.

One line of language research closely related to this axiom of cultural interinfluence deals with "language contact" and borrowings from one language into another (Haugen, 1950; Heath, 1984; McMahon, 1994). For example, American English has influenced Cuban Spanish; yet, Cubans living in the United States remain loyal to Spanish and what it symbolizes about cultural identity.

IMPLICATIONS

Together, these axioms point to elaborate and intricate cultural relations among many different groups in the United States. The Language-Centered Perspective on Culture leads us to think in complex ways about the discourses we hear and the cultural practices underlying these language variables. When discourses differ from one another, underlying codes of meaning differ too. As we consider some of the major cultural groupings in the United States, the discursive implications of cultural multiplicity will become evident.

References

Bhachu, P. (1985). *Twice migrants: East African Sikh settlers in Britain*. London; New York: Tavistock Publications.

Carbaugh, D. (Ed.). (1990). *Cultural communication and intercultural contact*. Hillsdale, NJ: Lawrence Erlbaum.

D'Andrade, R. G. (1984). Cultural meaning systems. In R. A. Shweder & R. A. LeVine (Eds.), *Culture theory: Essays on mind, self, and emotion* (pp. 88–119). Cambridge, England: Cambridge University Press.

Forgas, J. P. (1988). Episode representations in intercultural communication. In Y. Kim & W. Gudykunst (Eds.), *Theories in intercultural communication*. Newbury Park, CA: Sage.

Gangotena, M. (1994). The rhetoric of *la familia* among Mexican Americans. In A. González, M. Houston, & V. Chen (Eds.), *Our voices: Essays in culture, ethnicity, and communication* (pp. 69–80). Los Angeles: Roxbury.

Gee, J. P. (1993). *An introduction to human language*. Englewood Cliffs, NJ: Prentice Hall.

Geertz, C. (1973). *The interpretation of cultures*. New York: Basic Books.

Geertz, C. (1983). *Local knowledge: Further essays in interpretive anthropology*. New York: Basic Books.

Goodenough, W. H. (1981). *Culture, language, and society* (2nd ed.). Menlo Park, CA: Benjamin/Cummings.

Hannerz, U. (1989). Culture between center and periphery: Toward a macroanthropology. *Ethnos, 54,* 200–216.

Harding, S. (1993). Rethinking standpoint epistemology: What is "strong objectivity"? In L. Alcoff & E. Potter (Eds.), *Feminist epistemologies* (pp. 49–82). New York: Routledge.

Haugen, E. (1950). The analysis of linguistic borowing. *Language, 26,* 210–231.

Heath, J. G. (1984). Language contact and language change. *Annual Review of Anthropology, 13,* 367–384.

Hudson, R. A. (1980). *Sociolinguistics*. Cambridge, England: Cambridge University Press.

Hymes, D. (1971). Competence and performance in linguistic theory. In R. Huxley & E. Ingram (Eds.), *Language acquisition: Models and methods* (pp. 3–28). New York: Academic Press.

Johnson, F. L. (1979). Communicative competence and the Bernstein perspective. *Communication Quarterly, 26*, 12–19.

Johnson, F. L. (1989). Women's culture and communication: An analytical perspective. In C. M. Lont & S. A. Friedley (Eds.), *Beyond boundaries: Sex and gender diversity in communication* (pp. 301–316). Fairfax, VA: George Mason University Press.

Kachru, B. B. (1981). American English and other Englishes. In C. A. Ferguson & S. B. Heath (Eds.), *Language in the USA* (pp. 21–43). Cambridge, England: Cambridge University Press.

Kim, Y. Y. (1991). Intercultural communication competence: A systems-theoretic view. In S. Ting-Toomey & B. F. Korzenny (Eds.), *Cross-cultural interpersonal communication* (pp. 259–275). Newbury Park, CA: Sage.

McMahon, A. M. S. (1994). *Understanding language change.* Cambridge, England: Cambridge Univesity Press.

Mead, G. H. (1934). *Mind, self, and society.* Chicago: University of Chicago Press.

Philipsen, G. (1975). Speaking "like a man" in Teamsterville: Culture patterns of role enactment in an urban neighborhood. *Quarterly Journal of Speech, 61*, 13–22.

Schultz, E. A. (1990). *Dialogue at the margins: Whorf, Bakhtin, and linguistic relativity.* Madison: University of Wisconsin Press.

Shweder, R. A. (1984). Anthropology's romantic rebellion against the enlightenment, or There's more to thinking than reason and evidence. In R. A. Shweder & R. A. LeVine (Eds.), *Culture theory: Essays on mind, self, and emotion* (pp. 27–66). Cambridge, England: Cambridge Unviersity Press.

"Singapore: After the caning, 'Mike's in pain.'" (1994, May 16). *Newsweek,* p. 41.

Stewart, W. C., & Bennett, M. J. (1991). *American cultural patterns: A cross-cultural Perspective.* Yarmouth, ME: Intercultural Press.

West, C. (1993). *Keeping faith: Philosophy and race in America.* New York: Routledge.

Whorf, B. L. (1940/1956). *Language, thought, and reality: Selected writings of Benjamin Lee Whorf* (J. B. Carroll, Ed.). Cambridge, MA: MIT Press.

Concepts and Questions

1. What is the Language-Centered Perspective on Culture? How does it help you understand the relationship between culture and language?

2. How does Johnson distinguish between society and culture?

3. What does Johnson view as the origins of culture? What two dynamics contribute to the complexity of culture?

4. How do enlightenment and romantic literary views lead to an understanding of contemporary culture?

5. What differing views of the role of language in culture are discussed in this article?

6. What are cultural abstractions? Give an example of a cultural abstraction. How do cultural abstractions determine choices available within a culture?

7. What are cultural artifacts? How do these artifacts influence the relationship between culture and language?

8. What is the main purpose of the "system of cultural language and communication" discussed in this article?

9. What does Johnson set forth as the essential elements of intercultural communication competence?

10. What are the six axioms in the Language-Centered Perspective on Culture? How do they lead to an understanding of language as a cultural resource?

Fern L. Johnson Cultural Dimensions of Discourse **197**

The Nexus of Language, Communication, and Culture

MARY FONG

Throughout the centuries, scholars around the world have been interested in both oral and written languages and the role they serve in contributing to cultural societies. Confucius observed that proper human conduct maintains a civil society, and cautions: "If language not be in accordance with the truth of things, affairs cannot be carried on to success." Saint-Exupery's comment that "to grasp the meaning of the world of today we use a language created to express the world of yesterday," and the Biblical injunction "may the words of my mouth and the meditation of my heart be acceptable in thy sight, oh Lord" also reflect this concern. In the current era, anthropologists, linguists, psychologists, philosophers, and communication scholars continue to try to fathom the role of language and communication in human activity and its nexus to culture.

In this essay, I first define language, communication, and culture. Then, I examine briefly some basic perspectives about the relationship between language, communication, and culture. In the course of this analysis, I begin with a description of the Sapir–Whorf hypothesis and then review the more current directions of language, communication, and culture research. Finally, in order to demonstrate some of the relationships between language, communication, and culture using qualitative methodologies, I draw from research on the Chinese culture to demonstrate the nexus of language, communication, and culture in examples from both cultural and intercultural interactions.

INTERRELATIONSHIP OF LANGUAGE, COMMUNICATION, AND CULTURE

Language, communication, and culture are intricately intertwined with one another. Language is a symbolic system in which meaning is shared among people who identify with one another. Both verbal and nonverbal aspects of language exist. In the study of language and culture, the verbal aspect of both written and spoken communications has been the predominant focus of research.

Spoken language is a vehicle for people to communicate in social interaction by expressing their experience and creating experience. Words reflect the sender's attitude, beliefs, and points of view. Language expresses, symbolizes, and embodies cultural reality (Kramsch, 1998). Communication cannot exist without language, and language needs the process of communication to engage people in social interaction.

Both language and communication reflect culture. For Sherzer (1987), culture is the organization of individuals who share rules for production and interpretation of behavior. Language and communication represent an individual's symbolic organization of the world. Language is a medium that reflects and expresses an individual's group membership and relationships with others. Both written and oral languages are shaped by culture, and in turn, these languages shape culture. As Kramsch points out:

> Culture both liberates and constrains. It liberates by investing the randomness of nature with meaning, order, and rationality and by providing safeguards against chaos; it constrains by imposing a structure on nature and by limiting the range of possible meanings created by the individual. (1998, p. 10)

With this same tenor, language and communication both liberate and constrain. Language and communication enable people to express themselves, while simultaneously constraining them to conform to shared cultural standards. Culture is a social system in which members share common standards of communication, behaving, and evaluating in everyday life.

PERSPECTIVES ON LANGUAGE AND CULTURE

A major proponent of linguistic relativity and one of the first modern observations of the relationship between language and culture is the Sapir–Whorf hypothesis. This notion proposes a deterministic view that language structure is necessary in order to produce thought. In other words, language and its categories—grammar, syntax, and vocabulary—are the only categories by which we can experience the world. Simply stated, language influences and shapes how people perceive their world, their culture. This vision dominated scholarly thinking as a point of discussion, research, and controversy for more than five decades.

The Sapir–Whorf hypothesis also holds that language and thought co-vary. That is, diversity in language categories and structure lead to cultural differences in thought and perceptions of the world. This position is known as *linguistic relativity*. Sapir (1951) believes that the "real world" is largely built on the unconscious language habits of the group. Benjamin Whorf was a student of Edward Sapir at Yale University from about 1931 (Carroll, 1992). Initial publications of Whorf's (1956) views about language and culture were printed in a series of articles in 1940–1941. He writes:

> We cut nature up, organize it into concepts, and ascribe significances as we do, largely because we are parties to an agreement to organize it in this way—an agreement that holds throughout our speech community and is codified in the patterns of our language. (p. 213)

Sapir and Whorf's ideas have been understood to mean that people who speak different languages segment their world differently. Thus, any language such as Russian, Chinese, or German structures a "Russian," "Chinese," or "German" reality by framing and screening what these cultural members pay attention to. If there is a word for "it," in their language, then cultural members know that "it" exists, and if not, "it" is nonexistent to them.

For instance, when I was five years old, I remember my mother asked me to stick out my tongue so that she could look at it. She looked at it briefly and said in Chinese Cantonese, "*Ni yao yi hay*," meaning "you have heat." My mother observed the texture, color, and coating of my tongue and lips. In the Chinese culture, it is common knowledge than an aspect of our physical health is viewed in terms of *yi hay* (heat) or *leung* (cool), which are extreme conditions that may be balanced through various types of foods and herbs. It is not the actual temperature of the food, but rather the *nature* of the food that produces a cool or warm effect on your body. If a person eats too many fried and baked foods and not enough cool foods such as particular fruits, vegetables, and liquids, then the person will eventually have a condition of too much heat in the body. If a person has a cool condition, one way to increase the heat in one's body is to lessen the consumption of cool foods and to increase one's diet to warm nature foods. This is one way that the Chinese strive to maintain a healthy physical balance.

This is an example of a "Chinese" reality of framing and screening what these cultural members pay attention to. On the other hand, the "American" reality promotes eating a well-balanced diet from the four main food groups: fruits and vegetables, meat and poultry, breads and grains, and dairy products. The American reality does not typically categorize food as warm or cold in nature in understanding and maintaining a balanced diet to increase one's health.

The system of labeling food, drink, medicines, herbs, illnesses, and medical procedures as either cold or hot is based on a system originating with the ancient Greeks and spreading to Central Asia (Dresser, 1996). For instance, as perceived in many Asian cultures, after a major surgery or childbirth, the body loses blood, energy, and heat. Therefore, the heat must be replenished, and avoidance of drinking cold water, eating cool foods, or taking showers is recommended. Middle Eastern and Latin American peoples also have a system of classifying foods, medicines, and procedures, but all cultural groups may differ in varying degrees depending on their principles (Dresser, 1996).

The situation of my mother observing my physical condition and the examples of foods, medicines, and procedures provide instances of how various cultural people segment their world and reality in varying ways. Furthermore, this natural cultural process of thinking and perceiving influences how members may communicate by accepting or rejecting particular foods, medicines, and procedures in certain circumstances. A person who is not familiar with another person's cultural ways will be likely to misinterpret the person's actions.

Another scholar, Brown (1958), in part disagreed with the Sapir–Whorf hypothesis and argued that a cultural member's worldview is not determined by language. He held, rather, that people categorize their world by attaching labels to what is out there. People use language to do what they need it to do. According to Brown, people will label an object, an idea, a process, and so forth based on the importance and utilization it has for them. For example, CDs, DVDs, cell phones, and the Internet are relatively new inventions that need labeling through language so that people can communicate their ideas about them. Because antiquated technology such as a record player, a rotary phone, and a slide rule is no longer important or used by people, the once common labels for these objects are now archived in museums and hardly referred to in conversation. Brown's position, however, supports the idea of linguistic relativity because the perceptual categories that are frequently used receive labels, whereas unused or insignificant categories may not be labeled.

Several research studies on color terms and color perception tested the Sapir–Whorf hypothesis (Berlin & Kay, 1967; Bruner, Oliver, & Greenfield, 1966; Greenfield & Bruner, 1966; Kay and Kempton, 1984). Eastman (1990) reviewed these studies that supported the idea of linguistic relativity and stated that: "[I]t appears to be the case that world view is a matter more of linguistic relativity than linguistic determinism" (p. 109).

Other researchers have found it difficult to test how strongly the structure of a language influences the worldview of people because reliable methods in assessing the worldview of a cultural people independently of the language they speak are needed (Brown, 1976; Carroll, 1967; Kay & Kempton, 1984). The deterministic view of the Sapir–Whorf hypothesis is not taken seriously (Kramsch, 1998). Carroll (1992) believes that researchers and theorists generally regard the Sapir-Whorf as either uncomfirmable or incorrect because the evidence offered in its support is viewed as being flawed. He further contends that if the hypothesis can be sus-tained, it would only suggest a weak influence of language structure on thought.

The linguistic-relativity view of the Sapir–Whorf hypothesis is its strength and contribution in understanding an aspect of the differences in language and culture. It is not so much if languages can be translated into one another, which they can, for the most part, if two speakers are of different languages; but rather, the two speakers coming from different cultures are operating under different language and communication systems that are designed differently, which influences their perceptions and interpretation of an event. As Kramsch (1998) suggests, speakers from different cultures define reality or categorize experience in different ways. Achieving understanding across languages is dependent on common conceptual systems rather than on structural equivalences. They may differ in terms of the meaning and value of a concept.

CURRENT RESEARCH TRENDS AND DIRECTIONS

In 1974, Hymes described the development of linguistic research in the first half of the 20th century, which was distinguished by a drive for the autonomy of language as an object of study and a focus on description of [grammatical] structure, and in the second half of the century, which was distinguished by a concern for the integration of language in sociocultural context and a focus on the analysis of function (p. 208).

Hymes's description was accurate because the second half of the 20th century has marked several research methods, such as discourse analysis, pragmatics, ethnography of communication, rhetorical analysis, and quantitative analysis, as ways to investigate the linkages of language, communication, and culture. Examples of themes of interest to researchers are the relationship between language and context, the relationship between language and identities (i.e., personal identity, social role identity, and cultural/ethnolinguistic identity), and multiple functions and meanings of language and communication in relationship to culture (Ting-Toomey, 1989).

Current approaches to the study of language, communication, and culture are developmental, interactional, and social psychological. The *developmental* approach focuses on language acquisition and cultural communication practices simultaneously in the language development stages of a child. Developmental theorists are interested in understanding the connection between the cognitive processing in a culture (Ting-Toomey, 1989). The *interactional* approach investigates what people are doing with speech as they interact face to face in a particular interactional context. Interactional theorists are interested in identifying appropriate communication styles and norms in various cultures (Ting-Toomey, 1989). The *social psychological* approach explores the underlying factors that influence language choices in multilingual communication contexts. For example, group comparison factors, identity salience factors, and attitudinal and motivational factors have significant association to the language accommodations process in intergroup communication situations. Social psychological theorists are interested in delineating specific social psychological conditions that account for first-language or second-language usage in majority and minority groups in cultural communities globally (Ting-Toomey, 1989).

For some researchers, the controversy over whether language determines or reflects thought or thought determines or reflects language is not the primary concern. According to Sherzer (1987), what is at issue is the analysis of discourse as the "embodiment of the essence of culture and as constitutive of what language and culture relationship is all about." Sherzer (1987) also views discourse as the intersection where language and culture interrelate. He states: "It is discourse that creates, recreates, focuses, modifies, and transmits both culture and language and their intersection" (p. 295).

For Sherzer (1987), culture is the organization of individuals who share rules for production and interpretation of behavior. Language represents an individual's symbolic organization of the world. Language is a medium that reflects and expresses an individual's group membership and relationships with others. Discourse analysis derives from pragmatics and speech act theory (Saville-Troike, 1989). *Pragmatics* or *speech act theory* refers to the study of the connotative (inner) and denotative (outer) meanings of "expressions when used in a conversation or a written work" (Paul, 1987, p. 101). According to Silverstein (1976), pragmatics is "the study of the meaning of linguistic signs relative to their communicative functions" (p. 20). Pragmatics also entails cultural members applying their knowledge of the world to the interpretation of what is said and done in interaction (Fromkin & Rodman, 1983; Gumperz, 1982).

The ethnography of communication provides the researcher with a framework of observation and interviewing techniques to facilitate capturing the interlocutors' meanings in various communicative acts both culturally and interculturally. The ethnographer endeavors to describe the communicative choices that interlocutors make. This involves describing and accounting for the interpretive systems and practices through which members construct actions and deal with behaviors.

Hymes (1962), the originator of the ethnography of communication, states that the "study of speech as a factor in cognitive and expressive behavior leads to concern with the ethnographic patterning of the uses of speech in a community" (p. 102). Investigating language, communication, and culture is discovering not only linguistic structural regularities, but also regularities of usage that have motives, emotions, desires, knowledge, attitudes, and values attached to them. An essential aim of studies on language, communication, and culture using the ethnography of communication approach is to make implicit cultural beliefs, attitudes, values, norms of interpretation, rules of speaking, norms of interaction, and so forth explicit in order to understand and to practice communication competence within a particular culture, and eventually in intercultural interactions.

LANGUAGE STUDIES

Some of the sample findings in the cultural and intercultural studies that follow are illustrations of language and culture analysis. The qualitative methods—discourse analysis, pragmatics, and ethnography of communication—jointly provide tools and perspectives to make possible an in-depth examination of the communicative phenomena.

A Cultural Study

An ethnographic study of the Chinese New Year celebration in Hong Kong (Fong, 2000) provides one instance of the manner in which the Chinese employ language to reverse bad luck. By examining a speaking pattern that is used when someone makes a negative comment during the Chinese New Year, it is possible to understand how Chinese people are prepared to avoid arguments and negative talk during the Chinese New Year. It is possible to understand how Chinese are prepared to handle a rule violation committed. Chinese people engage in positive talk and try to avoid arguments and negative talk during the Chinese New Year. Spoken words are carefully watched to avoid saying words that signify death, sickness, poverty, or anything else unlucky. All of the participants in this cultural study agreed with the same ideas as the following participant, who explains why negative comments during the New Year celebrations are avoided:

> Of course you don't say unlucky things. Always be positive. Chinese New Year is supposed to be a happy occasion. Try not to say something unlucky, like mentioning death or misfortune. Say it after the New Year. Perhaps some people may even think that saying those things during Chinese New Year will bring bad luck in the coming year. Those things may happen.

If someone accidentally talks about something unfortunate or utters a negative comment during this holiday, the rule of positive speaking is violated in this context. The hearer of the message may say:

/tou³ hæu² sæy² dzɔi³ gɔŋ² gwɔ³/

("Spit out your saliva; speak once more")

Another expression that participants in the study reported is:

/tsɔi¹/ or /tsɔi¹, dai⁶ gæt⁷ lei⁶ si⁶/

("lucky" or "very lucky, auspicious")

These expressions are said in order to reverse the bad luck that has been invited into good luck.

To understand what linguistic devices the Chinese employ, it is necessary to understand a few rules of behavior and speaking. Shimanoff (1980) proposes an "If . . . then . . ." method of concisely stating a rule of behavior. To develop Shimanoff's method of stating behavioral rules, I will add a "because . . . meaning . . ." sequence in order to add a meaning component to a formulation of a communication rule.

In this situation, the sequential rule statement begins with the initial linguistic "If . . ." slot that provides information on the particular context, condition, or situation, like a speech event, speech act, or genre. It is followed by the "then . . ." slot, which refers to the speaking and/or behavioral interaction pattern discovered from the researcher's ethnographic data analysis.

The third linguistic device, the "because . . ." slot, provides a concise rationale for why people of a particular culture behave the way they do. Here, an underlying belief or value system or cultural principle may be revealed to provide an explanation for a people's way of communicating. The final linguistic device, the "meaning . . ." slot, serves the same function as Hymes's component norm of interpretation of a symbol, the speaking and/or behavioral interaction pattern, a particular speech act, speech event, scene, and so forth.

These sequential rules statement provide the following formula:

If . . . (context, condition, or situation like a speech event, speech act, or genre) . . . then . . . (speaking and/or interaction pattern) . . .
because . . . (belief or value system or cultural principle) . . .
meaning . . . (norm of interpretation of a symbol, speaking pattern, interaction pattern, a particular speech act, speech event, scene, etc.)

Applying these sequential rules to the Chinese custom of reversing the negative comments can be expressed in a concise rule statement using the following formula:

If a person makes a negative comment on Chinese New Year Day, *then* a Hong Kong Chinese person who hears it should say:

/tsɔi¹/ or /tsɔi¹, dai⁶ gæt⁷ lei⁶ si⁶/

("lucky" or "very lucky, auspicious")

/tou³ hæu² sæy² dzɔi³ gɔŋ² gwɔ³/

("Spit out your saliva; speak once more")

because this is believed to counteract the bad luck and create good luck, *meaning* that the negative comments will not come true in the coming new year.

An Intercultural Study

An intercultural study on compliment interactions between Chinese immigrants and European Americans from the perspective of Chinese immigrants (Fong, 1998) found that both cultural groups have differing ways of speaking in compliment interactions (Chen, 1993; Chiang & Pochtrager, 1993; Fong, 1998). European Americans on the West Coast and in the Midwest generally accept a compliment (Chen, 1993; Chiang & Pochtrager, 1993; Fong, 1998).

On the other hand, the literature reports that Chinese have the tendency to deny compliments in order to give an impression of modesty (Chen, 1993; Chiang & Pochtrager, 1993; Gao, 1984; Zhang, 1988). In one study (Fong, 1998), an informant from Mainland China explained the primary difference and the internal similarity between two cultural groups:

> On the surface I say "no, no, no.". . . But inside I accept it. I feel really excited. In western culture, they say "yes" means accept the compliment. But in China, people say "no," but really, really accept the compliment. Different [speaking] way, but the feeling is the same. (p. 257)

Four adaptations by Chinese immigrant participants (CIPs) to European-American compliments were found. An orientation is a state or condition that is changeable from one interaction to another depending on the CIP's adaptation to intercultural communication differences. Four orientations in which the CIP can be located are (1) intercultural shock state, (2) intercultural resistance state, (3) intercultural accommodation state, and (4) bi-cultural competence state. For the purpose of this essay, we will capture a glimpse of one of the orientations, the intercultural shock state, in order to have a sense of Chinese immigrants' thinking and speaking patterns.

Affectively, CIPs reported feeling uncomfortable, unnatural, uneasy, nervous, stressed, embarrassed, surprised, shocked, or afraid when a European American complimented them. The situational outcome of the intercultural compliment interaction for CIPs, however, was an appreciation in receiving praise because they felt accepted, liked, and welcomed by European Americans. CIPs reported that compliments helped them reduce some of their stress as a newcomer to the United States.

Cognitively, CIPs in the intercultural shock state have minimum knowledge of the intercultural communication differences in compliment interactions with European Americans. Before coming to the United States, CIPs reported that they were not familiar with the European Americans' generosity in giving (1) compliments, (2) compliments containing strong positive adjectives, (3) compliments intended to encourage a person after an unsatisfactory performance, and (4) compliments on a wide variety of topics; and they were unfamiliar with (5) accepting compliments and (6) face-to-face compliments in all types of relationships.

Behaviorally, five speaking patterns were found; two examples are provided here. One type of a compliment response that Chinese immigrants used was the Direct Denial + Verbal Corrective/Prescriptive response. Following is a reported intercultural compliment interaction:

(AMERICAN) BOYFRIEND: You're the most beautiful person that I've seen.

(HONG KONG) GIRLFRIEND: Oh gaaa. Oohh. Please don't say that.

Because Chinese immigrants value indirectness and modesty, the compliment was interpreted as being direct (e.g., face-to-face, expressing openly with positive adjectives on the complimentee's appearance), which is contrary to the reported Chinese way of compliment interactions. The response was made to avoid self-praise and to suggest to the complimenter not to make such a direct compliment.

CIPs who were in the intercultural shock state were also found to use the Silence response. The following intercultural compliment interaction is reported to have occurred at work:

(AMERICAN FEMALE) BOSS: I want to thank you for doing a wonderful job. You're very, very nice.

(CHINESE FEMALE) WORKER: [silence]

Chinese immigrant interlocutors value modesty highly, but they are also aware of one of the American values of directly accepting and appreciating compliments. The compliment was interpreted as direct (i.e., face-to-face, expressing openly their positive thoughts with positive adjectives), which is contrary to the reported Chinese way of compliment interactions. The response was made because Chinese immigrant recipients reported that they felt ambivalent about which cultural response to use, thus the Chinese immigrant recipient remained silent.

CONCLUSION

The excerpt from the cultural study (Fong, 2000) illustrates the Chinese way of thinking and speaking. When a negative comment is made during the Chinese New Year holiday, the Chinese way of thinking is interpreting the incident as forthcoming bad luck in the coming new year. Through speech, however, the perceived bad luck is reversed to good luck.

The intercultural compliment interaction study (Fong, 1994) sheds light on the way Chinese immigrants in the intercultural shock state reveal patterns of thinking and speaking. The denial response is a pattern of speaking that is commonly used in the intercultural shock state. CIPs in this orientation essentially perceive European Americans as being generous in giving compliments with relatively strong positive adjectives, and in accepting compliments.

Current ethnographic methods hold that the best way to capture a view of language, communication, and culture is to observe the communicative phenomenon in a naturalistic setting and to have cultural members identify and classify the interaction or event as being culturally significant. The crossroads of language, communication, and culture is found in the culturally shared meaning of ideas and behaviors that are voiced as symbolic utterances, expressions, dialogue, and conversations in such various contexts as interpersonal and group interactions, research interviews, and public speaking forums.

In the two qualitative studies described in this essay, the ways of speaking and thinking were the two primary interrelated foci that reveal and reflect the outer and inner shared substances of communications that primarily make up a speech community. To examine a speech community's patterns of speaking without also discovering the norms of interpretation or the shared sociocultural knowledge of cultural members is to silence their cultural humanness as a speech community. To study only the shared sociocultural knowledge of cultural members and not attend to how it is relevant to their way of speaking is to lose an opportunity to understand more about different cultural communication styles. In accomplishing this goal, potential sources at borderlines and intersections of cultural differences are able to richly understand and resolve intercultural conflicts.

Both examples of findings from the mentioned qualitative studies illuminate, in part, what Hymes (1974) has suggested:

> It has often been said that language is an index to or reflection of culture. But language is not simply passive or automatic in its relation to culture. . . . Speaking is itself a form of cultural behavior, and language, like any other part of culture, partly shapes the whole; and its expression of the rest of culture is partial, selective. That selective relation, indeed, is what should be interesting to us. Why do some features of a community's life come to be named—overtly expressible in discourse—while others are not? (p. 127)

Note

*The International Phonetic System was used in transcribing this and other Chinese dialogue.

References

Berlin, B., & Kay, P. (1967). *Universality and evolution of basic color terms.* Working Paper #1, Laboratory for Language Behavior Research, University of California, Berkeley.

Bruner, J., Oliver, R. R., & Greenfield, P. M. (1966). *Studies in cognitive growth.* New York: John Wiley & Sons.

Brown, R. (1958). *Words and things.* New York: The Free Press.

Brown, R. (1976). In Memorial Tribute to Eric Lennenberg. *Cognition, 4,* 125–153.

Carroll, J. B. (1967). Bibliography of the Southwest Project in Comparative Psycholinguistics. In D. Hymes (Ed.), *Studies in southwestern ethnolinguistics* (pp. 452–454). The Hague: Mouton.

Carroll, J. B. (1992). Anthropological linguistics: An overview. In W. Bright (Ed.), *International encyclopedia of linguistics.* New York: Oxford University Press.

Chen, R. (1993). Responding to compliments: A contrastive study of politeness strategies between American English and Chinese speakers. *Journal of Pragmatics, 20,* 49–75.

Chiang, F., & Pochtrager, B. (1993). A pilot study of compliment responses of American-born English speakers and Chinese-born English speakers. (Available in Microfiche only, ED 356649).

Dresser, N. (1996). *Multicultural manners.* New York: John Wiley & Sons.

Eastman, C. M. (1990). *Aspects of language and culture* (2nd ed.). Novato, CA: Chandler & Sharp Publishers.

Fong, M. (1994). Patterns of occurrence of compliment response types. In a doctoral dissertation, *Chinese immigrants' interpretations of their intercultural compliment interactions with European-Americans.* Seattle: University of Washington.

Fong, M. (1998). Chinese immigrants' perceptions of semantic dimensions of direct/indirect communication in intercultural compliment interactions with North Americans. *The Howard Journal of Communications, 9,* 3.

Fong, M. (2000). 'Luck talk' in celebrating the Chinese New Year. *Journal of Pragmatics, 32,* 219–237.

Fromkin, V., & Rodman, R. (1983). *An introduction to language* (3rd ed.). New York: CBS Publishing and Holt, Rinehart, & Winston.

Gao, W. (1984). *Compliment and its reaction in Chinese and English cultures.* Working papers in discourse in English and Chinese. Canberra: Canberra College of Advanced Education, 32–37.

Greenfield, P. M., & Bruner, J. S. (1966). Culture and cognitive growth. *International Journal of Psychology, 1,* 89–107.

Gumperz, J. J. (1982). *Discourse strategies.* New York: Cambridge University Press.

Hymes, D. (1962). The ethnography of speaking. In T. Gladwin & W. Sturtevant (Eds.), *Anthropology and human behavior* (pp. 99–137). Washington, DC: Anthropological Society of Washington.

Hymes, D. (1964). Toward ethnographies of communication: The analysis of communicative events. *American Anthropologist, 66,* 21–41.

Hymes, D. (1974). *Foundations in sociolinguistics: An ethnographic approach.* Philadelphia: University of Pennsylvania Press.

Kay, P., & Kempton, W. (1984). What is the Sapir-Whorf Hypothesis? *American Anthropologist 86,* 65–79.

Kramsch, C. (1998). *Language and culture.* London, England: Oxford University Press.

Paul, A. (1987). Review of Joseph H. Greenberg, *Language in the Americas.* In "In Brief Books," *The Chronicle of Higher Education,* July 15, 6.

Sapir, E. (1951). The status of linguistics as a science. In D. Mandelbaum (Ed.), *Selected writings.* Berkeley: University of California Press.

Saville-Troike, M. (1989). *The ethnography of communication* (2nd ed.). New York: Basil Blackwell.

Sherzer, J. (1987). A discourse-centered approach to language and culture. *American Anthropologist, 89,* 295–309.

Shimanoff, S. B. (1980). *Communication rules: Theory and research.* Beverly Hills: Sage.

Silverstein, M. (1976). Shifters, linguistics categories, and cultural description. In K. H. Basso & H. A. Selby (Eds.), *Meaning in anthropology* (pp. 11–56). Albuquerque: University of New Mexico Press.

Ting-Toomey, S. (1989). Language, communication, and culture. In S. Ting-Toomey & F. Korzenny (Eds.), *Language, communication, and culture* (pp. 9–15). Newbury Park: Sage.

Whorf, B. L. (1940/1956). *Language, thought, and reality: Selected writings of Benjamin Lee Whorf* (J. B. Carroll, Ed.). Cambridge, MA: MIT Press.

Zhang, Z. (1988). A discussion of communicative culture. *Journal of Chinese Language Teacher Association, 23,* 107–112.

Concepts and Questions

1. What does Fong mean when she writes: "Language and thought vary with one another"? Do you agree?

2. Can you think of specific examples that illustrate the link between culture and language?

3. Can you explain what Fong means when she states that language influences and shapes how people perceive their world and their culture?

4. What is meant by the following phrase: "People who speak different languages segment their world differently"?

5. How do Chinese immigrants and Americans differ in their ways of compliment interactions?

6. When referring to Sherzer, what does Fong means when she writes: "Culture is the organization of individuals who share rules for production and interpretation of behavior"?

7. How do the Chinese use language to reverse bad luck?

8. In what ways do the Chinese and the Americans express themselves differently?

Mary Fong The Nexus of Language, Communication, and Culture **205**

Contemporary Social and Political Movements and their Imprints on the Chinese Language

Mei Zhong

In the 50s, people love people;
In the 60s, people hate people;
In the 70s, people fight people;
In the 80s, people cheat people;
In the 90s, people eat people.*
　　　　— **Chinese Folk Rhyme (Lee, 1997, p. 359)**

The mutually penetrating relation between culture and language has been stressed a great deal in the study of intercultural communication. From the early days of the Sapir–Whorf hypothesis (Whorf, 1956) to recent studies of cultures (Carbaugh, 1997; Ting-Toomey & Korzenny, 1989; Zormeier & Samovar, 1997), we have come to realize that culture has an enormous influence on language. Culture has been generally defined as a set of norms for a group of people over a relatively long period of time. Porter and Samovar (1985) maintained that culture includes "language, friendships, eating habits, communication practices, social acts, economic and political activities" (p. 19). Thus, the main elements in a culture should include such elements as political structures, social institutions, economic capacities, education systems, artistic expressions, daily practices, and other cultural issues.

Because China is becoming increasingly visible and important in the global community, there has been a growing interest and need to study the Chinese culture. At the same time, because the country is undergoing perhaps the most drastic changes in its history, the culture is changing too. These changes in the Chinese culture are consequently reflected in the Chinese language. This essay examines these language changes and the evolving trends in Chinese that result from the series of cultural changes, especially from the powerful influences of social and political movements in the contemporary timeframe.

Chronologically, I will distinguish five main eras of Chinese history in order to discuss the Chinese language: (1) the New Culture Era, (2) the New China Era, (3) the Cultural Revolution Era, (4) the Economic Reform Era, and (5) the All-around Opening and Western Influences Era. For each of these eras, I will explain the social and political events that influenced the language, discuss the characteristics of the language styles, and demonstrate each with examples. Cultural analyses will be applied along with these discussions.

The language examples are collected through interviews of many Chinese native-speakers over the years as well as based on the author's (a Chinese-English bilingual) personal experiences and observations. I will cover the Chinese language briefly and then go on to discuss each era.

THE CHINESE LANGUAGE

Chinese is a very old language, more than 3,000 years old. No other known language has existed and retained its structure over such a long history; it is still comprehensible in its oldest form. As Chang and Chang (1978) maintained, the Chinese language "unites more human beings than any other language of mankind" (p. 3). Moreover, because of China's influential history in Asia, "[a] knowledge of Chinese has for centuries been essential to scholars all over Asia, as Latin was to scholars and diplomats of Renaissance Europe" (Chang & Chang, 1978, p. 5).

It has been considered that Chinese literature includes four main periods. The first period is based on the very rich traditional literature from the early Qin Dynasty (approximately 100 B.C.) to the end of the Qing Dynasty (1911 A.D.). The second period is called the May Fourth New Culture period. This represents the unique literature that blossomed from around the time of the Opium war to the ruling of the Chinese Communist Party. The third period is represented by the literature style set by Mao Zedong in his Talks on Literature and Arts at the Yanan Conference in 1942 and the years following the founding of the People's Republic of China until 1966. Finally, the fourth period is symbolized by the infamous Cultural Revolution literature until the present time (Flowers, 1997).

Historically, the Chinese language is developed from an agricultural, feudalistic society. It reflects the structure of the society—collectivistic, hierarchical, male-dominant, and generally not very explicit in style. Traditionally, the written language had been an elite language that only the nobles had the opportunity to learn. It also carried a formal and not readily comprehensible format called "the ancient literature style" (*gu wen*). It was used primarily by the elite group associated with the ruling powers as entertainment (in the form of poetry and literature) or as a tool to record history. As such, it divorces itself from the spoken language.

Although the language had evolved slowly over 3,000 years, it had been serving the same functions. It was not until the 20th century that the Chinese language experienced many drastic changes. Many of the changes resulted from the many political and social movements that took place over the past 100 years or so. Therefore, this author is particularly interested in examining the social and political influences on the Chinese spoken language in the most recent century. For this purpose, I will discuss the language chronologically in the following five eras, and I will do this with (1) a discussion of social and political movements that took place during each era; (2) a summary of language characteristics that bear imprints of the corresponding movement; and (3) examples to demonstrate these imprints.

The New Culture Era

The New Culture Era started around the early 20th century, marked first by the Xinhai Revolution (the Chinese bourgeois democratic revolution led by Dr. Sun Yat-Sen, which overturned the Qing Dynasty, China's last dynasty) in 1911 and followed by the May Fourth New Culture Movement in 1919. The time is largely recognized as the beginning of contemporary Chinese history.

This period represents the first wave of Western influences being introduced to China. They came by way of Chinese intellectuals who studied overseas and returned to China, bringing with them ideas they had learned from these countries. It is recognized that the two most significant sources were British and American influences. These ideas indicate an understanding of revolutions, individualism, and democracy. The movement went on in China for almost half a century, and the most recognizable person in the promotion of the "plain literature style" was Lu Xun, a revolutionary writer.

As a result of this movement, contemporary history has seen drastic changes in both the form and substance of the Chinese language. In form, Chinese was able to do away with the "ancient literature style" and replaced it with a new and fresh written style that is coherent with spoken language, called the "plain literature style" (*bai hua wen*). This great movement allowed the masses to learn and comprehend the Chinese written language and changed the outlook of education tremendously. Therefore, the biggest change in the Chinese language at this time is its ability to inform.

In terms of substance, the Chinese language was introduced to terms representing "the British and American thoughts," "Marxism," "revolutionism," "individualism," "symbolism," and so forth. The notions of "left wing" and "right wing" were used from this period (Flowers, 1997). It is obvious that most of these terms are politically oriented because of the change of eras in Chinese history. Soon, the Chinese Communist Party was to take power in China, starting the era of their rule.

The New China Era

In 1942, Mao Zedong, in his talks at the Yanan Literature and Arts Conference, emphasized the necessity of mass literature, new literature movements, and mass movements. The use of the term *mass* is very frequent in Mao's literature. He gained power through military actions and established the People's Republic of China (PRC) in October 1949. So he said: "Literature and arts should serve the workers, farmers, and soldiers." He encouraged intellectuals, whom he called "literature and art workers," to "let a hundred flowers bloom and let a hundred voices be heard."

The first decade or so after the founding of the PRC was regarded as the New China Era. Carried by his victory from military battles, Mao started political and literary movements, often using military strategies and naming them with military terms. In his writings, he claimed that "[p]olitical power comes from guns." Therefore, language in this period used many military and revolutionary phrases. For example, the country was divided up into several classes (e.g., landlord, rich farmers, poor peasants), and the whole country was engaged in "class struggles." Apparently, Mao considered it a successful strategy. He believed that "[c]lass struggle works magically."

In the cities, residents were assigned into "work units," which could mean companies, factories, government departments, offices, and the like. "Organization" is used as a synonym of "the Chinese Communist Party." In each work unit, there is a branch "organization," complete with a secretary and a committee. It was encouraged that each person reports to the "organization" regularly (e.g., once a month) about what they thought of—practically anything from opinions of the political and national events to personal relationships. Under Mao's assertion that "the Party leads," it was understood that in any work unit, the Party leader, translated in English as the "Party Secretary," is the top rank and above any other leaders in the work unit, including the president of the company.

I was amazed to hear a story about a Chinese delegation visiting a university department in the United States in the 1990s. The delegation was introduced to the department chair, professors, and the department secretary. From that point on, the delegation followed the secretary around for directions, assuming that the "Secretary" was in charge of the department.

Other terms used in political movements and adopted in daily life include "persistence is victory," and "perish the enemy," which can be used to mean "finishing a dish" at the dinner table. If someone asked a question, such as "What are you doing?" the response could be, "I'm doing revolution, of course," to mean, "I'm working, of course." If one is successful in a task and wants to advance, the term to use was "expand the outcome of the victory" (*kuo da zhan guo*).

Interpersonal relationships were changed by the blanket use of "comrade," replacing the traditional "Mr.," "Mrs.," and "Miss." Thus, in a traditionally hierarchical society, suddenly everyone was equal in title—"revolutionary comrade," with the exception of the "class enemy." "Comrade" was used commonly in plural form as well, for instance, "worker comrades," "farmer comrades," "teacher comrades," "men comrades," "women comrades," and so on. Intimate terms, such as "husband" and "wife," were replaced by "lover" (*ai ren*) in order to diminish the status differences associated with the traditional male-dominated language connotations. A husband may have introduced his wife as: "This is my lover, Comrade Chen." These terms were the only way to address anyone formally during those years, and "comrade" and "lover" are still used habitually by some people in China today.

On an informal level, however, out of the need to express respect for age, perhaps because of the hierarchical tradition of the Chinese culture, people address each other according to their ages before their last names. I have been aware of four levels: "*xiao*" (little, for young people around 20 and 30), "*da*" (big, for middle-aged people around 40 up to 50), "*lao*" (old, for older people over 50), and finally, "*lao*" used after the last name. This last form is used only for those who are extremely well established and have earned high respect, and mostly, high-ranking political figures, intellectuals, or military *taikoons*. Take the last name Wang as an example; if he is a young man, his colleagues typically refer him to as "*Xiao Wang*." When he reaches around 40, he becomes "*Da Wang*." Then, when he turns over 50, he would be addressed as "*Lao Wang*." And if he became, say, a nationally known writer in his old age, he would be addressed as "*Wang Lao*."

It should be noted that these names are only relative to the person who is addressing the addressee. If *Xiao Wang* started working under a boss at a young age, he is likely to stay *Xiao Wang* to that boss, even when he is in his fifties. So the status relationship also determines the address.

Soon after the effort to build and advance the economy by the "Great Leap Forward" (*da yue jin*), Mao thought it was time to start a series of political movements in order to cleanse the "revolutionary troop." The most significant political movement during this period is the "anti-rightist" movement that started in 1957, in which Mao invited intellectuals to criticize the Communist Party. A year later, in 1958, "having, in Mao's words, enticed the snakes (his critics and opponents) out of their holes, Mao launched an anti-rightist campaign in June, purging 550,000 intellectuals as anti-Party, anti-Socialist rightists, most of whom were sent to the countryside and deprived of their jobs and civil rights" (Lee, 1990, pp. xix–xx; cited in Schnell, 1999, p. 43).

Mao expressed his military style not only in domestic politics, but also in international affairs. During the 1950s and 1960s, China found its ally in the former Soviet Union, and regarded the United States as the enemy. People who lived through that time still vividly remember his famous sayings about the United States: "The American imperialists are but paper tigers" and "It is not the west wind that prevails the east wind; but the east wind that prevails the west wind" (the United States is west and China is east). If a person worked hard and performed well on the job, he or she was praised as being "progressive" (*ji ji*). It may have been applied to "work progressively" (*ji ji gong zuo*) or "progressively participate in revolution" (*ji ji ge ming*). But if someone was not so "progressive," then he or she was said to be "fallen behind the troop" (*luo hou, or luo wu*). If something needed to be done or was considered necessary to have, then it was of "revolutionary need" (*ge ming xu yao*).

At the beginning of this essay, I quoted a folk rhyme from China that indicates how the Chinese feel about the changes in people's mentality in recent decades. It reflects the consequences of social changes in general (please see the endnote for a full explanation). Folk rhyme in China, as a cultural phenomenon, has a long history. It is primarily a form of expression by the masses through unofficial channels. Zheng (1993) believes that the rhythmic form of literature has existed since approximately the first century in the Western calendar. In the past, it has served the function of fanning flames among rebellious groups against the government. In contemporary history, however, it has been spread across China as a way for people to voice their opinions or distaste about corruption, injustice, and as catharsis among friends and social groups (Zheng, 1993). All translations are by this author and, for

lack of appropriate rhymes, they are translated mostly by meaning. In the 1950s, there was a rhyme that says:

> *Learn about math, physics, and chemistry,*
> *Walk through the whole world with no fear.* (Zheng, 1993, p. 152)

This was a rather innocent rhyme that simply indicates the importance of studying science and technology, in line with the political objectives of the in-power government. This rhyme was to evolve and change years later along with societal changes.

The Cultural Revolution Era

The era that follows next is the Cultural Revolution, formally known as the "Great Proletarian Cultural Revolution," from 1966 to 1976. It was started by Mao, led by his wife, Jiang Qing, and ended shortly after Mao's death in September 1976. Many believe that it represents the darkest period in Chinese contemporary political history. Because of its fierce coercive nature and widespread effects, it penetrated through all levels and affected just about everybody in China. It has been estimated that about two-thirds of the entire country—and it is a huge country—were either charged with some form of "counter-revolutionary crimes" or had family members who were.

Continuing from the previous decade of class and political struggles, Mao wanted to make sure that he banished all potential enemies. The then first lady, Jiang Qing, in her own wish to gain political power in the Party, decided to "progressively" assist Mao in order to please him. As such, she made an effort to make Mao out to be a God-like figure who was inviolable. Indeed, Mao was considered nothing short of a God in those years. A person would swear the truth by saying, "I promise to Chairman Mao that . . ." It is comparable to "I swear to God . . ." in English.

Because most of those who followed his call and criticized him in the 1950s were intellectuals, the target of the revolution naturally fell on them. Therefore, anti-intellectual and class struggle were the themes of the movement. Intellectuals were called "stinky ninth class" (*chou lao jiu,*) which is the lowest possible class. They belonged to the category of "bad elements" (*huai fen zi*). These "bad elements" were sorted into five different kinds based on their "counter-revolutionaryness," and they were called the "black five kinds" (*he wu lei*). Then there were the "red five kinds" (*hong wu lei*), who were considered revolutionary, plus "red successors," meaning young people with great promise; "red guards," a term with which the Western world is familiar; and "little red soldiers," the younger kids who were to become "red guards," and so on. These are but a few examples of the Cultural Revolution vocabulary.

During the Cultural Revolution, Jiang Qing and her associates invented extreme terms in their political slogans. Never in history was there such strong, hateful profanity in formal media. Zheng (1993) stated that many of these terms appeared in the Party's official publication, the *People's Daily*. For example, the younger generation of class enemies was called "sons of bastards"; the class enemies' words were referred to as "dog fart" (comparable to "bullshit" in English); and the revolution was to "crash the dog heads," meaning perish the class enemy and then "stepping on them a million times and never let them overturn," and so on. The newspaper was the most prestigious and most widely distributed in China.

On the other hand, Mao was called the "Red Sun" and the "Great Captain of the Revolutionary Ship"; his words were the "highest commands" of the day; and the Cultural Revolution was the great historical movement that is "unprecedented" and happened "never before and never after." The Party was called "The great, glorious, ever-correct Chinese Communist Party." Again, these terms were not just used in political and public settings but were also integrated into ordinary people's daily life during those years.

Another important political movement was the "up the mountain and down to the countryside" movement, which affected an entire generation of young people and produced lasting effects on the lives of those people until even today. Mao believed that young students were not receiving the right education from schools and wanted them to learn from the working mass. Consequently, large groups of students in junior high and high schools were sent to the countryside to work on the farms. The exact theme of the movement was for "intellectual youth to go up the mountain and down to the countryside to receive re-education from the poor peasants."

These individuals' formal education was interrupted, and many of them stayed in the countryside for many years until the end of the Cultural Revolution. They are now referred to as "the old three classes" (including three classes in junior high and three classes in high school in 1966).

Some of these intellectual youths became "bearfoot doctors" (not systematically trained doctors who help people with medical needs in remote areas). Some of them, toward the end of the Cultural Revolution, joined the enviable group that was to become college students; however, these students were selected primarily based on their family's class status and political background, rather than academic qualifications. They were called "worker, peasant, and soldier students." These people are considered the lucky few who were able to obtain a diploma (equivalent to a college degree) out of that generation. Again, these terms were imprinted in Chinese language and are often used even today. For example, students who left China to study abroad today are referred to as "going to the countryside abroad" (a rough translation) to mean the hard life these students had to endure being away from their families and friends.

One of the side effects of the Cultural Revolution movement was the promotion of women's status against thousands of years of the old tradition. Because of Jiang Qing's ambition to gain power in the Party—and it was not easy for a woman to be in power in China—she wanted to change the image of women. Everyone who lived through those years would remember the famous quote: "Time is different now, men and women are just the same." Another very popular slogan was "women can support half of the sky." Consequently, a woman might be referred to as a "half sky." I have heard a man talk about his wife with his friends, saying: "Last week, the other half sky in my home told me . . ." In order to prove the equal capability that women possess, women were assigned to labor-intensive jobs just like men. If they were able to endure the physical challenge, then they may have been awarded the title "iron girls" (*tie gu niang*). There was absolutely no negative connotation or any trace of sarcasm, but rather only positive praise in this phrase.

Another range of expressions should be noted, which are from the "Model Opera Plays." These were eight revolutionary stories that were re-created and made into the Peking Opera style. They were produced directly under Jiang Qing's command. For about 10 years, they were the primary source of cultural entertainment across the whole country. People were organized to see these plays over and over, and dialogues from these plays took on real-life functions after a while. Terms such as "ladies troop" (*niang zi jun*) are from these operas. Based on the storyline, people use the term "Party Representative" (*dang dai biao*) of the "ladies troop" to mean the only man who leads a group of women.

Some of the lines from these model operas have become daily expressions. Very often, people may joke about someone blushing using a dialogue from one of the model operas:

"Why are you blushing?"

"Because of good health."

"Then why are you turning pale now?"

"Because of the wax I applied to keep warm."

It is almost like form language in daily practice. Furthermore, the revolutionary expressions were not only used in daily language but also implemented into textbooks at schools. For example, a question in a math book may use a scenario between classes as the background: "In the old society, a landlord harvested an X amount of crops and only distributed a Y amount of it to the poor peasants. How much did he deprive from the peasants?"

Even in English education, the standard textbook used across high schools in China during the 1970s provides a vivid example of the "revolutionary focus." The textbook contained the following lessons:

1. Long Live Chairman Mao
2. The English Alphabet
3. We Wish Chairman Mao a Long, Long Life
4. Our National Flag
5. China
6. The Red Sun
7. Workers and Peasants Work for the Revolution
8. The Best Weapon is Mao Tse-tung Thought
9. Our Party
10. Mao Tse-tung Thought is the Beacon Light
11. Learn from the Working Class
12. Good Fighters of Chairman Mao
13. We are Chairman Mao's Red Guards (Lehmann, 1975, pp. 78–79)

At the end of the last section, I introduced a folk rhyme. During the Cultural Revolution, to express people's distaste in distribution of power through social connections rather than competence, the rhyme evolved into the following:

Learn math, physics, and chemistry,
but it won't compare to having a well-connected daddy.
(Zheng, 1993)

The uniform address of "comrade" during the 1950s continued to be used, but around the 1970s, another address term was created. "*Shifu*" (master) was originally used in martial arts for the instructor and among handicraft workers to refer to the one who teaches the pupils. During the political movement, the term was used to address senior workers in the factories. Because workers and peasants were praised while intellectuals were condemned in those years, "*shifu*" took on a new meaning to become a respect form of addressing someone. It was adopted because it would not violate the political correctness code even in those years; yet it subtly showed respect for someone, rather than the cold "comrade."

Mao died in 1976, ending the 10-year-long political disaster. The Maoist Cultural Revolution left abundant imprints on the Chinese language. Because it was such an unforgettably painful part of Chinese history, it was amazing that some people started a wave in popular culture to remember the Model Operas in the mid-1990s, knowing that they remind people of the miserable years of their lives. To those who experienced hardship during the movement, the operas bring back horrible memories about that chaotic time in their lives, and they argue that it is wrong for the government to even allow such products to circulate (Yao, 1997). But in the late 1970s, China was about to lunge into recovery and face a new challenge.

The Economic Reform Era

Two years after Mao died, Deng Xiao-Ping gained power in China. The country was in chaos, and he inherited a destroyed economy, a broken higher-education system, and crises in most other areas. Some scholars (Flowers, 1997) identify that the 1980s was a period of denigration of the Cultural Revolution. Many literature works reflecting the painful experiences that people, especially intellectuals, went through were published during this decade. They were rightly labeled "The Scar Literature" (*shang hen wen xue*).

To lift the country's spirit and rebuild its system, Deng immediately jump-started the higher-education system by re-establishing the college entrance examination system, which allowed young people to take examinations regardless of class status or family background. Young people were most grateful for this change. Then came the challenge of the economy. Deng started by allowing farmers to own lands rather than keeping them in communes, which was a system established after the founding of the PRC. In the cities, people were allowed to own small businesses and keep profits for themselves, compared to almost 30 years of state ownership of all businesses.

On the other hand, Deng used political campaigns in an effort to rebuild civilization and, of course, to keep people in line with the government, as the policy had always been for the Chinese Communist Party. Because of these movements, the language style reflects the healing sensation from the Cultural Revolution and a somewhat uplifting spirit in looking forward to a better life.

Typical terms in the language include "individual business family" and "land ownership" to reflect the new economic policies. People were at the waking period to realize that no political reform would make life better than having money. People turned from talking about political ideologies to talking about money and realized that being rich is not such a bad thing. The government asked people to "look forward," and people secretly altered it to "look money" ("forward" and "money" sound the same in Chinese).

The country was setting out to "realize the four modernizations" of agriculture, industry, national defense, and science and technology. The process of this movement is called "the new long march," in reference to the "Long March" by the Red Army in 1927 in its battle during the Chinese Civil War. To praise those who exerted excellent performance

at work, they were awarded the title, "the pioneers on the road of the new long march."

The movement to rebuild civilization was called the "spiritual civilization movement." Under the movement in 1981, people were expected to recognize "five attentions, four beautifications, and three loves." The "five attentions" meant giving attention to civilization, courtesy, cleanliness, orderliness, and morality. The "four beautifications" referred to beautifying the heart, the language, the behavior, and the environment. Finally, the "three loves" signified love of the country, socialism, and the Communist Party. These slogans were printed in the newspapers, broadcast in the news, painted on the walls, and talked about at meetings. People adopted these terms in their daily lives and would joke or seriously accuse someone about "How come you don't pay attention to spiritual civilization?"

With the focus on economic reform, some people's needs were ignored. The idea of "spiritual civilization" sounds wonderful but was one-dimensional. When the Chinese people got a taste of reform, they developed an appetite for more. People longed for political reform to go along with economic reform. Therefore, this time, there was a need from the people for a movement. Events of smaller scale scattered in the 1980s, but the most significant took place in 1989 at the Tiananmen Square in the capital city. Started by university students and intellectuals in Beijing and joined later by workers and spectators, the world-known demonstration called for faster and all-around reform in China. Needless to report, the demonstration ended in dispersion in the strongest sense. It is believed that most people were silenced by the result of the movement and decided to forget about politics and concentrate on business activities.

At the beginning of Deng's economic reform, people passed around his famous saying "a black cat or a white cat; a good cat is one that catches the mouse." Even though the reform was successful on a small scale, Deng did not have a systematic theory to support it. So it was very much an experiment. The following rhyme suggests how people worry about how the policy was going to succeed. In the 1980s, a popular song from Taiwan was well-received in mainland China. Its title is "Follow your feelings." So, one folk rhyme in the economic reform era went like this:

The ordinary person follows local [government],
Local follows central [government],
Central follows Deng, and
Deng follows his feelings. (Lee, 1997, p. 225)

The All-Around Open and Western Influence Era

In 1992, three years after the Tiananmen Square movement, Deng Xiao-ping visited southern China, where he had experimented with "special economic zones" and saw tremendous success there. He then issued the policy to grant an "all-around open" policy. This created a safe environment and a favorable atmosphere for more advanced development, hence, taking the initial economic reform to a higher level. The policy gave green lights to most international businesses to invest in Chinese businesses either in the form of sole foreign capital or duo- or trio-capital investments as in joint ventures. The important implication of this policy was that most of these capital investments were made by Western companies. With the capital and technology, came ideas and Western popular cultures. China's young generation in urban areas consists primarily of only-children. They possess the most consuming power and are most vulnerable to new ideas. Therefore, Chinese language was about to experience a second wave of Western influences and, this time, it was much closer to home.

Compared to Japanese, Chinese had adopted fewer loan words from other languages, especially from Western languages; however, since the open-door policy in the late 1970s, especially in the 1990s, there has been a trend to accept many Western words in their original forms into the Chinese language. These include Western languages, Japanese, and expressions in Chinese variations from Hong Kong and Taiwan.

Moreover, during the first wave of Western influences in the early 20th century, the loan words were mostly those that were difficult to translate because these objects or ideas did not exist in China. Examples of these terms include "opium," "sofa," "cocoa," "coffee," "chocolate," "engine," "motor," "radar," "humor," "club" (by way of Japanese 'Kurabu'), "shock," "gene," "car," "card," "copy," and so forth. It is obvious that most of these words are nouns that originated outside of China. Therefore, to save the trouble of inventing some new words in Chinese, it was easier to adopt the original pronunciation and use the phonetic translation.

All Western words that were being accepted in the 1990s, however, are not necessarily retained in their Western form. Words such as "T-shirt," "cool," "cracker," "cookie," "call" (used as in "I'll call you"), "talk show," "e-mail," "Internet," and so on may also be expressed in Chinese or have Chinese equivalents. For many Chinese, it just seems more fashionable and, therefore, preferable to use the original form. For example, when the computer was invented, the Japanese took "kum pu- ta-" out of "computer," but the Chinese translated it into *"dian nao"* (meaning electronic brain). When "e-mail" and "Internet" came along, however, even though they were first translated into Chinese terms with accurate meanings, most people now simply use the Westernized version of *"yi mei er"* (direct phonetic translation) and *"in ter wang"* (*wang* means net).

Other examples include loan words from Japan meaning "to create" (*qi hua*); from Hong Kong, "moble phone" (*da ge da*), "to take a taxi" (*da di*); from Taiwan, "to present" (*chu tai*), "to do a show" (*zuo xiu*, "show" is from English), and "lunch box" (*bian dan*, originally from Japanese).

Finally, in addition to these loan words, there are also newly coined words direct from mainland China that are the result of economic development. With the large scale of reform, many state-owned work units could not afford to keep so many employees. Therefore, many employees were being laid off. Instead of calling these people "unemployed," however, the government invented the word that means "off-duty" (*xia gang*). So, there are many "off-duty workers" (*xia gang gong ren*) in China's major cities since the 1990s. On the other hand, many people rode on the advantageous reform policy and became very rich. These people are called "big-money" (*da kuan*). If a man is extremely rich, then he becomes "big-money grandfather" (*kuan ye*). As soon as there were rich people, there were many young women who began to live with them and serve their needs. This situation is called "big-money companion" (*ban da kuan*). There are also women who work for the rich men under the disguise of being a secretary. These women are called "little honey" (*xiao mi*, "mi" is said to stem from the English "Miss").

The term used to address everybody from the New China Era went full circle from "comrade" (*tong zhi*) to "master" (*shi fu*) during the Cultural Revolution, and then back to "Mr." (*xian sheng*, along with Mrs. and Miss) again in the 1990s.

The rhyme that existed in the 1950s and 1960s about studying sciences took on a new dimension of meaning. It now reads:

> Learn about ABC [meaning English],
> but it won't compare to prostitution;
> Learn about math, physics, and chemistry,
> but it won't compare to a well-connected daddy. (Lee, 1997, p. 317)

This change shows the sad reality that some people have turned to focus so much on money and that nothing else matters, including basic principles. Similar to political satire in the West, most Chinese folk rhymes reflect how people feel about their political leaders, although they usually do not point directly at individuals. They exist because there is not an open channel for political satires.

A novelist, Wang Shuo, became very famous in the 1990s for his novels that reflect the reality of the ordinary people who live in urban Chinese society. Much of this reality is derived as a result of contemporary political movements. His extremely sarcastic style is believed to have influenced modern Chinese language, perhaps only second to Lu Xun. Many of his works are quickly produced as movies and television series, reaching millions of people in China, and therefore, changing and adding to their daily vocabulary. Words such as *"kan"* (meaning to chat and boast) and *"wan zhu"* (meaning someone who is good at nothing but fooling around) are popular and are already an integral part of the modern Chinese language. Whereas Lu Xun brought Chinese language from the ancient literature style to the plain literature style so that the written language is understandable to ordinary people, Wang Shuo took a step further and made ordinary people's language an acceptable form in literature.

Through examinations of the contemporary social and political movements over the past century, we can see that the Chinese language has experienced much change considering its relatively steady form over thousands of years of history. Political movements and social changes have had their share in making such changes.

DISCUSSION

I have attempted to look at Chinese history in order to explain the evolution of the Chinese language in contemporary history. I investigated the issue by examining social and political movements during five eras in the past century, focusing on the influences of these movements on the characteristics of the Chinese language at each time period and demonstrating them with examples.

With the new generation of Chinese today being a group of largely only-children (in the cities), there is a tendency for them to move toward a more individualistic mentality. There are more references concerning the self and individual rights than ever before (Zhong, 1996). There are also indicators toward a smaller power differential in terms of future language interactions. Already, it is common for children today to address their parents with *"ni"* (you, for equals and peers) instead of *"nin"* (you, for the elder and with respect). As well, while young people are certainly becoming more expressive with language, the high-text tradition of the Chinese culture (Hall, 1976) may possibly see a sway toward more low-context in the future.

In addition, the simple fact that the generation consists of only-children points at the future generations who will be without cousins, uncles, and aunts. Thus, a great part of the whole range of addresses for extended family members will diminish. For example, terms that distinguish a mother's younger brother (*jiu*) or father's younger brother (*shu*), or a term for a father's sister's oldest daughter (*da biao jie*) versus the second younger son of the father's brother (*er biao di*) are rapidly falling into disuse. It will be up to the future generations to re-learn the concepts and their meanings. This may also change the pattern by which people relate to each other in a close society such as China. There may not be, for instance, terms to the effect of "brotherly loyalty" or "dragging along a family of many members" (*la jia dai ko*). It will also be difficult to achieve the highest family reunion, "four generations under one roof" (*si shi tong tang*).

Whatever the future generations will become is yet to be foreseen. Many other factors may influence these tendencies as suggested. It is a worthwhile issue to be studied and deserves attention from scholars who are interested in communication in and about China. Hopefully, through this analysis, I have been able to present an overview of the evolution of the Chinese language, especially during the recent decades.

Endnote

*The People's Republic of China was founded in 1949, and the task of the first decade was to revive the spirit from the wars and rebuild the country. Carried by great victories, the country was overjoyed by an extremely uplifting atmosphere. It appeared that people loved each other. The 1960s was the beginning of political movements. Everyone was suspicious of everyone else, and there was a hateful air around people. The 1970s represented the peak of the Cultural Revolution, and it seemed that everyone was fighting with each other. The 1980s saw a turn in people's focus from the distaste of a series of political movements to practical matters, such as building the economy. Therefore, people focused on making money more than anything else. At the beginning of the economic development, it was recognized that some businesspeople cheated each other and consumers in order to make money. The economic competition was becoming more and more severe in the 1990s, to the extent that it appeared as if no moral standards existed anymore and people could "eat" (or kill) each other to get ahead.

References

Carbaugh, D. (1997). Finnish and American linguistic patterns: A cultural comparison. In L. A. Samovar & R. E. Porter (Eds.). *Intercultural communication: A reader* (8th ed.) (pp. 221–226). Belmont, CA: Wadsworth.

Chang, R., & Chang, M. S. (1978). *Speaking of Chinese.* New York: W.W. Norton & Company.

Flowers, N. (1997). *China's cultural wealth.* Available: E-mail Newsgroup: alt.chinese.text.

Hall, E. T. (1976). Beyond culture. Garden City, NY: Anchor/Doubleday.

Lee, C. C. (1990). *Voices of China: The interplay of politics and journalism.* New York: Guilford Press.

Lee, J. (1997). *The wisdom of the ordinary people: Appreciation and analysis of contemporary mainland [China] fold rhymes.* Monterey Park, CA: Evergreen Books.

Lehmann, W. P. (1975). *Language & linguistics in the People's Republic of China.* Austin: University of Texas Press.

Porter, R. E., & Samovar, L. A. (1985). Approaching intercultural communication. In L. A. Samovar & R. E Porter (Eds.), *Intercultural communication: A reader* (7th ed.) (pp. 15–13). Belmont, CA: Wadsworth.

Schnell, J. A. (1999). *Perspectives on communication in the People's Republic of China.* Boulder, CO: Lexington Books.

Ting-Toomey, S., & Korzenny, F. (Eds.) (1989). *Language, communication, and culture.* Newbury Park, CA: Sage.

Whorf, B. L. (1956). *Language, thought, and reality.* Cambridge, MA: MIT Press.

Yao, D. F. (1997, October 10). The revitalization of the dead "Cultural Revolution" standard operas caused major debates in China. E-Magazine: *Hua Xia Wen Zhai [China Digest]*, volume 341. Available: www.cnd.org:8014/HXWZ/CM97.

Zheng, Y. (1993). *Liyu, zhouchi, guanqiang, hehua* [Polite language, curse words, official tone, black jargon.] Beijing, China: Guangming Daily Press.

Zhong, M. (1996). *Analysis of cultural and social factors and their influences on communication of the urban only-child generation of the People's Republic of China.* Unpublished doctoral dissertation, Kent State University, Ohio.

Zormeier, S. M., & Samovar, L. A. (1997). Language as a mirror of reality: Mexican American proverbs. In L. A. Samovar & R. E. Porter (Eds.), *Intercultural communication: A reader* (8th ed.) (pp. 235–239). Belmont, CA: Wadsworth.

Concepts and Questions

1. How do changes in the social structure of a culture affect the language of that culture?
2. How does Zhong's approach to the relationship between language and culture differ from that of Johnson and Fong?
3. How has the Chinese language historically reflected the structure of society?
4. How has contemporary Chinese history caused changes in both the form and substance of the Chinese language?

5. What ramifications would you expect in a hierarchical society when the traditional terms of address (e.g., Mr., Mrs., Miss) were replaced by the universal term of address "Comrade"?

6. How did the changes in the social structure of Chinese society affect language during the era of the Cultural Revolution?

7. What changes in Chinese language usage occurred during the Economic Reform Era? How did these changes in language usage reflect the new ideas being presented during that period?

8. What influences on the Chinese language occurred during the All-Around Open and Western Influence Era? Give some examples of how technical terms in the English language were interjected into Chinese usage.

Discriminating Attitudes Toward Speech

AARON CASTELAN CARGILE

The term *intercultural communication* typically invokes visions of people from two (or more) different nations interacting with one another. Such a situation could be an American customs officer speaking with a Mexican tourist. In many such instances, participants may not use the same language, thus the challenge presented by differences in speech is obvious. Intercultural communication also describes interactions between people from the same nation, but from different co-cultures, as in the case of exchanges between many Asian Americans and African Americans. On these occasions, it may seem that the challenge of coping with differences in speech is minimal, if not nonexistent. Yet, it must be realized that even when people speak the same language, such as English, they don't always speak the same "language."

Consider, for example, a New York businesswoman interviewing a West Virginian job candidate who answers questions with an Appalachian drawl. She may comprehend with little, if any, difficulty what is being said; however, she may not feel completely at ease during the interaction, or afterward, when she decides the person's fate of employment. Sadly, these feelings may come regardless of what the applicant has said: The applicant may be thoroughly qualified for the job, and he may answer all interview questions satisfactorily, but the words running through the businesswoman's mind may be the same as those heard by June Tyler during a closed-door meeting with a senior partner in a law firm: "be careful about hiring anyone with a mountain accent" (Pasternak, 19, p. A16). The discomfort felt by the businesswoman when faced with this fully qualified job applicant illustrates a special sort of difficulty faced by intercultural communicators—a difficulty of fair evaluation and equal treatment. Unlike more obvious difficulties of comprehension, this sort of difficulty presents a greater challenge to intercultural communication because people tend to ignore or minimize language-based prejudices.

In this example, it may be the case that the New York businesswoman is consciously aware of her decision to discriminate against the job applicant based on his Appalachian accent. Although such discrimination is illegal, many people freely admit that a Southern accent is often inappropriate and suggest that it should be abandoned in favor of other accents. For example, soon after Atlanta was awarded the 1996 summer Olympics, a column appeared in the *Atlanta Business Chronicle* encouraging citizens to "get the South out of our mouth" in order to impress the expected visitors (reported in Pearl, 1991). Unlike the open prejudice in this example however, it is more likely that the businesswoman would not be aware of her discriminatory motives. Instead, she would likely experience only some general sense that the applicant was not quite as "sharp" as the others, and that he or she somehow did not "seem right" for the job, even though these impressions could unknowingly be fostered by her own prejudice against the speaker's accent. Because, as in this example, episodes of intercultural communication are often spontaneously shaped by participants' language-based prejudices, it is important that we learn to deal effectively with the challenges they present. Before this can be done, however, we must first understand both the nature of and reasons for our attitudes toward speech.

ATTITUDES TOWARD SPEECH

Despite the previous example, skeptics might think that what we say remains far more important than how we say it, thus our attitudes toward speech are not "that big of a deal"; they don't ever really encourage people to act in a prejudice or discriminatory manner, do they? Fortunately, social scientists, including linguists, psychologists, and communication scholars, have developed a field of study called "language attitudes" in order to find out if and when

language influences our impressions of, and reactions to, others. It is beyond the scope of this chapter to review this entire field (see Bradac, Cargile, & Halett, in press). Thus instead, provided a predominantly American (U.S.) readership, I will describe some of the research investigating attitudes toward speech held by American listeners.

Although people hold attitudes toward many different features of speech (e.g., speech rate or speech style), one of the most salient features is accent. Research has shown that listeners make ready and regular judgments regarding the personal and social characteristics of speakers based simply on the way they sound. In the case of most standard-speaking Americans, they consistently prejudge others with "Appalachian," "Spanish," "German," or "African-American vernacular" accented speech as less intelligent, poorer, less educated, and less status possessing than standard-accented speakers (Bradac & Wisegarver, 1984; Johnson & Buttny, 1982; Luhman, 1990; Ryan & Bulik, 1982; Ryan & Carranza, 1975; Tucker & Lambert, 1969). For example, Bishop (1979) found that white female respondents evaluated African-American colleagues as less responsible and less desirable co-workers when they spoke "black" as opposed to "white" English. Similarly, Giles, Williams, Mackie, and Rosselli (1995) discovered that Anglo respondents rated the same bidialectical speaker as less literate and more lower class when he spoke English with a "Hispanic" accent, compared to an "Anglo" accent.

Surprisingly though, standard-accented listeners are not the only ones who look down on many nonstandard-accented speakers. Even listeners who themselves speak with a nonstandard accent often judge others who sound like themselves to have low social standing. For example, a study by Doss and Gross (1992) revealed that African-American respondents perceived same-race Standard English speakers as more competent than those who spoke African-American vernacular English. As this last example suggests, the complex reality of intercultural communication is not that we think badly of *everyone* who speaks differently. Indeed, research indicates that there are some "foreign"-accented speakers who Americans *don't* perceive to be less competent or inferior (e.g., British-accented English speakers; Stewart, Ryan, & Giles, 1985). Similarly, listeners who speak with a standard accent sometimes judge nonstandard-accented speakers to be equal to standard-accented speakers along some dimensions (e.g., being "friendly" and "good natured"; see Ryan, Hewstone, & Giles, 1984). Even so, this language attitudes research demonstrates that we often prejudge others in unflattering and potentially harmful ways based on their accent alone.

LANGUAGE-BASED DISCRIMINATION

In addition to prejudgment, our attitudes toward speech may also result in discriminatory actions against speakers. There are perhaps few contexts in which someone else's behavior is more important for our own well-being than in the courtroom or in an employment interview. In both instances, evidence shows that unfair treatment can be provoked by a speaker's use of language. For example, Seggie (1983) presented standard- or nonstandard-accented voices to listeners and told them that the speaker stood accused of one of several crimes. On the audiotapes, the speakers were heard protesting their innocence regarding the crime of which they had been accused. Listeners were then asked to make a decision regarding the probable guilt or innocence of the speaker. The results showed that standard-accented speakers were more often seen as guilty when the crime was embezzlement, whereas nonstandard-accented speakers were more often judged guilty when the crime was physical assault. Listeners thus more often associated white-collar crimes with standard-sounding defendants and crimes of violence with nonstandard-sounding defendants. Although these listeners were not actual jury members, the results plainly suggest that people can be treated differently based on their accent alone; treatment that is particularly unfair can result in the case of a nonstandard-accented speaker accused of a violent crime.

In the case of a job interview, language attitudes research has extended beyond the campus laboratory to investigate the ways in which actual employees of real companies respond to accented speakers. In an important study by Henry and Ginzberg (1985), individuals with different ethnic/racial accents made telephone inquires about jobs advertised in a newspaper. Job applicants who spoke with a nonstandard accent were most often told that the jobs had been filled. Applicants with a standard accent, however, were most often invited to appear for a personal interview, even after the nonstandard speakers were informed that applications for the position were no longer being accepted! In a similar study, de la Zerda and Hopper (1979) asked employers from San Antonio, Texas, to predict the likelihood of a speaker being hired for each of three positions: supervisor, skilled technician, and semiskilled laborer. A comparison of standard American and (Mexican American) Spanish-accented speakers revealed that standard speakers were favored for the supervisor position, whereas Spanish-accented speakers were more likely to be hired for the semiskilled position. It would thus be doubly hard for a Spanish-accented speaker to be hired as a supervisor because he or she would not only be seen as less appropriate for this position but also as more appropriate for the lower skilled (and lower waged) job. Sadly, these and other results (e.g., Giles, Wilson, & Conway, 1981; Kalin & Rayko, 1978) clearly illustrate that people can not only be prejudiced against others who sound different, but they can also discriminate against these speakers in ways that may jeopardize both the speakers' livelihoods and their lives.

WHY DO WE HAVE DISCRIMINATING ATTITUDES?

Having explored the potential dangers of attitudes toward speech, an important question to consider now is why do we have these attitudes in the first place? Quite simply, attitudes exist because people have to cope with a world full of uncertainty. Life often requires us to respond to others even though we lack complete information about their character or intentions. When a uniformed stranger rings your doorbell, or a student in the library takes your chair, what are you supposed to do? Before you can respond to the person, you must first evaluate him or her. If you think the uniformed stranger is kind, honest, and responsibly doing her job as a government census worker, you should cooperate with her request for information. If you think the student is lazy, mean, and rude, you should firmly insist that he find another chair to use. Behavior demands evaluation, but we rarely, if ever, have the time, the opportunity, or the ability to base these instant evaluations on thoroughly collected or completely tested information. On what basis, then, can we behave in these situations? On the basis of prejudgments. We call on our attitudes about properly uniformed, polite, "well-spoken" individuals as a basis to evaluate and respond to the uniformed stranger at our door. And we call on our stereotypes of sloppily dressed, heavy metal music–listening, loud-talking individuals as a basis to evaluate and respond to the student in the library. Although these prejudgments may, in fact, be incorrect in these situations, without them we would have no basis for behaving spontaneously and life would quickly come to a halt.

Attitudes provide us with a sense of certainty and some basis for behavior. As such, they are absolutely natural and necessary for our survival in an otherwise uncertain world. Even so, they are especially problematic because they are mostly biased and discriminatory. As human beings, we far more often prejudge different-sounding others in unflattering ways. Although many specific reasons for this stuation have been described (see Mackie, Hamilton, Susskind, & Rosselli, 1996), the underlying motive is that humans and human groups are naturally competitive; evolution has designed us with social competition in mind. We can be cooperative, obviously, but cooperation normally occurs only when it is in our interests—immediate or otherwise (see Cosmides & Tooby, 1992). Social group interaction is more often characterized by competition than cooperation (see Worchel & Austin, 1986), thus discriminatory attitudes are one way in which people maintain a competitive edge.

DISCRIMINATING ATTITUDES IN CULTURE

Of course, the complex reality of intercultural communication is not that we are predisposed to think badly of everyone who speaks differently. As described earlier, there are occasions when we think worse of people who sound like us and better of peo-

ple who sound different. How can this happen if we are supposed to develop unfavorable attitudes about *others'* ways of speaking? It usually happens when one social group dominates another to a point where competition ends. At this point, the dominant social group clearly controls the spaces in which the two groups co-exist (e.g., the workplace) and often greatly influences even the subordinate group's privates spaces (e.g., the home). In these circumstances, dominant and subordinate group members alike receive the dominant group's culture—the one that includes its own discriminating attitude. Consequently, members of both groups may learn to discriminate against subordinate group speech.

In the case of the United States, the most salient social groups are those identified by race or ethnicity, and among these different groups, Anglo-Americans have clearly been dominant. As a result, mainstream American culture has socialized attitudes toward speech that favor Anglo-Americans and discriminate against all other forms of American English. For example, the CBS Evening News aired a national broadcast in which a reporter clearly passed along this bias by commenting about a program in accent reduction: "The idea is to teach them how to speak English so that it sounds like English, and not, as Henry Higgins might put it, warmed-over grits. Think of them as prisoners—prisoners of their own accent" (Fagar, 1984).

Similarly, a reporter in a regional newspaper wrote: "No matter how qualified a person is, a voice twisted by regional or ethnic influences can be a stumbling block socially and professionally" (Kerr, 1994). With ideas like these promoted not only in the media but also in school and in the workplace (see Lippi-Green, 1997), it is little wonder that many non-Anglo speakers have developed unfavorable attitudes toward their own, otherwise native, way of speaking. As one African American wrote:

> Although we were surrounded in New York by a number of poorly spoken and frequently stereotypical black . . . dialects, my siblings and I soon learned to hear it for what it was—the language of the street, the language of black trash. The language that went right along with Saturday-night knife fights to settle a grudge. (Hamblin, 1995, p. B8)

To make matters worse, not only do we internalize the discriminating attitudes that saturate our culture, but we also rarely give them up. Although the use of attitudes is both natural and unavoidable, they are typically used far too often, and far too long, to really benefit communicators. As discussed earlier, attitudes are useful in situations in which we must respond to others, but lack the time, the opportunity, and the ability to base our behavior on thoughtfully collected information. Sadly though, once we have developed attitudes to help get us through these pressing situations, we become lazy and use these prepackaged evaluations even when we can collect more accurate and personalized information about the person with whom we are interacting. Collecting this information is absolutely critical to fair and effective interaction, but it requires us to spend a great deal of cognitive energy; in other words, we have to think (and we all know how effortful that can be sometimes!). So instead, because it is easier, we carelessly rely on our attitudes far more often than is justifiable.

Relatedly, people also tend to rely on their attitudes far too long. By this I mean that once we have applied an attitude-based evaluation, it becomes increasingly difficult to change it despite information to the contrary because there are many different ways in which we work unknowingly to ensure the survival (and supposed accuracy) of our attitudes. For example, because attitudes affect what information we attend to (Fazio, Roskos-Ewoldsen, & Powell, 1994), we often perceive only those facts about another person that are consistent with our attitude and ignore other important, contradictory information. To illustrate, I may deem a job applicant unsuitable for a managerial position based on her accent, and then pay attention to information on her résumé that supports this evaluation (e.g., lack of managerial experience), while ignoring conflicting information (e.g., high GPA or leadership experience). In this way, I can continue to rely on my original attitude-based evaluation long after I should have revised it. When this happens, we are reminded that even though attitudes are natural, the biases with which they are typically developed and applied can create substantial difficulties for fair and effective communication.

WHAT SHOULD BE DONE ABOUT OUR DISCRIMINATING ATTITUDES?

Whether we like it or not, and whether we admit it or not, we all possess discriminating attitudes toward speech. Attitudes are an essential feature of social life, so what should responsible intercultural communicators do about them?

First, the most important thing is to recognize your own attitudes toward speech. Despite the generalizations offered throughout this reading, each one of us has a distinct profile of attitudes developed over a unique life history. Figure out what your attitudes are and then notice when you use them. For example, in universities across America, students often respond unfavorably to foreign-born teaching assistants and professors. Specifically, on some campuses, more than two of five students withdraw or switch from a class when they find out their teacher is a non-native speaker of English (Rubin & Smith, 1988). In addition, many of the rest of students in classes taught by these professors make complaints of the variety that forced the state of Illinois to pass a fluency law for college instructors (Secter, 1987). Who is responsible for such student dissatisfaction? In some cases, it may in fact be an instructor with verifiably poor language skills. In many other cases, though, it may in fact be the students themselves.

On first hearing an instructor's accent, students will often unknowingly make assumptions about the instructor's personality and (language) skills based solely on their own attitudes toward foreign-accented speakers (e.g., "this teacher isn't too friendly, too smart, and he doesn't speak proper English"). The instructor may, in fact, be or do none of the things that the student assumes. Even so, because attitudes toward speech have the power to initiate selective perceptions, the students may create, in their own minds, evidence to support their views. In particular, they may "hear" the instructor make grammatical mistakes that he or she has not really made (indeed, this has been demonstrated in a study by Cargile and Giles, 1998). Students can then, in turn, point to these "mistakes" as justification for their attitudes and a reason for responding unfavorably to the instructor. Thus, a class may end up with an instructor who is in fact friendly, smart, and who speaks grammatically correct and comprehensible English, but because students have based their responses, unknowingly, on their attitudes toward foreign-accented speech alone, they may feel dissatisfied with their instruction.

As the previous scenario illustrates, in the end, the evaluations we make of others may be more a product of our own attitudes than others' behaviors. The trouble is that we rarely realize this situation, and thus act as if the other is entirely responsible for our reactions. Consequently, we must begin to manage our attitudes by recognizing their existence. Ask yourself: "Am I thinking this about the person only because of the way that he or she speaks?" You may answer "no" to this question, thus indicating that the role attitudes are playing is minimal and perhaps justified. You may, however, answer "yes," suggesting that your attitudes about language use are exerting an undue and likely problematic influence on your behavior.

Once you learn to recognize the role attitudes toward speech play in your responses, a second thing to do is to seek out and integrate additional information into the evaluation process—especially when you answer "yes" to the aforementioned question. Your attitudes may lead you to believe one thing about a speaker, but your job as a responsible intercultural communicator is to test out, to the best of your abilities, whether your evaluation is accurate and appropriate. For example, in the case of a non–native English–speaking instructor, find out about his or her educational background, prior teaching experience, and real English competency through patient listening (and perhaps some careful questioning) before passing the easy, ready-made judgment that this person lacks the intelligence and ability to be a successful teacher. Of course, this kind of "fact checking" and follow-up is effortful and never easy; however, it is critical to managing our attitudes well.

Although these first two suggestions are enough to occupy all of us for a lifetime, there is a third, even more challenging, thing to do—change our discriminating attitudes. Of course, any attitude is difficult to change because it has likely developed over a lifetime and meets many our needs, like providing a sense of certainty or competitive edge. Despite this feeling, however, it is possible to remold our discriminating attitudes into *more* accurate, less biased ones.

For example, consider the teacher who is annoyed by her African-American students' pronunciation of the word "ask" [a:ks]. She reprimands them for speaking "incorrectly" and justifies this action (and her attitude) by claiming that such linguistic "sloppiness" will ruin American English—a homogeneous language that assures mutual intelligibility within the United States. In response, one of her students patiently explains that the homogeneity of American English is a myth. American English resulted from a confluence of many languages, not just British English, and has always been subject to significant regional variation. Moreover, because all human languages are equally sophisticated (as Steven Pinker claims, "there is no such thing as a Stone Age language," p. 27, 1994), variation does not represent error, but instead marks different identities within and understandings of the world. The real reason that she corrects the students, he explains, is because of her discriminatory attitudes. Otherwise, why would she preach homogeneity of pronunciation [a:sk] while accepting one variation as correct (the one associated with wealthy white Easterners [æsk]) and rejecting another as incorrect (the one associated with African Americans (a:ks])? Indeed, this is what dictionaries do!

Faced with the facts about her attitude, it is possible for the teacher to change her reactions to African-American Vernacular English speakers. Rather than hearing them as "uneducated," she can relearn to hear them as claiming a place in society that is different from her own. Of course, this will require tremendous effort, patience, and practice, but it is the more accurate, less biased attitude to adopt. If we hope to follow in her footsteps of becoming responsible and fair-minded participants in intercultural interaction, we must begin, as she does, by recognizing the attitudes toward speech we currently possess. With luck, such action will set us on a path toward managing our discriminating attitudes.

References

Bishop, G. D. (1979). Perceived similarity in interracial attitudes and behaviors: The effects of belief and dialect style. *Journal of Applied Social Psychology, 9,* 446–465.

Bradac, J. J., Cargile, A. C., & Halett, J. (2001). Language attitudes: Retrospect, conspect, and prospect. In H. Giles & P. Robinson (Eds.), *The New Handbook of language and social psychology* (2nd ed., pp. 137–155). Chichester, England: John Wiley & Sons.

Bradac, J. J., & Wisegarver, R. (1984). Ascribed status, lexical diversity, and accent: Determinants of perceived status, solidarity, and control of speech style. *Journal of Language and Social Psychology, 3,* 239–255.

Cargile, A. C., & Giles, H. (1998). Language attitudes toward varieties of English: An American-Japanese context. *Journal of Applied Communication Research, 26,* 338–356.

Cosmides, L., & Tooby, J. (1992). Cognitive adaptations for social exchange. In J. H. Barkow, L. Cosmides, and J. Tooby (Eds.), *The adapted mind: Evolutionary psychology and the generation of culture* (pp. 163–228). New York: Oxford University Press.

de la Zerda, N., & Hopper, R. (1979). Employment interviewers' reactions to Mexican-American speech. *Communication Monographs, 46,* 126–134.

Doss, R. C., & Gross, A. M. (1992). The effects of Black English on stereotyping in intraracial perceptions. *The Journal of Black Psychology, 18,* 47–58.

Fazio, R. H., Roskos-Ewoldsen, D. R., & Powell, M. C. (1994). Attitudes, perception, and attention. In P. M. Niedenthal & S. Kitayama (Eds.), *The heart's eye: Emotional influences in perception and attention* (pp. 197–216). Orlando, FL: Academic Press.

Fagar, I. (Executive Producer) (1984, October 10). *The CBS Evening News.* New York: CBS Corporation.

Giles, H., Williams, A., Mackie, D. M., & Rosselli, F. (1995). Reactions to Anglo- and Hispanic-American accented speakers: Affect, identity, persuasion, and the English-only controversy. *Language and Communication, 114,* 102–123.

Giles, H., Wilson, P., & Conway, A. (1981). Accent and lexical diversity as determinants of impression formation and employment selection. *Language Sciences, 3,* 92–103.

Hamblin, K. (1995, April 7). Speaking well has its merit. *Ann Arbor News,* Opinion Page: B8.

Henry, F., & Ginzberg, E. (1985). *Who gets the work: A test of racial discrimination in employment.* Toronto: Urban Alliance on Race Relations and Social Planning Council of Metropolitan Toronto.

Johnson, F. L., & Buttny, R. (1982). White listeners' responses to "sounding black" and "sounding white": The effects of message content on judgments about language. *Communication Monographs, 49,* 33–49.

Kalin, R., & Rayko, D. (1.978). Discrimination in evaluative judgments against foreign-accented job candidates. *Psychological Reports, 43,* 1203–1209.

Kerr, B. (1994, April 18). Voice of success silences dialect: Program helps people shed tell-tale tones. *Providence Journal-Bulletin,* p. B1.

Lippi-Green, R. (1997). *English with an accent: Language, ideology, and discrimination in the United States.* New York: Routledge.

Luhman, R. (1990). Appalachian English stereotypes: Language attitudes in Kentucky. *Language in Society, 19,* 331–348.

Mackie, D. M., Hamilton, D. L., Susskind, J., & Rosselli, F. (1996). Social psychological foundations of stereotype formation. In C. N. Macrae, C. Stangor, & M. Hewstone (Eds.), *Stereotypes and Stereotyping,* (pp. 41–78). New York: The Guilford Press.

Pasternak, J. (1994, March 29). Bias blights life outside Appalachia. *Los Angeles Times,* pp. A1, A16.

Pearl, D. (1991, December 13). Hush mah mouth! Some in South try to lose the drawl. *Wall Street Journal,* p. A1.

Pinker, S. (1994). *The language instinct.* New York: Harper Collins.

Rubin, D. L., & Smith, K. A. (1988). Effects of accent, ethnicity, and lecture topic on undergraduates' perceptions of nonnative English-speaking teaching assistants. *International Journal of Intercultural Relations, 14,* 337–353.

Ryan, E. B., & Bulik, C. (1982). Evaluations of middle-class and lower-class speakers of standard American and German-accented English. *Journal of Language and Social Psychology, 1,* 51–61.

Ryan, E. B., & Carranza, M. A. (1975). Evaluative reactions of adolescents toward speakers of standard English and Mexican-American accented English. *Journal of Personality and Social Psychology, 31,* 855–863.

Ryan, E. B., Hewstone, M., & Giles, H. (1984). Language and intergroup attitudes. In J. Eiser (Ed.), *Attitudinal judgment* (pp. 135–160). New York: Springer.

Secter, B. (1987, September 27). Foreign teachers create language gap in colleges. *Los Angeles Times,* pp. A1, A26–A27.

Seggie, I. (1983). Attribution of guilt as a function of ethnic accent and type of crime. *Journal of Multilingual and Multicultural Development, 4,* 197–206.

Stewart, M. A., Ryan, E. B., & Giles, H. (1985). Accent and social class effects on status and solidarity evaluations. *Personality and Social Psychology Bulletin, 11,* 98–105.

Tucker, G. R., & Lambert, W. E. (1969). White and Negro listeners' reactions to various American-English dialects. *Social Forces, 41*, 463–468.

Worchel, S., & Austin, W. G. (Eds.) (1986). *Psychology of intergroup relations.* Chicago: Nelson-Hall.

Concepts and Questions

1. Do you believe Cargile is correct when he asserts that people tend to like others who possess attitudes and traits similar to their own and to dislike others with dissimilar attitudes and traits?

2. How do language differences compound the problems associated with ethnocentrism?

3. According to Cargile, what are examples of situations in which language accents influenced someone's perception of another person? Has accent ever influenced your perception of another person? How?

4. Can you think of examples in your own life when a speaker's choice of words or grammatical phrases may have contributed to some harmful and erroneous prejudgments?

5. How may language attitudes affect job interviews?

6. Under what circumstances might speaking rate become a variable in intercultural communication? Can you think of examples where you have interacted with someone from another culture who used a speaking rate different from your own? Did that factor influence your encounter with that person?

7. In what settings do we most often see discrimination based on speech differences?

8. If, as Cargile asserts, it is true that not only do we internalize the discriminating speech attitudes that saturate our culture, but we also rarely give them up, how can you learn to interact successfully who have people with differing speech patterns?

9. According to Cargile, how should responsible intercultural communicators manage language attitudes?

Dialogue and Cultural Communication Codes Between Israeli-Jews and Palestinians

DONALD G. ELLIS
IFAT MAOZ

Even a casual observer of contemporary political events knows that Israeli-Jews and Palestinian Arabs are locked in severe conflict that often becomes violent. The origins of the conflict between Israeli-Jews and Palestinian-Arabs can be traced to the end of the 19th century with the appearance of political Zionism and the resulting waves of Jewish immigration to Palestine. Zionism sought to establish a Jewish State in Palestine. On the same land, however, lived Arabs, with a Palestinian national identity. This resulted in a clash between the Jewish and Palestinian communities over the ownership of the land, the right for self-determination, and statehood. Violence between the two communities first erupted in the 1920s and has pervaded the relationship in various forms, and with varying degrees of intensity, since that time (Kelman, 1997; Rouhana & Bar-Tal, 1998).

The communal clash that characterized the first decades of the 20th century escalated into a war that involved the neighboring Arab states. This war erupted after the United Nations (UN) declared, in November 1947, the partition of Palestine into two states—one Arab and one Jewish. The Palestinians rejected the UN partition plan, and an independent Jewish state was established in 1948. Israel won the war, and most Palestinians who lived in the portion of Palestine on which Israel was now established

This original essay appears here for the first time. All rights reserved. Permission to reprint must be obtained from the publisher and the authors. Donald G. Ellis teaches at School of Communication at the University of Hartford, West Hartford, Connecticut. Ifat Maoz teaches in the Department of Communication at The Hebrew University, Mt. Scopus Campus, Jerusalem, Israel.

were dispersed to the neighboring Arab countries, partly having fled war zones and partly having been expelled by Israeli forces (Maoz, 1999).

Other historical turning points in the relationship between Israelis and Palestinians include the 1967 war between Israel on one side, and Egypt, Jordan, and Syria on the other, which brought the remainder of Palestine under Israeli control. The first *intifada*, or uprising, was an uprising of the Palestinians in the West Bank and Gaza strip territories, expressing resistance to the Israeli occupation of these territories. It began in 1987 and lasted until 1993 (Rouhana & Bar-Tal, 1998).

In 1993 peace accords were signed in Oslo, Norway, which signaled a breakthrough in the relations between Israelis and Palestinians. This dramatic agreement included an exchange of letters of mutual recognition between representatives of the two peoples, which was followed by a declaration of principles that stipulated the establishment of a Palestinian authority in Gaza and Jericho as a first step in Palestinian self-rule (Kelman, 1997). At this point, which was indeed historic, prospects for the success of the peace process seemed exceptionally good. There was hope that the peace accords would end violence and lead to reconciliation; however, a few years after signing the accords, it became clear that this optimism was premature.

A chain of violent incidents began in November 1995 with the assassination of the then Israeli Prime Minister and continued with several terrorist attacks in the first half of 1996. These events signaled a slowdown in the Israeli–Palestinian peace process. Increasingly, the adversaries presented obstacles and impediments to the peace process, posed problems for the implementation of the different stages of the agreements, and violated the agreements. In October 2000, the Al Aqsa *intifada* broke out, and the relationship between the Israelis and the Palestinians again took a violent turn.

Yet, political leaders from both sides continue to try and return to peace making and peace building. Although the conflict centers on the issue of land, and who has legitimate rights to the land—an issue that has strong historical, religious, and emotional significance—it is also a cultural conflict, a conflict over identities and recognition. The political and cultural differences between Israeli-Jews and Palestinians involve negative stereotypes, mutual delegitimization, and severe miscommunication. Dialogue and group encounters are one way to cope with these difficult problems. Dialogue sessions between Israeli-Jews and Palestinians involve a process of transformative communication aimed at improving the relations between the sides (Maoz, 2000a).

TRANSFORMATIVE COMMUNICATION BETWEEN GROUPS IN CONFLICT

Intergroup dialogues are useful venues for growth, change, and conflict management. Transformative dialogue between cultural groups in conflict helps reduce prejudice and hostility and foster mutual understanding (Gergen, 1999). Such dialogue experiences have been successful at helping groups cope with conflict in Northern Ireland, South Africa, and the Middle East.

The notion of transformative contact or dialogue, when used in the context of intergroup conflict, draws heavily from the contact hypothesis in social psychology. This theory was first presented by Allport (1954) and since has been the subject of numerous studies (Amir, 1976; Pettigrew, 1998). The *contact hypothesis* states that under certain conditions, contact between groups in conflict reduces prejudice and changes negative intergroup attitudes. The contact hypothesis is optimal under certain conditions:

1. The two groups should be of equal status, at least within the contact situation. Contact of unequal status, where the traditional status imbalance is maintained, can act to perpetuate existing negative stereotypes.
2. Successful contact should involve personal and sustained communication between individuals from the two groups.
3. Effective contact requires cooperative interdependence, where members of the two groups engage in cooperative activities and depend on one another in order to achieve mutual goals.
4. Social norms favoring equality must be the consensus among the relevant authorities.

TRANSFORMATIVE DIALOGUES BETWEEN ISRAELIS AND PALESTINIANS

The first attempts to address the dispute between Israelis and Palestinians by means of structured communication events were in interactive problem-solving workshops developed by Herbert Kelman from Harvard University in the early 1970s and have been conducted since then by him and his colleagues (Kelman, 1997). These workshops brought together politically active and influential Israelis and Palestinians for private, direct communication facilitated by unofficial third-party mediators (Kelman, 1995, 1997). Since the Oslo peace agreements in 1993, numerous Israeli–Palestinian dialogue events are conducted each year that are targeted at grassroots populations from both sides (Adwan & Bar-On, 2000). These dialogue events typically last two to three days and are aimed at building peace and reconciliation through processes of constructive communication (Maoz, 2000b). Both Israelis and Palestinians facilitate the dialogues. In some sessions all of the participants meet, and in others they are divided into smaller groups. There are also several uni-national meetings where participants meet only with members of their own group. Dialogues are conducted either in English, or Hebrew and Arabic that is translated.

The concept of "dialogue" as discussed by scholars such as Martin Buber, Carl Rogers, and Mikhail Bakhtin is the general guiding principle of these groups. That is, the goal of the communication is to avoid "monologue," or the pressure of a single authoritative voice, and to strive for "dialogue," which emphasizes the interplay of different perspectives where something new and unique emerges. At its best, dialogue is a search for deep differences and shared concerns. It asks participants to inquire genuinely about the other person and avoid premature judgment, debate, and questions designed to expose flaws.

The process of change and transformation during dialogue is difficult, complex, and slow. Many issues enter the mix of politics, psychology, culture, and communication. In our work we have found that the communication process remains central. There is simply no possibility for reconciliation and peace without sustained interaction. Therefore, we direct our attention to the issues in culture and communication that characterize these groups. The remainder of this article is devoted to explaining the cultural communication codes that typify interactions between Israeli-Jews and Palestinians and how these speech codes are expressed in actual dialogues when Israeli-Jews and Palestinians are arguing.

SPEECH CODES

Whenever groups of people live in a culture, they have certain characteristics and behaviors in common. We know, for example, that people in cultures dress similarly, share tastes in food preparation, and have many common attitudes, but they also share orientations toward communication. Members of cultural communities share principles of language use and interpretation. This simply means that your use of language (word choice, slang, accents, syntax) and your tendencies to interpret and understand this language in a certain way depend on your cultural membership. For example, assume you overhead the following conversation (Ellis, 1992):

JESSE: Yea, I'm thinkin' 'bout getting some new ink.

GENE: Really, where you gonna put it?

JESSE: Oh, I don' know. I've still got some clean spots.

For the moment, this conversation is probably pretty confusing and odd. What does it mean to "get new ink"? Why is Gene concerned about where to put it? What do "clean spots" refer to? Who are these people, and what cultural functions is this conversation serving? Is Jesse thinking about buying a new bottle of ink for his fountain pen and Gene does not think there will be room for it on his messy desk?

This is a conversation between two tattoo enthusiasts who live and work among others in a tattoo culture that has developed norms of speaking. If you were a member of the culture and understood the "speech code," then you could participate in this conversation easily and competently. You would know that "new ink" refers to a "new tattoo" and that "clean spots" were places on the body that had no tattoos. You would understand the personal identity satisfaction that members of this culture gain from their unique code of communication.

Jesse and Gene are speaking in a cultural code, and you can only understand and participate in the conversation if you understand the code. The concept of speech codes has been studied by Bernstein (1971), Ellis (1992, 1994), and Philipsen (1997). Philipsen's treatment is most thorough in communication, and it is the perspective we rely on here. But first we describe two cultural communication codes termed *dugri* and *musayra* known to characterize Israeli-Jews and Arabs, respectively. This discussion will be followed by an elaboration of the concept of speech codes and an explanation of their role in intercultural communication dialogues for peace.

Israeli-Jewish and Arab cultures have emerged from the special circumstances of their history, and different norms of communication emerge from this history. These contrasting speech codes can make for difficult and uncoordinated communication. Several researchers have described an Arab communication coded called *musayra* (e.g., Feghali, 1997; Katriel, 1986). *Musayra* means "to accommodate" or "go along with." It is a way of communicating that orients the speaker toward a harmonious relationship with the other person. *Musayra* emerges from the core values of Arab culture that have to do with honor, hospitality, and collectivism. An Arab speaker who is engaging in the code of *musayra* is being polite, indirect, courteous, and nonconfrontive to the other member of a conversation.

More specifically, *musayra* is composed of four communication features. The first is *repetition* in which the communication is characterized by repetitive statements that are formulaic in nature. Repetition is used primarily for complimenting and praising others, which is an important communication activity when you are trying to be gracious and accommodating. Repetition is also used as an argumentative style where repeated phrases are used to influence beliefs rather than Western-style logic. *Indirectness* is a second feature of the *musayra* code. This communication strategy reflects the cultural tendency to be interpersonally cautious and responsive to context. By being indirect, one can shift positions easier to accommodate the other person. Indirectness also facilitates politeness and face saving. *Elaboration* is a third feature, which pertains to an expressive and encompassing style. It leads to a deeper connection between speakers and affirms relationships. The final characteristic is *affectiveness* or an intuitive and emotional style. Again, this allows for identification with the other person and the maintenance of an engaged relationship.

The speech code of Israeli-Jews is a sharp contrast to *musayra*. Israeli-Jews employ a direct, pragmatic, and assertive style. This style has been termed *dugri* by Katriel (1986). *Dugri* means "straight talk" and is a well-documented code used by Israeli-Jews. *Dugri* is the opposite of *musayra*. *Dugri* speech is "to the point," with the communication of understanding and information as the most important communicative goals. Emotional appeals and personal niceties are of secondary importance. In *musayra* it is important to maintain the face or positive image of the other speaker. In *dugri* speech the speaker is more concerned with maintaining his or her own image of clarity and directness.

Dugri and *musayra* are excellent examples of speech codes. Philipsen (1997) describes five main ideas that characterize cultural speech codes. We can see how these ideas are powerfully ingrained in the communication of cultural members and are often responsible for misunderstanding and problems in intercultural communication. We further elaborate on *dugri* and *musayra* by explaining them within the context of the five principles of speech codes.

Speech Codes Are Culturally Distinctive

Speech codes are identified with a specific people in a specific place. When you first listen to someone speak, you often ask or wonder, "Where are they from?" Language is always identified with locations such as countries (e.g., American English, British English, or Australian English), regions (e.g., the South, East), or neighborhoods. Israeli *dugri* speech is associated with native-born Israelis of Jewish heritage in the land of Israel. The code is unique to Jews primarily of European heritage, and the code became crystallized in the pre-state period of the 1930s and 1940s (Katriel, 1986). *Musayra* is culturally distinct for speakers of Arabic and members of Arabic cultures; however, its geographic location is more complex than *dugri* because Arabic cultures are more geographically diverse. In both cases, however, when speakers of a code change geographic locations, they modify their code use.

Speech Codes Result From a Psychology and Sociology Unique to the Culture

Speech codes are intimately connected to the psychological qualities of a culture. They are related to how people see themselves. In other words, certain attitudes, values, and states of mind are more descriptive of one culture than another. For example, an Arab using a *musayra* code is maintaining consistency with his culture's expectations of honor. Honor is a controlling psychological value that legitimates a modesty code and the hospitality that one bestows. To use a *musayra* code—to be indirect, affective, and polite—is to maintain honor and express a distinct psychology of Arabs. Israeli-Jews, on the other hand, use *dugri* to express their strong native identity. This identity is rooted in the pride and strength they feel with respect to the state of Israel. Historically, Jews were a dislocated and oppressed people, but the establishment of the state of Israel altered this historical condition. *Dugri* speech is a communicative expression of this pride.

The Meaning and Significance of Messages Fundamentally Depend on Codes

You may be familiar with the maxim that "meanings are in people, not words." This means that true understanding of a communication depends on the people speaking and the code they use. When people communicate, they are performing some type of action, and others interpret that action. The interpretation relies on the speech code. When an Arab speaker deploys a *musayra* code and is polite, indirect, and courteous, a non–code user might interpret this speech as being weak, obsequious, or manipulative. This interpretation can lead to communication problems. Israeli-Jews have a reputation for being rude and aggressive. The *dugric* code contains a directness of style that includes bluntness and forthrightness. It is not uncommon to hear Israeli-Jews in

a meeting say things like "you are wrong" or "not true." This kind of directness is considered rude by many people, but not if you understand the code. A listener who "speaks" the *dugri* code will not come to any hasty conclusions about the dispositions of the other speaker because the same code is used to define the communicative act. In other words, bold utterances such as "you are wrong" are understood as normal ways of speaking rather than a rude way of speaking.

Speech Codes Are Located in the Language and Communication of Native Speakers

This simply means that speech codes are on display in the language of others. These codes are not inside the heads of others or contained in the generalities about culture. They are empirically observable in the communication of cultural members. Thus, when a native Israeli speaks directly and bluntly, the *dugri* code is very apparent. Speech codes are also found in the ritualized functions of communication. These are the known and repeated ways of organizing interaction, and they have code-specific symbolic forms. A greeting ritual is an example. An African American will greet another African American differently than he would a white person. These people might use certain vocabulary and body movements to signal a bond or friendship. The same is true for *dugri* and *musayra*. Both have symbolic forms that project and affirm an identity. By studying these symbolic forms and communication patterns, we can discover how the cultural world is orderly rather than chaotic.

Speech Codes Can Be Used to Understand, Predict, and Control Communication

The artful understanding and use of speech codes can be used to improve communication. People do not communicate like machines. Even if they are steeped in cultural codes, they often think reflectively about the code and alter typical patterns. This means there is potential for change and opportunities to avoid the more troublesome aspects of codes. An Israeli who is being very *dugri* can learn to recognize how others perceive him or her and perhaps alter certain patterns of communication. Moreover, situations can alter speech codes. In the next section of this essay, we explain how codes are influenced by particular communication situations.

ARGUMENT BETWEEN ISRAELI-JEWS AND PALESTINIANS

Argument is a persistent characteristic of the relationship between Israeli-Jews and Palestinians. In fact, argument is important to these groups because at least it is an acceptable mechanism of conflict resolution. We would rather these two groups argue than shoot at each other. We might expect from the previous discussion that *dugri* speech would be characteristic of Israeli-Jews and the mode of speech preferred by them during argument since Israeli-Jews have a speech code that includes an argumentative style. *Musayra*, on the other hand, is not argument oriented at all. Interestingly, the little research that exists on Arab argument patterns is consistent with *musayra*. Hatim (1991), in a study devoted to this issue, found that argumentation in modern Arabic is related to politeness and saving face.

Group status is one of the problems for groups in dialogue situations. When cultural groups are different in status, the arguments produced by the high-status groups can carry more weight. Israeli-Jews, given their military and economic advantages, carry considerably more status into dialogues. Moreover, their speech codes are more conducive to argument. But dialogue groups that work to promote open discussion and equal relations can help lessen status differences. They become a context that levels differences. Even though Arabs come from a cultural background where argument is considered disrespectful, there are situations where this difference can be diminished.

In our studies (Maoz & Ellis, in press; Ellis & Maoz, 2001), we found that the arguments during political dialogues between Israeli-Jews and Palestinians were not necessarily consistent with expectations from cultural speech codes. In other words, the Israeli-Jews do not necessarily use more assertive arguments, and the Arabs are not necessarily less

overtly aggressive. It appears that the dialogue context of communication does alter speech codes and provides an environment for more equal status discussion. Palestinians are more assertive during these dialogues than speech code theory would suggest. They speak more and engage in more reasoning and elaboration. This means that they state propositions and then support them with evidence in the classic tradition of argument.

The Israeli-Jews are somewhat consistent with the *dugri* code because they are quick to object to allegations and challenge assertions made by the Palestinians. Their experience with the *dugri* code makes it easy for them to sharply deny charges and demand justifications. But these dialogues do provide an environment for transformative communication because they afford the Palestinians an opportunity to accuse the Israeli-Jews of historical injustices. This is why the Israeli-Jews are typically on the defensive with objections and challenges to various statements. But, interestingly, the Israeli-Jews are also more hesitant and submissive in these dialogues. They qualify their arguments, backtrack, and provide context. Again, they are being challenged and responding in an accommodating and yielding manner rather than in a style associated with *dugri*. The dialogue context, and its transformative qualities, is probably responsible for these changes because typical roles are altered.

This dialogue context may also strengthen the sense of unity for groups with minority status, and the communication patterns reflect this fact. The Palestinians argue in such a way that they elaborate and provide evidence for arguments in a manner much more akin to *dugri* than their own *musayra*. They clearly use the context to transform themselves into a power coalition. The Palestinians engage in a form of "tag-team" argument (Brashers & Meyers, 1989). This is where one's own group engages in a repetitive elaboration of a point to produce the perception of unity. Following is an example of a tag-team argument. The Palestinians are expressing their anger about being prevented from entering Jerusalem. The Israelis say it is because of security, but the Palestinians "gang up" on the Israelis saying that the security measures— which are check points that the Palestinians must pass and are monitored by the Israeli military—do not work and it is just harassment.

PAL: If we go into Jerusalem not through the *Machsom* (Hebrew word for "checkpoint"), I can go in. They see me, and they don't care. It is that they want to make it difficult for me.

PAL: There are three ways to go from Bethlehem to Jerusalem.

PAL: If I want to go to Jerusalem, I am there in five minutes.

PAL: Sixty thousand Palestinians every day go to Israel without permission, every day; forty thousand with permission. So it's not security, it's politics. This is the information. I am not saying this to support.

The Palestinians are emboldened. The dialogue context helps transform the indigenous code of each group. This is an important matter with respect to the power relationship between each group. It suggests that the speech codes are pliant and that situations and activities can be found that reduce the cultural strength of these codes and make change and growth more possible. Moreover, these communication experiences balance the relationship between hostile and unequal groups in order to promote egalitarianism and make future interactions more productive.

CONCLUSION

In this article we have explained and illustrated cultural communication patterns between Israeli-Jews and Palestinians. These two groups are in bitter conflict and experiencing tremendous pressures and tensions for reconciliation and change. Clearly, national leaders and negotiators for peace need to solve the legal and legislative issues with respect to land, sovereignty, and other legal obligations. But true peace and prosperity "on the ground" will come only when these two groups learn to work together and improve communication. We have shown in this essay that each national group has evolved a different code and orientation to communication. These codes can be bridges or barriers to communication. Although communication codes are rela-

tively firm, they are not unyielding. We have shown that there are contexts and situations in which codes do not predict communication behavior. But more important, a thorough understanding of codes is necessary for dialogue and negotiation. Even words that are translated the same from different languages carry additional cultural baggage that is lost in the translation. Words are not neutral. They acquire their meaning from a culturally charged set of symbols that make up a speech code. The task for the future is to continually explore the nature of speech codes and their role in dialogue and conflict management.

References

Adwan, S., & Bar-On, D. (2000). *The Role of non-governmental organizations in peace building between Palestinians and Israelis*. Jerusalem: PRIME (Peace Research Institute in the Middle East), with the support of the World Bank.

Allport, G. (1954). *The nature of prejudice*. Reading, MA: Addison-Wesley.

Amir, Y. (1976). The role of intergroup contact in change of prejudice and ethnic relations. In P. Katz, (Ed.), *Towards the elimination of racism* (pp. 245–308). New York: Pergamon.

Bernstein, B. (1971). *Class, codes and control.* Volume 1. London: Routledge & Kegan Paul.

Brashers, D. E., & Meyers, R. A. (1989). Tag-team argument and group decision making: A preliminary investigation. In B. E. Gronbeck (Ed.), *Spheres of argument: Proceedings of the sixth SCA/AFA conference on argumentation* (pp. 542–550). Annandale, VA: Speech Communication Association.

Ellis, D.G. (1992). Syntactic and pragmatic codes in communication. *Communication Theory, 2,* 1–23.

Ellis, D.G. (1994). Codes and pragmatic comprehension. In S. A. Deetz (Ed.), *Communication yearbook 17* (pp. 333–343). Thousand Oaks, CA: Sage Publications.

Ellis, D. G., & Maoz, I. (2001). *Cross-cultural argument interactions in dialogues between Israeli-Jews and Palestinians*. Unpublished manuscript.

Feghali, E. (1997). Arab cultural communication patterns. *International Journal of Intercultural Relations, 21,* 345–378.

Hatim, B. (1991). The pragmatics of argumentation in Arabic: The rise and fall of a text type. *Text, 11,* 189–199.

Gergen, K. (1999). *Toward transformative dialogue*. A paper presented to the 49th Annual Conference of the International Communication Association, San Francisco, CA, May 27–31 1999.

Katriel, T. (1986). *Talking straight: Dugri speech in Israeli sabra culture*. London, England: Cambridge University Press.

Kelman, H. (1995). Contributions of an unofficial conflict resolution effort to the Israeli-Palestinian breakthrough. *Negotiation Journal, 11*, 19–27.

Kelman, H. (1997). Group processes in the resolution of international conflicts: Experiences from the Israeli-Palestinian case. *American Psychologist, 52*, 212–220.

Maoz, I. (2000a). Multiple conflicts and competing agendas: A framework for conceptualizing structured encounters between groups in conflict—The case of a coexistence project between Jews and Palestinians in Israel. *Journal of Peace Psychology, 6*, 135–156.

Maoz, I. (2000b). An experiment in peace: Processes and effects in reconciliation aimed workshops of Israeli and Palestinian youth. *Journal of Peace Research, 37*, 721–736.

Maoz, M. (1999). From conflict to peace? Israel's relations with Syria and the Palestinians. *Middle East Journal, 53*, 393–416.

Maoz, I., & Ellis, D. G. (in press). Going to ground: Argument in Israeli-Jewish and Palestinian encounter groups. *Research on Language and Social Interaction*.

Philipsen, G. (1997). A theory of speech codes. In G. Philipsen & T. L. Albrecht (Eds.), *Developing communication theories* (pp. 119–156). Albany: State University of New York Press.

Pettigrew, T. (1998). Intergroup contact theory. *Annual Review of Psychology, 49*, 65–85.

Rouhana, N., & Bar-Tal, D. (1998). Psychological dynamics of intractable ethnonational conflicts: The Israeli-Palestinian case. *American Psychologist, 53*, 761–770.

Concepts and Questions

1. What roles do land rights, religion, and cultural conflict play in defining the communicative dynamics of Israeli-Jews and Palestinian Arabs?

2. What do Ellis and Maoz mean when they refer to "transformative communication"?

3. How does transformative communication help improve the communication between groups in conflict?

4. What conditions must be met between two groups in conflict before the contact hypothesis will help reduce prejudice and negative inter-group attitudes?

5. How does the concept of "dialogue" as discussed by Martin Buber, Carl Rogers, and Mikhail Bakhtin provide guiding principles for transformative diaglogue?

6. How do cultural differences in speech codes affect communication between Israeli-Jews and Palestinian Arabs? Provide some examples of differences in speech codes for each of these groups.

7. What have been the major circumstances that have led to the development of the unique speech codes among Isreali-Jews and Palestinian Arabs?

8. *Musayra*, which means "to accommodate," or "to go along with" plays a major role in the speech codes of Palestinian Arabs. What are the four communicative features of *musayra*?

9. How do the speech codes of Israeli-Jews differ from those of the Palestinian Arabs?

10. What do Ellis and Maoz mean when they assert that the meaning and significance of Messages fundamentally depend on speech codes?

Mexican *Dichos*: Lessons Through Language

CAROLYN ROY

MEXICAN CULTURE AND ITS REFLECTED IMAGES

The late Octavio Paz, one of Mexico's most renowned writers, asserts in his classic *The Labyrinth of Solitude: Life and Thought in Mexico* that the Mexican's "face is a mask" (Paz, 1961, p. 29). Paz thereby implies that knowing *the* Mexican national character might be impossible. Carlos Fuentes, another of Mexico's most esteemed men of letters, employs the imagery of dark, ancient Aztec polished hematite mirrors reflecting the soul of Mexico when he writes: "Is not the mirror both a reflection of reality and a projection of the imagination?" (Fuentes, 1992, p. 11). Despite the self-confessed inscrutable nature of Mexican national character, *dichos*—popular sayings including, but not limited to, *proverbios*/proverbs, *adagios*/adages, and *refranes*/refrains—open an avenue for exploring the attributes most esteemed and salient in Mexican popular culture. Using Fuentes' metaphor, however, our understanding of Mexican culture remains but a darkly reflected image. Our understanding is further obscured by the difficulty of precise idiomatic translation of the complex Mexican language that hybridizes the Spanish brought from Europe with the intricately nuanced indigenous languages, predominantly Nahuatl, of Mexico's native peoples. Nevertheless, popular sayings heard from the northern reaches of the Chihuahuan desert to the highlands of southern Chiapas do provide insight into some commonly held values in Mexican culture.

Such popular sayings transmit "what a culture deems significant" (Samovar & Porter, 2001, p. 36). Examination of these orally transmitted traditional values offers an excellent means of learning about another culture because these oft-repeated sayings fuse past, present, and future. These sayings focus our attention on basic principles accepted within the culture. The premise of this present exercise is that we can learn much about Mexican values through scrutiny of these distilled lessons of life transmitted through their language.

While some of these popular sayings are uniquely Mexican, many more of them were brought to Mexico by Spaniards after 1519; therefore, they reflect the fusion of cultures, especially Castillian and Muslim, found in recently "reconquered" and unified early 16th-century Spain. Because many values are universally human, similar sayings may be found just as often in cultures around the globe. For example, most cultures attribute some responsibility for a child's character or nature to the parents; hence, in the United States one might hear, "like father, like son," or "a chip off the old block," while in Mexico the close approximation is *de tal palo, tal astilla* (from such a stick, such a splinter). But the proverb *Al nopal nomás lo van a ver cuando tiene tunas* (One only goes to see the cactus when it has prickly pear fruit) derives specifically from the Mexican milieu. However, one might readily overhear a parent in the United States complaining to an adult child: "You only come to see me when you want something." So the principle of the saying is universal, while the expression relates uniquely to its culture. Although some sayings are culturally unique and others universal, our purpose here is to focus on specific Mexican sayings that reflect some of the values of that culture.

MEXICAN *DICHOS*

Popular sayings—*dichos*—reflect many of the basic values of contemporary Mexican society, although the roots of these expressions of popular culture extend far back into both European and pre-Columbian Native American civilizations. Although many of these expressions demonstrate the universality of proverbs generally, many uniquely mirror Mexican reality. Yolanda Nava writes about Latin American culture in general, but her observation applies equally well to Mexican sayings in particular. She notes:

This original essay, while written for this edition, draws on principles discussed in an article written by Shelly Zormeier and Larry A. Samovar and published in the eighth edition. All rights reserved. Permission to reprint must be obtained from the author and the publisher. Carolyn Roy teaches in the Department of History at San Diego State University, California.

"*Dichos* feel good on the tongue . . . they are, after all, a verbal shorthand which . . . elders used countless times to remind [one] . . . to behave wisely" (Nava, p. 35). *Dichos* may be pithy condensations of wisdom gained through centuries of experience. They are one form of transmitting folk wisdom. The sayings selected here might be heard in any Mexican household.

Many of the proverbs in the following sections may be readily consulted in Sellers (1994), but caution must be exercised in reviewing Sellers' interpretations of these *dichos*. One must always maintain cognizance of the cultural context. While a Mexican might playfully jest, saying, *No hagas hoy lo que puedas hacer mañana* (Don't do today what you can put off until tomorrow), such should not be taken literally (as Sellers apparently does, p. 26). This inverted *dicho* merely jocularly reminds the listener that one should *No dejar para mañana lo que se puede hacer hoy* (Not put off until tomorrow what can be done today), a well-known adage in many cultures.

The Mexican tradition of playfulness with words, as in the previous example, or the use of double meaning [*doble sentido*] (often with obscured sexual undertones—most frequently heard with such apparently innocuous words as *huevos*/eggs, *aguacates*/avocados, and so on, used as anatomical designations), or in using a word for its exact opposite, has ancient roots in pre-Columbian Mexican linguistic practices. Among the Aztecs, it was proper practice to refer to an older person as "my dear young one," much as a Mexican mother today may call her toddler "my dear father" [*mi papito*]. Those expressions chosen for discussion here reflect some of the values central to Mexican popular culture. These values include cheerful acceptance of the "will of God," the need to place trust with great care, the significance of appearances, the necessity to guard one's privacy and not breach that of others, prescribed gender roles, a communal spirit, and the importance of family.

Acceptance of "God's Will"

No hay mal que por bien no venga. (There is no bad that good does not accompany.) Mexicans have often been characterized as fatalistic, but their nature seems more than merely accepting of the in-evitable. Much of Mexican folk wisdom relates to acceptance of poverty and even laughing at it. Mexican folk seem to relish the challenge of finding happiness in the face of adversity. Some of the most frequently heard proverbs reflect that optimism. This proverb might be equated to: "It's an ill wind that brings nobody good," but that does not carry the same positive outlook that the Spanish phrase indicates. Closer to the Mexican concept might be: "Every cloud has a silver lining."

Mejor reír que llorar. (Better to laugh than to cry.) If one laughs at adversity, whether that is a simple upset of plans or that which is most inevitable—death—then there is nothing that can disturb one's happiness. Much of Mexican art reflects the duality of life and death, as can be seen in art from pre-Columbian times to the present. The very popular woodcuts of José Guadalupe Posada depicting skeletons in scenes that range from the mundane to the hilariously outrageous clearly demonstrate the Mexican's friendly attitude toward death. If one can laugh, then there is no need for lament.

El hombre propone y Dios dispone. (Man proposes and God disposes.) Few Mexican women would dare to make plans, whether it be meeting for lunch tomorrow or making plans for a child's future, without adding before concluding those plans, *Si Dios quiere* (If God wills). It would be presuming much to think that one could control the future; that is viewed as in God's hands alone. In the South of the United States, one hears a similar expression made popular by Southern folklorists: "If the Lord's willing and the creek don't rise," but this seems less an attitude of fatalistic acceptance than an almost humorous excuse in the event of inclement weather in the backwoods. Whereas *Si Dios quiere* is an expression used almost exclusively by Mexican women, "If the Lord's willing" may be used by males or females.

No por mucho madrugar amanece más temprano. (No matter how early one rises, the sun will not come up any sooner.) One must simply accept what one cannot change. Nothing is accomplished by unnecessary effort. Only the foolish will attempt to defy the forces of nature.

Cuando el pobre tiene para carne sea vigilia. (When the poor have [money] to buy meat, it must be

Lent.) The poor must accept that when they have the good fortune to have money, then it will be a time of fasting [not eating meat]. The poor must accept that they will not have good luck. This is an instance of making fun of—of laughing at—adversity. If I am poor, I should expect to eat beans and tortillas, not meat.

Quien canta su mal espanta. (He who sings frightens away his grief.) By singing, the individual can dispel sadness and drive away gloom. Singing and other forms of music accompany most private Mexican gatherings, but can also be heard in the Metro stations and on street corners of metropolitan centers.

Sparing Bestowal of Trust

En confianza está el peligro. (There is danger in trust.) For the Mexican to place trust in another, particularly anyone who is not a blood relative, is very high esteem. But when one does bestow trust, then the greatest harm possible would be to betray that trust. It is a great risk to have faith in another; therefore, trust must never be granted lightly.

La confianza tambien mata. (Trust also kills.) Betrayal of trust kills the spirit as surely as a bullet might kill the body. And the betrayal of trust would be the gravest ill that one friend could commit against another. Another *dicho* conveys the gravity of betrayal of trust: *Ni te fíes de amigo reconciliado, ni de manjar dos veces guisado¡* (Do not trust a reconciled friend nor a dish twice cooked.) If a trust has been betrayed, the lost trust can never be recovered.

Del dicho al hecho hay mucho trecho. (From said to done, there is a great gap.) One should not trust that promises will be fulfilled. Even with the best of intentions, circumstances intervene, thus one should always be prepared to accept less than is promised, thereby avoiding disappointment.

Músico pagado toca mal son. (The musician who has been paid plays bad music.) The most foolish act that an employer could commit would be to pay the worker before the task is completed. Such an employer would not be viewed as kind or generous, merely foolish. If a worker is paid in advance, then the foolish employer deserves to be treated

with contempt. One of the first lessons to be learned when interacting within Mexican culture is that easy trust is not valued. Trust/*confianza* must be given sparingly and only after being earned. Reserving payment until the work is completed is viewed as prudent. The lesson of the saying is that paying for a job before it is completed produces bad results.

The Importance of Appearances

Díme con quien andas y te diré quien eres. (Tell me with whom you associate [walk, travel], and I will tell you who you are.) Whom you choose as your companions and associates reflects your quality. If you associate with "common people," then you will be judged common. It follows that one always seeks to associate with people of higher status in order to improve on one's station in life. In English one hears, "Birds of a feather flock together," but that does not fully convey the idea that one can rise in status by associating with a better class of people.

Quien anda con lobos a aullar se aprenda. (One who goes around with wolves learns to howl.) In this same vein is the Biblical principle in English: "Evil companions corrupt good morals." If you run with the wolves, you will learn their wild ways; therefore, one should avoid such savages and associate with cultured society. One must choose associates with great care. They not only reflect one's position, but they also influence one's character.

El que es buen gallo dondequiera canta. (A good rooster can crow anywhere.) Despite the previous admonitions, quality is quality no matter the circumstance. A person of true character will show that character in all circumstances, but a person of poor character will not be able to measure up in difficult circumstances.

Respect for Privacy

Agua que no has de beber, déjala correr. (Water that you do not have to drink, leave it to flow.) Aranda translates this as: "Don't meddle in others' affairs; don't start trouble." If you stir up the water, then it will be undrinkable for anyone. So let everyone tend to their own problems and thus avoid spreading them to others.

Bueno aconsejar, mejor remediar. (It is good to give advice, but it is better to solve the problem.) When there is a problem, it is good to give advice when it is sought, but it would be better to solve the problem. If you cannot solve the problem, then refrain from giving advice. And there are even times when the truth is better left unsaid, as attested by the proverb: *Si dices la verdad no pecas, pero no sabes los males que suscitas* (If you tell the truth you do not sin, but you don't know the troubles you cause. So keep your own counsel).

En boca cerrada no entran moscas. (Flies do not enter a closed mouth.) If you keep your mouth shut, then you will not have to worry about "putting your foot in it." Be careful of what you say, because *Un resbalón de lengua es peor que el de los pies¡* (A slip of the tongue is worse than a slip of the foot.) The foot will heal, but damage done by words will not. Also, *Rezarle sólo a su santo¡* (Pray only to your saint); that is, only someone who can help you should know of your problems.

Gender Roles

Mejor quedarse para vestir los santos que tener que desvestir un borracho. (It is better to remain to dress the saints than to have to undress a drunk.) Women who do not marry are often referred to as "those who stay to dress the saints"; that is, they spend their lives caring for the images of the saints, which often involves making new garments for the images or painting and refurbishing them. Thus, single women often justify their unmarried state by suggesting that they prefer dressing the saints' images to having to undress a drunken husband.

Más vale solo que mal acompañado. (It is better to remain single than to be disagreeably accompanied.) In a society in which women are viewed as weak and vulnerable, single women must justify their unmarried state, so that women most often cite the refrain that it is better to be single than to have an unbearable spouse.

A la mujer ni todo el amor ni todo el dinero. (To a woman neither all your love nor all your money.) A "real" Mexican male must maintain control of himself and his money. Men make a practice of

allocating a certain portion of their income to women for maintaining the household, but the rest of their earnings belong to them. One of the great enigmas of Mexican culture is the dichotomy of *machismo* [strong, dominant male] versus *marianismo* [long-suffering, submissive female]. This concept is most readily seen in the fact that *cantinas*/bars are exclusively for males (and women of ill-repute).

Triste está la casa donde la gallina canta y el gallo calla. (Sad is the house where the chicken crows and the rooster is quiet.) The proper role for a man is as the master of his house, and the woman should be silent. It is a reversal of proper roles for the Mexican woman to make the decisions and the man to allow her to do so. In English a similar refrain is: "A whistling girl and a crowing hen always come to some sad end." Women are assigned their proper roles and men theirs. A sad state results when these roles are reversed.

Communalism

Mucha ayuda, poco trabajo. (Much help, little work.) When many work together, it is little work for any of them. When work is shared, it goes quickly and is not much effort for anyone. The tradition of communal work precedes European contact with the New World. Among the Aztecs, taking turns at doing community service was widely practiced.

Vida sin amigos, muerte sin testigos. (Life without friends, death without witnesses.) [Life without friends, no mourners when it ends.] If one does not live so as to have many friends, then death will come with no one there to mourn that death. In Mexican culture it is extremely important that there be mourners to accompany the deceased. It has long been common practice to pay mourners so that the dead will be accompanied to the cemetery. Again, this reflects the importance of one's public persona, one's appearance to the rest of the world, even in death.

Family

¿A dónde vas que valgas más? (Where are you going that you are worth more?) Where would you be valued more than at home? The Mexican family

is extended, but still very close. When an individual needs help, the family is expected to supply it. The understanding is that you are always better off at home.

Amor de padre o madre, lo demás es aire. (The love of mother or father, everything else is air.) Compared to a mother or father's love, there is nothing else of importance. Father and mother will love and support their children when everyone and everything else fails. It is not unusual to encounter adult children living in the home of their parents and even rearing their own children in that same home. At times this is done out of economic necessity, but just as often it is because of the bond of the extended family. Grandparents become the caregivers for the offspring and take a hand in their upbringing.

SUMMARY

Popular sayings reflect basic cultural values. They do not even require literacy because they transmit the values orally to all who hear them. They metaphorically condense timeless lessons into readily recalled phrases. Through *dichos* we are reminded that our experiences are not unique; others have experienced the same things in other times and other places and left us messages to guide us. By reviewing a selection of Mexican *dichos*, one readily perceives some of that culture's more significant values: cheerful acceptance of one's lot in life, the need to exercise caution when placing trust, the importance of appearances, the sanctity of privacy, proper gender roles, communalism, and family.

References

Aranda, C. (1977). *Dichos: Proverbs and sayings from the Spanish.* Santa Fe: Swanstone Press.

Ballesteros, O. (1979). *Mexican proverbs: The philosophy, wisdom, and humor of a people.* Burnet, TX: Eakin Press.

Burciaga, J. (1997). *In few words/en pocas palabras: A compendium of Latino folk wit and wisdom.* San Francisco: Mercury House.

Fuentes, C. (1992). *The buried mirror: Reflections on Spain and the New World.* New York: Houghton Mifflin.

Nava, Y. (2000). *It's all in the frijoles: 100 famous Latinos share real-life stories, time-tested* dichos, *favorite folktales, and inspiring words of wisdom.* New York: Fireside.

Paz, O. (1961). *The labyrinth of solitude: Life and thought in Mexico.* New York: Grove Press.

Samovar, L. A., & Porter, R. E. (2001). *Communication between cultures* (4th ed.). Belmont, CA: Wadsworth.

Sellers, J. M. (1994). *Folk wisdom of Mexico.* San Francisco: Chronicle Books.

Concepts and Questions

1. How does the study of familiar sayings help us understand some of the important values of a particular culture?

2. Which Mexican sayings discussed by Roy are heard in other cultures?

3. Can you think of some sayings from your own culture and relate the specific values they represent?

4. What are your favorite familiar sayings? Why have you selected these?

5. What sayings in the United States stress the value of individualism?

6. What Mexican sayings reflect the underlying religious philosophy of the culture?

chapter 5

Nonverbal Interaction: Action, Sound, and Silence

I t is indeed a truism that you communicate not only with your words but also with your actions. Successful participation in intercultural communication therefore requires that you recognize and understand culture's influence on both verbal and nonverbal interaction. Your nonverbal actions constitute a second symbol system that enables other people to gain insight into your thoughts and feelings. Because nonverbal symbols are derived from such diverse behaviors as body movements, postures, facial expressions, gestures, eye movements, physical appearance, the use and organization of space, the structuring of time, and vocal nuances, these symbolic behaviors vary from one culture to another. An awareness of the role nonverbal behaviors play during interaction is therefore crucial if you are to appreciate all aspects of intercultural communication.

Nonverbal behavior is largely unconscious. You use nonverbal symbols spontaneously, without thinking about what posture, what gesture, or what interpersonal distance is appropriate to the situation. Nonverbal behavior is critically important in intercultural communication because, as with other aspects of the communication process, these behaviors reflect cultural diversity. In other words, culture largely determines which posture, which gesture, or which interpersonal distance is appropriate in a host of social situations. This influence of culture on nonverbal behavior can be considered from two perspectives.

In the first perspective, culture tends to determine the specific nonverbal behaviors that represent specific thoughts, feelings, or states of the communicator. Thus, what might be a sign of greeting in one culture might very well be an obscene gesture in another. Or what is considered a symbol of affirmation in one culture could be meaningless or even signify negation in another. In the second perspective, culture determines when it is appropriate to display or communicate various thoughts, feelings, or internal states; this is particularly evident in the display of emotions. Although there seems to be little cross-cultural difference in the nonverbal behaviors that represent emotional states, there can be significant cultural differences in the specification of which emotions may be displayed, the degree to which they may be displayed, who may display them, and when or where they may be displayed.

As important as verbal language is to a communication event, nonverbal communication is just as, if not more, important. Nonverbal messages can stand alone or they can tell you how other messages are to be interpreted. For example, they often indicate whether verbal messages are true, were uttered in jest, are serious or threatening, and so on. Nonverbal communication is especially important because as much as 90 percent of the social content of a message is transmitted paralinguistically—that is, nonverbally.

Chapter 5 deals with nonverbal interaction. More specifically, it deals with how one's culture influences both the perception and use of nonverbal actions. These readings will demonstrate the diversity of culturally derived nonverbal behaviors and the underlying value structures that produce these behaviors.

We begin this chapter with an essay by Peter Andersen titled "In Different Dimensions: Nonverbal Communication and Culture." Andersen offers an overview of the topic of nonverbal communication rather than a critique of a single culture. Embedded in Andersen's article is the idea that nonverbal codes, like verbal languages, shift from culture to culture. To help us appreciate and understand these codes, Andersen begins by briefly summarizing the basic codes of nonverbal communication: physical appearance (attire), proxemics (space and distance), chronemics (time), kinesics (facial expressions, movements, gestures), haptics (touch), oculesics (eye contact and gaze), vocalics (paralanguage), and olfactics (smell). After his discussion of these basic codes, Andersen moves to an analysis of how these codes can differ from one culture to another. He explores these differences as they apply to high and low contexts, individualism and collectivism, power distance, uncertainty, immediacy and expressiveness, and gender.

Our next essay moves us from a discussion of cultures in general to an analysis of a specific culture. Edwin R. McDaniel, in his piece titled "Japanese Nonverbal Communication: A Reflection of Cultural Themes," examines some nonverbal communication patterns found in the Japanese culture. As a means of demonstrating the link between culture and communication, McDaniel examines the communication behaviors of the Japanese culture and traces the reasons for these behaviors. By presenting what he refers to as "cultural themes," McDaniel explains how Japan's social organizations, historical experiences, and religious orientations are directly connected to Japanese nonverbal behavior. In a propositional survey, McDaniel presents a series of 11 propositions that tie various cultural themes to how the Japanese perceive and use kinesics (movement), oculesics (eye contact), facial expressions, proxemics, touch, personal appearance, space, time, vocalics or paralanguage, silence, and olfactics (smell).

In our next essay, "Monochronic and Polychronic Time," anthropologist Edward T. Hall looks at the conscious and unconscious ways in which cultures use time. Hall maintains that cultures organize and respond to time in two very different ways; he has labeled them as *polychronic* (P-time) and *monochronic* (M-time). These chronological systems are not either–or categories, but the extremes of a concept dimension that offers two distinct approaches to the notion of time. People from cultures such as those found in the Mediterranean, Africa, and South America operate near the P-time end of the dimension. As the term *poly*chronic suggests, they do many things simultaneously, are more concerned with people and the present moment than with schedules, and believe that they are in command of time rather than are being controlled by it. Cultures that operate near the M-time end of the time dimension, such as those found in Northern Europe and North America, are *mono*chronic and tend toward doing only one thing at a time. They emphasize schedules, the segmentation of time, and promptness. It is easy to imagine the potential for misunderstanding when people from these diverse time orientations come together. Hall's essay helps us avoid communication problems by introducing us to the many forms these two interaction patterns may take.

As we have seen, a great deal of difference exists between cultures in terms of their nonverbal behavior. Yet, within cultures we can find, to a lesser degree, diversity in nonverbal behavior among co-cultures. One of the most important, if not *the* most important, sources of nonverbal communication diversity within a culture is gender. In our final essay, "Gender and Nonverbal Communication," Deborah Borisoff and Lisa Merrill introduce us to the role gender plays in influencing nonverbal behavior. Through an examination of women's and men's use and interpretation of space, height, touch, gestures, facial expressions, and eye contact, they explore some of the assumptions and controversies about the nonverbal aspects of gender. They provide us with rich insight into gender-based differences in the perception of nonverbal behavior by detailing how men and women differ in their awareness and interpretation of nonverbal communication.

In Different Dimensions: Nonverbal Communication and Culture

PETER A. ANDERSEN

Long ago, before the Internet, before the global economy, before even the television and the airplane, most people spent their lives within their own cultures. Only rarely across the generations did sojourners, traders, or warriors encounter people from other cultures. Not so today. Cultures are colliding and communicating at an ever-accelerating rate. For several decades international travel has been increasing, and international trade is at an all-time high (Brown, Kane, & Roodman, 1994). Countries throughout the world encounter new immigrants from dramatically different cultural backgrounds. Moreover, the technological revolution and especially the Internet "will blur national boundaries and it will transform the nation state in a way humans have not witnessed for a millennium" (Andersen, 1999b, p.540). The probability of communicating with people from other cultures in our daily interactions is greater than ever before.

On the streets of London, Los Angeles, Sydney, or Singapore dozens of languages are being spoken. Although language differences are highly apparent, they are only the tips of a very large cultural iceberg. Culture is primarily an implicit nonverbal phenomenon because most aspects of one's culture are learned through observation and imitation rather than by explicit verbal instruction or expression. The primary level of culture is communicated implicitly, without awareness, chiefly by nonverbal means (Andersen, 1999a; Hall, 1984; Sapir, 1928). In most situations, intercultural interactants do not share the same language. But languages can be

learned, and larger communication problems occur in the nonverbal realm. Nonverbal communication is a subtle, nonlinguistic, multidimensional, and spontaneous process (Andersen, 1999a). Indeed, individuals are little aware of their own nonverbal behavior, which is enacted mindlessly, spontaneously, and unconsciously (Andersen, 1999a; Burgoon, 1985; Samovar & Porter, 1985).

Because we are not usually aware of even our own nonverbal behavior, it becomes extremely difficult to identify and master the nonverbal behavior of another culture. At times we feel uncomfortable in other cultures because we intuitively know something isn't right. "Because perceptions of nonverbal behaviors are rarely conscious phenomena, it may be difficult for us to know exactly why we are feeling uncomfortable" (Gudykunst & Kim, 1992, p. 172). Sapir was among the first to note that "[w]e respond to gestures with an extreme alertness and, one might almost say, in accordance with an elaborate and secret confused with human nature itself.

This article first will briefly explore eight codes of nonverbal communication: *physical appearance, proxemics, chronemics, kinesics, haptics, oculesics, vocalics,* and *olfactics*; briefly define and situate culture; and finally discuss six primary dimensions of cultural variation, including *immediacy, individualism, gender, power distance, uncertainty–avoidance,* and *cultural contextualization,* that help explain the thousands of cross-cultural differences in nonverbal behavior.

NONVERBAL CODES

Most discussions of nonverbal intercultural communication have been anecdotal, descriptive, and atheoretical, where numerous examples of intercultural differences for each nonverbal code are discussed in detail. Recapitulation of the various nonverbal codes of intercultural communication is not a primary purpose here. Thus, the basic codes of nonverbal communication will be discussed only briefly, along with references that provide detailed and excellent analyses of how each nonverbal code differs interculturally.

The most externally obvious code of nonverbal behavior is *physical appearance*—the most important code used during initial encounters. Cultural attire is obvious and leads to ethnic stereotypes. During a field study of touch conducted at an international airport, I witnessed Tongans in multicultural ceremonial gowns, Sikhs in white turbans, Hasidic Jews in blue yarmulkes, and Africans in white dashikis—all alongside Californians in running shorts and halter tops. Little formal research has been conducted on the impact of physical appearance on intercultural communication. Discussions of intercultural differences in appearance are provided by Scheflen (1974) and Samovar, Porter, and Stefani (1998). Although blue jeans and business suits have become increasingly accepted attire internationally, local attire still abounds. Preoccupation with physical appearance is hardly a new phenomenon. Since the dawn of culture, humans from the upper Paleolithic period (40,000 years ago) to the present have adorned their bodies in great variety of ways (Samovar et al., 1998).

Perhaps the most fundamental code of nonverbal behavior is *proxemics*, communication via interpersonal space and distance. Research has documented that cultures differ substantially in their use of personal space, their regard for territory and the meanings they assign to proxemic behavior (Gudykunst & Kim, 1992; Hall, 1959, 1976; Scheflen, 1974). For example, people from Mediterranean and Latin cultures maintain close distance, whereas people from Northern European and Northeast Asian cultures maintain greater distances. But this behavior also is highly contextual. At rush hour in Tokyo the normally respectful, distant Japanese are literally jammed into subways and trains.

Chronemics—or the study of meanings, usage, and communication of time—is probably the most discussed and well-researched nonverbal code in the intercultural literature (Bruneau, 1979; Gudykunst & Kim, 1992; Hall, 1959, 1976, 1984). These analyses suggest that cultural time frames differ so dramatically that if only chronemic differences existed, then intercultural misunderstandings would still be considerable. In the United States, time is viewed as a commodity that can be wasted, spent, saved, and used wisely (Andersen, 1999a). Of course, many cultures have radically different concepts of time. In most less developed countries, life moves to the rhythms of nature, the day, the seasons, the year. Such human inventions as seconds, minutes, hours,

and weeks have no real meaning. Things are experienced polychronically and simultaneously, whereas in Western culture time is modularized and events are scheduled sequentially, not simultaneously.

People's *kinesic* behavior differs from culture to culture, including some aspects of their facial expressions, body movements, gestures, and conversational regulators (Gudykunst & Kim, 1992; Hall, 1976; Samovar et al., 1998; Scheflen, 1974). Gestures differ dramatically in meaning, extensiveness, and intensity. Stories abound in the intercultural literature of gestures that signal endearment or warmth in one culture but may be obscene or insulting in another.

Tactile communication, called *haptics*, also shows considerable intercultural variation (Andersen & Leibowitz, 1978; Ford & Graves, 1977; McDaniel & Andersen, 1998; Samovar et al., 1998). Recent research has shown vast differences in international and intercultural touch in amount, location, type, and public or private manifestation (Jones, 1994; McDaniel & Andersen, 1998).

One important code of nonverbal communication that has attracted considerably less intercultural research attention is *oculesics*, the study of messages sent by the eyes—including eye contact, blinks, eye movements, and pupil dilation (Gudykunst & Kim, 1992; Samovar et al., 1998). Because eye contact has been called an "invitation to communicate," its variation cross-culturally is an important communication topic.

Vocalics, or *paralanguage*, the nonverbal elements of the voice, also has received comparatively little attention from intercultural researchers (Gudykunst & Kim, 1992; LaBarre, 1985; Samovar et al., 1998; Scheflen, 1974). Music and singing, universal forms of aesthetic communication, have been almost completely overlooked in intercultural research, except for an excellent series of studies (Lomax, 1968) that identified several groups of worldwide cultures through differences and similarities in their folk songs.

Finally, *olfactics*, the study of interpersonal communication via smell, has been virtually ignored in intercultural research despite its importance (Samovar et al., 1998). Americans are the most smell-aversive culture in the world (Andersen, 1998). While most of the world's people emit natural body smells, the cultures in the most developed parts of the world use an array of cosmetics to eliminate body odor or to replace it with natural smells.

SITUATING AND DEFINING CULTURE

Along with traits, situations, and states, culture is one of the four primary sources of interpersonal behavior (Andersen, 1987; see Figure 1). Culture is the enduring influence of the social environment on our behavior, including our interpersonal communication behavior. Culture is a learned set of shared perceptions about beliefs, values, and needs that affect the behaviors of relatively large groups of people (Lustig & Koester, 1999). Culture exerts a considerable force on individual behavior through what Geertz (1973) called "control mechanisms—plans, recipes, rules, instructions (what computer engineers call 'programs')—for the governing of behavior" (p. 44). Culture has similar and powerful, though not identical, effects on all residents of a cultural system. As another group of researchers explains: "Culture can be behaviorally observed by contrasting intra-group homogeneity with intergroup heterogeneity" (Andersen, Lustig, & Andersen, 1986, p. 11).

Personal traits and culture are sometimes confused because both are enduring phenomena (Andersen, 1987). Traits have multiple causes (Andersen, 1987), only some of which are the result of culture. Culture has also been confused with situation because both are part of one's social environment; however, culture is an enduring phenomenon, whereas situation is a transient one with an observable beginning and end. Culture, along with genetics, is the most enduring, powerful, and invisible shaper of our communication behavior.

Dimensions of Cultural Variation

Thousands of anecdotes regarding nonverbal misunderstandings between persons from different cultures have been reported. Although it may be useful to know that Arabs stand closer during communication than Americans, the Swiss are more time conscious than Italians, and Asians value silence more than Westerners, we need more than this basic approach. Because the number of potential pairs of cultures are huge and the number of possible non-

Figure 1 *Sources of influence on interpersonal behavior*

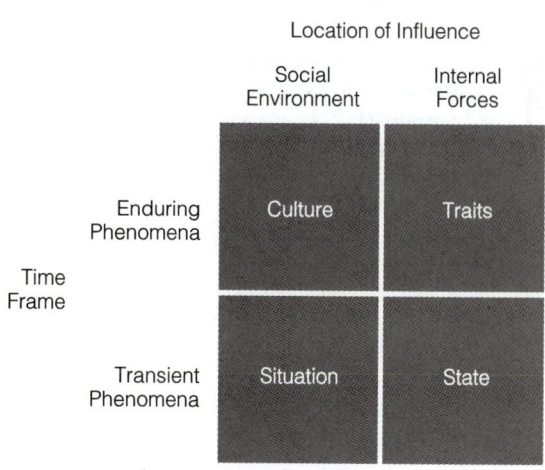

verbal misunderstandings between each pair of cultures is similarly large, millions of potential intercultural anecdotes are possible (Andersen, 1999a). What is needed is some way to organize, explain, and understand this plethora of potential problems in intercultural communication. Some initial research has shown that cultures can be located along dimensions that help explain these intercultural differences. Most cultural differences in nonverbal behavior are a result of variations along the dimensions discussed as follows.

High and Low Context. The first cultural dimension of communication proposed decades ago is *context*—the degree to which communication is explicit and verbal or implicit and nonverbal. Hall (1976, 1984) has described high-context cultures in considerable detail: "A high context (HC) communication or message is one in which most of the information is either in the physical context or internalized in the person, while very little is in the coded, explicit, transmitted parts of the message" (Hall, 1976, p. 91). Another group of researchers explains: "In a high-context culture such as that of Japan, meanings are internalized and there is a large emphasis on nonverbal codes" (Lustig & Koester, 1999, p. 108). Married couples or old friends skillfully use HC or implicit messages that are nearly impossible for an outsider to understand. The situation, a smile, or a glance provides implicit meaning that does not need to be articulated. In HC situations or cultures, information is integrated from the environment, the context, the situation, and nonverbal cues that give the message meaning that is unavailable in the explicit verbal utterance.

Low-context (LC) messages are the opposite of HC messages; most are communicated via explicit code usually via verbal communication (Andersen, 1999a; Hall, 1976). LC messages must be detailed, unmistakably communicated, and highly specific. Unlike personal relationships, which are high-context message systems, institutions such as courts of law and formal systems such as mathematics and computer languages require explicit LC systems because nothing can be taken for granted (Hall, 1984).

There is vast cultural variation in the degree of context used in communication. Research suggests that the lowest-context cultures are Swiss, German, North American, and Scandinavian (Gudykunst & Kim, 1992; Hall, 1976, 1984). In these cultures, literal meaning, specific details, and precise time schedules are valued at the expense of context. Low-context cultures employ cognitive and behavioral systems based on Aristotelian logic and linear thinking (Hall, 1984) and may be pathologically verbal. Cultures that have some characteristics of both HC and LC systems would include the French, English, and Italian (Gudykunst & Kim, 1992), which are less explicit than Northern European cultures.

The highest HC cultures are found in Asia, especially China, Japan, and Korea (Elliott et al., 1982; Hall, 1976, 1984; Lustig and Koester, 1999). Although most languages are explicit, LC communication systems, in China even the language is an implicit, high-context system. To use a Chinese dictionary, one must understand thousands of characters that change meaning in combination with other characters. Zen Buddhism, a major influence in Asia, places a high value on silence, lack of emotional expression, and the unspoken, nonverbal parts of communication (McDaniel & Andersen, 1998). Americans often complain that the Japanese never "get to the point," but they fail to recognize that HC culture must provide a context and setting and let the point evolve (Hall, 1984). In a recent study of airport farewell episodes, McDaniel and Andersen (1998) found Asians to be the least tactile

of any cultural group on earth. The influence of Buddhism and the value placed on context rather than emotional expression probably explains this finding. American Indian cultures with ancestral migratory roots in East Asia are remarkably like contemporary Asian culture in several ways, especially in their need for high context (Hall, 1984). Latin American cultures—a fusion of Iberian (Portuguese–Spanish) and Indian traditions—are also high-context cultures. Likewise, southern and eastern Mediterranean people and people from the Persian Gulf, including Persians, Arabs, Greeks, and Turks, are HC cultures as well.

Communication is used very differently in HC and LC cultures. Andersen, Hecht, Hoobler, and Smallwood (in press) suggest that these differences between HC and LC communication can be explained by four principles.

1. *Verbal communication and other explicit codes are more prevalent in low-context cultures such as the United States and Northern Europe.* People from LC cultures are often perceived as excessively talkative, belaboring of the obvious, and redundant. People from HC cultures may be perceived as nondisclosive, sneaky, and mysterious.

2. *HC cultures do not value verbal communication the same way that LC cultures do.* Elliot et al. (1982) found that more verbal people were perceived as more attractive in the United States, but less verbal people were perceived as more attractive in Korea, which is an HC culture.

3. *HC cultures are more reliant on and tuned in to nonverbal communication.* In LC cultures, most people, particularly men, fail to perceive as much nonverbal communication as do members of HC cultures. Nonverbal communication provides the context for all communication (Watzlawick, Beavin, & Jackson, 1967), but people from HC cultures are particularly affected by these contextual cues. Thus, facial expressions, tensions, movements, speed of interaction, location of the interaction, and other subtle forms of nonverbal communication are likely to be more easily perceived by and have more meaning for people from HC cultures.

4. *In HC cultures, interactants expect more than in LC cultures* (Hall, 1976). People in HC cultures anticipate that communicators will understand

unspoken feelings, implicit gestures, and environmental clues that people from LC cultures do not process. Given that both cultural extremes fail to recognize these basic communication differences, intercultural attributions about behavior are often incorrect.

In conclusion, HC cultures rely more on nonverbal communication and less on verbal communication. Generally, HC cultures are also somewhat more collectivistic and less individualistic than LC cultures (Gudykunst et al., 1996; Andersen et al., in press). Given this fact, it is appropriate that the next dimension of culture to be examined is individualism/collectivism.

Individualism/Collectivism. A culture's degree of individualism versus collectivism is one of the most extensively researched dimensions of culture. Individualism/collectivism determines how people live together: alone, in families, or tribes (Hofstede, 1980), their values, and how they communicate. Americans are extreme individualists for better or worse. Americans take individualism for granted and are blind to its impact until travel brings us into contact with less individualistic, more collectivistic cultures.

Individualism has been applauded as a blessing and has been elevated to the status of a national religion in the United States. Indeed, the best and worst in our culture can be attributed to individualism. Proponents of individualism have argued that it is the basis of liberty, democracy, freedom, and economic incentive and serves as protection against tyranny. Conversely, individualism has been blamed for our alienation from one another, loneliness, selfishness, and narcissism. Indeed, Hall (1976) has claimed that as an extreme individualist, "Western man has created chaos by denying that part of his self that integrates while enshrining the part that fragments experience" (p. 9). There can be little doubt that individualism is one of the fundamental dimensions that distinguishes cultures. Western culture is individualistic, so people rely on personal judgments to a greater degree than group decisions. Eastern cultures emphasize harmony among people, between people and nature, and value collective judgments (Andersen et al., in press). Tomkins

(1984) demonstrated that an individual's psychological makeup is the result of this cultural dimension. Western civilization has tended toward self-celebration, positive or negative. In Asian culture, another alternative is represented, that of harmony among people and between people and nature.

In a landmark intercultural study of individualism in 40 noncommunist countries, Hofstede (1980) reported that the 10 most individualistic nations (starting with the most) were the United States, Australia, Great Britain, Canada, the Netherlands, New Zealand, Italy, Belgium, Denmark, and Sweden, all of which primarily derive from European cultures. The least individualistic nations (starting with the least) were Venezuela, Colombia, Pakistan, Perú, Taiwan, Thailand, Singapore, Chile, and Hong Kong, all of which are Asian or South American cultures. Likewise, Sitaram and Codgell (1976) reported that individuality is a primary value in Western cultures, of secondary importance in African cultures, and of little importance in Eastern and Muslim cultures.

Even though the United States is the most individualistic country on earth (Andersen, 1999a; Hofstede, 1982), some of its regions and ethnic groups diverge in their degree of individualism. Elazar (1972) found that the central Midwest and the Mid-Atlantic states have the most individualistic political culture, whereas the Southeast is the most traditional and least individualistic; however, this relationship is all relative and, by world standards, even Alabama is an individualistic culture. As Bellah and colleagues (1985) stated: "Individualism lies at the very core of American culture. . . . Anything that would violate our right to think for ourselves, judge for ourselves, make our own decisions, live our lives as we see fit, is not only morally wrong, it is sacrilegious" (p. 142). Likewise, different ethnic groups may vary within a culture. African Americans, for example, greatly emphasize individualism (Hecht, Collier, & Ribeau, 1983), whereas Mexican Americans emphasize group and relational solidarity more (Andersen et al., in press). Indeed, our extreme individualism makes it difficult for Americans to interact with and understand people from other cultures. We are unique; all other cultures are less individualistic. As Condon and Yousef (1983) stated: "The fusion of individualism and equality is so valued and so basic that many Americans find it most difficult to relate to contrasting values in other cultures where interdependence greatly determines a person's sense of self" (p. 65).

The degree to which a culture is individualistic or collectivistic affects the nonverbal behavior of that culture in every way. First, people from individualistic cultures are more remote and distant proximally. Collectivistic cultures are interdependent; as a result, the members work, play, live, and sleep in proximity to one another. One recent study reports that people in individualistic cultures are more distant proximally than collectivists (Gudykunst et al., 1996). Hofstede (1980) cites research suggesting that, as hunters and gatherers, people lived apart in individualistic, nuclear families. When humans became agricultural, the interdependent extended family began living in proximity in large families or tribal units. Urban–industrial societies returned to a norm of individualism, nuclear families, and a lack of proximity to one's neighbors, friends, and co-workers.

Kinesic behavior tends to be more coordinated in collectivistic cultures, where people match one another's facial expressions, and body movements are in sync with each other. Where families work collectively, movements, schedules, and actions need to be highly coordinated (Argyle, 1975). In urban cultures, family members often do their "own thing," coming and going, working and playing, eating and sleeping on different schedules. People in individualistic cultures also smile more than do people in normatively oriented cultures (Tomkins, 1984). Individualists are responsible for their relationships and their own happiness, whereas normatively or collectively oriented people regard compliance with norms as a primary value and personal or interpersonal happiness as a secondary value (Andersen, 1999a). Matsumoto (1991) reports that "collective cultures will foster emotional displays of their members that maintain and facilitate group cohesion, harmony, or cooperation, to a greater degree than individualistic cultures" (p. 132). Porter and Samovar (1998) report that people in individualistic cultures display a wider range of emotions particularly to out-groups than are displayed by collectivists, who are discouraged from showing a range

of positive and/or negative emotions outside of the immediate in-group.

In a similar vein, Lustig and Koester (1999) maintain that "people from individualistic cultures are more likely than those from collectivistic culures to use confrontational strategies when dealing with interpersonal problems; those with a collectivist orientation are likely to use avoidance, third-party intermediaries, or other face-saving techniques" (p. 123). In collectivistic cultures, people suppress both positive and negative emotional displays that are contrary to the mood of the group, because maintaining the group is a primary value (Andersen, 1999a). Bond (1993) found the Chinese culture to be lower in frequency, intensity, and duration of emotional expression than other cultures. Bond asserts that "the expression of emotion is carefully regulated out of a concern for its capacity to disrupt group harmony and status hierarchies" (p. 245).

People in individualistic cultures are encouraged to express emotions because individual freedom is a paramount value. Research suggests that people in individualistic cultures are more nonverbally affiliative. Intuitively, the reason for this is not obvious because individualism does not require affiliation; however, Hofstede (1982) explained:

> In less individualistic countries where traditional social ties, like those with extended family members, continue to exist, people have less of a need to make specific friendships. One's friends are predetermined by the social relationships into which one is born. In the more individualistic countries, however, affective relationships are not socially predetermined but must be acquired by each individual personally. (p. 163)

In individualistic countries such as the United States, affiliativeness, dating, flirting, small talk, smiling, and initial acquaintance are more important than in collectivistic countries where the social network is more fixed and less reliant on individual initiative. Bellah et al. (1985) maintain that for centuries in the individualistic and mobile North American society, people could meet more easily and their communication was more open; however, their relationships were usually more casual and transient than those found in more collectivistic cultures.

In an impressive study of dozens of cultures, Lomax (1968) found that a country's song and dance styles were related to its level of social cohesion and collectivism. Collectivistic cultures are higher in "groupiness" and show both more cohesiveness in singing and more synchrony in their dance style (Lomax, 1968). It isn't surprising that rock dancing, which emphasizes separateness and "doing your own thing," evolved in individualistic cultures such as England and the United States. These dances may serve as a metaphor for the whole U.S. culture, where individuality is more prevalent than in any other place (Andersen, 1998).

Power Distance. Another basic dimension of intercultural communication is *power distance*—the degree to which power, prestige, and wealth are unequally distributed in a culture. Power distance has been measured in many cultures using Hofstede's (1980) Power Distance Index (PDI). Like individualism, power distance varies greatly among cultures. Cultures with high PDI scores have power and influence concentrated in the hands of a few rather than more equally distributed throughout the population. Condon and Yousef (1983) distinguish among three cultural patterns: democratic, authority-centered, and authoritarian. The PDI is highly correlated (.80) with authoritarianism, as measured by the F scale (Hofstede, 1980).

High PDI countries, from highest to lowest, are the Philippines, Mexico, Venezuela, India, Singapore, Brazil, Hong Kong, France, and Colombia (Hofstede, 1982), all of which, except for France, are southern countries located near the equator. Likewise, Gudykunst and Kim (1992) report that both African and Asian cultures generally maintain hierarchical role relationships characteristic of high power distance. Asian students are expected to be modest and deferent nonverbally in the presence of their instructors. Likewise, Vietnamese people consider employers to be their mentors and will not question orders.

The lowest PDI countries are, respectively, Austria, Israel, Denmark, New Zealand, Ireland, Sweden, Norway, Finland, Switzerland, and Great Britain (Hofstede, 1980), all of which are European or of European origin, middle-class, democratic, and located at high latitudes. The United States is slightly lower than the median in power distance, indicating smaller status differentials than in many

other countries. Cultures differ in terms of how status is acquired. In many countries, such as India, class or caste determines one's status. In the United States, power and status is typically determined by money and conspicuous material displays (Andersen & Bowman, 1999).

As suggested previously, the latitude of a country is an important force in the determiner of power distance. Hofstede (1980) claims that latitude and climate are one of the major forces shaping a culture. He maintains that the key intervening variable is that technology is needed for survival in a colder climate, which produces a chain of events in which children are less dependent on authority and learn from people other than authority figures. Hofstede (1982) reports a high, .65 correlation between PDI and latitude. In a study conducted at 40 universities throughout the United States, Andersen, Lustig, and Andersen (1990) report a −.47 correlation between latitude and intolerance for ambiguity, and a −.45 correlation between latitude and authoritarianism. This suggests that residents of the northern United States are less authoritarian and more tolerant of ambiguity. Northern cultures may have to be more tolerant and less autocratic to ensure cooperation and survival in harsher climates.

It is obvious that power distance would affect a culture's nonverbal behavior. In high PDI cultures, such as India, a rigid caste system may severely limit interaction, as in the case of India's "untouchables." More than 20% of India's population are untouchables who lie at the bottom of India's five-caste system (Chinoy, 1967). Any contact with untouchables by members of other castes is strictly forbidden and considered "polluting." Certainly, tactile communication among people of different castes is greatly curtailed in Indian culture. High PDI countries with less rigid stratification than India may still prohibit free interclass dating, marriage, and contact, all of which are taken for granted in low PDI countries.

Social systems with large power discrepancies also produce unique kinesic behavior. Cultures with high power distance encourage emotions and nonverbal displays that reveal status differences. For instance, in high-power-distance cultures, people are expected to show only positive emotions to high-status others and only negative emotions to low-status others (Matsumoto, 1991). According to Andersen and Bowman (1999), subordinates' bodily tension is more obvious in power-discrepant relationships. Similarly, Andersen and Bowman (1999) also report that in power-discrepant circumstances, subordinates smile more in an effort to appease superiors and appear polite. The continuous smiles of many Asians are a culturally inculcated effort to appease superiors and smooth social relations—behaviors that are appropriate to a high PDI culture.

The power distance of a culture also affects vocalic and paralinguistic cues. Citizens of low PDI cultures are generally less aware that vocal loudness may be offensive to others. American vocal tones are often perceived as noisy, exaggerated, and childlike (Condon & Yousef, 1983). Lomax (1968) has shown that in countries where political authority is highly centralized, singing voices are tighter and the voice box is more closed, whereas more permissive societies produce more relaxed, open, and clear sounds.

Uncertainty. Some cultures value change and ambiguity, whereas others value stability and certainty. Uncertainty is a cultural predisposition to value risk and ambiguity (Andersen et al., in press; Hofstede, 1980). At the individual level, this quality is called tolerance for ambiguity (Martin & Westie, 1959). People with intolerance of ambiguity have high levels of uncertainty avoidance and seek clear, black-and-white answers. People with tolerance of ambiguity have low levels of uncertainty avoidance and tend to be more tolerant, to accept ambiguous answers, and to see many shades of gray. Similarly, Hofstede (1980) reports that a country's neuroticism or anxiety scores are strongly correlated with uncertainty avoidance. High uncertainty avoidance is negatively correlated with risk taking and positively correlated with fear of failure.

Countries vary greatly in their tolerance for uncertainty. In some cultures, freedom leads to uncertainty, which leads to stress and anxiety. Hofstede (1980) maintained that intolerance of ambiguity and dogmatism are primarily a function of the uncertainty-avoidance dimension rather than the power-distance dimension. The 10 countries with the highest levels of uncertainty avoidance are Greece, Portugal, Belgium, Japan, Perú, France, Chile, Spain, Argentina,

and Turkey (Hofstede, 1980). Countries whose culture originated in the Mediterranean region, especially southern European and South American countries, dominate the list. The 10 countries lowest in uncertainty avoidance and highest in tolerance are Singapore, Denmark, Sweden, Hong Kong, Ireland, Great Britain, India, the Philippines, the United States, Canada, and New Zealand. This list is dominated by Northern European and South Asian cultures, many of which were countries that were originally part of the British Empire. Not surprisingly, these low-uncertainty-avoidant countries have a long history of democratic rule that is likely to be the cause and an effect of uncertainty avoidance. Catholic countries are higher in uncertainty avoidance, whereas Protestant, Hindu, and Buddhist countries tend to be more accepting of uncertainty (Hofstede, 1980). Eastern religions and Protestantism tend to be less "absolute," whereas Catholicism is a more "absolute" and certain religion. Andersen, Lustig, and Andersen (1990) report that intolerance for ambiguity is much higher in the American South than in the Northern states, tending to reflect the international pattern of latitude and tolerance.

Few studies have examined nonverbal behavior associated with uncertainty. Hofstede (1980) maintains that countries high in uncertainty avoidance tend to display emotions more than do countries that are low in uncertainty avoidance. Furthermore, he reports that the emotional displays of young people are tolerated less in countries with high uncertainty avoidance. Certainly, disagreement and nonconformity are not appreciated if uncertainty avoidance is high. Nonverbal behavior is more likely to be codified and rule-governed in countries with high uncertainty avoidance. This seems to fit a country such as Japan, but the hypothesis remains to be tested and is somewhat speculative. Hofstede (1980) found that nations high in uncertainty avoidance report more stylized and ritual behavior, so we should expect that nonverbal behavior is more prescribed in these cultures. When people from the United States communicate with people from a country such as Japan or France (both high in uncertainty avoidance), the Americans may seem unruly, nonconforming, and unconventional, whereas their Japanese or French counterparts might seem too controlled and rigid to the Americans (Lustig & Koester, 1999).

During the past decade, research on uncertainty reduction and avoidance has been extended from interpersonal communication to the study of intercultural communication (Berger & Gudykunst, 1991; Gao & Gudykunst, 1990; Gudykunst, 1993, 1995; Gudykunst & Hammer, 1988), resulting in Gudykunst's Anxiety/ Uncertainty Management Theory. The theory seeks to explain attitudes and behaviors toward strangers and member of other cultures (Gudykunst, 1995). Interacting with people outside of our group induces physiological arousal that is experienced as anxiety. This is consistent with the work of Hofstede (1980), who has shown that people in uncertainty-avoidant countries experience and show more anxiety than in other countries. The theory suggests that more secure, uncertainty-tolerant groups are more positive and accepting toward people from another group or culture. Of course, much of this takes place at subtle nonverbal levels. People from cultures that embrace uncertainty are much more likely to treat strangers with positive nonverbal behaviors such as smiles and other indications of immediacy and warmth.

Immediacy. Immediacy behaviors and interpersonal warmth are actions that signal closeness, intimacy, and availability for communication rather than avoidance and greater psychological distance (Andersen, 1985, 1998). Examples of immediacy behaviors are smiling, touching, eye contact, closer distances, and more vocal animation. Some scholars have labeled these behaviors as "expressive" (Patterson, 1983). Cultures that display considerable interpersonal closeness or immediacy have been labeled "contact cultures" because people in these countries stand closer together and touch more (Hall, 1966). People in low-contact cultures tend to stand apart and touch less. According to Patterson (1983):

> These habitual patterns of relating to the world permeate all aspects of everyday life, but their effects on social behavior define the manner in which people relate to one another. In the case of contact cultures, this general tendency is manifested in closer approaches so that tactile and olfactory information may be gained easily. (p. 145)

Interestingly, contact cultures are generally located in warmer countries nearer the equator and low-contact cultures are found in cooler climates farther from the equator. Explanations for these latitudinal variations have included energy level, climate, and metabolism (Hofstede, 1980; Andersen, Lustig, & Andersen, 1990). Evidently, cultures in cooler climates tend to be more task-oriented and interpersonally "cool," whereas cultures in warmer climates tend to be more interpersonally oriented and interpersonally "warm." Even within the United States, the warmer latitudes tend to be higher-contact cultures. Andersen, Lustig, and Andersen (1990) report a .31 correlation between latitude of students' university and touch avoidance. These data indicate that students at universities located in the so-called Sunbelt are more touch-oriented. Pennebaker, Rimé, and Sproul (1994) found a correlation between latitude and expressiveness within dozens of countries. Northerners are more expressive than southerners, according to their data, in Belgium, Croatia, France, Germany, Italy, Japan, Serbia, Spain, Switzerland, and the United States, with an overall difference within the entire Northern Hemisphere. Pennebaker et al. (1994) conclude:

> Logically, climate must profoundly affect social processes. People living in cold climates devote more time to dressing, to providing warmth, to planning ahead for food provisions during the winter months. . . . In warm climates, people are more likely to see, hear, and interact with neighbors year around. Emotional expressiveness then would be more of a requirement. (pp. 15–16)

Similarly, Andersen, Lustig, and Andersen (1990) conclude:

> In Northern latitudes societies must be more structured, more ordered, more constrained, and more organized if the individuals are to survive harsh weather forces. . . . In contrast, Southern latitudes may attract or produce a culture characterized by social extravagance and flamboyance that has no strong inclination to constrain or order their world. (p. 307)

Traditionally, research has shown that high-contact cultures comprise most Arab countries, including North Africa; the Mediterranean region, including France, Greece, Italy, Portugal, and Spain; Jews from both Europe and the Middle East; Eastern Europeans and Russians; and virtually all of Latin America (Condon & Yousef, 1983; Jones,

1994; Jones & Remland, 1982; Mehrabian, 1971; Patterson, 1983; Samovar, Porter, & Jain, 1981; Scheflen, 1972). Australians are moderate in their cultural contact level, as are North Americans (Patterson, 1983). Research generally found that low-contact cultures comprise most of Northern Europe, including Scandinavia, Germany, and England; British Americans; white Anglo-Saxons (the primary culture of the United States); and virtually every Asian country, including Burma, China, Indonesia, Japan, Korea, the Philippines, Thailand, and Vietnam (Andersen, Andersen, & Lustig, 1987; Heslin & Alper, 1983; Jones, 1994; Jones & Remland, 1982; McDaniel & Andersen, 1998; Mehrabian, 1971; Patterson, 1983; Remland, 2000; Samovar, Porter, & Jain, 1981; Scheflen, 1972). Recent research reported by Remland (2000) suggests that people do touch significantly more in southern Europe than in northern Europe.

Other recent research suggests that the biggest differences in immediacy are not between North America and Europe, both of which are probably moderate to high contact cultures. Compared to the rest of the world, Asia is an extreme noncontact culture (McDaniel & Andersen, 1998; Remland et al., 1991). These two studies question whether Hall's (1966) original designation of some cultures as "low contact" is an oversimplification. Whether a generational shift or internationalization may have produced this change is unclear, but much of the Western world, including the United States, appears to be a contact culture. Indeed, McDaniel and Andersen's (1998) study of public touch suggests that the biggest difference is between Asians, who rarely touch in public, and virtually every other culture, which all manifest higher degrees of public touching. These findings are consistent with other research suggesting that China and Japan are distinctly nontactile cultures (Barnland, 1978; Jones, 1994).

Without a doubt, cultures differ in their immediacy. In general, people living in northern countries, northern parts of individual countries, and traditional cultures, as well as Asians, are the least immediate and expressive. Conversely, people living in the south, modern countries, and non-Asian cultures are the most expressive and immediate. Obviously, these findings are painted with a fairly broad brush and will await a more detailed cultural portrait.

Gender. Perhaps the most researched issue in social science during recent decades is gender. While humans can be viewed as masculine or feminine, so can nations and cultures. The gender orientation of culture has an impact on many aspects of nonverbal behavior. This includes the nonverbal expressions permitted by each sex, occupational status, nonverbal aspects of power, the ability to interact with strangers or acquaintances of the opposite sex, and all aspects of interpersonal relationships between men and women. According to one research group: "Numerous studies have examined gender as an individual characteristic, but gender has been neglected as a cultural dimension" (Andersen et al., in press). *Gender*, as discussed in this article, refers to the rigidity of gender rules. In masculine cultures, gender rules are more rigid and traits such as strength, assertiveness, competitiveness, and ambitiousness are valued. In more feminine or androgynous cultures, attributes such as affection, compassion, nurturance, and emotionality are valued (Bem, 1974; Hofstede, 1980). In less rigid cultures, both men and women can express more diverse, less stereotyped sex-role behaviors.

Cross-cultural research shows that girls are expected to be more nurturant than boys, although there is considerable variation from country to country (Hall, 1984). Hofstede (1980) has measured the degree to which people of both sexes in a culture endorse masculine or feminine goals. Masculine cultures regard competition and assertiveness as important, whereas feminine cultures place more importance on nurturance and compassion. Not surprisingly, the masculinity of a culture is negatively correlated with the percentage of women in technical and professional jobs and positively correlated with segregation of the sexes in higher education (Hofstede, 1980).

Countries with the 10 highest masculinity index scores, according to Hofstede (1980), are Japan, Austria, Venezuela, Italy, Switzerland, Mexico, Ireland, Great Britain, Germany, and the Philippines. The 10 countries with the lowest masculinity scores are Sweden, Norway, the Netherlands, Denmark, Finland, Chile, Portugal, Thailand, and Perú. Not surprisingly, high-masculinity countries have fewer women in the labor force, have only recently afforded voting privileges to women, and are less likely to consider wife rape a crime than are low masculinity countries (Seager & Olson, 1986).

Not surprisingly, the Scandinavian countries, with their long history of equal rights for women, are at the top of the list of feminine countries. But why would South American cultures be less masculine and not manifest the Latin pattern of machismo? Iberian countries like Spain and Portugal have relatively feminine cultures, as do their South American cultural descendents like Chile and Perú. Hofstede (1980) suggests that machismo is more present in the Caribbean region than in the remainder of South America. In fact, South America, as compared to Central America, has a much higher percentage of working women, much higher school attendance by girls, and more women in higher education (Seager & Olson, 1986).

Considerable research suggests that androgynous patterns of behavior (that is, both feminine and masculine) result in more self-esteem, social competence, success, and intellectual development for both males and females (Andersen, 1999). Nonverbal styles where both men and women are free to express both masculine traits (such as dominance and anger) and feminine traits (such as warmth and emotionality) are likely to be both healthier and more effective. Buck (1984) has demonstrated that males may harm their health by internalizing emotions rather than externalizing them as women usually do. Internalized emotions that are not expressed result in more stress and higher blood pressure. Not surprisingly, more masculine countries show higher levels of stress (Hofstede, 1980).

Considerable research has demonstrated significant vocal differences between egalitarian and nonegalitarian countries. Countries in which women are economically important and where sexual standards for women are permissive show more relaxed vocal patterns than do other countries (Lomax, 1968). Moreover, those egalitarian countries show less tension between the sexes, more vocal solidarity and coordination in their songs, and more synchrony in their movement (Lomax, 1968).

The United States tends to be a masculine country, according to Hofstede (1982), although it is not among the most masculine. Intercultural communicators should keep in mind that other countries may be either more or less sexually egalitarian than the United States. Because most countries are more feminine (that is, nurturant and compassionate), Americans of both sexes often seem loud, aggressive, and competitive by world standards. Likewise, Americans' attitude toward women may seem sexist in extremely feminine locations such as Scandinavia.

Most important, in relatively more feminine countries, both men and women can engage in either masculine or feminine nonverbal behaviors. In masculine countries, the nonverbal behavior of men and women is carefully proscribed and must adhere to a narrower sexual script. So, for example, in feminine countries like Sweden and Norway, women can engage in more powerful speaking styles, wear masculine clothing, and be more vocally assertive. Similarly, men in feminine countries can show emotions such as sadness or fear and engage in more nurturant and less dominant behaviors.

CONCLUSIONS

Studying these six cultural dimensions cannot ensure competence in intercultural communication. The beauty of international travel and even travel within the United States is that it provides a unique perspective on one's own and others' behavior. Combining cognitive knowledge from intercultural readings and courses with actual encounters with people from other cultures is the best way to gain intercultural competence.

A full, practical understanding of the dimensions along which cultures differ—along with knowledge of how specific communication acts differ cross-culturally—has several practical benefits.

1. *Such knowledge will highlight and challenge assumptions about our own behavior.* The structure of our own behavior is invisible and taken for granted until it is exposed and challenged through study of cultures and actual intercultural encounters. Indeed, Hall (1976) stated that ethnic diversity in interethnic communication can be a source of strength and an asset from which one's self can be discovered.

2. *This discussion should make it clear that attributions about the nonverbal communication of people from other cultures are bound to be wrong.* No dictionary

or code of intercultural behavior is available. You cannot read people like books, not even people from your own culture. Understanding that someone is from a masculine, collectivistic, or high-context culture, however, will make his or her behavior less confusing and more interpretable.

3. *Despite the Internet and global media, intercultural diversity is likely to persist for centuries.* Indeed, some countries are still discovering or rediscovering their ethnic identity. Global migrations and a global economy mean that diverse intercultural interactions will be increasingly common. If you enjoy living in a diverse world, you have come to the right planet in the right century. Let us hope that we celebrate this great, diverse, intertwined tapestry of diversity we call the human race.

References

Andersen, J. F., Andersen, P. A., & Lustig, M. W. (1987). Opposite-sex touch avoidance: A national replication and extension. *Journal of Nonverbal Behavior, II,* 89–109.

Andersen, P. A. (1985). Nonverbal immediacy in interpersonal communication. In A. W. Siegman & S. Feldstein (Eds.), *Multichannel integrations of nonverbal behavior* (pp. 1–36). Hillsdale, NJ: Lawrence Erlbaum.

Andersen, P. A. (1987). The trait debate: A critical examination of the individual differences paradigm in intercultural communication. In B. Dervin & M. J. Voigt (Eds.), *Progress in communication sciences,* Vol. VIII (pp. 47–82). Norwood, NJ: Ablex.

Andersen, P. A. (1998). The cognitive valence theory of intimate communication. In M. T. Palmer & G. A. Barnett (Eds.), *Progress in communication sciences, Volume XIV: Mutual influence in interpersonal communication: Theory and research in cognition, affect, and behavior.* (pp. 39–72). Stamford, CT: Ablex.

Andersen, P. A. (1999a). *Nonverbal communication: Forms and functions.* Mountain View, CA: Mayfield.

Andersen, P. A. (1999b). 1999 WSCA Presidential address. *Western Journal of Communication, 63,* 339–543.

Andersen, P. A., & Bowman, L. (1999). Positions of power: Nonverbal influence in organizational communication. In L. K. Guerrero, J. A. DeVito, & M. L. Hecht (Eds.), *The nonverbal reader* (pp. 317–334). Prospect Heights, IL: Waveland Press.

Andersen, P. A., Hecht, M. L., Hoobler, G. D., & Smallwood, M. (2002). Nonverbal communication across culture. In B. Gudykunst and B. Mody (Eds.), *Handbook of international and intercultural communication.* Thousand Oaks, CA: Sage.

Andersen, P. A., & Leibowitz, K. (1978). The development and nature of the construct touch avoidance. *Environmental Psychology and Nonverbal Behavior, 3,* 89–106.

Andersen, P. A., Lustig, M. W., & Andersen, J. F. (1986). *Communication patterns among cultural regions of the United States: A theoretical perspective.* Paper presented at the annual convention of the International Communication Association, Chicago.

Andersen, P. A., Lustig, R., & Andersen, J. F. (1990). Changes in latitude, changes in attitude: The relationship between climate and interpersonal communication predispositions. *Communication Quarterly, 38,* 291–311.

Argyle, M. (1975). *Bodily communication.* New York: International Universities Press.

Barnland, D. C. (1978). Communication styles in two cultures: Japan and the United States. In A. Kendon, R. M. Harris, & M. R. Key (Eds.), *Organization of behavior in face to face interaction* (pp. 427–456). The Hague: Mouton.

Bellah, R. N., Madsen, R., Sullivan, W. M., Swidler, A., & Tipton, S. (1985). *Habits of the heart: Individualism and commitment in American life.* New York: Harper & Row.

Bem, S. L. (1974). The measurement of psychological androgny. *Journal of Consulting and Clinical Psychology, 42,* 155–162.

Berger, C. R., & Gudykunst, W. B. (1991). Uncertainty and communication. In B. Dervin & M. Voigt (Eds.), *Progress in communication sciences* (vol. 10, pp. 21–66). Norwood, NJ: Ablex.

Bond, M. H. (1993). Emotions and their expression in Chinese culture. *Journal of Nonverbal Behavior, 17,* 245–262.

Brown, L. R., Kane, H., & Roodman, D. M. (1994). *Vital signs 1994: The trends that are shaping our future.* New York: W. W. Norton.

Bruneau, T. (1979). The time dimension in intercultural communication. In D. Nimmo (Ed.), *Communication yearbook 3* (pp. 423–433). New Brunswick, NJ: Transaction Books.

Buck, R. (1984). *The communication of emotion.* New York: Guilford Press.

Burgoon, J. K. (1985). Nonverbal signals. In M. L. Knapp & G. R. Miller (Eds.), *Handbook of interpersonal communication* (pp. 344–390). Beverly Hills, CA: Sage.

Chinoy, E. (1967). *Society.* New York: Random House.

Condon, J. C., & Yousef, F. (1983). *An introduction to intercultural communication.* Indianapolis, IN: Bobbs-Merrill.

Elazar, D. J. (1972). *American federalism: A view from the states*. New York: Thomas P. Crowell.

Elliot, S., Scott, M. D., Jensen, A. D., & McDonough, M. (1982). Perceptions of reticence: A cross-cultural investigation. In M. Burgoon (Ed.), *Communication yearbook 5* (pp. 591–602). New Brunswick, NJ: Transaction Books.

Ford, J. G., & Graves, J. R. (1977). Differences between Mexican-American and white children in interpersonal distance and social touching. *Perceptual and Motor Skills, 45*, 779–785.

Gao, G., & Gudykunst, W. B. (1990). Uncertainty, anxiety, and adaptation. *International Journal of Intercultural Relations, 14*, 301–317.

Geertz, C. (1973). *The interpretation of cultures*. New York: Basic Books.

Gudykunst, W. B. (1993). Toward a theory of effective interpersonal and intergroup communication: An anxiety/uncertainty management (AUM) perspective. In R. L. Wiseman & J. Koester (Eds.), *Intercultural communication competence* (pp. 33–71). Newbury Park, CA: Sage.

Gudykunst, W. B. (1995). Anxiety/Uncertainty Management (AUM) Theory: Current status. In R. L. Wiseman (Ed.), *Intercultural communication theory* (pp. 8–58). Thousand Oaks, CA: Sage.

Gudykunst, W. B., & Hammer, M. R. (1988). Strangers and hosts. In Y. Kim & W. Gudykunst (Eds.), *Cross-cultural adaptaion* (pp. 106–139). Newbury Park, CA: Sage.

Gudykunst, W. B., & Kim, Y. Y. (1992). *Communicating with strangers: An approach to intercultural communication*. New York: Random House.

Gudykunst, W. B., Matsumoto, Y., Ting-Toomey, S., Nishida, T., Kim, K., & Heyman, S. (1996). Influence of cultural individualism-collectivism, self-construals, and individual values on communication styles across cultures. *Human Communication Research, 22*, 510–543.

Hall, E. T. (1959). *The silent language*. New York: Doubleday.

Hall, E. T. (1966). A system of the notation of proxemic behavior. *American Anthropologist, 65*, 1003–1026.

Hall, E. T. (1976). *Beyond culture*. Garden City, NY: Anchor.

Hall, E. T. (1984). *The dance of life: The other dimension of time*. Garden City, NY: Anchor.

Hecht, M. L., Collier, M. J., & Ribeau, S. A. (1993). *African-American communication: Ethnic identity and cultural interpretation*. Newbury Park, CA. Sage.

Heslin, R., & Alper, T. (1983). "Touch: A bonding gesture." In J. M. Wiemann & R. Harrison (Eds.), *Nonverbal Interaction* (pp. 47–75). Beverly Hills, CA: Sage.

Hofstede, G. (1980/1982). *Culture's consequences* (abridged ed.). Beverly Hills, CA: Sage.

Jones, S. E. (1994). *The right touch: Understanding and using the language of physical contact*. Cresshill, NJ: Hampton Press.

Jones, T. S., & Remland, M. S. (1982, May). *Cross-cultural differences in self-reported touch avoidance*. Paper presented at the annual convention of the Eastern Communication Association, Hartford, CT.

LaBarre, W. (1985). Paralinguistics, kinesics, and cultural anthropology. In L. A. Samovar & R. E. Porter (Eds.), *Intercultural communication: A reader* (pp. 272–279). Belmont, CA: Wadsworth.

Lomax, A. (1968). *Folk song style and culture*. New Brunswick, NJ: Transaction Books.

Lustig, M. L., & Koester, J. (1999). *Intercultural competence: Interpersonal communication across culture*. New York: HarperCollins.

Martin, J. G., & Westie, F. R. (1959). The intolerant personality. *American Sociological Review, 24*, 521–528.

Matsumoto, D. (1991). Cultural influences on facial expressions of emotion. *Southern Communication Journal, 56*, 128–137.

McDaniel, E. R., & Andersen, P. A. (1998). Intercultural variations in tactile communication. *Journal of Nonverbal Communication, 22*, 59–75.

Mehrabian, A. (1971). *Silent messages*. Belmont, CA: Wadsworth.

Patterson, M. L. (1983). *Nonverbal behavior: A functional perspective*. New York: Springer-Verlag.

Pennebaker, J. W., Rimé, B., & Sproul, G. (1994). *Stereotype of emotional expressiveness of Northerners and Southerners: A cross-cultural test of Montesquieu's hypotheses*. Unpublished paper, Southern Methodist University, Dallas, TX.

Porter, R. E., & Samovar, L. A. (1998). Cultural influences on emotional expression: Implications for intercultural communication. In P. A. Andersen & L. K. Guerrero (Eds.) *Handbook of communication and emotion: Research theory, applications and contexts* (pp. 451–472). San Diego, CA: Academic Press.

Remland, M. S., Jones, T. S., & Brinkman, H. (1991). Proxemic and haptic behavior in three European countries. *Journal of Nonverbal Behavior, 15*, 215–232.

Remland, M. S. (2000). *Nonverbal communication in everyday life*. Boston, MA: Houghton Mifflin.

Samovar, L. A., & Porter, R. E. (1985). Nonverbal interaction. In L. A. Samovar & R. E. Porter (Eds.), *Intercultural communication: A reader*. Belmont, CA: Wadsworth.

Samovar, L. A., Porter, R. E., & Jain, N. C. (1981). *Understanding intercultural communication*. Belmont, CA: Wadsworth.

Samovar, P. A., Porter, R. E., & Stefani, L. A. (1998). *Communication between cultures*. Belmont, CA: Wadsworth.

Sapir, E. (1928). The unconscious patterning of behavior in society. In E. S. Drummer (Ed.), *The unconscious* (pp. 114–142). New York: Knopf.

Scheflen, A. E. (1972). *Body language and the social order*. Englewood Cliffs, NJ: Prentice-Hall.

Scheflen, A. E. (1974). *How behavior means*. Garden City, NY: Anchor.

Seager, J., & Olson, A. (1986). *Women in the world atlas*. New York: Simon & Schuster.

Sitaram, K. S., & Codgell, R. T. (1976). *Foundations of intercultural communication*. Columbus, OH: Charles E. Merrill.

Tomkins, S. S. (1984). Affect theory. In K. R. Scherer & P. Ekman (Eds.), *Approaches to emotion* (pp. 163–195). Hillsdale, NJ: Lawrence Erlbaum.

Watzlawick, P., Beavin, J. H., & Jackson, D. D. (1967). *Pragmatics of human communication*. New York: W. W. Norton.

Concepts and Questions

1. What does Andersen mean when he writes that "the primary level of culture is communicated implicitly, without awareness, by primarily nonverbal means"?

2. Do you agree with Andersen that two of the most fundamental nonverbal differences in intercultural communication involve space and time? From your experiences, what two nonverbal areas have you found most troublesome when interacting with people from different cultures?

3. From your personal experiences, can you think of different ways in which people in various cultures greet, show emotion, and beckon?

4. Do you believe that intercultural communication problems are more serious when they involve nonverbal communication or verbal communication?

5. What is *kinesic* behavior? How does it vary from one culture to another? What types of communication problems can be caused by cultural differences in *kinesic* behavior?

6. The term *hoptics* refers to patterns of tactile communication. How does tactile communication differ between cultures? Can you think of examples of how tactile communication differs among members of co-cultures? What type of communication problems might arise when people with different touching orientations interact?

7. How does physical appearance affect first impressions during interaction? How are expectations of physical appearance related to the informal–formal dimension of culture?

8. How does immediacy affect interpersonal interaction? What differences in behaviors would you expect from high- and low-contact cultures? In what way would violations of immediacy expectations affect intercultural communication?

9. How is the degree of individualism within cultures manifest in nonverbal behavior?

10. What is the relationship between power distance and kinesic behavior? How is high-power distance displayed? How is low-power distance displayed?

Japanese Nonverbal Communication: A Reflection of Cultural Themes

EDWIN R. MCDANIEL

Modern technological advances have made the world a much smaller place, promoting increased interactions between peoples of different nations and cultures. Growing international economic interdependencies and expanding multinational security alliances have significantly increased the importance of effective intercultural encounters. Individuals from diverse cultures are interacting with each other more and more frequently—in professional, diplomatic, and social venues.

The most critical aspect of this burgeoning transnational intercourse is, of course, communication. The ability to understand and be understood is central to successful cross-cultural activities. Comprehension, however, must go beyond a topical awareness of another culture's communicative practices and behaviors. An appreciation of the cultural antecedents and motivations shaping an individual's communication conventions is necessary for understanding *how* and *why* a particular practice is used.

An established method of explaining the cultural motivations of human behavior is to identify and isolate consistent themes among a social grouping. Anthropological writings have posited that each culture manifests a "limited number of dynamic affirmations" (Opler, 1945, p. 198), referred to as *themes*. According to Opler (1945), these cultural themes promote and regulate human behavioral activities that are societally encouraged and condoned. To illustrate this approach, Opler (1945) used an examination of the social relations of the Lipan Apaches to

demonstrate how thematic study could provide insight into cultural beliefs and behaviors.

In communication studies, the concept of thematic commonality has been used by Burgoon and Hale (1984, 1987) to help explicate relational communications. They conceptualized a series of "interrelated message themes" (Burgoon & Hale, 1987, p. 19), which have been purported to have application to both verbal and nonverbal exchanges. These proposed themes, or *topi*, have become a supposition cited in studies of interpersonal relations communication (e.g., Buller & Burgoon, 1986; Coker & Burgoon, 1987; Spitzberg, 1989).

Burgoon and Hale's (1984) concept of identifying consistent themes to assist in the explanation of a communication process possesses significant utility for additional, more comprehensive employment. The innovation has clear application to the study of culture-specific communication predispositions.

Using the Japanese as a cultural model, this essay makes practical application of the thematic consistency concept advanced by Opler (1945, 1946) and Burgoon and Hale (1984, 1987). The objective is to illustrate how nonverbal communication practices function as a reflection, or representation, of societal cultural themes. Employing a standard taxonomy of nonverbal communication codes and addressing each individually, cultural themes influencing and manifested by the code are discussed in a propositional format. Additionally, the essay strives to demonstrate how cultural influences can subtly shape a society's communication conventions.

JAPANESE CULTURAL THEMES

Japan's predominantly homogeneous population embodies a particularly rich array of cultural themes. The more prevalent themes include group affiliation (collectivism), hierarchy, social balance or harmony (*wa*), empathy, mutual-dependency, perseverance and sacrifice (*gaman*), humility, and formality (ritual, tradition, and protocol) (Caudill, 1973; Lebra, 1976; Reischauer, 1988).

Confucian-based collectivism exerts a significant influence on Japanese communication patterns. The nation's racial and cultural homogeneity creates a strong identity bond and facilitates intragroup and interpersonal familiarity. This societal closeness promotes an instinctive, nonverbal understanding among Japanese people. Their cultural similitude abets an intuitive, nonverbal comprehension by diminishing the requirement to orally specify numerous details (Barnlund, 1989; Ishii, 1984; Kinosita, 1988; Kitao & Kitao, 1985; Morsbach, 1988a; Nakane, 1970; Westwood & Vargo, 1985; Yum, 1988).

The Japanese concept of collectivism is epitomized by their usage of the term *nihonjinron* to express self-perceived uniqueness as both a nation and a people. This idea of distinctive originality provides the Japanese with a focus for social cohesiveness. Their propensity for group affiliation has created a social context referred to as *uchi-soto*, or inside–outside. This context can also be viewed as in-group (possessing membership) and out-group (no involvement). Within the security of their respective in-group (*uchi*), the Japanese can be quite expressive and display considerable nonverbal affiliation with other members. Much less interaction will occur in an out-group (*soto*) situation (Gudykunst & Nishida, 1984; Gudykunst, Nishida, & Schmidt, 1989; Gudykunst, Yoon, & Nishida, 1987; Lebra, 1976, 1993).

The hierarchical nature of Japanese society and an inexorable compulsion for social balance or harmony (*wa*) increases the reliance on nonverbal behaviors and concomitantly discourages verbal exchanges. A hierarchy exists in every instance of group or interpersonal interaction. In this superior–subordinate environment, the junior is socially compelled to assume a passive role, awaiting and hopefully anticipating the senior's desires or actions. The senior, desiring to exemplify humility and avoid any social or personal discord, will endeavor to nonverbally ascertain the junior's expectations.

The cultural pressure for social balance dictates the course of all Japanese activities and creates a pervasive acceptance of ambiguity and vagueness during any communication endeavor. Reluctant to arbitrarily advance personal opinions or attitudes, the Japanese will draw on the situational context and attempt to instinctively discern what the other person is thinking (Hall & Hall, 1990; Ishii, 1984; Ishii & Bruneau, 1991; Kitao & Kitao, 1985; Lebra, 1976; Morsbach, 1988a; Munakata, 1986; Reischauer, 1988).

The cultural trait of empathy (*omoiyari*) also lessens the Japanese reliance on verbal exchanges. In Japan, considerable value is placed on an individual's ability to empathetically determine the needs of another person. During interpersonal encounters, the Japanese often use indirect or vague statements and depend on the other person's sensitivity to ascertain the desired meaning of the interaction (Doi, 1988; Ishii, 1984; Lebra, 1976).

PROPOSITIONAL SURVEY

Considered in isolation, a nonverbal code normally provides only partial interpretation of the intended message. This study, however, is not concerned with the code's proposed message, but instead attempts to demonstrate how the code is culturally based and motivated. To this end, in each of the following propositions (denoted as P1, P2, etc.), specific nonverbal communication codes are shown to reflect one or more cultural themes common to Japanese society.

P1: *Japanese kinesics reflect the cultural themes of (1) group orientation, (2) hierarchy, (3) social balance, (4) formality, and (5) humility.*

The Japanese enjoy a wide array of kinesic activities, especially gestures (Caudill & Weinstein, 1969; March, 1990; Seward, 1983). Usage, however, is situational and often limited to males (Richie, 1987). A Japanese manager, for instance, might rely on gestures to communicate with work subordinates (Sethi, 1974), thereby demonstrating the cohesive familiarity common among in-group (*uchi*) members.

The Japanese are more relaxed and expressive within their in-group. Away from the in-group, however, the use of body language is usually remarkably restrained (Cohen, 1991; Ishii, 1975). In public, it is common to see both Japanese men and women sitting quietly and unobtrusively, with hands folded (March, 1990). This self-restraint of body movement in out-group (*soto*) environments is designed to avoid attention and maintain situational harmony or balance.

As another example of concern for social balance, Japanese hand gestures are never used in reference to a person who is present at the time. Instead, they are employed when referring to some absent party (Richie, 1987). This behavior, quite naturally, reduces the opportunity for offending anyone present and helps sustain contextual harmony.

The most common activity associated with Japanese kinesics is the bow, which is an integral and repetitive part of daily social interaction. The Japanese bow is used when meeting someone, when asking for something, while apologizing, when offering congratulations, when acknowledging someone else, and when departing, to mention just a few instances. Historically a sign of submission, the bow is a contemporary ritual that continues to convey respect and denote hierarchical status. The junior person bows first, lowest, and longest. An improperly executed bow can be interpreted as a significant insult (Hendry, 1989; Ishii, 1975; Kitao & Kitao, 1987, 1989; Morsbach, 1988b; Ramsey, 1979; Richie, 1987; Ruch, 1984).

Traditional Japanese women exhibit a distinct kinesic activity by obscuring facial areas with their hands or some object[1] (Ishii, 1975; Ramsey, 1981). Ramsey's (1981) investigation of this phenomenon concluded that women utilized these adaptors for impression management. An explicit intent of these actions is to evoke a perception of humility when in the presence of a social superior.

P2: *Japanese oculesics reflect the cultural themes of (1) hierarchy, (2) social balance, and (3) humility.*

In Japan, prolonged eye contact is considered rude, threatening, and disrespectful.[1] The Japanese are taught, from childhood, to avert their gaze or look at a person's throat. When one is part of an audience, looking away or simply sitting silently with eyes closed indicates attention to, and possibly agreement with, the speaker. Direct, sustained eye contact is normally avoided, unless a superior wants to admonish a subordinate (Hall & Hall, 1990; Ishii, 1975; Kasahara, 1986; Kitao & Kitao, 1987, 1989; March, 1990; Morsbach, 1973; Richie, 1987; Ruch, 1984; Watson, 1970).

By avoiding eye contact, the participants in communication simultaneously evince an air of humility and sustain situational *wa*. The employment of direct eye contact by a superior is a clear exercise of hierarchical prerogative (March, 1990).

P3: *Japanese facial expressions reflect the cultural themes of (1) social balance and (2) gaman.*

As is common to all aspects of their social behavior, the Japanese do not normally evince any significant emotion through public facial displays. The most commonly observed expressions are either a placid, unrevealing countenance or a nondescript smile, whose actual meaning or intent may be totally indecipherable. A smile can indicate happiness or serve as a friendly acknowledgement. Alternatively, it may be worn to mask negative emotions, especially displeasure, anger, or grief (Gudykunst & Nishida, 1993; Kitao & Kitao, 1987, 1989; Matsumoto, 1996; Morsbach, 1973).

For the Japanese, the smile is simply a part of social etiquette, designed to help sustain harmony. In a social environment, the Japanese would consider it unpardonable to burden someone else with an outward show of elation, irritation, or anguish. Eschewing any external display of negative emotion is an example of perseverance or self-sacrifice (*gaman*) to avoid disrupting the social balance (*wa*). The smile is also used to avoid conflict; a Japanese person might simply smile in order to avoid answering an awkward question or giving a negative answer (Ishii, 1975; Kitao & Kitao, 1987, 1989; Nakane, 1970; Ruch, 1984; Seward, 1972).

P4: *Japanese proxemic behaviors reflect the cultural themes of (1) in-group affinity, (2) hierarchy, and (3) balance.*

The Japanese attitude toward personal space is, on the surface, complex and often seemingly contradictory. In uncrowded situations, they assiduously strive to maintain personal space intervals that are even greater than those maintained by Americans. Conversely, when on a train or bus they offer no resistance to frequent or even prolonged body contact with total strangers. Personal space is also close among friends or family members (Hall, 1990; Richie, 1987).

This apparent dichotomy is the result of their societal group orientation, vertical structure, and constant concern for social balance. In an uncrowded out-group environment, the Japanese maintain their personal space, which also provides a psychological barrier against the unknown, such as the hierarchical status and group affiliation of others (Ishii, 1975; Morsbach, 1973; Watson, 1970). If forced into proximity with an out-group member, the Japanese will assume a façade of unperturbable passivity in an effort to maintain situational harmony. I have often observed the Japanese projecting an air of composed detachment while being subjected to suffocating conditions in a crowded Tokyo subway car.

Among in-group members, where strong social ties exist, personal space is dramatically reduced. Traditionally, family members commonly slept in the same room, within easy touching distance of each other (Caudill & Plath, 1966). Male white-collar co-workers (salarimen) sitting close together and patting each other on the back during after-work drinking excursions are a common sight in Japanese bars.

Japanese proxemic behavior has been the subject of several investigations. In a study involving status manipulation, Japanese subjects exhibited signs of anxiety in reaction to an interviewer's forward lean (Bond & Shiraishi, 1974). Iwata's (1979) study of Japanese female students disclosed that individuals with high self-esteem evinced a negative reaction to crowding. This behavior is consistent with the Japanese concept of hierarchy. Self-esteem would be proportional with social status, which would predicate greater interpersonal distance in out-group situations.

P5: *Japanese tactile conventions reflect the cultural themes of (1) in-group affinity and (2) social balance.*

Studies of Japanese maternal care have disclosed that children experience considerable touch from their mothers (Caudill & Plath, 1966; Caudill & Weinstein, 1969). Even today, parents and their young children often share the same bed. The amount of public tactile interaction drops dramatically, however, after childhood, and the individual is expected to conform to societal nontouch standards (Barnlund, 1975; McDaniel & Andersen, 1998; Montague, 1978). Indeed, adult Japanese actively avoid public displays of interpersonal physical expressiveness[1] (Barnlund, 1989; Malandro & Barker, 1983) unless in a close-knit in-group setting.

For adults, in-group (uchi) touching is acceptable (Lebra, 1976). This is especially evident when male co-workers are drinking (Miyamoto, 1994). In an out-group (soto) situation, touch is uncommon unless it results inadvertently from crowding, and then it is simply ignored (Ishii, 1975; Morsbach, 1973;

Ramsey, 1985). These conventions again indicate the value placed on group affiliation and harmony.

P6: *Japanese personal appearance reflects the cultural themes of (1) collectivism, (2) group affiliation, (3) social balance, and (4) hierarchy.*

The central theme of Japanese external appearance is, quite simply, group identity and status. The ubiquitous dark suit dominates the business world, and everyone, men and women alike, normally opts for conservative styles. Small lapel pins or badges identifying the individual's company are frequently worn.[2] Blue-collar workers normally wear a uniform (such as coveralls or smocks) distinctive to their corporation (Condon & Yousef, 1983; Hall, 1981; Harris & Moran, 1979; March, 1990; Morsbach, 1973; Ruch, 1984).

The general proclivity for conservative dress styles and colors emphasizes the nation's collectivism and, concomitantly, lessens the potential for social disharmony arising from nonconformist attire. Lapel pins and uniforms signal a particular group affiliation, which in turn helps determine a person's social position.

Although not specifically nonverbal, the Japanese business card, or *meshi*, must be discussed. It exerts considerable influence on Japanese nonverbal behavior and communication in general. The initial impression of an individual is derived from his or her *meshi*. The card must be of the appropriate size and color and, in addition to the individual's name, list the person's company and position. This facilitates rapid determination of the individual's group affiliation and personal station, which dictates the correct deportment and appropriate speech levels for participants engaging in interpersonal dialogue (Craft, 1986; Morsbach, 1973; Ruch, 1984).

P7: *Japanese use of space reflects the cultural themes of (1) hierarchy and (2) group orientation.*

The Japanese hierarchical contextualization of space is best exemplified by the standard spatial array of governmental and corporate offices. Numerous desks, occupied by lower-level employees, are lined, facing each other, hierarchically in rows in a large, common room, absent of walls or partitions. The supervisors and managers are positioned at the head of each row. This organization encourages the exchange of information, facilitates multitask accomplishment, promotes group cooperation and solidarity, and facilitates rapid discernment of the work-center rank structure. Seating arrangements at any formal or semi-formal function are also based on hierarchy (Hamabata, 1990; Ramsey, 1979; Ramsey & Birk, 1983; Ruch, 1984; Takamizawa, 1988).

In explaining the Japanese perception of space as a hierarchical concept, Hall (1990) offers an insightful illustration. Neighborhood houses in Japan are numbered in the order they are constructed, regardless of actual location along the street.

P8: *Japanese use of time reflects the cultural themes of (1) hierarchy, (2) group orientation, and (3) social balance.*

Hall and Hall (1990) have indicated that the Japanese use time polychronically among themselves and monochronically when conducting business with foreigners. The rigid adherence to schedules when dealing with foreigners is in contrast with the temporal flexibility exhibited during interactions with other Japanese. This demonstrates an ability to adjust to dynamic situations. For example, schedules may have to be altered in order to accommodate the desires of a senior, which reflects hierarchical sensitivities.

The Japanese decision-making process characterizes the influence of group orientation and social balance on the usage of time. In almost every interpersonal context, it is necessary to build a consensus before announcing a decision. This process, concerned with maintaining social balance among group members, can take days, weeks, or even months (Hall, 1988; Nakane, 1970; Stewart, 1993).

P9: *Japanese vocalics reflect the cultural themes of (1) hierarchy, (2) social balance, and (3) empathy.*

The Japanese make ample use of paralanguage in their conversations. During interpersonal discussions, the Japanese will constantly use small, culturally unique, gestures (*aizuchi*) and utterances (e.g., *hai, soo, un,* or *ee*) to demonstrate their attentiveness (Harris & Moran, 1979; Nishida, 1996). These vocalics possess a cultural motivation. Hierarchy is demonstrated by the adjustment of voice tone and pitch to fit the speaker's position of junior or senior (Morsbach, 1973). Additionally, the feedback stream indicates that the listener is paying attention

to the speaker, which helps maintain positive social relations (*wa*) between the two individuals.

For the Japanese, laughter can possess a variety of meanings. Laughter can signal joy, of course, but it is also used to disguise embarrassment, sadness, or even anger (Seward, 1972). Use of laughter in the latter modes is designed to maintain situational harmony and avoid any potential for interpersonal discord.

In a 1989 study, White analyzed tape-recorded English-language conversations of Americans and native Japanese. The Japanese participants employed significantly more feedback responses than did the Americans. Unable to ascertain a linguistic reason for this greater use of vocalics, White (1989) concluded it was a cultural influence. The listener was believed to be exhibiting a sensitivity to the speaker's viewpoint and feelings (in other words, was expressing empathy).

P10: *Japanese use of silence reflects the cultural themes of (1) hierarchy, (2) social balance, and (3) empathy.*

The salient role of silence in the Japanese communication process is attributed to a general mistrust of spoken words and an emphasis on emotionally discerning the other person's intentions (empathy). Silence is considered a virtue as well as a sign of respectability and trustworthiness (Buruma, 1985; Cohen, 1991; Hall & Hall, 1990; Ishii, 1975, 1984; Lebra, 1976, 1993; Morsbach, 1988a).

A pronounced feature of Japanese conversations is the many short pauses or breaks, referred to as *ma*. According to Matsumoto (1988), the Japanese closely attend to these brief conversational breaks. The pauses may convey meaning, demonstrate respect, or be an attempt to assess the other person or the situation (Di Mare, 1990; Doi, 1973, 1988).

Instances of *ma* in Japanese discourse can impart a variety of messages, with the context supplying the actual meaning. Silence is employed to tactfully signal disagreement, nonacceptance, or an uncomfortable dilemma. A period of silence can be used to consider an appropriate response or formulate an opinion. Also, a junior may remain silent in deference to a senior (Graham & Herberger, 1983; Morsbach, 1973; Ramsey & Birk, 1983; Ueda, 1974).

P11: *The Japanese use of olfactics reflects the cultural theme of social balance.*

Little information is available concerning the Japanese attitude toward odors. Kasahara (1986) asserted that the Japanese propensity for cleanliness creates a preference for an environment totally absent of odors. Although there is no supporting evidence, the near-ritualistic tradition of taking frequent baths and the desire to refrain from personal offense lends credence to this supposition.

CONCLUSIONS

The preceding propositions suggest that the use of and reliance on nonverbal communication is actually a part of Japanese behavioral psychology motivated by cultural imperatives. If this concept is accepted, the benefits of employing cultural motivations to investigate a society's nonverbal communication habits, or other communication patterns, becomes self-evident. Application of cultural themes to communicative dispositions could provide a salient methodology for examining and better understanding both cultural-specific and intercultural communication phenomena.

Potential benefits derived from practical application of this approach are especially promising. Greater appreciation of the cultural imperatives behind communicative behaviors would directly enhance intercultural communication competence. An individual engaged in an intercultural communication exchange would better understand both *what* the other person was doing and *why* he or she was doing it.

The suggested design is not, however, free of limitations. Several perceived impediments exist that require additional investigation and clarification before implementation of wider theoretical application.

A particularly important aspect that demands greater inquiry relates to the identification of cultural themes. As discussed earlier, Japan presents an unusually homogeneous culture when compared with other nations. This societal similitude facilitates discernment of both cultural themes and their motivations. Moreover, the cultural themes can then be reliably applied across almost all dimensions of Japanese society.[3]

Other societies, such as the United States, do not have the degree of cultural congruency extant in Japan. For these cases, identification and application of consistent cultural themes to the composite ethnicities is fraught with considerable difficulty and potential peril. Any motivation to stereotype themes across an entire heterogeneous populace must be tempered by a resolve to treat ethnic divisions as both separate entities and as integral parts of the greater societal whole.

Another dilemma requiring meditation concerns units of measurement. The nonverbal communication patterns of a culture are largely observable and measurable. Culture, as an entity itself and as a motivator of communication behaviors, is not, however, readily quantifiable. Most studies dealing with cultural influences have relied on recounts of personal experiences and observations (anecdotal documentation).

Many studies incorporate "culture" as a somewhat ethereal, abstract manifestation of humankind's imagination. Others have approached "culture" empirically and attempted to employ scientific measurements. Hofstede, for instance, used survey questionnaires and statistical analysis in an effort to determine the role of culture in the formation of value systems that affect "human thinking, organizations, and institutions in predictable ways" (1980, p. 11). Similarly, Osgood, May, and Miron have made noteworthy progress in statistically quantifying intangible attributes, what they term "subjective culture" (1975, p. 4).

The progress of Hofstede (1980) and Osgood, May, and Miron (1975) suggests that culture is not entirely beyond the scope of objective quantification. Their achievements provide benchmarks for empirical examination of the influence of cultural themes on communication behaviors.

Thematic universality is also an area of potential peril for theoretical application of cultural themes to communicative practices. Specifically, the investigator must not axiomatically assume that similar themes beget similar behaviors when moving among cultures. A theme prompting a specific behavioral action in one culture may generate an entirely different pattern in another cultural environment. To obviate this possible pitfall, each culture must be examined as a unique entity. The identification of common cultural themes and communication practices across a substantial number of societies is needed before theoretical application can be made on unexamined cultures.

Further investigation is also needed to determine if any of the cultural themes are codependent. For example, if hierarchy is manifested by a culture, will formality or another theme also be present?

The preceding constraints should not be interpreted as a repudiation of the proposed approach to explaining communicative practices. Rather, they are simply areas of concern that must be investigated and clarified before cultural themes can be reliably employed to help discern and understand societal communication predispositions. Resolution of these concerns will instill the concept with increased application, additional rigor, and greater parsimony.

Notes

1. Although sometimes moving at a seemingly glacial pace, culture is actually a dynamic process, as individuals avail themselves of modern technologies they are exposed to and often adopt different social practices. This diffusion of cultural behaviors can and does exert change. With this in mind, we must recognize that the nonverbal communicative behaviors of the Japanese, as discussed in this article, are undergoing change. For example, except in rural areas, one seldom sees young Japanese women place their hand over their mouth. Direct eye contact is becoming increasingly common, especial in interactions with Westerners. Public touch is becoming more acceptable, and young Japanese couples can be seen cuddling in Tokyo's parks.
2. Even this established tradition is undergoing change. A recent article in a Japanese business newspaper bemoaned the fact that many of the younger employees were eschewing the company's lapel pins.
3. This is not to suggest that the Japanese are a wholly homogenous group uninfluenced by other cultures. For example, Japan has three large minority groups—Koreans, Ainu, and Burakumin—which possess distinct cultural characteristics. In recent years, the urban areas of Japan have also experienced a growing influx of foreign workers, coming from all parts of the globe. These immigrants bring their own values, beliefs, and behaviors, some of which are diffused, in varying degrees, into the Japanese culture.

References

Barnlund, D. (1975). *Public and private self in Japan and United States*. Tokyo: Simul.

Barnlund, D. (1989). *Communicative styles of Japanese and Americans*. Belmont, CA: Wadsworth.

Bond, M. H., & Shiraishi, D. (1974). The effect of body lean and status of an interviewer on the nonverbal behavior of Japanese interviewees. *International Journal of Psychology, 9*(2), 117–128.

Buller, D. B., & Burgoon, J. K. (1986). The effects of vocalics and nonverbal sensitivity on compliance. *Human Communication Research, 13*, 126–144.

Burgoon, J. K., & Hale, J. L. (1984). The fundamental topi of relational communication. *Communication Monographs, 51*, 193–214.

Burgoon, J. K., & Hale, J. L. (1987). Validation and measurement of the fundamental themes of relational communication. *Communication Monographs, 54*, 19–62.

Buruma, I. (1985). *A Japanese mirror*. New York: Penguin Books.

Caudill, W. (1973). General culture: The influence of social structure and culture on human behavior in modern Japan. *The Journal of Nervous and Mental Disease, 157*, 240–257.

Caudill, W., & Plath, D. (1966). Who sleeps with whom? Parent–child involvement in urban Japanese families. *Psychiatry, 29*, 344–366.

Caudill, W., & Weinstein, H. (1969). Maternal care and infant behavior in Japan and America. *Psychiatry, 32*, 12–43.

Cohen, R. (1991). *Negotiating across cultures*. Washington, DC: U.S. Institute of Peace.

Coker, D. A., & Burgoon, J. K. (1987). The nature of conversational involvement and nonverbal encoding patterns. *Human Communication Research, 13*, 463–494.

Condon, J. C., & Yousef, F. (1983). *An introduction to intercultural communication*. Indianapolis, IN: Bobbs-Merrill.

Craft, L. (1986). All in the cards: The mighty *meishi*. *TOKYO Business Today*, May, 61–64.

Di Mare, L. (1990). *Ma* and Japan. *Southern Communication Journal, 55*, 319–328.

Doi, T. (1973). The Japanese patterns of communication and the concept of *amae*. *The Quarterly Journal of Speech, 59*, 180–185.

Doi, T. (1988). Dependency in human relationships. In D. I. Okimoto & T. P. Rohlen (Eds.), *Inside the Japanese system: Readings on contemporary society and political economy* (pp. 20–25). Stanford, CA: Stanford University Press.

Graham, J. L., & Herberger, R. A. (1983). Negotiations abroad: Don't shoot from the hip. *Harvard Business Review, 83*, 160–168.

Gudykunst, W. B., & Nishida, T. (1984). Individual and cultural influences on uncertainty reduction. *Communication Monographs, 51*, 23–36.

Gudykunst, W. B., & Nishida, T. (1993). Interpersonal and intergroup communication in Japan and the United States. In W. B. Gudykunst (Ed.), *Communication in Japan and the United States* (pp. 149–214). Albany: State University of New York Press.

Gudykunst, W. B., Nishida, T., & Schmidt, K. (1989). The influence of culture, relational, and personality factors on uncertainty reduction processes. *Western Journal of Speech Communication, 53*, 13–29.

Gudykunst, W. B., Yoon, Y. C., & Nishida, T. (1987). The influence of individualism–collectivism on perceptions of communication in ingroup and outgroup relationships. *Communication Monographs, 54*, 295–306.

Hall, E. T. (1981/1976). *Beyond culture*. New York: Anchor Books, Doubleday.

Hall, E. T. (1988). The hidden dimensions of time and space in today's world. In F. Poyatos (Ed.), *Cross-cultural perspectives in nonverbal communication* (pp. 145–152). Lewiston, NY: C. J. Hogrefe.

Hall, E. T. (1990/1966). *The hidden dimension*. New York: Anchor Books, Doubleday.

Hall, E. T., & Hall, M. R. (1990/1987). *Hidden differences: Doing business with the Japanese*. New York: Anchor Books, Doubleday.

Hamabata, M. M. (1990). *Crested kimono: Power and love in the Japanese business family*. Ithaca, NY: Cornell University Press.

Harris, P. R., & Moran, R. T. (1979). *Managing cultural differences*. Houston, TX: Gulf Publishing.

Hendry, J. (1989/1986). *Becoming Japanese: The world of the pre-school child*. Honolulu: University of Hawaii Press.

Hofstede, G. (1980). *Culture's consequence: International differences in work-related values*. Newbury Park, CA: Sage.

Ishii, S. (1975). Characteristics of Japanese nonverbal communicative behavior. *Occasional Papers in Speech*. Honolulu: Department of Speech, University of Hawaii.

Ishii, S. (1984). *Enyro–Sasshi* communication: A key to understanding Japanese interpersonal relations. *Cross Currents, 11*, 49–58.

Ishii, S., & Bruneau, T. (1991) Silence and silences in cross-cultural perspective: Japan and the United States. In L. A. Samovar and R. E. Porter (Eds), *Intercultural communication: A reader* (6th ed.) (pp. 314–319). Belmont, CA: Wadsworth.

Iwata, O. (1979). Selected personality traits as determinants of the perception of crowding. *Japanese Psychological Research, 21*, 1–9.

Kasahara, Y. (1986). Fear of eye-to-eye confrontation among neurotic patients in Japan. In T. S. Lebra & W. P. Lebra (Eds.), *Japanese culture and behavior: Selected readings* (Rev. ed.) (pp. 379–387). Honolulu: University of Hawaii Press.

Kinosita, K. (1988). Language habits of the Japanese. *Bulletin of the Association for Business Communication, 51*, 35–40.

Kitao, K., & Kitao, S. K. (1985). *Effects of social environment on Japanese and American communication*. (ERIC Document Reproduction Service, No. ED 260 579).

Kitao, K., & Kitao, S. K. (1987). *Differences in the kinesic codes of Americans and Japanese*. East Lansing, MI: Department of Communication, Michigan State University. (ERIC Document Reproduction Service, No. ED 282 400).

Kitao, K., & Kitao, S. K. (1989). *Intercultural communication between Japan and the United States*. Tokyo: Eichosha Shinsha Co. (ERIC Document Reproduction Service, No. ED 321 303).

Lebra, T. S. (1976). *Japanese patterns of behavior*. Honolulu: University of Hawaii Press.

Lebra, T. S. (1993). Culture, self, and communication in Japan and the United States. In W. B. Gudykunst (Ed.), *Communication in Japan and the United States* (pp. 51–87). Albany: State University of New York Press.

Malandro, L. A., & Barker, L. L. (1983). *Nonverbal communication*. Menlo Park, CA: Addison-Wesley.

March, R. M. (1990/1989). *The Japanese negotiator: Subtlety and strategy beyond Western logic*. New York: Kondansha.

Matsumoto, D. (1996). *Unmasking Japan: Myths and realities about the emotions of the Japanese*. Stanford, CA: Stanford University Press.

Matsumoto, M. (1988). *The unspoken way: "Haragei": Silence in Japanese business and society*. New York: Kondansha. (Original work published in 1984 in Japanese under the title *Haragei*.)

McDaniel, E. R., & Andersen, P. A. (1998). International patterns of tactile communication: A field study. *Journal of Nonverbal Behavior, 22*, 59–75.

Miyamoto, M. (1994). *Straitjacket society: An insider's irreverent view of bureaucratic Japan*. New York: Kodansha International.

Montague, A. (1978). *Touching: The human significance of the skin* (2nd ed.). New York: Harper & Row.

Morsbach, H. (1973). Aspects of nonverbal communication in Japan. *Journal of Nervous and Mental Disease, 157*, 262–277.

Morsbach, H. (1988a). The importance of silence and stillness in Japanese nonverbal communication: A cross-cultural approach. In F. Poyatos (Ed.), *Cross-cultural perspectives in nonverbal communication* (pp. 201–215). Lewiston, NY: C. J. Hogrefe.

Morsbach, H. (1988b). Nonverbal communication and hierarchical relationships: The case of bowing in Japan. In F. Poyatos (Ed.), *Cross-cultural perspectives in* nonverbal communication (pp. 189–199). Lewiston, NY: C. J. Hogrefe.

Munakata, T. (1986). Japanese attitudes toward mental illness and mental health care. In T. S. Lebra & W. P. Lebra (Ed.), *Japanese culture and behavior: Selected readings* (Rev. ed.) (pp. 369–378). Honolulu: University of Hawaii Press.

Nakane, C. (1970). *Japanese society.* Berkeley: University of California Press.

Nishida, T. (1996). Communications in personal relationships in Japan. In W. B. Gudykunst, S. Ting-Toomey, & T. Nishida (Eds.), *Communication in personal relationships across cultures* (pp. 102–117). Thousand Oaks, CA: Sage.

Opler, M. E. (1945). Themes as dynamic forces in culture. *American Journal of Sociology, 51,* 198–206.

Opler, M. E. (1946). An application of the theory of themes in culture. *Journal of the Washington Academy of Sciences, 36,* 137–166.

Osgood, C. E., May, W. H., & Miron, M. S. (1975). *Cross-cultural universals of affective meaning.* Urbana: University of Illinois Press.

Ramsey, S. J. (1979). Nonverbal behavior: An intercultural perspective. In M. K. Asante, E. Newmark, & C. A. Blake (Eds.), *Handbook of intercultural communication* (pp. 105–143). Beverly Hills, CA: Sage.

Ramsey, S. J. (1981). The kinesics of femininity in Japanese women. *Language Sciences, 3,* 104–123.

Ramsey, S. J. (1985). To hear one and understand ten: Nonverbal behavior in Japan. In L. A. Samovar & R. E. Porter (Eds.), *Intercultural communication: A reader* (4th ed.) (pp. 307–321). Belmont, CA: Wadsworth.

Ramsey, S. J., & Birk, J. (1983). Training North Americans for interaction with Japanese: Considerations of language and communication style. In D. Landis & R. W. Brislin (Eds.), *The handbook of intercultural training, Vol. III: Area studies in intercultural training* (pp. 227–259). New York: Pergamon Press.

Reischauer, E. O. (1988). *The Japanese today: Change and continuity.* Cambridge, MA: Belknap Press of Harvard University.

Richie, D. (1987). *A lateral view: Essays on contemporary Japan.* Tokyo: The Japan Times.

Ruch, W. (1984). *Corporate communication: A comparison of Japanese and American practices.* Westport, CT: Quorum Books.

Sethi, S. P. (1974). Japanese management practices: Part I. *Columbia Journal of World Business, 9,* 94–104.

Seward, J. (1972). *The Japanese.* New York: William Morrow.

Seward, J. (1983). *Japanese in action* (Rev. ed.). New York: Weatherhill.

Spitzberg, B. H. (1989). Issues in the development of a theory of interpersonal competence in the intercultural context. *International Journal of Intercultural Relations, 13,* 241–268.

Stewart, L. P. (1993). Organizational communication in Japan and the United States. In W. B. Gudykunst (Ed.), *Communication in Japan and the United States* (pp. 215–248). Albany: State University of New York Press.

Takamizawa, H. (1988). *Business Japanese: A guide to improved communication.* New York: Kondansha International.

Ueda, T. (1974). Sixteen ways to avoid saying "no" in Japan. In J. C. Condon & M. Saito (Eds.), *Intercultural encounters with Japan* (pp. 185–192). Tokyo: Simul Press.

White, S. (1989). Backchannels across cultures: A study of Americans and Japanese. *Language in Society, 18,* 59–76.

Watson, M. O. (1970). *Proxemic behavior: A cross-cultural study.* The Hague: Mouton.

Westwood, M. J., & Vargo, J. W. (1985). Counselling double-minority status clients. In R. J. Samuda (Ed.), *Intercultural counselling and assessment: Global perspectives* (pp. 303–313). Lewiston, NY: C. J. Hogrefe.

Yum, Y. (1988). The impact of Confucianism on interpersonal relationship and communication patterns in East Asia. *Communication Monographs, 55,* 374–388.

Concepts and Questions

1. What are "cultural themes," and how may we benefit from their study?

2. What are the major Japanese cultural themes that influence intercultural communication?

3. Can you think of any American cultural themes that might influence how Americans use nonverbal communication?

4. How does Confucian-based collectivism help control Japanese nonverbal communication?

5. What cultural themes are seen as the basis for Japanese kinesic behavior? Are the same or different themes active in U.S. American nonverbal behavior?

6. What are the most obvious activities associated with Japanese kinesic behavior? What would be a U.S. American counterpart?

7. How does culture influence personal appearance in Japanese and U.S. American culture?

8. What are the cultural underpinnings of silence in Japan? How does the Japanese manipulation of silence affect intercultural communication?

9. Describe differences in the use of *vocalics* or paralanguage in Japan and the United States. How might these differences lead to misunderstandings during intercultural communication?

Monochronic and Polychronic Time

EDWARD T. HALL

Lorenzo Hubbell, trader to the Navajo and the Hopi, was three quarters Spanish and one quarter New Englander, but culturally he was Spanish to the core. Seeing him for the first time on government business transactions relating to my work in the 1930s, I felt embarrassed and a little shy because he didn't have a regular office where people could talk in private. Instead, there was a large corner room—part of his house adjoining the trading post—in which business took place. Business covered everything from visits with officials and friends, conferences with Indians who had come to see him, who also most often needed to borrow money or make sheep deals, as well as a hundred or more routine transactions with store clerks and Indians who had not come to see Lorenzo specifically but only to trade. There were long-distance telephone calls to his warehouse in Winslow, Arizona, with cattle buyers, and to his brother, Roman, at Ganado, Arizona—all this and more (some of it quite personal), carried on in public, in front of our small world for all to see and hear. If you wanted to learn about the life of an Indian trader or the ins and outs of running a small trading empire (Lorenzo had a dozen posts scattered throughout northern Arizona), all you had to do was to sit in Lorenzo's office for a month or so and take note of what was going on. Eventually all the different parts of the pattern would unfold before your eyes, as eventually they did before mine, as I lived and worked on that reservation over a five-year period.

I was prepared for the fact that the Indians do things differently from [Anglo-European] (AE) cultures because I had spent part of my childhood on the Upper Rio Grande River with the Pueblo Indians as friends. Such differences were taken for granted. But

this public, everything-at-once, mélange way of conducting business made an impression on me. There was no escaping it, here was another world, but in this instance, although both Spanish and Anglos had their roots firmly planted in European soil, each handled time in radically different ways.

It didn't take long for me to accustom myself to Lorenzo's business ambiance. There was so much going on that I could hardly tear myself away. My own work schedule won out, of course, but I did find that the Hubbell store had a pull like a strong magnet, and I never missed an opportunity to visit with Lorenzo. After driving through Oraibi, I would pull up next to his store, park my pickup, and go through the side door to the office. These visits were absolutely necessary because without news of what was going on, life could become precarious. Lorenzo's desert "salon" was better than a newspaper, which, incidentally, we lacked.

Having been initiated to Lorenzo's way of doing business, I later began to notice similar mutual involvement in events among the New Mexico Spanish. I also observed the same patterns in Latin America, as well as in the Arab world. Watching my countrymen's reactions to this "many things at a time" system, I noted how deeply it affected the channeling and flow of information, the shape and form of the networks connecting people, and a host of other important social and cultural features of the society. I realized that there was more to this culture pattern than one might at first suppose.

Years of exposure to other cultures demonstrated that complex societies organize time in at least two different ways: (1) events scheduled as separate items—one thing at a time—as in North Europe, or (2) following the Mediterranean model of involvement in several things at once. The two systems are logically and empirically distinct. Like oil and water, they don't mix. Each has its strengths and its weaknesses. I have termed doing many things at once: polychronic, P-time. The North European system—doing one thing at a time—is monochronic, M-time. P-time stresses involvement of people and completion of transactions rather than adherence to preset schedules. Appointments are not taken as seriously and, as a consequence, are frequently broken. P-time is treated as less tangible than M-time. For polychronic people, time is seldom experienced as "wasted," and is

Edward T. Hall, *The Dance of Life: The Other Dimension of Time* (New York: Doubleday and Company, 1983), pp. 42–54. Copyright ©1983 by Edward T. Hall. Used by permission of Doubleday, a division of Bantam, Doubleday, Dell Publishing Group, Inc.

apt to be considered a point rather than a ribbon or a road, but that point is often sacred. An Arab will say, "I will see you before one hour," or "I will see you after two days." What he means in the first instance is that it will not be longer than an hour before he sees you, and in the second instance, it will be at least two days. These commitments are taken quite seriously as long as one remains in the P-time pattern.

Once, in the early 1960s, when I was in Patras, Greece, which is in the middle of the P-time belt, my own time system was thrown in my face under rather ridiculous but still amusing circumstances. An impatient Greek hotel clerk, anxious to get me and my ménage settled in some quarters that were far from first-class, was pushing me to make a commitment so he could continue with his siesta. I couldn't decide whether to accept this rather forlorn "bird in the hand" or take a chance on another hotel that looked, if possible, even less inviting. Out of the blue, the clerk blurted: "Make up your mind. After all, time is money!" How would you reply to that at a time of day when literally nothing was happening? I couldn't help but laugh at the incongruity of it all. If there ever was a case of time not being money, it was in Patras during siesta in the summer.

Although M-time cultures tend to make a fetish out of management, there are points at which M-time doesn't make as much sense as it might. Life in general is at times unpredictable; and who can tell exactly how long a particular client, patient, or set of transactions will take? These are imponderables in the chemistry of human transactions. What can be accomplished one day in 10 minutes may take 20 minutes on the next. Some days people will be rushed and can't finish; on others, there is time to spare, so they "waste" the remaining time.

When traveling in Latin America and the Middle East, North Americans are often psychologically stressed. Immersed in a polychronic environment in the markets, stores, and souks of Mediterranean and Arab countries, one is surrounded by other customers all vying for the attention of a single clerk who is trying to wait on everyone at once. There is no recognized order as to who is to be served next, no queue or numbers to indicate who has been waiting the longest. To the North European or American, it appears that confusion and clamor abound. In a different context, the same patterns can be seen operating in the governmental bureaucracies of Mediterranean countries: A typical office layout for important officials usually includes a large reception area (an ornate version of Lorenzo Hubbell's office) outside the private suite, where small groups of people can wait and be visited by the minister or his aides. These functionaries do most of their business outside in this semipublic setting, moving from group to group conferring with each in turn. The semiprivate transactions take less time and give others the feeling that they are in the presence of the minister and other important people with whom they may also want to confer. Once one is used to this pattern, it is clear that there are advantages, which often outweigh the disadvantages of a series of private meetings in the inner office.

Particularly distressing to Americans is the way in which polychronic people handle appointments. Being on time simply doesn't mean the same thing as it does in the United States. Matters in a polychronic culture seem in a constant state of flux. Nothing is solid or firm, particularly plans for the future; even important plans may be changed right up to the minute of execution.

In contrast, people in the Western world find little in life exempt from the iron hand of M-time. Time is so thoroughly woven into the fabric of existence that we are hardly aware of the degree to which it determines and coordinates everything we do, including the molding of relations with others in many subtle ways. In fact, social and business life, even one's sex life, is commonly schedule-dominated. By scheduling, we compartmentalize; this makes it possible to concentrate on one thing at a time, but it also reduces the context. Since scheduling by its very nature selects what will and will not be perceived and attended, and permits only a limited number of events within a given period, what gets scheduled constitutes a system for setting priorities for both people and functions. Important things are taken up first and allotted the most time; unimportant things are left until last or omitted if time runs out.

M-time is also tangible; we speak of it as being saved, spent, wasted, lost, made up, crawling, killed, and running out. These metaphors must be taken seriously. M-time scheduling is used as a classification system that orders life. The rules apply to everything except birth and death. It should be mentioned that without schedules or something similar to the M-time system, it is doubtful that our industrial civilization could have developed as it has, but there are other consequences. Monochronic time seals off one or two people from the group and intensifies relationships with one other person or, at most, two or three people. M-time in this sense is like a room with a closed door ensuring privacy. The only problem is that you must vacate the "room" at the end of the allotted 15 minutes or an hour, a day, or a week, depending on the schedule, and make way for the next person in line. Failure to make way by intruding on the time of the next person is not only a sign of extreme egocentrism and narcissism, but also just plain bad manners.

Monochronic time is arbitrary and imposed—that is, learned. Because it is so thoroughly learned and so thoroughly integrated into our culture, it is treated as though it were the only natural and logical way of organizing life. Yet, it is not inherent in man's biological rhythms or his creative drives, nor is it existential in nature.

Schedules can and often do cut things short just when they are beginning to go well. For example, research funds run out just as the results are beginning to be achieved. How often have you had the experience of realizing that you are pleasurably immersed in some creative activity, totally unaware of time, solely conscious of the job at hand, only to be brought back to "reality" with the rude shock of realizing that other, often inconsequential previous commitments are bearing down on you?

Some Americans associate schedules with reality, but M-time can alienate us from ourselves and from others by reducing context. It subtly influences how we think and perceive the world in segmented compartments. This is convenient in linear operations but disastrous in its effect on nonlinear creative tasks. Latino peoples are an example of the opposite. In Latin America, the intelligentsia and the academicians commonly participate in several fields at once—fields that the average North American academician, business, or professional person thinks of as antithetical. Business, philosophy, medicine, and poetry, for example, are common, well-respected combinations.

Polychronic people, such as the Arabs and Turks, who are almost never alone, even in the home,

make very different uses of "screening" than Europeans do. They interact with several people at once and are continually involved with each other. Tight scheduling is therefore difficult, if not impossible.

Theoretically, when considering social organization, P-time systems should demand a much greater centralization of control and be characterized by a rather shallow or simple structure because the leader deals continually with many people, most of whom stay informed as to what is happening. The Arab *fellah* can always see his *sheik*. There are no intermediaries between man and *sheik* or between man and God. The flow of information as well as people's need to stay informed complement each other. Polychronic people are so deeply immersed in each other's business that they feel a compulsion to keep in touch. Any stray scrap of a story is gathered in and stored away. Their knowledge of each other is truly extraordinary. Their involvement in people is the core of their existence, but this approach has bureaucratic implications. For example, delegation of authority and a buildup in bureaucratic levels are not required to handle high volumes of business. The principal shortcoming of P-type bureaucracies is that as functions increase, there is a proliferation of small bureaucracies that really are not set up to handle the problems of outsiders. In fact, outsiders traveling or residing in Latin American or Mediterranean countries find the bureaucracies unusually cumbersome and unresponsive. In polychronic countries, one has to be an insider or have a "friend" who can make things happen. All bureaucracies are oriented inward, but P-type bureaucracies are especially so.

There are also interesting points to be made concerning the act of administration as it is conceived in these two settings. Administration and control of polychronic peoples in the Middle East and Latin America is a matter of job analysis. Administration consists of taking each subordinate's job and identifying the activities that contribute to make up the job. These are then labeled and indicated on the elaborate charts with checks to make it possible for the administrator to be sure that each function has been performed. In this way, it is believed that absolute control is maintained over the individual. Yet scheduling how and when each activity is actually performed is left up to the employee. For an employer to schedule a subordinate's work for him would be considered a tyrannical violation of his individuality—an invasion of the self.

In contrast, M-time people schedule the activity and leave the analysis of the activities of the job to the individual. A P-type analysis, even though technical by its nature, keeps reminding the subordinate that his or her job is not only a system but also part of a larger system. M-type people, on the other hand, by virtue of compartmentalization, are less likely to see their activities in context as part of the larger whole. This does not mean that they are unaware of the "organization"—far from it—only that the job itself or even the goals of the organization are seldom seen as a whole.

Giving the organization a higher priority than the functions it performs is common in our culture. This is epitomized in television, where we allow the TV commercials, the "special message," to break the continuity of even the most important communication. There is a message all right, and the message is that art gives way to commerce—polychronic advertising agencies impose their values on a monochronic population. In monochronic North European countries, where patterns are more homogeneous, commercial interruptions of this sort are not tolerated. There is a strict limit regarding the number as well as the times when commercials can be shown. The average American TV program has been allotted one or two hours, for which people have set aside time, and is conceived, written, directed, acted, and played as a unity. Interjecting commercials throughout the body of the program breaks that continuity and flies in the face of one of the core systems of the culture. The polychronic Spanish treat the main feature as a close friend or relative who should not be disturbed and let the commercials mill around in the antechamber outside. My point is not that one system is superior to another, it's just that the two don't mix. The effect is disruptive and reminiscent of what the English are going through today, now that the old monochronic queuing patterns have broken down as a consequence of a large infusion of polychronic peoples from the colonies.

Both M-time and P-time systems have strengths as well as weaknesses. There is a limit to the speed with which jobs can be analyzed, although once analyzed, proper reporting can enable a P-time administrator to handle a surprising number of subordinates. Nevertheless, organizations run on the polychronic model are limited in size; they depend on having gifted people at the top; and they are slow and cumbersome when dealing with anything that is new or different. Without gifted people, a P-type bureaucracy can be a disaster. M-type organizations go in the opposite direction. They can and do grow much larger than the P-type model; however, they combine bureaucracies instead of proliferating them (e.g., with consolidated schools, the business conglomerate, and the new superdepartments we are developing in government).

The blindness of the monochronic organization is to the humanity of its members. The weakness of the polychronic type lies in its extreme dependence on the leader to handle contingencies and stay on top of things. M-type bureaucracies, as they grow larger, turn inward; oblivious to their own structure, they grow rigid and are apt to lose sight of their original purpose. Prime examples are the Army Corps of Engineers and the Bureau of Reclamation, which wreak havoc on our environment in their dedicated efforts to stay in business by building dams or aiding the flow of rivers to the sea.

At the beginning of this chapter, I stated that "American time is monochronic." On the surface, this is true, but in a deeper sense, American (AE) time is both polychronic and monochronic. M-time dominates the official worlds of business, government, the professions, entertainment, and sports; however, in the home—particularly the more traditional home in which women are the core around which everything revolves—one finds that P-time takes over. How else can one raise several children at once, run a household, hold a job, and be a wife, mother, nurse, tutor, chauffeur, and general fixer-upper? Nevertheless, most of us automatically equate P-time with informal activities and with the multiple tasks and responsibilities and ties of women to networks of people. At the preconscious level, M-time is male time and P-time is female time, and the ramifications of this difference are considerable.

In the conclusion of an important book, *Unfinished Business*, Maggie Scarf vividly illustrates this point. Scarf addresses the question of why depression (the hidden illness of our age) is three to six times more prevalent in women than it is in men. How does time equate with depression in women? It so happens that the time system of the dominant culture adds another source of trauma and alienation to the already overburdened psyches of many American women. According to Scarf, depression comes about in part as a consequence of breaking significant ties that make up most women's worlds. In our culture, men as a group tend to be more task-oriented, whereas women's lives center on networks of people and their relations with people. Traditionally, a woman's world is a world of human emotions, of love, attachment, envy, anxiety, and hate. This concept is a little difficult for twenty-first-century people to accept because it implies basic differences between men and women that are not fashionable at the moment. Nevertheless, for most cultures around the world, the feminine mystique is intimately identified with the development of the human relations side of the personality rather than the technical, cortical left-brain occupational side. In the United States, AE women live in a world of people and relationships, and their egos become spread out among those who are closest to them by a process we call *identification*. When the relationships are threatened or broken or something happens to those to whom one is close, there are worries and anxieties, and depression is a natural result.

Polychronic cultures are by their nature oriented to people. Any human being who is naturally drawn to other human beings and who lives in a world dominated by human relationships will be either pushed or pulled toward the polychronic end of the time spectrum. If you value people, you must hear them out and cannot cut them off simply because of a schedule.

M-time, on the other hand, is oriented to tasks, schedules, and procedures. As anyone who has had experience with our bureaucracies knows, schedules and procedures take on a life all their own without reference to either logic or human needs. And this set of written and unwritten rules—and the consequences of these rules—is at least partially responsible for the reputation of American business being cut off from human beings and unwilling to recognize the importance of employee morale. Morale may well be the deciding factor in whether a given company makes a profit or not. Admittedly, American management is slowly, very slowly, getting the message. The problem is that modern management has accentuated the monochronic side at the expense of the less manageable, and less predictable, polychronic side. Virtually everything in our culture works for and rewards a monochronic view of the world. But the antihuman aspect of M-time is alienating, especially to women. Unfortunately, too many women have "bought into" the M-time world, not realizing that unconscious sexism is part of it. The pattern of an entire system of time is too large, too diffuse, and too ubiquitous for most to identify its patterns. Women sense there is something alien about the way in which modern organizations handle time, beginning with how the workday, the week, and the year are set up. Such changes as flextime do not alter the fact that as soon as one enters the door of the office, one becomes immediately locked into a monochronic, monolithic structure that is virtually impossible to change.

There are other sources of tension between people who have internalized these two systems. Keep in mind that polychronic individuals are oriented toward people, human relationships, and the family, which is the core of their existence. Family takes precedence over everything else. Close friends come next. In the absence of schedules, when there is a crisis the family always comes first. If a monochronic woman has a polychronic hairdresser, there will inevitably be problems, even if she has a regular appointment and is scheduled at the same time each week. In circumstances like these, the hairdresser (following his or her own pattern) will inevitably feel compelled to "squeeze people in." As a consequence, the regular customer, who has scheduled her time very carefully (which is why she has a standing appointment in the first place), is kept waiting and feels put down, angry, and frustrated. The hairdresser is also in a bind because if he does not accommodate his relative or friend regardless of the schedule, the result is endless repercussions within his family circle. Not only must he give preferential treatment to relatives, but the degree of accommodation and who is pushed aside or what is pushed aside is itself a communication!

The more important the customer or business that is disrupted, the more reassured the hairdresser's polychronic Aunt Nell will feel. The way to ensure the message that one is accepted or loved is to call up at the last minute and expect everyone to rearrange everything. If they don't, it can be taken as a clear signal that they don't care enough. The M-time individual caught in this P-time pattern has the feeling either that he is being pressured or that he simply doesn't count. There are many instances where culture patterns are on a collision course, and there can be no resolution until the point of conflict is identified. One side or the other literally gives up. In the instance cited above, the hairdresser usually loses a good customer. Patterns of this variety are what maintain ethnicity. Neither pattern is right, only different, and it is important to remember that they do not mix.

Not all M-times and P-times are the same. There are tight and loose versions of each. The Japanese, for example, in the official business side of their lives where people do not meet on a highly personalized basis, provide us an excellent example of tight M-time. When an American professor, businessperson, technical expert, or consultant visits Japan, he may find that his time is like a carefully packed trunk—so tightly packed, in fact, that it is impossible to squeeze one more thing into the container. On a recent trip to Japan, I was contacted by a well-known colleague who had translated one of my earlier books. He wanted to see me and asked if he could pick me up at my hotel at twelve-fifteen so we could have lunch together. I had situated myself in the lobby a few minutes early because the Japanese are almost always prompt. At twelve-seventeen, I could see his tense figure darting through the crowd of arriving businesspeople and politicians who had collected near the door. Following greetings, he ushered me outside to the ubiquitous black limousine with chauffeur, with white doilies covering the arms and headrests. The door of the car had hardly closed when he started outlining our schedule for the lunch period by saying that he had an appointment at three o'clock to do a TV broadcast. That set the time limit and established the basic parameters in which everyone knew where he would be at any given part of the agenda. He stated these limits— a little over two hours—taking travel time into account.

My colleague next explained that not only were we to have lunch, but he wanted to tape an inter-

view for a magazine. That meant lunch and an interview, which would last thirty to forty minutes. What else? Ah, yes. He hoped I wouldn't mind spending time with Mr. X, who had published one of my earlier books in Japanese, because Mr. X was very anxious to pin down a commitment on my part to allow him to publish my next book. He was particularly eager to see me because he missed out on publishing the last two books, even though he had written me in the United States. Yes, I did remember that he had written, but his letter arrived after my agent had made the decision on the Japanese publisher. That, incidentally, was the very reason why he wanted to see me personally. Three down and how many more to go?

Oh, yes, there would be some photographers there, and he hoped I wouldn't mind if pictures were taken? The pictures were to be both formal group shots, which were posed, and informal, candid shots during the interview, as well as pictures taken with Mr. X. As it turned out, there were at least two sets of photographers as well as a sound man, and while it wasn't "60 Minutes," there was quite a lot of confusion (the two sets of photographers each required precious seconds to straighten things out). I had to hand it to everyone—they were not only extraordinarily skilled and well organized, but also polite and considerate. Then, he hoped I wouldn't mind, but there was a young man who was studying communication who had scored over 600 on an examination, which I was told put him 200 points above the average. This young man would be joining us for lunch. I didn't see how we were going to eat anything, much less discuss issues of mutual interest. In situations such as these, one soon learns to sit back, relax, and let the individual in charge orchestrate everything. The lunch was excellent, as I knew it would be—hardly leisurely, but still very good.

All the interviews and the conversation with the student went off as scheduled. The difficulties came when I had to explain to the Japanese publisher that I had no control over my own book—that once I had written a book and handed it in to my publisher, the book was marketed by either my publisher or my agent. Simply being first in line did not guarantee anything. I had to try to make it clear that I was tied into an already existing set of relationships with attached obligations and that other people made these decisions. This required some explaining, and I then spent considerable time trying to work out a method for the publisher to get a hearing with my agent. This is sometimes virtually impossible because each publisher and each agent in the United States has its own representative in Japan. Thus an author is in their hands, too.

We did finish on time—pretty much to everyone's satisfaction, I believe. My friend departed on schedule as the cameramen were putting away their equipment and the sound man was rolling up his wires and disconnecting his microphones. The student drove me back to my hotel on schedule, a little after 3 P.M.

The pattern is not too different from schedules for authors in the United States. The difference is that in Japan the tightly scheduled monochronic pattern is applied to foreigners who are not well enough integrated into the Japanese system to be able to do things in a more leisurely manner, and where emphasis is on developing a good working relationship.

All cultures with high technologies seem to incorporate both polychronic and monochronic functions. The point is that each does it in its own way. The Japanese are polychronic when looking and working inward, toward themselves. When dealing with the outside world, they have adopted the dominant time system, which characterizes that world. That is, they shift to the monochronic mode and, characteristically, since these are technical matters, they outshine us.

Concepts and Questions

1. How might cultural differences in time conceptualization lead to intercultural communication problems?
2. How have you seen Hall's concept of monochronic time reflected in your culture?
3. What difficulties might an M-time–oriented person experience when interacting with someone who follows a P-time orientation? What feelings might emerge during this interaction?
4. What difficulties might a P-time–oriented person experience when interacting with someone who follows an M-time orientation? What feelings might emerge during this interaction?
5. What does Hall imply by the statement "there are points at which M-time doesn't make as much sense as it might seem"?
6. How does an M-time orientation affect perception?
7. What problems arise in a P-time–oriented society as bureaucratic levels increase? How does a P-time society adjust to a bureaucratic buildup?
8. How is administrative scheduling affected by M-time and P-time orientations?
9. What does Hall mean by his statement that "European-American (EA) time is both polychronic and monochronic"?
10. Hall notes that "both M-time and P-time systems have strengths as well as weaknesses." What are some of these strengths and weaknesses?

Gender and Nonverbal Communication

DEBORAH BORISOFF
LISA MERRILL

The effect of gender is produced through the stylization of the body and, hence, must be understood as the mundane way in which bodily gestures, movements, and styles of various kinds constitute the illusion of an abiding gendered self.

JUDITH BUTLER, *Gender Trouble*

There's language in her eye, her cheek, her lip; Nay, her foot speaks; Her wanton spirits look out at every joint and motive of her body.

WILLIAM SHAKESPEARE, *Troilus and Cressida*

According to Judith Butler (1990), what we know as gender is a set of "acts" or social performances that people are repeatedly compelled to enact so that, over time, they "produce the appearance of substance, of a natural sort of being" (p. 33). For example, young girls are intentionally taught to "sit like a lady" with legs close together; young boys are instructed not to cry or express fear. Erving Goffman (1979) has called these nonverbal behaviors a form of "gender display." There are often severe social penalties for those who act in violation of their culture's accepted gender "script." The gender-differentiated nonverbal behaviors that result from this socialization are learned rather than innate, and they become part of an individual's experience as a "gendered self." As a result, many people conclude that men "naturally" take up more space than do women or that women are "naturally" more emotionally expressive than men, although the prescriptions for how men and women should act vary from culture to culture.

Nonverbal messages have a *presentational dimension*; through demeanor, gestures, expressions, and artifacts, communicators present aspects of their socially constructed—and gendered—selves to others. Through our nonverbal behaviors, we express and display our emotions and our experience of gender, ethnicity, sexuality, and socioeconomic class identifications. Each of these variables influences the others. For example, every culture formulates its own display rules that dictate when, how, and with what consequences nonverbal expressions will be exhibited. In some cultures, heterosexual male friends, family members, or colleagues routinely walk hand-in-hand and kiss each other upon greeting and leave-taking; but in other cultures men who engage in these behaviors are considered homosexual. In some cultures, women are taught that it is not "ladylike" to run, to meet a man's gaze directly, or to expose one's arms, legs, or face to the gaze of male strangers in public. In other cultures, women engage in athletics and wear slacks and shirts with short sleeves, clothing that is not differentiated from that worn by men.

In this article, we will examine some of the assumptions and controversies about the nonverbal performance of gender and explore women's and men's use and interpretation of such nonverbal variables as space, height, touch, gesture, facial expressions, and eye contact. Further, because sensitivity to the nonverbal messages of others is both a learned skill and related to a given society's gender expectations, we will consider whether men and women differ in their perception of and ability to decode nonverbal messages accurately.

SPACE, OR "BIGGER IS BETTER"

In North American culture, space is a signifier of power, and individuals who have command over greater amounts of space and territory are often considered to have greater power. Women and lower-status persons of both sexes are afforded and expected to take up less space than males and higher-status persons. In addition, people in subordinate positions cannot control others from entering the space available to them. The boss can enter the worker's space, lean on the employee's desk, or tower over the subordinate. Only with the supervisor's invitation can the subordinate enter into the supervisor's space. In pub-

Reprinted by permission of Waveland Press, Inc. from Deborah Borisoff and Lisa Merrill, *The Power to Communicate: Gender Differences as Barriers*, 3d ed. (Prospect Heights, IL: Waveland Press, Inc., 1998). All rights reserved. Deborah Borisoff teaches at New York University, and Lisa Merrill teaches at Hofstra University.

lic and in private, in the workplace and in the streets, women constantly experience space encroachment. Gender-differentiated proxemic patterns appear even in childhood when young boys are encouraged and permitted to play outdoors, whereas play for young girls is more commonly centered within the home (Graebner, 1982; Harper and Sanders, 1975; Thorne, 1993; Valentine, 1997).

Learned behavior patterns inform beliefs about entitlement to space and affect how individuals interpret the use of space—especially when expected spatial norms are violated. In the animal kingdom and among human beings, subordinates yield space to dominants. Frank Willis (1966) performed studies in which he measured the initial distance set by an approaching person. He established that both sexes approach women more closely than they do men. In a review of many such research studies on nonverbal sex differences in interpersonal distance, Judith Hall (1984) also found that females are approached more closely than are males. When women's space is intruded upon, they are apt to acquiesce to the intrusion—just as they frequently acquiesce to interruptions. Jeanette Silveira's research (1972) indicated that when men and women walked toward each other on the sidewalk, the woman moved out of the man's way in 12 of 19 cases. Knapp and Hall (1997) speculate that acquiescing or ceding space to males may be linked, in part, to associating male behavior with the potential for threatening aggression. They further hypothesize that acquiescence to "invasions" of personal space may be attributed to societal norms for maintaining "appropriate" distance: "people expect men to keep larger distances, and when they do not, it may be disturbing" (p. 168). Yet as we have seen, societal norms and expectations serve dominant interests.

Women are encouraged to sit and move in ways that intensify the lesser amount of space available to them. For example, when involved in a dyadic or small-group communication interaction, women may sit poised on the edge of a chair, eagerly leaning forward rather than "taking up" space. "Feminine" clothes also contribute to a nonverbal image of female weakness and reconfigure the bodies that wear them. Tight skirts and tight slacks restrict movement. High heels force women to take small steps. In the late 1800s economist Thorstein Veblen

(1899) asserted that "the high heel, the skirt, the impracticable bonnet, the corset, and the general disregard of the wearer's comfort which is an obvious feature of all civilized women's apparel, are so many items of evidence to the effect that in the modern civilized scheme of life the woman is still, in theory, the economic dependent of the man." Veblen noted that middle-class women were not just restricted in their movements, they, and their relative powerlessness, were literally "on display" (pp. 126–127).

In the United States, contemporary women are still socialized to take up less space than men. They are taught to sit with their legs together and elbows to their sides and to walk with smaller steps. Contemporary women's fashion, such as tight clothing, short skirts, and high heels, discourages women who wear it from sitting and moving expansively, as do men. While seated, men spread their legs and put their arms on the armrests of chairs. They walk with longer strides. We know that these stereotypical ways of moving are not anatomically based, because men in Asia, for example, sit with their legs as closely together and cross their legs as do Western women. Yet in the United States, men who retreat into such little available space may not be considered "masculine," whereas women who sit and stand with open movements and walk with long strides may be regarded as "unfeminine."

Culture as well as gender exerts a determining force on the degree of personal space individuals use in interaction with each other. Members of many cultures tend, in general, to interact at closer distances than do white North Americans. As Carol Zinner Dolphin (1988) has established, "use of personal space as influenced by the sex(es) of interacting individuals tends to differ dramatically from one culture to another" (p. 28). Dolphin found that proximity was influenced by a given culture's expectations for male or female behavior. Thus, while one culture may expect physical closeness and contact between men, in another this may be largely forbidden. Some cultures may expect women to maintain larger distances from each other than are expected of men from each other, whereas members of other cultures may interpret such behavior between women as a sign of coldness or disinterest. Although some cultures allow for a degree of physical proximity in mixed-sex interactions, others prohibit it and proscribe greater amounts of distance between men and women.

Jeffrey Sanders and his colleagues (1985) studied the degrees of personal distance maintained between same-sex and mixed-sex dyads of North American and Arab students. Sanders found that mixed-sex pairs of Arab women and men interacted at a much greater distance than did either same-sex pairs of Arab students or same-sex or mixed-sex North American pairs. Robert Shuter's (1976) study of proxemics and touch in men and women from three Latin American cultures (Costa Rica, Colombia, and Panama) found that same-sex female dyads in all three cultures interacted the most closely—at significantly smaller distances and with greater amounts of physical contact—than same-sex male or opposite-sex dyads. In these two cases, respectively, the greater distance between men and women and the greater closeness between women are cultural expectations, constituting part of the construction and performance of gender in the cultures studied.

Within most cultures, the closer people feel to each other emotionally, the more they are likely to allow each other to be in proximity. Thus, the distance between communicators in an interaction may be influenced by gender, culture, power, and the degree of intimacy and reciprocity. There is no one meaning for any given nonverbal message. In some cases, close interpersonal distances between people are a result of warmth and affiliation; in others, they reflect an abuse of status differences. Distance between partners in an interaction may be an expression of respect and deference—or disinterest and hostility.

Lombardo's (1986) study of sex roles and personal distance has led him to suggest that the sex of communicators and their orientation toward particular sex roles exerts a considerable impact over how individuals use space, their perceptions of spatial needs, and the invasions of their personal space. For example, if the feeling of emotional closeness or affiliation between individuals is not reciprocal, an undesired intrusion into others' personal space may be considered a gross abuse of power. Our discussion of sexual harassment will be informed by an awareness of the complex components involved in such nonverbal behavior as negotiating personal space. According to Bochner (1982), the "meanings" attached to the use of personal space are determined by a range of variables, including the relationship between the individuals involved, their relative status and power, their degree of intimacy, and the type of activity in which they are engaged.

TOUCH, OR "JUST A FRIENDLY PAT ON THE BACK"?

Touch, like physical closeness, may be considered an expression of affection, support, or sexual attraction; however, touch may be used to express and maintain an asymmetrical relationship as well as a reciprocal one. For example, as a gesture of comfort, the doctor may touch the patient, but the patient may not initiate physical contact with the doctor. Similarly, upon entering the secretary's cubicle, the department head might pat the secretary on the back and inquire about her or his family. This apparently "friendly" gesture is not as benign as it appears, however, as long as the secretary does not have an equal right to initiate the same pat on the back and elicit similar personal information from the department head.

In the mid-1970s, Nancy Henley performed observational studies investigating the relationship between touch and socioeconomic status, sex, and age. Henley (1973, 1977) found that, in interactions between people not romantically involved with each other, higher-status persons (individuals of higher socioeconomic status, male, and older) touched lower-status persons significantly more often. In their review of gender and touching behavior between romantic partners, Knapp and Hall (1997) report "inconsistent" findings on "which sex touches the other more, overall" (p. 303). In these situations, as a relationship becomes more intimate and committed, sex differences in the initiation of touch between partners appears less evident. Yet even in such relationships, Knapp and Hall contend that "observers seem to *perceive* the initiator [of touch] as the person with greater power" (p. 304). These findings have important implications for both women and men. Individuals of both sexes should guard against using touch to assert authority. We should avoid initiating touch in situations where either the other individual is not desirous of the gesture or where the higher-status person would not accept a reciprocal touch.

What about when the gesture is reciprocal? Co-workers must be aware of outsiders possibly misconstruing the sexual implications of touch. In the 1984 Mondale–Ferraro campaign for the U.S. presidency, newscasters mentioned a distinction from previous campaigns. Whereas male candidates for president and vice president traditionally linked inner arms and waved their raised outer arms, Mondale and Ferraro waved outer arms with their inner arms at their sides. They did not touch each other. The sexism and heterosexism in our society impose restrictions on behavior. Until people become accustomed to perceiving women as competent professionals in their own right rather than as potential sexual objects, they will have difficulty imagining a collegial relationship between men and women without sexual implications. Consequently, at present, women and men who work together will continue to be subject to greater scrutiny than same-sex pairs.

Within same-sex dyads in the United States, women are generally much freer than men to touch one another. Women friends and relatives may walk arm-in-arm, dance together, and hug one another. Touch between heterosexual males is generally more restricted. As Barrie Thorne (1993) found in her ethnographic study of elementary school boys and girls, young girls regularly engage in such gestures of intimacy with each other as stroking or combing their friends' hair, whereas touch among boys is rarely relaxed and affectionate—limited primarily to a ritual handslap and the mock violence of pushing, poking, and grabbing (p. 94). Outside of the sporting arena, many North American men do not feel free to exchange much more than a slap on the back without their behavior being construed as having sexual connotations.

It is important to remember that the notion of "appropriate" touch, like that of "comfortable" interpersonal distance between communicators, is largely culturally determined. In some cultures same-sex male dyads have a greater latitude of haptic expression with each other. They may commonly hug or kiss each other on both cheeks, for example, whereas women friends or family members are much more restricted in their socially sanctioned ability to touch one another. In some cultures, all touch between men and women who are not related to each other by family or by marriage is strictly forbidden. In these circumstances, uninvited touch may be experienced as an abuse of power that takes the form of cultural and sexual oppression.

HEIGHT, OR "WHOM DO YOU LOOK UP TO?"

Height is also a nonverbal variable that may be manipulated, thereby either empowering or impeding an individual. We say "I look up to you" to indicate respect or admiration. "Higher," like "bigger," is often used to mean "better" or "more" (as in "higher class," "high opinion").

In hierarchies, the individual with greater power is often perceived as taller than he or she is. Paul R. Wilson (1968) reported that undergraduates who were asked to estimate the height of a man who was described as any one of five academic ranks increased their estimation of his height when his ascribed status was increased. In some environments (e.g., in courtrooms, in the military, in some religious practices) deference is enforced by norms of courtesy and respect that dictate, for example, who may sit and who may stand when status unequals interact.

Although men as a group may be somewhat taller than women, in individual mixed-sex dyads, these differences may be minimal or reversed; however, there are behaviors that make males appear taller. Social dyads in which the woman is appreciably taller than the man are often subject to ridicule, as though they are subverting gender and power expectations. In a world in which height equals power and women are not supposed to be more powerful than men, taller women may attempt to diminish themselves, to slouch and round their shoulders so as to retreat or to occupy as little space as possible.

Traditional female facial expressions of coyness and flirtation may reinforce the height and power differential between the sexes. For example, women often exhibit their femininity by tilting their heads to the side and looking upward when talking to male conversational partners. Although the head tilt is a gesture that indicates attentive listening in either sex, women are apt to employ this more frequently in mixed-sex pairs than men, thus reinforcing the notion that, in addition to listening, the woman is "looking up to" the man.

We must guard against using height to control or to influence. Superiors need not tower over subordinates in the workplace. Tall individuals should be encouraged neither to use their height in an intimidating fashion nor to attempt to diminish themselves by denying their personal power. Power need not be used as power *over* others.

FACIAL EXPRESSIONS, OR "YOU LOOK SO PRETTY WHEN YOU SMILE"

White, middle-class women in the United States are expected to be highly expressive emotionally. One of the hallmarks of the feminine stereotype for this group is to be facially expressive, and a woman's face is believed to reflect her emotional state. The most common and easily discernible facial expression is the smile.

From childhood, white female children are admonished to smile. They are taught to smile not as an expression of their own pleasure, but because it is pleasing to others. Hence a smile may be considered a gesture of appeasement or deference. Women are told that they are more attractive when they smile and appear happy. The key word in the previous sentence is *appear*. As long as women and other subordinates are concerned with pleasing others, they are not considered threatening to their superiors. African-American women are not expected to perform their "femininity" within their cultures in exactly the same manner. As a result, Halberstadt and Saitta (1987) found African-American women to be less deferential than white women and, therefore, less inclined to smile merely because it is expected of them. Consequently, some of the racism to which women of color are exposed is a result of whites misinterpreting an absence of facial gestures of deference as hostility, arrogance, unfriendliness, or disinterest. As long as one *seems* to be satisfied with the position that has been allotted, the hierarchical system is reinforced. Smiles, therefore, can function as genuine or artificial signs of satisfaction.

In addition to functioning as an expression of pleasure, pleasantness, or a desire for approval, smiling may also reflect the smiler's nervousness. In some service occupations, smiling is not only preferred

behavior, it is *required*. In Arlie Russell Hochschild's (1983) article "Smile Wars: Counting the Casualties of Emotional Labor," she discussed the emotional labor required of flight attendants. According to Hochschild, the flight attendant, receptionist, server, and salesperson often pay a psychological price for their requisite smiles. When a smile is an *expected* part of the job, it becomes a commodity to be given. Women in these and other occupations are often required to "give" male patrons or superiors a smile. The constant feigned smile is an expression of duplicity. (And it must be feigned, for obviously no one can be happy all the time.) An individual engaging in this behavior cuts himself or herself off from the expression of his or her own emotions. The smile becomes a mask, a form of "makeup," constructed to gain the approval of one who has power. Subordinates are expected to smile at superiors. When the boss walks into the room, the secretaries are expected to smile and warmly greet him or her.

Moreover, dominant members of a hierarchy are less likely to smile or disclose their feelings nonverbally. They typically withhold verbal and nonverbal expressions of emotions. Instead, they are often encouraged to maintain a "poker face," to appear neutral and impassive, and to disclose as little about themselves as possible. In some contexts, however, rather than smiling to gain others' approval, superiors are apt to assume facial expressions that imply that they are judging others. One such example, according to Gerald I. Nierenberg and Henry H. Calero (1971), is the disapproving attitude conveyed by raised eyebrows, a partially twisted head, and a look of doubt. (According to Webster's Dictionary, the word *supercilious* comes from Latin meaning "disdain or haughtiness as expressed by raising the eyebrows.")

Little difference has been found in the smiling behavior of female and male infants and young children; however, as white North American girls grow up, they smile significantly more often than do white North American boys. In one study, preschool boys' spontaneous facial expressions were found to decrease dramatically from age four to six (Buck, 1977). According to Hall (1984), "this suggests that socialization, pressure or modeling induces boys during this period to reduce expression of emotion via the face" (p. 54). The social pressure to present a "more masculine" face (less smiling) may be operative for boys at this age because they are likely to be in school starting at age four or five.

As we stated earlier, women are believed to be more facially expressive (Hall, 1984; Leathers, 1986) than men. In analyses of numerous studies of expression accuracy, Hall (1984) found that "females were better expressors, that is their expressions were more accurately judged by decoders" (p. 53). Perhaps one of the ways to account for women's greater expressiveness is to consider to what extent the performance of femininity in the United States depends on heightened or exaggerated facial expression.

Zuckerman and colleagues (1982) conducted three separate studies that related the legibility of an individual's facial expressions to signifiers of masculinity and femininity. The studies revealed that the very concept of femininity implies clear and willing expression of nonverbal cues. According to Marianne LaFrance and Nancy Henley (1994) the pressure on women to develop and to "perform" these nonverbal cues is reinforced and perpetuated by men's "greater social power relative to women in everyday social interactions" (p. 290). Borisoff and Hahn (1997) contend that to the extent that initial attractiveness and heterosexual relationship satisfaction remain associated with women's nonverbal expressiveness, women "are destined to be the arbiters of affective nonverbal display" (p. 65). Of course, nonverbal signifiers of "masculinity" or "femininity" are culturally determined, rather than innate. In those cultures and subcultures in which being facially expressive is an integral component in the collection of behaviors that are seen as markers of "femininity," males may resist both the nonverbal display of expression and attentiveness to others in order to appear more masculine.

As Buck (1977) has noted, people whose faces express their emotional states have lower levels of electrothermal response than do people whose faces do not display emotion. Higher electrothermal responses indicate suppressed emotions and have been considered possible contributors to heart disease and other stress-related conditions that are more prevalent in men than women. Thus, men may be paying with their lives for withholding emotional expression (see Borisoff and Merrill, 1991).

In homes, schools, and workplaces, we need to be aware of ways in which expressions of emotions establish or maintain a power differential. Women and other subordinates should evaluate the need to engage in overeager smiles for approval or to offer smiles that are expected of them. Men and dominant members of hierarchies should also reevaluate their tendency to withhold or mask emotional expressiveness and equate the appearance of pleasing expressions with compliance that is due them. They might also allow themselves to engage more openly in genuine, mutual expressions of pleasure and approval.

GAZE, OR "ARE YOU LOOKING AT ME?"

Direct eye contact between individuals may be interpreted in several different ways. Looking directly into another person's eyes can connote an aggressive threat, a sexual invitation, or a desire for honest and open communication. For many contemporary theorists, the "gaze" is a metaphor for power, where a seeing subject—often assumed to be male—takes the position of an active spectator when regarding another person as a passive object. This notion of objectification, where one person looks while another "is looked at," is at the root of many interpretations of and reactions to eye contact.

Several years ago, actor Robert DeNiro portrayed a psychopathic murderer in the film *Taxi Driver*. Posed in front of a mirror, DeNiro glared at his own reflection, taunting an imaginary assailant whom he envisioned to be staring at him. Menacingly, he asked: "You talkin' to me? Who do you think you're talkin' to?" DeNiro's character interpreted a glance as an attempt at dominance. Researchers Ellsworth, Carlsmith, and Henson (1972) tell us that a stare may have this function. Ellsworth and colleagues have reported studies that relate staring in humans to primate threat displays. For most individuals, a glance that catches another person's eye for several seconds is relatively insignificant. If, however, eye contact is maintained beyond several seconds, a nonverbal power contest may ensue in which the person with less power ultimately averts her or his eyes.

Thus, gaze has been proven to be related to status and power as well as to gender. In some cultures, children are taught that to look adults in the eyes is a sign of disrespect. Submission is indicated by a bowed head and an averted glance. In mixed-sex pairs, women are more likely than men to avert their eyes. Judith Hall's (1984) analysis established that "the more dominant individual gazes more while speaking and relatively less while listening; while the less dominant individual gazes more while listening and relatively less while speaking" (p. 73). Further, Ellyson and colleagues' 1980 study on visual dominance behavior in female dyads found that while women with relatively high status gazed an equivalent amount of time while speaking and listening, lower-status female subjects gazed significantly more while listening than when speaking. In her book *Body Politics*, Nancy Henley attempted to differentiate between subordinate attentiveness and dominant staring. Henley (1977) claimed that women and other subordinates look at others more but avert their eyes when looked at. Both of these behaviors are indicative of submissiveness. Status exerts a powerful influence on gaze and affects the behavior of research subjects of both sexes. Knapp and Hall (1997) reported that in studies where the variable of assigned status was removed, "the male tends to use the gaze pattern typically used by higher-status people, while the female tends to use the gaze pattern typically used by lower-status people" (p. 456).

In any discussion of nonverbal communication, it is important not to interpret behavior in an ethnocentric fashion. Eye contact, like all other nonverbal behavior, has different connotations in different cultural contexts. There are cultures in which direct eye contact between men and women is regarded as a sexual invitation and is, therefore, to be avoided in "polite" society. For individuals from these backgrounds, averting one's eyes in a mixed-sex dyad may be a sign of respect, modesty, or disinterest, rather than inattentiveness or submissiveness. In Curt and Nine's (1983) study of nonverbal communication among Hispanic couples, they found that many Puerto Rican wives never looked directly at their husbands.

Because of differing expectations and interpretations for behavior, there is the potential for much misunderstanding in mixed-sex and intercultural communication exchanges. Women and men need to be able to identify precisely those behaviors that seem intrusive or inappropriate and their connection with power inequities in specific social contexts.

GESTURE AND DEMEANOR, OR "ACT LIKE A LADY"

Through our bearing, demeanor, and gestural mannerisms, we perform much of the behavior that is associated with gender identities. But the gestures of communicators, the ways they "carry themselves," and the meanings associated with those nonverbal behaviors are also, in part, culturally specific, and they have changed over time.

In a nineteenth-century English etiquette manual entitled *The Habits of Good Society: A Handbook for Ladies and Gentlemen* (1870), readers who desired "good manners" were warned that "[f]oreigners talk with their arms and hands as auxiliaries to the voice. The custom is considered vulgar by us calm Englishmen. . . . You have no need to act with the hands, but if you use them at all, it should be very slightly and gracefully, never bringing down your fist upon the table, nor slapping one hand upon the other, nor poking your fingers at your interlocutor" (pp. 284–285). Yet, while appearing "calm" and "graceful" might signify appropriate "manly" gentility to the Englishman of one hundred years ago, those same qualities of graceful restraint are liable to be read as "feminine" to contemporary North American communicators who have been taught to equate forcefulness with "masculinity" rather than vulgarity. Class and cultural biases are apparent in this warning not to "talk with one's hands." Similar gender biases and stereotypes are operative when women are told that it is "ladylike" to stand up straight and hold one's body rigid, rather than to appear to be "loose" and "easy," as if a woman's deportment signified her sexual availability.

ARTIFACTUAL MESSAGES, OR "WHAT YOU WEAR SPEAKS VOLUMES"

Artifacts are objects. When worn, they have been used to signify a wearer's gender, culture, and socioeconomic class. From the moment at which families or hospitals assign infants pink or blue blankets, artifacts announce and contribute to the shaping of children's experience of gender. As Julia Wood (1994) has noted, clothing is a form of artifactual communication that "manifest[s] and promote[s] cultural definitions of masculinity and femininity" (p. 159). In earlier centuries sumptuary laws regulated "appropriate" dress, and it was literally against the law for women to wear men's breeches, for men to appear in women's dress, or for anyone to dress above their appropriate "station" in life by wearing the clothes of others more privileged than they, except in the special province of the theatre (Borisoff and Merrill, 1998).

Elizabeth Grosz (1994) has asserted that "through exercises and habitual patterns of movement, through negotiating its environment . . . and through clothing and make-up, the body is more or less marked, constituted as an appropriate, or, as the case may be, inappropriate body for its cultural requirements." Grosz contends that these procedures are more than adornment; rather, the "norms and ideals governing beauty and health" in a given culture and time literally shape the bodies of those who ascribe to them (p. 142). Consider the nineteenth-century woman tightly lacing herself into a corset designed to reduce her waist to a then-fashionable eighteen inches, and so transforming her body into an artificial hourglass shape, or the contemporary man using steroids to build his muscles into a body type currently fashionable. In both cases norms of "beauty" and people's complicity in or resistance to them send complex messages about gender and cultural values. What do the bodies of bodybuilders or anorexics "communicate" about the desirability of hard, pumped-up muscles or excessively thin, childlike bodies to those who witness them?

Like other forms of nonverbal communication, our bodies and the ways we clothe them are liable to be interpreted to signify things that the communicator may not have intended. For example, women are often seen and evaluated largely in terms of how they appear to others. Whether or not women's bodies are clothed in such a way as to intentionally draw attention to female body parts, sex-differentiated clothing (such as low-cut blouses, tightly fitted garments, short skirts, and high heels), rather than merely reflecting an individual's taste and sense of personal aesthetics, reinforces cultural values. Men's looser-fitting clothing, ample pockets, and flat shoes afford those who wear them a greater freedom of movement than most women's clothes.

DECODING NONVERBAL MESSAGES, OR "I CAN SEE WHAT YOU MEAN"

In Judith Hall's (1984) extensive review of studies of differences in decoding nonverbal messages, women were found to be significantly better decoders of nonverbal cues than were men. Women were found to be most skilled in decoding facial expressions. Hall based her review on 75 studies of sex differences in nonverbal decoding skills and 50 subsequent studies (1984) as well as her work with Robert Rosenthal on the design of the PONS (Profile of Nonverbal Sensitivity) Test. Regardless of age, white and African-American women exceeded men in the ability to ascertain emotions expressed nonverbally. Although differences in men's and women's scores on the PONS Test were small, they were consistent. Recent research, according to Knapp and Hall (1997) suggests no discernible differences in the ability to determine solely from nonverbal cues whether an individual is lying. The only emotion Knapp and Hall found men to be more adept at identifying was anger in other men.

To what can we attribute this facility? Several different hypotheses have been offered. Rosenthal and his colleagues (1979) hypothesized that women's greater accuracy in decoding facial expressions may be related to the fact that women gaze at others' faces more in interaction and that "one decodes better what one is paying attention to at the moment" (cited in Hall, 1984, p. 34). Related to this is the claim that women's experience with young children and their sensitivity as caregivers necessitate their accurate reading of nonverbal messages (Rosenthal et al., 1979).

Hall proposed a relationship between the amount of time that women gaze at their conversational partners and women's greater accuracy in decoding facial expressions. She suggested that "women may seek cues of approval or disapproval or cues that indicate how contented others are from moment to moment as part of a general motive to maintain harmonious relationships" (1984, pp. 34–35). Furthermore, research findings support a positive correlation between an individual's successful decoding of nonverbal cues and that individual's own expression accuracy in depicting messages nonverbally. Thus, women, who themselves are expected to be more nonverbally expressive, may be more accurate in reading the messages of others.

Nancy Henley (1973, 1977) offered the "oppression" theory. She posited that women, and others who have less power, must learn to "read" the nonverbal messages of those who have power over them. People who are oppressed have heightened needs to anticipate and to understand others' nonverbal messages. Henley claims that this is the reason for the greater interpersonal sensitivity of women and other less dominant persons. We suspect, therefore, that as women and men continue to negotiate and redefine their social roles and economic positions in society, these changes are likely to influence acuity in decoding nonverbal messages. At this point, however, Hall and her colleagues' findings that women far exceeded men in their ability to ascertain emotions expressed nonverbally remains largely uncontested in the research literature.

It appears impossible to provide one definitive explanation for women's greater facility with decoding nonverbal messages. Basically, all of the explanations offered to date fall into two categories: (1) theorists who relate women's greater nonverbal decoding skills to needs that arise out of their subordinate status and (2) theorists who attribute women's nonverbal skills to their greater tendency toward affiliation with others. However, as Hall contends:

> it is . . . difficult to disentangle these two basic explanations—dominance and affiliation—because of the possibility that women's lower status reduces their ability to challenge or threaten anyone, which in turn enables or requires them to act warm and nice. (1984, p. 84)

In any case, nonverbal factors such as touch, space, height, gaze, and facial expressions exert a potent influence on our interactions with others. Although often unacknowledged, many of our notions of masculinity and femininity rest on the nonverbal messages we display and those we decode. We are often unaware of our nonverbal behavior and of how it is being interpreted by others. This can present obstacles in professional as well as personal settings. Certainly one cannot work effectively if being ogled or ignored, leered at or laughed at. We need to monitor our own behavior responsibly and to provide feedback to others about what we perceive to be their reactions to us.

References

Bochner, S. (1982). The social psychology of cross-cultural relations. In S. Bochner (Ed.), *Cultures in contact* (pp. 5–44). New York: Pergamon Press.

Borisoff, D., and Hahn, D. F. (1997). The mirror in the window: Displaying our gender biases. In S. J. Drucker and G. Gumpert (Eds.), *Voices in the street: Explorations in gender, media, and public space* (pp. 101–107). Cresskill, NJ: Hampton Press.

Borisoff, D., and Merrill, L. (1991). Gender issues and listening. In D. Borisoff and M. Purdy (Eds.), *Listening in everyday life: A personal and professional approach* (pp. 59–85). Lanham, MD: University Press of America.

Borisoff, D., and Merrill, L. (1998). *The power to communicate: Gender differences as barriers*, 3rd ed. Prospect Heights, IL: Waveland Press.

Buck, R. (1977). Nonverbal communication of affect in preschool children: Relationships with personality and skin conductance. *Journal of Personality and Social Psychology, 35,* 225–236.

Butler, J. (1990). *Gender trouble: Feminism and the subversion of identity.* New York: Routledge.

Curt, C., and Nine, J. (1983). Hispanic-Anglo conflicts in nonverbal communication. In I. Albino (Ed.), *Perspectives pedagogicas.* San Juan: Universidad de Puerto Rico.

Dolphin, C. Z. (1988). Beyond Hall: Variables in the use of personal space. *Howard Journal of Communications, 1,* 23–38.

Ellsworth, P. C., Carlsmith, J. M., and Hensen, A. (1972). The stare as a stimulus to flight in human subjects: A series of field experiments. *Journal of Personality and Social Psychology, 21,* 302–311.

Ellyson, S. L., Dovidio, J. F., Corson, R. L., and Vinicur, D. L. (1980). Visual dominance behavior in female dyads: Situational and personality factors. *Social Psychology Quarterly, 42,* 328–336.

Goffman, E. (1979). *Gender Advertisements.* New York: Harper & Row.

Graebner, A. (1982). Growing up female. In L. A. Samovar and R. E. Porter (Eds.), *Intercultural communication: A reader.* Belmont, CA: Wadsworth.

Grosz, E. (1994). *Volatile bodies: Toward a corporeal feminism.* Bloomington: Indiana University Press.

Halberstadt, A., and Saitta, M. (1987). Gender, nonverbal behavior and perceived dominance: A test of the theory. *Journal of Personality and Social Psychology, 53,* 257–272.

Hall, J. (1984). *Nonverbal Sex Differences: Communication Accuracy and Expressive Style.* Baltimore, MD: Johns Hopkins University Press.

Harper, L. V., and Sanders, K. M. (1975). Preschool children's use of space: Sex differences in outdoor play. *Developmental Psychology, 11*, 119.

Henley, N. M. (1973). Status and sex: Some touching observations. *Bulletin of the Psychonomic Society, 2*, 91–93.

Henley, N. M. (1977). *Body politics: Power, sex, and nonverbal communication*. Englewood Cliffs, NJ: Prentice-Hall.

Hochschild, A. H. (1997, April 20). There's no place like work. *New York Times Sunday Magazine*, 51–55, 81, 84.

Knapp, M. L., & Hall, J. A. (1997). *Nonverbal communication in human interaction*, 4th ed. Ft. Worth: Harcourt Brace College Publishers.

LaFrance, M., and Henley, N. M. (1994). On oppressing hypotheses: Or differences in nonverbal sensitivity revisited. In H. L. Radke and H. J. Stam (Eds.), *Power/gender: Social relations in theory and practice* (pp. 287–311). Thousand Oaks, CA: Sage.

Leathers, D. (1986). *Successful nonverbal communication*. New York: Macmillan.

Lombardo, J. P. (1986). Interaction of sex and sex role response to violations of preferred seating arrangements. *Sex Roles, 15*, 173–183.

Nierenberg, G. I., and Calero, H. H. (1971). *How to read a person like a book*. New York: Hawthorne.

Rosenthal, R., Hall, J., DiMatteo, M. R., Rogers, R. S., and Archer, D. (1979). *Sensitivity to nonverbal communication: The PONS Test*. Baltimore, MD: Johns Hopkins University Press.

Sanders, J., et al. (1985). Personal space amongst Arabs and Americans. *International Journal of Psychology, 20*, 13–17.

Shuter, R. (1976). Nonverbal communication: Proxemics and tactility in Latin America. *Journal of Communication, 26*, 46–52.

Silveira, J. (1972, February). Thoughts on the politics of touch. *Women's Press, 1*, 13.

Thorne, B. (1993). *Gender play: Girls and boys in school*. New Brunswick, NJ: Rutgers University Press.

Valentine, G. (1997). "My son's a bit ditzy." "My wife's a bit soft": Gender, children and cultures of parenting. *Gender, Place and Culture, 4*, 37–62.

Veblen, T. (1953/1899). *Theory of the leisure class*. New York: New American Library.

Willis, F. (1966). Initial speaking distance as a function of the speaker's relationship. *Psychonomic Science, 5*, 221–222.

Wilson, P. R. (1968). Perceptual distortion of height as a function of ascribed academic status. *Journal of Social Psychology, 74*, 97–192.

Wood, J. T. (1994). *Gendered lives: Communication, gender, and culture*. Belmont, CA: Wadsworth.

Zuckerman, M., DeFrank, R. S., Spiegel, N. H., and Larrance, D. T. (1982). Masculinity–femininity and the encoding of nonverbal cues. *Journal of Personality and Social Psychology, 42*, 548–556.

Concepts and Questions

1. How is gender manifested as a set or series of social acts? What implications can you draw from this perspective?

2. What do Borisoff and Merrill mean when they say that nonverbal messages have a *presentational* dimension?

3. How does space define power? How does the use of space by men and women affect perceptions of power and influence behavior by women and men?

4. How do gender differences in the use of personal space during interaction affect individual behavior?

5. What feelings may be evoked by touch? Are these feelings the same for women as they are for men? How might misperceptions of touch affect communication between men and women?

6. How does individual height function as a nonverbal variable? How does height reflect power status between men and women?

7. In what manner does smiling behavior differ between women and men among white, middle-class Americans? Do the same behaviors hold for African-American women and men? If not, why?

8. How do facial expressions function to signify masculinity or femininity? In what manner might gender differences in the facial expressions of males and females affect communication between men and women?

9. How may direct eye contact between individuals be interpreted? Is it the same for women as for men? What might be the consequences of eye aversion rather than direct eye contact in a male–female dyadic interaction?

10. In the decoding of nonverbal messages, which gender tends to be the better decoder? Why does this seem to be the case?

chapter 6

Cultural Contexts: The Influence of the Setting

All human interaction takes place within a social setting or context that affects the communication event. Whether you are in a classroom, dance hall, doctor's office, business meeting, or church, the context or social environment influences how you communicate. How you dress, what you talk about, to whom you talk, and even the volume level of your voice are in some way determined by the context in which you find yourself. We call attention to the concept of social context because the setting is never neutral; it always influences, to some degree, how the communication participants behave. We have all learned appropriate patterns of communicative behavior for the various social contexts in which we normally find ourselves. But, as with other aspects of intercultural communication, the patterns of behavior appropriate in various social contexts are culturally diverse. When you find yourself in an unfamiliar context without an internalized set of rules to govern your behavior or when you are interacting with someone who has internalized a different set of rules, communication problems often arise. This chapter is about those communication problems and how you can learn to resolve them.

As indicated, the readings in this chapter deal with cultural diversity in communication contexts. In order for you to engage better in intercultural communication, we will focus on a combination of international and domestic settings in which knowledge and appreciation of cultural diversity are important if successful intercultural communication is to occur. To this end, we will examine the influence of contextual dynamics as they apply to business, health care, and educational settings.

The growth of international business during the last 30 years has been astonishing. Overseas transactions that annually generated millions of dollars just a few decades ago are now multibillion-dollar operations. Furthermore, many national companies have become multinational, multicultural companies with offices and production or service facilities located throughout the world. This trend toward multinationalism/multiculturalism has come about for several reasons. One is the imposition of regulations that require some aspect of production to be done within a country if the product is to be marketed in that country, such as the assembly of Japanese automobiles in U.S. factories. A second way this trend has occurred is through mergers and acquisitions where one company may buy or merge with another across national boundaries, such as the recent merger of the U.S. Chrysler and German Daimler-Benz automobile companies. A third impetus for the trend is the recognition that productivity increases come about with local presence.

Finally, changes have occurred within the United States. In many geographic areas of the country, society has become pluralistic and multicultural. The resulting cultural diversity of the U.S. population has created a multicultural workforce employed by most companies, whether they are local, regional, national, or international organizations.

Because of this worldwide economic growth and the internationalization of business, people no longer have the comfort of dealing exclusively with those who possess the same cultural background and experiences. One's associates, clients, subordinates, and even supervisors are often from different countries and cultures. Such aspects of business life as methods of negotiation, decision making, policy formulation, marketing techniques, management structure, human resource management, gift giving, and patterns of communication are now influenced by cultural diversity.

Your understanding of how communication operates in the multicultural business setting is becoming increasingly important becasuse you may find yourself engaged in intercultural communication in a variety of international and domestic workplace contexts. In order for you to function successfully in these arenas, you will have to learn effective intercultural communication approaches to business dealings that are often quite different from those with which you are most familiar.

We begin with three essays that involve a setting that is truly international—the world of business. It is obvious that all business activities encompass many forms of communication, and those forms reflect the attitudes, values, and communication patterns unique to each culture. Hence, our first three essays examine how cultural diversity touches and alters organizational communication, managerial styles, negotiation strategies, human relations, and interpersonal relations.

Business between the United States and Asia has been an important element in the American economy for several decades. Recent economic difficulties in Asia, especially in Japan, Hong Kong, Indonesia, Taiwan, and South Korea, have affected the U.S. economy and stock market. Future successful economic dealings in Asia will require an increased understanding of how Asian culture affects business practices. To this end, we begin with an essay that focuses on business communication within Japanese culture.

In our first essay on international business, Steve Quasha and Edwin R. McDaniel offer their experiences gained from more than 30 years of living, studying, and working with the Japanese. In their essay "Reinterpreting Japanese Business Communication in the Information Age," they reveal how traditional Japanese culture has influenced the protocols of communication that occur within business organizations. By examining historical events, social circumstances, and Japanese values and beliefs, they provide an excellent description of current organizational communication practices in Japan. They hold, however, that these communication procedures are "presently endangered by the expanding influence of globalization which is largely driven by information technology." In the second portion of their article, Quasha and McDaniel discuss the impact that information technology will have on Japanese business communication practices. They envision that these practices will affect corporate structures, the hierarchical or *sempai-kohai* system, the immigration of information technology workers, and the method of decision making in Japanese business organizations.

Although there is major American involvement in both European and Asian marketplaces, there are still many intercultural communication concerns relative to the business world closer to home. With the advent of the North American Free Trade Agreement (NAFTA), working relationships between the United States and Mexico have increased dramatically. Both in terms of trade negotiations between the United States and Mexico and in the operation of U.S. businesses in Mexico, the need for better understanding of Mexican culture and the differences in U.S.–Mexican business practices increases daily. The importance of this relationship and the effect it is having on the cultures of both Mexico and the United States was examined in detail in a special issue of *Time* magazine in which the editors suggest that "along the U.S.-Mexican border, where hearts and minds and money and culture merge, the Century of the Americas is born" (June 11, 2001). In their essay "U.S. Americans and Mexicans Working Together: Five Core Concepts for Enhancing Effectiveness," Sheryl Lindsley and Charles Braithwaite provide us with valuable insights into Mexican culture as it applies to the business environment. Here Lindsley and Braithwaite discuss five shared cultural patterns or core concepts common to doing business in Mexico. These are *confianza, simpatía, palanca, estabilidad,* and *mañana,* which are not mutually exclusive categories, but rather overlapping concepts reflecting deeply held values for many Mexicans. As these shared values make their way into the business environment, effective U.S. business managers and representatives must become aware of the influences these values have on behavior and communication.

One of the major communicative acts associated with business is negotiation. Similar to other forms of communication, negotiation is affected by cultural diversity. In her article "Culture and Negotiation," Jeanne M. Brett leads you through the development of a conceptual model of intercultural negotiation. She begins with a review of negotiation as a form of social interaction in which she discusses cultural influences on the negotiation process. She ends her article with a discussion of what happens when cultures clash during negotiation and offers ideas about how cultural clash may be avoided.

A multicultural society strongly affects the health care setting because cultural beliefs about health, disease, and caregiver–patient communication can differ significantly. In the next essay, Nagesh Rao reports the initial findings of an ongoing investigation into physician–patient communication across cultures. Through interviews conducted worldwide, Rao seeks to develop a base of information that will ultimately lead to a model of intercultural health care communication.

In his article "'Half-truths' in Argentina, Brazil, and India: An Intercultural Analysis of Physician–Patient Communication," Rao provides an insightful view of how physicians from these cultures view the diversity within their countries. In addition, Rao shows how these physicians operating with a collectivist cultural environment would choose to reveal news of serious or terminal illness to patients.

Education in a multicultural society is the final context we will consider. Classrooms are an important setting where the sway of culture must be considered. Although educational practices at any educational level of a multicultural society are affected by the cultural diversity found in each classroom, we believe that the practice of communication in the multicultural classroom is paramount. Traditional approaches to education and the use of unicultural communication strategies are inadequate in a multicultural context. Cultural diversity affects thinking habits and strategies, communication patterns and styles, approaches to learning, and classroom behavior—to name but a few cultural influences found in the educational setting.

In her article "Culture and Communication in the Classroom," Geneva Gay introduces the semiotic relationship that exists among communication, culture, teaching, and learning. She discusses some of the critical features and pedagogical potentials for different ethnic groups of color. Her discussion of culture and communication in this article first outlines some key assertions about culture and communciation in teaching and learning in general. Gay then presents some of the major characteristics of the communicative modes of African, Native, Asian, and European Americans. Her focus throughout is on discourse dynamics; that is, who participates in communication, under what conditions, and how participation patterns are affected by culture.

Reinterpreting Japanese Business Communication in the Information Age

Steve Quasha
Edwin R. McDaniel

INTRODUCTION

Contemporary Japanese communicative behaviors are the product of a broad array of cultural antecedents. Historical events and social circumstances, coupled with geographical and environmental factors, shaped the nation's culturally instilled values and beliefs and formed current Japanese communication practices. The results of these influences are particularly evident in the communication procedures characterizing modern Japanese commercial activity.

But these culturally established communication protocols are presently endangered by the expanding influence of globalization, which is largely driven by information technology (IT) astride a Silicon Valley organizational model (Delbecq & Weiss, 1988). The pervasive influence of the IT industry and the concomitant emphasis on cross-border market penetration, transparency, and conformity carry the potential to create immense turbulence and, ultimately, effect dramatic change in Japan's business communication standards.

In the IT era, Japan's traditional harmonious, hierarchical networks will ultimately create corporate bottlenecks. The ideal of the company providing lifetime employment in return for complete loyalty and unwavering adherence to traditional corporate communication practices is incongruent with established IT organizational structures.

Japanese organizations will have to adjust to the requirements of a rapid-paced IT environment, which promotes near-constant change and optimum flexibility. Japanese business communication practices, built around social stability and communitarianism, will impede normative IT operations. In short, Japan's adaptation to IT business practices presages an acceleration of culture's normally glacial-paced evolution.

The objective of this essay is to explain how traditional Japanese modes of business communication will be jeopardized by the nation's economic push to become a global power in the IT field. The initial section provides an historical overview of the formation of Japan's modern-day hierarchical social structure and selected cultural patterns that formed the nation's 20th-century corporate communication practices. The second part discusses the potential effect of information technology on the Japanese corporate environment and the accompanying changes in business communication protocols.

HISTORICAL FORMATION OF CONTEMPORARY JAPANESE CULTURAL PATTERNS

Japan is a relatively small, insular, densely populated nation, with a somewhat homogeneous society.[1] This physical setting, along with a variety of historical forces and social circumstances, gave rise to a collection of culturally instilled beliefs, values, and behaviors that are often unique to Japan.

Events that originated or further developed many of the cultural values evident in contemporary Japan can be traced to the Tokugawa era (1600–1868). In the early 1600s, Japan was politically unified under the leadership of a military-style governor (*shogun*). Most of the population resided in or near castle towns and was divided into four distinct, hierarchical groups (i.e., *samurai*, farmer, artisan, and merchant), each with its own set of subgroups and intragroup hierarchy. The central government proscribed strict protocols regulating the conduct of every aspect of personal and public life. The objective of these conventions, grounded in Confucian orthodoxy, was to ensure external peace and internal group harmony by subordinating the individual to the greater social order. Social stability was the paramount objective (Hirschmeire & Yui, 1981).

The distinct geographical conditions, demographics, and historical circumstances that shaped contemporary Japanese social order also gave rise to culturally patterned beliefs, values, and behaviors, which have been further influenced by intergenerational evolution. Japan's early experience under Tokugawa rule, for example, instilled a continuing sense of collectivism, or group orientation, and hierarchy. Regimentation of the population into distinct groupings with separate social standings inculcated the Japanese with an acceptance of status differentiation. Proscribed protocols (i.e., a single correct way of doing things) for nearly every aspect of social conduct have been translated into an enduring dedication to social and organizational formality.

The emphasis that Tokugawa rulers placed on social stability has exerted a continuing influence on contemporary Japanese deportment. Today, this desire to maintain social balance is referred to as *wa*, most commonly translated as "harmony." The meaning of this term, however, is much more complex and can be extended to include social balance, stability, teamwork, or group spirit (Goldman, 1994; Gudykunst & Nishida, 1994). At the core of *wa* lays the philosophy of subordinating the individual to the needs of the greater whole: family, in-group, organization, nation.

Japan's historical influences coalesced to create cultural patterns that foster philosophies and values that presently guide the conduct of business and communication within Japanese organizations. For example, profit is, of course, a salient consideration in Japanese businesses, but it is often a secondary concern. Gaining market share and protecting the well-being of company employees are the primary motivations for traditional Japanese businesspeople, who see corporate–employee relations and corporate–government interactions as a series of mutual obligations, the fulfillment of which benefits everyone. Accordingly, Japanese business executives sometimes subordinate corporate profit in order to maintain harmony within the organization, the market, or the nation (De Mente, 1993; "Japan on the brink," 1998).

COMMUNICATION IN CORPORATE JAPAN

Integration of the cultural patterns of collectivism, hierarchy, formality, face, and social stability (*wa*) has created a distinct form of business communication in Japan. The Japanese tradition of group orientation, coupled with the relatively homogenous populace, has perpetuated a communication environment in which individuals are less reliant on verbal interactions. Strong, lasting in-group affiliation permits individuals to know each other intimately and to become proficient at intuitive understanding. This affiliation is abetted by a high degree of societal formality, which prescribes exacting standards of social deportment. Thus, one's actions, desires, and ambitions are normally channeled into socially accepted activities that adhere to established behavioral protocols. This structure enables the Japanese, especially other in-group members, to anticipate each other's social and communication deportment in a variety of situated contexts, thereby reducing the requirement for explicit communicative interaction. As a result, the Japanese value an individual's ability to intuitively or nonverbally discern another's desires and to draw meaning from the situational context (Ishii, 1984; Matsumoto, 1988). This approach is quite in contrast to the importance U.S. Americans place on oratory skills. The influence of the five cultural patterns can be further isolated in any number of varying commercial contexts, as this section will illustrate.

Language and Respect

The Japanese language operates on multiple hierarchical levels that depend on social context and participants. Communication patterns are based on social status and dictate the proper way to address another person. Daily conversations among friends, family members, and people of equal status use an informal variation of the language, which puts aside polite verb endings and honorific forms. Once the language migrates away from this familiar setting, however, it takes on an entirely different aura and is characterized by subtle nuances, different levels of politeness, and a plethora of status codes.

In the business environment, office workers must learn to speak honorific or polite speech (*keigo*) when they join a company. For many workers, it is their first experience using polite speech on a daily basis, and, most will admit, it can be quite challenging and takes some time to adapt. The new employee has to master a wide assortment of honorific phrases and terms that must be exercised properly to address customers, superiors, and others within particular contexts of the social hierarchy. A key consideration is that when speaking with a superior, respectful language must be used, and when referring to one's self, humble verb forms are customary (Yamada, 1997). Such a communication dynamic is dissimilar to American English, which is generally direct, has limited degrees of politeness, and often relies on voice inflection to invoke a favor or register displeasure.

The complexity and degree of difficulty of the Japanese language has also contributed to Japan's delayed entry into the global IT market. The employment of three distinct syllabaries (*hiragana*, *katakana*, and *romaji*) and a complicated system of integrated ideograms (*kanji*) tends to impede universal usage of Japanese-based software. Additionally, the subtle nuances, indirectness, and intuitiveness that characterize Japanese interpersonal interactions are difficult to transfer to an electronic medium (Hodgson, Sano, & Graham, 2000).

Rank and Status

Relative status among the Japanese people is determined by a combination of factors, such as age, sex, rank, social position, and favors performed or owed. Interpersonal communication patterns are based on the status differential and dictate the proper way to address another person.

Historically, age has played a major role in Japanese society. Filial piety forms the basis for Japan's vertical society (*tate-shakai*), and elder superiors are addressed with respect. For the post–World War II generation, this cultural notion was kept intact by the *sempai* (senior mentor)–*kohai* (junior) system. New company employees learned loyalty and diligence, while patiently awaiting their turn to climb the proverbial corporate ladder. Only when their *sempai* had retired or they had logged enough work experience did their own managerial career arrive.

From a communication perspective, March (1992) has described Japan as a "culture of command" (p. 219), which follows a vertical track. Japanese businesspeople work in an environment that places little value on verbal give-and-take between seniors and juniors. Subordinates are expected to obey post-decision directives issued by superiors without the need for discussions or justifying rationale. The subordinates are, however, allowed considerable latitude in devising appropriate measures for implementing the directive.

Sempai–Kohai Relations

The cycle of social obedience and conformance to societal expectations, largely based on the *sempai–kohai* relationship, is an integral part of Japanese society. Beginning in the K–12 educational system, the structured relationship between upper and lower classmates functions as a social apprenticeship program that permeates all school club activities, sports teams, and other extracurricular programs. University-bound students begin the process anew when they enter academic social life. After graduation, young corporate entrants quickly acquire a new *sempai*, usually someone who graduated from the same university (*gakubatsu*). The corporate sempai serves as both guide and mentor along the pathways of the chosen organization.

As part of their early corporate training, *kohai* are expected to tolerate a certain level of "hazing" from their *sempai*. A comparable analogy in the West is military officer training, during which harried new recruits quickly learn to submit to the directions of a superior officer and acquiesce to the directives of an omnipotent organization. The Japanese corporate world operates in a similarly intimidating manner. Only with proper discipline and a pure mind can honorable company troops take to the battlefields of commerce. Most young employees rapidly discern that adherence to company policy and respect for their *sempai* is critical in order to achieve upward mobility within the system.

This belief in perseverance, or the need to stoically bear the adversities of life, is a widely held Japanese cultural attribute known as *gaman*. Company employees who endure the hardships usually find corporate success because the Japanese truly believe that hard work can overcome all shortcomings (Whiting, 1990). More important, others ultimately grow to respect a *kohai* for his fighting spirit. They know that someday the *kohai* will become a *sempai* and the cycle will continue.

A glaring weakness of this socioeconomic climate, however, is that individual initiative and personal achievement is frowned upon. Instead, people within the system learn that not making waves and remaining loyal to their superiors are the best attributes to ensure success in the Japanese workforce. Company loyalty is a keystone of the post-war generation's enculturated value system. Some look at their employment, which often includes grinding 70-hour-plus workweeks, as vaguely similar to the way noble samurai stoically represented their retainers. Thus, those who persevere rise up through the ranks and are socially admired as modern-day corporate samurai.

The Corporate Setting

The influence of Japan's cultural patterns can also be isolated in varying commercial contexts, as demonstrated in the following examples.

Office Arrangements. A fundamental difference between office settings in Japan and the United States is that all Japanese workers, ranging from managers to secretaries, sit near one another. The small cubicles and partitions, which frequently corral U.S. workers into confined spaces and mark territorial boundaries, are essentially nonexistent in Japanese offices. At the middle-management level, rows of desks are positioned side-by-side or across from each other in spacious, unobstructed rooms, and employees sit in hierarchical order.

In the United States, climbing the corporate ladder has historically equated to a private office and other individual-based perks. This is not so in Japan. Other than the director of large corporations, no one within the company normally has a separate office. Instead, those in power sit among the division or section subordinates and act as role models. The Japanese believe this arrangement promotes and eases collaboration, and because everyone in a workgroup is in view of each other, employees feel compelled to perform at an optimum level. The arrangement also facilitates horizontal and vertical information

exchange among fellow in-group employees, replicating the communal nature of the traditional village-based social organization (*mura-shakai*).

Aisatsu. Yet another traditional Japanese corporate practice is the preference for, and reliance on, an initial face-to-face meeting (*aisatsu*) (Japan External Trade Organization [JETRO], 1999). Certainly, other cultures value an icebreaker meeting to help foster nascent business relationships, but the Japanese place great importance on these meetings. Japanese corporations consider entering into joint business ventures as tantamount to establishing a long-term social bond between the involved parties. Although telephone calls, e-mail, or faxes can more expediently initiate a commercial endeavor, it is customary for participants to have an *aisatsu*. Even though the parties may live on opposite ends of the Japanese archipelago or distant parts of the globe, the Japanese derive a sense of security by engaging in this human-relations-building procedure (Clark, 1983).

Many non-Japanese, especially Westerners, regard the seemingly endless *aisatsu*—which often serves as a meeting before a meeting—as a waste of time. Raised on Western linear logic, they see no need to engage in activities that hold little promise of immediate, tangible results. Nevertheless, *aisatsu* exists because interpersonal relationships are extremely important among the Japanese. For the Japanese businessman, *aisatsu* represents a critical process because the extent and content of future communication, regardless of the medium, will depend on the interactants knowing and trusting each other. The Japanese consider *aisatsu* to be the first step on the road to a long and productive relationship.

Decision Making and the Ringi System. The Japanese collective nature and desire for social stability is reflected in the group-centered corporate decision-making process.[2] The Japanese employ a bottom-up, or more accurately middle-up, procedure (*ringi seido*), which usually begins at the middle-management level, in which a few employees prepare a memo (*ringi sho*) suggesting a new venture or direction for the organization. The document is then circulated through all appropriate branches of the company, and at each level, managers and subordinates have the opportunity to examine and discuss (*nemawashi*) the potential impact of the suggestion. If a manager and his subordinates agree with the proposal, the manager endorses the document and sends it to one of his counterparts. If approved, the document will ultimately circulate to the upper management and executive levels. When a clear consensus emerges, the proposal becomes policy (Donnelly, 1993; Goldman, 1994; JETRO, 1992). If a consensus fails to emerge, the project will simply languish in someone's in-box until it is either forgotten or overtaken by events.

This communal process requires considerable time and employee involvement. Detailed, in-depth information relating to all aspects of the proposal must be acquired, widely disseminated, studied, and thoroughly discussed. When dissent is encountered, discussions and consultations are conducted in an effort to reach a consensual agreement. These deliberations may commence in the office as part of the workday routine and extend into after-work gatherings in restaurants and bars.

Once a consensual decision is achieved, however, implementation is rapid and encompassing, a result of broad employee involvement in the decision process from inception to finish. Everyone has had the opportunity to voice his or her opinion and to discuss the various options before the proposal is agreed upon. Thus, employees are already familiar with the decision, its ramifications, and the actions required for execution.

Diffused Responsibility. Characterized by information sharing through frequent meetings and discussions (*nemawashi*), the Japanese collective decision-making process (*ringi*) is also a means to ensure that no single individual has to shoulder responsibility in the event that a project does not achieve the desired or anticipated results. A Japanese corporate vice-president provided this account:

> I think that in Japan, the *ringi* system is often used to spread the responsibility and risks. If everyone puts stamps [seals or *inkan*] on the *ringi* then people get the impression that if anything goes wrong they can say, "Well, I thought it was a good idea, but so did all the other people." So you kind of spread the responsibility.

The desire to avoid individual responsibility is also noted by Hayashi (1988) in his explication of the role of communication in Japanese organizational decision making. By sharing information and achieving a consensus, no one in the Japanese organization can be blamed if the project fails. The risk is spread among everyone, thereby reducing uncertainty, contributing to in-group cooperation and cohesion, and concomitantly sustaining collective harmony by lessening the potential for personal embarrassment.

Conflict Management. How conflict is viewed and managed within a society is also a function of cultural values. For example, Japan's collectivistic inclinations and desire for social stability have inculcated the population with an aversion to open, direct conflict. Because conflict is seen as socially disruptive, detrimental to group cohesion, and a threat to one's face, measures have been spun and woven into the social fabric to help mitigate the potential for discord. This is not to say that Japanese society wholly lacks conflict, but it has been found to be less prevalent and intense than in the United States (Krauss, Rohlen, & Steinhoff, 1984).

Japanese organizations are especially sensitive to the perils of disharmony and employ a variety of means to help obviate or reduce the potential for disagreement. These measures include programs to socialize employees into considering the organization as part of their "professional and personal fulfillment" (Krauss, Rohlen, & Steinhoff, 1984, p. 382). Indeed, the most important in-group in contemporary Japanese society is the workgroup, which has become a locus of Japanese self-identity, status, loyalty, achievement, and friendship (Kashima & Callan, 1994).

Because the individual's identity will be partly derived from the organization, there is little incentive toward disruptive organizational activities. Japanese companies also incorporate small group discussions, personal communication, and trusted intermediaries to help preclude or resolve conflicts (Krauss, Rohlen, & Steinhoff, 1984). Other means include the use of consultation before meeting formally and an unquestioning acceptance of authority (Befu, 1990).

On an interpersonal level, the Japanese strive to avoid conflict or, if it is inevitable, to search for avenues of accommodation. Areas of agreement are emphasized and points of disagreement are minimized (Barnlund, 1989). Communicative strategies, detailed previously, and a complex system of reciprocal obligations (*giri* and *on*), are used as an effective impediment to interpersonal strife. Criticism, a potent source of disagreement, is expressed indirectly, using passive, accommodating styles. Confronted with the specter of conflict and potential loss of face, the Japanese might well choose to remain silent or employ nonverbal actions to express disapproval. Complaints are often channeled through humor, jokes, or via a third person.

THE INFORMATION TECHNOLOGY EFFECT

In January 2001, the Japanese government implemented a national information technology strategy designed to make Japan the world's leading IT nation within five years. The program advocates a "drastic reform of the social structure," calls for eliminating the vertical divisions in government administration, and promises that the Japanese will be "able to do the work of their choice regardless of age and sex" (Basic IT Strategy, 2000). The government's frenetic push to create an IT society could very well alter Japan's established business communication model, which rests on the culturally based social hierarchy, and usher in a period of significant change for Japanese corporate structure and communicative practices.

New Corporate Structures

A modern IT society could force Japan to create new corporate structures. According to Cairncross (1997), the traditional approach to management will no longer be effective in an IT environment. Corporations will gravitate toward a more diffuse, loosely coupled, and informal organizational structure, characterized by employees working in small groups or even alone. The company's relationship with suppliers and customers will be less personal as everyone becomes more reliant on IT communication equipment and procedures.

IT industries are also distinguished by advanced computer systems, which normally include large databases connected to intranets available to a preponderance of employees, regardless of division or section (Cairncross, 1997). This portends a weakening of Japanese corporate divisions, where it is common to use information secrecy (*maruhi*) to gain an advantage over rivals within the same organization (Yoshimura & Anderson, 1997).

State-of-the-art communication, such as e-mail, also carries the potential to erode Japanese corporate hierarchies by providing junior employees with direct access to senior executives, skirting middle managers. A story widely circulated in Tokyo in late 1999 concerned a first-year employee who had sent an e-mail message directly to the president of a major Japanese company, and the president had responded. Many of the company's middle-level managers had begun to openly question their role and purpose in the hierarchal, vertical communication chain.

Not only do IT developments provide avenues to circumvent middle managers, but they also allow creative and industrious junior employees to advance ideas without having to endure the cumbersome, and potentially initiative-suppressing, processes of *nemawashi* and *ringi* (Nakasako, 1998). This can promote an erosion of Japan's autocratic institutions and heighten the opportunity to achieve a more merit-based system.

Yet another convention of IT industries is the virtual workgroup, where employees are selected for their individual skills regardless of physical location, electronically merge to fulfill the requirements of a specific project, and then return to their parent division without ever actually meeting face-to-face. Virtual workgroups, along with telecommuters, can seriously undermine Japan's entrenched concept of the workgroup as the primary source of personal identity and basis for social interaction. How, for example, can a geographically separated virtual workgroup meet at a bar or restaurant after work to continue their discussions (*nemawashi*) or express complaints to the section (*kacho*) or division (*bucho*) head?

Generation Gap

Until recently, Japan's long-established *sempai–kohai* system depended on an age-based seniority relationship, complemented by perceived expertise, or skills and experiences, that correlated to the number of employment years. The normative procedure was to graduate from a university, secure a corporate position, and stoically accept the drudgery of a salary man's (*sarariman*) life, while patiently waiting one's turn for advancement.

Rather than following the status quo of their fathers' generation, however, some young Japanese are breaking new ground by starting companies with only a year or two of personal work experience or, in some instances, straight out of university. Their opportunities are facilitated by the IT industry, which makes business start-ups easier to get off the ground by reducing initial overhead costs and relying on small, flexible organizations (Cairncross, 1997; Delbecq & Weiss, 1988; Sprague & Mutsuko, 2000).

A reduction in the total number of Japanese company employees occurred in 1999, partly because of young people's aversion to becoming "salary men" (Sprague & Murakami, 2000). Job-hopping for the sake of gaining personal experience and diverse expertise is also growing in popularity among younger workers. Many see few reasons to log endless hours for the sake of company loyalty, as their fathers' generation did, and instead seek to secure a job that promises a better quality of life. During an interview with one of the authors, a Western executive in the Tokyo subsidiary of a major U.S. corporation reported that it had become much easier to hire young Japanese workers because employment with the U.S. company allowed them greater freedom and more opportunity to pursue hobbies and other recreational interests. Unlike working for a Japanese corporation, they are not required to devote all of their waking hours and energies to the company.

This seemingly minor shift in employment patterns portends a sea change for traditional Japanese business communication conventions. Until recently, age was the pivotal factor in the hierarchical structure of Japanese corporate communication, but a successful IT-based environment creates opportunities for a more merit-based system. Age, social status, or socioeconomic positions are not considered to be impediments in the IT field (Delbecq & Weiss, 1988). If this system evolves in Japan, the traditional corporate communication practices would rapidly become obsolete. How, for example, would the middle-aged salary-men speak to younger, more talented people in their field?

Based on the tenets of Japan's present hierarchical society, elders would be forced to defer to those with higher social status. A young corporate president or vice-president, for instance, would have to be addressed in honorific language because he or she would be superior in employment rank. Japan's rapidly aging society, shrinking labor pool, and current social dynamics suggest a more mobile workforce, with younger company presidents and executives eventually managing large numbers of people much older than themselves. Can the *sempai–kohai* system endure such a reversal of age-based roles? Employees who are still wedded to the cultural notion of the company protecting its workforce because of loyalty or longevity will have difficulty adjusting to the new IT environment.

Immigration of IT Workers

Japan's rapidly graying population and declining birthrate is creating an ever-diminishing national workforce, which has become especially acute in the IT industry. To compensate, Japan is being forced to open its doors to foreign immigration. This was illustrated by the government's acceleration of the process to grant residence status to Indian IT engineers ("Japan to streamline," 2001).

The introduction of significant levels of foreign workers will send shock waves through Japan's relatively homogeneous population and significantly impact current business communication conventions. Because the inherent complexities of the Japanese language make it difficult for foreigners to achieve high levels of fluency, the Japanese will be denied the use of intuitive understanding and the language's more subtle references when communicating with foreign employees. International employees are also less likely to attempt to master the many honorific forms (*keigo*) of polite speech. This situation will, of course, prove to be a source of misunderstanding and difficulty that adversely affects societal harmony (*wa*).

Equally important is that highly educated and talented foreign workers will be far less inclined to attach their identities to the company or to patiently wait for their turn to advance. Those workers coming from individualistic cultures will demand greater self-recognition and personal rewards for their creative efforts. The time-consuming process of *nemawashi* and *ringi* will be eschewed for more rapid and individualistic decision making. *Aisatsu* will be perceived as too time consuming, insufficiently productive, and just simply unnecessary.

Long-Term Relations

The role of interpersonal relations has long been a cornerstone of Japanese corporate endeavors. Companies promote long-term relationships with other organizations through a gradual, continual process, in which mutual trust and cooperation is paramount. The process also requires significant time and effort for the relationship to reach a mature level. When a business relationship transpires, companies initially place small trial orders to test both the sincerity of the agreement and quality of the merchandise. This may occur quite a few times until the purchasing party feels that mutual trust has been established and both parties understand one another. Once this level of relationship has been attained, the parties expect to enjoy a long and productive relationship.

Since its inception on the other side of the Pacific, the IT industry has tended to follow the Silicon Valley organizational model. In this model, corporate decision making must be swift in order to respond to emergent or shifting market conditions. The cooperative relationship-building process that exists in Japan becomes secondary to the shorter-term reality of recognizing and capitalizing on profit-promoting opportunities.

This creates a cultural chasm between current IT practices and traditional Japanese business conventions. The time-consuming Japanese communication protocols (i.e., *aisatsu*, *nemawashi*, and *ringi*) associated with relationship building and maintenance rapidly become an impediment in the dynamic IT environment, where companies will often form temporary relations in order to enhance their position in a particular market. These unions are usually designed around a particular opportunity and are dissolved when the opportunity is realized or passes. In these dynamic situations, relationships become secondary and communication must accommodate the rapid pace of events.

Decision Making in the IT Environment

As it has evolved in the United States, the IT industry demands constant innovation and rapid response to dynamic global market conditions. Success requires individual initiative and quick decisions, often based on a minimum of information. This scenario is the antithesis of traditional Japanese corporate practices.

An inability to promptly institute or alter corporate decisions, even in the wake of changing economic conditions, is a byproduct of Japanese communication style. Circulating proposals within the *ringi* system requires time and countless deliberations by the participants. As previously discussed, once a decision has been reached, it is etched in stone. Compared to the United States, Japanese proposals take a longer time to ratify because a clear group consensus must be attained to help ensure social stability and diffused personal responsibility. U.S. businesspeople, on the other hand, are more reliant on intuitive judgments and tend to hastily cobble together ideas with the full expectation that further revisions, based on market-driven conditions, are necessary to optimize the final result or product (Kagawa, 1997).

These are two quite different decision-making models. Although each one certainly fits the cultural framework of its participants, it appears that Japan is at a disadvantage in the fast-paced nature of today's IT-based economy. Rapid introduction of products and quick shifts in manufacturing lines are endemic to the current global IT industry. To date, this situation has not boded well for Japanese businesspeople, whose inherently slow decision making prevents larger organizations from staying nimble and hinders their ability to capture positions in emergent or changing markets.

The necessity to make rapid decisions will also have an unsettling influence on the assignment of responsibility. If Japanese IT employees are expected to make quick judgments, without benefit of the time-consuming *ringi* or *nemawashi* processes, decision making will become more individual based. In those instances where the chosen course of action results in unfavorable outcomes, the decision maker will be forced to accept greater personal responsibility, along with the inevitable loss of face and resultant potential for intragroup conflict. This scenario begs the question of whether the culturally ingrained concern for face and the desire to avoid open conflict can be overcome.

CONCLUSIONS

In the past, Japan's corporate framework relied on a diligent workforce that unquestioningly adhered to the company's philosophy, which often meant maintaining the status quo. Lifetime employment with a large, well-known company was the dream for all graduates from Japan's best universities, and years of service equated to incremental increases in wages. With the development of a merit-based IT system, however, the potential for social transformation looms large. Japan's harmonious, hierarchical corporate structure becomes a bottleneck when used as a template for contemporary IT industries, which have developed and honed the Silicon Valley organizational model of small, informal, flexible companies.

Intragenerational communication will be altered as younger people in power attempt to resuscitate the long-ailing economy. The inherent difficulty of the Japanese language, compounded by its indirect, nonconfrontational nature, will become an impediment when dealing with foreign IT workers. The rise of a young entrepreneurial class carries the potential for eroding the well-established *sempai–kohai* system, along with its concomitant communication conventions. The IT industry's demand for expedient decisions will clash with the entrenched *ringi* system and force greater individual responsibility for corporate choices.

According to Rogers & Shoemaker (1971), the adoption of technological advances depends on the "compatibility with the cultural beliefs of the social system" (1971, p. 5). This prerequisite does not bode well for Japan, which has long demonstrated a preference for continuity over change. In order to achieve its stated desire to become the world's leading IT nation, Japan will have to enact sweeping alterations to the traditional corporate structure and communication model in a relatively short time frame. The long-enduring penchants for group orientation and group-associated communication behaviors will become an enervating obstruction (Fukukawa, 2000). The ability to achieve a new communication model will depend on the degree of difficulty in changing the current culturally based model. In the end, it will prove to be a test of the Japanese businesspeople's desire and ability to accelerate the normally glacial pace of cultural change in order to achieve new corporate structures and communication conventions.

Endnotes

1. The homogeneity of Japanese society is often overstated. Although the population is characterized by greater similitude than is found in most other nations, there is considerable diversity within Japan. This diversity has also become a topic of scholarly inquiry. Michael Weiner (1997) and his colleagues, for example, provide an analysis of six distinct Japanese minorities (*Ainu, Burakumin,* Chinese, Koreans, *Nikkeijin,* and Okinawans). Our own experience has disclosed variety in regional customs, norms, and language usage (e.g., Tokyo versus *Kansai* dialect).
2. The decision-making process described here is greatly simplified and has traditionally been employed in large Japanese corporations (*kaisha*), especially the trading companies. Moreover, "major decisions on investment and financing are made or carefully reviewed by top management and the 'consensus' approach is not applied" (Japan External Trade Organization, 1992, p. 3). In smaller, individually owned companies, it is not unprecedented for the company president/owner to make unilateral decisions.

References

Barnlund, D. C. (1989). *Communicative styles of Japanese and Americans.* Belmont, CA: Wadsworth.

Basic IT Strategy (2000, November 27). IT Strategy Council. Available at www.kantei.go.jp/foreign/it/council/basic_it.html. Accessed February 16, 2001.

Befu, H. (1990). Four models of Japanese society and their relevance to conflict. In S. N. Eisenstadt & E. Ben-Ari (Eds.), *Japanese models of conflict resolution* (pp. 213–238). New York: Kegan Paul International.

Cairncross, F. (1997). *The death of distance: How the communications revolution will change our lives.* Cambridge, MA: Harvard Business School.

Clark, G. (1983). *Understanding the Japanese.* Tokyo: Kinseido Press.

Clark, R. (1979). *The Japanese company.* New Haven, CT: Yale University Press.

Delbecq, A. L., & Weiss, J. (1988). The business culture of Silicon Valley: Is it a model for the future? In J. Hage (Ed.), *Futures of organizations: Innovating to adapt strategy and human resources to rapid technological change* (pp. 124–141). Lexington, MA: Lexington Books.

De Mente, B. L. (1993). *Behind the Japanese bow: An in-depth guide to understanding and predicting Japanese behavior*. Chicago: Passport Books.

Donnelly, M. (1993). On political negotiation: America pushes to open up Japan. *Pacific Affairs, 66*, 329–350.

Fukukawa, S. (2000). Awaking to the IT revolution. *Japan Quarterly, 47*, 16–22.

Goldman, A. (1994). *Doing business with the Japanese*. Albany: State University of New York Press.

Gudykunst, W. B., & Nishida, T. (1994). *Bridging Japanese/North American differences*. Thousand Oaks, CA: Sage.

Hayashi, S. (1988). *Culture and management in Japan* (F. Baldwin, Trans.). Tokyo: University of Tokyo Press.

Hirschmeire, J., & Yui, T. (1981). *The development of Japanese business* (2nd ed.). Boston: George Allen & Unwin.

Hodgson, J. D., Sano, Y., & Graham, J. L. (2000). *Doing business with the new Japan*. Lanham, MD: Rowman & Littlefield.

Ishii, S. (1984). *Enryo-sashi* communication. A key to understanding Japanese interpersonal relations. *Cross Currents, 11*, 49–58.

Japan External Trade Organization. (1992). *Japanese corporate decision making*. JETRO Business Information Series. Tokyo: Author.

Japan External Trade Organization. (1999). *Doing business in Japan*. JETRO Marketing Series. Tokyo: Author.

"Japan on the brink." (1998, April 11). *The Economist*, 15–17.

"Japan to streamline immigration for Indian engineers." (2001, February 9). *Jiji Press English News Service*. Tokyo.

Kagawa, H. (1997). *The inscrutable Japanese*. Tokyo: Kodansha International.

Kashima, Y., & Callan, V. J. (1994). The Japanese work group. In H. C. Triandis, M. D. Dunnette, & L. M. Hough (Eds.) *Handbook of industrial and organizational psychology: Vol. 4* (2nd ed., pp. 609–645). Palo Alto, CA: Consulting Psychologist Press.

Krauss, E. S., Rohlen, T. P., & Steinhoff, P. G. (1984). Conflict and its resolution in postwar Japan. In E. S. Krauss, T. P. Rohlen, & P. G. Steinhoff (Eds.), *Conflict in Japan* (pp. 375–397). Honolulu: University of Hawaii Press.

March, R. M. (1992). *Working for a Japanese company*. Tokyo: Kodansha.

Matsumoto, M. (1988). *The unspoken way: Haragei – silence in Japanese business and society*. Tokyo: Kodsansha.

Nakasako, S. (1998). Japan. *Business Communication Quarterly, 61*, 101–106.

Rogers, E. M., & Shoemaker, F. F. (1971). *Communication of innovations: A cross-cultural approach*. New York: The Free Press.

Sprague, J., & Mutsuko, M. (2000). Japan's new attitude. *AsiaWeek, 26*. Available at www.asiaweek.com/asiaweek/magazine/2000/1020/cover1.html.

Weiner, M. (Ed.). (1997). *Japan's minorities: The illusion of homogenity*. New York: Routledge.

Whiting, R. (1990). *You gotta have* Wa. New York: Vintage Books.

Yamada, H. (1997). *Different games, different rules*. New York: Oxford Press.

Yoshimura, N., & Anderson, P. (1997). *Inside the Kaisha: Demystifying Japanese business behavior*. Boston: Harvard Business School Press.

Concepts and Questions

1. What aspects of traditional Japanese business communication practices are not directly suited for an IT-based business climate?

2. How do the cultural patterns of collectivism, hierarchy, formality, face, and social stability influence communication within Japanese businesses?

3. What dynamics of the Japanese language reflect respect during interaction?

4. How does rank and status affect communication within Japanese businesses?

5. What is the *sempai–kohai* relationship in Japanese culture? How does it affect communication practices in Japanese companies?

6. How does the arrangement of offices in Japan differ from those in the United States? How does each form of office arrangement influence communication in Japan and the United States?

7. What are the differences in decision-making processes found in Japanese and U.S. businesses?

8. In what way might IT-based communication affect the corporate structure of Japanese companies?

9. How might IT-based communication impinge on the hierarchical structure of Japanese corporations?

10. The development of long-term interpersonal relationships has been a cornerstone of Japanese corporate activities. How might information technology affect these relationships?

292   Chapter 6 Cultural Contexts: The Influence of the Setting

U.S. Americans and Mexicans Working Together: Five Core Mexican Concepts for Enhancing Effectiveness

SHERYL L. LINDSLEY
CHARLES A. BRAITHWAITE

I was disadvantaged when I first came down here [to Mexico] because I didn't have the class [multicultural training]. I'm probably still doing some things wrong now. When I go to business meetings, I was raised in a culture where you just get out your reports and start talking about them and that's not how it is here. Here you talk about family and other things first. I often forget this and so one of my Mexican colleagues will remind me that I am violating this tradition by saying, "So, [name], how is your dog?" When I hear this then I know I'm not supposed to be talking about business. (Lindsley, 1995, p. 239)

This account by a U.S. American who lives and works in Mexico reflects the importance of adapting cultural behaviors to achieve communication competency in organizational settings. As an administrator who was transferred to Mexico more than eight years ago without any intercultural training, he's learned the hard way that lack of cultural knowledge and skills negatively affects organizational relationships, goals, and productivity. In this account, it appears that he still struggles to put aside that U.S. American "Let's get right down to business" orientation in order to prioritize personal relationships in meetings with his Mexican associates. A look at the literature on U.S. American experiences abroad tells us that his problems in intercultural communication are not unique.

Although U.S. American organizations are increasingly reliant on international liaisons to compete in the global economy, many have suffered failures as a result of inadequate managerial training for work abroad (Albert, 1994). These problems have resulted in tremendous financial losses to organizations as well as human costs by undermining job successes and increasing personal and familial suffering (Mendenhall et al., 1987). These international experiences demonstrate that one cannot simply export U.S. American ways of doing business to other countries. Rather, personnel in international organizations must understand the histories, cultures, and languages of the people with whom they work. This essay will review recent events affecting U.S.–Mexican economic relationships and then examine five Mexican cultural concepts influencing organizational effectiveness.

The historical ratification of the North American Free Trade Agreement (NAFTA) between the United States, Canada, and Mexico embodies both promises and problems. Government leaders who supported the bill promised increased competitiveness with other trade blocs such as the European Economic Community (EEC) and the Pacific Rim nations, along with larger consumer markets for good and services and, ultimately, increased prosperity (Weintraub, 1991). At the same time, this alliance created new problems and highlighted old ones that remain unresolved (Davidson, 2000). Critics have charged that the agreement promotes the interests of only large international and multinational firms, at the expense of smaller businesses and ordinary people in all three nations (Castañeda, 1995). In the United States, domestic manufacturers have problems competing with products made with inexpensive Mexican labor, and many citizens have lost jobs when factories relocated south of the border. In Mexico, many people fear increased national dependency on the United States for employment (Hansen, 1981; Sklair, 1993) and difficulties in competing with large U.S. multinationals in many service and product sectors (Batres, 1991; Hellman, 1994).

Finally, critics on both sides of the border have pointed to problems with several U.S.-owned assembly plants in Mexico that have exploited inexpensive labor (Prieto, 1997), failed to provide adequate health and safety conditions for workers, and polluted the borderlands and waterways (Fernandez-Kelly, 1983; Pena, 1997). Although a comprehensive review of international relationships between these two countries is beyond the scope of this article, it is important to understand these issues because they contribute to the conditions in which businesses operate and the way people from both countries interpret each other's behavior in everyday work relationships.

In an environment characterized by anxiety about ongoing economic changes, the need for mutual understanding and respect is critical. One way for those who are unfamiliar with Mexican culture to begin to understand it is to examine some of the core cultural concepts that guide organizational relationships. Of course, it is essential to keep in mind that diversity exists within both U.S. American and Mexican societies related to socioeconomic class, ethnic origin, regional affiliation, gender, personal ideologies, and character. Thus, when the term *U.S. American* or *North American* culture is used, it refers to the dominant cultural characteristics—typically, middle-class, of the European American male. Among Mexicans, too, it is important to recognize that adherence to dominant cultural characteristics varies within the population, and although most Mexicans are *mestizos*, of both Spanish and indigenous origin, several ethnic groups have maintained aspects of their precolonial traditions. For example, more than 600,000 people who live on the Yucatan peninsula today speak predominantly Mayan languages among their family, friends, and community members. Because many Mayans learn Spanish as a second language to interact with other Mexicans, they often do not speak it with the same fluency as their first tongue, which likely influences satisfaction and effectiveness in interethnic work relationships (Love, 1994). Regional and ethnic differences also affect the structures of modern-day businesses. Although indigenous Mayans from Mexico's southern highlands emphasize corporate organization, northern Mexican businesses embody characteristics of traditional patronage systems (Alvarez & Collier, 1994).

Diversity notwithstanding, many behaviors that are typical of dominant cultural patterns in each country provide a useful starting point for developing intercultural awareness. These shared cultural patterns have been referred to as *core concepts*. Core concepts provide us with knowledge about appropriate and inappropriate cultural interactions in specific relationships and contexts (Lindsley, 1999a). Through an understanding of these concepts, one can choose from a myriad of ways of behaving in order to enhance intercultural work relationships and goals. Core concepts derived from research on doing business in Mexico include *confianza, simpatía, palanca, estabilidad*, and *mañana*. Throughout the discussion, it will be apparent that these are not mutually exclusive categories, but rather overlapping concepts that reflect deeply held values for many Mexicans.

CONFIANZA

In an interview with a Mexican production manager about communication with U.S. home office personnel, I asked her what she does when she thinks someone is wrong. She responded:

> Well, it's hard at first if someone is new, but after you establish trust and confidence, then it's easier. . . . I just make suggestions about things, but I don't tell people they are wrong. I just give them information to make the decisions and then they are grateful and the relationship benefits from this. . . . When you just make suggestions and don't tell people what to do and let them learn and make decisions for themselves, then more confidence in the relationship develops and then they owe you. You didn't confront them, you treated them well, with respect, and now they owe you. (Lindsley & Braithwaite 1996, p. 215)

According to this account, indirectness is appropriate in a situation in which another's face (of self-presentation) is vulnerable. Because relationships are generally more central to Mexican than U.S. American organizations, it is no surprise that relationships are carefully nurtured and safeguarded. One of the core aspects of a good relationship is the co-creation of *confianza*, or "trust," which is built through communicative behaviors that adhere to cultural norms for face saving. In addition, the aforementioned production manager's account reveals cultural norms for mutual obligation. There is an explicit reference to reciprocity—each party should protect the other's positive face in interaction.

The kinds of situations in which face concerns are primary include those that could possibly be threatening to one's own image or the other party with whom one is interacting. This means that communication of negative information (e.g., I don't understand; I made a mistake; I disagree with you; You made a mistake) is avoided or communicated indirectly. For example, a person's tone of voice may indicate they he or she is reticent to adopt a new plan, even though this is not stated explicitly. Among the ways that U.S. American managers can adapt their own behaviors are avoiding displays of negative emotions, especially direct criticism, conveying receptivity to negative information, asking how they can help their employees, and paying close attention to nonverbal behaviors.

SIMPATÍA

In an interview with another Mexican production manager, he stated that the importance of good communication between managers and employees is not only in maintaining positive working relationships, but also in meeting productivity goals. He explained:

> When I have to discipline an employee, I start off by talking about the person's place in the corporation and what they are there for . . . what their role is in the plant. Then I talk to them about what they need to do. It is important not to hurt the employee, because once you do— [he shrugs, as if to say, "it's the end."] (Lindsley, 1999a, p. 32)

It is evident that this situation, in which the employee's behavior was not meeting organizational standards, was potentially face threatening. In addressing the situation, the manager demonstrated adherence to the cultural script of *simpatía*, which emphasizes emotional support and self-sacrifice for the good of the group (Triandis et al., 1984). The norm for "good communication" is evaluated through the types of interpersonal linkages that connect people in their familial, social, and organizational lives. Communication competency is described as developing over the course of long-term relationships, through interaction occurring both within and outside the plant. One Hermosillan manufacturing manager explained:

> Our communication is really good here. The informal communication is really the most important thing. A number of people here knew each other in high school, for example, I knew [name] in high school, I also knew the trainer [name] in high school, so we had known each other for a long time and done things together outside the plant. This is really important in contributing to the communication at the plant. (Lindsley, 1999b, p. 12)

The effects of this cultural script on communication include culturally normative behaviors that stress commitment to harmony and cooperation. Thus, communication that stresses the positive and minimizes negative feedback is emphasized. In this case, criticism is couched in terms of the individual's importance to the group (his or her role in the organization), which is stated in positive terms, showing concern for the employee's feelings. In Mexico, a person who is considered *simpático* "is sympathetic, understanding, pleasing, friendly, well-behaved, (and) trustworthy" (DeMente, 1996, p. 278). Being *simpático* is something to strive for in organizational relationships and is demonstrated through communication behaviors that show positive emotional connection with others.

PALANCA

The concept of *palanca* refers to leverage, or power derived from affiliated connections. It affects organizational relationships in terms of one's ability to get things done by virtue of one's official authority as well as through one's contacts with extensive networks of relationships among family members, relatives, former classmates, friends, and business associates. These connections are often built over many years and enable one to obtain favors that may transcend institutional rules and procedures or overcome scarcity of resources and services (Archer & Fitch, 1994). For example, interpersonal connections may allow one to receive "special" consideration for business transactions, faster service in obtaining government services, and personal recommendations for new jobs.

U.S. Americans may tend to evaluate these practices negatively as "corrupt" without reflecting on the similarities with their own organizational behaviors or without understanding the rationale for why these behaviors are functional in Mexican culture. It is typical in the United States for businesspeople to say, "Who you know is just as important, if not more so, than what you know," and to rely on personal affiliations for special introductions, advice, and information to promote their business goals. In Mexico, the importance of these interpersonal affiliations in business have been described as evolving from a history in which official authority was held for hundreds of years by descendants of Spanish colonial conquerors and government that were not representative of the majority of the people, but which served the interests of a small elite. Even today, one of the challenges of all Presidential administrations is to establish a true representative democracy (Castañeda, 1995). Therefore, one of the ways that people work to protect themselves and promote their interests is through informal systems of affiliated connection. U.S. Americans often rely on a system of written laws and rules, but history has taught Mexicans that it is often more effective to rely on personal connections for social negotiation of written laws and rules to accomplish desired objectives.

Although the use of *palanca* is typical throughout Central and Latin America, it is important to differentiate from *mordida* (paying a bribe) and to understand that both Mexican laws and U.S. American international laws (e.g., the Foreign Corrupt Practices Act) prohibit payments for certain kinds of services. Although the differentiation is murky, *palanca* embodies a system of mutual obligation and reciprocated favors, not necessarily money or gifts. In this matter, like all other aspects of culture, Mexican business practices are changing. In addition, there are differences among Mexicans in the way any particular behavior is evaluated.

For example, some individuals perceive that giving a small fee to a government worker for processing paperwork expeditiously is something positive and similar to the U.S. practice of tipping a food server for good service. Others might think it is inappropriate to give a "tip" but appropriate to reward good service by giving a gift afterward or simply making a point to tell that person's boss about how satisfied they are with the employee (Lindsley, 1995). In consideration of these issues, U.S. Americans need to be aware not only of the power of affiliated connections, but also of current laws and Mexicans' individual attitudes about special favors and consideration.

ESTABILIDAD

A common sentiment among many Mexicans is, "The family is our first priority and must remain so for the future stability of our country" (Kras, 1989, p. 27). The need for *estabilidad* or "stability" reinforces the value of personal relationships and permeates organizational behaviors. It is reflected in the tendency for Mexicans to place relationships before tasks. This view is communicated through a wide range of behaviors, including asking questions about colleagues' families, discussing personal matters before business (e.g., at the beginning of a meeting), taking action to promote employees' personal well-being, including families in organizational activities, taking time off work to assist family members in need, and establishing, developing, and maintaining long-term interconnected networks of personal relationships. One Mexican manager explained the positive nature of familial stability as an adaptive force in an uncertain world. He said, "Families give us stability in Mexican culture. Men want stability in families because the Mexican economy and politics are sometimes not stable. In Mexico the family is the stable foundation" (Lindsley, 1995, p. 129).

Some of the ways that managers show responsibility for employees' well-being may be through *compradrazgo* and *comadrazgo* systems in which they become godfathers, godmothers, and mentors for their employees' children. This type of relationship, which dates back to the 16th century, is viewed as mutually beneficial because young people can rely on their mentors for advice, guidance, and financial, spiritual, and social support. In return, mentors can count on the loyalty of the young people throughout their lives.

These types of relationships exemplify the extent to which Mexican personal and organizational roles overlap in contrast to U.S. roles that are typically more separate. American managers often criticize the reluctance to separate personal life from work life in Mexico. Kopinak (1996) describes an American manager being bothered by this characteristic because "I could argue with a person at work and still have a beer with him after work (in the U.S.) whereas the Mexicans wouldn't do this" (p. 55). The often-blurred distinction between familial and organizational life also means that Mexicans may give preference to hiring relatives over strangers, helping employees get a better education, or giving them small personal loans. These favors are often reciprocated with strong employee support and loyalty to the manager. For example, during financial hardships, the employee might continue working for his or her manager without a pay check (Alvarez & Collier, 1994). Like other aspects of culture, this is an adaptive mechanism in Mexico—building stability through interconnected networks of familial and organizational relationships provides "social insurance" against the vagaries of uncertainty in economic and political structures.

Concerns for stability are also manifest in some Mexicans' negative attitudes about U.S. American investment in Mexico. Historically, U.S. Americans have often acted in ways that promoted their own interests at the expense of Mexicans, which has led to criticism that U.S. involvement in Mexico threatens Mexican economic, political, and cultural stability. When U.S. American organizational personnel go to Mexico with attitudes of cultural superiority (e.g., "We're going to teach Mexicans how to do business"), negative stereotypes are reinforced about U.S. Americans as arrogant, exploitive, and self-centered. In this case, fear about threats to stability may emerge when U.S. Americans are in higher-power positions and try to use their authority to change Mexican culture, laws, policies, and so on. To establish positive working relationships, these stereotypes and the behaviors that reinforce them must be addressed. Although there are no guaranteed ways to combat stereotypes, a good beginning is awareness that these stereotypes exist. The next step, of course, is developing intercultural awareness and skills in order to adapt behaviors in ways that show an understanding and respect for Mexican culture and language. Mexicans and U.S. Americans can and do learn to appreciate aspects of each other's cultures, but this cannot be accomplished

without mutual openness and trust based on true respect and understanding, not one-sided opportunistic motives.

MAÑANA

In intercultural interaction in organizations, Mexicans and U.S. Americans often find themselves at odds over different understandings and attitudes surrounding the concept of time. Misunderstandings may arise in intercultural interpretations of language:

> Spanish language dictionaries say that *mañana* means "tomorrow," and that is the meaning taught to foreign students in the language. But "tomorrow" is a literal translation, not the true cultural meaning of the word. In its normal cultural context *mañana* means "sometime in the near future, maybe." Behind the term are such unspoken things as "If I feel like it," "If I have the time," or "If nothing unexpected happens." (DeMente, 1996, p. 183)

U.S. Americans have the tendency to think about mañana as referring to some specific time period beginning at 12 A.M. and running for 24 hours because of a primarily external orientation toward time (clocks guide activities). Most Mexicans use time clocks but also consider time to be more interpersonally negotiable (relationships guide activities), and what counts as being "on time" can be mediated by unexpected events beyond one's control. In Mexico, organizational tasks are often not accomplished as quickly as in the United States because of infrastructural conditions (e.g., telephone service, roads, electricity, water, mail) and other structural elements (e.g., government bureaucracy) that can slow progress. Moreover, beyond the physical world, metaphorical forces influence people's lives. For example, events occur "*Si Dios quiere*" (God willing). Therefore, for Mexicans it is very adaptive in interaction to acknowledge that events occur that one cannot control and that influence the flow of organizational processes.

In addition, Mexicans' attitudes toward time differ from that of U.S. Americans because of relatively differing values that influence how one organizes one's behaviors. One Mexican manager explained to me, "In Mexico we have a saying, '*Salud, dinero, amor y tempo para disfrutarlos'* (Health, wealth, love and time for enjoying them)." He contrasted this concept with such American sayings as "Time is money." Thus, while Mexicans perceive time as functioning in a way that allows one to engage in behaviors that are part of a desirable life, U.S. Americans quantify time as a commodity that is most importantly viewed as related to profits. As one writer on border communication has noted:

> You may take much longer establishing a relationship with your Mexican prospects, and you may spend hours talking about anything except the details of the purchase; but once you're in the door, you're likely to be their supplier for a long time . . . don't expect to get right down to business until you've established at least the beginnings of a friendship. (Webber, 1993, p. 20)

These contrasts in cultural orientation toward time can exacerbate problems in intercultural interaction. When U.S. Americans do not take time to develop and maintain good interpersonal relationships in business, Mexicans may think they do not care about people, only money. Likewise, when Mexicans do not complete tasks "on time," U.S. Americans may think they're lazy. To overcome these misunderstandings, U.S. Americans need to adapt their behaviors to respond to the recognition that personal relationships are the foundation of good business in Mexico and adjust their attitudes to recognize that Mexicans work very hard but have other priorities in life, too.

SUMMARY

U.S. organizations often have given employees foreign assignments based on technical expertise; however, experience shows that intercultural communication competency is critical to organization success. Through an understanding of the concepts of *confianza, simpatía, palanca, estabilidad,* and *mañana,* one can better adapt to working in Mexico. In business, cultural diversity can be a strength that managers can build on when personnel understand the ways that culture affects organizational lives. Thus, cultural contrasts in ways of doing business should not be viewed as simply a

problem, but rather as an advantage in contributing to new understandings about ways of conducting business.

Significantly, U.S. Americans who learn to adapt their behaviors have reported enjoying the closeness of Mexican relationships, their emphasis on family values, as well as their hard work ethic and employee loyalty. Mexicans working in U.S. organizations have reported enjoying their career opportunities, learning efficiency in developing schedules, and training in new kinds of management philosophies. And many Mexicans understand the importance of such adaptation, as reflected in this common tale told by a Mexican administrator in a U.S.-owned Maquiladora, which is an industry located along the border between the United States and Mexico:

> There is a mouse, a cat, and a dog that live together in the same house. The mouse has a child and is trying to teach the baby mouse how to survive. So the mom mouse tells her baby, "Listen before you go outside, and if you hear *meow-meow,* then don't go outside because it's the cat, and if you hear *hrrr-hrrr,* you can go outside because it's the dog." So one day, the baby mouse is listening at the door and it hears *hrrr-hrrr,* so, confident that it's the dog, he goes outside. . . . Unfortunately, it's the cat. The cat grins and says, "Isn't it great to be bilingual?" (Lindsley, 1995, p. 210)

References

Albert, R. D. (1994). Cultural diversity and international training in multinational organizations. In R. L. Wiseman & R. Shuter (Eds.), *Communicating in multinational organizations* (pp. 153–165). Thousand Oaks, CA: Sage.

Alvarez, R. R., & Collier, G. A. (1994). The long haul in trucking: Traversing the borderlands of the North and South. *American Ethnologist, 21,* 606–627.

Archer, L., & Fitch, K. L. (1994). Communication in Latin American multinational organizations. In R. L. Wiseman & R. Shurer (Eds.), *Communicating in multinational organizations* (pp. 75–93). Thousand Oaks, CA: Sage.

Batres, R. E. (1991). A Mexican view of the North American Free Trade Agreement. *Columbia Journal of Business, 26,* 78–81.

Casteñeda, J. G. (1995). *The Mexican shock: The meaning for the U.S.* New York: The New Press.

Davidson, M. (2000). *Lives on the line: Dispatches from the U.S.–Mexico Border*. Tucson: University of Arizona Press.

DeMente, B. L. (1996). *NTC's Dictionary of Mexican cultural code words*. Lincolnwood, IL: NTC Publishing Group.

Fernandez-Kelly, M. P. (1983). *For we are sold, I and my people: Women and industry in Mexico's frontier*. Albany: State University of New York Press.

Hansen, N. (1981). *The border economy*. Austin: University of Texas Press.

Hellman, J. A. (1994). *Mexican lives*. New York: The New Press.

Kopinak, K. (1996). *Desert capitalism: Maquiladoras in North America's western industrial corridor*. Tucson: University of Arizon Press.

Kras, E. S. (1989). *Management in two cultures*. Yarmouth, ME: Intercultural Press.

Lindsley, S. L. (1995) *Problematic communication: An intercultural study of communication competency in maquiladoras*. Unpublished doctoral dissertation. Tempe: Arizona State University.

Lindsley, S. L. (1999a). A layered model of problematic intercultural communication in U.S.-owned Maquiladoras in Mexico. *Communication Monographs, 66*, 145–167.

Lindsley, S. L. (1999b). Communication and "The Mexican way": Stability and trust as core symbols in maquiladoras. *Western Journal of Communication, 63*, 1–31.

Lindsley, S. L., & Braithwaite, C. A. (1996). "You should wear a mask": Facework norms in cultural and intercultural conflict in maquiladoras. *International Journal of Intercultural Relations, 20*, 199–225.

Love, B. (1994). *Mayan culture today*. Valladolid, Yucatan: ServiGraf Peninsular.

Mendenhall, M. E., Dunbar, E., & Oddou, G. R. (1987). Expatriate selection, training, and career-pathing: A review and critique. *Human Resource Management, 26*, 331–345.

Pena, D. G. (1997). *The terror of the machine: Technology, work, gender, and ecology on the U.S.–Mexico border*. Austin, TX: Center for Mexican American Studies.

Prieto, N. I. (1997). *Beautiful flowers of the Maquiladora: Life histories of women workers in Tijuana*. (Michael Stone with Gabrielle Winkler, Trans.) Austin: University of Texas Press.

Sklair, L. (1993). *Assembling for development: The maquila industry in Mexico and the United States*. San Diego: Center for the U.S. Mexican Studies, University of California at San Diego.

Triandis, H. C., Marin, G., Lisansky, J., & Berancourt, H. (1984). Simpatía as a cultural script of Hispanics. *Journal of Personality and Social Psychology, 47*, 1363–1375.

Webber, T. (1993, August). It's about time! *Twin Plant News, 18*.

Weintraub, S. (1991). *Trade opportunities in the Western hemisphere*. Washington, DC: Woodrow Wilson Center for International Scholars.

Concepts and Questions

1. Describe some aspects of cultural diversity you may find in Mexico.
2. How is the core value of *confianza* or trust manifested in Mexican human resources management?
3. How can an American manager manifest *confianza* when dealing with Mexican workers?
4. What role does *simpatía* play in interpersonal relations among Mexicans?
5. What communication behaviors must an American manager display to establish that he or she is *simpático*?
6. *Palanca* refers to one's power derived from extensive networking among family members, relatives, former classmates, friends, and business associates. How, if at all, does the Mexican *palanca* differ from the American concept of the "good old boys" network?
7. How can an American manager in Mexico develop the relationships necessary to employ *palanca* as a management tool?
8. How does *estabilidad* or stability reinforce the value of personal relationships and affect organizational behavior?
9. How do Mexican and American concepts toward time differ?
10. List several ways in which an American manager might misconstrue Mexican workers' behavior that reflects the cultural value of *mañana*.

Culture and Negotiation

JEANNE M. BRETT

Breakdowns in negotiations when parties are from different cultures are invariably attributed to cultural differences. Though some of these breakdowns may not fairly be attributable to culture, others undoubtedly have cultural origins. This article develops a conceptual model to explain how culture impacts negotiation. It draws on previous research on culture and on negotiation to develop an understanding of how culture affects negotiation processes and outcomes. The article begins with a review of fundamental concepts in the literature on negotiation and culture. These concepts provide a language for what we know and what we do not know about culture and negotiation and allow us to build a model of factors affecting intercultural negotiation process and outcome.

A MODEL OF INTERCULTURAL NEGOTIATION

Negotiation

Negotiation is a form of social interaction. It is the process by which two or more parties try to resolve perceived incompatible goals (Carnevale & Pruitt, 1992). In order to understand the effect of culture on negotiation, it is useful to have a mental model of negotiation. What is it that people mean when they say they negotiate? What is involved in negotiating? What is a good outcome in negotiation? What does it take to get a good outcome? What goes wrong in a negotiation that has a poor outcome? However, if culture has an effect on negotiation, the mental models of negotiators from one culture may not map onto the mental models of negotiators from another culture, making the specification of a single mental model problematic. There are two ways to approach this problem of specifying a mental model

of negotiation. One is to specify the model in use in one culture and then compare and contrast its elements with elements of models of negotiation from other cultures.

Alternatively, we can specify the mental models of negotiation in many different cultures and aggregate their common and unique elements. The latter approach is less likely to overlook culturally unique aspects of negotiation, but requires the prior existence or current construction of many culturally emic (unique) models of negotiation. (See Brett et al., 1997 for a discussion of these two approaches to designing cross-cultural research.) This article relies on the first approach because there is a well-specified model of negotiation grounded in Western theory and empirical research by scholars such as Howard Raiffa, Morton Deutsch, Dean Pruitt, Peter Carnevale, and Max Bazerman and Margaret Neale. In taking the Western mental model of negotiation as a starting point, no assumption is made that the Western model is etic (generalizable to all cultures).

Direct Confrontation. Negotiation involves direct confrontation, either face-to-face, or electronic, of principles and/or their agents. This is clearly the first of many Western biases in the model. Negotiations can be, and in many cultures frequently are, carried out indirectly through third parties. These third parties may act as agents (representatives of the principles), or mediators (neutral third parties trying to facilitate an agreement), or they may act as go-betweens, conveying information among parties and others with interests in the outcome. This is not to say that such indirect third-party activity never occurs in cultures like the United States, only that it is not usually what cultural members think about when they think about negotiation.

Types of Negotiations. Negotiations may be transactional with buyers and sellers, or directed toward the resolution of conflict or disputes. Both types of negotiation revolve around a perceived incompatibility of goals (Carnevale & Pruitt, 1992). Negotiators engaged in a transaction are determining whether, despite this anticipated incompatibility of goals, they can negotiate the terms of a relationship that is more favorable than any they believe they can negotiate with alternative buyers or sellers.

Conflict or dispute resolution negotiations imply that some blocking of goal attainment has already occurred. Negotiators resolving disputes are determining what can be done about the blocked goal. A dispute is a rejected claim (Felstiner, Abel, & Sarat, 1980–1981), distinguished from the more general term, *conflict* (perceived goal incompatibility), by its explicit nature.

Another difference between transactional and conflict management negotiations is the degree to which the negotiators bring emotion to the table. In transactional negotiations, negotiators may try to use positive emotion, such as ingratiation, or feign emotional irrationality to influence outcomes. Negotiators may also become angry during the course of the negotiation. When conflict is the reason for the negotiation, however, negative emotion precedes the negotiation.

Conflict within relationships and transactions to construct relationships occur in and between all cultures. However, every culture has evolved its own ways of managing conflict and transactions.

Distributive and Integrative Agreements. The result of a transactional or conflict resolution negotiation may be a purely distributive agreement or an integrative agreement or an impasse. Distributive agreements divide a fixed set of resources among the parties. The division can be equal, which is sometimes what is meant by the term "compromise," or unequal. Integrative agreements distribute an enhanced set of resources. Few negotiations are pure win-lose situations (Deutsch, 1973). In most situations there are opportunities to expand the resources to be divided, or to integrate, either by adding issues to the table or fractionating a single negotiation issue into parts. With multiple issues, negotiators may be able to trade low-priority issues for high-priority issues, or identify compatible issues that bring value to both parties.

Why should negotiators care about integrative agreements when most fail to realize integrative potential (Thompson, 1998)? There are two important reasons. First, integration can help parties avoid impasse. Second, when parties reach agreements that are suboptimal, they leave resources on the table that neither party is able to recover (Walton & McKersie, 1965).

Processes that Lead to Distributive and Integrative Agreements. The processes by which distributive and integrative agreements are negotiated differ slightly in transactions and the resolution of disputes. To understand these negotiation processes we need to understand how power and information are used in negotiation.

Power is the ability to make the other party concede when that party prefers not to concede (Ury, Brett, & Goldberg, 1993). In transactional negotiations power is typically the economic power of alternatives. Parties' economic power is a function of their dependency on each other (Emerson, 1962). The party with the best alternative to a negotiated agreement (BATNA) (Fisher, Ury, & Patton, 1991) is the more powerful. Economic power may vary as a function of the market (free market economy cultures) and of each party's social status within the market (controlled economy cultures). Normative standards of fairness (Fisher et al., 1991) may also be used to reach distributive agreements. Examples of standards of fairness include relying on past practice or the agreements reached with other buyers or suppliers. In the resolution of disputes, in addition to economic and social power, and normative standards of fairness, legal standards may be the dominant standard used to determine the distribution of resources.

Two types of information are relevant in negotiation: information about parties' power and information about parties' interests, or the reasons why they take the positions they do (Fisher et al., 1991). Information about power is relevant to both distributive and integrative agreements, because in any integrative agreement, there is still a distribution. Information about interests is relevant to constructing integrative agreements.

With information about relative power, the negotiator can judge (a) when to walk away from a negotiation with confidence that no deal is possible, (b) when to press for more in a negotiation, or (c) when to accept an offer. However, acquiring such information may not be a simple task. First, power is a perception, a psychological representation of the strength of one's position in the negotiation. Like other perceptions, perceptions of power are likely to be biased by egocentrism (thinking you have more power than you would be assigned as having by a neutral observer), anchoring (being influenced by the persuasive arguments the other side uses about its power), and framing (being influenced by role, for example buyer or seller, or some other contextual variable) (Neale & Bazerman, 1991). Second, perceptions of power are subject to influences such as persuasion, ingratiation, substantiation, and appeals to sympathy (Lewicki, Saunders, & Minton, 1997; Weingart et al., 1990).

The creation of resources that is the hallmark of integrative agreements rests on the identification of trade-offs and mutually beneficial alternatives. To realize integrative potential, negotiators need to know both their own and the other party's priorities and interests. Priority information identifies what issues are more and what issues are less important to a negotiator. Interest information identifies why an issue is important or unimportant (Fisher et al., 1991). When different interests are uncovered, trade-offs can be negotiated. When mutual interests are uncovered, both parties can gain. There are two ways to acquire such information leading to integrative agreements. Parties can engage in reciprocal information sharing about preferences, priorities, and interests underlying positions (Pruitt, 1981). Alternatively, parties can engage in heuristic trial-and-error processing, during which they may propose alternative deals, slowly working their way toward an integrative agreement (Pruitt, 1981).

Recent empirical research suggests that cultures differ with respect to the basis of power in negotiation (Brett & Okumura, 1998) and appropriate standards of fairness (Leung, 1997). Cultures also differ with respect to information sharing, both in the extent to which information is viewed as important in negotiation (Brett et al., 1998), and in the approach to sharing information relevant to reaching integrative agreements (Adair, Okumura, & Brett, 1998c). Some cultures share the information about interests and priorities needed to reach integrative agreements directly, while others share that information indirectly, and still others not at all (Adair et al., 1998a). Other research shows cultural differences in the emphasis placed on interests, rights, and power in dispute resolution (Tinsley, 1997, 1998).

Culture

Culture is the unique character of a social group. It encompasses the values and norms shared by members of that group. It is the economic, social, political, and religious institutions that direct and control current group members and socialize new members (Lytle et al., 1995). All of these elements of culture can affect social interactions such as negotiations. Cultural values direct group members' attention to what is more and less important. Cultural norms define what is appropriate and inappropriate behavior. Cultural values and norms provide the philosophy underlying the society's institutions. At the same time cultural institutions preserve cultural values and norms, give them authority, and provide a context for social interaction.

There are many different cultural values, norms, and institutions. Not all relate to negotiation. However, many do because they provide a basis for interpreting situations (this is a negotiation, therefore I behave) and a basis for interpreting the behaviors of others (he or she threatened me, therefore I should . . .) (Fiske & Taylor, 1991). Cultural values that our research indicates are relevant to norms and strategies for negotiation include individualism versus collectivism, egalitarianism versus hierarchy, and direct versus indirect communications. Other values, no doubt, are also relevant.

Individualism versus Collectivism. Individualism versus collectivism refers to the extent to which a society treats individuals as autonomous, or as embedded in their social groups (Schwartz, 1994). In individualistic cultures, norms and institutions promote the autonomy of the individual. Individual accomplishments are rewarded and revered by economic and social institutions, and legal institutions protect individual rights. In collectivist cultures, norms and institutions promote interdependence of individuals through emphasis on social obligations. Sacrifice of personal needs for the greater good is rewarded, and legal institutions place the greater good of the collective above the rights of the individual. Political and economic institutions reward classes of people as opposed to individuals.

The way a society treats people affects the way people self-construe and the way they act toward and interact with each other. People in all cultures distinguish between in-groups, of which they are members, and out-groups, of which they are not (Turner, 1987). In collectivist cultures self-identity is interdependent with in-group membership, but in individualistic cultures self-identity consists of attributes that are independent of in-group membership (Marcus & Kitayama, 1991). Perhaps because collectivists identify more strongly with their in-groups, they are said to be more attuned to the needs of others than individualists (Schweder & Bourne, 1982) and to make stronger in-group–out-group distinctions than individualists (Gudykunst et al., 1992). Individualism versus collectivism, according to Schwartz (1994, p. 140), reflects cultures' basic preferences and priorities for "some goals rather than others." Goals are motivating; they direct behavior and sustain effort (Locke & Latham, 1990). We have found that individualists, because of their strong self-interests, set high personal goals in negotiation (Brett & Okumura, 1998). We think these goals motivate individualists to reject acceptable, but suboptimal, agreements and to continue to search among alternative possible agreements for one that best meets the individualists' self-interests.

Because of their identification with in-groups, collectivists' goals should be aligned with their in-groups' goals. If the other negotiator is an in-group member, goal alignment should generate cooperative behavior in negotiations, whereby parties search together for a mutually satisfying agreement. However, if the other negotiator is an out-group member, as is likely in any intercultural negotiation, goals are unlikely to be aligned and competitive behavior may ensue. In Prisoners' Dilemma games, negotiators with individualistic motivational orientations do not change their behavior depending on with whom they are interacting (Kelley & Stahelski, 1970). However, in some recent multiparty negotiation research, some individualists changed to a cooperative strategy, perhaps because they were confronted with the possibility of an impasse (Weingart & Brett, 1998), suggesting that individualists may be pragmatic. Negotiators with cooperative motivational orientations vary their behavior, depending on the orientation of the other negotiator (Kelley & Stahelski, 1970). They cooperate when they are dealing with other cooperative negotiators, but in dyads will compete when dealing with negotiators with individualist or competitive orientations.

The distinction between individualistic and competitive behavior is important. The individualist goes his or her own way regardless of the behavior of the other, but may be affected by the structure of the situation. The competitor, like the cooperator, is sensitive to the needs of others, and the competitor seeks to maximize the difference between his or her own and other's outcomes (Messick & McClintock, 1968). This is a very different orientation from the individualist, who essentially is unconcerned with how well or how poorly the negotiation is going for the other party, so long as it is going well for him or herself.

Egalitarianism versus Hierarchy. Egalitarianism versus hierarchy refers to the extent to which a culture's social structure is flat (egalitarian) versus differentiated into ranks (hierarchical) (Schwartz, 1994). In hierarchical cultures, social status implies social power. Social superiors are granted power and privilege. Social inferiors are obligated to defer to social superiors and comply with their requests. However, social superiors also have an obligation to look out for the needs of social inferiors (Leung, 1997). No such obligation exists in egalitarian societies, where social boundaries are permeable and superior social status may be short-lived.

Conflict within hierarchical cultures poses a threat to the social structure, since the norm in such a culture is not to challenge the directives of high-status members. Thus, conflict between members of different social ranks is likely to be less frequent in hierarchical than egalitarian cultures (Leung, 1997). Conflict between members of the same social rank is more likely to be handled by deference to a superior than by direct confrontation between social equals (Leung, 1997). So, hierarchy reduces conflict by providing norms for interaction, primarily by channeling any conflict that does break out to superiors. The decision by the high-status third party reinforces his or her authority without necessarily conferring differentiated status on the contestants, as would be the case in a negotiation in which one party won and the other lost.

Conflict within egalitarian cultures also poses a threat to the social structure, but the egalitarian nature of the culture empowers conflicting members to resolve the conflict themselves. Egalitarian cultures support direct, face-to-face negotiations, mediation or facilitation by a peer, and group decision making to resolve conflict. An agreement between two disputing parties may not distribute resources equally. One party may claim more and the other less. Yet, differentiated status associated with successful claiming in one negotiation may not translate into permanent changes in social status. There are two reasons for this. First, there are few avenues in egalitarian societies for precedent setting. Second, social status is only stable until the next negotiation.

Thus, one implication for negotiations of the cultural value of egalitarianism versus hierarchy is the way conflict is handled in a culture. A second implication is the view of power in negotiations.

Negotiators from egalitarian and hierarchical societies have rather different views of the bases of power in negotiations (Brett & Okumura, 1998). Consistent with the transitory notion of social structure that is characteristic of egalitarian societies, power in negotiations in egalitarian cultures tends to be evaluated with respect to the situation under negotiation and the alternatives if no agreement can be reached. Every negotiator has a BATNA (best alternative to negotiated agreement). BATNAs are not fixed. If, in analyzing the alternatives, the negotiator is dissatisfied with his or her BATNA, he or she may invest in action to improve the BATNA by seeking another alternative. In transactional negotiations, parties' BATNAs are frequently unrelated. The buyer has an alternative seller with whom to negotiate and the seller has an alternative buyer with whom to negotiate. However, in dispute resolution negotiations, one party may be able to impose its BATNA on the other. For example, in a dispute over the terms of a contract, the defendant may not simply be able to walk away from a negotiation that has reached an impasse, but will have to defend him or herself in court, which is the claimant's BATNA.

Negotiators in egalitarian cultures refer to BATNA or any other source of power in transactional negotiations relatively infrequently, so long as negotiations are moving toward agreement (Adair et al., 1998c). These negotiators prefer to focus on the issues under negotiation, sharing information about priorities and interests, and noting similarities and differences (Adair et al., 1998a).

In hierarchical societies, interpersonal relationships are vertical. In almost all social relationships a difference in status exists based on age, sex, education, organization, or position in the organization (Graham, Johnston, & Kamins, 1998). Social status confers social power, and knowledge of status dictates how people will interact. In within-culture negotiations, when parties' social status is known, there may be little need to negotiate the relative distribution of resources. However, when relative status is in doubt, negotiators must somehow determine each party's relative status, and thus the distribution of resources. Research on transactional negotiations shows that negotiators from hierarchical cultures are more likely than negotiators from egalitarian cultures to endorse as normative and to use all types of power in negotiation: status, BATNA, and persuasion (Adair et al., 1998a; Brett et al., 1998).

High- versus Low-context Communication. High- versus low-context communication refers to the degree to which within-culture communications are indirect versus direct (Hall, 1976; Ting-Toomey, 1988). In high-context cultures little information is in the message itself. Instead, the context of the communication stimulates preexisting knowledge in the receiver. In high-context cultures meaning is inferred rather than directly interpreted from the communication. In low-context cultures information is contained in explicit messages, and meaning is conveyed without nuance and is context free. Communication in low-context cultures is action oriented and solution minded. The implications of the information are laid out in further detailed communications.

Information is the central factor affecting the degree to which negotiated agreements are integrative. Differences between parties in priorities and interests provide one source of integrative potential. Compatibility with respect to issues provides another. If parties are going to realize integrative potential, they must learn about the other party's interests, preferences, and priorities. Negotiation research has shown that integrative agreements may result from information sharing about preferences and priorities (Olekalns, Smith, & Walsh, 1996; Pruitt, 1981; Weingart et al., 1990), or from heuristic trial-and-error search (Pruitt & Lewis, 1975; Tutzauer & Roloff, 1988). Information sharing about preferences and priorities is a direct information-sharing approach. Questions are asked and answered in a give-and-take fashion as both sides slowly develop an understanding of what issues are mutually beneficial, what issues are more important to one side than the other, and what issues are purely distributive.

Heuristic trial-and-error search is an indirect information-sharing approach. It occurs in negotiations when parties trade proposals back and forth across the bargaining table. When one party rejects the other's proposal, and offers its own, the first party may infer what was wrong with the proposal from the way the second party changed it in making its own proposal. Multi-issue proposals provide a great deal of indirect information about preferences and priorities because the integrative trade-offs are contained within the proposal. Our research shows that negotiators from low-context cultures who share information directly are as capable of negotiating integrative agreements as negotiators from high-context cultures who share information indirectly (Brett & Okumura, 1998).

The cultural value for high- versus low-context communication may also be related to the willingness of parties in conflict to confront and negotiate directly versus to avoid confrontation and conceal ill feelings, or to confront indirectly by involving third parties (Leung, 1997; Ting-Toomey, 1988; Tinsley, 1997). Most of the research regarding confrontation versus avoidance is survey research of preferences for conflict management processes or descriptions of actual conflict management behaviors. Attributions for these preferences are as frequently made to collectivism as to high-context communication. (See Leung, 1997, for a review.) The cultural value for egalitarianism versus hierarchy also serves as a context for confrontation versus nonconfrontation in negotiations. In research comparing Hong Kong Chinese and U.S. intracultural negotiators, we placed parties in a simulated, face-to-face dispute resolution setting, perhaps an uncomfortable setting for the Hong Kong Chinese (Tinsley & Brett, 1998). We found that during the 45-minute negotiation, the Hong Kong Chinese negotiators resolved fewer issues and were more likely to involve a third party than were the U.S. negotiators (Tinsley & Brett, 1998).

MODEL OF CULTURE AND NEGOTIATION

When people from two different cultural groups negotiate, each brings to the table his or her way of thinking about the issues to be negotiated and the process of negotiation. Some of that thinking is affected by the negotiator's cultural group membership and the ways in which issues are typically assessed and negotiations carried out within that cultural group. Figure 1 represents intercultural negotiations as a function of differences between parties with respect to preferences on issues and negotiation strategies.

Cultural values may result in preferences on issues that are quite distinct. For example, negotiators from cultures that value tradition may be less enthusiastic about economic development that threatens to change valued ways of life than negotiators from cultures that value change and development. The same values that generate cultural differences in preferences may also act as cultural blinders. Members of one culture expect preferences to be compatible, and cannot understand the rationality of the other party, whose views on the same issue are at odds with their own. It is generally unwise in negotiation to label the other party as irrational. Such labeling encourages persuasion to get the other party to adopt the first's view of the situation, rather than the search for trade-offs that are the foundation of integrative agreements. There is opportunity in differences, or what is represented in Figure 1 as integrative potential.

Figure 1 *A Model of Intercultural Negotiation*

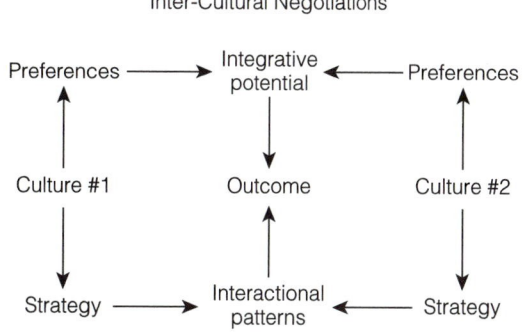

Inter-Cultural Negotiations

Cultural values and norms may also affect negotiators' strategic negotiation processes. For example, negotiators from cultures where direct, explicit communications are preferred may share information by stating and reciprocating preferences and priorities, by commenting on similarities and differences, and by giving direct feedback. Negotiators from cultures where the norm is to communicate indirectly and infer meaning may share information by making multi-issue proposals and inferring priorities from subtle changes in proposals. In our research contrasting U.S. and Japanese negotiators, we found that the Japanese were using a relatively large number of proposals, compared to the U.S. negotiators, and the U.S. negotiators were using a whole array of direct communications relatively more frequently than the Japanese (Adair et al., 1998c).

Figure 1 suggests that when the strategies negotiators bring to the table clash, the negotiation process is likely to be less efficient, and agreements are likely to be suboptimal. We found, for example, that Japanese intracultural negotiators, using indirect communications, and U.S. intracultural negotiators, using direct communications, reached similarly efficient agreements. However, when Japanese expatriate managers negotiated with U.S. managers, agreements were suboptimal. Japanese intercultural negotiators understood the U.S. negotiators' priorities, because the U.S. negotiators were sharing information directly. The U.S. negotiators did not understand the Japanese negotiators' priorities, even though the intercultural Japanese negotiators shut down their culture's normative indirect approach to information sharing and tried to adapt to the U.S. strategy of direct information sharing (Adair et al., 1998c; Brett & Okumura, 1998).

There is not much research on what happens when negotiators' initial strategic approaches to bargaining are different, much less when those strategies are linked to cultural differences. In the negotiations literature, there is generally more theorizing than empirical research on incompatible negotiation strategies. This theorizing tends to argue that negotiators must adapt to each other and develop a common "frame" or approach to negotiations, if an agreement is to be reached (Drake & Donohue, 1996; Pinkley & Northcraft, 1994). Weiss (1994) argues that the party who is most familiar with the other's culture should adapt. This pattern of adaptation is consistent with our U.S.–Japanese research. However, we note that the adaptation was not sufficient to generate joint gains. Weiss's perspective also ignores other criteria, such as parties' relative power, that might be used as a basis for adaptation. Then again there is the problem of how much adaptation is necessary. Research has identified cultural differences with respect to power, goals, and information sharing in negotiation. Is adaptation uniform across all areas of cultural differences, or is it easier to adapt information sharing strategies than power strategies? Is the adaptation short-lived for the single negotiation, or does the enhanced negotiation strategy continue to be available to the adapting negotiator? Do negotiators even realize that they are adapting?

WHEN CULTURES CLASH IN NEGOTIATION

The practical questions for the cross-cultural negotiator are how the party across the bargaining table is likely to construe the issues and what strategies he or she is likely to use. Culture can provide some insight into these questions. At the same time there are pitfalls of over-reliance on cultural expectations.

Research has shown that there are fundamental differences among cultures with respect to norms for negotiation (Brett et al., 1998) and behavior in negotiations (Adair et al., 1998a; Tinsley, 1997, 1998). Furthermore, these differences in norms and behavior are correlated with cultural values (Brett et al., 1998; Tinsley, 1997). Knowing the links between culture and negotiation strategies and knowing the other party's cultural background may help reduce uncertainty about issue construal and strategy. Several sources provide descriptive information about culture and cultural values, including Hall (1976), Hofstede (1980), Morrison, Conaway, and Borden (1994), and Schwartz (1994). There are also descriptive accounts of how people from different cultures negotiate (e.g., March, 1990). The best of these is the new edited volume by Leung and Tjosvold (1998), describing negotiation norms in cultures around the Pacific Rim.

These sources agree that there is a major cultural divide between East and West, with the West's profile generally being individualism, egalitarianism, and low-context communication, and the East's profile being collectivism, hierarchy, and high-context communication. However, East–West distinctions at the level of cultural values grossly oversimplify more fine-grained cultural differences in negotiation norms. There are distinct normative differences within regions (Leung & Tjosvold, 1998).

On the other hand, just because negotiators are from different cultures does not necessarily mean that their negotiation strategies will clash and their agreements will be suboptimal. Distinct social groups may have similar cultural values, and members may find the intercultural negotiation process trouble-free. In addition, not all members of a cultural group with a distinct value profile believe and act consistently with the cultural norm. There is a distribution of cultural traits within a culture. Two negotiators from cultures with distinct but overlapping distributions of cultural characteristics may find that they have very similar cultural values and norms, despite the differences in their cultures. If these negotiators are naive about cultural differences, they may not anticipate differences in the negotiation process and not experience them. On the other hand, if they hold cultural stereotypes, their ability to recognize their fundamental compatibility may be biased by their stereotypes and make the negotiation process more difficult than it otherwise would be.

This observation raises the troubling issue of whether knowing about the other party's cultural approach to negotiation is useful information or not. Such knowledge is harmful if it stimulates biased perceptions and inappropriate adjustments of negotiation strategy. It is useful to the extent that it facilitates accurate attributions and allows a negotiator to take the perspective of the other negotiator and adjust his or her strategy.

When parties are motivated to reach an agreement, much can go on during the course of a negotiation to overcome individual, contextual, and cultural differences in negotiation strategy. Our research has identified three key factors leading to successful integrative and distributive agreements that are affected by culture: (1) a value for information sharing, (2) a means of searching for information, and (3) the motivation to search for information. Cultures vary in the importance negotiators place on

information sharing, in negotiators' normative approaches to information search, and in what motivates negotiators to search for information that may lead them to alternatives and better outcomes (Adair et al., 1998a, 1998c; Brett et al., 1998; Brett & Okumura, 1998). As a result, negotiating interculturally may pose a significant strategic challenge. Yet, if negotiators remain motivated to search for information on which to build acceptable agreements and are flexible in how that search is conducted, cultural differences can be bridged (Adair et al., 1998b).

References

Adair, W., Brett, J., Lempereur, A., Okumura, T., Tinsley, C., & Lytle, A. (1998a). *Culture and negotiation strategy*. Evanston, IL: Dispute Resolution Research Center, Northwestern University.

Adair, W., Kopelman, S., Gillespie, J., & Brett, J. M. (1998b). *Compatible cultural values and schemas in US/ Israeli negotiations; Implications for joint gains*. Evanston, IL: Dispute Resolution Research Center, Northwestern University.

Adair, W., Okumura, T., & Brett, J. M. (1998c). *Culturally bound negotiation scripts and joint gains in US and Japanese intra- and inter-cultural dyads*. Evanston, IL: Dispute Resolution Research Center, Northwestern University.

Brett, J. M., et al. (1998). Culture and joint gains in negotiation. *Negotiation Journal, 14,* 55–80.

Brett, J. M., & Okumura, T. (1998). Inter- and intra-cultural negotiation: US and Japanese negotiators. *Academy of Management Journal, 41,* 495–510.

Brett, J. M., Tinsley, C. H., Janssens, M., Barsness, Z. I., & Lytle, A. L. (1997). New approaches to the study of culture in industrial/organizational psychology. In P. C. Earley & M. Erez (Eds.), *New perspectives on international industrial organizational psychology* (pp. 75–129). San Francisco, CA: New Lexington.

Carnevale, P., & Pruitt, D. G. (1992). Negotiation and mediation. *Annual Review of Psychology, 43,* 531–582.

Deutsch, M. (1973). *The resolution of conflict.* New Haven, CT: Yale University Press.

Drake, L. E., & Donohue, W. A. (1996). Communicative framing theory in conflict resolution. *Communication Research, 23,* 297–322.

Emerson, R. M. (1962). Power dependence relations. *American Sociological Review, 27,* 31–41.

Felstiner, W. L. F., Abel, R. L., & Sarat, A. (1980–1981). The emergence and transformation of disputes: Naming, blaming and claiming. *Law and Society Review, 15,* 631–654.

Fisher, R., Ury, W., & Patton, B. (1991). *Getting to yes: Negotiating agreement without giving in.* New York: Penguin.

Fiske, S. T., & Taylor, S. E. (1991). *Social cognition.* New York: McGraw-Hill.

Graham, J. L., Johnston, W. J., & Kamins, M. A. (1998). *A multi-method examination of buyer-seller interactions among Japanese and American business people.* Irvine, CA: Graduate School of Management, University of California.

Gudykunst, W. B., et al. (1992). The influence of individualism-collectivism, self-monitoring, and predicted outcome value on communication in ingroup and outgroup relationships. *Journal of Cross-Cultural Psychology, 23,* 196–213.

Hall, E. T. (1976). *Beyond culture.* Garden City, CA: Anchor.

Hofstede, G. (1980). *Culture's consequences: International differences in work-related values.* Beverly Hills, CA: Sage.

Kelley, H., & Stahelski, A. J. (1970). Social interaction basis of cooperators' and competitors beliefs about others. *Journal of Personality and Social Psychology, 16,* 66–91.

Leung, K. (1997). Negotiation and reward allocations across cultures. In P. C. Earley & M. Erez (Eds.), *New perspectives on international industrial organizational psychology.* San Francisco, CA: Jossey Bass.

Leung, K., & Tjosvold, D. (1998). *Conflict management in the Asia Pacific.* Singapore: Wiley.

Lewicki, R. J., Saunders, D. M., & Minton, J. W. (1997). *Essentials of negotiation.* Chicago: Irwin.

Locke, E. A., & Latham, G. P. (1990). *A theory of goal setting and task performance.* Englewood Cliffs, NJ: Prentice Hall.

Lytle, A., Brett, J. M., Barsness, Z., Tinsley, C., & Janssens, M. (1995). A paradigm for confirmatory cross-cultural research in organizational behavior. *Research in Organizational Behavior, 17,* 167–214.

March, R. M. (1990). *The Japanese negotiator.* New York: Kodansha International.

Marcus, H., & Kitayama, S. (1991). Culture and the self: Implications for cognition, emotion, and motivation. *Psychological Review, 98,* 224–253.

Messick, D., & McClintock, C. (1968). Motivational bases of choice in experimental games. *Journal of Experimental Social Psychology, 4,* 1–25.

Morrison, T., Conaway, W. A., & Borden, G. A. (1994). *Kiss, bow, and shake hands.* Holbrook. MA: Adams Media.

Neale, M. A., & Bazerman, M. (1991). *Cognition and rationality in negotiation.* New York: Free Press.

Olekalns, M., Smith, P. L., & Walsh, T. (1996). The process of negotiating: Strategies, timing and outcomes. *Organizational Behavior and Human Decision Processes, 68,* 68–77.

Pinkley, R., & Northcraft, G. B. (1994). Conflict frames of reference: Implications for dispute resolution processes and outcomes. *Academy of Management Journal, 37,* 193–205.

Pruitt, D. G. (1981). *Negotiation behavior.* New York: Academic Press.

Pruitt, D. G., & Lewis, S. (1975). Development of integrative solutions in bilateral negotiation. *Journal of Personality and Social Psychology, 31,* 621–633.

Schwartz, S. H. (1994). Beyond individualism/collectivism: New cultural dimensions of values. In U. Kim, H. C. Triandis, & G. Yoon (Eds.), *Individualism and collectivism* (pp. 85–117). London: Sage.

Schweder, R. A., & Bourne, E. J. (1982). Does the concept of the person vary cross-culturally? In A. J. Marsella & G. M. While (Eds.), *Cultural conceptions of mental health and therapy* (pp. 97–137). London: Reidel.

Thompson, L. (1998). *The mind and heart of the negotiator.* Englewood Cliffs, NJ: Prentice Hall.

Ting-Toomey, S. (1988). Intercultural conflict styles: A face negotiation theory. In Y. Kim & W. Gudykunst (Eds.), *Theories in intercultural communication* (pp. 213–235). Newbury Park, CA: Sage.

Tinsley, C.H. (1997). *Culture's influences on conflict management behaviors in the workplace.* Unpublished doctoral dissertation. Evanston, IL: Northwestern University.

Tinsley, C.H. (1998). Models of conflict resolution in Japanese, German, and American cultures. *Journal of Applied Psychology, 83,* 316–323.

Tinsley, C., & Brett, J. M. (1998). *Managing work place conflict in the US and Hong Kong.* Evanston, IL: Dispute Resolution Research Center, Northwestern University.

Turner, J. C. (1987). *Rediscovering the social group: A self categorization theory.* New York: Basil Blackwell.

Tutzauer, F., & Roloff, M. E. (1988). Communication processes leading to integrative agreements: Three paths to joint benefits. *Communication Research, 15,* 360–380.

Ury, W. L., Brett, J. M., & Goldberg, S. B. (1993). *Getting disputes resolved: Designing a system to cut the costs of conflict.* Cambridge, MA: Harvard Program on Negotiation.

Walton, R. E., & McKersie, R. B. (1965). *A behavioral theory of labor negotiations: An analysis of a social interaction system.* New York: McGraw-Hill.

Weingart, L. R., & Brett, J. M. (1998). *Mixed motive orientations in negotiating groups: Convergence and reaching agreement.* Evanston, IL: Dispute Resolution Research Center, Northwestern University.

Weingart, L. R., Thompson, L. L., Bazerman, M. H., & Carroll, J. S. (1990). Tactical behavior and negotiation outcomes. *International Journal of Conflict Management*, *1*, 7–31.

Weiss, S. E. (1994). Negotiating with the Romans, Parts I & II. *Sloan Management Review, Winter/Spring*, 51–99.

Concepts and Questions

1. What is negotiation?
2. How does negotiation involve direct confrontation? In what ways do some cultures try to avoid direct confrontation when negotiating?
3. What are the differences between transactional and conflict-resolving negotiations?
4. Distinguish between distributive and integrative agreements.
5. How are power and information used in negotiation?
6. How does information about relative power help a negotiator?
7. Which cultural dynamics are most likely to inject themselves into the negotiation process?
8. How do cultural values affect a negotiator's negotiation strategy?
9. How does knowing the links between culture and negotiation strategies help avoid cultural clashes during negotiation?
10. What types of strategies can be employed to avoid cultural clashes during intercultural negotiations?

"Half-truths" in Argentina, Brazil, and India: An Intercultural Analysis of Physician–Patient Communication

Nagesh Rao

Mr. Akbar Ali, a 60-year-old Muslim from Pakistan, has been diagnosed as having insulin-dependent diabetes. Dr. Martin has prescribed insulin for him and instructed his family on how to administer it. However, when Mr. Ali returns for a checkup, Dr. Martin notices little improvement. Careful questioning of Mr. Ali's son reveals that Mr. Ali has not been taking his insulin, and when asked why, Mr. Ali sternly replies, "I am an Orthodox Muslim and would rather die than disobey Islam." Dr. Martin is puzzled and has no idea what Mr. Ali means. (Gropper, 1996)

Such instances are not uncommon when physicians[1] in the United States treat patients from diverse cultural backgrounds. In this case, it is likely that Mr. Ali has heard that insulin is made from the pancreas of a pig. A Muslim is expected to avoid any product of swine because it is considered unclean. Dr. Martin needs to explain that insulin can come from sheep or oxen too, and she would take care to make sure the insulin is not from a pig. This kind of problem, however, is not limited to situations where the caregiver and the patient speak different languages and come from two different countries.

Helman (1994) aptly notes that, "Physicians and patients, even if they come from the same social and cultural background, view ill-health in very different ways. Their perspectives are based on very dif-

This original article appears here in print for the first time. All rights reserved. Permission to reprint must be obtained from the author and the publisher. An earlier version of this paper was presented at the Health Communication Division of the International Communication Association, Washington D.C., 2001. Nagesh Rao teaches in the School of Interpersonal Communication, Ohio University, Athens, Ohio.

ferent premises, employ a different system of proof, and assess the efficacy of treatment in a different way" (p. 101). The following anecdote narrated by a patient named "Chris" is not uncommon even when the physician and patient perceive the other as having the same cultural background[2]:

> I was a sergeant in the army. I had been in the hospital, sick with fever for a week. I had lost 24 pounds (15% of my body weight) and the physicians could not find the cause of the illness. The physician read the results of some blood work that had been run the day before. Without preparing me for it, he casually said, "hmm . . . people with your white blood count normally have leukemia." He then started walking away. When I tried to stop him to ask questions, he reprimanded me for not calling him "sir!".

In this paper, we argue that the interaction between a physician and patient is inherently an *intercultural*[3] encounter even when the two parties *perceive* they are from the same culture. The distinction between illness and disease helps explain why every encounter between a physician and patient is intercultural. Rosen et al. (1982) define disease "as the malfunctioning of biological and/or psychological processes whereas illness may be defined as the perception, evaluation, explanation, and labeling of symptoms by the patient and his family and social network" (p. 496). Traditionally, physicians focus on the disease while patients are concerned with the illness. As du Pré (2000) adds, patients are operating with feelings while physicians are addressing evidence. Thus, in our anecdote, the physician is keen to diagnose the disease (possibly leukemia), while "Chris" is dealing with the psychological implications of having leukemia. This disparity in the physician's and patient's beliefs and value structures could create miscommunication between them and lead to ineffective medical care.

Recent research on physician–patient interaction also suggests the need to study the intercultural aspects of physician–patient communication. Physician–patient research generally falls into one of two broad areas: (1) research focusing on the interpersonal communication aspects of physician–patient interactions and identifying specific interpersonal skills for physicians to learn (e.g., see Burgoon, Birk, and Hall, 1991; O'Hair, 1989;

Ong et al., 1995; Roter, 2000; Sharf, 1990), and (2) scholarship focusing on the cross-cultural aspects of physician-patient communication to assist caregivers in being more culturally sensitive toward their patients (e.g., see Baylav, 1996; Greengold and Ault, 1996; Rosenbaum, 1995; Young & Klingle, 1996). Both of these areas of research, however, fail to bring communication and culture together; the first area of research concentrates on communication and not culture, and the second area focuses on culture, but cross-culturally rather than interculturally. Kim et al. (2000) begin the quest to create an intercultural approach to physician–patient communication by analyzing how a patient's self-construal impacts his or her verbal communication with a physician. Further, Geist (2000) offers an insightful analysis of the health challenges faced in dealing with co-cultural differences in the United States. In this chapter, as part of a five-year study to develop an *intercultural* model of physician–patient communication, we offer data from our interviews with physicians in Argentina, Brazil, and India.

In this essay, we begin with a literature review on the impact of culture on physician–patient communication and summarize the key findings. After offering a brief description of our methodology (see Rao & Beckett, 2000, for further information), we offer three key findings from our interviews with 91 physicians in Argentina, Brazil, and India. Finally, we highlight our main findings and discuss the implications for future research.

IMPACT OF CULTURE ON PHYSICIAN–PATIENT COMMUNICATION

Traditional medical literature increasingly stresses the importance of good physician communication skills (Burgoon, Birk, and Hall, 1991; Cegala, McGee, and McNeils, 1996; O'Hair, 1989; Ong et al., 1995; Roter, 2000). Many factors that inhibit physician–patient communication have previously been documented. Although time limitations remain the number one reason given by providers for lack of communication, some posit that the qualities that earn respect from colleagues are very different from those that earn respect from patients (Welsbacher, 1998). With the exception of several key areas (e.g., care for refugees, using interpreters), the influence of culture(s) in health-related interactions has been largely glossed over. Considering the high rates of global migration, physicians from many different sociocultural backgrounds will find themselves serving an increasingly diverse patient population. Thus, it would seem that a major gap exists within mainstream medical literature.

However, there is one notable exception within the medical arena. Researcher-practitioners within the field of nursing have long advocated that health care providers become familiar with how patients of different cultures conceptualize the notions of "health" and "care." In particular, Madeline Leininger (1991) has been at the forefront of research dedicated to extrapolating these differences. According to her Theory of Culture Care Diversity and Universality, all cultures express care but attach different meanings to health-related practices. Within the health care context, meaning is shaped by technology, religion, cultural norms, economics, and education. Her work is critical in reminding providers that there is far more to culture than simple geography.

Several themes emerge from the nursing research. We are reminded that just as diversity exists across cultures, it also exists within cultural groups (Rosenbaum, 1995). These differences can be intensified by factors such as ethnicity, religion, education, age, sex, and acculturation. As Herselman (1996) aptly states, perceptions are influenced by individual experiences as well as cultural background. Thus, there is a great danger in relying on excessive generalizations (Meleis, 1996). For example, Denham (1996) explains that medical practitioners tend to believe that rural Appalachians are fatalistic in their outlook and in their health practices. However, Denham (1996) adds that a lot of variability occurs in rural Appalachians' fatalistic beliefs and health practices. Finally, if a health care provider is to understand how these variables influence a patient's ways of thinking and behaving, he or she must first be familiar with the patient's cultural background. One must also be aware of how the patient's cultural heritage intersects with the culture of the particular health care organization.

Language can provide a major barrier to culturally appropriate care because exploring goals and expectations can become difficult (Baylav, 1996). In her thesis, "When Yes Means No," Katalanos (1994) argues convincingly that South-East Asian (SEA) patients who are recent immigrants have health beliefs that are different from those held by the health care professionals in the United States, and these differences are manifested in the communication behaviors of the two parties. Katalanos's (1994, p. 31) analyses of the communication patterns (see following section) show that there is significant misunderstanding between SEA patients and U.S.-trained health care providers, sometimes with serious consequences.

PHYSICIAN ASSISTANT: "Are you happy here in America?"

VIETNAMESE PATIENT: "Oh yes" [meaning: I am not happy at all, but I do not want to hurt your feelings. After all, your country took me in].

Further, "yes" may simply mean, "I hear you, and I will answer your question," as the following exchange illustrates:

PHYSICIAN ASSISTANT: "Did you take your medicine?"

VIETNAMESE PATIENT: "Yes [I hear you]. No [I did not take it]."

PHYSICIAN ASSISTANT: "You did not take your medicine?"

VIETNAMESE PATIENT: "Yes [I hear you]. Yes [I did not take it. The medicine was too strong]."

PHYSICIAN ASSISTANT: "Ah, so you did not take it!"

VIETNAMESE PATIENT: "Yes. No."

These responses leave both the health care provider and the patient frustrated, as each person is operating out of her or his own paradigm—the U.S. provider paradigm of diagnosing the specific cause of illness and providing medication, and the SEA paradigm of being polite and not wanting to hurt the provider's feelings.

Medical jargon exacerbates linguistic barriers even further. Some measures that nurses have taken to compensate for these barriers include the use of interpreters, health education sessions run in conjunction with local service providers, ethnic recruiting, alternative medical services, cultural sensitivity training, multicultural videos/fliers, and cultural health care fairs (Baylav, 1996; Kothari and Kothari, 1997).

Research in nursing has also acknowledged the importance of culture in understanding a patient's attitudes toward birth, death, sex, relationships, and ritual (Mullhall, 1996). Treatments that are based on assumptions of how a patient regards such issues could potentially result in miscommunication, if not outright noncompliance. Spitzer et al. (1996) assert that expecting a patient to conform to a health care provider's orders is simply a cultural imposition rather than a joint process of discovering the best ways to treat certain ailments. Charonko (1992) also argues that the term "noncompliant" is biased toward preserving the power of the health care provider at the expense of his or her patient. From Charonko's perspective, it is the provider's responsibility to help patients live as productively as possible within *their* choices. Patient satisfaction, which depends heavily on communication, has been strongly correlated with compliance (Eraker, Kirscht, and Becker, 1984).

The traditional medical literature in the United States, however, is beginning to acknowledge the increasing diversity of the United States. Between 1990 and 1996, growth in Latino, African American, and Asian American populations accounted for almost two-thirds of the increase in the U.S. population (Bureau of the Census, 1996). While the patient population in the United States is growing more diverse, there is little being done to prepare our physicians to work more effectively with these patients (Baylav, 1996; Greengold and Ault, 1996; Rao & Beckett, 2000; Rosenbaum, 1995).

For example, Drake and Lowenstein (1998) hold that California is an interesting case study because "minorities" (e.g., Latinos, Asians) will soon outnumber Caucasians.[4] Texas has also attracted attention as of late because of its ranking as the fifth most culturally diverse state (Kothari and Kothari, 1997). In either case, pronounced disparities exist between ethnicity and level of access to health care. The researchers do note that education, language, and literacy are major reasons why access to health care is limited among certain populations. Studies such as this dance around the issue of culture but stop short of providing culturally specific care based on systematic research.

One area of medical research where culture is central, however, concerns health care for refugees. Although Kang, Kahler, and Tesar (1998) assert that there are 26 million refugees in the world, the crisis in Kosovo has surely increased these numbers. And the current problems in Afghanistan are creating additional refugees. Keeping this in mind, physicians will find themselves dealing with these issues increasingly often. Similarly, Obmans, Garret, and Treichel (1996) write that immigrants and refugees are often over-represented in emergency room care. Interpreters are often necessary for physicians to provide care for refugees, yet many communication problems have been documented from this activity. Regardless of strategy, Obmans et. al (1996) write that negotiation and compromise will remain critical to culturally appropriate treatment.

Our succinct review suggests that culture impacts physician–patient communication in several significant ways. The key findings from research on physician–patient communication can be summarized as follows. First, most physicians follow the biomedical approach where they focus more on the disease rather than on the person. Roter (2000) argues, rather persuasively, that as molecular and chemistry-oriented sciences gained prominence in the 20th century, the focus on communication as a central tenet in physician–patient relationships has declined. Second, there has been considerable research emphasizing the importance of several communication skills like empathy, active listening, and so on in physician–patient communication (Burgoon, Birk, and Hall, 1991; Ong et al., 1995; Roter and Hall, 1992). Third, research in nursing and counseling has emphasized the usefulness of focusing on the patient's culture in creating more effective encounters (Leininger, 1991). Fourth, patients are most satisfied when both task and relational dimensions of the relationship are addressed effectively in the physician–patient communication (Helman, 1991; Lochman, 1983; Stewart, 1995). Fifth, while most medical students enter medical school with an idealism to save lives, they often leave with "detached concern" because of the biomedical nature of the training (Miller, 1993). Finally, some medical schools train their students to communicate more effectively with their patients, but such models still focus on general communication and not on intercultural communication (Marshall, 1993).

It can be argued, therefore, that the research on physician–patient communication has focused on how to improve a physician's interpersonal and cross-cultural skills. Since there is limited research on the intercultural nature of this encounter, we are working on a systematic research program to create an intercultural communication model of physician–patient communication. In this next section, we focus on the first phase of our research project to answer the following research question: How do physicians in different countries communicate with culturally diverse patients? We administered the Medical Provider Questionnaire (MPQ) to 29 physicians in Campinas, Brazil; 30 physicians in Madras, India; and 32 physicians in Cordoba, Argentina.[5] Each interview was tape recorded and ranged between 45 to 90 minutes in length. The MPQ had several parts: (1) What motivated these physicians to join this profession; (2) What they liked and disliked about this profession; (3) How they communicated with culturally diverse patients; (4) The physician's response to the case study described in the first part of this article; (5) How physicians defined a successful encounter with a patient; and (6) What the physicians would change in the medical system if they were to go through medical school again. In this next section, we focus on the physicians' responses to questions 3 and 4. We first begin with how physicians defined cultural diversity in their context. Then, we focus on the three key findings—"half-truths," family as patient, and how physicians defined success.

Physicians' Definition of Culture

Almost without exception, the physicians in Argentina, Brazil, and India saw their countries as heterogeneous. This was not surprising by itself. However, what was surprising was how physicians defined diversity in these three countries. In Brazil, a few physicians divided patients along traditional race, ethnic, and national origin lines. One of our respondents, a resident in cardiology, explained:

> Oh, of course. No doubt about it because mainly the kind of settlement of people here in Brazil was in periods over these five centuries. So in the South region

you have mostly a European settlement in the last century so Italians, Germans, many of these people. So in the North and Northeast mainly Portuguese and Indians and the slaves that were brought from Africa, so they are totally different.

Most of our Brazilian respondents, however, felt that their main cultural diversity was based on socioeconomic status. Brazil, according to them, had two distinctive cultures, the rich and the poor. For example, a cardiology resident, summarized it rather succinctly:

> Oh, no, we have many cultures here. We have a statesman, a former minister of industry, economics, I don't know, and he always said Brazil is—was Belindia, I don't know if you ever heard of it—it's part of Belgium and part of India. You have many countries inside a country. I don't know if you have traveled for many states here. I don't know if you know the state of Maranhao. The Northeast region is the poorest region in the country. So our country is a mosaic, so if we are having problems here, you can imagine what they are having in the Northeast or the North region where we have the Amazon forest and many people don't have hospitals, don't have many roads because all of the transport system is water, it's rivers and boats and all of this, so the country is extremely, it's not homogeneous like you said.

Similarly, the physicians in Argentina saw their culture as heterogeneous. One senior female cardiologist noted:

> It [Argentina] is heterogeneous. People who formed this country have different origins, different customs, different traditions, and at the same time there were people who were from here.

Most Argentinean physicians focused primarily on education and socioeconomic status to describe the diversity in their country. One internist explained:

> No, it is heterogeneous. We have people very intellectual and with a lot of knowledge and people with a complete lack of education.

An ophthalmologist described Argentina with passion:

> I would say that it is heterogeneous but mainly because we have a huge difference between social

classes. Instead of paying 20 dollars to go to a theater, you just think that you need food and clothing.

There are many people here who are right now experiencing those kinds of problems.

Physicians in India also saw their country as diverse, but focused on different aspects of diversity—religion, language, socioeconomic status, north-south differences, and so on. A senior female general practitioner described India in the following manner:

We have patients from all spectrums of life. When the patient's language is different, it is almost like they are from a different country. Their dress is different, language is different, and habits are different. The people in the south are much more humane.

A senior oncologist, working for a large private hospital, explained:

In our setup here, we see really a cross section both geographically and culturally and even to some extent economically. It is not that only rich people come here. Here patients know that there is better treatment available. So people come here selling all their belongings. Secondly, we see a lot of patients from the northeast. At least 30% of the patients come from that region.

It is intriguing that while Argentina, Brazil, and India have significant diversity based on immigration patterns, religion, languages, and so on, the physicians in Argentina and Brazil focused mainly on socioeconomic status and education as the main indicators of diversity. The Indian physicians represented the various aspects of India's diversity, including language, socioeconomic status, and the like. A physician in Brazil explained that because they speak Portuguese throughout the country, even though there is diversity, the common language takes care of cultural differences. This explanation is also viable in Argentina where Spanish is spoken throughout the country.

India, however, has 18 official languages, and it is difficult to ignore the cultural diversity. An Indian colleague often uses this analogy, "Think of India as a mini-Europe. You can travel 100 miles and speak a completely new language!" Thus, it is not surprising that the physicians in these cultures focused on different aspects of their country's diversity. These cultural differences also played a significant role in how they communicated with their patients.

"Half-truths"

As part of the interview, we asked our respondents to read the following case study (cited previously) and asked them if the physician had responded appropriately.

I was a sergeant in the army. I had been in the hospital, sick with fever for a week. I had lost 24 pounds (15% of my body weight) and the physicians could not find the cause of the illness. The physician read the results of some blood work that had been run the day before. Without preparing me for it, he casually said, " hmm . . . people with your white blood count normally have leukemia." He then started walking away. When I tried to stop him to ask questions, he reprimanded me for not calling him "sir!".

All 91 respondents indicated that the physician in this case study had responded inappropriately. We then asked the physicians to explain what they would have done if they had to tell a patient that he or she is terminally ill. Our data suggest that 90 percent of the physicians in these three countries engaged in what we have termed "half-truths," where physicians did not disclose the diagnosis immediately, described the diagnosis in doses over several visits, or informed a family member of the diagnosis first before telling the patient. In all these cases, the physicians explained that hearing such life-threatening news immediately would psychologically harm the patient, which, in turn, would reduce the patient's ability to fight the illness. In other words, the type of "half-truth" used was based on the psychological readiness of the patient. In 10% of the cases, the physicians insisted that they would tell the patient directly and immediately because that is what they would have liked. A cardiologist from India described his strategy:

If I knew a patient had a terminal illness like leukemia, I would tell him that we have to do more tests before we can really be sure. If I tell him directly, he could die of the shock. If I think he is stronger, I may tell him that there are several possibilities and one could be cancer. If he is not strong, I would see which family member he has come with and take them aside to tell them the news. We are very family oriented, and he has to get their support. So, better to tell them first. Also, they may have to make preparations.

A Brazilian physician, in response to the case study, offered a more direct example of "half-truths":

> It's completely crazy—unacceptable. First of all, because a blood exam is not enough to make a diagnosis of leukemia. It's more complicated; there are no justifications to answer this question in this way. I think the physician could hide the diagnosis in the start. If I was the physician I would try to hide my scared face. I would try not to reveal to the patient the situation and I would think more about it. I would ask for more tests, and when the diagnosis was certain, I would talk to the patient about the disease and about the treatment. Leukemia is not lethal and can be cured through chemotherapy.

A rheumatologist from Argentina described what he would do in this situation:

> One patient never comes alone, so I think that if I know the background and I recognize that the patient is unable to hear anything about himself, I first talk with the family if the background allows me to do that. If there is no family here, in the case of leukemia, sometimes you have to wait, just one day, two days, one week until you say to the patient, to know him better to know which words to use.

One Argentinean doctor, however, indicated that he would prefer to tell the patient directly:

> You have to tell the truth to a patient and tell what the patient wants to know. If the patient has leukemia, you have to explain to him that if you follow the treatment, you will be better. The patient knows that because you tell him about the several studies on this topic. You have to motivate the patient to do the treatment and keep on living.

In each of these cases, most of the physicians from Argentina, Brazil, and India chose to use "half-truths" to tell a patient that he or she is terminally ill. This phenomenon can be best explained by understanding collectivism and face-saving behaviors. Argentina, Brazil, and India are collective cultures where "[a] 'we' consciousness prevails: Identity is based on the social system; the individual is emotionally dependent on organizations and institutions; the culture emphasizes belonging to organizations; organizations invade private life and the clans to

which individuals belong; and individuals trust group decisions even at the expense of individual rights" (Samovar & Porter, 2001, p. 67–68). In these three cultures, the physicians are thinking of the patient's well-being within the context of his or her family and the larger community.

It is common to use face-saving behaviors like "half-truths" to comfort the patient and sustain the harmony of the group. Face-saving behaviors focus less on the veracity of a statement than what is culturally appropriate for the context. In our preliminary interviews in the United States, physicians were clear that they would tell only the patient and tell him or her directly. This is consistent with the individualistic nature of the United States where direct and explicit communication is preferred. Du Pré (2000) notes that therapeutic privilege was a practice in the United States when physicians withheld information if they thought sharing the information would hurt the patient. However, Veatch (1991) argues that if we wish for patients to be informed partners in their health care, therapeutic privilege is counterproductive. Consistent with current legal expectation in medicine, there is an expectation that physicians in the United States inform the patient as soon as they know the diagnosis.

Family as Patient

Our analysis of "half-truths" indicated that physicians often chose to tell a family member rather than tell the patient. Further investigation suggested that even in regular health care visits, the physician had to treat the "family as patient," rather than focus just on the patient. When a patient was ill, the family members felt ill. When a patient recovered, the family members felt better too. We had explained earlier that Argentina, Brazil, and India are collectivistic cultures. People from these cultures also tend to have an interdependent self-construal (Markus & Kitayama, 1991) where a person's identity is intrinsically connected with his or her family's identity. A person with an interdependent self-construal often makes decisions taking into consideration the needs of his or her family members, and family members often make decisions for him or her. Physicians described this interconnectedness in several ways. A cardiologist in India noted:

> Patients rarely come alone to the clinic. There are always two or three family members with them. I have to be careful to understand the family dynamics and understand how I should share the information. I will share certain kinds of information with the wife, some with the son, and may decide not to share anything with the uncle. I also know that the wife and the son feel the pain the patient is suffering from. When the patient feels better, I feel good too.

A senior cardiologist in Brazil explained how he would include the family so that they can make decisions for the patient:

> If the family were there, I would tell them together. If it were just the patient, I would contact the family. Why? The patient may not need to say anything. I would try to talk to the patient's spouse or child or parents. I would say, your son, your husband, your wife has this illness and we are going to treat it. In this situation, I would tell because the family has to prepare, there is going to be therapy, days when the patient is not feeling well, his diet will change, his hair will fall out. He needs the family's help.

An obstetrician in Argentina described how he would share the news with a patient that the baby in her womb is dead:

> The most common situation is to tell the news that the baby inside of the womb is dead. If I made the diagnosis, I won't tell her immediately. I will take a patient aside and, if she is alone, I will try to call the family so she begins to suspect something is wrong. I allow that to happen because it helps me. If you tell her directly her baby is dead, she will be very hurt. Now she guesses and asks if her baby is dead. So the baby is dead, but that word might come from her mouth and not mine. Then I stay with her, I hold her arms and help her cry for a little while. If the husband comes later, which happens very often, I repeat the same exercise.

In all these cases, the family is an integral part of the healing process, being constantly present, making decisions, seeking advice, and protecting the patient. Our initial conversations with physicians in the United States suggest that patients generally come alone and, if family members are present, they respect the patient's space. Occasionally, the family member may seek clarification on behalf of the patient on certain issues.

Defining Success

We asked the physicians to explain when they had a successful interaction with a patient. In about two-thirds of our interviews, we asked the physician if it was a failure if their patient died. Every one of these physicians indicated that it was not a failure if the patient died, as long as they had done everything possible for the patient. Our preliminary conversations with physicians in the United States suggest that they would see it as a failure if the patient died. It is likely that the U.S. physicians trained in the biomedical perspective are focusing on curing the disease. If they cannot cure the patient, they have failed. Death is the ultimate failure with this perspective. Physicians in Argentina, Brazil, and India focused mostly on relational issues or relational plus task issues to define success, with a limited few focusing only on task-related issues (curing the patient). An emergency room physician summarized the task-oriented perspective by saying:

> I think I am always successful because I always give them a favorable solution. I try to help them. For example, when I am in the emergency room, I am there to give all I can so that a patient can leave the hospital with a treatment or with any response to her problem.

Most physicians, however, described the importance of building trust and strengthening the relationship with a patient as a key part of being successful. A second-year nuclear resident in Brazil defined success as follows:

> When he comes back with another patient. When he brings his uncle or daughter or wife. They would come over and say, "Oh, I knew that you were here; that is why I brought my grandmother. I wanted you to take a look at her." Probably the grandmother

didn't have anything, but he wanted me to look at her. That is when I know a patient likes me.

A family practice physician in Madras described how she looked at both task and relational issues to define success:

> Early diagnosis. When we are able to pick up on traits and/or behaviors that might possibly cause illness. Success is also when a patient comes to you and says that they are happy with the treatment you have given them. You are building trust with a patient that will definitely help with the cure.

A senior physician of legal medicine in Argentina summarized the need to be aware of the patient's multiple needs by defining success as follows:

> In many moments, but especially when you have to transmit [to] a patient the information of an incurable disease, but not terminal. When sharing this information with the patient, if it ends up in improving the patient's wish to fight for his/her life and it has given the patient the possibility of living wonderful experiences that s/he has never lived before, I have allowed the patient a certain quality of life.

THE INTERCULTURAL JOURNEY CONTINUES

"The doctor is mean and the patient is dumb" (du Pré, 2000, p. 48) is a common response in the United States. In this essay, we have argued that it is not fruitful to assign blame to the physician or the patient when communication fails between these two parties. While there is significant research on the interpersonal and cross-cultural aspects, there is little focus on the *intercultural* aspects of physician–patient communication. Our overall goal is to create such an intercultural model, drawing on literature from several disciplines and from original research. Our interviews with physicians in Argentina, Brazil, and India suggest that their collective orientation influences them to use unique communication strategies to deal with culturally diverse patients. They use "half-truths" to share challenging diagnoses, treat the family as the patient, and define success mostly along relational or relational and task objectives.

Our results have several significant implications for studying the role of culture in physician–patient communication.

First, as Lienenger (1991) pointed out in her work, there is more to culture than just geography. Our respondents in Argentina and Brazil defined the country's cultural diversity mainly through socioeconomic and educational differences. Many of our respondents noted that having a common language (Portuguese or Spanish) reduced the impact of other cultural differences such as gender, age, ethnicity, religion, and so on. This is a particularly important finding since Bennett (1998) points out that people from most countries generally tend to focus on race, ethnicity, religion, and language when discussing cultural diversity.

Second, it is important to understand the communication strategies used by physicians in individualistic cultures. Toward this end, we are presently interviewing physicians in the United States to understand how they communicate with patients from culturally diverse backgrounds. Finally, since there are at least two people involved in a physician–patient communication, there are at least two cultural perspectives interacting in their communication. Therefore, it is no longer sufficient to conduct research from only the physician's or the patient's perspective; rather, the physician–patient communication must be analyzed as an *intercultural* phenomena.

To achieve this goal, in addition to our interviews with physicians, we have administered our Multicultural Health Beliefs Inventory (MBHI) to 600 patients in Argentina, Brazil, India, and the United States to explicate how they define good health (Rao, Beckett, & Kandath, 2000). The MBHI assesses respondents' perceptions of good health along five dimensions of health—physical, psychological, relational, spiritual, and lifestyle/environmental. Du Pré (2000) explains how the physician and the patient bring two opposing worldviews when they interact; the physician focuses on the disease (task) only, while the patient focuses on the illness (task plus relational dimension). By combining our data from physicians and patients from several cultures, our goal is to create an *intercultural* model of physician–patient communication that will have both theoretical and practical implications.

Endnotes

1. In our paper, the term *physicians* includes only Doctors of Medicine trained in the allopathic tradition.
2. We used this case study as a part of our Medical Provider Questionnaire to interview physicians.
3. Lustig and Koester (1999) explain that the term *intercultural* "denotes the presence of at least two individuals who are culturally different from each other on such important attributes as value orientations, preferred communication codes, role expectations and perceived rules of social relationships" (p. 60).
4. Since this research was conducted, Caucasians have become a minority in California.
5. We chose these three countries to compare how physicians in collectivistic cultures treated their patients as compared to physicians in the United States, an individualistic culture. For a more detailed explanation of our methodology, see Rao and Beckett (2000).

References

Baylav, A. (1996). Overcoming culture and language barriers. *The Practitioner, 240,* 403–406.

Bennett, M. J. (1998). *Basic concepts of intercultural communication.* Yarmouth, ME: Intercultural Press.

Bureau of the Census. (1996). *Statistical abstract of the United States* (116th ed.). Washington, DC: Author.

Burgoon, M., Birk, T. S., & Hall, J. R. (1991). Compliance and satisfaction with the physician-patient communication: An expectancy theory interpretation of gender differences. *Human Communication Research, 18,* 177–208.

Cegala, D. J., McGee, D. S., & McNeils, K. S. (1996). Components of patients and physicians perceptions of communication competence during a primary care medical interview. *Health Communication, 8,* 1–27.

Charonko, C. V. (1992). Cultural influences in "noncompliant" behavior and decision making. *Holistic Nursing Practice, 6,* 73–78.

Denham, S. (1996). Family health in a rural Appalachian Ohio county. *Journal of Appalachian Studies, 2,* 299–310.

Drake, M. V., & Lowenstein, D. H. (1998). The role of diversity in the health care needs of California. *Western Journal of Medicine, 168,* 348–354.

Du Pré, A. (2000). *Communication about Health.* Mountain View, CA: Mayfield Publishing Company.

Eraker, S. A., Kirscht, J. P., & Becker, M. H. (1984). Understanding and improving patient compliance. *Annals of Internal Medicine, 100,* 258–268.

Geist, P. (2000). Communicating health and understanding in the borderlands of co-cultures. In L. A. Samovar & R. E. Porter (Eds.) *Intercultural communication: A reader* (9th ed., pp. 341–354). Belmont, CA: Wadsworth.

Greengold, N. L., & Ault, M. (1996). Crossing the cultural physician-patient barrier. *Academic Medicine, 71,* 112–114.

Gropper, R. C. (1996). *Cultural and the clinical encounter: An intercultural sensitizer for the health professions.* Yarmouth, ME: Intercultural Press.

Helman, C. G. (1991). Limits of biomedical explanation. *Lancet, 337,* 1080–1083.

Helman, C. G. (1994). *Culture, health and illness.* Boston: Butterworth–Heinemann.

Herselman, S. (1996). Some problems in health communication in a multi-cultural clinical setting: A South African experience. *Health Communication, 8,* 153–170.

Kang, D. S., Kahler, L. R., & Tesar, C. M. (1998). Cultural aspects of caring for refugees. *American Family Physician, 57,* 1245–1255.

Katalanos, N. L. (1994). "When yes means no: Verbal and nonverbal communication of southeast Asian refugees in the New Mexico health care system" (pp. 10–54). Unpublished Masters Thesis. Albuquerque: University of New Mexico.

Kim, M., Klingle, R. S., Sharkey, W. F., Park, H., Smith, D. H., & Cai, D. (2000). A test of a cultural model of patients' motivation for verbal communication in physician-patient interactions. *Communication Monographs, 67,* 262–283.

Kothari, M. P., & Kothari, V. K. (1997). Cross-cultural healthcare challenges: An insight into small American community hospitals. *Journal of Hospital Marketing, 12,* 23–32.

Leininger, M. (1991). *Culture care diversity and universality: A nursing theory.* New York: National League for Nursing Press.

Lochman, J. E. (1983). Factors related to patients' satisfaction with their medical care. *Journal of Community Health, 9,* 91–109.

Lustig, M. W., & Koester, J. (1999). *Intercultural competence: Interpersonal communication across cultures* (3rd ed.). New York: Longman.

Markus, H. R., & Kitayama, S. (1991). Culture and the self: Implications for cognition, emotion, and motivation, *Psychological Review, 98,* 224–253.

Marshall, A. A. (1993). Whose agenda is it anyway? Training medical residents in patient-centered interviewing techniques. In E. B. Ray (Ed.). *Case Studies in Health Communication* (pp. 15–30). Hillsdale, NJ: Lawrence Erlbaum.

Meleis, A. I. (1996). Culturally competent scholarship: Substance and rigor. *Advances in Nursing Science, 19,* 1–16.

Miller, K. I. (1993). Learning to care for others and self: The experience of medical education. In E. B. Ray (Ed.). *Case Studies in Health Communication* (pp. 3–14). Hillsdale, NJ: Lawrence Erlbaum.

Mullhall, A. (1996). The cultural context of death: What nurses need to know. *Nursing Times, 92,* 38–40.

Obmans, P., Garrett, C., & Treichel, C. (1996). Cultural barriers to health care for refugees and immigrants: Provider perceptions. *Clinical and Health Affairs, 79,* 26–30.

O'Hair, D. (1989). Dimensions of relational communication control during physician-patient interactions. *Health Communication, 1,* 97–115.

Ong, L. M. L., De Haes, J. C. J. M., Hoos, A. M., and Lammes, F. B. (1995). Physician-patient communication: A review of the literature. *Social Science and Medicine, 40,* 903–918.

Rao, N., & Beckett, C.S. (2000). "Half-truths" and analogies in doctor-patient communication: Dealing with culturally diverse patients in Brazil. Paper presented at the Health Communication Division of the International Communication Association Conference, Washington, DC.

Rao, N., Beckett, C. S., & Kandath, K. (2000). What is good health? Exploratory analyses of a multidimensional health beliefs scale in Brazil and in India. Paper presented at the Health Communication Division of the National Communication Association Conference, Seattle, Washington.

Rosen, G., Kleinman, A., & Katon, W. (1982). Somatization in family practice: A biopsychosocial approach. *Journal of Family Practice, 14,* 493–502.

Rosenbaum, J. N. (1995). Teaching cultural sensitivity. *Journal of Nursing Education, 4,* 188–198.

Roter, D. (2000). The enduring and evolving nature of patient-physician relationship. *Patient Education and Counseling, 39,* 5–15.

Roter, D., & Hall, J. A. (1992). *Physicians talking with patient, patients talking with physicians.* Westport, CT: Auburn House.

Samovar, L. A., & Porter, R. E. (2001). *Communication between cultures.* (4th ed.). Stamford, CT: Wadsworth Thomson Learning.

Sharf, B. (1990). Physician-patient communication as interpersonal rhetoric: A narrative approach. *Health Communication, 2,* 217–231.

Spitzer, A., Kesselring, A., Ravid, C., Tamir, B., Granot, G., & Noam, R. (1996). Learning about another culture: Project and curricular reflections. *Journal of Nursing Education, 35,* 323–328.

Stewart, M.A. (1995). Effective physician-patient communication and health outcomes: A review. *Canadian Medical Association Journal, 152,* 1423–1433.

Veatch, R. M. (1991). *The patient-physician relation: The patient as partner* (Part 2). Bloomington: Indiana University Press.

Welsbacher, A. (1998). The give and take of physician-patient communication: Can you relate? *Minnesota Medicine, 81,* 15–20.

Young, M., & Klingle, R. S. (1996). Silent partners in medical care: A cross-cultural study of patient participation. *Health Communication, 8,* 29–53.

Concepts and Questions

1. How does Rao distinguish between the dynamics of illness and disease? In what manner may these dynamics be influenced by culture and affect physician–patient communication?

2. Describe several ways in which culture might inhibit physician–patient communication.

3. In what ways might cultural diversity in language affect physician–patient communication?

4. Rao makes the argument that effective physician–patient communication requires cultural knowledge as well as well-developed interpersonal communication skills. What justification is there for this position?

5. How do physician perceptions of cultural diversity in Argentina and Brazil seem to differ from those found in India?

6. What effect does the cultural dynamic of collectivism have on physician–patient communication in Argentina, Brazil, and India?

7. How does the collectivistic concept of family as patient differ from the individualistic approach often found in the United States?

8. In what way does building trust between physician and patient in Argentina, Brazil, and India differ from how it is achieved in the United States?

9. What does Rao mean when he refers to the *intercultural* aspects of physician–patient communication?

10. In what ways do the communication strategies of physicians in collectivistic cultures seem to differ from those of physicians in individualistic cultures?

Culture and Communication in the Classroom

GENEVA GAY

A semiotic relationship exists among communication, culture, teaching, and learning, and it has profound implications for implementing culturally responsive teaching. This is so because "what we talk about; how we talk about it; what we see, attend to, or ignore; how we think; and what we think about are influenced by our culture. . . . [and] help to shape, define, and perpetuate our culture" (Porter & Samovar, 1991, p. 21). Making essentially the same argument, Bruner (1996) states, "learning and thinking are always situated in a cultural setting and always dependent upon the utilization of cultural resources" (p. 4). Culture provides the tools to pursue the search for meaning and to convey our understanding to others. Consequently, communication cannot exist without culture, culture cannot be known without communication, and teaching and learning cannot occur without communication or culture.

INTRODUCTION

The discussions in this article explicate some of the critical features and pedagogical potentials of the culture–communication semiotics for different ethnic groups of color. The ideas and examples presented are composites of group members who strongly identify and affiliate with their ethnic group's cultural traditions. They are not intended to be descriptors of specific individuals within ethnic groups, or their behaviors in all circumstances. If, how, and when these cultural characteristics are expressed in actual behavior, and by whom, are influenced by many different

factors. Therefore, the ethnic interactional and communication styles described in this article should be seen as *general and traditional referents of group dynamics* rather than static attributes of particular individuals.

Students of color who are most traditional in their communication styles and other aspects of culture and ethnicity are likely to encounter more obstacles to school achievement than those who think, behave, and express themselves in ways that approximate school and mainstream cultural norms. This is the case for many highly culturally and ethnically affiliated African Americans. In making this point, Dandy (1991) proposes that the language many African Americans speak "is all too often degraded or simply dismissed by individuals both inside and outside the racial group as being uneducated, illiterate, undignified or simply non-standard" (p. 2). Other groups of color are "at least given credit for having a legitimate language heritage, even if they are denied full access to American life" (p. 2).

Much of educators' decision-making on the potential and *realized* achievement of students of color is dependent on communication abilities (their own and the students'). If students are not very proficient in school communication, and teachers do not understand or accept the students' cultural communication styles, then their academic performance may be misdiagnosed or trapped in communicative mismatches. Students may know much more than they are able to communicate, or they may be communicating much more than their teachers are able to discern. As Boggs (1985, p. 301) explains, "The attitudes and behavior patterns that have the most important effect upon children . . . [are] those involved in communication." This communication is multidimensional and multipurposed, including verbal and nonverbal, direct and tacit, literal and symbolic, formal and informal, grammatical and discourse components.

The discussions of culture and communication in classrooms in this article are organized into two parts. The first outlines some key assertions about culture and communication in teaching and learning in general. These help to anchor communication within culturally responsive teaching. In the second part of the article, some of the major characteristics of the communication *modes* of African,

Native, Latino, Asian, and European Americans are presented. The focus throughout these discussions is on discourse dynamics; that is, who participates in communicative interactions and under what conditions, how these participation patterns are affected by cultural socialization, and how they influence teaching and learning in classrooms.

RELATIONSHIP AMONG CULTURE, COMMUNICATION, AND EDUCATION

In analyzing the routine tasks teachers perform, B. Smith (1971) declares that "teaching is, above all, a linguistic activity" and "language is at the heart of teaching" (p. 24). Whether making assignments, giving directions, explaining events, interpreting words and expressions, proving positions, justifying decisions and actions, making promises, dispersing praise and criticism, or assessing capability, teachers must use language. And the quality of the performance of these tasks is a direct reflection of how well teachers can communicate with their students. Smith admonishes educators for not being more conscientious in recognizing the importance of language in the performance and effectiveness of their duties. He says, "It could be that when we have analyzed the language of teaching and investigated the effects of its various formulations, the art of teaching will show marked advancement" (p. 24). Dandy (1991) likewise places great faith in the power of communication in the classroom, declaring that "teachers have the power to shape the future, if they communicate with their students, but those who cannot communicate are powerless" (p. 10). These effects of communication skills are especially significant to improving the performance of underachieving ethnically different students.

Porter and Samovar's (1991) study of the nature of culture and communication, the tenacious reciprocity that exists between the two, and the importance of these aspects to intercultural interactions provides valuable information for culturally responsive teaching. They describe communication as "an intricate matrix of interacting social acts that occur in a complex social environment that reflects the way people live and how they come to interact with and get along in their world. This social environ-ment is culture, and if we are to truly understand communication, we must also understand culture" (p. 10). Communication is dynamic, interactive, irreversible, and invariably contextual. As such, it is a continuous, ever-changing activity that takes place between people who are trying to influence each other; its effects are irretrievable once it has occurred, despite efforts to modify or counteract them.

Communication is also governed by the rules of the social and physical contexts in which it occurs (Porter & Samovar, 1991). Culture is the rule-governing system that defines the forms, functions, and content of communication. It is largely responsible for the construction of our "individual repertories of communicative behaviors and meanings" (p. 10). Understanding connections between culture and communication is critical to improving intercultural interactions. This is so because "as cultures differ from one another, the communication practices and behaviors of individuals reared in those cultures will also be different," and "the degree of influence culture has on intercultural communication is a function of the dissimilarity between the cultures" (p. 12).

Communication entails much more than the content and structure of written and spoken language, and it serves purposes greater than the mere transmission of information. Sociocultural context and nuances, discourse logic and dynamics, delivery styles, social functions, role expectations, norms of interaction, and nonverbal features are as important as (if not more so than) vocabulary, grammar, lexicon, pronunciation, and other linguistic or structural dimensions of communication. This is so because the "form of exchange between child and adult and the conditions in which it occurs will affect not only what is said, but how involved the child will become" (Boggs, 1985, p. 301). Communication is the quintessential way in which humans make meaningful connections with each other, whether as caring, sharing, loving, teaching, or learning. Montague and Matson (1979, p. vii) suggest that it is "the ground of [human] meeting and the foundation of [human] community."

Communication is also indispensable to facilitating knowing and accessing knowledge. This is the central idea of the Sapir–Whorf hypothesis about the relationship among language, thought, and behavior. It says that, far from being simply a means for reporting experience, language is a way of defining experience, thinking, and knowing. In this sense, language is the semantic system of meanings and modes of conveyance that people habitually use to code, analyze, categorize, and interpret experience (Carroll, 1956; Hoijer, 1991; Mandelbaum, 1968). In characterizing this relationship, Sapir (1968) explains that "language is a guide to 'social reality' . . . [and] a symbolic guide to culture. . . . It powerfully conditions all of our thinking about social problems and processes" (p. 162). People do not live alone in an "objectified world" or negotiate social realities without the use of language. Nor is language simply a "mechanical" instrumental tool for transmitting information. Instead, human beings are "very much at the mercy of the particular language which has become the medium of expression for their society" (p. 162). The languages used in different cultural systems strongly influence how people think, know, feel, and do.

Whorf (1952, 1956; Carroll, 1956), a student of Sapir, makes a similar argument that is represented by the "principle of linguistic relativity." It contends that the structures of various languages reflect different cultural patterns and values, and, in turn, affect how people understand and respond to social phenomena. In developing these ideas further, Whorf (1952) explains that "a language is not merely a reproducing instrument for voicing ideas but rather is itself the shaper of ideas, the program and guide for the individual's mental activity, for his analysis of impressions, for his synthesis of his mental stock in trade" (p. 5). Vygotsky (1962) also recognizes the reciprocal relationship among language, culture, and thought. He declares, as "indisputable fact," that "thought development is determined by language . . . and the sociocultural experience of the child" (p. 51).

Moreover, the development of logic is affected by a person's socialized speech, and intellectual growth is contingent on the mastery of social means of thought, or language. According to Byers and Byers (1985), "[t]he organization of the processes of human communication in any culture is a template for the organization of knowledge or information in that culture" (p. 28). This line of argument is applied specifically to different ethnic groups by theorists, researchers, and school practitioners from a

variety of disciplinary perspectives, including social and developmental psychology, sociolinguistics, ethnography, and multiculturalism. For example, Ascher (1992) applied this reasoning to language influences on how mathematical relationships are viewed in general. Giamati and Weiland (1997) connected it to Navajo students' learning of mathematics, concluding that the performance difficulties they encounter are "a result of cultural influences on perceptions rather than a lack of ability" (p. 27). This happens because of the reciprocal interactions among language, culture, and perceptions. Consistently, when these scholars refer to "language" or "communication," they are talking more about discourse dynamics than structural forms of speaking and writing.

Thus, languages and communication styles are systems of cultural notations and the means through which thoughts and ideas are expressively embodied. Embedded within them are cultural values and ways of knowing that strongly influence how students engage with learning tasks and demonstrate mastery of them. The absence of shared communicative frames of reference, procedural protocols, rules of etiquette, and discourse systems makes it difficult for culturally diverse students and teachers to genuinely understand each other and for students to fully convey their intellectual abilities. Teachers who do not know or value these realities will not be able to fully access, facilitate, and assess most of what these students know and can do. Communication must be understood to be more than a linguistic system.

CULTURALLY DIFFERENT DISCOURSE STRUCTURES

In conventional classroom discourse, students are expected to assume what Kochman (1985) calls a *passive-receptive* posture. They are told to listen quietly white the teacher talks. Once the teacher finishes, then the students can respond in some prearranged, stylized way—by asking or answering questions; validating or approving what was said; or taking individual, teacher-regulated turns at talking. Individual students gain the right to participate in the conversation by permission of the teacher. The verbal discourse is accompanied by nonverbal attending behaviors and speech-delivery mechanisms that require maintaining eye contact with the speaker and using little or no physical movement. Thus, students are expected to be silent and look at teachers when they are talking and wait to be acknowledged before they take their turn at talking. Once permission is granted, they should follow established rules of decorum, such as one person speaking at a time, being brief and to the point, and keeping emotional nuances to a minimum (Kochman, 1981; Philips, 1983).

These structural protocols governing discourse are expressed in other classroom practices as well. Among them are expecting students always to speak in complete sentences that include logical development of thought, precise information, appropriate vocabulary, and careful attention to grammatical features such as appropriate use of vocabulary and noun-verb tense agreement. Student participation in classroom interactions is often elicited by teachers asking questions that are directed to specific individuals and require a narrow range of information-giving, descriptive responses. It is important for individuals to distinguish themselves in the conversations, for student responses to be restricted to only the specific demands of questions asked, and for the role of speaker and audience to be clearly separated.

In contrast to the passive-receptive character of conventional classroom discourse, some ethnic groups have communication styles that Kochman (1985) describes as *participatory-interactive*. Speakers expect listeners to engage them actively through vocalized, motion, and movement responses *as they are speaking*. Speakers and listeners are action-provoking partners in the construction of the discourse. These communicative styles have been observed among African Americans, Latinos, and Native Hawaiians. As is the case with other cultural behaviors, they are likely to be more pronounced among individuals who strongly identify and affiliate with their ethnic groups and cultural heritages. For example, low-income and minimally educated members of ethnic groups are likely to manifest group cultural behaviors more thoroughly than those who are middle class and educated. This is so because they have fewer opportunities to interact with people different from themselves and to be af-

fected by the cultural exchanges and adaptations that result from the intermingling of a wide variety of people from diverse ethnic groups and varied experiential backgrounds.

ETHNIC VARIATIONS IN COMMUNICATION STYLES

Among African Americans the participatory-interactive style of communicating is sometimes referred to as *call-response* (Asante, 1998; Baber, 1987; Kochman, 1972, 1981, 1985; Smitherman, 1977). It involves listeners giving encouragement, commentary, compliments, and even criticism to speakers *as they are talking*. The speaker's responsibility is to issue the "calls" (making statements), and the listeners' obligation is to respond in some expressive, and often auditory, way (e.g., smiling, vocalizing, looking about, moving around, "amening") (Dandy, 1991; Smitherman, 1977). When a speaker says something that triggers a response in them (whether positive or negative; affective or cognitive), African American listeners are likely to "talk back." This may involve a vocal or motion response, or both, sent directly to the speaker or shared with neighbors in the audience. Longstreet (1978) and Shade (1994) describe the practice as "breaking in and talking over." This mechanism is used to signal to speakers that their purposes have been accomplished or that it is time to change the direction or leadership of the conversation. Either way, there is no need for the speaker to pursue the particular discourse topic or technique further.

African Americans "gain the floor" or get participatory entry into conversations through personal assertiveness, the strength of the impulse to be involved, and the persuasive power of the point they wish to make, rather than waiting for an "authority" to grant permission. They tend to invest their participation with personality power, actions, and emotions. Consequently, African Americans are often described as verbal performers whose speech behaviors are fueled by personal advocacy, emotionalism, fluidity, and creative variety (Abrahams, 1970; Baber, 1987). These communication facilities have been attributed to the oral-aural nature of African American cultural and communal value orientations (Pasteur & Toldson, 1982; Smitherman, 1977). Many teachers view these behaviors negatively, as "rude," "inconsiderate," "disruptive," and "speaking out of turn," and they penalize students for them.

Native Hawaiian students who maintain their traditional cultural practices use a participatory-interactive communicative style similar to the call-response of African Americans. Called "talk-story" or "co-narrative," it involves several students working collaboratively, or talking together, to create an idea, tell a story, or complete a learning task (Au, 1980, 1993; Au & Kawakami, 1985, 1991, 1994; Au & Mason, 1981; Boggs et al., 1985). After observing these behaviors among elementary students, Au (1993) concluded that "what seems important to Hawaiian children in talk-story is not individual . . . but group performance in speaking" (p. 114). These communication preferences are consistent with the importance Native Hawaiian culture places on individuals' contributing to the well-being of family and friends instead of working only for their own betterment (Gallimore, Boggs, & Jordon, 1974; Tharp & Gallimore, 1988).

A communicative practice that has some of the same traits of call-response and talk-story has been observed among European American females. Tannen (1990) calls it "cooperative overlapping" and describes it as women "talking along with speakers to show participation and support" (p. 208). It occurs most often in situations where talk is casual and friendly. This *rapport-talk* is used to create community. It is complemented by other traditional women's ways of communicating, such as the following:

- Being "audience" more often than "speaker" in that they are recipients of information provided by males
- De-emphasizing expertise and the competitiveness it generates
- Focusing on individuals in establishing friendships, networks, intimacy, and relationships more than exhibiting power, accomplishment, or control
- Negotiating closeness in order to give and receive confirmation, support, and consensus
- Avoiding conflict and confrontation (Belensky et al., 1986; Klein, 1982; Maltz & Borker, 1983; Tannen, 1990)

While these habits of "communal communication and interaction" are normal to the users, they can be problematic to classroom teachers. On first encounter, they may be perceived as "indistinguishable noise and chaos" or unwholesome dependency. Even after the shock of the initial encounter passes, teachers may still consider these ways of communicating socially deviant, not conducive to constructive intellectual engagement, rude, and insulting. They see them as obstructing individual initiative and preempting the right of each student to have a fair chance to participate in instructional discourse. These assessments can prompt attempts to rid students of the habits and replace them with the rules of individualistic, passive-receptive, and controlling communication styles predominant in classrooms.

Teachers may not realize that by doing this they could be causing irreversible damage to students' abilities or inclinations to engage fully in the instructional process. Hymes (1985) made this point when he suggested that rejecting ethnically different students' communication styles might be perceived by them as rejection of their personhood. Whether intentional or not, casting these kinds of aspersions on the identity and personal worth of students of color does not bode well for their academic achievement.

Problem Solving and Task Engagement

Many African American, Latino, Native American, and Asian American students use styles of inquiry and responding that are different from those employed most often in classrooms. The most common practice among teachers is to ask convergent (single-answer) questions and use deductive approaches to solving problems. Emphasis is given to details, to building the whole from the parts, to moving from the specific to the general. Discourse tends to be didactic, involving one student with the teacher at a time (Goodlad, 1984). In comparison, students of color who are strongly affiliated with their traditional cultures tend to be more inductive, interactive, and communal in task performance. The preference for inductive problem solving is expressed as reasoning from the whole to parts, from the general to the specific. The focus is on the "big picture," the pattern, the principle (Boggs et al., 1985; Philips, 1983; Ramirez & Castañeda, 1974; Shade 1989).

Although these general patterns of task engagement prevail across ethnic groups, variations do exist. Some teachers use inductive modes of teaching, and some students within each ethnic group of color learn deductively. Many Asian American students seem to prefer questions that require specific answers but are proposed to the class as a whole. While many Latino students may be inclined toward learning in group contexts, specific individuals may find these settings distracting and obstructive to their task mastery.

In traditional African American and Latino cultures, problem solving is highly contextual. One significant feature of this contextuality is creating a "stage" or "setting" prior to the performance of a task. The stage setting is invariably social in nature. It involves establishing personal connections with others who will participate as a prelude to addressing the task. In making these connections, individuals are readying themselves for "work" by cultivating a social context. They are, in effect, activating their cultural socialization concept that an individual functions better within the context of a group. Without the group as an anchor, referent, and catalyst, the individual is set adrift, having to function alone.

These cultural inclinations may be operating when Latino adults begin their task interactions with colleagues by inquiring about the families of other participants and their own personal well-being or when African American speakers inform the audience about their present psychoemotional disposition and declare the ideology, values, and assumptions underlying the positions they will be taking in the presentation (i.e., "where they are coming from"). This "preambling" is a way for the speakers to prime the audience and themselves for the subsequent performance. Students of color may be setting the stage for their engagement with learning tasks in classrooms (e.g., writing an essay, doing seatwork, taking a test) when they seem to be spending unnecessary time arranging their tests, sharpening pencils, shifting their body postures (stretching, flexing their hands, arms, and legs, etc.), or socializing with peers rather than attending to the assigned task. "Preparation before performance" for these stu-

dents serves a similar purpose in learning as a theater performer doing yoga exercises before taking the stage. Both are techniques the "actors" use to focus, to get themselves in the mood and mode to perform.

For those Asian Americans who prefer to learn within the context of groups, it is accomplished through a process of *collaborative and negotiated problem solving*. Regardless of how minor or significant an issue is, they seek out opinions and proposed solutions from all members of the constituted group. Each individual's ideas are presented and critiqued. Their merits are weighed against those suggested by every other member of the group. Discussions are animated and expansive so that all parties participate and understand the various elements of the negotiations. Eventually, a solution is reached that is a compromise of several possibilities. Then more discussions follow to ensue that everyone is in agreement with the solution and understands who is responsible for what aspects of its implementation. These discussions proceed in a context of congeniality and *consensus building* among the many, not with animosity, domination, and the imposition of the will of a few.

A compelling illustration of the positive effects of this process on student achievement occurred in Treisman's (1985; Fullilove & Treisman, 1990) Mathematics Workshop Program at the University of California, Berkeley. He observed the study habits of Chinese Americans to determine why they performed so well in high-level mathematics classes and if he could use their model with Latinos and African Americans. He found what others have observed more informally—the Chinese American students always studied in groups, and they routinely explained to each other their understanding of the problems and how they arrived at solutions to them. Treisman attributed their high achievement to the time they devoted to studying and to talking through the solution with peers. When he simulated this process with African Americans and Latinos, their achievement improved radically. Treisman was convinced that "group study" made the difference. Given other evidence that compatibility between cultural habits and teaching-learning styles improves student performance, this is probably what occurred. Communal problem solving and the communicative impulse were evoked, thus producing the desired results.

These are powerful but challenging pedagogical lessons for all educators to learn and emulate in teaching students of color. Collective and situated performance styles require a distribution of resources (timing, collective efforts, procedures, attitudes) that can collide with school norms; for instance, much of how student achievement is assessed occurs in tightly scheduled arrangements, which do not accommodate stage setting or collective performance. Students of color have to learn different styles of performing, as well as the substantive content to demonstrate their achievement. This places them in potential double jeopardy—that is, failing at the level of both procedure and substance. Pedagogical reform must be cognizant of these dual needs and attend simultaneously to the content of learning and the processes for demonstrating mastery. It also must be bi-directional—that is, changing instructional practices to make them more culturally responsive to ethnic and cultural diversity, while teaching students of color how to better negotiate mainstream educational structures.

Organizing Ideas in Discourse

In addition to mode, the actual process of discourse engagement is influenced by culture and, in turn, influences the performance of students in schools. Several elements of the dynamics of discourse are discussed here to illustrate this point; they are how ideas are organized, taking positions, conveying imagery and affect through language, and gender variations in conversational styles. How ideas and thoughts are organized in written and spoken expression can be very problematic to student achievement. Two techniques are commonly identified—*topic-centered* and *topic-associative* or *topic-chaining* techniques. European Americans seem to prefer the first while Latinos, African Americans, Native Americans, and Native Hawaiians (Au, 1993; Heath, 1983) are inclined toward the second.

In *topic-centered* discourse, speakers focus on one issue at a time; arrange facts and ideas in logical, linear order; and make explicit relationships between facts and ideas. In this process, cognitive processing moves deductively from discrete parts to a cumula-

tive whole with a discernible closure. Quality is determined by clarity of descriptive details, absence of unnecessary or flowery elaboration, and how well explanations remain focused on the essential features of the issue being analyzed. The structure, content, and delivery of this discourse style closely parallel the expository, descriptive writing, and speaking commonly used in schools. A classic example of topic-centered discourse is journalistic writing, which concentrates on giving information about who, what, when, where, why, and how as quickly as possible. Its purpose is to convey information and to keep this separate from other speech functions, such as persuasion, commentary, and critique. Another illustration is the thinking and writing associated with empirical inquiry, or critical problem solving. Again, there is a hierarchical progression in the communication sequence, beginning with identifying the problem, collecting data, identifying alternative solutions and related consequences, and selecting and defending a solution. There is a clear attempt to separate facts from opinions, information from emotions.

A *topic-associative style* of talking and writing is episodic, anecdotal, thematic, and integrative. More than one issue is addressed at once. Related explanations unfold in overlapping, intersecting loops, with one emerging out of and building on others. Relationships among segments of the discourse are assumed or inferred rather than explicitly established (Cazden, 1988; Lee & Slaughter-Defoe, 1995). Thinking and speaking appear to be circular and seamless rather than linear and clearly demarcated. For one who is unfamiliar with it, this communication style sounds rambling, disjointed, and as if the speaker never ends a thought before going to something else.

Goodwin (1990) observed topic-chaining discourse at work in a mixed-age (4- to 14-year-olds) group of African Americans in a Philadelphia neighborhood as they told stories, shared gossip, settled arguments, and negotiated relationships. She noted the ease and finesse with which a child could switch from a contested verbal exchange to an engaging story and dramatically reshape dyadic interactions into multiparty ones. Using a single utterance, the children could evoke a broad history of events, a complex web of identities and relationships that all participants understood without having elaborate details on any of the separate segments. The talk-story discourse style among Native Hawaiians operates in a similar fashion, which explains why Au (1993) characterizes it as a "joint performance, or the cooperative production of responses by two or more speakers" (p. 113).

Two other commonplace examples are indicative of a topic-chaining or associative discourse style. One is used by many African Americans who literarily try to attach or connect the sentences in a paragraph to each through the prolific use of conjunctive words and phrases; for example, frequently beginning sentences with "consequently," "therefore," "however," thus," "moreover," "additionally," and "likewise." These sentences are in close proximity to each other—sometimes as often as four of every five or six.

The second example illuminates the storytelling aspect of topic-chaining discourse. African Americans (Kochman, 1981, 1985; Smitherman, 1997) and Native Hawaiians (Boggs, 1985) have been described as not responding directly to questions asked. Instead, they give narratives, or tell stories. This involves setting up and describing a series of events (and the participants) loosely connected to the questions asked. It is as if ideas and thoughts, like individuals, do not function or find meaning in isolation from context. A host of other actors and events are evoked to assist in constructing the "stage" upon which the individuals eventually interject their own performance (i.e., answer the question). This narrative-response style is also signaled by the attention given to "introductions" and preludes in writing. They are extensive enough to prompt such comments from teachers as, "Get to the point" or "Is this relevant?" or "More focus needed" or "Too much extraneous stuff" or "Stick to the topic." The students simply think that these preludes are necessary to setting the stage for the substantive elements of the discourse.

Storytelling as Topic-Chaining Discourse

Speaking about the purposes and pervasiveness of storytelling among African Americans, Smitherman (1977) surmises that they allow many different things to be accomplished at once. These include relating information, persuading others to support the speaker's point of view, networking, countering opposition, exercising power, and demonstrating one's own verbal aestheticism. She elaborates further:

> An ordinary inquiry [to African American cultural speakers] is likely to elicit an extended narrative response where the abstract point or general message will be couched in concrete story form. The reporting of events is never simply objectively reported, but dramatically acted out and narrated. The Black English speaker thus simultaneously conveys the facts and his or her personal sociopsychological perspective on the facts. . . . This meandering away from the "point" takes the listener on episodic journeys and over tributary rhetorical routes, but like the flow of nature's rivers and streams, stories all eventually lead back to the source. Though highly applauded by blacks, this narrative linguistic style is exasperating to whites who wish you'd be direct and hurry up and get to the point. (pp. 161, 148)

It takes African American topic-chaining speakers a while to get to the point—to orchestrate the cast of contributors to the action. The less time they have to develop their storylines, the more difficult it is for them to get to the substantive heart of the matter. Frequently in schools, the time allocated to learning experiences lapses while African Americans are still setting up the backdrop for "the drama"— their expected task performance—and they never get to demonstrate what they know or can do on the proposed academic task.

Posed to an African American student who routinely uses a topic-chaining discourse style, a simple, apparently straightforward question such as, "What did you do during summer vacation?" might prompt a response such as the following:

> Sometimes, especially on holidays, you know, like July 4, or maybe when a friend was celebrating a birthday, we go to the amusement park. It's a long ways from where I live. And, that is always a big thing, because we have to get together and form car caravans. Jamie and Kelly are the best drivers, but I preferred to ride with Aisha because her dad's van is loaded, and we be just riding along, chilling, and listening to tapes and stuff. Going to the amusement

park was a kick 'cause we had to drive a long way, and when we got there people would stare at us like we were weird or something. And we would just stare right back at them. All but Dion. He would start to act crazy, saying things like, "What you lookin' at me for? I ain't no animal in no zoo. I got as much right to be here as you do." You see, Dion gets hyped real quick about this racist thing. And we be telling him, "Man, cool it. Don't start no stuff. We too far from home for that." Then, we just go on into the park and have us a good time. We try to get all the rides before everything closes down for the night. Then, there's the trip home. Everybody be tired but happy. We do this three or four times in the summer. Different people go each time. But, you know something— we always run into some kind of funny stuff, like people expecting us to make trouble. Why is that so? All we doing is out for a good time. Dion, of course, would say it's a racist thing.

The narrator does eventually answer the question, but it is embedded in a lot of other details. In fact, there are stories within stories within stories (e.g., celebration rituals, friendships, drivers, the drive, racism, risk taking, activities at the amusement park, similarities and differences, continuity and change, etc.). These elaborate details are needed to convey the full meaning of the narrator's answer to the initial question. But to culturally uninitiated listeners or readers (such as many classroom teachers), the account sounds like rambling and unnecessarily convoluted information, or Smitherman's (1977) notion of "belabored verbosity" (p.161).

Teachers seeking to improve the academic performance of students of color who use topic-associative discourse styles need to incorporate a storytelling motif into their instructional behaviors. This can be done without losing any of the substantive quality of academic discourses. Gee (1989) believes topic-associative talking is inherently more complex, literary, and enriching than topic-centered speech. The assertions are verified by the success of the Kamehameha Early Elementary Program, which produced remarkable improvement in the literacy achievement of Hawaiian students by employing their cultural and communication styles in classroom instruction. Boggs (1985) found that the performance of Native Hawaiian stu-

dents on the reading readiness tests correlated positively with narrative abilities. The children who told longer narratives more correctly identified the picture prompts than those who responded to individually directed questions from adults.

Yet, topic-associative discourse is troubling to many conventional teachers. Michaels and Cazden's (1986) research explains why. The European American teachers who participated in their study found this discourse style difficult to understand and placed little value on it. African American teachers gave equal positive value to topic-centered and topic-associative discourse. We should not assume that this will always be the case. Some African American teachers are as troubled by topic-chaining discourse among students as teachers from other ethnic groups. The ethnicity of teachers is not the most compelling factor in culturally responsive teaching for ethnically diverse students. Rather, it is teachers' knowledge base and positive attitudes about cultural diversity, as well as their ability to teach ethnically diverse students, contributions, experiences, and perspectives effectively.

Taking Positions and Presenting Self

In addition to significant differences in the *organization* of thinking, writing, and talking, many ethnically diverse students *relate* differently to the materials, issues, and topic discussed or analyzed. Most of the information available on these patterns deals with African and European Americans. Not much research has been done on the discourse dynamics of Latinos and Native Americans. Deyhle and Swisher (1997) concluded their historical view of research conducted on Native Americans with a strong conviction that there are fundamental and significant linkages among culture, communication, and cognition that should help shape classroom instruction for ethnically diverse students. But they do not provide any descriptions of the discourse dynamics of various Native American groups. Fox (1994) examined the thinking, writing, and speaking behavior of international students from different countries in Africa, Asia, Latin America, and the Middle East studying in U.S. colleges and universities. She found that their cultural traditions valued indirect and holistic communication, wisdom of the past, and the importance of the group. Their cultural socialization profoundly affects how these students interact with professors and classmates, reading materials, problem solving, and writing assignments. How they write is especially important to their academic performance because, according to Fox (1994), "writing touches the heart of a student's identity, drawing its voice and strength and meaning from the way the student understands the world" (p. xiii).

Personalizing or Objectifying Communications

Kochman (1972, 1981, 1985), Dandy (1991), and Smitherman (1977) point out that African Americans (especially those most strongly affiliated with the ethnic identity and cultural heritage) tend to take positions of advocacy and express personal points of view in discussions. Facts, opinions, emotions, and reason are combined in presenting one's case. The worth of a particular line of reasoning is established by challenging the validity of oppositional ideas and by the level of personal ownership of the individuals making the presentations. Declaring one's personal position on issues, and demanding the same of others, is also a way of recognizing "the person" as a valid data source (Kochman, 1981). Publication is not enough to certify the authority of ideas and explanations, or the expertise of the people who author them. They must stand the test of critical scrutiny and the depth of personal endorsement.

Consequently, Kochman (1981) proposes that African Americans are more likely to challenge authority and expertise than students from other ethnic groups. He suggests the following reason for this:

> Blacks . . . consider debate to be as much a contest between individuals as a test of opposing ideas. Because it is a contest, attention is also paid to performance, for winning the contest requires that one outperform one's opponents; outthink, outtalk, and outstyle. It means being concerned with art as well as argument. . . . [B]lacks consider it essential for individuals to have personal positions on issues and assume full responsibility for arguing their validity. Otherwise, they feel that individuals would not care enough about truth or their own ideas to want to

struggle for them. And without such struggle, the value of ideas cannot be ascertained. (pp. 24–25)

According to Kochman (1981), the discourse dynamics of European Americans are almost the opposite of African Americans. He says they relate to issues and materials as spokespersons, not advocates, and consider the truth or merits of an idea to be intrinsic, especially if the person presenting it has been certified as an authority or expert. How deeply individuals personally care about the idea is irrelevant. Their responsibility is to present the facts as accurately as possible. They believe that emotions interfere with one's capacity to reason and quality of reasoning. Thus, European Americans try to avoid or minimize opposition in dialogue (especially when members of ethnic-minority groups are involved) because they assume it will be confrontational, divisive, and lead to intransigence or the further entrenchment of opposing viewpoints. They aim to control impulse and emotions, to be open-minded and flexible, and to engage a multiplicity of ideas. Since no person is privy to all the answers, the best way to cull the variety of possibilities is to ensure congeniality, not confrontation, in conversation. As a result of these beliefs and desires, the European American style of intellectual and discourse engagement "weakens or eliminates those aspects of character or posture that they believe keep people's minds closed and make them otherwise unyielding" (Kochman, 1981, p. 20).

"Playing with and on" Words

African American cultural discourse uses repetition for emphasis and to create a cadence in speech delivery that approximates other aspects of cultural expressiveness such as dramatic flair, powerful imagery, persuasive effect, and polyrhythmic patterns (Baber, 1987; Kochman, 1981; Smitherman, 1977). Some individuals are very adept at "playing on" and "playing with" words, thereby creating a "polyrhythmic character" to their speaking. It is conveyed through the use of nonparallel structures, juxtaposition of complementary opposites, inclusion of a multiplicity of "voices," manipulation of word meanings, poetic tonality, creative use of word patterns, and an overall playfulness in language usage. Although decontextualized, this statement written by a graduate student illustrates some of these tendencies: "The use of culturally consistent communicative competencies entails teachers being able to recognize the multitude of distinct methods of communication that African American students bring to the classroom." Another example of these discourse habits is the frequent use of verb pairs. Following are some samples selected from the writings of students:

- a number of public issues to be explored and represented
- numerous factors have impacted and influenced
- make an attempt to analyze and interpret
- no model is available to interpret and clarify
- many ways of explaining and understanding
- a framework that will enable and facilitate
- validity was verified and confirmed
- he will describe and give account

Two other examples are helpful in illustrating the dramatic flair and poetic flavor of playing with words that characterize African American cultural discourse. One comes from Smart-Grosvenor (1982), who describes African American cultural communication as "a metaphorical configuration of verbal nouns, exaggerated adjectives, and double descriptives" (p. 138). She adds (and in the process demonstrates that which she explains) that "ours is an exciting, practical, elegant, dramatic, ironic, mysterious, surrealistic, sanctified, outrageous and creative form of verbal expression. It's a treasure trove of vitality, profundity, rhythm—and, yes, style" (p. 138). Smitherman (1972) provides a second example of African American discourse style and aestheticism. She writes:

> The power of the word lies in it enabling us to translate vague feelings and fleeting experiences into forms that give unity, coherence, and expression to the inexpressible. The process of composing becomes a mechanism for discovery wherein we may generate illuminating revelations about a particular idea or event. (p. 91)

Ambivalence and Distancing in Communication

Classroom experiences and personal conversations with Asian international and Asian American college students and professional colleagues reveal some recurrent communication features. These individuals tend not to declare either definitive advocacy or adversarial positions in either oral or written discourse. They take moderate stances, seek out compromise positions, and look for ways to accommodate opposites. They are rather hesitant to analyze and critique but will provide factually rich descriptions of issues and events. They also use a great deal of "hedges" and conciliatory markers in conversations; that is, "starts and stops," affilitative words, and apologetic nuances interspersed in speech, such as "I'm not sure," "maybe . . .," "I don't know, but . . .," "I may be wrong, but . . ." These behaviors give the appearance of tentative, unfinished thinking, even though the individuals using them are very intellectually capable and thoroughly prepared academically. And many Asian and Asian American students are virtually silent in classroom discussions.

I have observed Asian and Asian American students frequently interjecting laughter into conversations with me about their academic performance. This happens in instructional and advising situations in which students are having difficulty understanding a learning task that is being explained by the teacher. Rather than reveal the full extent of their confusion, or lack of understanding, students will interject laughter into the conversations. It functions to diffuse the intensity of their confusion and give the impression that the problem is not as serious as it really is. Teachers who are unaware of what is going on may interpret these behaviors to mean the students are not taking their feedback or advice seriously. Or they may assume that the students understand the issue so completely that they have reached a point in their intellectual processing where they can relax and break the mental focus (signaled by laughter). When queried about this practice, students invariably say, "It's cultural" and often add an explanation for it that invokes some rule of social etiquette or interpersonal interaction that is taught in their ethnic communities. Interestingly, Japanese, Chinese, Korean, Taiwanese, and Cambodians offer similar explanations about the motivation behind and meaning of this shared behavior. These students explain that "ritualized laughter" is a means of maintaining harmonious relationships and avoiding challenging the authority or disrespecting the status of the teacher.

These communication behaviors among students of Asian origin are consistent with those reported by Fox (1994). Hers were gleaned from observations, interviews, and working with students from non-Western cultures and countries (Fox refers to them as "world majority students") on their analytical writing skills in basic writing courses at the Center for International Education at the University of Massachusetts. Data were collected over three years. Sixteen graduate students from several different disciplines participated in the formal interviews. They represented 12 countries: Korea, Japan, the People's Republic of China, Nepal, Indonesia, Brazil, India, Chile, Sri Lanka, Cote d'Ivoire, Somalia, and Cape Verde. Faculty members who worked closely with these students were also interviewed. Additional information was derived from informal conversations and interactions with other students; analyzing writing samples; the teacher's notes about how she and the students worked through writing difficulties; and students' explanations about what they were trying to say in their writing, why assignments were misunderstood, and connections among language, culture, and writing.

Several common writing habits among these students from different countries emerged that conflict with formal writing styles of academe, known variously as academic argument, analytical or critical writing, and scholarly discourse (Fox, 1994). The characteristics and concerns included:

- Much background information and imprecise commentary
- Exaggeration for effect
- Prolific use of transitional markers, such as "moreover," "nevertheless," and "here again"
- Preference for contemplative instead of action words
- Much meandering around and digressions from the primary topic of discussion
- Emphasis on surrounding context rather than the subject itself
- Being suggestive and trying to convey feelings instead of being direct and concise and providing proof or specific illustrations, as is the expectation of academic writing in the United States
- Tendency to communicate through subtle implications

- Great detail and conversational tonality
- Elaborate and lengthy introductions
- Reticence to speak out, to declare personal positions, and to make one's own ideas prominent in writing

Although all the students shared these communication tendencies, according to Fox's (1994) study, how they were expressed in actual behaviors valued widely. Culturally different meanings of "conversational tone" illustrate this point. Fox notes:

> In Spanish or Portuguese . . . speakers and writers may be verbose, rambling, digressive, holistic, full of factual details, full of feeling, sometimes repetitious, sometimes contradictory, without much concern for literal meanings. In many Asian and African languages and cultures, metaphor, euphemism, innuendo, hints, insinuation, and all sorts of subtle nonverbal strategies—even silence—are used both to spare the listeners possible embarrassment or rejection, and to convey meanings that they are expected to grasp. (p. 22)

These descriptions of Asian American and non-Western student discourse are based on observations and conversations with a small number of people, in college classes and professional settings. How widespread they are across other educational settings, ethnic groups, generations of immigrants, and social circumstances is yet to be determined. Much more description and substantiation of these communicative inclinations are needed.

The explanations of Asian students that their discourse styles are cultural is elaborated by S. Chan (1991), Kitano and Daniels (1995), and Nakanishi (1994). They point to traditional values and socialization that emphasize collectivism, saving face, maintaining harmony, filial piety, interdependence, modesty in self-presentation, and restraint in taking oppositional points of view. Leung (1998) suggests some ways these values translate to behavior in learning situations, which underscore the observations made by Fox. Students socialized in this way are less likely to express individual thoughts, broadcast their individual accomplishments, and challenge or disagree with people in positions of authority, especially in public arenas. These interpretations echo the connections between Asian American culture and communicative styles provided by B. Kim (1978). She suggests that one of their major functions is to promote social harmony and build community. Consequently, many Asian American students may avoid confrontations as well as the expression of negative feelings or opinions in classroom discourse.

GENDER VARIATIONS IN DISCOURSE STYLES

Most of the detailed information on gender variations in classroom communication involves European Americans. Some inferences can be made about probable gender discourse styles among African, Latinos, Native, and Asian Americans from their cultural values and gender socialization, since culture and communication are closely interrelated.

Females Communicate Differently from Males

Lakoff (1975) was among the first to suggest that different lexical, syntactical, pragmatic, and discourse features existed for females and males. She identified nine speech traits prolific among females that are summarized by L. Crawford (1993) as specialized vocabulary for homemaking and care giving, mild forms of expletives, adjectives that convey emotional reactions but no substantive information, tag comments that are midway between questions and statements, exaggerated expressiveness, super polite forms, hedges or qualifiers, hypercorrect grammar, and little use of humor.

Other research indicates that European American females use more affiliating, accommodating, and socially bonding language mechanisms, while males are more directive, managing, controlling, task-focused, and action-oriented in their discourse styles. Girls speak more politely and tentatively, use less forceful words, are less confrontational, and are less intrusive when they enter into conversations. By comparison, boys interrupt more; use more commands, threats, and boast of authority; and give information more often (Austin, Salem, & Leffler, 1987; M. Crawford, 1995; Grossman & Grossman, 1994; Hoyenga & Hoyenga, 1979; Maccoby, 1988; Simkins-Bullock & Wildman, 1991; Tannen, 1994).

Because of these gender patterns, Maccoby (1988) concludes that "speech serves more egotistic functions among boys and more socially binding functions among girls" (p. 758).

These general trends were substantiated by Johnstone (1993) in a study of spontaneous conversational storytelling of men and women friends. The women's stories tended to be about groups of people (women and men) engaged in supportive relationships and the importace of community building. The men's stories were more about conquests (physical, social, nature) in which individuals acted alone. Invariably, the characters were nameless men who did little talking but engaged in some kind of physical action. More details were given about places, times, and things than about people. Based on these findings, Johnstone suggests that women are empowered through cooperation, interdependence, collaboration, and community. For men, power comes from individuals "conquering" and acting in opposition to others.

Research by Gray-Schlegel and Gray-Schlegel (1995/1996) on the creative writing of third- and sixth-grade students produced similar results. They examined 170 creative writing samples of 87 students to determine if differences existed in how control, outcomes, relationships, and violence were used. Clear gender patterns emerged. Both boys and girls placed male characters in active roles more often than females, but this tendency increased with age only for the males. Females were more optimistic about the fate of their characters, while males were inclined to be cynical. Boys usually had their protagonists acting alone, while girls had them acting in conjunction with others. Regardless of age or the gender of the story character, boys included more crime and violence in their narrative.

Gender Communication Patterns Established Early in Life

These kinds of gender-related discourse patterns are established well before third grade, as research by Nicolopoulou, Scales, and Weintraub (1994) revealed. They examined the symbolic imagination of four-year-olds as expressed in the kinds of stories they told. The girls' stories included more order and social realism. These concepts were conveyed through the use of coherent plots with stable characters, continuous plot lines, and social and familial relationships as the primary topics of and contexts for problem solving. Their stories emphasized cyclical patterns of everyday domestic life, along with romantic and fairy tale images of kings and queens, princesses and princes. They were carefully constructed, centered, and coherent, with elaborate character and theme development, and were invariably directed toward harmonious conflict resolution.

Whenever threatening disruptive situations occurred, the girls were careful to reestablish order before concluding their stories. The boys' stories contained much more disorder and a picaresque, surrealistic aesthetic style. These traits were apparent in the absence of stable, clearly defined characters, relationships, and plots; large, powerful, and frightening characters; violence, disruption, and conflict; and a series of loosely associated dramatic images, actions, and events. The boys were not concerned with resolving conflicts before their stories ended. Instead, action, novelty, excess, defiance, destruction, and often escalating and startling imagery drove their plots.

In summarizing differences between how boys and girls construct stories, Nicolopoulou and associates (1994) made some revealing observations that should inform instructional practices. They noted that the stories produced by girls focused on "creating, maintaining, and elaborating structure." In comparison, the stories boys told emphasized "action and excitement" and involved a restless energy that is often difficult for them to manage (p. 110). Furthermore, the boys and girls dealt with danger, disorder, and conflict very differently. The girls' strategy was *implicit avoidance* while the boys' techniques was *direct confrontation*.

Another fascinating verification of theorized gender differences in communication is provided by Otnes, Kim, and Kim (1994). They analyzed 344 letters written to Santa Claus (165 from boys and 179 from girls). Although the age of the authors was not specified, they were probably eight years old or younger, since children stop believing in Santa Claus at about this time. The content of the letters was analyzed to determine the use of six kinds of semantic units, or meaning phrases: (1) polite or socially accepted forms of ingratiation, (2) context-oriented references, (3) direct requests, (4) requests accompanied by qualifiers, (5) affectionate appeals, and (6) altruistic requests of gifts for someone other than self. For the most part, results of the study confirmed the hypothesized expectations. Girls wrote longer letters, made more specific references to Christmas, were more polite, used more indirect requests, and included more expressions of affection. By comparison, boys made more direct requests. There were no differences between boys and girls in the number of toys requested or the altruistic appeals made. Findings such as these provide evidence about the extent and persistence of patterns of culturally socialized communicative behaviors.

Early gender patterns of communication may transfer to other kinds of social and educational interactions. They also can entrench disadvantages that will have long-term negative effects on student achievement. Interventions to achieve more comparable communications skills for male and female students should begin early and continue throughout the school years. Efforts also should be undertaken in both research and classroom practices to determine if or how communicative styles are differentiated by gender in ethnic groups other than European Americans. Undoubtedly some differences do exist, since discourse styles are influenced by cultural socialization, and males and females are socialized to communicate differently in various ethnic groups.

Problems with Gendered Communication Styles

The "gendered" style of communication may be more problematic than the gender of the person per se doing the communicating. If this is so, then a female who is adept at using discourse techniques typically associated with males will not be disadvantaged in mainstream social interactions. Conversely, males who communicate in ways usually ascribed to females will lose their privileged status. Hoyenga and Hoyenga (1979) offer some support for this premise. In their review of research on gender and communication, they report that "feminine communication styles" are associated with less intelligence, passivity, and submissiveness, while "masculine styles" evoke notions of power, authority, confidence, and leadership.

However, M. Crawford (1995) suggests that some of the claims about female–male communication differences need to be reconsidered. For example, indirectness and equivocation in communication are not inherently strategies of female subordination or dominance. They can be tools of power or powerlessness as well. Interpretations of speech behaviors may depend more on the setting, the speaker's status and communicative ability, and the relationship to listeners rather than the person's gender per se (Tannen, 1994). Sadker and Sadker (1994) propose that males may be at greater *emotional risk* than females because of their role socialization. Girls are encouraged to be caring and emotionally expressive, but boys are taught to deny their feelings and to be overly cautious about demonstrating how deeply they care. Thus, male advantages in conventional conceptions of academic discourse may be countered somewhat by the psychoemotional and social advantages that females have in interpersonal relations.

CONCLUSION

Communication is strongly culturally influenced, experientially situated, and functionally strategic. It is a dynamic set of skills and performing arts whose rich nuances and delivery styles are open to many interpretations and instructional possibilities. Ethnic discourse patterns are continually negotiated because people talk in many different ways for many different reasons. Sometimes the purpose of talking and writing is simply to convey information. It is also used to persuade and entertain; to demonstrate sharing, caring, and connections; to express contentment and discontentment; to empower and subjugate; to teach and learn; and to convey reflections and declare personal preferences. In imagining and implementing culturally responsive pedagogical reform, teachers should not merely make girls talk more like boys, or boys talk more like girls, or all individuals within and across ethnic groups talk like each other. Nor should they assume that all gender differences in communication styles are subsumed by ethnicity or think that gender, social class, and education obliterate all ethnic nuances. Instead, we must be mindful that communication styles are multidimensional and multimodal, shaped by many different influences. Although culture is paramount among these, other critical influences include ethnic affiliation, gender, social class, personality, individuality, and experiential context.

The information in this chapter has described some of the patterns, dynamics, and polemics of the discourse styles of different ethnicities and groups. Since communication is essential to both teaching and learning, it is imperative that it be a central part of instructional reforms designed to improve the school performance of underachieving African, Native, Asian, and European American students. The more teachers know about the discourse styles of ethnically diverse students, the better they will be able to improve academic achievement. Change efforts should attend especially to discourse dynamics as opposed to linguistic structures. The reforms should be directed toward creating better agreement between the communication patterns of underachieving ethnically diverse students and those considered "normal" in schools.

Knowledge about general communication patterns among ethnic groups is helpful, but it alone is not enough. Teachers need to translate it to their own particular instructional situations. This contextualization might begin with some self-study exercises in which teachers examine their preferred discourse modes and dynamics, and determine how students from different ethnic groups respond to them. They should also learn to recognize the discourse habits of students from different ethnic groups. The purposes of these analyses are to identify (1) habitual discourse features of ethnically diverse students; (2) conflictual and complementary points among these discourse styles; (3) how, or if, conflictual points are negotiated by students; and (4) features of the students' discourse patterns that are problematic for the teacher. The results can be used to pinpoint and prioritize specific places to begin interventions for change.

Whether conceived narrowly or broadly, and expressed formally or informally, communication is the quintessential medium of teaching and learning. It also is inextricably linked to culture and cognition. Therefore, if teachers are to better serve the school achievement needs of ethnically diverse students by implementing culturally responsive teaching, they must learn how to communicate differently with them. To the extent they succeed in doing this, achievement problems could be reduced significantly.

References

Abrahams, R. D. (1970). *Positively black*. Englewood Cliffs, NJ: Prentice-Hall.

Asante, M. K. (1998). *The afrocentric idea* (rev. and exp. ed.). Philadelphia: Temple University Press.

Ascher, M. (1992). *Ethnomathematics*. New York: Freeman.

Au, K. H. (1980). Participation structures in a reading lesson with Hawaiian Children: Analysis of a culturally appropriate instructional event. *Anthropology and Education Quarterly, 11*, 91–115.

Au, K. H. (1993). *Literacy instruction in multicultural settings*. New York: Harcourt Brace.

Au, K. H., & Kawakami, A. J. (1985). Research currents: Talk story and learning to read. *Language Arts, 62*, 406–411.

Au, K. H., & Kawakami, A. J. (1991). Culture and ownership: Schooling of minority students, *Childhood Education, 67*, 280–284.

Au, K. H., & Kawakami, A. J. (1994). Cultural congruence in instruction. In E. R. Holling, J. E. King, & W. C. Hayman (Eds.). *Teaching diverse populations: Formulating a knowledge base* (pp. 5–23). Albany: State University of New York Press.

Au, K. P., & Mason, J. M. (1981). Social organizational factors in learning to read: The balance of rights hypothesis. *Reading Research Quarterly, 17*, 115–152.

Austin, A. M. B., Salehi, M., & Leffler, A. (1987). Gender and developmental differences in children's conversations. *Sex Roles, 16*, 497–510.

Baber, C. R. (1987). The artistry and artifice of Black communication. In G. Gay & W. L. Baber (Eds.), *Expressively Black: The cultural basis of ethnic identity* (pp. 75–108). New York: Praeger.

Belensky, M. F., Clinchy, B. M., Goldberger, N. R., & Tarule, J. M. (1986). *Women's ways of knowing: The development of self, voice, and mind*. New York: Basic Books.

Boggs, S. T. (1985). The meaning of questions and narratives to Hawaiian children. In C. B. Cazden, V. H. John, & D. Hymes (Eds.), *Functions of language in the classroom* (pp. 299–327). Prospect Heights, IL: Waveland.

Boggs, S. T., Watson-Gegeo, K., & McMillen, G. (1985). *Speaking, relating, and learning: A Study of Hawaiian children at home and at school*. Norwood, NJ: Albex.

Bruner, J. (1996). *The culture of education*. Cambridge, MA: Harvard University Press.

Byers, P., & Byers, H. (1985). Nonverbal communication and the education of children. In C. B. Cazden,

V. P. John, & D. Hymes (Eds.), *Functions of language in the classroom* (pp. 3–31). Prospect Heights, IL: Waveland.

Carroll, J. B. (Ed.). (1956). *Language, thought, and reality: Selected writings of Benjamin Lee Whorf*. Cambridge, MA: MIT Press.

Cadzen, C. B. (1988). *Classroom discourse: The language of teaching and learning*. Portsmouth, NH: Heinemann.

Chan, S. (Ed.). (1991). *Asian Americans: An interpretative history*. Boston: Twayne.

Crawford, L. W. (1993). *Language and literacy learning in multicultural classrooms*. Boston: Allyn & Bacon.

Crawford, M. (1955). *Talking difference: On gender and language*. Thousand Oaks, CA: Sage.

Dandy, E. B. (1991). *Black communications: Breaking down the barriers*. Chicago: African American Images.

Deyhle, D., & Swisher, K. (1997). Research in American Indian and Alaska native education: From assimilation to self-determinations. In M. W. Apple (Ed.). *Review of research in education* (Vol. 22) (pp. 113–194). Washington, DC: American Educational Research Association.

Fox, H. (1994). *Listening to tht world: Cultural issues in academic writing*. Urbana, IL: National Council of Teachers of English.

Fullilove, R. E., & Treisman, P. U. (1990). Mathematics achievement among African Americans undergraduates at the University of California, Berkeley: An evaluation of the Mathematics Workshop Program. *Journal of Negro Education, 59*, 463–478.

Gallimore, R., Boggs, J. W., & Jordon, C. (1974). *Culture, behavior and education: A study of Hawaiian Americans*. Beverly Hills, CA: Sage.

Gee, J. P. (1989). What is literacy? *Journal of Education, 171*, 18–25.

Giamati, C., & Weiland, M. (1997). An exploration of American Indian students' perceptions of patterning, symmetry, and geometry. *Journal of American Indian Education, 36*, 27–48.

Goodlad, J. I. (1984). *A place called school: Prospects for the future*. New York: McGraw-Hill.

Goodwin, M. H. (1990). *He-said she-said: Talk as social organization among Black children*. Bloomington: Indiana University Press.

Gray-Schlegel, M. A., & Gray-Schlegel, T. (1995/1996). An investigation of gender stereotypes as revealed through children's creative writing. *Reading Research and Instruction, 35*, 160–170.

Grossman, H., & Grossman, S. H. (1994). *Gender issues in education*. Boston: Allyn & Bacon.

Heath, S. B. (1983). *Ways with words: Language, life, and work in communities and classrooms*. Cambridge, England: Cambridge University Press.

Hoijer, H. (1991). The Sapir-Whorf hypothesis. In L. A. Samovar & R. E. Porter (Eds.), *Intercultural communication: A reader* (6th ed.) (pp. 244–251). Belmont, CA: Wadsworth.

Hoyenga, K. B., & Hoyenga, K. T. (1979). *The question of sex differences: Psychological, cultural, and biological issues*. Boston: Little Brown.

Hymes, D. (1985). Introduction. In C. B. Cazden, V. P. John, & D. Hymes (Eds.), *Functions of language in the classroom* (pp. xi–xvii). Prospect Heights, IL: Waveland.

Johnstone, B. (1993). Community and contest: Midwestern men and women creating their worlds in conversational storytelling. In D. Tannen (Ed.), *Gender and conversational interaction* (pp. 62–80). New York: Oxford University Press.

Kim, B. L. (1978). *The Asian Americans: Changing patterns, changing needs*. Montclair, NJ: Association for Korean Christian Scholars of North America.

Kitano, H., & Daniels, R. (1995). *Asian Americans: Emerging minorities* (2nd ed.). Englewood Cliffs, NJ: Prentice-Hall.

Klein, S. S. (Ed.). (1982). *Handbook for achieving sex equity through education*. Baltimore: Johns Hopkins University Press.

Kochman, T. (Ed.). (1972). *Rappin' and stylin' out: Communication in urban Black America*. Urbana: University of Illinois Press.

Kochman, T. (1981). *Black and White styles in conflict*. Chicago: University of Chicago Press.

Kochman, T. (1985). Black American speech events and a language program for the classroom. In C. B. Cazden, V. P. John, & D. Hymes (Eds.), *Functions of language in the classroom* (pp. 211–261). Prospect Heights, IL: Waveland.

Lakoff, R. (1975). *Language and women's place*. New York: Harper & Row.

Lee, C. D., & Slaughter-Defoe, D. T. (1995). Historical and sociocultural influences on African American education. In J. A. Banks & C. A. M. Banks (Eds.), *Handbook of research on multicultural education* (pp. 348–371). New York: Macmillan.

Leung. B. P. (1998). Who are Chinese American, Japanese American, and Korean American children? In V. O. Pang & L-R. L. Cheng (Eds.), *Struggling to be heard: The unmet needs of Asian Pacific American children* (pp. 11–26). Albany: State University of New York Press.

Longstreet, W. (1978). *Aspects of ethnicity: Understanding differences in pluralistic classrooms*. New York: Teachers College Press.

Maccoby, E. E. (1988). Gender as a social category. *Developmental Psychology, 24,* 755–765.

Maltz, D. N., & Borker, R. A. (1983). A cultural approach to male-female miscommunication. In J. J. Gumperz (Ed.), *Communication, language, and social identity* (pp. 196–216). Cambridge, England: Cambridge University Press.

Mandelbaum, D. G. (Ed.). (1968). *Selected writings of Edward Sapir in language, culture and personality*. Berkeley: University of California Press.

Michaels, S., & Cazden, C. B. (1986). Teacher/child collaboration as oral preparation for literacy. In B. B. Schieffelin & P. Gilmore (Eds.), *The acquisition of literacy: Ethnographic perspectives* (pp. 132–154). Norwood, NJ: Ablex.

Montague, A., & Matson, F. (1979). *The human connection*. New York: McGraw-Hill.

Nakanishi, D. (1994). *Asian American educational experience*. New York: Routledge.

Nicolopoulou, A., Scales, B., & Weintraub, J. (1994). Gender differences and symbolic imagination in the stories of four-year-olds. In A. H. Dyson & C. Genishi (Eds.), *The need for story: cultural diversity in classroom and community* (pp. 102–123). Urbana, IL: National Council of Teachers of English.

Otnes, C., Kim, K., & Kim, Y. C. (1994). Yes, Virginia, there is a gender difference: Analyzing children's requests to Santa Claus. *Journal of Popular Culture, 28,* 17–29.

Pasteur, A. B., & Toldson, I. L. (1982). *Roots of soul: The psychology of Black expressiveness*. Garden City, NY: Anchor Press/Doubleday.

Philips, S. U. (1983). *The invisible culture: Communication in classroom and community on the Warm Springs Indian Reservation*. Prospect Heights, IL: Waveland.

Porter, R. E., & Samovar, L. A. (1991). Basic principles of intercultural communication. In L.A. Samovar and R. E. Porter (Eds.), *Intercultural communication: A reader* (6th ed.) (pp. 5–22). Belmont, CA: Wadsworth.

Ramírez, M. III, & Castañeda, A. (1974). *Cultural democracy, bicognitive development and education*. New York: Academic Press.

Sadker, M., & Sadker, D. (1994). *Failing at fairness: How our schools cheat girls*. New York: Touchstone.

Sapir, E. (1968). The status of linguistics as a science. In D. G. Mandelbaum (Ed.), *Selected writings of Edward Sapir in language, culture and personality* (pp. 160–166). Berkeley: University of California Press.

Shade, B. J. (Ed.). (1989). *Culture, style, and the educative process*. Springfield, IL: Thomas.

Shade, B. J. (1994). Understanding the African American learner. In E. R. Hollins, J. E. King, & W. C. Hayman (Eds.), *Teaching diverse populations* (pp. 175–189). Albany: State University of New York Press.

Simkins-Bullock, J. A., & Wildman, B. G. (1991). An investigation into the relationship between gender and language. *Sex Roles, 24*, 149–160.

Smart-Grosvenor, V. (1982). We got a way with words. *Essence, 13*, 138.

Smith, B. O. (1971). On the anatomy of teaching. In R. T. Hyman (Ed.), *Contemporary thought on teaching* (pp. 20–27). Englewood Cliffs, NJ: Prentice-Hall.

Smitherman, G. (1972). Black power is black language. In G. M. Simmons, H. D. Hutchinson, & H. E. Summons (Eds.), *Black culture: Reading and writing Black* (pp. 85–91). New York: Holt, Rinehart & Winston.

Smitherman, G. (1977). *Talkin' and testifyin': The language of Black America*. Boston: Houghton Mifflin.

Tannen, D. (1990). *You just don't understand: Women and men in conversation*. New York: Morrow.

Tannen, D. (1994). *Gender and discourse*. New York: Oxford University Press.

Tharp, R. G., & Gallimore, R. (1988). *Rousing minds to life: Teaching, learning, and schooling in social context*. Cambridge, England: Cambridge University Press.

Treisman, P. U. (1985). *A study of the mathematics achievement of Black students at the University of California, Berkeley*. Unpublished doctoral dissertation. Berkeley: University of California.

Vygotsky, L. S. (1962). *Thought and language* Cambridge, MA: MIT Press.

Whorf, B. L. (1952). *Collected papers on metalinguistics*. Washington, DC: Department of State, Foreign Service Institute.

Whorf, B. L. (1956). Language, mind, and reality. In J. B. Carroll (Ed.), *Language, thought and reality: Selected writings of Benjamin Lee Whorf* (pp. 246–270). Cambridge, MA: MIT Press.

Concepts and Questions

1. In what ways do students' communication abilities affect teachers' perceptions of students?

2. How important is language in the performance and effectiveness of teachers?

3. Beyond the transmission of information, what other purposes does Gay suggest that language serves?

4. What does Gay mean when she says "language and communication styles are systems of cultural notation and the means through which thought and ideas are expressed and embodied"?

5. What does Gay mean when she uses the term "discourse structures"?

6. Distinguish between *passive-receptive* and *participatory-interactive* styles of discourse.

7. Describe the methods employed by many African American students to gain entry into conversations. How does this style differ from the communication styles of Native Hawaiian students?

8. Describe differences in problem-solving styles among African Americans, Latinos, Native Americans, and Asian American students.

9. Distinguish between *topic-centered*, *topic-associative*, and *topic-chaining* techniques in organizing ideas in discourse. Which methods are associated with which cultural groupings of students?

10. How does the African American storytelling style function as topic-chaining discourse?

11. Distinguish between female and male communication styles.

Geneva Gay Culture and Communication in the Classroom **337**

part 4

Intercultural Communication: Seeking Improvement

Happy are they that hear their detractions and can put them to mending.

WILLIAM SHAKESPEARE

Understanding is the beginning of approving.

ANDRÉ GIDE

In a sense, this entire volume has been concerned with helping you become competent in the practice of intercultural communication. We have introduced you to many diverse cultures and a host of communication variables that operate when people from different cultures attempt to interact. Our analysis thus far, however, has been more theoretical than practical. Previous selections have concentrated primarily on the task of understanding the nature of intercultural communication. We have not yet dealt with the act of practicing intercultural communication.

We have already pointed out many of the difficulties that cultural diversity introduces into the communication process. And we have shown how awareness not only of other cultures but also of one's own culture can help mediate some of those difficulties. But intercultural communication is not exclusively a single-party activity. Like other forms of interpersonal communication, intercultural communication requires the reciprocal and complementary participation of all parties to the communication event in order to achieve its highest and most successful practice.

When elevated to its highest level, interpersonal communication becomes an act in which participants make simultaneous inferences not only about their own roles but also about the role of the other. This act of mutual role taking must exist before people can achieve a level of communication that results in mutual understanding. In intercultural communication, this means that you must know about both your own culture and the culture of the one with whom you are communicating. And that person also must know about his or her own culture and about your culture as well. Unless there is mutual acknowledgment of each other's cultures and a willingness to accept those cultures as a reality governing communicative interactions, then intercultural communication cannot rise to its highest potential.

In this final section, we have slightly modified our orientation to discuss the activity of communication. The readings in this portion of the book will still increase your understanding, but their main purpose is to improve your behavior during intercultural communication.

The motivation for this particular section grows out of an important precept found in the study of human communication. It suggests that human interaction is a behavior in which people engage to change their environment. Inherent in this notion is the idea that communication is something people do—it involves action. Regardless of how much you understand the concepts of intercultural communication, when you are communicating with someone from another culture, you are part of a behavioral situation. You and your communication counterpart are doing things that affect each other. This final part of the book deals with that "doing." In addition, these readings are intended to help your communication become as effective as possible.

As you might well imagine, personal contact and experience are the most desirable methods for improvement. Knowledge and practice tend to work in tandem. The problem, however, is that we cannot write or select readings that substitute for this personal experience. Therefore, our contribution by necessity must focus on the observations of those who have practiced intercultural communication with some degree of success.

GO ONLINE

to the *Intercultural Communication: A Reader* website

at the Wadsworth Communication Café,
www.wadsworth.com/communication_d.

From the home page, select "Course Materials," then "Speech Communication," and then "Intercultural Communication." From the textbook menu, select *Intercultural Communication: A Reader* to access the book's website. Click on "…For Students" and use the drop-down menus at the top of the page to select a chapter and select a study aid resource. A practice quiz and an InfoTrac College Edition activity are included for each chapter.

You can complete the InfoTrac College Edition Activities by using the passcode that came free with each new copy of this text. InfoTrac College Edition is an easy-to-use database of reliable, full-length articles from hundreds of top academic journals and popular sources. You can expand your learning about the concepts illustrated in each reading by completing the InfoTrac College Edition activities.

chapter 7

Communicating Interculturally:
Becoming Competent

A
s you approach the last two chapters of this book, we need to remind you that our primary purpose is to help you become a competent intercultural communicator. To this end, the readings throughout the text have offered you material that will increase your knowledge about culture in general and introduce you to the diversity found in many specific cultures. In this chapter we continue these two themes by offering you advice and counsel that applies both to all cultures and to specific cultures. That is to say, the essays in Chapter 7 were selected specifically because the suggestions they advance are both universal and specific. Most of the selections discuss problems as well as solutions. Being alert to potential problems is the first step toward achieving intercultural communication competence. Once problems have been identified, it is easier to seek means of improvement—and improvement is at the heart of this chapter.

We begin this chapter with an essay that addresses the issue of intercultural awareness because we, as do the authors, see such awareness as the first step toward intercultural communication competency. The authors hold that intercultural awareness is one of three interrelated components of intercultural communication competence. In their essay "Intercultural Awareness," Guo-Ming Chen and William J. Starosta demonstrate that you must be able "to acknowledge, respect, tolerate, and integrate cultural differences" in order to become an enlightened global citizen. They define intercultural awareness as the "cognitive aspect of intercultural communication competence that refers to the understanding of cultural conventions that affect thinking and behavior." They identify three levels of intercultural awareness: *superficial cultural traits, awareness of significant and subtle cultural traits that contrast markedly with another's,* and *awareness of how another culture feels from the insider's perspective.* After discussing the components of intercultural awareness, Chen and Starosta provide examples of how you can study intercultural awareness and become cognizant of the various cultural dimensions that affect cultural awareness.

The catastrophic events at the World Trade Center in New York on September 11, 2001 vividly revealed how hate and intolerance can lead to massive death and devastation. Hate, intolerance, and their devastating outcomes are world-wide problems. Whether it is Catholics and Protestants in Ireland, Taliban warriors in Afghanistan, Israeli and Palestinian forces in the Middle East, or racial- and ethnic-based intolerance in the United States, the results of terrorism are disruptive to society and often lead to serious injury, death, and destruction.

In their article "Unpacking Group-Based Intolerance: A Holographic Look at Identity and Intolerance," John R. Baldwin and Michael Hecht approach the study of hate and intolerance as a continuation of Social Identity Theory, which posits that our perceptions of others are based on broad demographic categories with which we categorize others and ourselves into groups and then compare our own group with that of the other, usually in a way that makes our own group look more favorable.

Focusing on the communicative dynamics between African Americans and White Americans, Baldwin and Hecht point out seven issues that are important to African Americans as they interact with White Americans: (1) negative stereotyping, (2) acceptance, (3) emotional expressiveness, (4) authenticity, (5) understanding, (6) goal attainment, and (7) powerlessness. Baldwin and Hecht then take their discussion into the realm of intolerance and apply their views to other forms of interethnic communication.

We continue our investigation of how to become more effective intercultural communicators with an article by Anita S. Mak, Marvin J. Westwood, F. Ishu Ishiyama, and Michell C. Barker titled "Optimising Conditions for Learning Sociocultural Competencies for Success." These authors bring an international perspective to our inquiry because they are from the countries of Australia, Canada, and New Zealand. Their main thesis is that there are may benefits "immigrants and sojourners may reap from learning skills for intercultural competence (that is, developing sociocultural competence)." Mak et al. discuss several psychological barriers to developing these skills, including limited practice and coaching opportunities and conscious or unconscious resistance to developing competent social skills.

The authors then identify the optimal conditions for the development of these competencies and provide a theoretical basis for learning sociocultural competencies. This theoretical basis includes operant conditioning, classical conditioning, social cognitive learning, role-based training, and the relevant conditions for effective learning of intercultural social skills.

In our next reading, "Managing Intercultural Conflicts Effectively," Stella Ting-Toomey moves us from a general analysis of intercultural awareness to a specific topic associated with intercultural communication—intercultural conflict. The rationale behind this selection is clearly stated in the opening line of the essay: "Conflict is inevitable in all social and personal relationships." To preempt the problems created by interpersonal disharmony, particularly in the intercultural setting, Ting-Toomey maintains that conflict must be defined and managed. To help us improve our capacity to clarify and regulate conflict, the author explains three significant features of intercultural conflict. First, a framework that uses low-context versus high-context and monochronic and polychronic time is advanced to demonstrate why and how cultures are different and similar. Second, some basic assumptions and factors that contribute to conflict are discussed. Finally, Ting-Toomey offers a series of skills that can help individuals manage conflict when it develops in the intercultural encounter.

Conflict is an inevitable aspect of the human condition. One factor that leads to conflict is cultural diversity, whether it be among the major cultures of the world or among co-cultures found within the United States. Harmonious relationships are necessary in all aspects of human endeavor if people are to get along with one another and accomplish the requirements of life and society. When conflict arises among members of co-cultures, its resolution is paramount if peaceful relations are to be achieved. James Manseau Sauceda, in his article "Effective Strategies for Mediating Co-Cultural Conflict," narrates you through some of his experiences as a co-cultural conflict mediator and presents you with some of the strategies he has found to be effective in his role of a mediator. He draws on his experiences in mediating conflict in the arenas of police/community relations, mental health services, the workplace, and the educational setting to develop strategies you will find useful in becoming an effective intercultural communicator with people from the various co-cultures in the United States.

When we travel to a foreign culture, we often encounter for the first time a new and often-confusing environment. Our ability to interact effectively in a new cultural environment depends on our abilities to adapt. In our next article, "Sojourner Adaptation," Polly Begley draws on her extensive international travel experiences to offer insights and strategies for living, learning, and adapting in global communities. After introducing us to both the characteristics and the effects of culture shock and the challenges associated with adapting to another cultural environment, she reviews the changes and adaptations one must make as a sojourner in another culture. Begley suggests that ethnocentrism, language disequilibrium, length of stay, and level of knowledge are the major factors that affect our ability to adapt to a foreign culture. She then provides us with several useful strategies to assist in cultural adaptation.

Our next selection by Mary Jane Collier seeks to promote and facilitate the understanding and practice of intercultural communication. Collier contributes to that understanding by offering a "Ten Step Inventory" that takes the form of a series of relevant questions. Collier answers each question by reviewing important literature in the field, illuminating the issues that must be considered by anyone attempting to improve their intercultural communication skills. In addition, Collier encourages you to take the information in her article and apply it to current social problems and yoru own intercultural experiences.

Two themes recurring throughout this book have been the notions that our world is figuratively shrinking and that the U.S. population is rapidly becoming more diverse and multicultural. Worldwide, as the figurative distance among diverse cultures continues to decrease, and as our own population continues to reflect greater cultural diversity, our proximity to cultural differences grows closer. This nearness demands that we develop intercultural understanding and sensitivity if we are to live peacefully among and interact successfully with others who reflect unique and different cultures.

Intercultural Awareness

Guo-Ming Chen

William J. Starosta

Globalization creates a world in which people of different cultural backgrounds increasingly come to depend on one another. Understanding and accepting cultural differences becomes an imperative in order to become an effective intercultural communicator in a global society. According to Chen and Starosta (1997, 2000), technology development, especially communication and transportation technology, over the last decades is the main reason the world now engages in intercultural communication on a daily basis. Communication and transportation technology not only enable people to easily and efficiently move from continent to continent to encounter others in face-to-face communication, but also bring about other impacts, including increasing domestic cultural diversity and globalization of the economy. As a result, the need for intercultural knowledge and skills that lead to intercultural communication competence becomes critical for leading a productive and successful life in the 21st century.

Interculturally competent persons know how to elicit a desired response in interactions and to fulfill their own communication goals by respecting and affirming the worldview and cultural identities of the interactants. In other words, intercultural communication competence is the ability to acknowledge, respect, tolerate, and integrate cultural differences that qualifies one for enlightened global citizenship. Intercultural communication competence comprises three interrelated components: intercultural sensitivity, intercultural awareness, and intercultural adroitness (Chen & Starosta, 1996).

This original article appears here in print for the first time. All rights reserved. Permission to reprint must be obtained from the author and the publisher. An earlier version of this paper appeared in the Winter 1998/Spring 1999 edition of *Human Communication*, a journal of the Pacific and Asian Communication Association. Guo-Ming Chen teaches at the University of Rhode Island, Kingston, Rhode Island. William J. Starosta teaches at Howard University, Washington, D.C.

Intercultural sensitivity is the affective aspect of intercultural competence, and refers to the development of a readiness to understand and appreciate cultural differences in intercultural communication. *Intercultural awareness* is the cognitive aspect of intercultural communication competence that refers to the understanding of cultural conventions that affect thinking and behavior. *Intercultural adroitness* is the behavioral aspect of intercultural communication competence that stresses these skills that are needed for us to act effectively in intercultural interactions.

Unfortunately, although the three concepts are closely related, most research tends to mingle them without clearly distinguishing them from each other. This chapter attempts to alleviate this problem of conceptual ambiguity and confusion by conceptualizing and operationalizing intercultural awareness through synthesizing existing literature.

INTERCULTURAL AWARENESS: WHY AND WHAT?

Globalization of the world community inevitably leads to cultural diversity or multiculturalism in all aspects of life. In other words, the changing cultural characteristics of neighborhoods, schools, the workforce, and social and political life make cultural diversity the norm rather than the exception of life in most countries, especially the United States. According to Belay (1993), the trend will nourish multiple identities for citizens in terms of culture, race, ethnicity, gender, religion, and nationality. To be aware of the relevant multiple identities of another is the first step to becoming an enlightened global citizen who tolerates cultural differences and shows mutual respect among cultures in order to practice a multicultural coexistence in a "global civic culture" (Boulding, 1988). Thus, intercultural awareness functions as the minimum condition for an interculturally competent individual in the global society.

The importance of intercultural awareness in the modern world is reflected in the increasing demands of intercultural training programs. Scholars and experts have developed numerous intercultural training programs to develop intercultural awareness (Landis & Bhagat, 1996; Yum, 1989). A common goal of intercultural training is to increase awareness of cultural differences in order to develop one's communication skills while lessening the likelihood of misunderstandings in intercultural interactions (Seidel, 1981). Among the six most common intercultural training programs, including affective training, cognitive training, behavioral training, area simulation training, cultural awareness training, and self-awareness training, only cognitive training, cultural awareness, and self-awareness are directly concerned with intercultural awareness (Brislin, Landis, & Brandt, 1983; Gudykunst & Hammer, 1983).

According to Gudykunst, Ting-Toomey, and Wiseman (1991), cognitive training promotes understanding of cultural differences and similarities. Cultural awareness training requires participants to understand the aspects of culture that are universal and specific. Finally, self-awareness training helps participants identify attitudes, opinions, and biases embedded in their own culture that influence the way they communicate. Thus, intercultural awareness requires individuals to understand, from their own cultural perspective, that they are cultural beings and to use this understanding as a foundation to further figure out the distinct characteristics of other cultures in order to effectively interpret the behavior of others in intercultural interactions (Triandis, 1977). It refers to the understanding of cultural conventions that affect how people think and behave.

Intercultural awareness is, therefore, the cognitive perspective of intercultural communication. It emphasizes the changing of personal thinking about the environment through the understanding of the distinct characteristics of one's own and the other's cultures (Triandis, 1977). It furnishes an opportunity to develop an understanding of cultural dynamics by reducing the level of situational ambiguity and uncertainty in intercultural interactions. With little visible discomfort, little confusion, and little nervousness in a new environment, individuals can adapt to situational demands with no noticeable personal, interpersonal, or group consequences and can cope with the changing environment rapidly and comfortably (Ruben, 1976; Ruben & Kealey, 1979).

Thus, understanding the dimensions of cultural variability provides ways to identify how communication differs across cultures. Because each culture tends to favor certain forms of processing surrounding data, problems occur in intercultural communication when newcomers misunderstand such thought patterns. Therefore, learning the preferences of a culture for supporting arguments and determining knowledge becomes one key to effective intercultural interaction (Glenn & Glenn, 1981; Harris & Moran, 1989; Oliver, 1962). In other words, one must understand cultural variability in order to modify communication patterns to be congruent with the cues of unfamiliar interactants (Hall, 1959, 1976; Hall & Whyte, 1963). Changing behaviors to be congruent with that of our counterparts helps in reaching a mutual understanding and maintaining a multicultural coexistence.

Finally, intercultural awareness resembles the ideas of "cultural map," (Kluckhohn, 1948), "cultural theme" (Turner, 1968), or "cultural grammars" (Colby, 1975) that emphasize the importance of cultural knowledge for being competent in intercultural communication. Kluckhohn (1948) asserts that cultural awareness requires understanding the "cultural map"; "if a map is accurate, and you can read it, you won't get lost; if you know a culture, you'll know your way around in the life of a society" (p. 28). If a point in reality consistently corresponds to points on a mental map, the map is said to be "isomorphic" with reality. Thus, isomorphic attribution becomes a level of cognitive awareness. Turner (1968) indicates that to be aware of a culture means to catch the "culture theme"—the thread that goes through a culture and organizes a culture as a recognizable system. It acts as a guideline to people's thinking and behavior, and appears repeatedly in daily life.

LEVELS OF INTERCULTURAL AWARENESS

Intercultural awareness can be considered as a process of attitudinally internalizing "insights about those common understandings held by groups that dictate the predominant values, attitudes, beliefs, and outlooks of the individual" (Adler, 1987). This process can be integrated into three levels: (1) awareness of superficial cultural traits, (2) awareness of significant and subtle cultural traits that contrast markedly with another's, and (3) awareness of how another culture feels from the insider's perspective (Hanvey, 1987).

The first level is the understanding of another culture based mainly on stereotypes. The awareness in this level tends to be superficial and often partial. Information about the culture comes from the media, tourism books, textbooks, or the first impression. For example, U.S. Americans are perceived as outgoing, friendly, loud, hard working, wasteful, wealthy people by foreigners (Kohls, 1988). Chen and Starosta (1998) also report some of the first impressions of U.S. Americans made by Japanese visitors. They include that Americans walk very fast, are always in a hurry, always try to talk everything out, and don't respect teachers in school. In this level, one tends to understand a culture or its people by the most visible characteristics it possesses. Then some of these characteristics are applied to the whole group. For example, Asian students with a high GPA in American colleges are often incorrectly considered as science and math majors because the media reports that Asian students often do better in those areas. Finally, the same treatment is given to each member of the group by saying, for example, "You are Japanese, you must be smart."

The second level of intercultural awareness shows how significant and subtle cultural traits differ sharply from one's own through direct or second-hand experience. This level has two phases. The first phase approaches intercultural awareness through culture-conflict situations and the second through intellectual analysis. Although the media, tourism books, or textbooks may provide contrasting information, one does not fully feel or grasp the real meaning of the cultural differences except through experience by direct or indirect interactions with people of another culture. In the first phase of this level, the experience of cultural conflict may lead to depression, helplessness, hostility, anxiety, withdrawal, or disorientation, but at the same time it provides the chance to further recognize and understand another's culture. The feeling in this phase resembles culture shock in the process of intercultural adjustment (Oberg, 1960).

Many sojourners, such as Peace Corps volunteers and foreign students, experience stress during this phase of intercultural awareness. If they are unable to overcome the symptoms of culture shock, then development of intercultural awareness will be halted in this frustrating stage, and culture-conflict situations will continue to exist in which they feel alienated and marginalized (Mansell, 1981). At this point, the conflict situations that lead to culture shock may impede the process of being aware of the host culture. For example, as Draguns (1977) indicates, experiencing something unbalancing may be detrimental to the psychological growth of some learners or sojourners. Moreover, cognitively and perceptually, some sharp cultural differences are considered bizarre or idiosyncratic. It may take a long time or may prove impossible for learners or sojourners to sort through their feelings about cultural differences. This, in turn, leads them to judge the unfamiliar more harshly and irrationally than they did in the first level of intercultural awareness.

In the second phase of the second level of intercultural awareness, through rational and intellectual analysis, one comes to understand that cultural differences can be justified from the other culture's perspective. In other words, differences in cultural traits begin to make sense. Differences then become believable and acceptable (Bennett, 1986). This believability through understanding helps sojourners fully adjust to the host culture. In this phase sojourners begin to appreciate and respect the new culture and to develop sensitivity toward cultural differences. Cultural differences in this phase are processed with a positive affect. This provides motivational force to move one forward to a higher level of intercultural awareness. In addition, intercultural understanding in this phase results from drawing comparisons and contrasts. This practice promotes the learning of cultures that have not yet been experienced (Adler, 1987; Hall, 1976; Stewart & Bennett, 1991). While a few scholars argue that some people reach this kind of intellectual understanding even before they move into the first phase of this level (Hanvey, 1987), research on intercultural adjustment portrays it as a process that all sojourners must experience, although the duration of each phase may vary.

Finally, the third level of intercultural awareness requires the ability to see the culture from an insider's perspective through empathy. The believability through understanding explicated in phase two of the second level is enhanced by intellectual analysis and by subjective familiarity (Hanvey,

1987). In other words, one needs to foster the power of flexibility to make psychic shifts. The power of flexibility is nourished by empathy and "transspection." Empathy helps one to estimate what is inside another's mind and to share their experience (Barnlund, 1989). This selfless and affectively or telepathically sensitive process helps one to more accurately estimate behaviors or internal states of mind in counterparts that are different from one's own (Campbell, Kagan, & Drathwohl, 1971; Gardner, 1962). The latent capacity of empathy can be activated through the process of "transspection." The term was coined by Maruyama (1970), who indicates that "transspection" is an understanding by practice.

Empathy is the ability to project feelings to others with a shared epistemology, whereas "transspection" is a trans-epistemological process of temporarily believing whatever counterparts believe by trying to learn their beliefs, their assumptions, their perspectives, their feelings, and the consequences of such feelings in their context. This parallels the stage of duality or biculturalism in the intercultural adjustment process through which the fully developed autonomy provides us with the freedom and ability to approach dual cultural identity, awareness of being in control of creative enjoyment, aesthetic appreciation for the contrasts of cultures, development of satisfactory interpersonal relationships, and a high level of commitment toward both cultural contexts (Mansell, 1981). Whether this stage can be fully achieved or only approximated is still an open question (Chen & Starosta, 1988).

The developmental levels show that intercultural awareness is a learning process by which one becomes aware of his or her own cognitive growth, learning, and change regarding a set of cultural situations and cultural principles stemming from intercultural communication. It is a part of cognitive function regarding the knowing of how people's outlook, attitudes, values, and behavior are based on cultural dispositions. Thus, intercultural awareness involves change and movement from one cultural frame of reference to another and provides unlimited opportunity for contrast and comparison resulting from cultural differences. A clearer picture of cultural maps, cultural themes, or cultural grammars emerges through this process.

APPROACHES TO THE STUDY OF INTERCULTURAL AWARENESS

Culture-general and culture-specific are two approaches used to demystify the process of intercultural awareness. A culture-general approach aims to understand culture's global influence on human behavior. Through different learning techniques, one comes to know the possible variations in culture. For example, cultural assimilators and baFà baFà simulation (Shirts, 1973) are common techniques used in intercultural training programs to help participants learn about the general influence of culture. Cultural assimilators require participants to answer a question by selecting the best from the four or five possible answers about a critical incident regarding a specific culture. The critical incident has been demonstrated to produce variant cultural interpretations. This kind of attribution training not only helps participants recognize that the way they think is not always the way other cultural groups think, but also helps them understand that certain experiences are common to all intercultural interactions (Albert, 1986; Cushner, 1989; Cushner & Brislin, 1995).

BaFà baFà is a simulation game that divides participants into Alphas and Betas—cultural groups representing two distinct sets of values and communication patterns. Members in each group are sent to the other group to collect information about the culture. The ensuing exchange gives participants a chance to play a new role in a different cultural setting and to experience the inevitable communication frustration, confusion, and anxiety caused by the different cultural orientations. An understanding of the general influence of culture on its members is therefore reached.

The culture-specific approach aims to impart information about specific culture and cultural guidelines for interacting with people in a specified culture. In addition to cultural assimilators that can help participants learn about the specific characteristics of a culture, role plays and area studies are commonly used to enhance culture-specific understandings. Role plays allow participants to gain insight into the experiences of people of different cultures. Through playing a role of a host national in a situation that is problematic because of cultural differences, learners are transformed from observers of a culture into participants in another culture. The process can develop great understanding of the thinking and behavioral patterns of people from different cultures and can further augment and enhance intercultural communication skills (Barnak, 1980; Seidel, 1981). Area studies usually employ a lecture to present information about a particular country and its people and culture. For example, environmental briefings or cultural orientations are used to describe facts such as the locale, history, politics, or economics of a particular cultural group. A "do's and don'ts" format is often used to help learners obtain specific data that can be assembled to develop a holistic picture of the culture.

Both culture-specific and culture-general approaches indicate that intercultural awareness can be reached through didactic and experiential learning. Didactic learning is implemented through traditional academic methods in which, for example, the lecture format is used to disseminate cultural information and characteristics of another culture to learners. Didactic learning is commonly used in the first level of intercultural awareness. Experiential learning involves participants intellectually, emotionally, and behaviorally in a simulated environment of role play (Cargile & Giles, 1996). It aims to reach intercultural awareness through interactions. The second level of intercultural awareness, especially the second phase, demands that participants learn, respect, and accept sharp cultural differences through this kind of interactional experience with people from or representing the target culture.

MODELS FOR THE STUDY OF INTERCULTURAL AWARENESS

What constitutes the components of "cultural map," "cultural theme," or "cultural grammars" that embody a comprehensive knowledge of a culture? From the discussions of the levels of and approaches to the study of intercultural awareness are derived two categories of cultural components: basic factual information and deep structured cultural values. The basic factual information concerns the profile of the culture or nation regarding history, geography, family and social organization, art, or political system. It concerns the "what" aspect of the culture that can

be obtained through reading, didactic learning, or other media without the need to interact with people from the target culture for collecting the information. For example, Saville-Troike (1978) proposed 20 categories for learning about the basic factual information of a culture. Such learning also proceeds incidentally and stereotypically from viewing mass media productions. Fact learning includes asking general questions about what are "traditional" or "typical" cultural beliefs or behaviors, family structure and relationships, food, dress, and personal appearance. Similar to this approach, Kohls (1988) also pointed out 10 basic areas that constitute foundational cultural factual information.

In addition, *Culturegram*, a series published by the David M. Kennedy Center for International Studies, classifies the understanding of a nation into four categories: customs and courtesies, the people, the lifestyle, and the nation. Harris and Moran (1989), by contrast, used a coordinated systems approach to divide the unitary whole of a culture into eight systems: kinship system, educational system, economic system, political system, religious system, association system, health system, and recreational system.

Although the basic factual information of a culture tends to be easier to approach and acquire, the deep structure of the culture is much more difficult to attain. Cultural values are the most fundamental framework of the deep structure of a culture. They concern the "why" aspect of a culture. They justify why people of the culture think or practice as learned in the "what" aspect: why do people of the culture dress like that, celebrate that, communicate in that way, or have that kind of religious belief? Cultural values dictate what one ought or ought not to do. In other words, they are a set of explicit or implicit conceptions that distinguish an individual or characteristic of a group from another and according to Sitaram and Haapanen (1979), cultural values are communicated through verbal and nonverbal symbols. For example, the proverb "A man's home is his castle" explicates the U.S. American emphasis on "privacy" and hints at male dominance, while the custom of exchanging gifts in Japanese society reflects the cultural values of reciprocity and generosity. Moreover, cultural values determine our communication patterns. For example, the emphasis on "harmony" in the Chinese culture leads Chinese people to exhibit minimal displays of public emotion and to avoid saying "no" in interactions (Chen, in press). Thus, understanding cultural values through direct and indirect experience with people is the key to the awareness, respect, and acceptance of the contrasting cultural practices.

Much research has been conducted to examine cultural values. Among them, models developed by Parsons, Kluckhohn and Strodbeck, Condon and Yousef, Hall, Hofstede, and Schwartz are commonly mentioned. Parsons' (1951) model consisted of five categories: (1) The gratification-discipline dilemma: affectivity vs. affective neutrality, (2) the private vs. collective interest dilemma: self-orientation vs. collectivity-orientation, (3) the choice between types of value-orientation standards: universalism vs. particularism, (4) the choice between "modalities" of the social object: achievement vs. ascription, and (5) the definition of scope of interest in the object: specificity vs. diffuseness.

Kluckhohn and Strodbeck's (1961) model indicated that all human societies must face universal problems, and the ways used to solve these universal problems are limited and different for each society. Based on this assumption, they proposed five universal problems faced by human societies that form the basic dimensions of cultural values: human nature, human-nature relationship, sense of time, activity, and social relations.

Based on Kluckhohn and Strodbeck's model, Condon and Yousef (1975) extended the categories of cultural values to cover the six basic spheres of human societies, including the self, the family, society, human, nature, and the supernatural, and attached four or five universal problems to each sphere, which makes the model a highly comprehensive one. Hall (1976) classified culture into high-context culture and low-context culture, in which people demonstrate different thinking patterns and communication styles. Hofstede's (1983, 1984) model stipulated five dimensions of cultural values from the organizational perspective: individualism/collectivism, power distance, uncertainty avoidance, masculinity/femininity, and Confucian dynamism.

Finally, aiming to improve the problem of dichotomous categorization of cultural values, Schwartz (1990, 1992), Schwartz & Bilsky (1987, 1990), and Schwartz & Sagiv (1995) argued that many universal values, such as power, achievement, and hedonism, exist in different cultures. In other words, in order to reach intercultural awareness, one must also seek universal commonalities of human behaviors. In sum, the study of cultural values is the most important gateway to reach intercultural awareness. The models discussed not only provide us with a structured way to tackle the complexity of cultural values, but they also offer the potential for further examining different aspects of human society.

Nevertheless, the great potential for the application of cultural values to reach intercultural awareness is not without its limitations and inherent problems. In addition to the misperception of the dichotomy of cultural values such as high-context versus low-context culture and individualism versus collectivism, we must understand that all models used for the study of cultural values are incomplete and show the scholars' biases. Furthermore, the categories used to explain the models tend to break the concepts and components of cultural values into fragments. In other words, the cultural values approach to cultural classification is only for the purpose of illustration. In real-life situations, cultural values are meaningful only when the categories are treated or examined in combination rather than in isolation (Condon & Yousef, 1975) and are viewed within specified contexts.

ASSESSMENT OF INTERCULTURAL AWARENESS

Because intercultural awareness aims to unveil the "cultural map," "cultural theme," or "cultural grammar," the next question will be how to extract empirical indicators from the process of operationalization. In other words, the question is about how to measure or assess intercultural awareness. Although a thorough literature review shows that presently there is no instrument used to directly measure intercultural awareness in the field, there are measurements developed to assess our understanding of the basic factual information of the culture and cultural values.

Four measurements regarding the basic factual information or knowledge of a culture include Saville-Troike's Questions to Ask about Culture, Kitao's Test of American Culture, Kohl's Fifty

Questions about Culture, and Harris and Moran's Pre-deployment Area Questionnaire.

Saville-Troike (1978) proposed 20 categories for learning about the basic factual information of a culture. For each category, the author created three to ten open-ended questions that reflect the understanding of the basic information of the category. For example, the category of communication asks "What languages, and varieties of each language, are used in the community? By whom? When? Where? For what purposes?" One hundred and twenty-eight questions are attached to the 20 categories. Kitao's (1981) Test of American Culture is a specific measurement used to test participants' knowledge of basic traits of American culture. The test contains 100 multiple-choice questions about 49 different areas of American culture. Examples of questions include "The Gettysburg Address was given by: (a) Abraham Lincoln, (b) Patrick Henry, (c) Daniel Boone, (d) Martin Luther King, Jr." And "Common speaking distance is: (a) 1 ft, (b) 1.5 ft, (c) 2 ft, (d) 3 ft."

Kohls's (1984) Fifty Questions were developed to help sojourners better know their host country and culture. The author claims that if sojourners know the answers of the 50 open-ended questions, they have moved well beyond the beginner stage of intercultural adaptation. Representative questions include "Who are the country's national heroes and heroines?" and "What are the most important religious observances and ceremonies? How regularly do people participate in them?"

Finally, Harris and Moran's (1989) questionnaire was designed to help a global manager, who is planning to go abroad on an extensive foreign assignment, be familiar with the host culture. Ninety-two "yes" or "no" questions were used to reflect different aspects of the culture that are closely related to the business interaction. For example, one question asks about an aspect of social structure, "Does dress reflect social or economic status?" and a question about the roles of men and women queries: "Are there differences between male and female roles in business?"

While these measurements can be used to assess and help people understand the basic cultural information or traits, they suffer from two main weaknesses. First, the complexity of a culture requires a large volume of questions to catch different nuances of cultural characteristics. It is not uncommon to have more than 100 items in a single measurement. This often leads to the problem of efficiency in the process of measurement. Thus, these tools are more appropriate to be applied to the didactic learning settings in which participants are gradually learning to know the basic information or traits of a culture, rather than to assess a person's ability in terms of the degree of understanding a specific culture. Second, culture is dynamic. Some of the basic information or traits of a culture tend to change in a short period of time. This leads to the problem of content validity of the measurement. For example, the answer for a question such as "Minimum wage per hour: (1) $1.60, (b) $2.00, (c) $2.20, (d) not specified" in Kitao's Test may be subject to change several times in a few years.

Studies that measure values are not scarce in the literature. Two of the representative measurements are Allport, Vernon, and Lindzey's study of values (1960) and Rokeach's (1967, 1973) value survey. The two measurements are highly reliable and valid and have been widely used to assess values. Unfortunately, the measurements approach values from the psychological rather than the cultural perspective. Their applications to the assessment of intercultural awareness are limited. Three measurements are more helpful for the assessment of intercultural awareness. First, Kluckhohn and Strodbeck's (1961) categories of cultural value orientations were used as an index for deriving instruments in written questionnaires (Platt, 1985; Triandis et al., 1985). For each universal problem, a case is created and explanations for the three value orientations are listed. Participants are then asked to choose which explanation is the most appropriate for answering the case.

This kind of questionnaire can reflect value orientations of a culture in terms of human nature, humans and nature, time perception, human activity, and social relation. The weakness is that it takes too much time and energy to create a case for each universal problem and explanations of the three value orientations attached to each universal problem. It is also a time-consuming process for participants to answer all of the questions. Second, Gilgen and Cho (1979) revised and simplified Kluckhohn and Strodbeck's original measures by using a Likert scale to answer statements that represent all cultural value orientations. For example, participants were asked to answer how much they agree or disagree with each of the statements, such as "I do not believe in a personal god," and "Man should strive to free himself from the uncompromising forces of nature," by using a five-point scale.

Finally, Chen (1995) generated 15 items of cultural value orientations from Kluckhohn and Strodbeck's and Condon and Yousef's models. Participants were also asked to use five-point Likert scales to answer the degree to which they agree or disagree with each of the statements, such as "*Americans* see themselves as individualists," and "*Americans* tend to express their opinions openly and directly." The instrument has been applied to assess participants' degree of intercultural awareness in international electronic communication settings. The nation underlined in the instrument can be changed to any nation to fit the purpose of the study. Both Gilgen and Cho's and Chen's instruments have a great potential for the assessment of intercultural awareness because of their preciseness and ease of operation. However, more empirical testing is needed to assess the validity of the instruments before they are widely applied.

CONCLUSION

The trend of global interdependence has created an ever-shifting cultural, economic, ecological, and technological reality that defines the shrinking world of the 21st century. Globalization demands the enhancement of intercultural communication among people from diverse cultures in order for us to survive in the 21st century. As a component of intercultural communication competence, intercultural awareness is an indispensable element for us to reach this global mindset. This article makes an effort to synthetically delineate the concept.

This article first conceptualizes and explains why it is important to develop intercultural awareness in the global society. Three levels of intercultural awareness are discussed. Then two approaches for the study of intercultural awareness and models for learning the basic cultural knowledge and cultural values are explicated and evaluated. Finally, instruments used to assess intercultural awareness are discussed and appraised. In conclusion, the indispensability of intercultural awareness for living meaningfully in global society demands that intercultural communication scholars further explore and expand the scope and functions of the concept. Understanding a culture through cognitive learning should be the foundation for individuals to reach intercultural communication competence. Accompanied with the abilities of intercultural sensitivity and intercultural adroitness, intercultural awareness can help us develop multiple cultural identities that transform us from single-culture-minded beings into "multiple persons." This approach will, in turn, ensure our ability to integrate various communication demands in the web of culture, ethnicity, race, gender, and religion.

References

Adler, P. S. (1987). Culture shock and the cross-cultural learning experience. In L. F. Luce & E. C. Smith (Eds.), *Toward internationalism* (pp. 24–35). Cambridge, MA: Newbury.

Albert, R. D. (1986). Conceptual framework for the development and evaluation of cross-cultural orientation programs. *International Journal of Intercultural Relations, 10,* 197–213.

Allport, G. W., Vernon, P. E., & Lindzey, G. (1960). *Study of values: Manual and test booklet.* Boston, MA: Houghton Mifflin.

Barnak, P. (1980). Role-playing. In D. S. Hoopes & P. Ventura (Eds.), *Intercultural sourcebook: Cross-cultural training methodologies* (pp. 7–10). Washington D. C.: Society for Intercultural Education, Training, and Research.

Barnlund, D. S. (1989). *Communication styles of Japanese and Americans: Images and reality.* Belmont, CA: Wadsworth.

Belay, G. (1993). Toward a paradigm shift for intercultural and international communication: New research directions. In S. A. Deetz (Ed.), *Communication Yearbook 16* (pp. 437–457). Newbury Park, CA: Sage.

Bennett, M. J. (1986). A developmental approach to training for intercultural sensitivity. *International Journal of Intercultural Relations, 10,* 179–196.

Boulding, E. (1988). *Building a global civic culture.* New York: Teachers College Press.

Brislin, R. W., Landis, D., & Brandt, M. E. (1983). Conceptualizations of intercultural behavior and training.

In D. Landis and R. W. Brislin (Eds.), *Handbook of intercultural training*, Vol. 1 (pp. 1–35). New York: Pergamon.

Campbell, R. J., Kagan, N., & Krathwohl, D. R. (1971). The development and validation of a scale to measure affective sensitivity (empathy). *Journal of Counseling Psychology, 18*, 407–412.

Cargile, A. C., & Giles, H. (1996). Intercultural communication training: Review, critique, and a new theoretical framework. *Communication Yearbook, 19*, 385–424.

Chen, G. M. (1995). *International e-mail debate and intercultural awareness*. Manuscript prepared for the grant project sponsored by FIPSI.

Chen, G. M. (in press). Towards transcultural understanding: A harmony theory of Chinese communication. In V. H. Milhouse, M. K. Asante, and P. O. Nwosu (Eds.), *Transculture: Interdisciplinary perspectives on cross-cultural relations*. Thousand Oaks, CA: Sage.

Chen, G. M., & Starosta, W. J. (1996). Intercultural communication competence: A synthesis. *Communication Yearbook, 19*, 353–384.

Chen, G. M., & Starosta, W. J. (1997). Chinese conflict management and resolution: Overview and implications. *Intercultural Communication Studies, 7*, 1–16.

Chen, G. M., & Starosta, W. J. (1998). *Foundations of intercultural communication*. Boston, MA: Allyn & Bacon.

Chen, G. M., & Starosta, W. J. (2000). Communication and globalization: An overview. In G. M. Chen and W. J. Starosta (Eds.), *Communication and globalization* (pp. 1–16). New York: Peter Lang.

Chung, J. (1992, November). *Electronic mail usage in low-context and high-context cultures*. Paper presented at the annual meeting of Speech Communication Association, Chicago, Illinois.

Colby, B. N. (1975). Culture grammars. *Science, 187*, 913–919.

Condon, J. C., & Yousef, F. (1975). *An introduction to intercultural communication*. Indianapolis: Bobbs-Merrill.

Cushner, K. (1989). Assessing the impact of a culture-general assimilator. *International Journal of Intercultural Relations, 13*, 125–146.

Cushner, K., & Brislin, R. W. (1995). *Intercultural interactions: A practical guide*. Thousand Oaks, CA: Sage.

Draguns, J. G. (1977). Problems of defining and comparing abnormal behavior across cultures. In L. L. Adler (Eds.), *Issues in cross-cultural research* (pp. 664–675). New York: New York Academy of Science.

Gardner, G. H. (1962). Cross-cultural communication. *Journal of Social Psychology, 58*, 241–256.

Gilgen, A. R., & Cho, J. H. (1979). Questionnaire to measure eastern and western thought. *Psychological Reports, 44*, 835–841.

Glenn, E. S., & Glenn, C. G. (1981). *Man and mankind: Conflict and communication between cultures*. New Jersey: Norwood.

Gudykunst, W. B., & Hammer, M. R. (1983). Basic training design: Approaches to intercultural training. In D. Landis and R. W. Brislin (Eds.), *Handbook of intercultural training*, Vol. 1 (pp. 118–154). New York: Pergamon.

Gudykunst, W. B., & Ting-Toomey, S. (1988). *Culture and interpersonal communication*. Newbury Park, CA: Sage.

Gudykunst, W. B., Ting-Toomey, S., & Wiseman, R. (1991). Taming the beast: Designing a course in intercultural communication. *Communication Quarterly, 40*, 272–286.

Hall, E. T. (1959). *Silent language*. Garden City, NY: Doubleday.

Hall, E. T. (1976). *Beyond culture*. Garden City, NY: Anchor.

Hall, E. T., & Whyte, W. F. (1963). Intercultural communication: A guide to men of action. *Practical anthropology, 9*, 83–108.

Hanvey, R. G. (1987). Cross-culture awareness. In L. F. Luce & E. C. Smith (Eds.), *Toward internationalism* (pp. 13–23). Cambridge, MA: Newbury.

Harris, R. H., & Moran, R. T. (1989). *Managing cultural differences*. Houston, TX: Gulf.

Hofstede, G. (1983). National cultures in four dimensions. *International Studies of Management and Organization, 13*, 46–74.

Hofstede, G. (1984). *Culture's consequences*. Beverly Hills, CA: Sage.

Kaplan, R. B. (1966). Cultural thought pattern in intercultural education. *Language Learning, 16*, 1–20.

Kitao, K. (1981). The test of American culture. *Technology & Mediated Instruction, 15*, 25–45.

Kluckhohn, F. K. (1948). *Mirror for man*. New York: Harper Collins.

Kluckhohn, F. K., & Strodbeck, F. L. (1961). *Variations in value orientations*. Evanston, IL: Row, Peterson.

Kohls, L. R. (1984). *Survival kit for overseas living*. Yarmouth, ME: Intercultural Press.

Kohls, L. R. (1988). Models for comparing and contrasting cultures. In J. M. Reid (Ed.), *Building the professional dimension of educational exchange* (pp. 137–153). Yarmouth, ME: Intercultural Press.

Landis, D., & Bhagat, R. S. (1996). A model of intercultural behavior and training. In D. Landis & S. Bhagat (Ed.), *Handbook of intercultural training* (pp. 1–16). Thousand Oaks, CA: Sage.

Mansell, M. (1981). Transcultural experience and expressive response. *Communication Education, 30*, 93–108.

Maryuma, M. (1970). *Toward a cultural futurology.* Cultural Futurology Symposium, American Anthropology Association national meeting, Training Center for Community Programs, University of Minnesota.

Oberg, K. (1960). Culture shock: Adjustment to new cultural environments. *Practical Anthropology, 7,* 177–182.

Oliver, R. T. (1962). *Culture and communication: The problem of penetrating national and cultural boundaries.* Springfield, IL: Thomas.

Parsons, T. (1951). *The social system.* Glencoe, IL: Free Press.

Platt, S. D. (1985). A subculture of parasuicide? *Human Relations, 38,* 257–297.

Rokeach, M. (1967). *Value survey.* Sunnyvale, CA: Halgren Tests.

Rokeach, M. (1973). *The nature of human values.* New York: Free Press.

Ruben, B. D. (1976). Assessing communication competency for intercultural adaptation. *Group & Organization Studies, 1,* 334–354.

Ruben, B. D., & Kealey, D. J. (1979). Behavioral assessment of communication competency and the prediction of cross-cultural adaptation. *International Journal of Intercultural Relations, 3,* 15–47.

Saville-Troike, M. (1978). *A guide to culture in the classroom.* Rosslyn, VI: InterAmerica Research Associates.

Schwartz, S. (1990). Individualism-collectivism. *Journal of Cross-Cultural Psychology, 21,* 139–157.

Schwartz, S. (1992). Universals in the content and structure of values: Theoretical advances and empirical tests in 20 countries. In M. Zanna (Ed.), *Advances in experimental social psychology* (pp. 1–65). Orlando, FL: Academic Press.

Schwartz, S., & Bilsky, W. (1987). Toward a psychological structure of human values. *Journal of Personality and Social Psychology, 53,* 850–862.

Schwartz, S., & Bilsky, W. (1990). Toward a theory of the universal content and structure of values: Extensions and cross-cultural replications. *Journal of Personality and Social Psychology, 58,* 878–891.

Schwartz, S., & Sagiv, L. (1995). Identifying culture-specifics in the content and structure of values. *Journal of Cross-Cultural Psychology, 26,* 92–116.

Seidel, G. (1981). Cross-cultural training procedures: Their theoretical framework and evaluation. In S. Bochner (Ed.). *The mediating person: Bridge between cultures.* Cambridge, MA: Schenhman.

Shirts, G. (1973). *BAFA BAFA: A cross-cultural simulation.* Delmar, CA: Simile.

Sitaram, K. S., & Haapanen, L. W. (1979). The role of values in intercultural communication. In M. K. Asante & C. A. Blake (Eds.), *The handbook of intercultural communication* (pp. 147–160). Beverly Hills, CA: Sage.

Stewart, E. C., & Bennett, M. J. (1991). *American cultural patterns.* Yarmouth, ME: Intercultural Press.

Triandis, H. C. (1977). Theoretical framework for evaluation of cross-cultural training effectiveness. *International Journal of Intercultural Relations, 1,* 195–213.

Triandis, H. C., Leung, K., Villareal, M. J., & Clark, F. L. (1985). Allocentric versus idiocentric tendencies: Convergent and discriminant validation. *Journal of Research in Personality, 19,* 395–415.

Turner, C. V. (1968). The Sinasina "big man" complex: A central cultural theme. *Practical Anthropology, 15,* 16–22.

Yum, J. O. (1989). *Communication sensitivity and empathy in culturally diverse organizations.* Paper presented at the 75th Annual Conference of Speech Communication Association, San Francisco.

Concepts and Questions

1. How do Chen and Starosta define intercultural communication competence? What are the three interrelated components of intercultural communication competence?

2. Why is intercultural awareness important to intercultural communication competence? How might you learn to increase your level of intercultural awareness?

3. What do Chen and Starosta mean when they say "intercultural awareness is, therefore, the cognitive perspective of intercultural communication?

4. What are the three levels of intercultural awareness? How do you achieve the highest of the three levels?

5. How do understanding the dimensions of cultural variability provide ways to identify how communication differs across cultures?

6. How might the experiential level of developing intercultural awareness lead to depression, helplessness, hostility, or disorientation?

7. Which do you believe would be the most useful means of developing intercultural awareness: experiential means or intellectual means? Why?

8. What are the differences between culture-general and culture-specific approaches to developing intercultural awareness?

9. What models are available for the study of intercultural awareness? How might these various models help you develop such awareness?

Unpacking Group-Based Intolerance: A Holographic Look at Identity and Intolerance

JOHN R. BALDWIN

MICHAEL HECHT

Recent reports in newspapers across the United States reveal that "race" is still an American obsession. We find that Blacks and Latinos are twice as likely to be stopped by police or to receive "undue force" as Whites; major cities report that "racial profiling," or stopping those

who are not White with less than likely cause, is a relatively common practice; there is debate about the use of Native American mascots for universities and the Confederate standard on state flags; movies and shows such as *The Sopranos* are accused of propagating ethnic stereotypes. News of some sort of ethnic or racial strife seems to surround us. Indeed, in an age of supposed tolerance, we find that hate crimes still continue in the United States with alarming proportions. In 1995, law enforcement agencies reported 7,947 hate crimes. That number remained consistent at around 8,000 (after peaking at nearly 9,000 in 1986) up through 1999.

These statistics (Table 1) reveal two facts. First, racial hate crimes are committed in large proportion, but not exclusively, by Whites. Second, race or ethnicity is only one axis of intolerance. Many offenders commit hate crimes for a variety of other reasons as well. These statistics demonstrate that group-based intolerance—of a variety of different types—is a social problem that merits our attention. In this chapter, we will present a theoretical approach to understanding intolerance that is based on our view of identity. We propose that intolerance

Table 1 *Hate Crimes in 1999**

Group of Target	Incidents	Offenses	Victims	Known Offenders
TOTAL	7,876	9,301	9,802	7,271
Race:	**4,295**	**5,240**	**5,485**	**4,362**
Anti-White	781	970	996	1,011
Anti-Black	2,958	3,542	3,679	2,861
Anti-Amer-Indian/Alaskan Native	47	79	50	40
Anti-Asia/Pacific Islander	298	363	379	288
Anti-Multi-Racial Group	211	316	381	162
Religion	**1,411**	**1,532**	**1,686**	602
Sexual Orientation	**1,317**	**1,487**	**1,558**	**1,376**
Ethnicity	829	**1,011**	**1,040**	**904**
Anti-Hispanic	466	576	588	562
Anti-Other Ethnicity	363	435	452	342
Disability	19	21	23	21
Multiple-Bias	5	10	10	6

*Adapted from Table 1, FBI Hate Crimes Statistics report, 1999 (FBI, 2001). Race and ethnicity provide breakdowns for the purposes of the present chapter. Original report also provides subcategories of crimes by religion, sexual orientation, and disability.

is multifaceted, and any solution to addressing or reducing intolerance will require the work of people in a variety of social spheres and academic disciplines.

INTERGROUP AND INTERCULTURAL COMMUNICATION

Many intercultural writers have developed models for trying to parse out the elements that influence intercultural communication, including the editors of the present book, most of which allow for the inclusion of prejudice (Porter & Samovar, Chapter 1, this book). Our view of intercultural communication can be best understood as a continuation of Social Identity Theory (SIT) (Tajfel & Turner, 1986). In its original conception, SIT suggested that we see people on a continuum between intergroup and interindividual (we will use the term *interpersonal*) perception. This goes along with communication scholars who contended that we first perceive people in terms of broader demographic categories and then, ultimately, in individual terms. SIT suggests that all communication has some group-based element to it, as we naturally see ourselves in terms of social categories. This, they suggest, is a part of the categorization process that helps us make sense of the world; however, when it comes to people, we first categorize others and ourselves into groups, and then compare our own group with that of the other, usually in a way that makes our own group look more favorable. In war, we see the other person strictly in group-based terms. In the classroom, students and teachers might see each other as individuals, but the teacher/student role difference will always be in the background, even if subconsciously.

Gudykunst and Lim (1986) provided a helpful expansion of the intergroup–interpersonal model of communication, suggesting that these may be two separate dimensions of perception. For example, in a war situation, we see the other very low in interpersonal terms, but very high in intergroup terms. In a romantic situation with someone we perceive to be of our own group, the interpersonal element will be high and the intergroup element will be low. An interaction with someone in the registrar's office at the university might be low on both—we see the person only as meeting a specific need, but not high in either group-belonging or interpersonal perception. In interracial romance, however, we might make individual attributions but also recognize the group-based identity of the other.

We feel that a helpful extension of this model would add a third dimension (Figure 1). Thus, a three-dimensional model of intercultural–intergroup communication would allow for individual differences, intergroup perception, and intercultural differences. One could be low on all three dimensions (the registrar example) or high on all three (an interracial romance). The model would be helpful, however, because it would allow for the *perception* of differences based on the person's group *even when real differences in culture between the people are minimal.* Thus, a younger person could *think* of an older person in stereotypical terms, *imagining* that the person had different values and so on, when, in fact, the person did not. At the same time, two people could perceive themselves to be of the same group (e.g., two African Americans), when, in fact, they have *notable cultural differences*, such as regional or class-based differences, that might influence communication or relationships.

Intercultural communication, in this approach, refers to communication in which actual (objective, real) differences in values, norms, beliefs, behavior, and symbol systems are significant enough to influence the communication process, similar to what researchers of ethnolinguistic vitality call "objective vitality." Intergroup communication refers to communication in which the social identity (or "groupness") of the partners, regardless of any real cultural

Figure 1 *Model of Intergroup and Intercultural Communication (Baldwin, 2000).*

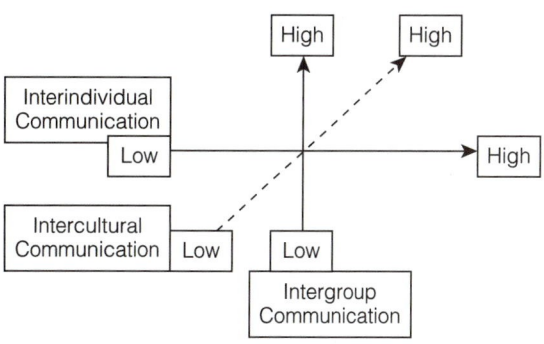

differences, influences the communication. Following Social Identity Theory, we believe that all face-to-face communication has some element of individual perception, group-perception, and cultural differences, even if those are at the microcultural level (Dodd & Baldwin, 1998).

GROUP AND INTERGROUP COMMUNICATION

If notions of both race and ethnicity are created in different societies' communication, we can make the assumption that supports the next section of this chapter, that social identities, including racial and ethnic identities, are inherently communicative. Many scholars from sociology, anthropology, and communication have taken this stance, following the notions of symbolic interactionism and "social construction." In essence, these approaches to social reality suggest that, by exchanging messages with each other, we create a view of which groups are important in a society and how those groups are defined, including the groups to which we belong. Where the original version of each of these theories, as well as the Communication Theory of Ethnic Identity, which one of us co-authored, emphasized face-to-face communication, we should also include mediated communication in the construction of identity.

Table 2 *Assumptions of the Communication Theory of Ethnic Identity*

1 Identities have individual, enacted, relational, and communal properties

2 Identities are both enduring and changing

3 Identities are affective, cognitive, behavioral, and spiritual

4 Identities have both content and relationship levels of interpretation

5 Identities involve both subjective and ascribed meanings

6 Identities are codes that are expressed in conversations and define membership in communities

7 Identities have semantic properties that are expressed in core symbols, meanings, and labels

8 Identities prescribe modes of appropriate and effective communication

9 Identities are hierarchically ordered meanings attributed to the self as an object in a social situation

10 Identities are meanings ascribed to the self by others in the social world

11 Identities are a source of expectations and motivations

12 Identities are emergent [in interaction and context]

13 Identities are enacted in social behaviors, social roles, and symbols

14 Identities emerge in relationship to other people

15 Identities are enacted in relationships

16 Relationships develop identities as social entities

17 Identities emerge out of groups and networks

From Hecht, Collier & Ribeau (1993, pp. 166–168).

The Communication Theory of Ethnic Identity

The Communication Theory of Ethnic Identity, or CTEI (Hecht, Collier, & Ribeau, 1993), proposes several ideas about African-American identity that can be expanded to any ethnic or racial identity, or even to other identities. Some of the assumptions of the theory are that identities have both enduring and changing aspects; that they include appropriate and effective ways of communicating to be a member of a particular group; that they have "affective, cognitive, behavioral, and spiritual" components; that they are "enacted in social behaviors, social roles, and symbols"; and that they can both be claimed (avowed) by the holder of the identity and ascribed by others (pp. 166–167; see Table 2).

One of the distinguishing features of the CTEI is the notion that "identities have individual, enacted, relational, and communal properties" (Hecht et al., 1993, p. 166). These refer to the different *frames of reference* of social behavior. These frames provide "means of interpreting reality that provide a perspective for understanding the social world" (p. 165). The levels should not be thought of as separate—if they were "circles" of identity, the circles would be sometimes concentric and sometimes overlapping because certain communications may bridge and cross the various levels of identity. In addition to the interpersonal dimensions mentioned previously, identity may also have mediated expressions, legal expressions, and so on. Although books, music videos, and laws are, ultimately, communicative acts of either individuals or groups of people, they merit their own focus as texts that pass on or challenge existing identities.

As an example of the different levels of identity, we can consider gender-based identity in the United States, especially in terms of marital roles of women and men. At the *individual* level, a specific woman has her perceptions of what the husband and wife do in the marriage, just as the man in the relationship has. When the partners are discussing with friends what they and their spouse do at night, or tell friends about some conflict, or discuss the notion of marriage in general, the *enactment* level (dyadic communication) is at work, although, as we can see, this level cannot exist apart from the individual perceptions at the individual level. When the partners interact to negotiate decision making, decide who cooks out on the grill and who diapers the baby, and argue about whose career will determine the next family move, they are negotiating gender identity at the *relational* level—defining their identity in relation to the other's identity. This level is distinct from *enactment* in that the enactment refers to any one-on-one communication we have in which identity is discussed or expressed (including subtle nonverbal expressions that mark one's social construction of gender). The *relationship* aspect refers to the ongoing connection between two people who interact on a regular basis, such as student–teacher, superior–subordinate, lovers, friends, and enemies.

One can see gender identity at the same time in a sort of "communal memory," as people engage in everyday and special rituals. For example, in the traditional Christian White American wedding ceremony, a groom stands at the right hand of a minister (the position of higher honor) and says the vows first. A bride is walked down the aisle, often with a veil (the groom is unveiled). A father (more recently, both parents) "gives" the bride to the groom. The minister pronounces them "man and wife" (or recently, husband and wife, but rarely "wife and husband," and never "woman and husband"). Finally, the groom is given permission to kiss the bride (the bride is not given such permission). In this case, embedded in the cultural memory and encoded in a ritual about which most people give little thought, are gender roles that may in turn become part of the re-

lational, dyadic, or personal identities. Coverage of female politicians, media portrayals of husbands and wives, and the representation of women and men in rap, country, or rock-and-roll videos, romance novels, as well as governmental legislation, research spending, and corporate wages and opportunities all also communicatively construct gender identity.

This same sort of analysis could be done for any specific identity—religious, ethnic, gender, sexual orientation, age cohort, social class—with the assumption that belonging to a specific group (women, African Americans, wealthy, elderly) does not necessarily give a person an identity of that group. Rather, identity is shared and developed only through communication, be that face-to-face (Friday morning Bingo) or mediated (AARP Newsletter for retired people). Because identities are communicative, groups within any particular larger identity group (e.g., African Americans) can have different identities. Thus, there might be several different Black ethnicities (Hecht & Ribeau, 1991), even if African-American groups share similar cultural roots and some historical experiences (Asante, 1987). Such a view of ethnic communication (or that of groups of other identities) would keep us from oversimplifying conclusions across groups of people, a criticism that is raised against research on racial communication (Orbe, 1995).

Research on Identity and Communication

Our ongoing research shows some specifics regarding particular identities and their enactment. In early research, for example, in same-ethnicity groups, Latinos (specifically, Mexican Americans) were more satisfied when they felt the other person genuinely wanted to know them, sought similar things in the interaction, and did not talk down to the person. Blacks and Whites were more satisfied when they felt the other person was listening to them and expressed interest in what they had to say. Other behaviors distinguished satisfaction of Whites from that of Blacks. For example, Black communicators were more satisfied if they felt they had helped the other person, if they got what they wanted in the conversation, and if they were not misunderstood, whereas Whites were more satisfied if they found similarities with the other person and were able to express their feelings (Hecht, Collier, & Ribeau, 1993).

The notion that different cultural and other identity groups have their own set of norms and meanings opens up a world of practical research implications. For example, recent research indicates that there are different rule sets involved in drug use. One study of 2,622 seventh graders in the Southwest United States finds that Mexican Americans are more likely than other groups to receive offers for drug use, and African Americans were the least likely group to be approached. Further, the most prominent location of where drugs were offered differs by group. Mexican Americans received more offers from family peers and at parties; African Americans received offers from boyfriends, girlfriends, or parents; and European Americans were offered drugs often by acquaintances, but were least likely to receive offers from brothers (Moon et al., 1999). Strategies for resisting drug use also varied— African Americans were more likely than the other two groups to explain (that is, directly confront the other) than the other groups, and males were more likely to use this strategy than females.

Further research into the meaning of ethnic labels to people finds that African, Mexican, and mixed-identity Americans with a high sense of ethnic pride (that is, their ethnicity has more symbolic meaning to them) received fewer offers for drug use and reported lower drug use. On the other hand, Whites with strong ethnic identity reported greater drug use (Marsiglia, Kulis, & Hecht, in press). These studies support the ideas of the CTEI in that both the labels one used for oneself and the actual sense of ethnic identity work together to provide the best prediction of drug exposure and rules for resistance. The knowledge of different cultural frameworks surrounding drug usage can be used to target drug resistance to specific communities, such as by building resistance through developing ethnic pride.

Identity and Intergroup Communication

If, as many theorists of social identity have argued (e.g., Gallois et al., 1995), our group belonging is intricately tied to how our group speaks, it only stands to reason that "identity," at its various levels of expression, would be at play in interethnic and other forms of intergroup communication. As noted previously, people of two different identity groups face (at least) three issues when they communicate: (1) individual differences; (2) cultural differences; and (3) differences pursuant to the groupness of the individuals involved. Much interethnic communication research has focused on the second aspect, that of cultural difference. Thus, breakdowns in communication are framed in terms of differences in eye contact (e.g., "visual dominance"), use of space, question patterns, views of conflict, and, as seen in our own research cited earlier, "satisfying communication." Unstated assumptions of this research are that (1) cultural differences exist between ethnic groups, and (2) problems occur in communication when people do not adapt to or recognize the rules of the other.

More recently, several research projects have investigated interethnic communication specifically (Hecht, Ribeau, & Alberts, 1989; Ribeau, Baldwin, & Hecht, 2000). One study finds several issues important to African Americans as they interact with White Americans:

1. *Negative stereotyping*: Has the communication partner treated the person as a member of a racial category, rather than as an individual?
2. *Acceptance*: Has the communication partner communicated in a way that accepts, confirms, and respects the person?
3. *Emotional expressiveness*: Have both partners been able to share their feelings both verbally and nonverbally?
4. *Authenticity*: Was the communication of both people perceived as being truthful and genuine?
5. *Understanding*: Did both partners perceive meaning to be conveyed successfully?
6. *Goal attainment*: Did both partners feel that desired ends were obtained through the interaction?
7. *Powerlessness*: Did the person feel manipulated or controlled by the communication partner?

Either the Black or the White partner in the interaction might adopt several strategies to improve the situation, such as asserting one's point of view, treating the other as an equal, avoiding the other person, regulating the amount and rate of talk (interaction management), and imagining the interaction from the point of view of the other person.

Later research found that Caucasian and African Americans preferred to use different strategies when different issues surfaced in interethnic interaction. For example, African Americans were more likely to use more assertive improvement strategies to improve the conversation, such as assertiveness, avoidance, and taking the role of the other. The Caucasian Americans were more likely to use more passive strategies, such as giving in or simply feeling there was nothing anyone could do to improve the interaction (Martin, Hecht, & Larkey, 1994). In one recent study (Martin et al., in press), 133 African Americans provided their open-ended responses to each of the seven strategies listed previously. The participants, as well as others in an additional in-depth interview study, listed a wide array of different strategies that could be useful in intergroup communication (See Table 3).

In sum, we believe the following summary best describes our approach to identity and communication. Identities are created socially through communication. An identity can emerge surrounding a political ideology, membership in a Greek organization, origin of one's ancestors, or supposed biological differences between people, but different bases of difference carry different meaning. For example, if difference is presumed to be biological, that can be much stronger in its communicative results than if it is seen only as cultural. Communication—both interpersonal and mediated—creates a sense of belonging and/or separation, and through these interactions we pervasively enact our own identities and "construct" the identities of others (at least in our own minds). We can feel identity, express it through our words and actions, develop it in relationships, participate in it communally, and pass it on or challenge it with media, books, and policies. Identities contain cultural elements (real differences), but as we see each other in terms of identity, there is also the component of *perception* of difference, even if such difference does not exist.

Table 3 *Strategies for Dealing with Problematic Intergroup Communication*

1 *Assertiveness*
- Assert one's point of view: Be straightforward about your opinion
- Confront: Be assertive in challenging stereotypes or false statements
- Inform/educate: Clarify or give more information to the other person

2 *Other Orientation*
- Other-orientation: Imagine yourself in the position of the other person
- Be friendly: Be tactful and polite, considerate of the other person
- Express genuineness: Be honest, real
- Positive self-presentation: Present one's self and group in a positive light

3 *Open-Mindedness*
- Treat the other as an individual

4 *Interaction Management*
- Interaction management: Talk more, ask questions, engage the other
- Language management: Avoid slang or jargon; talk the same language
- Internal management: Self-talk to manage attitudes during interaction

*These strategies were developed from an open-ended questionnaire and interview study with African Americans regarding their strategies for interacting with Whites (Martin et al., in press). They are not generalizable to all types of intergroup communication, though parallels may exist in other forms of communication, such as inter-class, inter-region, inter-age, and so on.

INTOLERANCE: EXTENDING THE CTEI

At this point, we move fully into a theory of intolerance. To track our thoughts so far, we first saw that different identity groups create different sets of rules and meanings. It was assumed that difference leads to misunderstanding; however, Rattansi (1992) suggests that this understanding is faulty. First, it assumes that people will respond rationally when presented with the proper information, and research does not support this idea. Second, and related to this concept, is the idea that this view of the prejudice aspect of intergroup communication is too simple. It leaves out too many other factors.

The CTEI work on intergroup communication described earlier hints at this weakness. Both African and Mexican Americans perceive both issues of misunderstanding *and* power in communication with Whites. Other research continues to point to the same notion. Orbe's (1994) ethnographic study of African-American males' views of communication with Whites reveals several strategies that point to power issues, to dealing with and having to adapt to an oppressive White culture ("clique"), to helping others learn the "system" and get along in an unfair world. Orbe (1998) expands his research to develop a theory that African Americans and other identity groups have their own standpoint that is determined not only by communication culture differences, but also by political, historical, and economic conditions. We cannot understand intergroup communication (such as African–Caucasian American interaction) without considering the years or centuries of history and politics between the groups (Hecht, Collier, & Ribeau, 1993).

Layers of Intolerance

If one is to fully understand intolerance, or prejudice, then one cannot remain in a single academic discipline. To this end, we have proposed an approach to intolerance that seeks to bring people from different disciplines together to understand how intolerance works (Baldwin & Hecht, 1995). This approach holds that, like identity, prejudice can exist at the personal, dyadic, relational, communal, and, we would add, rhetorical/mediated and political levels. At the *personal* level, a person may feel intolerant toward those who are perceived to be different in general or toward a specific group. At the *dyadic* (or *enactment*) level, intolerance can be reproduced in jokes, in speeches that one makes, or in subtle nonverbal behaviors. These subtle behaviors are especially important to consider because many authors argue that our society has buried overt racism and sexism under the guise of more subtle forms of intolerance. People can express intolerance at the *relational* level as they engage in relationships, even romantic relationships, with

people of groups about which they hold stereotypes or other prejudicial attitudes.

Further, the relationship we have with a person (e.g., a stranger versus an intimate, our roommate versus our mother or our priest or rabbi) may influence what forms of intolerance are acceptable to express. At the *communal* level, intolerance is built into the rituals, and into the collective memory of our society through textbooks, novels, movies, television, music, policies, and laws in ways that are not easily attributable to the individual. In some cases, an individual producer or songwriter might be expressing the intolerance (e.g., Eminem), which would be "dyadic" in a sense, except that the intolerance is broadcast across the airwaves and the Internet in a way that requires a different sort of analysis from one-on-one communication.

Although some prejudices exist only in a specific context (e.g., a rivalry between competing Greek organizations at a university or between pro-choice and pro-life groups), other intolerances run deeply to permeate the very fabric of American society, such as racism and sexism. This is to say, our very society, down to the structural level, is divided in terms of "race" and biological gender. As such, any attempt to deal with it only in terms of communication differences will ultimately end in failure. But then, so will any attempt to deal with intolerance at any other single level. Allport (1979) suggested that several factors might influence intolerance, including sociological factors, historical factors, personality factors, and so on, with the ultimate influence being the person's psychological perception of the individual. This view may be too linear and simple an explanation. So, in the Layered Perspective of Cultural Intolerance, we suggest that we must consider each of these areas as they relate to each other. The theory has four main components:

- *Stances:* Rather than think of people as either "tolerant" or "intolerant," we should expand our view of attitudes toward the other. Even the notion of "intolerance" sounds like we merely put up with others. We might include "appreciation." In some ways we might be intolerant and tolerant at the same time, or tolerant toward some groups but intolerant toward others.

- *Spheres*: Just as identity can revolve around a variety of different bases (political, biological, geographical, etc.), intolerance can also be exhibited toward those of any perceived group. The sphere of intolerance, then, is like a mirror to identity. It is the identity we ascribe, or give to, the other group, with all of the notions we hold toward that group. Common spheres of identity involve race/ethnicity, biological sex, sexual orientation, age cohorts, social class, nationality, and so on. In some cases, if one is a member of more than one group (e.g., African-American women), they might be perceived and treated by a dominant culture in ways that "compound" the intolerance based on group membership.
- *Levels of analysis*: This notion borrows the frames of analysis from the CTEI—personal, dyadic, relational, and communal, as noted earlier. Including the different levels would allow the perspective to inform those who look at attitudes (personal level), at intolerant behaviors (dyadic level), at intergroup relationships, at popular culture, and so on.
- *Types of analysis*: Because intolerance can be experienced or expressed at different levels, it must also be studied at different levels. There are both regularities in certain intolerances, which would require a more traditional scientific and statistical approach to study, and individual aspects and experiences of tolerance and intolerance, which would be best understood through open-ended research. In this final element, we urge people from different fields to study intolerance together and to seek solutions; however, because the problem of intolerance exists at different levels and across levels, solutions must be multifaceted.

A Holographic View

It is not realistic, of course, for any scholar or even any discipline to try to understand the entire puzzle of intolerance. Therefore, it may be best to think of intolerance (like identity), as a "hologram" (Hecht & Baldwin, 1998). Talbot (1991) makes two interesting points about how holographic photography works, and both of these apply to our understanding of intolerance. First, he points out that holographic film is different from normal photographic film in that every piece of film contains all the data. That is, if one takes a picture of a tree and cuts it in half, when one shines a laser through the film to obtain an image, the image will still be of the whole tree. So, one could cut the film into small pieces, but each piece still contains the image of the tree. As the piece of film gets smaller and smaller, however, the image loses fidelity, becoming increasingly blurred.

In terms of the study and treatment of intolerance, we can see the same phenomena. First, scholars from different fields—from literature to theatre to psychology to communication to urban studies—can look at a given intolerance, like racism. Even if the studies are on radically different aspects of the phenomenon, we will likely see a semblance of the same thing in each study; however, the more microscopic or limited the view, the less our fidelity. We gain the greatest understanding by looking across studies, across disciplines, across methodologies, even across assumptions about knowledge and the nature of social reality.

AN APPLICATION OF THE LAYERED PERSPECTIVE: VIOLENCE AGAINST ASIAN AMERICANS

In 1982, in a case that rocked the United States, a racist murdered Vincent Chen. In 1999, Buford Furrow gunned down Joseph Ileto, a letter carrier with the U.S. Postal Service. Between these incidents lies a long line of assault against Asian Americans, with five hate-related murders in the United States in 1998 alone ("The bloody legacy," 1999).

A specific anti-Asian (or Asian American) attack can be understood at the personal level. The attacker makes an individual decision to act on hatred. That hatred might be fueled by psychological drives, such as a need to feel superior, a need for structure, or ethnocentrism. At the same time, we find that acts of the most extreme aggression, such as killing, are rarely isolated from larger anti-immigrant sentiment. This sentiment might be expressed in terms of jokes about Asian Americans (and influenced by the inability or refusal of many people to differentiate among different Asian groups) at the dyadic level. Research could thus look at the subtle and overt behaviors of racism and ethnocentrism, how these are expressed or experienced, or at attitudes toward those perceived to be of Asian ancestry.

At the same time, acts of intolerance often surface more at times of economic insecurity, such as the mid-1970s or the late 1980s in the United States, or in areas where there is competition for resources. Researchers could, then, examine social factors such as immigration patterns, distribution of wealth and opportunity, joblessness, inflation, and group-competition in the late 1990s that might give rise to a spike in violence toward Asians and Asian Americans.

Even if there is competition and scarcity of resources, however, there must be some rhetorical element, some social construction of reality that determines which groups will be the target of violence, discrimination, segregation, or stereotyping. For example, in the 1980s and 1990s, when there was a flurry of buy-outs of American corporations by Japanese companies and a rise in the influence of the Japanese banking industry, many cartoonists and pundits poked "fun" at the Japanese, even complaining that America was being "sold out." However, little or no attention was paid to British, Dutch, or German multinational corporations that were doing the same thing. Just as newspapers frame the "immigration problem" as a "Mexican" problem (rather than a Canadian problem) and as a problem of the immigrants, rather than the employers who want to pay substandard wages or the average American citizens who want lower prices for products, so public rhetoric framed the Japanese as a key source of economic competition. Finally, anti-Asian sentiment cannot be divorced from the historical context of World War II, the Japanese internment camps in the United States, and other historical influences.

CONCLUSION

In sum, Asian American–bashing and other forms of anti-Asian sentiment have a long tradition at deep levels in the fabric of American society. Any solution that recommends merely "learning about our differences" will not be sufficient. Rather, intolerance should be perceived of as psychological, dyadic, relational, and communal. Strategies for change can begin with intercultural communication and studies of cultural difference. But at the end, we may have to rethink how we see group belonging because intolerance seems to be a distorted mirror of one's own identity. Researchers need to work together and read one another's writing to achieve a deeper, richer, "holographic" understanding of different types of group-based hatred.

If one wants to address any of the types of group-based intolerance or hatred described in this article, including racism, anti-"foreigner" sentiment (which is often also seen in racial terms), sexism, or ageism, the concepts of the Layered Perspective should be helpful. Solutions could consider the following:

- *Stances*: Our goal should not be simply tolerating (or putting up with) cultural and group-based differences, but should move toward appreciating the perspectives of other groups (both social and cultural). Attempts at cultural awareness, such as diversity fairs, must go beyond appreciating food, clothing, and music to look at the stuff beneath the surface, such as notions of status and respect, family structure, gender roles, value systems, and decision-making and logic patterns.

- *Spheres*: We need to continue to do research on the various types of intolerance that exist, both in terms of the behaviors that are intolerant, especially in an age when racism and sexism are expressed more subtly. We also need to do more research that opens up for us the perspectives of the recipients of intolerance to understand how the world is different for these recipients and to find strategies for resistance to intolerance.

- *Types of Understanding*: We need various types of research to understand intolerance, from literary and legal analysis to social scientific attitude and experience questionnaires, from in-depth interviews and ethnographies to analysis of everyday conversations. Only by looking at a variety of research from several academic disciplines can we really gain a more complete picture of a given group-based hatred.

- *Aiming Solutions at Multiple Sites*: Those who want to reduce a specific intolerance, such as sexism in the workplace, should avoid simplistic strategies that aim at only one aspect of intolerance (such as, for example, reducing misunderstanding). Some aspects can be aimed at attitude change, such as through role-playing. But advocates of change should also look to social policy and structure and whether those constructs reinforce the intolerant behaviors. In the workplace, for example, lack of norms to redress sexism or a culture that allows sexist jokes or language are more likely to produce environments that are more fertile for the growth of specific cases of sexist communication. Because segregation and perceived competition between groups may feed intolerance, efforts can be made to integrate workers in terms of proximity and to foster collaboration rather than cooperation. Certainly other strategies for change aimed at specific aspects of intolerance can be developed from the perspective.

Most important for students reading this chapter, individuals need to find where they fit into the picture of both identity and intolerance. As individuals, we might think about the ways we express and enact our own identity, and whether those actions in any way exclude or put down those of other identities. Finally, in terms of an approach that urges complex solutions for a complex problem, each of us may find ourselves addressing intolerance in different ways. Some of us will rethink the images we make for media and public relations organizations, attempting to spot the subtle assumptions of intolerance in our own work. Others will become activists, seeking to change political and educational structures that make for a better world. And probably most of us will need to find ways to address intolerance in a wholesome, constructive way that builds bridges for people to cross, rather than barriers to stand in their way.

References

Allport, G. A. (1979/1954). *The nature of prejudice*. Reading, MA: Addison-Wesley.

Asante, M. K. (1987). *The Afrocentric idea*. Philadelphia: Temple University Press.

Baldwin, J. R., & Hecht, M. L. (1995). The layered perspective of cultural (in)tolerance(s): The roots of a multidisciplinary approach. In R. Wiseman (Ed.) *Intercultural communication theory* (pp. 59–91). Thousand Oaks, CA: Sage.

"The bloody legacy of hate crime: From Vincent Chin to Joseph Ileto, the killing continues." (August 19, 1999). *Asian Week: AsianWeek.com*. Available at www.asianweek.com/081999/feature_intro.html.

Dodd, C. H., & Baldwin, J. R. (1998). Family culture and relationship differences as a source of intercultural communication. In J. Martin, T. Nakayama, & L. Flores (Eds.), *Readings in cultural contexts* (pp. 335–344). Mountain View, CA: Mayfield.

Federal Bureau of Investigation (2001). *Uniform crime reports*. Available at www.fbi.gov/ucr.htm, updated March 13, 2001.

Gallois, C., Giles, H., Jones, E., Cargile, A. C., & Ota, H. (1995). Accommodating intercultural encounters: Elaborations and extensions. In R. L. Wiseman (Ed.), *Intercultural communication theory* (pp. 115–147). Thousand Oaks, CA: Sage.

Gudykunst, W. B., & Lim, T.S. (1986). A perspective for the study of intergroup communication. In W. Gudykunst (Ed.), *Intergroup communication*. London: Edward Arnold.

Hecht, M. L., & Baldwin, J. R. (1998). Layers and holograms: A new look at prejudice. M. L. Hecht (Ed.), *Communication of prejudice* (pp. 57–84). Thousand Oaks, CA: Sage.

Hecht, M. L., Collier, M. J., & Ribeau, S. A. (1993). *African American communication: Ethnic identity and cultural interpretation*. Newbury Park, CA: Sage.

Hecht, M., & Ribeau, S. (1991). Socio-cultural roots of ethnic identity: A look at Black America. *Journal of Black Studies, 21*, 501–513.

Hecht, M.L., Ribeau, S., & Alberts, J.K. (1989). An Afro-American perspective on interethnic communication. *Communication Monographs, 56*, 385–410.

Marsiglia, F. F., Kulis, S., & Hecht, M. L. (in press). Ethnic labels and ethnic identity as predictors of drug use among middle school students in the Southwest. *Journal of Research on Adolescence*.

Martin, J. M., Hecht, M. L., & Larkey, L. K. (1994). Conversational improvement strategies for interethnic communication: African American and European American perspectives. *Communication Monographs, 61*, 236–255.

Martin, J. M., Hecht, M. L., Moore, S., & Larkey, L. K. (in press). African American conversational improvement strategies for interethnic communication. *Howard Journal of Communications*.

Moon, D. G., Hecht, M. L., Jackson, K. M., & Spellars, R. E. (1999). Ethnic and gender differences and similarities in adolescent drug use and refusals of drug offers. *Substance Use & Misuse, 34*, 1059–1083.

Orbe, M. P. (1994). "Remember, it's always whites' ball": Descriptions of African American male communication. *Communication Quarterly, 42*, 287–300.

Orbe, M. P. (1995). African American communication research: Toward a deeper understanding of interethnic communication. *Western Journal of Communication, 59*, 61–78.

Orbe, M. P. (1998). *Constructing co-cultural theory: An explication of culture, power, and communication.* Thousand Oaks, CA: Sage.

Rattansi, A. (1992). Changing the subject? Racism, culture, and education. In J. Donald & A. Rattansi (Eds.), *'Race,' culture & difference* (pp. 11-48). London: Sage.

Ribeau, S. A., Baldwin, J. R., & Hecht, M. L. (2000). An African American communication perspective. In L. A. Samovar & R. E. Porter (Eds.), *Intercultural communication: A reader* (9th ed.) (pp. 128–136). Belmont, CA: Wadsworth.

Tajfel, H., & Turner, J.C. (1986). The social identity theory of intergroup behavior. In S. Worchel & W.G. Austin (Eds.), *Psychology of intergroup relationships* (2nd ed.) (pp. 7–24). Chicago: Nelson-Hall.

Talbot, M. (1991). *The holographic universe.* New York: Harper Perennial.

Comments and Questions

1. What do Baldwin and Hecht infer by the term *group-based intolerance?*

2. How can people perceive themselves to be members of the same group when in actuality they have notable cultural differences? How does this influence intercultural communication?

3. Explain the Communication Theory of Ethnic Identity. How does this theory support the notion that identities have individual, enacted, relational, and communal properties?

4. What are the individual, enactment, and relational levels of identity? How does knowledge of these levels foster successful intercultural communication?

5. How do the rules of different cultural and other identity groups affect the manner in which group members may be approached for drug usage?

6. What are some of the issues important to African Americans as they interact with White Americans? What strategies might African Americans and/or Whites employ to help assuage some of these issues?

7. What do Baldwin and Hecht consider to be the personal level of intolerance?

8. What are the four main components of the CTEI?

9. What solutions to group-based ethnic intolerance are suggested by Baldwin and Hecht?

Optimising Conditions for Learning Sociocultural Competencies for Success

Anita S. Mak

Marvin J. Westwood

F. Ishu Ishiyama

Michelle C. Barker

Current trends in increasing world trade, globalisation of skilled labor, and internationalisation of education have meant an increasing number of people moving between countries as skilled immigrants or sojourners for overseas work or studies. A major challenge for highly qualified expatriate workers and immigrants, as well as international students, is to continue to be successful in their careers and/or studies. This challenge requires discrimination about what constitutes effective communication and learning ways of establishing interpersonal relations in the host society (Hammer et al., 1978; Spitzberg and Cupach, 1984).

Even among immigrants and sojourners with a high level of proficiency in the language spoken in the host country, variations in sociocultural rules are often baffling, the more so for people from a cultural background very different from that of the hosts. Newcomers may operate from a culturally conditioned basis, where behaviors performed would be effective in their original country, but ineffective in the new context. This is because cultures and societies differ in the values, roles, and rules that govern

From the *International Journal of Intercultural Relations, 23(1)*, 1999. Reprinted by permission of Elsevier Science, Ltd. All rights reserved. Anita S. Mak is affiliated with the University of Canberra, Australia. Marvin J. Westwood and F. Ishu Ishiyama are associated with the University of British Columbia, Vancouver, Canada. Michelle C. Barker is affiliated with Griffith University, Brisbane, New Zealand.

appropriate verbal and nonverbal behavior in social situations (Barker, 1993; Hofstede, 1980).

This article explains the benefits that immigrants and sojourners may reap from learning skills for intercultural competence (that is, developing sociocultural competence), which will improve individuals' opportunities for success in a foreign country. Psychosocial barriers to developing these desirable sociocultural skills are discussed. The optimal conditions for the development of intercultural social competencies are then identified, utilising instructional implications from various theoretical bases of human learning.

The extent to which highly qualified immigrants and expatriate workers are able to transfer their occupational skills and potential for career success often rests largely on whether they can continue to be socially effective in the new country. This is particularly the case for human services professionals, businesspeople, managers, and administrators, because much of their work involves building rapport and communicating with staff and clients and is conducted in the context of work organisations. Similarly, for international students to reap the maximum benefits from an unfamiliar educational system, they will need to establish interpersonal relations and communicate effectively with mainstream students, teachers, and homestay parents (Barker, 1993; McInnis and James, 1995; Westwood and Ishiyama, 1991). Newcomers from culturally different backgrounds will benefit greatly from learning appropriate ways of conducting some strategic social exchanges useful for a variety of interpersonal situations, such as seeking information and help, making social contacts and conversation, participation in group discussion, receiving and giving feedback, and refusing a request or expressing disagreement.

Satisfactory social relationships with host cultural members are important for general social purposes in daily living and for children of immigrant and expatriate families to integrate successfully in schools and the neighborhood. Being socially competent is vital for meeting the human needs for belonging, love, and esteem as the newcomers seek acceptance in a new work, educational, and social environment dominated by host nationals.

Most newcomers tend to have clear goals for continued career and educational success and are often prepared to work very hard to attain these goals in the new country. However, not all immigrants and sojourners recognize the importance of sociocultural competence in their pursuit of these goals. For example, an Asian professional immigrant in Canada may willingly work through most coffee breaks and so miss out on vital informal exchanges of work-related information and opportunities for building social relationships in the lunch room, which could in the future jeopardize his chances of career advancement.

Immigrants and sojourners who have been in the new country for some time often notice considerable differences in what constitutes social competencies, and many begin to realize how desirable it is to be interculturally effective. In a study with 111 Hong Kong professional and managerial immigrants in Australia, Mak (1996) found that the most frequently identified barrier (by close to two-thirds of the subjects) in transfer of their occupational skills was unfamiliarity with the Australian culture and society. When her subjects were asked to suggest training programs that could have been useful for facilitating their career development, the most common response spontaneously expressed was that of some form of intercultural communication training. It would seem that some immigrants who are acutely aware of cultural differences in the workplace are nonetheless puzzled as to how to bridge the differences.

These newcomers are looking for guidance in or at least the critical clues for going about their adventure in the new country. They are like strangers lost in a new city who are in need of a map to help them reach their destinations. They should be able to benefit from cultural learning presented as social skills training in the host country (Bochner, 1986, 1994; Brislin, 1994). Their clear goals for career and educational success should provide the motivation for acquiring and practicing these intercultural social skills.

PSYCHOSOCIAL BARRIERS TO DEVELOPING SOCIOCULTURAL COMPETENCE

Despite the drive for success among the immigrants and sojourners, several potential psychosocial barriers may impede the development of sociocultural competence in adults and adolescents. They may have limited coaching and practice opportunities for learning these skills, or may be consciously or unconsciously resisting to develop intercultural social competence in the new country for a variety of reasons.

Newcomers may not be ready to learn and practice social behaviors appropriate to the new culture in the initial period of settlement. It is not unusual for recent arrivals to be overwhelmed by the immediate demands and challenges in orienting to living in a new place (Pedersen, 1991; Stening, 1979). Some new arrivals could also be preoccupied with multiple losses and grieving (Anderson, 1994). Those who have left behind beloved family members or have given up established and prestigious careers in their original country may be particularly sad and homesick (Mak, 1991). Ishiyama (Ishiyama, 1989, 1995) suggested that newcomers tend to have heightened initial needs for self-validation, including the validation of the cultural self. Many will want to seek comfort and affirmation of their sense of self through interacting with familiar others, such as co-ethnics, and conducting familiar, rather than novel, activities.

Newcomers who are unfamiliar with the host cultural code may experience considerable interpersonal anxiety as they begin to interact with host nationals (Gudykunst and Hammer, 1988). In cases where strangers attempt to cope with their anxiety by opting for minimising contacts with hosts, this may lead to social avoidance. It is well known that while some forms of contact may reduce prejudice and lessen ethnocentrism, contact that is competitive or overly formal could reinforce existing negative stereotypes (Amir, 1969, 1976; Triandis and Vassilou, 1967). The larger the distance between the original and the host culture, the greater is the potential for social anxiety. This tendency may be accentuated where newcomers have access to co-ethnic community enclaves and the familiar lifestyle they could provide, and hence a reduced need to interact with host nationals and learn their strange customs.

The motivation to develop sociocultural competence is likely to be compromised when people's original cultural pride or identity is threatened (Bond, 1992; Mak et al., 1994). New immigrants and sojourners may resist learning the social presentation of host nationals when faced with a perceived pressure to abandon their own customs and replace them with those characteristic of the new country. Individuals forced to assimilate into the new society and to give up their home cultural values and familiar ways of relating to the world often feel devalued and resentful. They may be reluctant to adopt new ways of doing things. However, if these cultural adjustment tasks are presented as additions to their existing repertoire of social skills that are highly advantageous for performing the newly adopted roles acquired through living in a foreign country, most newcomers will probably find such an augmentational approach to be attractive and certainly more acceptable than a replacement model. The extended range of social competencies enables immigrants, international students, and expatriate workers to continue to be effective within their ethnic community and at the same time increases their chances of success in the new country.

Various dispositional, demographic, and other personal factors may explain individual differences in cross-cultural adjustments (Kealey and Ruben, 1983; Smith and Bond, 1993). For example, those who are introverted, anxiety-prone, authoritarian, hesitant to open up to new experiences, low in self-esteem, and have external locus of control beliefs may be less motivated or find it harder to develop intercultural social competencies. Furthermore, minority group members at the resistance and immersion stage of cultural identity development (Sue and Sue, 1990) may strongly resist an identification with the mainstream society and indicate a clear preference for completely belonging to the original racial group.

In summary, potential psychosocial barriers to developing sociocultural competence include lack of coaching and practice opportunities, a sense of being overwhelmed by the number of adjustments required, heightened needs for self-validation, interpersonal anxiety about how to relate to host nationals, threat to the newcomer's original cultural identity, and various personal factors. These barriers will need to be addressed in an effective intercultural social skills training program.

THEORETICAL BASES OF LEARNING SOCIOCULTURAL COMPETENCIES

Previous works (e.g., Brislin et al., 1983; Gudykunst and Hammer, 1983) have delineated different approaches to intercultural training, but have not presented a theoretical discussion of what makes cultural learning effective despite various potential psychosocial barriers. While Taylor (1994) has argued for a significant link between becoming interculturally competent and Mezirow's (1991) theory of perspective transformative learning, he has not provided a specific explanation of how sociocultural competence skills can be acquired or trained.

The present article argues that combining instructional implications from established paradigms of operant and classical conditioning and social cognitive learning in a group setting can provide intercultural communication trainers with an integrated framework for enhancing the development of sociocultural competence among new immigrants and sojourners, while simultaneously addressing the potential psychosocial barriers. The learning paradigms are not presented as being fundamentally adversarial, but have evolved over decades of observation and research to account for different aspects of the complex processes of human learning. The theoretical discussion will be helpful for understanding why some intercultural competence training is likely to be more effective than others.

Operant Conditioning

The principles of operant conditioning (Skinner, 1953, 1972) in shaping new behaviors and changing the likelihood of behaviors are well-established and widely applied in educational and therapeutic settings (e.g., Masters et al., 1987). Following these principles, recent immigrants and sojourners can be trained to develop new micro social skills for career and educational success appropriate to the new culture if the following conditions are met: (1) their correct responses to specific social cues are repeatedly rewarded by praises and successes; (2) their appropriate social behaviors are further reinforced by the reduction of embarrassment and anxiety about unfamiliar social interactions; and (3) coaching and opportunities for practice are provided to facilitate corrective feedback and perfection of new skills. Effective social behaviors for specific goals may later be generalized to other appropriate situations. Training can proceed according to a graded sequence of difficulties, progressing from dealing with direct and obvious social cues to the more subtle and intricate.

Classical Conditioning

The established paradigm of classical conditioning that can be traced back to the work of Pavlov (1927) is useful for understanding some foreigners' conditioned social anxiety in interacting with hosts. Initially neutral stimuli (e.g., a foreign accent, visibly different facial features, and unfamiliar gestures) may come to acquire a capacity to provoke anxiety.

Fortunately, extensive research has established the effectiveness of the counter-conditioning procedure (Masters et al., 1987; Wolpe, 1958, 1973) in helping individuals extinguish conditioned anxiety through repeatedly pairing the anxiety-provoking stimuli with the relaxation response. A critical component of the procedure is that the individual will need to be exposed to the anxiety-provoking cues, either in imagination or in real-life situations, and in increasing amounts of exposure, instead of being allowed to avoid them.

Applied to dealing with anxiety in cross-cultural encounters, this would mean the importance of opportunities for strangers to interact with hosts in a supportive and relaxed atmosphere with potentially rewarding outcomes. The acquisition of a few simple but effective micro social skills (e.g., introducing oneself, and making a request appropriate to the new culture) through the operant conditioning procedures described previously is likely to increase considerably the chances of having a rewarding social interaction.

Social Cognitive Learning

Bandura's (1977a) theory of social learning, which was refined in 1986 as the theory of social cognitive learning, has greatly broadened the understanding of the processes of human acquisition and maintenance of complex social behaviors. According to the theory, individuals have a tendency to model upon others' behaviors when the role models are similar to themselves and/or are respected and are observed to be obtaining rewards for their behaviors. Through observations alone, trainees develop expectations that specific behaviors in certain social situations will lead to rewarding consequences, a process known as *vicarious learning*. After being shown what to do in strategic situations by credible role models and given an explanation of the underlying rationale, trainees are likely to learn to perform similar behaviors when opportunities arise.

Observing successful social performances by others similar to oneself (e.g., a visibly different co-ethnic who also speaks with an accent) enhances the trainees' perceived self-efficacy, or belief in ability to carry out a particular behavior. Increased self-efficacy in a strategic action in turn increases the chance of attempting and mastering that task as well as the likelihood of appropriate goal-setting (Berry and West, 1993). Bandura (1977b, 1989) argued that the way that individuals think affects their performance and that efficacy beliefs can regulate human functioning through integrated cognitive, motivational, affective, and selection (of activities and environment) processes. Hence, there are adaptive benefits of optimistic efficacy beliefs. Culturally, different newcomers who are not shown ways of being socially effective by role models from a similar background may become discouraged and believe that they will never be socially effective in the new country given their minority group member and newcomer status.

Another relevant concept within the social cognitive theory is reciprocal determinism, which means that person variables, situation variables, and behavior continuously interact with one another (Bandura, 1986). This is an important augmentation to classical and operant conditioning theories that are focused on the effect of the environment on the individual's behavior. While the concept of reciprocal determinism recognizes the importance of the environment and specific situations, it is also believed that an individual's behavior can have an impact on the situation as well as feedback into personal variables. It follows that changes to more effective social behavior interculturally will lead to a more congenial social environment as well as a more socially efficacious person. Bandura's idea of a self-generated environment is consistent with Anderson's (1994) model of cross-cultural adaptation, which views the individual as an active agent in choosing how to respond in a foreign environment, and in so doing creating his or her own adjustment. For instance, when a previously quiet Asian student began to participate enthusiastically in discussion in a class, she actually helped to create a more interesting and lively classroom environment, and she also started to feel that she belonged to the group.

Recent conceptualisations of social learning and behavior changes by Bandura have continued to emphasize human agency and self-regulation (1989, 1992). The acquisition and maintenance of the social skills are facilitated by self-regulation, including self-reinforcement. Trainees can motivate themselves by setting their own standards of behaviors and responding to their own actions in self-rewarding or self-punishing ways.

Role-Based Training in Groups: An Integrated Instructional Model

Implications for developing sociocultural competence from the three models of learning reviewed so far can be integrated into an instructional model for role-based intercultural training in a group setting. A role-based approach to experiential learning in groups is action-oriented, while simultaneously providing a safe and supportive group setting. It focuses on having trainees model and repeatedly practice behaviors as an opportunity for skills acquisition and receiving feedback on the extent of skill mastery in the context of a group of individuals with similar needs (Johnson and Johnson, 1994).

Corey and Corey (1988) summarized three advantages of using role-plays in developing competencies in a group situation. The first advantage in applying role-based learning in developing sociocultural competencies is that it serves as a method of diagnosis, wherein the facilitator has ample opportunities to observe the trainee's performance and assess where competencies are already present and where additional skills acquisition is required. Second, role-play in group situations provides opportunities for observing a variety of ways to deal with problems or approach challenges. This facilitates the modeling of an approach to deal with intercultural situations, in a way that enables an individual trainee to feel most comfortable. Third, role-plays enable trainees to gain new insights that are important for cultural and self-understanding as well as into new interpersonal presentation styles.

There are several reasons why group-based sociocultural competence training is not only economical and efficient but also likely to be effective. Group development involves setting in place a safe and inclusive situation that helps members to relax, reducing social anxiety and defensiveness. The psychosocial needs of the trainees are best met when members have a sense of belonging or feel included and when the guidelines for participation are clearly outlined.

The group setting provides newcomers with opportunities for mutual validation. Individuals can affirm their cultural uniqueness and appreciate common struggles and frustrations resulting from their minority status and language and other cultural handicaps, while at the same time sharing a common desire for career and educational success in the host country.

A climate of trust can then form, and the willingness to undertake risk-taking, inherent in adopting different social behaviors, increases. With increased risk-taking, trainees will try out more roles and feel comfortable experimenting with new behaviors; the group will also tend to be supportive, and trust formation is further enhanced.

An additional advantage of group-based learning lies in the multiple opportunities for feedback from other group members. They can help one another by providing either role models or role enactments of significant others when needed. The group is also effective in reinforcing goal setting and contracting for action outside the individual sessions. Accountability to peers is often motivating for learners.

A useful byproduct to the preceding advantages comes about when group members begin practicing with others. Learning to speak up or presenting one's ideas or opinions to a group are key sociocultural competencies needed in most social or work-related situations.

Mak et al. (1994) have further argued that role-based learning in intercultural training groups represents an augmentational approach in acquiring cultural competencies rather than an assimilationist, replacement approach. The challenges facing newcomers can be conceived as novel social roles. Recent immigrants and sojourners are, therefore, encouraged to find out what those new roles entail and then to practice the new role behaviors required for successful encounters with host nationals, while choosing to retain customary social skills for interacting with co-ethnics. This way, the training is unlikely to threaten the newcomer's original cultural identity.

Experiential learning through practicing novel social roles has a behavioral focus in the sense that cognition and affect are of secondary importance in the early learning stages (Johnson and Johnson, 1994). However, once acquired, the new behavior contributes to a heightened perceived self-efficacy in sociocultural competence, which may enhance self-esteem generally. Integration of the newly learned skills facilitates changes in how individuals feel and think about themselves. The affective and cognitive aspects are not ignored, but focused on secondarily in terms of intervention. For instance, an individual can directly benefit from behavioral training on dating in the new culture.

Conditions for Effective Learning of Intercultural Social Skills

What then are the likely elements of effective sociocultural competence training for career and academic success? To begin with, trainers and funding sources should recognize that most culturally different newcomers are fairly overwhelmed in the first weeks of arrival by the unfamiliarity and novelty of the host physical and sociocultural environment. They may need to first orient themselves to the foreign surroundings, and many will take some extra time to grieve over the loss of a familiar lifestyle (Ishiyama, 1989), before they are ready to contemplate setting realistic goals for career and academic success and to figure out the culturally appropriate path to success. Psychosocial needs at this early stage of shock tend to be geared toward validation of the familiar cultural self. Some social awkwardness in relating to host nationals can be expected. It may, in some cases, turn into social avoidance.

Later, when the newcomers have set goals for success and realize that effectiveness in social encounters is an integral part of the path to success, they will be more interested in observing cultural differences in social interactions in dyads and groups and be intrigued by both the obvious and subtle differences. At this contemplative and preparatory stage, new immigrants and sojourners are likely to be ready for an introduction to sociocultural competence training presented as a course in intercultural social presentation and communication. For immigrant and sojourner workers, such a program can be offered as an educational course for job search and career advancement rather than one of remedial group counseling. For international students, the course can be described as pertaining to social and presentation skills for academic success. Expatriate workers who have already participated in predeparture intercultural communication training can benefit from follow-up sociocultural competence training after the initial period of settling in, when they have had a real taste of the novel culture and society.

For individuals to reap the maximum benefits from a sociocultural training program, it is most effective if the group is led jointly by a minority group member (as a credible role model for the enhancement of trainees' perceived self-efficacy) and a member of the dominant culture (for an authentic explanation of the host cultural code). Trainees will be encouraged to witness how someone with visibly different features and speaking with a foreign accent can successfully assume a leadership position and demonstrate effective intercultural social skills.

The social skills taught should be discrete in order to facilitate learning and mostly generic for wider applications to a range of social situations. Examples of relevant micro social skills are making a request, interrupting, giving a different opinion, and expressing a wish to be included in a group. Depending on the needs and circumstances of group members, context-specific social skills such as those required for job interviews and negotiating an extension to the due date of an academic assignment may also be taught.

It will be helpful to explain to trainees that social anxiety in intercultural interactions among newcomers is normal, and a goal of the program is to replace the anxiety with efficacy beliefs reinforced by mastery of basic social skills, including those useful for accessing the new culture (e.g., introducing oneself, asking questions, starting a conversation in the lunch room, and inviting host nationals to coffee).

There should be opportunities for observing live and videotaped role-plays of social situations, followed by coaching of appropriate social responses, which are refined through repeated practice and corrective feedback. Trainees are encouraged to discuss variations in appropriate social responses and to adopt a presentation style that they feel most comfortable identifying (e.g., appearing energetic and engaging in frequent use of gestures, or relatively reserved and formal). This approach increases participants' chances of visualising themselves as being socially effective despite their individual differences in levels of extroversion, anxiety, and openness.

The training program should be delivered in several sessions to allow for practice in real-life social situations and completion of relevant prescribed activities between sessions. This process provides repeated opportunities for corrective feedback and consolidation of learning. Trainees are requested to identify the relevance of the course to their individual goals for career and educational success in the first session. Then, toward the end of each session, trainees are encouraged to set their individual short-term goals for practicing in real life the strategic social skills learned in the session, and to visualize how the attainment of these specific short-term goals will contribute to their broader and longer-term goals for career and/or educational success. The goal-setting should encourage self-regulation processes, as participants motivate themselves by setting their own standards and responding to their own actions using self-reinforcement.

CONCLUSIONS

To undertake training for the development of sociocultural competence does not guarantee career or educational success. Nor does it replace the actual hard work necessary for attaining such success. Nevertheless, being socially effective in a new country will significantly enhance interpersonal communication, inclusion in networks, social presentation of self, and the individual's well-being. Teachers and prospective employers often favor these personal qualities. After the initial period of settling in, culturally different immigrants and sojourners often come to the realisation that unfamiliarity with the host culture and society is a major obstacle to their goals for success.

However, various psychosocial barriers may undermine the motivation of acquiring and practicing sociocultural competencies, hence reducing the effectiveness and efficiency of any intercultural training effort. These barriers include lack of coaching, practice, and correction opportunities, a sense of being overwhelmed by the number of adjustments required in the initial period, heightened needs for validation, cross-cultural social anxiety, threat to the individual's original cultural identity, and various personal factors. Combining the instructional implications from models of conditioning and social cognitive learning in a role-based group training program can provide insight into how these potential barriers may be addressed, and provide optimal conditions for the acquisition and extension of social competencies instrumental to success in the new culture (Furnham and Bochner, 1982).

References

Amir, Y. (1969). Contact hypothesis in ethnic relations. *Psychological Bulletin, 71*, 319–342.

Amir, Y. (1976). The role of intergroup contact in change of prejudice and ethnic relations. In P. A. Katz (Ed.), *Towards the elimination of racism* (pp. 245–308). New York: Pergamon.

Anderson, L. E. (1994). A new look at an old construct: Cross-cultural adaptation. *International Journal of Intercultural Relations, 18*, 293–328.

Bandura, A. (1977a). *Social learning theory*. Englewood Cliffs, NJ: Prentice-Hall.

Bandura, A. (1977b). Self-efficacy: Toward a unifying theory of behavioral change. *Psychological Review, 84*, 191–215.

Bandura, A. (1986). *Social foundations of thought and action: A social cognitive theory*. Englewood Cliffs, NJ: Prentice-Hall.

Bandura, A. (1989). Human agency in social cognitive theory. *American Psychologist, 44*, 1175–1184.

Bandura, A. (1992). Social cognitive theory. In R. Vasta (Ed.), *Six theories of child development: Revised formulations and current issues* (pp. 1–60). London: Jessica Kingsley.

Barker, M. (1993). *Perceptions of social rules in intercultural and intracultural encounters: A study of Australian and ethnic Chinese university students*. Unpublished doctoral thesis. Department of Psychology, University of Queensland, Australia.

Berry, J. M., & West, R. L. (1993). Cognitive self-efficacy in relation to personal mastery and goal setting across the life span. *International Journal of Behavioral Development, 16*, 351–379.

Bochner, S. (1986). Training intercultural skills. In C. R. Hollin & P. Trower (Eds), *Handbook of social skills training: Volume 4. Applications across the life span* (pp. 155–184). New York: Pergamon.

Bochner, S. (1994). Culture shock. In W. J. Lonner & R. S. Malpass (Eds), *Psychology and culture* (pp. 245–251). Boston: Allyn and Bacon.

Bond, M. H. (1992). The process of enhancing cross-cultural competence in Hong Kong organisations. *International Journal of Intercultural Relations, 16*, 395–412.

Brislin, R. W. (1994). Preparing to live and work elsewhere. In W. J. Lonner & R. S. Malpass (Eds), *Psychology and culture* (pp. 239–244). Boston: Allyn and Bacon.

Brislin, R. W., Landis, D., & Brandt, M. E. (1983). Conceptualisations of intercultural behaviour and training. In D. Landis and R. W. Brislin (Eds), *Handbook of intercultural training, Volume 1* (pp. 1–35). New York: Pergamon.

Corey, M., & Corey, G. (1988). *Groups: Process and practice*. (3rd ed.). Pacific Grove, CA: Brooks Cole.

Furnham, A., & Bochner, S. (1982). Social difficulty in a foreign culture: An empirical analysis of culture shock. In S. Bochner (Ed.), *Cultures in contact: Studies in cross cultural interaction* (pp. 161–198). New York: Pergamon.

Gudykunst, W. B., & Hammer, M. R. G. (1983). Basic training design: Approaches to intercultural training. In D. Landis & R. W. Brislin (Eds), *Handbook of intercultural training, Volume 1* (pp. 118–154). New York: Pergamon.

Gudykunst, W. B., & Hammer, M. R. G. (1988). Strangers and hosts: An uncertainty reduction based theory of intercultural adaptation. In Y. Y. Kim & W. B. Gudykunst (Eds), *Cross-cultural adaptation: Current approaches* (pp. 105–139). Newbury Park, CA: Sage.

Hammer, M. R., Gudykunst, W. B., & Wiseman, R. L. (1978). Dimensions of intercultural effectiveness: An exploratory study. *International Journal of Intercultural Relations, 2*, 382–393.

Hofstede, G. (1980). *Cultures consequences: International differences in work-related values*. Beverly Hills, CA: Sage.

Ishiyama, F. I. (1989). Understanding individuals in transition: A self-validation model. *Canadian Journal of School Psychology, 4*, 41–56.

Ishiyama, F. I. (1995). Culturally dislocated clients: Self-validation and cultural conflict issues and counselling implications. *Canadian Journal of Counselling, 29*, 262–275.

Johnson, D., & Johnson, F. (1994). *Joining together: Group theory and group skills* (5th ed.). Englewood Cliffs, NJ: Prentice Hall.

Kealey, D. J., & Ruben, B. D. (1983). Cross-cultural personnel selection criteria, issues, and methods. In

D. Landis and R. W. Brislin (Eds), *Handbook of intercultural training, Volume 1* (pp. 155–175). New York: Pergamon.

Mak, A. S. (1991). From elites to strangers: Employment coping styles of new Hong Kong immigrants. *Journal of Employment Counseling, 28,* 144–156.

Mak, A. S. (1996). *Careers in cross-cultural transitions: Experiences of skilled Hong Kong immigrants.* Canberra, Australia: Department of Immigration and Multicultural Affairs.

Mak, A. S., Westwood, M. J., & Ishiyama, F. I. (1994). Developing role-based social competencies for career search and development in Hong Kong immigrants. *Journal of Career Development, 20,* 171–183.

Masters, J. C., Burish, T. G., Hollon, S. D., & Rimm, D. C. (1987). *Behavior therapy: Techniques and empirical findings* (3rd ed.). San Diego: Harcourt Brace Jovanovich.

McInnis, C., & James, R. (1995). *First year on campus.* Canberra: Australian Government Publishing Service.

Mezirow, J. (1991). *Transformative dimensions of adult learning.* San Francisco: Jossey-Bass.

Pavlov, I. P. (1927). *Conditioned reflexes* (G. V. Anrep, trans.). London: Oxford University Press.

Pedersen, P. (1991). Counseling international students. *The Counseling Psychologist, 19,* 10–58.

Skinner, B. F. (1953). *Science and human behavior.* New York: Free Press.

Skinner, B. F. (1972). *Beyond freedom and dignity.* New York: Bantam.

Smith, P. B., & Bond, M. H. (1993). *Social psychology across cultures: Analysis and perspectives.* New York: Harvester Wheatsheaf.

Spitzberg, B. H., & Cupach, W. R. (1984). *Communication competence.* Beverly Hills, CA: Sage.

Stening, B. W. (1979). Problems in cross-cultural contact: A literature review. *International Journal of Intercultural Relations, 3,* 269–313.

Sue, D. W., & Sue, D. (1990). *Counseling the culturally different: Theory and practice* (2nd ed.). New York: Wiley.

Taylor, E. W. (1994). learning model for becoming interculturally competent. *International Journal of Intercultural Relations, 18,* 389–408.

Triandis, H. C., & Vassiliou, V. (1967). Frequency of contact and stereotyping. *Journal of Personality and Social Psychology, 7,* 316–329.

Westwood, M. J., & Ishiyama, F. I. (1991). Challenges in counseling immigrant clients: Understanding intercultural barriers to career adjustment. *Journal of Employment Counseling, 28,* 130–143.

Wolpe, J. (1958). *Psychotherapy by reciprocal inhibition.* Stanford, CA: Stanford University Press.

Wolpe, J. (1973). *The practice of behavior therapy* (2nd ed.). Oxford: Pergamon.

Concepts and Questions

1. Mak et al. assert that "newcomers may operate from a culturally conditioned basis, where behaviors performed would be effective in their original country, but ineffective in the new context." In an intercultural situation, what clues might be present in the social context that would let you know that this was occurring?

2. The internationalization of world skilled labor presents new challenges because people are likely to move from one cultural location to another. What must these people do in terms of being socially effective in their new country?

3. Do you believe that clear goals for developing sociocultural competence are as important as your goals for continued career and educational success? Why?

4. Describe some of the psychological barriers to developing sociocultural competence discussed by Mak et al.

5. How would you tend to deal with interpersonal anxiety if it was a problem in a new cultural setting?

6. What threats might there be to the development of sociocultural competence?

7. How does operant conditioning affect the development of sociocultural competence?

8. What is social cognitive learning? How does it apply to the development of sociocultural competence?

9. Why do Mak et al. believe that role-based traning is the key to developing sociocultural competence? Do you agree? Why?

10. Describe some of the conditions Mak et al. believe are necessary for the effective learning of intercultural social skills.

Managing Intercultural Conflicts Effectively

STELLA TING-TOOMEY

onflict is inevitable in all social and personal relationships. The Latin root words for conflict, "com" and "fligere," mean "together" and "to strike" or more simply, "to strike together." Conflict connotes a state of dissonance or collision between two forces or systems. This state of dissonance can be expressed either overtly or subtly. In the context of intercultural encounters, *conflict* is defined in this article as the perceived and/or actual incompatibility of values, expectations, processes, or outcomes between two or more parties from different cultures over substantive and/or relational issues. Such differences often are expressed through different cultural conflict styles. Intercultural conflict typically starts off with miscommunication. Intercultural miscommunication often leads to misinterpretations and pseudoconflict. If the miscommunication goes unmanaged or unclarified, however, it can become actual interpersonal conflict.

This article is developed in three sections: (1) A cultural variability perspective that emphasizes identity construal variations, low-context versus high-context, and monochronic and polychronic time patterns is presented; (2) assumptions and factors leading to conflict induced by violations of expectations are explained; and (3) effective conflict-management skills in managing intercultural conflicts are discussed.

A CULTURAL VARIABILITY PERSPECTIVE

To understand differences and similarities in communication across cultures, it is necessary to have a framework to explain why and how cultures are different or similar. A cultural variability perspective refers to how cultures vary on a continuum of variations in accordance with some basic dimensions or core value characteristics. While there are many dimensions in which cultures differ, one that has received consistent attention from both cross-cultural communication researchers and psychologists around the world is individualism–collectivism. Countless cross-cultural studies (Chinese Culture Connection, 1987; Gudykunst & Ting-Toomey, 1988; Hofstede, 1980, 1991; Hui & Triandis, 1986; Schwartz & Bilsky, 1990; Triandis, Brislin, & Hui, 1988; Wheeler, Reis, & Bond, 1989) have provided theoretical and empirical evidence that the value orientations of individualism and collectivism are pervasive in a wide range of cultures. Ting-Toomey and associates (Ting-Toomey, 1988, 1991; Ting-Toomey et al., 1991; Trubisky, Ting-Toomey, & Lin, 1991) related individualism–collectivism to conflict styles, providing clear research evidence that the role of cultural variability is critical in influencing the cross-cultural conflict negotiation process.

The cultural socialization process influences individuals' basic assumptions and expectations, as well as their process and outcome orientations in different types of conflict situations. The dimension of individualism–collectivism, as existing on a continuum of value tendency differences, can be used as a beginning point to understand some of the basic differences and similarities in individualistic-based or group-based cultures. Culture is defined as a system of knowledge, meanings, and symbolic actions that is shared by the majority of the people in a society.

Individualism–Collectivism Value Tendencies

Basically, *individualism* refers to the broad value tendencies of a culture to emphasize the importance of individual identity over group identity, individual rights over group rights, and individual needs over group needs. In contrast, *collectivism* refers to the broad value tendencies of a culture to emphasize the importance of the "we" identity over the "I" identity, group obligations over individual rights, and in-group–oriented needs over individual wants and desires. An *in-group* is a group whose values, norms, and rules are deemed as salient to the effective functioning of the group in the society, and these norms serve as the guiding criteria for everyday behaviors. On the other hand, an *out-group* is a group whose values, norms, and rules are viewed as inconsistent with those of the in-group, and these norms are assigned a low priority from the in-group standard. Macrolevel factors such as ecology, affluence, social and geographic mobility, migration, cultural background of parents, socialization, rural or urban environment, mass media exposure, education, and social change have been identified by Triandis (1988, 1990) as some of the underlying factors that contribute to the development of individualist and collectivistic values. High individualistic values have been found in the United States, Australia, Great Britain, Canada, the Netherlands, and New Zealand. High collectivistic values have been uncovered in Indonesia, Colombia, Venezuela, Panama, Ecuador, and Guatemala (Hofstede, 1991).

In intercultural communication research (Gudykunst & Ting-Toomey, 1988), Australia, Canada, and the United States have been identified consistently as cultures high in individualistic value tendencies, while strong empirical evidence has supported that China, Taiwan, Korea, Japan, and Mexico can be identified clearly as collectivistic, group-based cultures. Within each culture, different ethnic communities can also display distinctive individualistic and collectivistic value tendencies. For example, members of first-generation, Asian immigrant cultures in the United States may retain some basic group-oriented value characteristics.

The core building block of individualism–collectivism is its relative emphasis on the importance of the "autonomous self" or the "connected self" orientation. In using the terms "independent construal of self" and "interdependent construal of self" to represent individualist versus group-oriented identity, Markus and Kitayama (1991) argue that the placement of our sense of self-concept in our culture has a profound influence on our communication with others. They argue that the sense of individuality that accompanies this "independent construal of self" includes a sense of

oneself as an agent, as a producer of one's actions. One is conscious of being in control over the surrounding situation, and of the need to express one's own thoughts, feelings, and actions of others. Such acts of standing out are often intrinsically rewarding because they elicit pleasant, ego-focused emotions (e.g., pride) and also reduce unpleasant ones (e.g., frustration). Furthermore, the acts of standing out, themselves, form an important basis of self-esteem. (p. 246)

Conversely, the self-concept that accompanies an "interdependent construal of self" includes an

attentiveness and responsiveness to others that one either explicitly or implicitly assumes will be reciprocated by these others, as well as the willful management of one's other-focused feelings and desires so as to maintain and further the reciprocal interpersonal relationship. One is conscious of where one belongs with respect to others and assumes a receptive stance toward these others, continually adjusting and accommodating to these others in many aspects of behavior. Such acts of fitting in and accommodating are often intrinsically rewarding, because they give rise to pleasant, other-focused emotions (e.g., feeling of connection), while diminishing unpleasant ones (e.g., shame) and, furthermore, because the self-restraint required in doing so forms an important basis of self-esteem. (p. 246)

Thus, the cultural variability of independent versus interdependent construal of self frames our existential experience and serves as an anchoring point in terms of how we view our communicative actions and ourselves. For example, if we follow an independent construal of self-orientation, our communicative action will tend to be more self-focused, more ego-based, and more self-expressive. Concurrently, the value we place on particular self-conception also influences the criteria we use to perceive and evaluate others' communicative actions. To illustrate, if we follow an interdependent construal of self-orientation, we will tend to use group norms, group interests, and group responsibilities to interpret and evaluate others' conflict behaviors. Overall, the cultural variability dimension of individualism–collectivism and the independent and interdependent construal of self help us to "make sense" or explain why people in some cultures prefer certain approaches or modes of conflict negotiation than people in other cultures.

Low Context and High Context

In addition to individualism–collectivism, Edward T. Hall's (1976, 1983) low-context and high-context communication framework helps enrich our understanding of the role of communication in individualistic and collectivistic cultures. According to Hall (1976), human transaction can be basically divided into low-context and high-context communication systems:

> HC [High Context] transactions featured preprogrammed information that is in the receiver and in the setting, with only minimal information in the transmitted message. LC [Low Context] transactions are the reverse. Most of the information must be in the transmitted message in order to make up what is missing in the context. (p. 101)

Although no one culture exists exclusively at one extreme of the communication context continuum, in general, low-context communication refers to communication patterns of linear logic interaction approach, direct verbal interaction style, overt intention expressions, and sender-oriented value (Ting-Toomey, 1985). High-context communication refers to communication patterns of spiral logic interaction approach, indirect verbal negotiation mode, subtle nonverbal nuances, responsive intention inference, and interpreter-sensitive value (Ting-Toomey, 1985). Low-context (LC) communication patterns have been typically found in individualistic cultures and high-context (HC) communication patterns have been typically uncovered in collectivistic cultures.

For individualistic, LC communicators, the bargaining resources in conflict typically revolve around individual pride and self-esteem, individual ego-based emotions, and individual sense of autonomy and power. For collectivistic, HC interactants, the negotiation resources in conflict typically revolve around relational "face" maintenance and group harmony, group-oriented status and self-esteem, face-related emotions, and a reciprocal sense of favors and obligations. For individualistic, LC negotiators, conflict typically arises because of incompatible personalities, beliefs, or goal orientations. For collectivistic, HC negotiators, conflict typically arises because of incompatible facework or relational management.

The concept of face is tied closely to the need people have to a claimed sense of self-respect in any social interactive situations (Ting-Toomey, 1985, 1988, 1994; Ting-Toomey & Cole, 1990). As human beings, we all like to be respected and feel approved in our everyday communicative behaviors. However, how we manage face and how we negotiate "face loss" and "face gain" in a conflict episode differs from one culture to the next. As Cohen (1991) observes:

> Given the importance of face, the members of collectivistic cultures are highly sensitive to the effect of what they say on others. Language is a social instrument—a device for preserving and promoting social interests as much as a means for transmitting information. [Collectivistic], high-context speakers must weigh their words carefully. They know that whatever they say will be scrutinized and taken to heart. Face-to-face conversations contain many emollient expressions of respect and courtesy alongside a substantive element rich in meaning and low in redundancy. Directness and especially contradiction are much disliked. It is hard for speakers in this kind of culture to deliver a blunt "no." (p. 26)

M-Time and P-Time

Finally, the concept of time in the conflict-negotiation process also varies in accordance with the individualism–collectivism dimension. Time is reflective of the psychological and the emotional environment in which communication occurs. Time flies when two friends are enjoying themselves and having a good time. Time crawls when two enemies stare at each other and have nothing more to say to one another. Time influences the tempos and pacings of the developmental sequences of a conflict-negotiation session. It also influences the substantive ideas that are being presented in a conflict-bargaining episode.

Hall (1983) distinguished two patterns of time that govern the individualistic and collectivistic cultures: Monochronic Time Schedule (M-time) and Polychronic Time Schedule (P-time). According to Hall (1983):

> P-time stresses involvement of people and completion of transactions rather than adherence to preset sched-

ules. Appointments are not taken as seriously and, as a consequence, are frequently broken. P-time is treated as less tangible than M-time. For polychronic people, time is seldom experienced as "wasted," and is apt to be considered a point rather than a ribbon or a road, but that point is often sacred. (p. 46)

For Hall (1983), Latin American, Middle Eastern, African, Asian, French, and Greek cultures are representatives of P-time patterns, while Northern European, North American, and German cultures are representatives of M-time patterns. M-time patterns appear to predominate in individualistic, low-context cultures, and P-time patterns appear to predominate in group-based, high-context cultures. People who follow individualistic, M-time patterns usually compartmentalize time schedules to serve individualistic-based needs, and they tend to separate task-oriented time from socioemotional time. In addition, they are more future-conscious of time than centered in the present or the past. People who follow collectivistic, P-time patterns tend to hold more fluid attitudes toward time schedules, and they tend to integrate task-oriented activity with socioemotional activity. In addition, they are more past and present-conscious than future-oriented.

Members of individualistic, M-time cultures tend to view time as something that can be possessed, drained, and wasted, while members of collectivistic, P-time cultures tend to view time as more contextually based and relationally oriented. For individualistic, M-time people, conflict should be contained, controlled, and managed effectively within certain frames or within certain preset schedules. For collectivistic, P-time people, the clock time in resolving conflict is not as important as in taking the time to really know the conflict parties who are involved in the dispute. For P-time individuals, the time spent in synchronizing the implicit interactional rhythms between people is much more important than any preset, objective timetable.

In sum, in individualistic cultures, people typically practice "I" identity-based values, low-context direct interaction, and M-time negotiation schedules. In collectivistic cultures, people typically treasure "we" identity-based values, high-context indirect interaction, and P-time negotiation rhythms.

VIOLATIONS OF CONFLICT EXPECTATIONS

Drawing from the key ideas of the cultural variability perspective, we can now apply these concepts to understanding the specific conflict assumptions, conflict issues and process factors, and the conflict interaction styles that contribute to intercultural miscommunication or intercultural conflict.[1] When individuals from two contrastive cultures meet one another especially for the first time, they typically communicate out of their culturally based assumptions and beliefs, stereotypical images of each other, and habitual communication patterns. These assumptions create expectations for others' conflict behavior.

It is inevitable that we hold anticipations or expectations of how others should or should not behave in any communicative situation. These expectations, however, are grounded in the social norms of the culture and also depend on the symbolic meanings individuals assign to behaviors (Burgoon, 1991). Intercultural miscommunication or intercultural conflict often occurs because of violations of normative expectations in a communication episode. Expectation violations occur frequently, especially if one party comes from an individualistic-based culture and the other party comes from a collectivistic-based culture.

Cultural Conflict Assumptions

Different cultural value assumptions exist as the metaconflict issues in framing any intercultural conflict episode. Based on the individualism–collectivism dimension, we can delineate several cultural assumptions concerning LC and HC communicators' basic attitudes toward conflict. For individualistic, LC communicators, conflict typically follows a "problem-solving" model: (1) Conflict is viewed as an expressed struggle to air out major differences and problems; (2) conflict can be both dysfunctional and functional; (3) conflict can be dysfunctional when it is repressed and not directly confronted; (4) conflict can be functional when it provides an open opportunity for solving problematic issues; (5) substantive and relational issues in conflict should be handled separately; (6) conflict should be dealt with openly and directly;

and (7) effective management of conflict can be viewed as a win–win problem-solving game.

For the collectivistic, HC interactants, their underlying assumptions of conflict follow a "face maintenance" model: (1) Conflict is viewed as damaging to social face and relational harmony and should be avoided as much as possible; (2) conflict is, for the most part, dysfunctional; (3) conflict signals a lack of self-discipline and self-censorship of emotional outbursts, and hence, a sign of emotional immaturity; (4) conflict provides a testing ground for a skillful facework negotiation process; (5) substantive conflict and relational face issues are always intertwined; (6) conflict should be dealt with discreetly and subtly; and (7) effective management of conflict can be viewed as a win–win face negotiation game.

From the conflict as a "problem-solving" model, conflict is viewed as potentially functional, personally liberating, and an open forum for "struggling against" or "struggling with" one another in wrestling with the conflict issues at hand. From the conflict as a "face maintenance" model, conflict is viewed as primarily dysfunctional, interpersonally embarrassing and distressing, and a forum for potential group-related face loss and face humiliation. These fundamental cultural conflict assumptions influence the mindsets and attitudinal level of the conflict parties in terms of how they should approach an interpersonal conflict episode. Appropriate and inappropriate conflict behaviors, in short, are grounded in the basic value assumptions of the cultural conflict socialization process.

Conflict Issues and Process Violations

Every conflict entails both substantive and relational issues. Individualistic conflict negotiators typically attend to the objective, substantive issues more than the relational, socioemotional issues. Collectivistic conflict negotiators, in contrast, typically attune to the relational, affective dimension as the key issue in resolving task-related or procedural-related conflict. When collectivistic communicators are in sync with one another and their nonverbal rhythms harmonize with one another, peaceful resolutions can potentially follow. When individualistic communicators are able to rationalize the separation of the people from the problems, and emphasize compartmentalizing affective issues and substantive issues, conflict can be functional.

In reviewing diplomatic negotiation case studies between individualistic, low-context (United States) and collectivistic, high-context (China, Egypt, India, Japan, and Mexico) cultures, Cohen (1991) concludes:

> Individualistic, low-context negotiators can be described as primarily problem oriented and have the definition of the problem and the clarification of alternative solutions uppermost in their thoughts, [collectivistic] high-context negotiators are seen to be predominantly relationship oriented. For them, negotiation is less about solving problems (although, obviously, this aspect cannot be dismissed) than about attending a relationship. For interdependent cultures it is not a conflict that is resolved but a relationship that is mended. . . . In international relations the consequence is concern both with the international relationship and with the personal ties between the interlocutors. (p. 51)

In individualistic, LC cultures such as Australia and the United States, control of one's autonomy, freedom, territory, and individual boundary is of paramount importance to one's sense of self-respect and ego. In collectivistic, HC cultures such as Japan and Korea, being accepted by one's in-group members and being approved by one's superiors, peers, and/or family members is critical to the development of one's sense of self-respect. Thus, conflict issues in individualistic cultures typically arise through the violation of autonomous space, privacy, individual power, and sense of individual fairness and equity. In collectivistic cultures, conflict issues typically revolve around the violation of in-group or out-group boundaries, norms of group loyalty and commitment, and reciprocal obligations and trust.

In terms of different goal orientations in intercultural conflict, individualists' conflict-management techniques typically emphasize a win–win goal orientation and the importance of a tangible outcome action plan. For collectivists, typically time and energy are invested in negotiating face loss, face gain, and face protection issues throughout the various developmental phases of conflict. While individualists tend to be highly goal or result-oriented in conflict management, collectivists tend to emphasize heavily the relational or facework process of conflict resolution. This collectivistic conflict facework negotiation process can also take place beyond the immediate conflict situation.

Several writers (Cohen, 1991; Leung, 1987, 1988; Ting-Toomey, 1985) indicate that collectivists tend to display a stronger preference for informal third-party conflict mediation procedure than individualists. For example, for the Chinese culture, conflict typically is diffused through the use of third-party intermediaries. However, there exists a key difference in the use of third-party mediation between the individualistic, Western cultures and the collectivistic, Asian cultures. In the Western cultures, conflict parties tend to seek help with an impartial third-party mediator (such as a professional mediator or family therapist). In many Asian cultures, conflict parties typically seek the help of an older (and hence assumed to be wiser) person who is related to both parties. It is presumed that the informal mediator has a richer database to arbitrate the conflict outcome. Expectations may be violated when an individualistic culture sends an impartial third party to arbitrate an international conflict with no prior relationship-building sessions. Conflict-process violations also arise if an individualistic culture sends an intermediary who is perceived to be of lower ranking or lower status than the representative negotiators of the collectivistic culture. Conversely, a collectivistic culture tends to violate the individualistic fairness norm when it sends an "insider" or in-group person to monitor or arbitrate the conflict outcome situation.

The concept of power in a conflict-negotiation situation also varies from an individualistic culture to a collectivistic culture. Power, in the context of individualistic culture, often means tangible resources of rewards and punishments that one conflict party has over another. Power, in the context of collectivistic culture, often refers to intangible resources such as face loss and face gain, losing prestige or gaining reputation, and petty-mindedness versus benevolent generosity as displayed in the conflict anxiety-provoking situation.

Finally, the interpretation of conflict-resolution rhythm also varies along the individualism–collectivism dimension. For individualistic, M-time people, conflict-resolution processes should follow a clear agenda of opening, expressing conflicting interests, negotiating, and closing sequences. For collectivistic, P-time people, conflict facework processes have no clear beginning and no clear end. For M-time individuals, conflict-resolution time should be filled with decision-making activities. For P-time individuals, time is a "being" construct that is governed by the implicit rhythms in the interaction between people. While M-time negotiators tend to emphasize agenda setting, objective criteria, and immediate, future-oriented goals in the conflict-negotiation process, P-time negotiators typically like to take time to engage in small talk, to delve into family or personal affairs, and also to bring in the historical past to shed light on the present conflict situation. As Cohen (1991) observes:

> [North] Americans, then, are mostly concerned with addressing immediate issues and moving on to new challenges, and they display little interest in (and sometimes little knowledge of) history. The idea that something that occurred hundreds of years ago might be relevant to a pressing problem is almost incomprehensible. . . . In marked contrast, the representatives of non-Western societies possess a pervasive sense of the past. . . . This preoccupation with history, deeply rooted in the consciousness of traditional societies, cannot fail to influence diplomacy. Past humiliations for these societies (which are highly sensitive to any slight on their reputations) are not consigned to the archives but continue to nourish present concerns. (p. 29)

The arbitrary division of clock time or calendar time holds little meaning for collectivistic, P-time people. For them, a deadline, in one sense, is only an arbitrary human construct. For P-time individuals, a deadline is always subject to revision and renegotiation. Graceful handling of time pressure is viewed as much more important than a sense of forceful urgency. In sum, people move with different conflict rhythms in conflict-negotiation sessions. For M-time individuals, a sense of timeline and closure-orientation predominate their mode of conflict resolution. For P-time individuals, a sense of the relational commitment and synchronized relational rhythm signal the beginning stage of a long-term, conflict-bargaining process.

Expectation violations often occur when a person from an individualistic culture engages a person from a collectivistic culture in an interpersonal conflict situation. Different cultural conflict assumptions lead to different attitudes toward how to approach a basic conflict episode. Miscommunication often gives rise to escalatory conflict spirals or prolonged misunderstandings. While common feelings of anxiety, frustration, ambivalence, and a sense of emotional vulnerability typically exist in individuals in any conflict situation, how we go about handling this sense of emotional vulnerability varies from one culture to the next. Individualists and collectivists typically collide over their substantive orientation versus relational face maintenance orientation; goal orientation versus process orientation; formal versus informal third-party consultation process; tangible versus intangible power resources; and different time rhythms that undergird the conflict episode. In addition, the verbal and nonverbal messages they engage in, and the distinctive conflict styles they carry with them, can severely influence the overall outcome of the conflict dissonance process.

Cross-Cultural Conflict Interaction Styles

In a conflict situation, individualists typically rely heavily on direct requests, direct verbal justifications, and upfront clarifications to defend one's action or decision. In contrast, collectivists typically use qualifiers ("Perhaps we should meet this deadline together"), tag questions ("Don't you think we might not have enough time?"), disclaimers ("I'm probably wrong but . . ."), tangential responses ("Let's not worry about that now"), and indirect requests ("If it won't be too much trouble, let's try to finish this report together") to make a point in the subtle, conflict face-threatening situation. From the collectivistic orientation, it is up to the interpreter of the message to pick up the hidden meaning or intention of the message and to respond either indirectly or equivocally. In addition, in an intense conflict situation, many collectivists believe that verbal messages can often compound the problem. However, by not using verbal means to explain or clarify a decision, collectivists are often viewed as "inscrutable."

Silence is viewed as demanding immense self-discipline in a collectivistic conflict situation. On the other hand, silence can be viewed as an admission of guilt or incompetence in an individualistic culture. In addition, while open emotional expression during a stressful conflict situation often is viewed as a signal of caring in an individualistic culture, proper emotional composure and emotional self-restraint are viewed as signals of a mature, self-disciplined person in most collectivistic, Asian cultures. In comparing verbal and nonverbal exchange processes in Japan and the United States, Okabe (1983) summarizes:

> The digital is more characteristic of the [North] American mode of communication. . . . The Japanese language is more inclined toward the analogical; its use of ideographic characters . . . and its emphasis on the nonverbal aspect. The excessive dependence of the Japanese on the nonverbal aspect of communication means that Japanese culture tends to view the verbal as only a means of communication, and that the nonverbal and the extra-verbal at times assume greater importance than the verbal dimension of communication. This is in sharp contrast to the view of Western rhetoric and communication that the verbal, especially speech, is the dominant means of expression. (p. 38)

In short, in the individualistic cultures, the conflict-management process relies heavily on verbal offense and defense to justify one's position, to clarify one's opinion, to build up one's credibility, to articulate one's emotions, and to raise objections if one disagrees with someone else's proposal. In collectivistic conflict situations, ambiguous, indirect verbal messages often are used with the intention of saving mutual face, saving group face, or protecting someone else's face. In addition, subtle nonverbal gestures or nonverbal silence are often used to signal a sense of cautionary restraint toward the conflict situation. The use of deep-level silence can also reflect a sense of resignation and acceptance of the fatalistic aspect of the conflict situation. The higher the person is in positional power in a collectivistic culture, the more likely she or he will use silence as a deliberate, cautionary conflict strategy.

In terms of the relationship between the norm of fairness and cross-cultural conflict interaction style, results from past research (Leung & Bond, 1984; Leung & Iwawaki, 1988) indicate that individualists typically prefer to use the equity norm (self-deservingness norm) in dealing with reward allocation in group conflict interaction. In comparison, collectivists often prefer to use the equality norm (the equal distribution norm) to deal with in-group members and thus avoid group disharmony. However, like their individualistic cohorts, collectivists prefer the application of the equity norm (the self-deservingness norm) when competing with members of outgroups, especially when the conflict involves competition for scarce resources in the system.

Findings in many past conflict studies also indicate that individuals do exhibit quite consistent cross-situational styles of conflict negotiation in different cultures. While dispositional, relationship, or conflict salient factors also play a critical part in conflict-management patterns, culture assumes the primary role of conflict-style socialization process. Based on the theoretical assumptions of the "I" identity and the "we" identity, and the concern of self-face maintenance versus mutual-face maintenance in the two contrastive cultural systems, findings across cultures (China, Japan, Korea, Taiwan, Mexico, and the United States) clearly indicate that individualists tend to use competitive control conflict styles in managing conflict, while collectivists tend to use integrative or compromising conflict styles in dealing with conflict. In addition, collectivists also tend to use more obliging and avoiding conflict styles in task-oriented conflict situations (Chua & Gudykunst, 1987; Leung, 1988; Ting-Toomey et al., 1991; Trubisky, Ting-Toomey, & Lin, 1991).

Different results have also been uncovered concerning in-group and out-group conflict in the collectivistic cultures. For example, Cole's (1989) study reveals that Japanese students in the United States tend to use obliging strategies more with members of in-groups than with members of out-groups. They also tend to actually use more competitive strategies with out-group members than in-group members. In addition, the status of the in-group person plays a critical role in the collectivistic conflict process.

Previous research (Ting-Toomey et al., 1991) suggests that status affects the conflict-management styles people use with members of their in-group. For example, in a collectivistic culture, while a high-status person can challenge the position or opinion of a low-status person, it is a norm violation for a

low-status person to directly rebut or question the position or the opinion of the high-status person, especially in the public arena. Again, the issue of face maintenance becomes critical in high- versus low-status conflict interaction. The low-status person should always learn to "give face" or protect the face of the high-status person in times of stressful situations or crises. In return, the high-status person will enact a reciprocal face-protection system that automatically takes care of the low-status person in different circumstances.

Overall, the preferences for a direct conflict style, for the use of the equity norm, and for the direct settlement of disputes reflect the salience of the "I" identity in individualistic, HC cultures; while preferences for an indirect conflict style, for the use of the equality norm, and for the use of informal mediation procedures reflect the salience of the "we" identity in the collectivistic, HC cultures. In individualistic, LC cultures, a certain degree of conflict in a system is viewed as potentially functional and productive. In collectivistic, HC cultures in which group harmony and consultative decision making are prized, overt expressions of interpersonal conflict are highly avoided and suppressed. Instead, nonverbal responsiveness, indirect verbal strategies, the use of informal intermediaries, and the use of cautionary silence are some of the typical collectivistic ways of dealing with interpersonal conflict.

EFFECTIVE CONFLICT MANAGEMENT

Effective conflict management requires us to communicate effectively, appropriately, and creatively in different conflict interactive situations. Effective conflict management requires us to be knowledgeable and respectful of different worldviews and ways of dealing with a conflict situation. It requires us to be sensitive to the differences and similarities between low-context and high-context communication patterns and to attune to the implicit negotiation rhythms of monochronic-based and polychronic-based individuals.

Effective conflict management also requires the awareness of the importance of both goal-oriented and process-oriented conflict-negotiation pathways, and requires that we pay attention to the close relationship between cultural variability and different conflict communication styles. For both individualists and collectivists, the concept of "mindfulness" can serve as the first effective step in raising our awareness of the differences and similarities in cross-cultural conflict-negotiation processes. Langer's (1989) concept of mindfulness helps individuals to tune in conscientiously to their habituated mental scripts and expectations. According to Langer, if mindlessness is the "rigid reliance on old categories, mindfulness means the continual creation of new ones. Categorization and recategorization, labeling and relabeling as one masters the world are processes natural to children" (p. 63). To engage in a mindfulness state, an individual needs to learn to (a) create new categories, (b) be open to new information, and (c) be aware that multiple perspectives typically exist in viewing a basic event (Langer, 1989, p. 62).

Creating new categories means that one should not be boxed in by one's rigid stereotypical label concerning cultural strangers. One has to learn to draw out commonalties between self and cultural strangers and to appreciate the multifaceted aspects of the individuals to whom the stereotypical label is applied. In order to create new categories, one has to be open to new information. New information relies strongly on responsible sharing and responsive listening behavior.

Some specific suggestions can be made based on differences in individualistic and collectivistic styles of conflict management. These suggestions, however, are not listed in order of importance. *To deal with conflict effectively in the collectivistic culture, individualists need to:*

1. Be mindful of the face-maintenance assumptions of conflict situations that take place in this culture. Conflict competence resides in the strategic skills of managing the delicate interaction balance of humiliation and pride, and shame and honor. The face moves of one-up and one-down in a conflict episode, the use of same-status negotiators, and the proprieties and decorum of gracious "face fighting" have to be strategically staged with the larger group audience in mind.

2. Be proactive in dealing with low-grade conflict situations (such as by using informal consultation

or the "go-between" method) before they escalate into runaway, irrevocable mutual face-loss episodes. Individualists should try to realize that by helping their opponent to save face, they might also enhance their own face. Face is, intrinsically, a bilateral concept in the group-based, collectivistic culture.

3. "Give face" and try not to push their opponent's back against the wall without any room for maneuvering face loss or face recovery. Learn to let their opponent find a gracious way out of the conflict situation if at all possible, without violating the basic spirit of fundamental human rights. They should also learn self-restraint and try not to humiliate their opponent in the public arena or slight her or his public reputation. For collectivists, the concept of "giving face" typically operates on a long-range, reciprocal interaction system. Bilateral face-giving and face-saving ensures a continuous, interdependent networking process of favor-giving and favor concessions—especially along a long-term, historical time sense.

4. Be sensitive to the importance of quiet, mindful observation. Individualists need to be mindful of the historical past that bears relevance to the present conflict situation. Restrain from asking too many "why" questions. Since collectivistic, LC cultures typically focus on the nonverbal "how" process, individualists need to learn to experience and manage the conflict process on the implicit, nonverbal pacing level. Use deep-level silence, deliberate pauses, and patient conversational turn taking in conflict interaction processes with collectivists.

5. Practice attentive listening skills and feel the copresence of the other person. In Chinese characters, hearing or wun (聽) means "opening the door to the ears," while the word listening or ting (聞) means attending to the other person with your "ears, eyes, and heart." Listening means, in the Chinese character, attending to the sounds, movements, and feelings of the other person. Patient and deliberate listening indicates that one person is attending to the other person's needs even if it is an antagonistic conflict situation.

6. Discard the Western-based model of effective communication skills in dealing with conflict sit-

uations in the collectivistic, HC cultures. Individualists should learn to use qualifiers, disclaimers, tag questions, and tentative statements to convey their point of view. In refusing a request, learn not to use a blunt "no" as a response because the word "no" is typically perceived as carrying high face-threat value in the collectivistic culture. Use situational or self-effacing accounts ("Perhaps someone else is more qualified than I am in working on this project"), counterquestions ("Don't you feel someone else is more competent to work on this project?"), or conditional statements ("Yes, but . . .") to convey the implicit sense of refusal.

7. Let go of a conflict situation if the conflict party does not want to deal with it directly. A cooling period sometimes may help to mend a broken relationship, and the substantive issue may be diluted over a period of time. Individualists should remember that avoidance is part of the integral, conflict style that is commonly used in the collectivistic, LC cultures. Avoidance does not necessarily mean that collectivists do not care to resolve the conflict. In all likelihood, avoidance is strategically used to avert face-threatening interaction and is meant to maintain face harmony and mutual face dignity.

In sum, individualists need to learn to respect the HC, collectivistic ways of approaching and handling conflicts. They need to continuously monitor their ethnocentric biases on the cognitive, affective, and behavioral reactive levels; learn to listen attentively; and observe mindfully and reflectively.

Some specific suggestions also can be made for collectivists in handling conflict with individualists. *When encountering a conflict situation in an individualistic, LC culture, collectivists need to:*

1. Be mindful of the problem-solving assumptions. The ability to separate the relationship from the conflict problem is critical to effective conflict negotiation in an individualistic, LC culture. Collectivists need to learn to compartmentalize the task dimension and the socioemotional dimension of conflict.

2. Focus on resolving the substantive issues of the conflict, and learn to openly express opinions or points of view. Collectivists should try not to take the conflict issues to the personal level, and learn to maintain distance between the person and the conflict problem. In addition, try not to be offended by the upfront, individualistic style of managing conflict. Learn to emphasize tangible outcomes and develop concrete action plans in implementing the conflict-decision proposal.

3. Engage in an assertive, leveling style of conflict behavior. Assertive style emphasizes the rights of both individuals to speak up in a conflict situation and to respect each other's right to defend her or his position. Collectivists need to learn to open a conflict dialogue with an upfront thesis statement, and then develop the key point systematically, with examples, evidence, figures, or a well-planned proposal. In addition, collectivists need to be ready to accept criticisms, counterproposals, and suggestions for modification as part of the ongoing, group dialogue.

4. Own individual responsibility for the conflict decision-making process. Owning responsibility and using "I" statements to describe feelings in an ongoing conflict situation constitute part of effective conflict-management skills in an individualistic, LC culture. Collectivists need to learn to verbally explain a situation more fully and learn not to expect others to infer their points of view. Assume a sender-based approach to resolving conflict; ask more "why" questions and probe for explanations and details.

5. Provide verbal feedback and engage in active listening skills. Active listening skills, in the individualistic, LC culture, means collectivists have to engage in active verbal perception checking and ensure that the other person is interpreting points accurately. Collectivists need to use verbal paraphrases, summary statements, and interpretive messages to acknowledge and verify the storyline of the conflict situation. Learn to occasionally self-disclose feelings and emotions; they cannot rely solely on nonverbal, intuitive understanding to "intuit" and evaluate a situation.

6. Use direct, integrative verbal messages that clearly convey their concern over both the relational and substantive issues of a conflict situation. Collectivists should also not wait patiently for clear turn-taking pauses in the conflict interaction because individualistic conversation typi-

cally allows overlap talks, simultaneous messages, and floor-grabbing behavior. Collectivists also may not want to engage in too many deliberate silent moments because individualists will infer that as incompetence or an inefficient use of time.

7. Commit to working out the conflict situation with the conflict party. Collectivists should learn to use task-oriented integrative strategies and try to work out a collaborative, mutual goal dialogue with the conflict party. Work on managing individual defensiveness and learn to build up trust on the one-to-one level of interaction. Finally, confirm the conflict person through explicit relationship reminders and metacommunication talks, while simultaneously working on resolving the conflict substantive issues, responsibly and constructively.

In sum, collectivists need to work on their ethnocentric biases as much as the individualists need to work out their sense of egocentric superiority. Collectivists need to untangle their historical sense of cultural superiority—especially in thinking that their way is the only "civilized" way to appropriately deal with conflict. Both individualists and collectivists need to be mindful of the cognitive, affective, and behavioral blinders they bring into a conflict-mediation situation. They need to continuously learn new and novel ideas in dealing with the past, present, and the future for the purpose of building a peaceful community that is inclusive in all ethnic and cultural groups.

In being mindful of the potential differences between individualistic, LC and collectivistic, HC conflict styles, the intercultural peacemaking process can begin by affirming and valuing such differences as diverse human options in resolving some fundamental, human communication phenomenon. While it is not necessary that one should completely switch one's basic conflict style in order to adapt to the other person's behavior, mutual attuning and responsive behavior in signaling the willingness to learn about each other's cultural norms and rules may be a first major step toward a peaceful resolution process. In addition, conflicting parties from diverse ethnic or cultural backgrounds can learn to work on collaborative task projects and strive toward reaching a larger-than-self, community goal.

To be a peacemaker in the intercultural arena, one has to be first at peace with one's self and one's style. Thus, the artificial switching of one's style may only bring artificial results. Creative peacemakers must learn first to affirm and respect the diverse values that exist as part of the rich spectrum of the basic human experience. They may then choose to modify their behavior to adapt to the situation at hand. Finally, they may integrate diverse sets of values and behaviors, and be able to move in and out of different relational and cultural conflict boundaries. Creative peacemakers can be at ease and at home with the marginal stranger in their search toward common human peace. Peace means, on a universal level, a condition or a state of tranquility—with an absence of oppressed thoughts, feelings, and actions, from one heart to another, and from one nation state to another nation state.

Note

I want to thank Bill Gudykunst for his thoughtful suggestions on an earlier version of the manuscript.

1. Many of the ideas in this section are drawn from Ting-Toomey (in press).

References

Burgoon, J. (1991). Applying a comparative approach to expectancy violations theory. In J. Blumer, J. McCleod, & K. Rosengren (Eds.), *Communication and Culture Across Space and Time*. Newbury Park, CA: Sage.

Chinese Culture Connection. (1987). Chinese values and search for culture-free dimensions of culture. *Journal of Cross-Cultural Psychology, 18*, 143–164.

Chua, E., & Gudykunst, W. (1987). Conflict resolution style in low- and high-context cultures. *Communication Research Reports, 4*, 32–37.

Cohen, R. (1991). *Negotiating across cultures: Communication obstacles in international diplomacy*. Washington, DC: U.S. Institute of Peace.

Cole, M. (1989, May). Relational distance and personality influence on conflict communication styles. Unpublished Master's thesis. Tempe: Arizona State University.

Gudykunst, W., & Ting-Toomey, S. (1988). *Culture and interpersonal communication*. Newbury Park, CA: Sage.

Hall, E. T. (1976). *Beyond culture*. New York: Doubleday.

Hall, E. T. (1983). *The dance of life*. New York: Doubleday.

Hofstede, G. (1980). *Culture's consequences: International differences in work-related values*. Beverly Hills, CA: Sage.

Hofstede, G. (1991). *Cultures and organizations: Software of the mind*. London: McGraw-Hill.

Hui, C., & Triandis, H. (1986). Individualism-collectivism: A study of cross-cultural researchers. *Journal of Cross-Cultural Psychology, 17*, 225–248.

Langer, E. (1989). *Mindfulness*. Reading, MA: Addison-Wesley.

Leung, K. (1987). Some determinants of reactions to procedural models for conflict resolution: A cross-national study. *Journal of Personality and Social Psychology, 53*, 898–908.

Leung, K. (1988). Some determinants of conflict avoidance. *Journal of Cross-Cultural Psychology, 19*, 125–136.

Leung, K., & Bond, M. (1984). The impact of cultural collectivism on reward allocation. *Journal of Personality and Social Psychology, 47*, 793–804.

Leung, K., & Iwawaki, S. (1988). Cultural collectivism and distributive behavior. *Journal of Cross-Cultural Psychology, 19*, 35–49.

Markus, H., & Kitayama, S. (1991). Culture and the self: Implications for cognition, emotion, and motivation. *Psychological Review, 2*, 224–253.

Martin, J. N. (1993). Intercultural communication competence: A review. In R. L. Wiseman & J. Koster (Eds.), *Intercultural communication competence* (pp. 16–29). Newbury Park, CA: Sage.

Okabe, R. (1983). Cultural assumptions of East-West: Japan and the United States. In W. Gudykunst (Ed.), *Intercultural communication theory*. Beverly Hills, CA: Sage.

Schwartz, S., & Bilsky, W. (1990). Toward a theory of the universal content and structure of values. *Journal of Personality and Social Psychology, 58*, 878–891.

Ting-Toomey, S. (1985). Toward a theory of conflict and culture. In W. Gudykunst, L. Stewart, & S. Ting-Toomey (Eds.), *Communication, culture, and organizational processes* (pp. 71–86). Beverly Hills, CA: Sage.

Ting-Toomey, S. (1988). Intercultural conflict styles: A face-negotiation theory. In Y. Kim & W. Gudykunst (Eds.), *Theories in intercultural communication*. Newbury Park, CA: Sage.

Ting-Toomey, S. (1991). Intimacy expressions in three cultures: France, Japan, and the United States. *International Journal of Intercultural Relations, 15*, 29–46.

Ting-Toomey, S. (Ed.) (1994). *The challenge of facework: Cross-cultural and interpersonal issues*. Albany: State University of New York Press.

Ting-Toomey, S. (in press). *Intercultural communication process: Crossing boundaries*. New York: Guilford.

Ting-Toomey, S., & Cole, M. (1990). Intergroup diplomatic communication: A face-negotiation perspective. In F. Korzenny & S. Ting-Toomey (Eds.), *Communicating for peace: Diplomacy and negotiation*. Newbury Park, CA: Sage.

Ting-Toomey, S., et al. (1991). Culture, face maintenance, and styles of handling interpersonal conflict: A study in five cultures. *The International Journal of Conflict Management, 2*, 275–296.

Triandis, H. (1988). Collectivism vs. individualism: A reconceptualization of a basic concept in cross-cultural psychology. In G. Verma & C. Bagley (Eds.), *Cross-cultural studies of personality, attitudes and cognition*. London: Macmillan.

Triandis, H. (1990). Cross-cultural studies of individualism and collectivism. In J. Berman (Ed.), *Nebraska Symposium on Motivation*. Lincoln: University of Nebraska Press.

Triandis, H., Brislin, R., & Hui, C. H. (1988). Cross-cultural training across the individualism-collectivism divide. *International Journal of Intercultural Relations, 12*, 269–289.

Trubisky, P., Ting-Toomey, S., & Lin, S. L. (1991). The influence of individualism-collectivism and self-monitoring on conflict styles. *International Journal of Intercultural Relations, 15*, 65–84.

Wheeler, L., Reis, H., & Bond, M. (1989). Collectivism-individualism in everyday social life: The middle kingdom and the melting pot. *Journal of Personality and Social Psychology, 57*, 79–86.

Concepts and Questions

1. How does Ting-Toomey define conflict?

2. In what way does the cultural socialization process relate to different forms of intercultural conflicts?

3. From the perspective of intercultural conflict, how may in-group and out-group differences contribute to such conflict?

4. How can differences between high- and low-context cultures contribute to intercultural conflict?

5. How can an awareness of expectations help mediate intercultural conflict?

6. How do differences along the individualistic–collectivist scale of cultural differences contribute to intercultural conflict? What would you suggest to minimize these influences?

7. In what ways can differences in cross-cultural conflict interaction styles affect intercultural communication?

8. What role does silence play in intercultural conflict reduction?

9. What differences are there between individualistic and collectivist conflict management styles?

10. What does Ting-Toomey suggest is necessary for effective intercultural conflict management?

384 Chapter 7 Communicating Interculturally: Becoming Competent

Effective Strategies for Mediating Co-Cultural Conflict

JAMES MANSEAU SAUCEDA

Let me begin with an ending
With the last time I saw 'Her' face—
Gwendolyn Brooks
One of America's premiere poets
Took center-stage
And did something ... surprising ...
She...
Smiled—
(Now I mean smiled authentically)
Aimed her Spirit at each in the audience,
And smiled—
And only after she had completed
Her sweet survey of our faces
Did she speak
Just three words:
"Art
Urges
Voyages"
She paused, savoring the silence,
And then she took in a gigantic gulp
Of air, and in a Voice that was ripe
With jubilation—She Proclaimed:
"Art
Urges
Voyages"[1]

PREFACE

This short narrative has made a long journey. These days I perform it as an incantation or a conjuring—a way of opening up the heart as I begin a workshop on issues of our diversity and culture. It was born more than 20 years ago, however, on the daring day

that I met Gwendolyn Brooks. The gift of her compassion, then, has been in my bloodstream ever since; somehow her kindness and profound presence gave me reassurance, that there was a goodness that prevails against all storms. Yes, and a justice that no unjust law could ever stop. Freedom, ultimately it seemed, was a *personal* choice.

The great Gwendolyn Brooks is gone. But she remains—a living miracle—forceful *and* fragile—a dynamic dreamer. Born in the American Midwest, she lived, and will always live, everywhere. Everywhere a risk is taken to see *beyond* color, *beyond* predictable patterns, *beyond* easy labeling. Gwendolyn never used words to indoctrinate, rather she unlocked their transportational power; yes, "Art urges voyages," and the journey she invites never ends.

INTRODUCTION

You may not realize it, but I have just offered you several strategies for meditating co-cultural conflict. To discover these strategies for yourself, please look again at the preface. Only this time let your imagination inhabit the scene (perhaps slow down the pace of your reading, or even say the poetic opener aloud). Now, did you discern any strategies woven into the narrative? (If not, don't worry, part of our challenge is to see "old" issues with "new" eyes, and this takes both innovative training as well as a renewed commitment for serious examination of self and society.) So, here are some strategies, drawn from the preface. I invite you to consider that co-cultural conflict may be effectively mediated by the following:

- Our willingness to be vulnerable and authentic
- Creating openness for dissolving defensiveness
- Crisscrossing our cultural boundaries
- The practice of compassion

Our Willingness to Be Vulnerable and Authentic

This means "keeping it real" and, therefore, not hiding behind the easy masks of our authority, expertise, credentials, and so on. Now, realize that with Gwendolyn Brooks, here stood the first African

American writer (male or female) ever to win the auspicious Pulitzer Prize for Poetry.[2] Here was a famous member of the American Academy of Arts and Letters[3]; here was the Poet Laureate of the State of Illinois, and the recipient of prestigious Guggenheim Fellowships.

In short, she was a V.I.P. in every respect. Yet, we in the audience saw in her no arrogance, nor a haughty manner. In fact, we felt no distance from Gwendolyn at all. Rather, she was just able to be one of us. No, better still, she was one *with* us.[4]

It is instructive, also, to note that initially Ms. Brooks built this bridge of our interconnectedness while *in complete silence* (we have so much to learn about communicating *non*verbally.) Hence, one of the tools to use when exploring ways of being vulnerable and authentic is to employ "the freedom of silence" (before using "the freedom of speech").[5]

Creating Openness for Dissolving Defensiveness

*Inter*racial tension, as well as *intra*racial tension can produce a fearful reaction. So much so that we may deny or avoid co-cultural conflict at any cost. It is a pattern of our conditioning to want to run away from a crisis situation, rather than face the conflict head-on. Also, there may be a biological impulse that is triggered if we feel threatened or perceive an attack. No matter the source, the result of our pernicious penchant for flight is that we *continue* to be defensive, embarrassed, awkward, uneasy, suspicious, or even shamed around co-cultural conflict.

Gwendolyn's smile, in this regard, was truly disarming of defensiveness. Somehow, we instantly knew that it was safe to lay down our armor because in Gwendolyn there was no threat; only her caring heart and opened hand. I submit to you that our defenses begin to dissolve when we are authentically seen by another. We find "soul-safety" when we feel a spirit of kindliness coming toward us. We don't have to run, or fight, or fear, but still, we have *all* undertaken and pursued an "arms race." In fact, over the years, each one of us has built up a personal arsenal of defensive weapons. Chief among these tenacious tactical devices are anger, cynicism, apathy, sarcasm, indifference, physical and psychological abuse, as well as all forms of violence.

Now, I readily admit and acknowledge that summarily letting go of our defensiveness is exceedingly difficult (and this bone-crushing challenge is particularly problematic in a conflict situation). After all, in the heat of conflict we find ourselves lost in a confusing swirl of intense hurt and inflammatory rhetoric. Add to this volatile mix that our "buttons" are likely being pushed repeatedly, that the high-pitched emotional level quickly gets unbearably uncomfortable, and ultimately is seen careening out of control!

So (whew!) given all that (catch your breath) tell me, how does anyone *un*learn to react defensively? Well, I submit to you that the answer starts by accepting the proposition that *personal risk is a prerequisite*. That is, in order to break out of the reflex of our fear requires that we first must *embrace our fragility*. Put another way, the circuit of conflict can be effectively mediated if we source the suffering, and speak to the taproot of that suffering, and boldly declare that such suffering is indeed *shared* by all parties involved in the conflict. As Dr. Martin Luther King Jr. reminds us: "The basic tension is *not* between 'races'—the tension is between *justice* and *injustice*."[6]

Now, this is deep. If we let ourselves see that the issues of cultural conflict over "our" identity and diversity are really about "justice for *all*," then we will recognize that "our loyalties must *transcend* our race, our class, and our nation."[7] From a multicultural perspective, then, our allegiances must evolve, becoming "ecumenical, rather than sectional."[8]

Crisscrossing Our Cultural Boundaries

A crucial distinction needs to be made when considering issues of diversity; simply put, being "multiethnic" does *not* imply being "multicultural." For example, in the classrooms of Southern California we are, without question, "multiethnic." But from a speech originally delivered by the Reverend Dr. Martin Luther King Jr., we learn the secret and sad situation of today; we share "physical *proximity* without sharing spiritual *affinity*."[9] Oh, sure, our "elbows are together," but our "hearts are apart."[10] The point is, for all of our demographic diversity, the plain truth is that we are, most often, really just strangers stuck together in one place. Aside from our polite or civil interactions in and out of the classroom or workplace, we really don't know much about each other's cultural background (much less choose to *enrich our own* cultural background through direct contact with others).

Yet, it is to this ability of crisscrossing, in and outside of our personal cultural boundaries, that a philosophy of multiculturalism really takes hold and finds nourishment; where the national goal of creating cultural pluralism actually becomes an individual enactment—a daily behavior of the acceptance of others, (not at arm's length, but truly *into* one's self). In this view, my very sense of "me" is multiplied (through *direct* intercultural contact, not from intellectual or theoretical contemplation).

But let's return to our Gwendolyn for an apt illustration. Before I begin performing the preface, I "bless" the stage with a silent ritual (my movements being drawn from the spiritual traditions of indigenous peoples of the Americas). I close this "ritual of silence" with a sacred bow reflecting Cambodian culture.[11] Then, as I speak the first words of the preface, I metaphorically bring an African American on stage with me—Gwendolyn herself.

Now, usually, the audience becomes sweetly unhinged as they watch, not knowing what ethnic or cultural category to place me in, not sure what the point of my "silent ritual" was, not able to predict where I'll go next. In short, I seek to initiate a form of *constructive crisis*[12]; one that "dwells in possibility,"[13] one that signals "difference," *in itself*, and one that encourages individual discovery.

Another way to position the idea of crisscrossing our cultural boundaries is to contrast it to the prevailing pattern of cultural identity that is still widely promoted in America. Namely, the ill-conceived construct of "segregated, *mono*-culturalism" (which continues to pose as *multi*culturalism). For instance, on a college campus when we look at student programming for so-called multiculturalism, what we generally witness, in fact, are "Black" events that only Black students attend, "Asian" events that only Asians attend, "Latino" events just for Latinos, and so on. In short, *no* events that extend *beyond* the old cookie-cutter categories. Instead of offering us challenging, stimulating experiences that *cut across* cul-

tural boundaries, we receive only safe, sanitized, and predictable segregated, monocultural events.

This tired format never succeeds in promoting the interconnectedness of our collective cultural identities, but only replicates and ratifies ethnic and cultural isolationism (encouraging ever more distance and division).

The Practice of Compassion

Multiculturalism is not an argument to be won, not a catch phrase or a buzzword, and not some esoteric theory. Multiculturalism is also *not* anti-white, anti-male, or anti-European. It is, rather, *pro* "all of us" on this planet—it is, indeed, an international struggle for our collective soul wholeness; it is, and requires from us, a daily demonstration of compassion.

Now, the truth is that most of us were never taught much about compassion as we were growing up. And probably the same absence or emptiness exists on the subject in our adulthood. So, you might rightly exclaim: "How can I be expected to practice something that I know little to nothing about?" Well, perhaps my original question is in error. Maybe, it is not really so much a problem of knowing, but, instead, one of listening.

We could start by listening to our bodies for compassion. For example, there is a visceral truth we recognize whenever we give, or receive, touch that is compassionate. Such touch clearly conveys kindliness and warmth (without any ulterior motive), it creates connection (without any conditions). The result is that we feel closer to ourselves and to all others, in the very act of and experience in compassionate touch.

The opposite of such nonjudgmental empathetic listening is an action of abuse. Whether the abuse is physical, verbal, or psychological, our bodies recoil; we are jolted by surges of stress that reflexes throughout our body. At worst, our sense of "self" is shattered, thrown into fragments and competing conflicts. We want to retaliate. We want to escape the assault. We seek vengeance. We need justice.

But, *if we act out of our anger, we actually re-injure ourselves.* Then, of course, we bring additional violence and injury to others (and, remember that no matter our aim, often the others we injure are not even the target, but innocent loved ones and/or unfortunate bystanders). So, it is not our anger, but our capacity for compassion, that conciliates conflict (anger merely heightens our hurt, and incites the indiscriminate dispersal of more darkness and wounds).

A stirring illustration of compassion, and one uniquely imbedded in the body, may be found in Gwendolyn Brook's poem, "the mother."[14] This searching poem, this tragic soliloquy, this mythic voice of a woman's heartfelt and complex reflections over her abortion has been deemed controversial since July 1944 (when it was submitted as part of her first collection, *A Street in Bronzeville*).[15] Yet, even from today's vantage point, the volatility of its subject remains unabated.

As Gwendolyn moved forward to perform the poem, however, she shared something surprising. She told the audience that over the years *both* camps of the abortion issue had asked to use her poem "the mother" to promote *their* cause! What neither side apparently realized was that their opponent's views were as validly revealed as their own.

You see, the genius of compassion is that it has within its compass the power to dissolve our discrimination of dualism.[16] Compassion, therefore, *transcends* the very taking up of sides; it's touch travels *beyond* the simple skin of "pro" and "con." It asserts an ever-widening circle of concerns, achieving universality (but at no one's expense):

> Abortions will not let you forget
> you remember the children you got that you did not
> get . . .
> If I stole your births and your names . . .
> If I poisoned the beginning of your breaths
> Believe that even in my deliberateness I was not deliberate . . .
> You were never made
> But that too, I am afraid
> Is faulty: oh, what shall I say, how is the truth to be said?

The answer, which Gwendolyn's own performance gave me, is that "the truth" needs to be said with compassion. The poem ends both with pain and paradox, yet it still achieves affirmation and caring (even in the choice that appears so uncaring):

> Believe me, I loved you all.
> Believe me, I knew you, though faintly, and I loved I
> loved you
> All.[17]

HEADLINING THE HEART

The preface and introduction have served as an opening act, a "curtain up" experience, and a way to make our way more deeply, more fully feeling, into the difficult subject at hand. From this point forward I will seek to offer you practical and effective strategies for conciliating and mediating co-cultural conflict. I will do so by applying these strategies to the contexts of police/community relations, mental health care, the general workplace, and the classroom.

Police/Community Relations

When I was first asked to design and implement diversity workshops for the Long Beach California Police Department, I was, well, a little uneasy. OK, I'll admit it: I was a lot more than just "a little uneasy." I was really quite scared. After all, my own experiences with the "po-lease" in Compton (where I grew up) were certainly not positive. Truth is, I definitely had biases against the police, and I also had never before addressed an audience of law enforcement officers. Moreover, this invitation came in the aftermath of police brutality allegations (with angry charges, and countercharges, being hurled daily on the television and in the news media).

Still, we must not minimize the message from our recent past. Such incendiary events as the "Watts Rebellion" in 1965[18] and the "L.A. Rebellion" in 1992 establish a frightening regularity to the rupture of trust in police/community relations. Our challenge is not only to repair the breach, but also to conciliate police/community relations in an ongoing and *proactive* way ("crisis intervention" must, therefore, evolve into a year-round curriculum of compassion).

Here are some key strategies, born from personal experience, that help when mediating co-cultural conflict in police/community contexts.

Mutually Admitting Our Suspicions and Biases. I told you, a little earlier, that I had developed a bias "against the police" while living in Compton. But as I entered the conference room of the L.B. Police Academy, I decided to keep that bias to myself—and that was a mistake. For me not to admit, right up front, that I personally held negative stereotypes against my audience of law enforcement officers was like trying to ignore that 400-pound gorilla standing at the lectern!

So I came to realize that I, too, like you, needed to learn and apply the initial strategy opening this essay, namely, "Willingness to be Vulnerable and Authentic." Not easy. But without an admission of our biases, there simply can be no level playing field. Remember, though, admitting bias does *not* mean perpetuating bias. In fact, once we give an honest "voice" to the condition of our bias, then the second strategy comes into play: "Creating Openness for Dissolving Defensiveness."

If we source the suffering of our bias, we will discover that the bias itself is but a cover-up for our anger, the anger is but a cover-up for our hurt, and the hurt covers up the root of the wound—which is a deeply felt experience of abuse, violence, and injustice. Now, while this core hurt is indeed real and therefore truthful, the overgeneralizations creating our bias, however, are illusionary and false. That's because bias indicts *all* members of a group as equally guilty and responsible for our pain; bias closes us off from the fact that it was individuals and not entire communities that perpetrated injustice upon our person.

The permission we grant for creating a safe place to admit our bias, however, must always be even handed and presented in a mutual way. In other words, *all* sides need some support and opportunity to clear the air of what otherwise remains their suppressed bias. (And suppressed bias festers, building resentment, and dysfunctionally filtering out what we don't want to hear.)

Empathizing with the Hurt of the Police. To have "empathy" is to feel *into* the feelings of another (and *without* any judgment). In most cases, the police have entered the dialogue already indicted and have been labeled as the oppressor. Add to such a volatile and defense-arousing context the following:

- The police officers attending a community forum or diversity training seminar may feel *forced* to attend. Their appearance may have been required by the Chief of Police or mandated by the Mayor or City Council because of an incendiary event.
- The audience likely enters hostile and angry (possibly assuming guilt of the police officers present). The moderator likely is not perceived by the police officers to have an adequate understanding of what it means to be in law enforcement. And, the officers may feel that *no one* in the forum really represents *their* experience (whether the organizing body, the media, or the audience).
- People may not recognize the valid reasons that the police have for being suspicious.

In hindsight, I can see just how naïve it was of me not to realize that the officers attending my workshop had good reasons to be suspicious of me—suspicious of my intent, my agenda, my background, and my expertise. I submit that *you* can avoid creating more tension and can effectively diffuse defensiveness by realizing the following:

- Police officers put themselves in a life-or-death situation *daily*.
- The representatives of the community that police officers have the most contact with are, indeed, *criminals* (often murderers, rapists, and drug dealers).
- Police officers are seldom, if ever, portrayed positively in the media or even in the communities in which they serve.
- Police officers "of color" often feel caught in a double-bind or no-win situation. Their white counterparts or partners frequently do not accept them as equals. And, they often are not accepted by their *own* ethnic community, but rather are seen as "sell-outs," "tio tacos," or "uncle toms."
- Women officers "of color" face a no-win, *triple-bind* situation. Prevalent gender bias causes them to not be seen as equals by their white counterparts or their partners, as well as not being seen as equals by their *own* ethnic group, simply because they are female. Frequently, they are not seen as equals because of their race. And, finally, their own ethnic community may not accept them because they dare to redefine the cultural roles assigned to women.

Now, understand that all of the above issues are usually unmentioned or totally ignored in public settings (which means that the emerging dialogue that follows just glides on the surface, never approaching the underlying issues). Note, too, that *none* of the above conditions are being brought up in order to condone any injustice, or to offer excuses for the levels of distrust between police and the surrounding community. Rather, here is where another earlier strategy, "The Practice of Compassion," becomes integral to the mediation process (i.e., *we have to see the situation clearly before we can see our way to a solution*). And the situation for police officers, everywhere, is very, very difficult—fraught with danger—and they deserve our empathy and our appreciation. Then, from a compassionate center, we can all move forward to truly improving our relations.

Keeping Understanding, Not Advocacy, as Our Goal. In an article titled, "Nonviolence and Racial Justice," Dr. King establishes a crucial covenant: "We do *not* seek to defeat or humiliate our opponent, rather we seek to win their understanding and friendship."[19] Now, the sad and profound truth is that we have all been taught quite the opposite! Whether it is a national presidential debate or your next research paper in college, we measure "winning" by our efficiency in subverting, undermining, and humiliating our opponent (and we are rewarded mightily for the successful demolition of our opponent's ideas, beliefs, or desires).

In mediation we learn a different way, we admit to ourselves that we have to make a major move *away* from our well-worn pattern of argument and intellectual attack. Part of our present indoctrination is the idea that the true goal of discussion is to prove the rightness of *our* view; in short, advocacy. Yet, advocacy does *not* promote mediation or conciliation because it asserts that there is only one way—*my* way! In a police/community context, however, there are many co-cultural ways competing for attention, for redress of grievance, and for basic respect.

Here's an example of what I mean: "Police culture" typically speaks in, and responds to, a language of clear authority, a quasi-military tone with chain-of-command structures and a delivery conveying control. This is not wrong. This is not right. This simply is. But this very authority voice may, in itself, be heard by the community as aggression, intimidation, and lack of caring (*despite* the intent or content of the message being delivered). Such a clash of communication cultural styles worsens if the co-culture in question responds best to language and delivery that conveys a more supportive tone, a tender emotion, humbleness, and open heartedness.

What we need to do, then, is first recognize that there are different co-cultural communication styles dynamically interacting in police/community forums. Second, we have to diffuse our own defensiveness by learning to listen *without judgment* for understanding, not advocacy. Now here's an extreme example. I had an officer actually taunt, then yell at me: "Well, I have a question, Dr. Sauceda, why are *all* Mexicans drunks? And why do they *all* beat their wives?"

I'll tell you, when I heard this I wanted to lash out, to spit back some choice obscenities, then throw in the towel and quit! Instead, I called for a break and sat in my car quivering in anger and pain. I knew then how little I knew about mediation of conflict. Slowly, I intuitively sourced the suffering of the officer. He sees more domestic violence on a single Saturday night than I will see in my lifetime. He is frustrated and also put in danger when an assailant is high on drugs or intoxicated. He's assigned to patrol a Chicano/Latino community, so it seems as if the whole group of Latinos behaves this way.

Eventually, I returned saying I was ready now to answer his questions. I began: "The truth is you're right, alcoholism *is* a very real problem in the Latino community, but it is also a problem in *your* community and throughout the country. In fact, it's a pan-epidemic problem worldwide. And, sad to say, I also agree that all of the violence against women you see *is* a horrible problem in the Chicano community you patrol, but it is also a problem in *your* community and throughout America. And, just like alcoholism, it is truly a pan-epidemic problem worldwide." This was the start of widening the circle of compassion. Things improved.

Allow me now to close this topic with a quote that I find summarizes the goal of mediation and an improved sense of community:

> What is needed to support diversity and true community building is a methodology that allows for the lively interplay of *multiple* cultural perceptions—a community whose sophistication in traffic management permits it to sustain multiple borders.[20]

Mental Health Services

> I call upon you to be *maladjusted*, I *never* intend to adjust myself to segregation and discrimination. I *never* intend to adjust myself to mob rule. . . . I call upon you to be as maladjusted as Amos . . . As maladjusted as Abraham Lincoln . . . As maladjusted as Jesus of Nazareth . . . God grant that we will be so maladjusted that we will be able to go out and change our world and our civilization.[21]

Racism is a mental health issue. Indeed, racism may constitute a bona fide mental disorder, one that eventually may be added to the standard Diagnostic Statistical Manual. But whether racism's dysfunctionality or its symptomology is ever recognized in the DSM, of one thing we can be certain: *Racism poisons the mind.*

More and more in the vast arena of health care, professionals are seeking strategies to mediate cocultural conflict. A case in point is "Accepting the Challenge of Cultural Competency," the first conference of its kind sponsored by the California Institute for Mental Health (CIMH) (March 2001).[22] But whether it's in youth and family centers, departments of behavioral health, local clinics serving a specific ethnic community, crisis teams or various counseling associations, we find that health care is recognizing the need for multiculturalism.

The quote opening this section, however, clearly challenges and redefines our idea of what it means to be well adjusted. Dr. King spoke those words before an overflow crowd of activist students attending the University of California at Berkeley. His startling point was that, too often, *we accommodate ourselves to the disorder and disease of racism* (all the while accepting these accommodations as perhaps sad, but necessary, adjustments). The *healthy* response, by contrast, is therefore to be maladjusted.

Initially, this advice sounds off the mark, doesn't it? I mean, it sounds kind of crazy that we should actually seek to be maladjusted. Yet, after we realize that Dr. King means becoming maladjusted *only* to behaviors that create or perpetuate deep discord and unresolved conflict in others and ourselves does it indeed make sense (maladjustment in this sense actually leads to health and mental balance). For you see, as a nation, and as individuals, we have become far too adjusted to homelessness, child abuse, violence against women, hate crimes, teenage suicide, and police brutality; far too adjusted to oppression from racism and discrimination; far too adjusted to the despair in our families and friends; and the list goes on and on.

Yet, in order for us to *readjust* ourselves back to a compassionate response requires a painful and probing process. It is necessary first for us to examine and admit to ourselves just how "adjusted" to negative conditions we've allowed our hearts to become (and the result of this accommodation to darkness is that our hearts and minds grow ever more numb). Mental health care provides pathways for us to reenter the hurt, reenter the soul wounds, to discover and uncover and recover the conciliation and healing potential in all of us.

I will be offering some strategies that I hope provide greater access to effective mediation across cultures in the field of mental health care. The goal is for us to become more caring at the counseling level, at the clinical level, at the psychotherapy level, at the service delivery level, and at the educational and training level.[23]

The Counseling Level. Counseling services are intended to provide a safe place for us to express not only our hopes, but also our harms. Yet a common obstacle to creating such a support system is that clients from various co-cultures feel unseen, or worse still, feel erased by their counselors. In short, the counselor is perceived as being unaware of, or completely out of touch with, the client's value system, class consciousness, or cultural identity. A typical complaint and a source of conflict often sounds like this:

> "Yeah, so this know-it-all counselor just laughed in my face when I asked about going to college. She said I should be 'realistic' and go to a vocational school instead."

> "Yo, check this, the damn counselor kept saying I was too angry, too loud, and that I was the problem! Right, like this white man's ever been to the 'hood."

The strategy needed in both of these cases—one of the hardest to explore and to apply—is discussed as follows.

Putting your "whiteness" on the table is an effective strategy in this situation. We study "blackness," but we don't study "whiteness." We also study ethnic groups and refer to individuals as people of color (but, again, here whiteness is excluded from the very concept of color). Perhaps, then, a better approach is to say that power, class, and privilege are inextricably tied into the idea of "whiteness." Yet whiteness is so pervasive and its privileged status is so ubiquitous that it appears to be invisible. An example reflecting this invisibility might be the following:

> "Look, why do you always have to keep calling yourself 'Mexican' American? I mean, just get over it. Why can't you just be 'American,' like me?"

The answer might be:

> "Because, *my* 'Mexican-ness' is a vital part of my 'American-ness'; look at history, over half of Mexico was stolen in 1848 (in fact, 10 states of the U.S. *used to be Mexico!*). So, we didn't go anywhere, we didn't even cross a border; the border crossed us!"[24]

But beyond such history is the present reality of separate and unequal school systems, the daily inequalities experienced by non-whites (such as being followed in stores as if we were criminals, or not being picked up by cabs, or being profiled "racially" by police, etc.). It is to this contemporary gulf of opportunity that makes the simple phrase *American* really mean more like European American or White American (but the white remains assumed, *not* voiced).

Now, what a white counselor with a non-white client needs to remember, then, is that their very whiteness is often perceived as an intimidating power, a negative force, a belittling and judgmental attitude, all coming from a privileged source. This situation need *not*, however, become some permanent stumbling block, but rather can be turned into a valuable teaching moment!

Putting whiteness on the table means having a sense of humor about the stereotypes people carry regarding white folk: "Good morning, Tyrone, my name is John Sandy and I am a white man! Yes, I'm here to oppress you and basically undermine your value!" Such an obviously absurd introduction would really "trip out" the client and could be used to say, in a funny, nonthreatening way:

> "Look, I'll do my best *not* to stereotype you, my friend, and you can do the same for me, OK? Hey, I know it's not easy for people to see beyond the prejudiced picture, but I'm interested in the *real* you, and my goal is simply to offer help and support."

The Clinical Level. In the clinical setting, one of the easiest and most helpful strategies is to reflect the co-cultures you serve in the design and décor of your physical setting. Sometimes the word *clinical* is synonymous with "antiseptic" or "the absence of emotion." And for most everyone, clinical, in that sense, is anything but welcoming.

A good example of a clinical setting, however, that resonates to the co-cultures they serve is the East Los Angeles Mental Health Agency. Upon entering one notices that the reception area is more like a family living room (with a television and couches). Once inside, the hallways are filled with artwork, vivid prints featuring, for example, the Mexican Modernist Diego Rivera. Interspersed among the paintings are historic events, both local and national, that reflect the struggle for social justice of the Latino community (e.g., "The Huelga" or "Strikes" of Cesar Chavez and the United Farm Workers, etc.). The signage outside is subdued, easily missed as you pass by. (This is quite intentional, for it minimizes the embarrassment for clients entering the facility.)

Taking such steps adds heart and honoring to the space, transforming clinical into caring. Given that the crucial challenge faced by mental health care facilities is the underuse of their services by many co-cultures, this strategy is not merely ornamental, but rather constitutes a prerequisite for projecting acceptance and warmth.

The Psychotherapy Level. This situation is akin to the whiteness issue, in that its core, Eurocentrism, is so imbedded in its theories that it, too, seems invisible. (In both cases, it's like trying to separate wetness from water!) The key presumptions of psychotherapy come from Europe, as did its foundational practitioners. But once it was transplanted to America, the underlying assumptions of psychotherapy had repeated collisions with co-cultural traditions (many traditions that are completely antithetical to psychotherapy). For many Latinos, Asian Americans, and Native Americans, the very idea of speaking to a stranger about intimate and private feelings seems outrageous and like a violation in itself. There is little trust and much suspicion surrounding the entire process, especially if the client has been remanded by the criminal justice system or from social service agencies.

Add to this already difficult situation a deep sense of shame, a horrible burden of humiliation at the thought that you may have mental disorders or dysfunctional behaviors, and it all sounds like an evil or mean-spirited attack on our core sense of self. (And it also sounds like an insult against our entire family!)

In many cultures the idea of "saving face" or preserving the honor of the family is extremely important. Further complications arise depending on the cultural role expectations, say on a Latino male head of household. For them, it appears to be a sign of weakness or an emasculating experience to go into a mental clinic for help. Two strategies are especially helpful in the psychotherapy level.

1. *Weave co-cultural folk medicine practices into psychotherapy to establish rapport with clients.* In Latino co-cultures, the *curandera* or folk physician plays a significant and healing role in the community. There is great comfort and familiarity in the diagnosis and remedies from *curanderismo*. A counselor or therapist could link his or her assessment of a client's mental condition to that offered by a folk healer. Involving the sacred medicine man of the Native Americans or the addition of acupuncture to psychotherapy could also bridge the provinces of European ideas with those of different cultures.

2. *Weave interfaith dimensions into psychotherapy to reach the client's faith system.* Something I have discovered to be healing and helpful in diversity-training workshops is being conversant with the traditions of world religion. An individual's faith system is a powerful and empowering mirror to his or her humanity. These "wisdom songs" come from all cultures, and their insight, although ancient, often speaks with a startling clarity that in-

forms us of contemporary life. Here are but a few examples (when they are quoted or used in a public setting, or framed and put up in clinical environments, they stand and honor co-cultures from a deep place of the heart):

All From One Clay Are Made;
In All One Light Shines.
—Sikhism (*Adi Granth, Guri, M5*)

See The Self in Every Creature
And All Creation in the Self.
—Hinduism (*Bhagavad Gita, 6.28-32*)

The families of mankind shall not lord over the other with the claim 'of being from superior stock': All have their common kinship in the collective human family.
—Judaism (*Talmud, Tosefta Sanhedrin 8:4*)

O Mankind! We created you from a single soul, male and female and made you into nations and tribes, so that you might come to know each other.
—Islam (*Qur'an, 49.13*)

Spokes Share One Hub
To Make A Wheel.
—Taoism (*Tao Te Ching*)

The Service Delivery Level. We often find ourselves face to face with the following issues:

Discriminatory practices result from ways in which services are organized—selection procedures, points of comparison for promotion, etc. (in the case of staff) and diagnostic processes, selective criteria for types of treatment, indicators of "dangerousness," etc. (in the case of patients).[25]

I will focus on the patient side of this equation. As a former faculty member of the California School of Professional Psychology, I developed and taught several courses for master's and doctoral candidates in clinical psychology. In one of these courses, exploring Chicano culture, I role-played as a teenage youth from the *barrio* who was remanded by the courts to see a psychotherapist.

I would enter the room wearing a "street" outfit (i.e., bandana, dark sunglasses, Pendleton shirt, khaki pants). I would then strut around the room and glare at the therapist. When the therapist would ask me questions, I simply would not answer. After awhile I abruptly got up and left. The students were asked to write their diagnosis of this "juvenile offender." The results were stunning, frightening, and bewildering.

The consensus of the class was that this Chicano youth was indeed "dangerous," "violent" and "possibly sociopathic." When I asked what they based their assessment on (since I hadn't spoken a word), they pointed to two things: "his gang clothes" and "the intimidating way he moved." I then shared that what I was attempting to enact was an extremely *frightened* teenager, one who didn't understand English very well and felt stupid and helpless in the presence of the white therapist. It had never occurred to these students that maybe the tough street strut was just a pose, a mask for his unvoiced fear, or that maybe this was actually a good kid who had gotten into trouble (and needed their help).

An effective strategy here is to neutralize your impression based on exteriors: clothes, nonverbal behavior, and street styles. The media perpetuates a criminal picture of many co-cultures in America. And if a person seems to fit the TV's profile of a gang member, then it's easy for *any* of us (counselors and therapists included) to react from this negative stereotype when we see perceived gang clothes or threatening behavior. But beyond our prejudiced response is the fact that a person's clothing is *not* an indicator of that person's character; and what we may interpret as a behavior that's threatening may only be a street style of projecting dignity and self-worth.

The Education and Training Level. Ultimately, the best pathway to improve mediation, in a mental health context, is at the education and training level. As it was recently lamented, however:

> Mental health professionals, and psychologists more specifically, continue to be predominantly Caucasian; to be trained by predominantly Caucasian faculty members; and to be trained in programs in which ethnic issues are ignored, regarded as deficiencies, or included as an afterthought."[26]

Let me say upfront that being Caucasian does not, in any way, preclude one from being an effective diversity trainer (of course not!). But as I have discussed earlier, such effectiveness does require that one first put whiteness on the table, then move to dispel misinformation and the stereotypes surrounding whiteness. Yet, the key point remains that too often the trainers of the mental health professionals have had little personal experience in cross-cultural or multicultural practice—much less been exposed to multicultural pedagogy or philosophy in their own training as counselors and psychologists.

Let me close this section with an illustration that comes from a Chinese American psychiatrist I met, whose clinical practice was centered in the very heart of San Francisco's China Town. A cross-cultural collision occurred when his traditional Chinese practices (as well as those of the families he served) met with a negative assessment by the ethical standards board of the American Psychological Association.

A common way for these Chinese American families to thank and honor this psychiatrist was to arrive at his office with a fully cooked feast (such as Peking Duck). Now, for the therapist *not* to accept this "love offering" or to refuse to eat with them would constitute an insult of the highest order. Such blatant disrespect could create a breach of trust and summarily undermine the supportive rapport it had taken him so long to build.

Yet, the psychological establishment interpreted these heartfelt gestures of caring as direct violations of the APA's code of ethical conduct. The food constituted "monetary gifts," the psychiatrist was "unprofessional" for accepting the food, and, furthermore, he had blurred the clear line that should exist between client and therapist by informally eating with his patients. That such a situation arose at all indicates the gulf that still exists across the American cultural divide.

The Workplace

Let's hit the ground running with an important first strategy. *Managing diversity in the workplace requires that we differentiate between equal treatment and equity.* Here's how Dr. Carlos Cortes puts the matter: "The statement, 'I treat everyone alike' is actually a statement of *inequality*!"[27] Confused? Let's clear things up. The concept of equity is one of fairness and effectiveness, *not* one of sameness. Therefore, to treat everyone the same really means that only *one* standard is being applied, unilaterally, to all (regardless of whether this produces poor results, creates resentment, or lowers morale.) Given our ever-increasing workplace made up of so many co-cultural groups, fairness, then, requires that we explore multiple approaches to achieve equal opportunity for all.

Now fairness itself involves a question of balance. In the American Disabilities Act, the phrase "reasonable accommodation" is introduced. I think this is helpful so if, for example, the price of making a workplace wheelchair accessible would actually bankrupt a company, or nearly deplete its resources, then it is not fair, or reasonable, to expect the company to comply. (But, of course, the debate still hinges on one's definition of the term "reasonable accommodation.")

But that's an extreme case. Most workplaces are *not* practicing multiculturalism for another reason. That reason is that they continue to be encumbered by rules and traditions that are no longer serving the needs of the company. While the company's workforce has changed, and the consumers' demographics have changed, the company's policies have often remained frozen in time. The attitude is, "We've *always* done things this way, so why should we change now?" And the term "this way" may mean excluding women from higher management positions; seldom, if ever, promoting "people of color"; ostracizing, if not firing, gay and lesbian workers; or ignoring any number of other issues concerning racism or sexism.

A second strategy that promotes fairness and equity is to *make the workplace an "English plus" environment, not one that mandates "English only."* In my view there is an insidious and false logic behind "English-only" policies in the workplace (and beyond). That logic goes something like this:

> "Look, folks, since we have so many people here speaking different languages, I think that it's time the company instituted an "English-only" policy. See, by using English exclusively, we will bring unity and end confusion. English will also help us create a sense that we all are actually part of One America, and not from different countries."

The lesson of U.S. History has been ignored in this regard. People forget that the land we call America *has always been multilingual*—that is, until very recently. The nearly 2,000 different languages spoken by indigenous Indian Nations in the 16th century freely mixed first with Spanish, then French, then finally in the 17th century, with English. The English colonies were themselves highly multilingual. The Colony of New Amsterdam, in 1623, had citizens speaking Dutch, Polish, Italian, German, Danish, Norwegian, Swedish, Finnish, Portuguese, African languages, and English!

Also one should not forget that English is, itself, not some monolithic language, but rather one comprising an *extraordinary* number of varieties in dialect and accent. In the Colonial Period, for example, the English spoken reflected many regional dialects: London, Manchester, Birmingham, Liverpool, and so on. The English spoken also represented class-based accents such as Cockney, Scouse, and "King's English," as well as Pidgin.

Then, of course, came the different national varieties of English from countries within the British Isles: Scottish, Irish, and Welsh. Finally, one does well to remember too, that the impulse to eliminate all other languages but "one's own" stems from a segregated, monocultural mindset. To be more emphatic, it represents a nativist fear about being overrun by foreigners. This denial of difference, coupled with Eurocentrism, is what is behind asserting that "To be truly American, one must speak English *only*."

By contrast, *to practice multiculturalism is to embrace multilinguality.* Clearly, to be multilingual is valuable both personally and professionally. (Particularly if your company's clientele includes non-English speakers.) But presently bilingual education holds a very low priority for most Americans (in fact, the virtual elimination of bilingual education in California points to a growing *anti*-multilingual trend). Add to this the fact that about half of the states have already passed "English-only" laws (with national legislation coming up on the agenda of Congress soon). So when I say to practice multiculturalism is to embrace multilinguality, I do *not* mean we all must, by law, become bilingual or trilingual. (Though *all* of the industrialized countries, *except the United States*, are indeed *already* multilingual!) What it does mean is that one begins incorporating the "English-*plus*" philosophy. This idea states that "English" is in no threat of being undermined or lost in any way. (Of course it is of benefit for *everyone* to speak English! Of course English is, in fact, used as a "world currency.") We have no problem with English; its prevalence is actually its first "plus."

The second "plus," however, is that we enrich our experience by being opened to, and participating in, all facets of multilinguality. For instance, we can demonstrate a new level of respect and caring for others simply by pronouncing a person's name in a non-anglicized way. In short, attempting to learn friendship greetings, little sayings, or again, an individual's name, by pronouncing them as they sound in their *original language*. And here the multicultural honoring does *not* depend on precision or accuracy of pronunciation, so much as it does on the sincere gesture itself. (In short, people appreciate an honest attempt.)

In a workplace, inviting multilinguality to flourish enhances the self-esteem of co-cultural groups, who no longer feel embarrassed to share ideas, at times, in "their own languages." Posters on the wall, inspirational sayings, and the like reflecting the languages of the company's own diverse workforce can enliven the setting and conveys appreciation of co-cultures.

Viewing customer service from a cross-cultural perspective is a third strategy applicable to the workplace. Whether on the phone, at the counter, or in the field, companies need to adopt and explore better ways to communicate across the cultural divide. We have just mentioned one such strategy that can improve customer service—multilinguality. A company benefits by taking the time to translate key information, policies, and mission statements into the languages spoken by its workers and clientele. Also, committing resources in order to provide on-going professional diversity training to its staff helps ensure a long-term healthy relationship with its customers. More and more, it is to a company's advantage to view its mission from a multicultural philosophy.

Two of the strategies previously offered in the Mental Health Care section may also be applicable to the general workplace: *Reflect the co-cultures you serve in the design and décor of your physical setting* and *Weave interfaith dimensions*.

The first strategy is self-explanatory, but the second needs some elaboration. Say you intend to hold important strategy sessions on Friday afternoons. Attendance is crucial. Given the complex issues under discussion, the meetings might easily continue into the early evening.

This would not be unusual, but perhaps it never occurred to anyone that starting at sundown, *on every Friday*, is when the "Sabbath day" begins. And not only do Jewish people observe the Sabbath (where *no work* whatsoever is allowed), but many Christians do too (i.e., the denomination of Seventh-Day Adventists). Scheduling other office events, without consulting religious calendars, can also bring about division, rather than build unity.

Certainly most of us expect to have time off work on New Year's Day, but if you are Chinese American or Vietnamese American, January 24 is New Year's Day (not to mention that January 1 is also Independence Day for the Sudan and Haiti, and Liberation Day in Cuba).

A related aspect of interfaith sensitivity involves dietary laws of different religions. A Muslim, for instance, is prohibited from eating pork or drinking alcoholic beverages. So, if a Muslim co-worker tells his supervisor, "I can't attend the office party, or luncheon, because of the food and alcohol," the supervisor may simply say, "I understand, but just go and don't drink, and I'm sure there's some food there that's okay for you to eat." Here the supervisor is unaware that for some Muslims even attending a gathering that serves pork or alcohol is not permissible.

Add to this illustration the fact that during the month of Ramadan Muslims must fast from the break of dawn to the end of the day at sunset (not even drinking water). Therefore, various office events could definitely interfere with their religious practice (or simply make them feel embarrassed, unseen, or ostracized). Furthermore, it is to be remembered that the Islamic Calendar is purely lunar. This means that important Muslim festivals, while always falling in the same lunar month, can actually occur in different seasons (e.g., the hajji and Ramadan's fasting can take place in the summer as well as the winter).

Finally, an overall strategy for the workplace is *to develop the individual's potential, not just produce a product*. In some ways, this strategy is linked to an earlier statement regarding Mental Health Care—that is, that "the best pathway to improve mediation is at the educational and training level." Here, in all kinds of organizations and businesses, a new kind of training can be explored—multicultural leadership training. The business world and private-sector enterprises are indeed incorporating models that extend far beyond those of the status quo. A more holistic approach is being pursued, which opens the workplace to different communication styles and ensures that a company's goals are best met by enhancing the individual's overall well-being.

One interesting aspect of this new thinking is realizing that the physical fitness of the individual is important. Some companies are now inviting their workers to work out in sponsored athletic club programs (or even building in-house facilities for their key personnel). This concept reflects new cultural ideas (i.e., going outside traditional views of culture as well as ideas involving ethnicity).

More to the point, however, is the emerging idea that leadership in a company must itself be infused with cross-cultural understanding in order to maximize its effectiveness. The marketplace is increasingly multicultural, and the workplace must reflect an awareness and sensitivity to that reality.

The Classroom, Diversity, and You

I want you to imagine the following scene: It's the first day of class; you've had the usual frustrations (i.e., fighting traffic jams, the chaos of parking, and then double-checking if you've got the right room numbers in the class schedule, etc.). Finally, you arrive in the correct classroom and you wait, anxiously, for the professor to arrive. She sweeps into the room and almost immediately launches into the following speech:

> "This will be *the most important* course you will *ever* take in college! Unfortunately, we don't have an adequate textbook for it, there's no helpful grammar of practice or insightful vocabulary for the subject, and any definitions of terms we will use are *hopelessly confusing* and contradictory. Now, let's officially begin and, remember, there will be a mid-term exam in eight weeks."

Now, wouldn't you be just a little bit floored and suspicious about the nature and purpose of such a course? I mean, how can anyone expect clear thinking to emerge from such a blurry situation? Well, in many ways this is an all-too-accurate description of

where most of us are in regards to understanding of so-called race relations. For example, the debates are still raging over what the "M" word even means (that's "M" for "multicultural"). Some people think it means *anti*-white, *anti*-European, *anti*-male, even *anti*-American. Some argue that the term is, in itself, divisive. Others extol the same term as representing a pathway toward true democracy or as a philosophy of social justice and as a necessary mission of education.

Pretty bizarre, isn't it? Quite a range of meanings and associations. This essay's purpose, however, is not to end this debate over the "M" word. Rather, we'll keep our goal more practical and personal. Let's review what I mean when I use the term: *Multicultural education is teaching and learning about the equal human worth of distinctive groups of people.*

Now, let me state, in a clear voice, that multiculturalism then, is decidedly *not* anti-white, or anti-male, or anti-European. From my perspective, it is simply *pro-human*. (And that means that the struggle for compassion and appreciating difference is *shared* by everyone and goes *beyond* national or cultural boundaries.) The word *multicultural*, however, is a relatively new term, so it's instructive to review some pernicious older terms. Consequently, I will review some of the current approaches to diversity in education and reveal how older terminology continues to keep our vision distorted. Therefore, to create more effective classroom dialogues on diversity, we will focus on the following strategies: (1) confront the current langwedge/slanguage problems of race, (2) reveal the incorrectness of political correctness, (3) institute a style of cultural improvisation rather than one of enculturation, (4) include intraethnic conflict, not just interethnic conflict, and (5) move beyond the idea of tolerance into "acceptance."

The Langwedge/Slanguage Problem. "Langwedge" is when words create a split between truth and falsity. This forcing apart, or *wedge* between understanding and distortion, may be found in the present state of terms we use on race. The "slanguage" issue refers to the imprecise, but popular, use of terms describing ethnic cultures as well as in-groups, labels, phrases of cultural identity, and so on.[28]

To begin with, the racial categories we typically use in America actually date to Scandinavia in the 18th century. In that year, a Swedish botanist named

Carolus Linnaeus published the tenth edition of his foundational work *The System of Nature*. In that work Linneaus declared that while humanity is indeed a "single species" it can, nonetheless, still be divided into four distinct "varieties" (yes, the word "variety" would soon turn into the term "race"). According to Linneaus these four varieties of people represented the "four quarters of the globe" and the skin color of the people living there. This race/color scheme will undoubtedly look very familiar:

- *European* (white skin)
- *American Indian* (red skin)
- *Asian* (yellow skin)
- *African* (black skin)

The only problem, then and now, is that *Linneaus was wrong!* After all, under any reasonable standard of observation, we must conclude that there are, in fact, *no* humans whose skin is naturally "red." (Certainly, extreme radiation exposure or skin burns can artificially turn skin red, but no one is born with such a hue.)

Second, there are *no* people on earth whose skin is naturally "yellow" either. Yet, even today, people still say "the yellow man" to refer to individuals from Asian cultures. But here's one that may surprise you even more. There are indeed *no* people on earth whose skin is naturally "white"! If you apply the color standard say of white paint or white-out, then even the lightest, fairest skin is *not* "white." The only skin colors that at all reflect hues of real skin on earth are shades of "black," but even such color designations as "black" in the world today are hardly limited to cultures of Africa. One could be called "black" and yet be culturally British, Brazilian, East Indian, American, Persian, or Egyptian. Also, as is the case with "black," "white" is a vague term that does *not* indicate a specific culture, ethnicity, or nationality. (You could have "white" skin, blue eyes, and blonde hair and consider yourself to be full-blood Mexican.)

So, if all of these terms are so inaccurate, why then do we continue to use them? Doesn't it seem ridiculous to you that in the so-called new millennium, we are still stuck using terms created in the late 1700s? But the issue is far more serious than merely distorted designations of color. Sadly, Linnaeus also offered us concise, racist generalities to accompany his color scheme. That these lies *persist* is the real problem. Such lies undergird many of the cross-cultural conflicts we experience in everyday life and certainly in the classroom. Here are Linneaus' generalizations:

- *European*: "courageous, hopeful, amorous, inventive and gentle"
- *American Indian*: "irascible temper, obstinate, ruled by custom and superstition"
- *Asian*: "gloomy, severe, haughty and miserly"
- *African*: "dull, sluggish, indolent, and foolish"[29]

So, "objectively" speaking, does any group appear "superior" to the others? Also, according to Linneaus, does any "color" appear to be preferable to the others? A few years later, in 1775, the German natural history scholar Johann Friedrich Blumenbach reaffirmed the "correctness" of Linneaus's four racial categories. In his book *On the Natural Varieties of Mankind*, Blumenbach, however, reinforced Linneaus with the "white supremacist" idea that one group indeed rightfully stands out: "The first, largest, and most important is the whole of *Europe*."[30] Now, a simple look at a world map refutes his contention. The running order, in terms of size, is actually Africa, Asia, America, *then* Europe. The issue of importance is, of course, much more of a subjective assessment.

But Blumenbach also chose to change some of Linnaeus's original terms:

- "White" Europeans became "Caucasian"
- "Asians" became "Mongolian"
- A new category of race was introduced referring to peoples from the "islands of the South Ocean." He called them "Malay"; we call them "Pacific Islanders."

According to Blumenbach, Caucasian "nations are white in colour and compared to the rest, beautiful in form." Just as in Linnaeus's earlier description, "white" is placed *above* all other colors. Blumenbach's reason for choosing the term "Caucasian" also reflects his bias: "I have taken the name from Mount Caucasus because it produces the most beautiful race of men, I mean the Georgian."[31] Now, I'm sure that when people today use the term "Caucasian," they are *not* thinking of the former Soviet Republic of Georgia! Nor are they usually aware that "Caucasians" are actually people from a country bordered by Russia, Azerbaijan, Armenia, Turkey, and the Black Sea.

Yet in U.S. classrooms some 250 years *after* Linneaus and Blumenbach, these myths of race persist. We still use the *same* "race/color" scheme that they devised. We still use their flawed and inaccurate terminology. Fortunately, the ideas of race produced from those early pseudo-sciences have been summarily dismissed by current science. In part thanks to the Human Genome Project begun in 1990, we have conclusive empirical evidence that dismantles "race":

1. "Race has *no* genetic or scientific basis."
2. "Not only *do all people have the same set of genes*, but all groups of people also share the major variants of those genes."
3. "Every group overlaps genetically with every other."[32]

In summary, "all human beings are incredibly similar genetically," therefore, it is simply inaccurate to attribute "group behavioral differences to biology rather than culture."[33] But, contrast the negative stereotypes put forth by Linneaus in 1758 with those reported in 1998 from the study, *Intergroup Relations in the United States: Research Perspectives*: "Overall, blacks are viewed the most negatively . . . not ambitious, dishonest, unpatriotic, aggressive, and insular."[34] It is tragic how such stereotypes still stand against all the assaults from "the facts" (and again, such stereotypes are being perpetuated nearly 250 years *after* Linneaus).

The *slanguage* problem in a classroom is when we casually use terms that devalue, undermine, marginalize, or even mock co-cultural groups. Sometimes these words are ethnic "in-house" terms, such as "Gabacho" (for European Americans) or "Buddha Head" (for Asian Americans) or "Camel Jockey" (for Arab Americans). Such racial slurs, however, are not so much the problem as words that we use that we don't even consider as being insensitive. (The obvious racist terms above are clearly *not* appropriate, and students in a classroom, as well as in society at large, are duly outraged when such inflammatory and ugly words are expressed.)

Following are three of the well-used terms that are overlooked. I hope you will consider possibly *not* using them in the future (or at least contemplating their implications or choosing to educate others on their deeper meaning).

1. *Foreign/Foreigner.* "Belonging to others, *not* one's own; dissimilar, irrelevant, inappropriate, unfamiliar, a stranger, an outsider; at a distance from home, *not* domestic."[35] When you take in the extended definition of the word *foreign*, you realize just how unhelpful and inaccurate it is, for instance, to refer to movies not produced in the United States as "foreign films." Or, for that matter, to call any language other than English, a "foreign language." The truth is that there is nothing foreign about the languages or the people who speak German, Italian, Farsi, Arabic, Khmer, Tagalog, English, and so on. All the world's people and languages are valuable and "belong." As for students studying in the United States from another country, they are better referred to as "international students" (and films other than "American made" are simply "international films," *not* "foreign").

2. *Alien.* "Foreign, *not* of one's own; of a repugnant nature, adverse, opposed to; Belonging to another place—an extraterrestrial, not human."[36] There is simply no good reason to ever refer to *any* human being as "alien" (no matter their country of origin or their employment status). It is even more absurd to concoct the phrase "*illegal* alien" (that is, unless you are indeed referring to an extraterrestrial being marauding the universe "without papers").

3. *Minority.* "The condition of being smaller, inferior, or subordinate; The state of being *minor*."[37] You would never think of going up to someone and saying: "Hello, good to meet you. I hear you are one of those *diminished* people." Yet, you are saying as much when you refer to someone as a "minority." The term claims to refer to numbers, but in L.A. where Latinos form a numerical majority, Latinos are *still* called "minority–majorities." The good news is that everyone, no matter his or her ethnic background, is already major (therefore, *no* group of people should be considered "minor").

The Incorrectness of Political Correctness. Really, the last thing we need in the classroom is censorship of free speech. And no matter what the good intentions behind so-called political correctness are, the end result is just that, a stifling of expression, a muzzling of opinion, and the undermining of the First

Amendment. The real genius of our constitutional right to free speech is that even *hate speech is protected*! Yes, repellent speech, insensitive language, crude or rude terminology should *not* be censored (whether under the heading of political correctness or otherwise). The best and most democratic response to hate speech is *more speech*. That is, we should seek to find out *why* someone uses a term. We are free to challenge its appropriateness or question its intention, but we need *not* close down discussion for reasons of political correctness.

Dialogues in diversity, particularly in the classroom, must be built on honesty and authentic expression. Permission to say what you really feel is crucial. As for not saying the truth because you're afraid others will be hurt, I have two things to say. First, the real hurt we carry *precedes* our entering into a classroom. If someone's comment in class triggers our pain, then let's discuss *both* the source of the suffering and why the comment triggered the hurt (rather than instantly and negatively judging the comment or the person who made the comment).

The following is, for me, one of the most helpful and concise strategies for creating solutions to our race relations problem. It was asked of Brother Minister Malcolm X:

Q: What is your aim?

A: The only way the [race relations] problem can be solved—First, the White man and the Black man have to be able to sit down at the *same* table. The White man has to *feel free* to speak his mind without hurting the feelings of that Negro. And the so-called Negro has to *feel free* to speak his mind without hurting the feelings of the White man. Then, they can bring the issues that are *under* the rug out *on top* of the table, and take an intelligent approach to get the problem solved.

Now, after hearing such an insightful response, you'd think the journalist would comment on its substance. Sadly, however, the journalist remained mired in a stereotype of Malcolm X (one that many *still* hold today). That is, Malcolm X as the "angry black man" intent on "violence against whites." So instead of remarking on the deep vision offered, we hear instead:

Q: Do you consider yourself *militant*?

A: (Big smile) I consider myself *Malcolm*.[38]

Cultural Improvisation: Making New Music. Dr. Mary Catherine Bateson is an extraordinary individual whose life role models multiculturalism. Allow me to quote her from a personal conversation about culture we shared not too long ago:

> Culture is the way people invent their forms of humanness. Multiculturalism, then, provides us an opportunity to learn by opening up a library. A library not of books, but *versions of humanness*. Life is not so much "enculturation" as it is "improvisation." We must work together to sustain *joint performances* across our cultural differences—to appreciate diverse approaches to the canvas of human experience.[39]

Dr. Bateson offers us a fresh and dynamic strategy, one that can foster more effective cross-cultural communication, namely "cultural improvisation." An apt illustration can be seen in a jazz group. With improvisational jazz players, the music is *not* set in advance. That means there is no one version to perform, rather *every* outing produces a new rendition. This is possible because each player brings an *original voice* to the occasion. Yet, for the group to produce a unified and compelling sound, each player must also *listen intently* to what the other band members are producing. In this way, individual or solo efforts become *blended*, with the added ability to support, and even augment, the other players' contributions.

A supreme example, available in your local music stores, is the jazz album *Some Kind of Blue*. This performance marks, both literally and metaphorically, a "milestone" (having been done by none other than Miles Davis).[40] This masterwork emerged from a jazz session that still sets the standard for musical improvisation. Now, what Dr. Bateson suggests is for us to create "joint performances across our cultural difference," with all the openness and emotional risk taking of *Some Kind of Blue*.

The old model of enculturation runs the risk of assuming that a simple checklist of cultural traits and values exists. We might, for example, be taught that Asians are collectivist, not individualist like Americans and Europeans. But by using cultural improvisation, we forego any such lists and realize that *this* Asian person next to me is able to express his own complex cultural identity freely (and it may well *not* conform to any of my preset expectations). Be open to new music!

Airing Our Families' Dirty Laundry: Intraethnic Conflict. One of the reasons we stay stuck in an "us" versus "them" mindset is because co-cultural conflict is almost always presented as an interethnic issue. But the truth is that, in many cases, much of the problem may actually stem from intraethnic tensions. In other words, cross-cultural conflict is not located exclusively between different groups, but is quite often experienced within one's own group itself.

Now, believe me, I know just how uncomfortable it is to admit this out loud. It feels as if you are betraying yourself or putting down your own group. Yet, if we are honest with ourselves, and if we share the hurt that comes from intolerance and racism *within* our own families and culture, then something positive and powerful can occur. That is, people *not* of our cultural background will be able to relate. We *all* need to realize that the struggle for acceptance is a *universal one.* Moreover, we need to acknowledge how hard it is for everyone to face conflicts within their own families and communities.

For example, white students too often become easy scapegoats for racism, especially in a classroom. Remember, *everyone* is responsible for racism, so it is *not* restricted to any one group. But relating racism from an intraethnic perspective can be curative in this regard. If an African American student honestly shares how light-skinned blacks are treated differently from dark-skinned blacks *inside* the African American community, then an important lesson is learned. Issues of racial prejudice based on color are not a white man's issue, but can be found *throughout* co-cultures in America. As was stated early on, racism is *not* a blame or a shame game. Together we construct it, and to effectively deconstruct it, we also need to act together.

Teaching Transcendence, Not Tolerance. "Teaching Tolerance" is a nationwide project designed, implemented, and distributed by the Southern Poverty Law Center from its headquarters in Montgomery, Alabama. First, let me emphatically state that I find the "Teaching Tolerance" project to be an invaluable contribution to the health of the nation, one committed to guaranteeing civil rights for *all* in America, and one that fosters both healing and reconciliation on issues of race. I count myself as a stalwart supporter of their "National Campaign for

Tolerance" and actively promote the classroom use of their many films and materials, including "A Time For Justice: America's Civil Rights Movement" (1992), "The Shadow of Hate: A History of Intolerance in America" (1995), and "A Place At The Table: Struggles for Equality in America" (2000).[41] Moreover, one of the efforts I lead on campus, the "Students Talk About Race" (STAR) project, recently received an endorsement stating, in part, that STAR "would make an excellent complement to *Teaching Tolerance.*"[42] So, clearly, I am *not,* in any way, being negative regarding this multifaceted program called "Teaching Tolerance."

But I am *definitely* concerned about the implications of the term *tolerance,* not only in the phrase "Teaching Tolerance," but also in its use for other high-profile and ambitious efforts (e.g., "The Museum of Tolerance" in Los Angeles).[43] What concerns me is this:

- To "tolerate" someone is simply "to put up with" them.
- To be "tolerant" is to be "disposed to bear with" someone you dislike (or even hate).
- Having "tolerance" is "the practice or capacity for enduring or sustaining pain."[44]

In a world filled with *in*tolerance, a move toward tolerance is indeed a step forward, but it's a shaky step at best. After all, people are often tolerant only because laws *compel* them to be. Put another way, you could get into serious trouble or even go to jail for being intolerant. But remember, civil rights legislation often achieves compliance by its threat of reprisals, *not* because people have necessarily had a deep change of heart. So the idea of tolerance is, in my view, nothing but a temporary way station, or a rest stop, *not* the goal or destination.

I propose that instead of teaching tolerance, we teach "transcendence":

- To "transcend" is "to go beyond" or "get over the top of something."
- To be "transcendent" is to rise "above ordinary" experience.
- Practicing "transcendence" is "the action of surmounting or rising above ordinary limits."[45]

The goal of diversity initiatives, from this perspective, is to open up a pathway leading us *beyond* mere tolerance into three transcendent levels: *understanding*, *acceptance*, and, ultimately, *celebration*. You might visualize the destination in a spectrum of five steps: intolerance, tolerance, understanding, acceptance, and celebration.

1. *Intolerance* is at the far end of our spectrum or continuum. It entails an *active* hostility toward people who are different in any way. Examples of intolerance include KKK cross burnings or the religious persecution of Jews. (Intolerance can be a positive act when it is focused *against* injustice. You could be intolerant of racism, for instance.)
2. *Tolerance* might be placed on the spectrum just short of midway. Tolerance can be understood negatively and positively. Negatively, tolerance suggests that the persons being tolerated have something wrong with them that must be *endured*. Why should I be tolerated and not accepted? But usually tolerance is understood positively and entails a willingness to coexist with others without hostility and with a measure of patience. In this sense, as stated earlier, tolerance is a real step forward. One of the best historic examples is the emergence of religious tolerance. Throughout the centuries, tolerance of religious diversity was often characterized by warfare between different religions and between sects of the same religion. In the eighteenth century, the U.S. Constitution made religious tolerance a pillar of its democratic freedoms.
3. *Understanding* is about midway on our spectrum. Understanding entails acquiring information that satisfactorily explains other people's way of life to us. This knowledge can help defuse anxiety we might *otherwise* have about other groups. An example of understanding occurs when we learn that in certain Asian cultures (such as Korean), direct eye contact is considered disrespectful. Such understanding permits us to become more comfortable in their presence when otherwise we might interpret this behavior as snobbery or inattention.
4. *Acceptance* is about three-quarters of the way toward our goal of celebration. Acceptance entails a sense of resolve about the reality of diversity that is a permanent feature of American life. It is characterized by empathy, nonjudgment, and open-mindedness. An example of acceptance is positive interethnic interaction of any kind, from sharing a meal to marriage.
5. *Celebration* comes in the realization that people's uniqueness makes life interesting. Celebration is typified by gladness about that fact. Contemporary art often mirrors this ideal, whether in films, plays, or music, such as world beat music, which combines many different cultural traditions.

Now we do well to remember that *all of us* move both forward and backward on this continuum. In fact, we may display facets of *several* of these steps in a single day. But, with renewed commitment and caring, our progress becomes more steady and headed in the right direction. As far as co-cultural conflict goes, it is realistic to expect that we will continue to manage permanent tensions between ourselves and other cultural groups. This management is not a negative situation, but rather a lifelong struggle enlarging our capacity for compassion and hope.

EPILOGUE

Let me end with a beginning, by invoking renewal for both us and the nation at large. These words come from the Inaugural Poem "On the Pulse of Morning" by Maya Angelou:

> Lift up your faces, you have a piercing need
> For this bright morning dawning for you.
> History, despite its wrenching pain,
> Cannot be unlived, but if faced
> With courage, need not be lived again
> Lift up your eyes
> Upon this day breaking for you
> Give birth again
> To the dream[46]

APPENDIX: QUICK-GLANCE GUIDE

I. **Strategies that Establish a Firm Foundation for Mediating Co-Cultural Conflict**
   A. Our willingness to be vulnerable and authentic
   B. Crisscrossing our cultural boundaries
   C. Practicing compassion

Outcomes: Diffuses defensiveness, creates positive common ground for all participants. Sets up an honest, open channel for communication.

II. Strategies for Police/Community Relations

A. Publicly airing our bias

B. Establishing empathy for the dangers inherent in police work

C. Seeking understanding, not advocacy

Outcomes: A clearing up of stereotypes held by both the community for police and vice versa. A respect for challenges faced by police officers. A respect for the hurts and concerns of the community.

III. Strategies for Mental Health Services

A. Putting "whiteness" on the table

B. Reflecting the co-cultures served in the design and décor of your physical setting

C. Weaving co-cultural folk medicine practices into psychotherapy

D. Weaving interfaith dimensions into psychotherapy

E. Neutralizing impressions based on exteriors: clothes, nonverbal behavior, and "street" styles

Outcomes: Creates a context of shared power and shared responsibility. Dispels stereotypes of "whiteness." Reassures the client by validating his or her cultural background. Establishes a continuity for the client by linking his or her traditions to current therapies.

IV. Strategies for the Workplace

A. Making "equity" a priority

B. Establishing an "English-plus" environment

C. Viewing customer service cross-culturally

D. Developing each worker's potential

Outcomes: Builds morale by giving all workers a fair opportunity to succeed. Reduces tension and stress by validating workers' "home" language. Increases a company's customer base by respecting and reaching out to different cultures. Increases workers' satisfaction by providing them with professional and personal growth opportunities.

V. Strategies for the Classroom

A. Confronting the "langwedge/slanguage" problem of race

B. Revealing the incorrectness of political correctness

C. Expressing intraethnic conflicts

D. Teaching trancendence

Outcome: Establishes an accurate and current foundation for discussing diversity. Promotes inclusion by giving all students permission to share their experiences honestly. Creates common ground by making multiculturalism a shared responsibility. Gives students a long-term vision of the potentials of multiculturalism.

Endnotes

1. The "Preface" first appeared in print as the "Director's Column" in the *Multicultural News*, Volume 9, Issue 1, Spring 2001, pp. 1–3 (a publication of the Multicultural Center at California State University, Long Beach).

2. Gwendolyn Brooks won the Pulitzer Prize for Poetry in 1950 for her collection of poems entitled *Annie Allen.*

3. This academy, like the Pulitzer recipients, is made up of a rare and select group of artists.

4. This "spiritual" sense of connectedness that Gwendolyn exuded, to me, represents multiculturalism at its best. When I wrote to her expressing my gratitude for her performance, she took the time to write back. We create a true practice of compassion with such personal touches.

5. Our First Amendment right of "free speech" is crucial to democracy, but we must now enlarge this largely European idea with the power that comes from the "freedom of silence" (an idea that is highly valued in Asian and American Indian cultures).

6. "Nonviolence and Racial Justice," by Reverend Dr. Martin Luther King Jr. in *Christian Century*, 74 (February 6, 1957): 165–167. Reprinted in *A Testament of Hope: The Essential Writings and Speeches of Martin Luther King Jr.* (Harper San Francisco, 1991), pp. 5–9. The quote appears on p. 8.

7. "A Christmas Sermon on Peace," delivered by the Reverend Dr. Martin Luther King Jr. at Ebenezer Baptist Church on Christmas Eve, 1967. First published in *The Trumpet of Conscience* (New York: Harper and Row, 1967), pp. 67–78. Reprinted in *Testament*, pp. 253–258. The quote appears on p. 253.

8. "The Ethical Demands for Integration," a speech originally delivered by the Reverend Dr. Martin Luther King Jr. in Nashville, Tennessee, on December 27, 1962, before a church conference. Reprinted in *Testament*, pp. 117–125. The quote appears on p. 118.

9. "The Ethical Demands for Integration," in *Testament*, p. 118.

10. "The Ethical Demands for Integration," in *Testament*, p. 118.

11. There are approximately 50,000 Cambodians living in Long Beach, California, representing the single largest concentration of Cambodians anywhere in the United States.

12. "I am not afraid of the words 'crisis' and 'tension.' I deeply oppose violence, but *constructive crisis* and tension are necessary for growth." These words come from the Reverend Dr. Martin Luther King Jr., spoken during an extensive interview appearing in *Playboy* (January 1965): 117. Reprinted in *Testament*, pp. 340–377. The quote appears on p. 284.

13. The phrase "dwell in possibility" comes from a poem by Emily Dickinson, which reads in part:

I dwell in Possibility
A fairer House than Prose—
More numerous of Windows—
Superior—for Doors—

The Poems of Emily Dickinson: Variorum Edition, Volume I, edited by R. W. Franklin (Cambridge: The Belknap Press of Harvard University Press, 1998) Poem #466, p. 483–484.

14. "the mother," Gwendolyn Brooks in *Blacks* (Chicago: The David Company, 1987), p. 21.

15. The first to evaluate the manuscript of *A Street in Bronzeville* was Richard Wright, who "took exception to only one poem, 'the mother'" in *Gwendolyn Brooks: Poetry & The Heroic Voice*, D. H. Melhem (The University Press of Kentucky, 1987), p. 16.

16. In Buddhism this transcendence of dualism is called "the state of no-birth . . . the getting rid of the idea that things are caused, the removal of the dualism of imagined and imaging . . ." (see *Lankavatara Sutra* 78). Also, for "the freedom from dualism," see Holy Teaching of *Vimalakirtu*. 5. In Taoism a "state in which 'this' and 'that' no longer find their opposites is called the Hinge of the Way" (see *Chuang Tzu* 2).

17. *Blacks*, p. 21.

18. The revisionist term of "rebellion" over "riot" is becoming increasingly more common as time passes. See *Why L.A. Happened: Implications of the '92 Los Angeles Rebellion*, edited by Haki R. Madhubuti (Chicago: Third World Press, 1993).

19. "Nonviolence and Racial Justice" in *Testament*, p. 7.

20. From a speech given by Edgar F. Beckham, Education and Culture Program Director for the Ford Foundation. The speech was entitled "Cultural Transactions and the Changing Requirements for Educational Quality," presented at the 18th Annual Meeting of the Association of American Colleges, New York, January 11, 1992.

21. From a speech delivered June 4, 1957, by the Reverend Dr. Martin Luther King Jr., titled "The Power of Nonviolence." *Intercollegian* (May 1958): 8. Reprinted in *Testament*, pp. 12–15. The quote appears on pp. 14–15.

22. This conference is indicative of the need for Mental Health professionals nationwide to receive diversity training.

23. I am indebted to Derald Wing Sue and David Sue, authors of *Counseling the Culturally Different: Theory and Practice*, 3rd ed. (New York: John Wiley & Sons, 1999).

24. The phrase "we never crossed the border, the border crossed us" is used by Latinos throughout the Southwest.

25. *Counseling the Culturally Different: Theory and Practice*, p. 6.

26. *Counseling the Culturally Different*, p. 6.

27. From a question-and-answer session conducted by Dr. Carlos Cortez at the "Ethical Leadership in a Diverse Society" conference, held at California State University, Long Beach, May 12, 2001.

28. The terms "langwedge" and "slanguage" come from James Joyce's *Finnegan's Wake*; "langwedge," FW 073.01, and "slanguage" FW 421.17.

29. *Systema Naturae, Caroli Linnaei: A Photographic Facsimile of the First Volume of the Tenth Edition* (1758), (London: British Museum, 1958) pp. 20–23.

30. *On the Natural Varieties of Mankind*, Johann Friedrich Blumenbach, 1775.

31. *On the Natural Varieties of Mankind*.

32. "The Genetic Archaeology of Race," by Steve Olson, *The Atlantic Monthly* (April 2001) pp. 61–80.

33. "The Genetic Archaeology of Race," p. 69.

34. *Intergroup Relations in the United States: Research Perspectives*, edited by Wayne Winborne and Renae Cohen (New York: The National Conference for Community and Justice). See in particular "Intergroup Relations in Contemporary America: An Overview of Survey Research" by Tom W. Smith, pp. 69–155. The quote appears on p. 78.

35. *The Compact Edition of the Oxford English Dictionary* (London: Oxford University Press, 1971), p. 105.

36. *OED*, Vol. I, p. 55.

37. *OED*, Vol I, p. 1805.

38. Transcribed from a sequence appearing in the documentary film *The Life and Death of Malcolm X* (Simitor Entertainment, 1992).

39. The conversation took place at the Western Speech Communication Association Annual Convention, on February 23, 1992, in Boise, Idaho.
40. This watermark of jazz was originally recorded in March and April of 1959. Today, it is generally considered to be perhaps the most influential and best-selling jazz record ever made.
41. All of these films are extraordinarily well made and come with a highly informative press kit. They are ideal for conducting dialogues on diversity in the classroom.
42. Mr. Dee's recommendation is proudly featured on the cover of the *STAR: Students Talk About Race* curriculum manual.
43. In a real sense, this is much more a museum of "intolerance" rather than "tolerance," although it seeks, of course, to engender the latter in all who visit. This museum, it should be noted, does provide a powerful experience (and is of enormous importance for the community at large in our quest for compassion and humanity).
44. *OED*, Vol. II, p. 3343.
45. *OED*, Vol. II, p. 3378.
46. *The Inaugural Poem: On the Pulse of Morning*, Maya Angelou (New York: Random House, 1993).

Concepts and Questions

1. Sauceda asserts that being vulnerable and authentic fosters co-cultural communication. Do you agree? How difficult do you believe it is to be genuinely vulnerable and authentic?
2. What does Sauceda mean by dissolving defensiveness? Select a situation in your own life that involves co-cultural contact. How easy is it for you to dissolve your defensiveness?
3. What is entailed in crisscrossing cultural boundaries? How might this process result in experiences that will enrich co-cultural contact?
4. How does compassion function as a strategy for improving co-cultural communication? What steps must you take to become a more compassionate intercultural communicator?
5. Do you believe that it is practical to expect people to admit their suspicions and biases when engaged in co-cultural communication? How do you believe that members of other co-cultures would respond to your attempts to admit any suspicions and biases?
6. Although Sauceda discussed empathy in terms of police/community relationships, how might the concept be applied to any aspect of co-cultural communication? What is asked of you to be an empathetic participant in co-cultural communication?
7. How did you react to Sauceda's use of the term *maladjusted* in discussing the concepts of segregation, discrimination, and mob rule? Do you agree with him?
8. How easy is it for you to neutralize your impressions of others based on exterior factors such as nonverbal behavior and "street" styles?
9. How does Sauceda distinguish between equal treatment and equity? Do you agree with his position that equality involves only one standard and does not reflect the diversity of co-cultures?
10. In what ways does the use of language (i.e., *langwedge/slanguage*) affect co-cultural communication?
11. Sauceda proposes teaching transcendence instead of tolerance. Do you agree with him that this is a vital goal? How might this concept be advanced in the school classroom?

Sojourner Adaptation

POLLY A. BEGLEY

I am not an Athenian or a Greek,
but a citizen of the world.

SOCRATES

What does it mean to be a global citizen when world economic markets change by the minutes or seconds, rebels plot in online chat rooms to overthrow oppressive governmental regimes, and borders on a map mean nothing as deadly "greenhouse" gasses and diseases permeate the planet? Economic, political, environmental, and cultural interdependence have made humanity aware that no one nation can meet the challenges of the current global frontier alone.

Former Citicorp Chairman, Walter Wriston, described globalization as a world that is "tied together in a single electronic market moving at the speed of light" (A.T. Kearney Inc., 2001, p. 58). The economic statistics are staggering as we witness 1.5 trillion U.S. dollars moving around the world daily. Specifically, advanced technology allows bonds and equities to flow across U.S. borders at a rate 54 times faster than in 1970, 55 times faster in Japan, and 60 times faster in Germany.

Technology is also changing the landscape of global politics. Literally thousands of Internet sites have been created to disseminate information for "Free Tibet" and "Free Burma" campaigns. Nobel Peace Prize winner Aung San Suu Kyi was under house arrest in Burma, but everyone still had access to her letters and speeches on the Web. The Zapatista National Liberation Army fighting government oppression in southern Mexico shouted "Ya Basta!" (Enough is enough!) across the world through such Internet sites as "Zapatistas in Cyberspace" (2001).

The United Nations (UN) climate summit at The Hague in 2000 failed to produce an accord to decrease greenhouse gas emissions. The facts are disturbing, as scientists find more evidence of global warming and overall climate disruption caused by environmental pollution. "The United States, with its wasteful lifestyle, annually pours 5.4 tons of carbon dioxide per capita into the atmosphere—20 times what an African produces" (Radford, 2000, p. 9). Melting ice caps, droughts, and rising sea levels are just a few possible environmental disasters humanity can look forward to because of increasing global temperatures.

Diseases that know no boundaries also threaten the citizens of the planet. AIDS has caused 20 million deaths, and infection rates in some African countries have risen to more than 35% of the adult population (Singer, 2000, p. 50). Fidler notes the importance of "disease diplomacy" as people, "spread shigella and malaria while fleeing across borders to business travelers and vacationers who carry pathogenic microbes on intercontinental flights" (2001, p. 80). The global spread of infectious diseases has made communication across borders a necessity for human survival.

Global instability stems from clashes between cultures as humankind creates catastrophes that are far worse than natural disasters. Human beings have to cope with living in harmony on a planet with a volatile international economy, too many people arguing over shrinking resources, mounting environmental contamination, and epidemics without borders. International travelers and tourists represent "almost 3 million people daily—up from only one million per day in 1980" (A.T. Kearney Inc., 2001, p. 57). Global citizens must learn how to communicate effectively wherever they are in the world.

This article examines challenges and strategies for living, learning, and adapting in global communities. Specifically, this is a review of the changes or adaptations that occur when a sojourner crosses cultural boundaries. First, the terms *culture shock* and *adaptation* will be defined. Second, this review will focus on the challenges associated with adapting to another cultural environment, such as ethnocentrism, language barriers, disequilibrium, length of stay, and level of knowledge. Finally, previous preparation, certain personality characteristics, personal determination, and the amount of time spent communicating are presented as possible strategies for effective adaptation.

SOJOURNERS, CULTURE SHOCK, AND ADAPTATION

People who cross cultural boundaries are referred to as *sojourners*. This term includes immigrants, refugees, business executives, students, or tourists. People enter a cultural region with diverse experiences, backgrounds, knowledge, and goals, but every sojourner must adjust or adapt his or her communication for the particular cultural setting. The term *culture shock* was coined by Oberg (1960) and included a four-stage model of cultural adjustment. These stages referred to the progression of experiences throughout intercultural interactions. Culture shock occurs in the second stage and is characterized by hostility and stereotypes. Although it is generally accepted that individuals experience shocks or stress as they learn to communicate with people of another culture, the term *shock* had a negative connotation. Researchers began to utilize other terms that described the shocks, stress, rewards, and growth process of sojourners who work, travel, or live in another country.

Cross-cultural *adaptation* refers to how a sojourner chooses to cope with cultural changes. *Adaptation* is an umbrella term that encompasses culture shock, assimilation, adjustment, acculturation, integration, and coping. A sojourner's coping mechanism can include seeking out specific cultural knowledge, adopting a different style of communication, reserving judgment on unfamiliar cultural practices, or withdrawing from intercultural interactions (Witte, 1993). Adaptation is a complex and dynamic process that is an inevitable part of intercultural interactions. When a sojourner is faced with diverse cultural practices and habits, then his or her assumed cultural training and self-identity is questioned, reevaluated, and adapted for the cultural environment. For example, assertive and task-oriented communication is a positive attribute in the United States but may be considered rude or selfish in China. The process of learning new greetings, responses, or communication styles while maintaining a balanced cultural and personal identity is part of the adaptive challenges faced by a sojourner.

CHALLENGES

Challenges to sojourner adaptation include ethnocentrism, language barriers, disequilibrium, length of stay, and level of knowledge.

Ethnocentrism

A photographer uses a green or yellow filter to enhance the natural hues of a landscape. Similarly, humans have "cultural filters" that influence the ways in which they see the world around them. *Ethnocentrism* refers to a bias leading people to judge another culture's habits and practices as right or wrong, good or bad according to their own cultural attitudes, beliefs, and values. Patricia Nell Warren used another analogy to describe ethnocentric thinking. When researchers study, "the peoples of ancient times, they believe that they understand the 'circle' mind. But they underestimate that their thinking is square. So they translate everything through the square" (Krebs, 1999, p. 98). Americans are astonished that some people consume dogs or cats. Hindus in India are dismayed by societies who eat cows. Taiwanese favor jade talismans and are shocked to discover that some Americans carry a severed animal's foot in their pockets for good luck (e.g., rabbit's foot).

Likewise, expelling mucus on a public street corner in China is acceptable behavior, but the American practice of blowing the nose into a handkerchief, then saving it in the pocket would astound many Chinese. Islamic countries have been criticized for supposedly subordinating women (e.g., female veiling practices and segregation), but Turkey is a predominantly Muslim country where about half of all Turkish stockbrokers, doctors, lawyers, professors, and bankers are women. A young Turkish stockbroker, Esra Yoldas, jokes, "Maybe the abnormal situation is not here, but in Christian countries where stockbrokers are mostly male" (Pope, 1997, p. A8). Ethnocentric attitudes limit the mind, preventing people from seeing beyond perceptions of right and wrong when in fact there are countless appropriate ways to accomplish the same goal.

Sojourners must be willing to reserve judgment and to accept that different is not automatically negative when they encounter diverse customs and habits. People may choose to eat cows, dogs, cats, or no meat at all. The range of acceptable and unacceptable behavior and communication styles varies from culture to culture. Ethnocentric attitudes can become barriers to the development of international business deals, meaningful relationships, and intercultural understanding. A key to effective adaptation is for a sojourner to not allow his or her own cultural biases to influence communication with people from another culture.

Language Barriers

Learning to speak to someone in her or his native language is an indisputable part of the adaptation process. Previous research studies link language skills with adaptation effectiveness (DeVerthelyi, 1995). Long-term sojourners and immigrants in America who cannot speak English experience social isolation and are segregated "into fields that require less mastery of the English language and less interpersonal interaction" (Leong & Chou, 1994, p. 165). Many subtle nuances of life in a particular culture can be conveyed only through the unique words of the people living in the region. A friendly sojourner in northern Canada would be surprised when he or she cannot say "come to my place" in the Inuktitut language because Inuits never lived by themselves (Nolen, 2000, p. 37). Sojourners who do not take the time to learn and understand the words of others will experience more difficulty adapting their communication patterns to the environment.

Disequilibrium

Adaptation involves a choice of how or what to adapt to or change to fit into the host culture. An encounter with changing communication patterns, a new language, or ethnocentrism can be a stressful experience. "It is estimated that one in seven UK managers fail on international assignments and this figure is even higher for US managers, with an estimated failure rate of 25-40 percent" (Marx, 1999, p. xiii).

Sojourners are "at least temporarily, in a state of disequilibrium, which is manifested in many emotional 'lows' of uncertainty, confusion, and anxiety" (Kim, 1995, p. 177). The degree of anxiety depends on whether the person feels able to cope with a situation. A goal-oriented international manager

would feel frustrated when things do not run on a strict schedule at the factory. An ambitious new employee might experience anxiety when political undercurrents or previously established relationships prevent him or her from accomplishing a task. A sojourner would also have to relearn everyday jobs such as how to order a meat-free meal in Mexico City or how to turn on the phone in a Tokyo apartment. Learning proper ways to accept or reject requests, local greetings, and polite conversational behavior can be confusing. Our own cultural habits and practices are questioned and modified as we adapt and learn to interact effectively in a different context. The adaptation process is typically characterized by "ups" and "downs" or incidents of effective and ineffective communication as cultural learning advances.

Length of Stay

The length of time spent in a different culture influences the adaptation process. A person who plans a short-term sojourn acquires less specific cultural knowledge and practical interactive experience, and is less motivated to make drastic adaptive changes to fit into the dominant culture. Tourists on a two-week tour need to know an occasional phrase in the local language and only a few details about their destination. In contrast, individuals who seek long-term business relations, work, travel, or residence are motivated to make significant changes in their communicative styles. Longer sojourns are characterized by less "social difficulty" and increasingly effective adaptations (Ward & Kennedy, 1993). Shorter sojourns are characterized by more uncertainty, confusion, or mistakes concerning appropriate communication behavior and practices.

Level of Knowledge

Should I shake hands, bow, hug, or kiss when I meet someone? Should I show enthusiasm when I speak or control my facial expressions? What kinds of topics are appropriate for initial meetings? A sojourner needs to learn many cultural customs and norms before and during a sojourn. A person's level of general and specific cultural knowledge can contribute to the adaptation process. For example, a sojourner bargaining in the Middle East should understand when to start with a conservative quote (Bedouin style) or to begin with an outrageously high number (*suk*/market style). In China, a public altercation with witnesses is one way to preserve the reputation and respect of the concerned parties. Countless international marketing campaigns have failed because companies failed to understand local values and beliefs. Negotiations stall between leaders of nations because there is insufficient understanding of appropriate communication or differing interactive styles. Incorrect information, broad cultural generalizations, or stereotypes are also destructive and may lead to misunderstandings.

STRATEGIES

Possible strategies for effective adaptation include previous preparation, certain personality characteristics, personal determination, and the amount of time spent communicating.

Preparation

Previous examples show the importance of acquiring the appropriate knowledge before intercultural contact. Sojourners should never assume that their communicative behavior would be appropriate in every cultural environment. The culture-specific and culture-general are two commonly used approaches to understanding interactive customs and behavior. The culture-specific approach focuses on one or a limited number of cultures. A culture-general approach explores "cultural traits and behaviors that are common to all cultures" (Samovar & Porter, 1995, p. 277).

Communication competence across cultures can benefit from a more general approach. Milhouse (1996) argues that students learn from general discussions of cross-cultural differences and similarities, rather than unique cultural details. One must be aware that knowing when to bow or shake hands does not guarantee communicative competence, but understanding that greetings vary according to culture helps us speak with people from diverse backgrounds. The general approach provides students with a broader base of knowledge.

The general approach can also take the focus away from differences. An emphasis on teaching re-

gional differences perpetuates stereotypes and discourages people from realizing that each person is unique. A common focus during culture-specific intercultural training is the characteristics of the group, and individuality is ignored. It would be incorrect to assume that all Americans have blond hair, eat at McDonald's restaurants, wear jeans, and drink Coca-Cola. Every population is characterized by diversity, and generalizations can only represent certain tendencies (but not rules) within a group. Individuals are influenced by culture, as well as genetic makeup, personal experiences, and gender. The culture-general approach can teach us to reject false generalizations and to recognize the unique and exceptional characteristics of each person.

Language skills are crucial to learning and adapting to another culture. Too many people assume and fear that English has become too much of a world standard. For instance, the aboriginal languages of Canada have been reduced from 60 to 4 commonly spoken in the last century, and the Ministry of Culture has just begun several linguistic preservation projects (Nolen, 2000). Hope may be in the form of "millions of young men and women around the globe [who] have responded to the challenges of globalization by learning Japanese, German, Mandarin, Cantonese, Russian, and French" (Llosa, 2001, p. 70).

Classes, books, videotapes, or audiotapes are effective ways to study a new language; however, common words and slang terms may have to be learned in the country of origin. The common language and accent may differ slightly according to region. Taiwanese students study English for approximately 10 years, but they frequently admit that communication with speakers of English is difficult. The reason for this difficulty stems from the dichotomy between "textbook language" and the "everyday language" that contains inside references, slang, and other regional differences. The most successful communicators take every opportunity to learn new vocabulary, ask questions, and practice their new language skills. Sojourners also demonstrate an interest and appreciation for a culture by attempting to learn the language. For example, a well-timed response of "*Insha'allah*" (a common Arabic expression translated as: "If God wills it") can elicit applause, lower prices from merchants, or better business relations in Egypt.

Personality Characteristics

Personality characteristics such as openness and strength of personality are influential determinants of cross-cultural adaptation effectiveness. Openness, and the related concept of flexibility, refers to a willingness to suspend judgment regarding another group's communication habits or practices. This implies a flexible attitude toward change and diverse viewpoints. Openness and flexibility are the antithesis of ethnocentrism and are based on the assumption that there is more than one way to reach our goals. Sojourners must recognize that there is more than one path to truth or understanding. A person may choose to improve his or her life by hiring a *feng shui* (wind and water) expert to rearrange furniture or add elements of wood and water to achieve balance and harmony in the home. Another person buys a red convertible car and an expensive gold watch to improve his or her life. Both people chose different paths to reach the same goal, but only they can judge if their efforts were successful.

Personal Determination

Personal determination can stem from external factors or internal factors. *External factors* refer to the length of stay, the purpose of the visit, or the attitude of the local culture. These factors may or may not be under the control of the sojourner. Entry permits limit the amount of time for business or tourist purposes. Companies often decide the agenda for executives. In some cases, cultural differences are tolerated within a society, but in other countries the sojourner is pressured to adopt the melting pot ideology of cultural sameness. If the society exhibits high levels of conformity pressure, then visitors have little choice but to emulate communicative patterns to fit into that cultural group. A major disadvantage of the melting pot idea is that it does not allow people to "treasure their uniqueness, which, for many, evolves from ethnic, cultural or spiritual history" (Krebs, 1999, p. 16).

Internal factors include the ability to think across cultures and a value of multiculturalism. Anxiety or disequilibrium may cause sojourners to reduce stress by becoming overly critical of their surroundings and others, by attempting only monocultural solutions, or by withdrawing from the situation (e.g., locking themselves in a luxury hotel room or seeking out culturally similar people). The person who develops an ability to think across cultures meets "a complex foreign environment with an equally complex range of interpretations" (Marx, 1999, p. 61). This person does not withdraw when experiencing stress, but rather utilizes coping strategies to manage the situation and ultimately find alternative ways to communicate effectively. For example, international students who make friends with members of multiple cultural groups tend to develop a broader worldview and express higher levels of satisfaction with their exchange experiences. Multiculturalism is characterized by "understanding and accepting the values and perspectives of both [or multiple] cultures" (Marx, 1999, p. 68). Multiculturalism rejects the melting pot and isolation ideologies while embracing the idea that people do not have to choose between cultures. Finally, sojourners must understand that the adaptation process is not a predictable or linear experience. A sojourner may experience stressful conditions prompting her or him to withdraw from cross-cultural contact one day, and then the next day is able to devise more effective ways to interact with the local population.

Amount of Time Spent Communicating

The most important factor predicting adaptation is the frequency of host communication participation. The proverb "practice makes perfect" is never truer for the sojourner. Although insight and knowledge can be gained through prior intercultural study, additional practical wisdom is attained through everyday conversations with people from other cultures. Practical interactions or extroversion is associated with an increase in "opportunities for cultural learning" (Ward & Kennedy, 1993, p. 240). The implication is that information pertaining to cultural communicative rules, nonverbal cues, and common customs can be learned and used during communication. Practical communicative experiences contribute to overall understanding and effective adaptations.

Although there is no substitute for face-to-face interactions with locals, mediated communication can also be an important source of intercultural knowledge and language skills. A sojourner can watch TV programs or listen to radio to learn a language and gain experience about additional cultural situations or events. Popular local programs can be a good topic of conversation. Jordanians especially appreciate the soap opera *The Bold and the Beautiful* and are eager to discuss plot developments with visiting Americans. The Chinese kung-fu movie star, Jackie Chan, is well known in Hong Kong, Taiwan, and the United States. The royal family of Britain, World Cup soccer, video games, Pokemon cartoons, and internationally known pop singer Michael Jackson are all topics that have inspired conversations all over the world.

CONCLUSION

An economic recession in one country causes a financial downturn in other countries. The depletion of a rainforest in South America can influence the world's supply of clean air. A nuclear mishap creates a cloud that causes a path of destruction across the globe. Distance and seas no longer keep people at home as more of the world's population is on the move, seeking trade, work, knowledge, or adventure. Sojourners who cross cultural boundaries encounter challenges and initiate strategies to adapt to different cultural settings. This article reviewed the terms and concepts associated with the coping process during a sojourn as well as specific challenges and strategies to increase adaptation effectiveness. Intercultural adaptation is a crucial area of interest for people of every nation who wish to live in a healthy and harmonious world.

References

A.T. Kearney Inc. & The Carnegie Endowment for International Peace. (2001, January/February). Measuring globalization. *Foreign Policy*, 56–64.

DeVerthelyi, R. F. (1995). International students' spouses: Invisible sojourners in the culture shock literature. *International Journal of Intercultural Relations, 19*, 387–411.

Fidler, D. P. (2001, January/ February). The return of "microbialpolitik." *Foreign Policy*, 80–81.

Kim, Y. Y. (1995). Cross-cultural adaptation: An integrative theory. In R. L. Wiseman (Ed.), *Theories in inter-*

cultural communication (pp. 170–193). Thousand Oaks, CA: Sage.

Krebs, N. B. (1999). *Edgewalkers: Defusing cultural boundaries on the new global frontier*. Far Hills, NJ: New Horizon.

Leong, F. T., & Chou, E. L. (1994). The role of ethnic identity and acculturation in the vocational behavior of Asian Americans: An integrative review. *Journal of Vocational Behavior, 44*, 155–172.

Llosa, M.V. (2001, January/February). The culture of liberty. *Foreign Policy*, 66–71.

Marx, E. (1999). *Breaking through culture shock: What you need to succeed in International business*. London: Nicholas Brealey.

Milhouse, V. A. (1996). Intercultural communication education and training goals, content, and methods. *International Journal of Intercultural Relations, 20*, 69–95.

Nolen, S. (2000, July 25). Can the Inuit keep their voice? *The Globe and Mail*. In *World Press Review* (2001, February), 8–9.

Oberg, K. (1960). Culture shock: Adjustment to new cultural environment. *Practical Anthropology, 7*, 177–182.

Pope, H. (1997, March 14). The new middle: Turks add their voices to contest of generals and fundamentals. *The Wall Street Journal*, pp. A1, A8.

Radford, T. (2000, November 15). The future of global warming: A grim picture. *The Guardian*. In *World Press Review* (2001, February), 8–9.

Samovar, L. A., & Porter, R. E. (1995). *Communication between cultures* (2nd ed.). Belmont, CA: Wadsworth.

Singer, P. (2000). How are your morals? *The World in 2001: The Economist*, 50.

Ward, C., & Kennedy, A. (1993). Where's the "culture" in cross-cultural transition? Comparative studies of sojourner adjustment. *Journal of Cross-Cultural Psychology, 24*, 221–249.

Witte, K. (1993). A theory of cognition and negative affect: Extending Gudykunst and Hammer's theory of uncertainty and anxiety reduction. *International Journal of Intercultural Relations, 17*, 197–215.

"Zapatistas in cyberspace: A guide to analysis and resources." (2001). Available at: www.eco.utexas.edu/ Homepages/Faculty/Cleaver/zapsincyber.html.

Concepts and Questions

1. What does Begley mean by the term *sojourner*?
2. What is culture shock? How does it affect a sojourner?
3. In what ways can ethnocentrism affect the adaptation of a sojourner to a new cultural environment?
4. How does reserving judgment help a sojourner deal with her or his ethnocentrism?

5. It is unusual for a sojourner to be fully fluent in the language of another culture he or she may be visiting, so what steps may be taken to help overcome language barriers?
6. What characterizes a "state of disequilibrium"? How can a sojourner minimize the disequilibrium effect?
7. How does the intended length of stay in a new culture affect a sojourner's experiences in that culture?
8. What strategies does Begley recommend for a sojourner to prepare for entry into a different culture?
9. How does an individual's personality affect interpersonal interactions in another culture?
10. What role can personal determination play in adapting to another culture?

Understanding Cultural Identities in Intercultural Communication: A Ten-Step Inventory

MARY JANE COLLIER

Let me begin by introducing myself and characterizing my experiences and background. We are beginning a conversation about intercultural communication, so becoming familiar with the fundamental assumptions I'm making about it will help you better understand why I'm making particular arguments, as well as help you evaluate the utility of my approach for your own views and conduct.

My orientation to intercultural communication is based on where I come from and where I have been—just as yours is. I am a European American, white, middle-class, middle-aged female, and I've lived on a Navajo reservation in Arizona, in small towns, and in large cities in the United States. I have been a sojourner in South Africa. I have studied national, ethnic, and gender identity and intercultural communication dealing with ethnically diverse South Africans, various British ethnic groups in England, Israelis and Palestinians in the Middle East, and African, Asian, and Latino Americans in the United States. I have participated in protests and marched for political causes. My M.A. and Ph.D. in Communication are from the University of Southern California in Los Angeles.

I have come to believe that ignoring our cultural and intercultural communication processes has profound consequences. Unless we commit our hearts, minds, and spirits to understanding what happens when people with different group identities come together, we will be doomed to approach protracted

This original essay appeared for the first time in the ninth edition. All rights reserved. Permission to reprint must be obtained from the author and the publisher. Mary Jane Collier teaches at the University of Denver.

conflicts such as those in the Middle East, Bosnia, and Northern Ireland through violence and military action. U.S. Americans will continue political and social violence against recent immigrants and marginalized groups in California in the name of "native-born Americans," as I heard recently, and forget that the United States was founded by immigrants who took the land and destroyed the lives and cultures of the indigenous peoples. We'll go on denying the kind of racism, classism, and sexism that have become more insidious and damaging now that they are hidden behind language that we call "politically correct," and those of us who are more conservative will denounce "the liberals," while those of us who are more liberal will denounce "the conservatives." We'll continue to believe that our truth is the one and only truth, rather than remembering that truths are created and molded and shaped by individuals within religious, political, and social contexts and histories.

REQUEST TO ENGAGE THE DIALOGUE

Some things you read here and then talk about will validate and confirm your ideas and identities. Some things you read here will challenge your views of yourselves and the world.

When we begin inquiry about intercultural communication, we are studying how we do, be, and know ourselves and others as cultural beings. Communication, however, is a process that occurs unconsciously or mindlessly (Langer, 1989) much or at least some of the time. Learning about things we take for granted and seeing our lives from the perspective of people who don't live the same way or value the same things can teach us about alternative ways of interpreting and being in the world, and increase our own options. In this way, we can also know better how to engage in talk and actions that will be viewed as moral and ethical.

Please enter into this reading as if we are having a dialogue; agree, disagree, and note alternative views and examples in the margins as you read. Also, talk about the claims you read here and add or modify ideas in and outside of class.[1] Search for alternative interpretations, examples, and reactions as you discuss these issues. Please think about how your

behavior looks and sounds to strangers or outsiders, and take the time to develop an understanding of the words and actions of strangers until they become more familiar. I encourage you to continue the dialogue with each other as well as with me by using e-mail to send me your reactions and thoughts (mcollier@du.edu).

In this essay, I outline an inventory,[2] a series of steps you can use to build your understanding of an intercultural event that you observed or heard about, improve the quality of an intercultural relationship, work toward solving a social problem that is based in intercultural communication, or conduct a systematic research study. The inventory will help you focus on how people construct their cultural identities in particular situations. Some of the questions on the inventory may be more relevant to particular situations and events than others, but all questions apply and affect what you conclude.

A TEN-STEP INVENTORY

The inventory is a series of questions designed to help you understand and critically evaluate diverse intercultural situations. The questions can be asked before, during, or after an intercultural experience and can be applied to public or group meetings, interpersonal conversations, and what you see and hear in films or television shows, read in newspapers or magazines, or come across on the Internet. The following questions can be thought of as steps that are interrelated but not necessarily sequential. In other words, when you answer the questions in Step 7 about the context of your intercultural issue, you may need to go back and revise how you answered an earlier step about cultural identities. Each step in the inventory has to do with questions that you, the "problem solver," need to ask.

1. What do I believe about communication and culture?
2. What intercultural communication question do I want to answer? Specifically, what do I want to know, understand, or change?
3. What cultural identity issues are relevant to the intercultural communication problem in which I'm interested?

4. How do power and ideology emerge and affect the intercultural communication problem in which I'm interested?
5. What intergroup and interpersonal relationship processes are relevant to my intercultural problem?
6. What kind of communication messages will I examine? What will be my "data"?
7. What is the context? What situational, historical, institutional, and social factors affect my intercultural problem?
8. What perspective and procedures should I use to analyze or interpret the communication messages?
9. What are my preliminary interpretations and findings? What are alternative views and interpretations?
10. How can I apply my interpretations to improve the quality of my own and others' intercultural experiences?

To show how the inventory can be applied, each step will be explained and then examples will be given. Each step will be applied first to a particular intercultural problem, one based on one or more recent conflicts on college campuses across the United States. The inventory can be applied not only to analyzing a current social problem or issue but also to helping you answer a question about your own intercultural experiences or to guide a research project you conduct.

To apply the inventory to our specific campus problem, you need a little background. The current debate regarding affirmative action and policies regarding immigrants in the United States is evident in political campaigns, town meetings, television talk shows, and campus organizations. On many university campuses, the debate is fueling discussion regarding the need for ethnic studies and women's studies programs, a higher percentage of faculty from underrepresented groups, separate ethnic cultural centers or international houses on campus, and separate residence halls for international students. The debate is based on whether it is best to have programs and places in which students who have particular ethnic backgrounds or backgrounds from countries outside the United States may meet, socialize, and study in a safe environment of support;

or whether it is best to offer traditional programs that emphasize how to be successful in the United States; hire faculty without attention to race, ethnicity, or sex; close the cultural centers; and streamline funding by devoting resources only to student activities that welcome all students.

This issue is complex, and each campus is different depending on the demographics and the mission of the institution. On many campuses, funding for maintaining the cultural centers and student programs comes from both administrative sources and student fees. On many campuses, costs are increasing and administrators are looking for places to downsize and save money. Take a minute to think about your own campus. Is there an ethnic studies department or program? Is there a women's studies department or program? Are there cultural centers? If you have residence halls, are any designated only for international students?

Here is the specific problem to work with and apply the steps in the inventory. An administrator on your campus has proposed closing all the cultural centers (black student alliance, Hispanic center, Native American longhouse) and international house, as well as the women's studies program and the ethnic studies program, and opening the residence hall previously designated for international students to all students. The administrator argues that separatist organizations do not prepare students to live in a culturally diverse, global society, and the centers and programs are too costly to maintain.

Answering the inventory of questions about this campus problem can help you make sense of the multiple points of view and perhaps better understand why some group members feel as they do. In the rest of this essay, each step in the inventory will be illustrated by systematically analyzing the campus problem; it will also be applied by explaining similar steps in research studies about a range of cultural groups.

STEP 1: WHAT DO I BELIEVE ABOUT COMMUNICATION AND CULTURE?

There are many ways we all commonly think of culture, and each may be more or less useful to help us understand a certain process, event, or relationship.

Approaches to Culture

Culture as Place. Often when you meet someone, the first question asked is "Where are you from?" Sometimes this refers to a question about where the person grew up, and other times it's a question about where the person lived previously. Groups also are described in print and broadcast media, literature, and academic texts as people who are from or reside in a country or region of a country. These references become evident in everyday discourse as well when an individual says, "I'm from L. A. (Los Angeles), so . . ." implying that who she or he is can be understood through knowing where she or he lives—in this case, in Southern California, which is known for the entertainment industry, wealth, freeway commuting, and a warm coastal climate.

Places of origin or residence bring to mind different social hierarchies and norms, class distinctions, political orientations, and communication styles. Without thinking about it, we assume that people who are raised or live in a particular place probably speak the same language, hold many of the same values, and communicate in similar ways.

Culture as Ancestry and People. Another common way we think about culture is to define culture as the group of people who share the same ancestry. Ethnicity is often used as an indicator of culture. For instance, Japanese Americans are understood as a people who live in the United States whose Japanese ancestors or relatives taught them Japanese language, values, and traditions. During the Second World War, U.S. government representatives assumed that ancestry was a powerful enough force to determine their cultural alliance with Japan, and U.S. citizens of Japanese ancestry were evicted from their homes, their businesses were closed or taken over, and they were imprisoned in internment camps for the duration of the war.

An approach to culture that is also based on ancestry is that which is exemplified by linking race with culture. When people remark, "He's the white guy who lives next door to me," or when writers of newspaper accounts of crimes, for instance, include a description of the race of the alleged perpetrator, then the speaker and writer are making assumptions about racial appearance and ancestry as apparent indicators

of character and identity. Scholars point out that race is a social construct and that we cannot predict behavior, values, or beliefs—let alone the content of one's character—by skin color or hair texture (Martin, 1997; Omi & Wanant, 1986; Webster, 1992). As a social construct, however, racial appearance is an everyday shorthand way to stereotype others.

Culture as Art and Artifact. Creative endeavors and expressions that represent the heart, spirit, emotions, or philosophies of a group at a particular time and place are another way we think of culture. Examples include not only what can be seen in museums and galleries, but also the artifacts and remnants of pottery, jewelry, tools, weapons left behind by groups such as the Anasazi Indians, and what is left of their dwellings in Mesa Verde.

Culture as Capital or Economic Resource. Many countries and organizations are based on economic principles of capitalism. We often come to think of areas of the world in terms of their economic status and relative wealth. More specifically, countries or regions are thought of in terms of their buying power and developing markets; the CBS television network program "60 Minutes," for example, featured a segment on investment opportunities and expanding wealth in Russia. Approaching groups as buyers or as producers of products is to think of culture as an economic resource.

Culture as Product. We think about cultures as commodities or products when we think of the numerous toys, foods, films, videos, and music that are internationally exported and imported. The Barbie doll produced by Mattel in the United States is sold to young women all over the world. A colleague of mine who visited Beijing last year commented that the department store mannequins advertising women's clothing and accessories were, more often than not, tall and blond replicas of Barbie. When the same colleague lived with a single mother and two children in Costa Rica who were extremely poor, the daughter wanted a Barbie doll more than any other gift for the Christmas holiday.

Culture as Politics and Ideology. Another way to think of culture is to associate a country with a political ideology. In the United States, the Peace Corps was created in 1961 to give people in areas such as Central America and Africa new technologies, agricultural techniques, and democratic values. More recently, the export of U.S. democratic values through the Peace Corps has been criticized as actually exporting imperialism and colonialism.

Halualani (1998) notes that culture can be approached as the structures, ideologies, and master narratives of groups in power that are created through mediated and public forms to maintain and extend their power. The press coverage of U.S. involvement in the Persian Gulf War in 1991 has been cited as an example of government and military control of the press, and thus the coverage reflected a public-relations emphasis. The news featured the success of the United States and its allies, the spectacle of the missiles and technology, and the lack of casualties (Sturken, 1995); it did not include references to deaths caused by friendly fire or civilian casualties.

Culture as Psychology, Worldview, or Style of Thinking and Speaking. One of the ways in which we come to know who we are is to compare our own group identities with the character of other groups (Tajfel, 1978). Our everyday talk often includes references to *they* and *we*. We learn and attribute to others, based on their group memberships, particular styles of thinking and feeling. In short, we may begin to stereotype other group members by attributing particular psychological tendencies to them (Brislin, 1986). Katz (1960) found that stereotypes become prejudiced, evaluative prejudgments about group members so that we can knowledgeably predict or explain the conduct of people in other groups, as well as serving an ego-defensive function that allows us to blame others for the outcomes of events. For example, when a European American friend of mine called to tell me he was not hired for a job at a fire station, he blamed affirmative action policies that favored members of ethnic minority groups.

Culture as Performance. Sometimes we think of culture as a kind of role we are acting in a play. Goffman (1967) created a theory of communication as performance and noted that some of our identities are "front stage" and others are more "back stage" or private. The audience affects the quality of the performance as well. Many groups such as Native American Indians have a long-standing tradition of elders sharing the oral histories and origin myths of their people at social gatherings and celebrations.

Culture as Group Identity. We have experienced an exponential increase in access to international information because of computer technology and the Internet; far-away places and people have become more accessible through more affordable and available travel; corporations are told to be multinational to be successful; and our nations and communities have become characterized by increasing diversity. In winter 1998, we could see the tired faces and nonverbal cues of frustration during televised interviews with United Nations representatives and national leaders as they discussed the possibility of a U.S. military strike in Iraq. Through such public and private contact with others, we come to define ourselves as members of cultural groups.

When we approach culture as group character or identity, it is essential to recognize that each group is made up of a multitude of individuals and voices, and each individual has a range of group identities. McPhail (1997), for instance, discusses the range of voices and political standpoints and values making up the African American community. Halualani (1998) argues that the "American Dream" is an idealized myth that is not available to people like her who are Japanese, Hawaiian, and female. Thus, we need to recognize that cultural identities are complex and created, sustained, challenged, and contested in our contact with each other.

Culture and the Campus Problem

Stereotyping occurs on the basis of linking culture to ancestry or race, so students who experience discrimination on the basis of race may argue that they need separate cultural centers in order to have a place to meet where they can feel safe and know that people who look like them are welcome. On the other hand, European American students may argue that cultural centers or ethnic studies programs are not necessary because these students may not value ethnicity or see why ancestry and past traditions are more important than the current American orientation.

Defining culture as ideology and politics may help you understand why members of different groups are so committed to maintaining their own cultural centers and programs, or why they wish to replace such programs. The programs are not only a source of identity reinforcement but also a source of empowerment. Finally, consider that the resources allocated to groups and programs—as well as courses focused on ethnic history, philosophy, and art—are an acknowledgment of the contribution and legitimacy of ethnic members of the U.S. American community. Thus, such programs and designated places are the site in which cultural identities are reinforced, contested, modified, and celebrated.

In my own research, I combine several approaches to culture. Currently, I define *culture* as a historically based, interpretive, constitutive, creative set of practices and interpretive frames that demonstrate affiliation with a group. Culture as group identity is the way I most often think of culture, although I also study the politics and ideology and the performance of the enacted group identities. A communication event or interaction becomes intercultural when different cultural identities emerge in the text or talk of interactants. I'll give several examples of the cultural groups and identity issues I study throughout the remainder of this article.

STEP 2: WHAT INTERCULTURAL COMMUNICATION QUESTION DO I WANT TO ANSWER?

Specifically, what do you want to know about the communicative event, contact, discourse, text, and situation? What problem do you want to address? You may have had a personal experience or an intercultural conversation that left you puzzled or intrigued. Have you witnessed or been a part of an intercultural conflict that you might want to manage? Do you want to explain why members of one group seem to adapt to a new country more quickly than members of another group? Do you wish to critique how multinational corporations in developed countries influence developing nations by introducing technology and products and creating dependency? For the campus problem, you may ask: How does the social history of each "ethnic minority"

group affect the standpoint taken by spokespersons of that group in the campus newspaper? How can understanding the perspective of the administrator (who has more than one cultural identity) and the perspective of the women's studies faculty and students (who also have many cultural identities) help you identify common goals?

This is the step in which you should narrow your interests to a question that you can answer by analyzing specific messages, what you can read, see, and hear in mediated or person-to-person communication. You need to be able to answer your question through systematic empirical observation or analysis or critique of communication messages in conversations, groups, public venues, and all forms of print and broadcast media. You are acting on the premise that people construct their identities and relationships through their communication, and the study of communication messages can help us not only understand what is going on in our communication with each other, but also potentially how to improve the quality of our intercultural relationships.

STEP 3: WHAT CULTURAL IDENTITY ISSUES ARE RELEVANT?

The third set of questions points to cultural identities and how they are enacted, produced, reproduced, reinforced, contested, constructed, and reconstructed in your selected problematic situation. Listed as follows are several principles or assumptions about cultural identities that you may find helpful as you think about the campus problem and your own experiences and research.

Multiple Cultural Identity Types (CITs)

Many groups (although not all) form cultural systems. In some cases, shared history or geography provides commonality of worldview or lifestyle that helps create and reinforce a cultural system of communication. To create a culture, a group must first define itself as a group. This may be on the basis of nationality, ethnicity, gender, profession, geography, organization, community, physical ability or disability, or type of relationship, among others. Once the group defines itself as a unit, then a cultural system may develop. For instance, U.S. Americans define themselves as a group based on use of English as a shared code; reinforcement of democracy through political discussion and action; individual rights and freedoms of speech, press, religion, and assembly being explicitly described in the Bill of Rights and enforced in the courts; and so forth. Attorneys or sales clerks or homemakers may be linked by similarities in daily activities and standard of living.

National and Ethnic Cultures. To better understand the many different types of cultures, we can categorize them from the more general and more common to the more specific. National and ethnic cultures are fairly general. These kinds of groups base membership on heritage and history that have been handed down for generations. Their histories are based on traditions, rituals, codes of language, and norms.

Persons who share the same nationality were born in a particular country or spent a significant number of years and period of socialization in that country. Such socialization promotes and reinforces particular values, beliefs, and norms. Many people contribute to the creation of a national culture's symbols, meanings, and norms, so national culture is fairly abstract and predictions about language use and what symbols mean must be general. For instance, Japanese national culture has been described as collectivistic, high-context, high on power distance, and other-face–oriented (Gudykunst & Ting-Toomey, 1988). Not all Japanese people follow these norms in every situation; comparing Japanese to Germans, however, the Japanese as a group are more group-oriented and emphasize status hierarchies more than do the Germans as an overall group (Hofstede, 1980).

Ethnicity is a bit different in that ethnic groups share a sense of heritage and history, as well as origin from an area outside of or preceding the creation of the current nation-state of residence (Banks, 1984). In some but not all cases, ethnic groups share racial characteristics, and many have a specific history of having experienced discrimination. In the United States, ethnic groups include African Americans, Asian Americans (e.g., Japanese Americans, Chinese Americans, Vietnamese Americans), Mexican Americans, German Americans, Irish Americans, Native American Indians, and Jewish Americans.

Sex and Gender. Another common cultural group is that based on biological sex or socially constructed gender. There are many subcategories of gender cultures. Groups create, reinforce, and teach what it means to use a gender style and what is interpreted as feminine or masculine. Groups also reinforce what is appropriate or inappropriate for a good husband, good wife, feminist, chauvinist, heterosexual, gay, or lesbian. Parents, religious leaders, teachers, and what we read and see in the media all provide information about how to be a member of a particular gender culture.

Remember that nationality, ethnicity, race, and sex are cultural group affiliations based on citizenship, heritage, and biology, and such broad memberships do not guarantee that members of those groups will automatically behave or interpret messages in the same ways. Many individuals have parents and grandparents with different backgrounds and heritages and claim more than one ethnicity and may have lived in several different countries. From the CIT perspective, cultural identity is created when a group affiliation is enacted, when an individual or group members claim membership in one or more groups. Cultural identity is based on what members of a group or community say and do and think and feel as they affiliate with others who share their history, origins, or biology. For a cultural identity to be recognized, the identity needs to be claimed and communicated in some way.

Profession. Groups of professionals sometimes create their own culture. Politicians, physicians, field workers, sales personnel, maintenance crews, bankers, and consultants share common ways of spending time, earning money, communicating with others, and sharing norms about how to be a member of their profession. For instance, most health care professionals share a commitment to health, to helping others, and to improving others' quality of life. They also share educational background, knowledge about their aspect of health care, and standards of practicing their profession.

Geographic Area. Geographic area is sometimes a boundary that contributes to the formation of a cultural group. In South Africa, the area surrounding Cape Town has its own version of spoken Afrikaans, has a higher population of coloureds (those of mixed race), and is viewed by many as a cosmopolitan area in South Africa. The South in the United States has its own traditions, historical orientation, and Southern drawl.

Corporation. Organizational culture is yet another type of culture. The most common type is that created in large corporations such as IBM, Nike, and Xerox. Here individuals are taught the corporate symbols; the corporate myths, heroes, and legends; and what it means to be an employee. In addition, individuals are taught the proper chain of command, procedures, policies, and schedules. Finally, they are taught the norms in the corporation, who to talk to about what and at which time. Some corporations value "team players," whereas others value "individual initiative." Some corporations have mottoes like "Never say *no* to an assignment" or "Never be afraid to speak up if you don't have what you need."

Support groups also have their own version of organizational culture. Alcoholics Anonymous, Overeaters Anonymous, and therapy and support groups, among others, have their own sets of symbols and interpretations and norms. For example, "Let go and let God" is an important requirement in the anonymous groups, emphasizing that relinquishing individual control to a higher power is a tool in managing one's addictions. Social living groups also often create their own cultures, such as sororities and fraternities, international dormitories, and the like.

Physical Ability and Disability. Physical ability and disability is still another category of group that can become a basis for culture. Professional athletic teams teach rookies how to behave and what to do to be accepted members of the team. Persons who have physical handicaps share critical life experiences, and groups teach individuals how to accept and overcome their disabilities, as well as how to communicate more effectively with those who do not have the disability (Braithwaite, 1991).

Cultural Identification as Constituted in Communication

Cultural identity is the particular character of the group communication system that emerges when people claim group membership in a particular situation, event, or communication context. Cultural identities are negotiated, co-created, reinforced, and challenged through communication (Hecht, Collier, & Ribeau, 1993). In CIT, identity is approached from a communication perspective, which views identity as located in the communication process in which messages are constructed, reinforced, contested, and challenged. A communication perspective also includes attention to the creation of cultural identities through products or words and images that are transmitted through media or technological channels.

Group affiliation and membering occurs in multiple contexts in which insiders and outsiders enact what membership looks and sounds like. All cultures that are created are influenced by a host of social and psychological and environmental factors as well as by institutions, history, and context. Latinos who wish to maintain their cultural center may argue their position more strongly at private meetings attended by members of their group and change the intensity of their tone and persuasive appeals when interacting with community representatives on their board of advisors. Identities therefore are co-created in relationship to other people. Who we are and how we are differs and emerges depending on who we are with, the cultural identities that are important to us and others, the context, the topic of conversation, and our interpretations and attributions.

Multivocality and Interpellated Cultural Identities

From an individual perspective, each person has a range of groups and cultures to which she or he belongs in a constantly changing environment. Each individual participates in many cultural systems each day, week, and year. Cultures are affected not only by changing socioeconomic and environmental conditions, but also by other cultures. As poet and writer bell hooks (1989) reminds us, she is not only an African American, but also a woman and a college professor. To understand her conduct, one must recognize her multiple identities and voices, just as someone else must recognize *your* multiple voices and identities. It is also important to recognize that not all voices within a group sound alike.

Morgan (1996) uses the term *feminisms* to recognize multivocality within feminists as a group; some voices are more radical, some more conservative, and some both radical and conservative. *Interpellation* refers to the interrelationships among such cultural identities as sex, race, and class, and the point that one cannot understand sex without also studying race and class.

Several months ago, on my way to work, I drove by a local seminary. For several days I saw on the outside lawn a small group of women leading another larger group in prayer. I also read in the newspaper that these women were on a hunger strike and were protesting discrimination toward women faculty who were denied tenure or a voice in determining policy in the seminary. If I want an accurate picture of the issues and group standpoints, then identifying how the women leading the protest, the staff, the students, and the administrators of the seminary were defining religion, feminism, and political voice would be important, as would noticing that the individuals within each group constructed their identities and position on the issues in a unique way.

Avowal and Ascription Processes

I have used the term *multivocality* to point out that groups are made up of individuals with unique as well as similar voices. In addition, each individual may enact various cultural identities over the course of a lifetime, not to mention over the course of a day. Identities are enacted across contexts through *avowal* and *ascription* processes. Avowal has to do with what an individual portrays to others and is analogous to the face or image shown to others. In a way, avowal is the individual showing to others "This is who I am" as a member of this group or these groups.

Ascription is when individuals or group members come to know that others attribute particular identities to them as members of a group. Stereotypes and attributions that are communicated are examples. In part, identity is shaped by others' communicated views of us. For example, a black Zulu female's cultural identities in South Africa are not only shaped by her definition and image of what it means to be a black Zulu female but also by the communicated views of the white Afrikaners for whom she

works, her Zulu family and relatives, the township in which she lives in poverty, her white teachers who speak Afrikaans and English, and so forth.

Another way of thinking about this concept is to say that cultural identities have both subjective and ascribed meanings. Some cultures emphasize ascription or an orientation toward others. In Japan, a traditional philosophy sometimes reflected in practice is that of *amae*. Amae represents an other orientation and a sense of obligation to the group; an individual is expected to sacrifice individual needs and give to others, and others are expected to reciprocate. Thus, the harmony and cohesiveness of the group is maintained (Doi, 1989; Goldman, 1992).

Information about avowal and ascription can be useful in understanding the role others play in developing your own cultural identities. If you feel you are a member of a group that is marginalized and discriminated against or has a high need for status, then those aspects of identity may be influenced by the stereotypes or conceptions held and communicated by other groups.

Salience and Intensity Differences

Identities differ in their salience in particular contexts, and identities are enacted with different intensities at different times. The intensities provide markers of strong involvement and investment in the identity. As a white U.S. American female professor visiting Australia and being taken on a dream time walk by a male aborigine, at different times throughout the walk, I was aware of being a white minority, a U.S. American tourist who was stereotyped somewhat negatively, a college professor who was interested in culture, and an honored guest.

Salience refers to featuring one or more particular identities more strongly than others, and it certainly does not mean individuals have split personalities or need to give up one cultural identity to feature another. Some people also have less choice about what cultural identities they can feature. I have come to see that I have certain unearned privileges and choice about whether or not I choose to share my British German ethnic heritage.

Enduring and Changing Property of Identity

Cultural identities are both enduring and changing. As already mentioned, cultures have a history that is continually constructed and reconstructed with new members over time. Cultural identities change because of economic, political, social, psychological, and contextual factors, not to mention the influence of other cultural identities.

Enacting the cultural identity of being gay or lesbian in the 1990s has certain things in common with being gay in the 1980s and 1970s. Individuals who "come out of the closet" encounter similar stereotypes and ascriptions to those in earlier centuries. However, the political climate in some areas of the country in which ballot initiatives sought to limit the rights of gays or link gays with other groups such as sadomasochists also affects the cultural identity of the group. Sometimes context changes how one manifests identity and how intensely one avows an identity. For example, not all members of a gay, lesbian, and bisexual alliance may avow that identity outside of their support group.

STEP 4: WHAT IS THE ROLE OF POWER AND IDEOLOGY?

This leads us to the fourth set of questions you will want to ask about power and ideology. These include: What is power? Is it a process, a commodity, a perception or impression of influence, access, or ability to distribute resources? How do people lose or gain power?

I have noticed in my classes that members of marginalized groups are more likely to make statements such as "All intercultural communication is political" or "Power is always an issue in intercultural communication." The newer theoretical perspectives point us to identifying the extent to which power is constructed through history, institutions, and social practices; and for some of us to interrogate previous assumptions and benefits we accrue on the basis of being white or male or upper class.

There are days when individually I feel somewhat powerless, and yet I, as a white, middle-class professional benefit from institutional practices in higher education and the broader political system that maintain my rights and privileges and lead me to expect to be hired, treated with respect by staff, or waited on in a department store without being shadowed or suspected of being a shoplifter. Even with affirmative-action policies, across the United States I am more likely to be hired for a corporate position or a position in higher education than my Latina, African American, or Native American Indian counterparts.

On the other hand, assuming that groups are *either* "all powerful" and totally "imperialist" *or* "powerless" and "colonized" can be an inappropriate oversimplification. Consider international contexts in which new products or ideologies are introduced by corporate representatives from developed nations to people in less developed nations. When parents in a village in Nicaragua take a Barbie doll that was a gift from a U.N. visitor and stain the skin to be darker, dress her in indigenous clothing, and create a new ritual in which she is the voice of the ancestors sharing their stories, this is a redefinition of power.

As both group members and problem solvers, we ought to recognize that those who have some degree of power will seek to maintain it, and that there are many collective interpretations of power and resistance. McClintock (1995) notes that there exists a "diverse politics of agency, involving the dense web of relations between coercion, negotiation, complicity, refusal, dissembling, mimicry, compromise, affiliation, and revolt" (p. 15). There are also benefits to becoming aware of presumed sources of power that have become somewhat invisible to some of us, as well as engaging in what hooks calls intercultural dialogue between those who feel oppressed and those who "exploit, oppress and dominate" (1989, p. 129) because this opens opportunities and spaces for understanding of the structures and functions of domination (Foss, 1998).

There are many related questions you may ask about power and what has endured in order to understand the historical, social, and ideological context of your intercultural problem. Such questions may address the importance of the environment, history, and institutions such as education and religion in determining how cultural identities emerge. Our own socioeconomic class affects what we deem appropriate and what we expect from others, and histories of racism, sexism, and classism, for example, influence how we all behave.

The importance of acknowledging the historical and social context in which power emerges is illustrated by the following comments. On a visit to the Middle East in spring 1998, a young Palestinian woman asked me, "What do you think? I am Palestinian and I live in Gaza. The Israeli government laws deny me and my brothers the right I.D. [identity] card, so I can't work in Israel, visit my aunts and uncles, or visit holy sites in Jerusalem. How can this be?" A young Israeli woman told me, "We were raised to hate them [Palestinians], to think that the men are all terrorists and the women are abused by their husbands because of Islam."

You may want to ask a more specific set of questions with regard to the power and ideology of different cultural groups in their intercultural contact. Who makes important decisions in the group, determines when and where meetings or social gatherings will take place, or speaks for the rest of the group in intercultural meetings or in public presentations? How are decisions made to allocate resources or create policy and procedures? What kinds of values and ideologies are handed down to new members?

STEP 5: WHAT ARE THE INTERGROUP AND INTERPERSONAL RELATIONSHIP PROCESSES?

Our cultural identities are constructed in relationships with others inside our own groups and with members of other groups. *Relationship process* refers to the quality of connection or bond that emerges in communication. When persons communicate with each other, their messages carry not only information, but also cues about the relationship between individuals and groups. These cues indicate who is dominant or submissive throughout the conversation or event, how much intimacy or hostility is felt, how much each partner or party trusts one another, and how much they feel included or excluded.

You could analyze the campus newspaper coverage of the debate about closing the campus centers and programs, or attend the public forum on campus where students articulate their views. Using the newspaper articles or transcriptions of the public

meeting or both, you could look for relational messages that constitute the relationship, phrases that indicate friendliness such as "We support the need for safe places to meet and are open to designating additional spaces for intercultural dialogue"; or control, "How can redefining what used to be a separatist place into a place where all students can go possibly be a bad thing?"; or exclusion in the press headline "Provost Says, 'Student Input Has No Place in Closing Cultural Centers.'" You could ask intercultural friends to tape-record their informal talk about the campus problem and look for what Baxter and Montgomery (1996) and Martin, Nakayama, and Flores (1997) describe as dialectic tensions in the dialogue. For instance, intercultural friends may experience contradictory tendencies to be both independent and connected, private and public, and dominant and submissive. Looking for dialectic tensions may help you guard against making overly simplistic generalizations about a group's preferred mode of communication.

Sometimes people use their in-group language to reinforce their in-group status and establish distance from the out-group (Giles, Coupland, & Coupland, 1991). At other times, they may use the language of the out-group in order to adapt and align with the out-group. Some Mexican Americans speak Spanish when in neighborhood communities in order to preserve their history and roots and to reinforce their identification and bond as a people. The same persons may speak English at work because the supervisor and executives of the company demand it. They may also choose to speak Spanish in meetings to plan their response to close their cultural center, and choose English when meeting with the provost.

STEP 6: WHAT KINDS OF COMMUNICATIVE MESSAGES SHOULD I EXAMINE IN MY STUDY?

What kind of data or communication messages do you need to answer your questions? What types or forms of messages may be important? Are you interested in analyzing a series of meetings between diplomats over several years, or the speeches of one political figure in a particular period of time, or a relationship you have, or a conversation that took place yesterday? It is also important to think about what you need to examine in the way of functions or outcomes of those forms.

This set of questions deals with what kind and how much communicative data you wish to understand or explain. Some scholars study the rhetoric that is common in a century or decade, or in the letters written by an international traveler during his or her lifetime. Others choose a much more specific focus on a particular event in time or critical point in a relationship. For the campus problem, if you want to interview people from various groups, you must decide who you want to interview, what you want to ask, if you want answers to specific questions or you want to have more of a collaborative dialogue, and how many times you want to meet with them. Whether you are addressing a concrete problem or conducting a research study, you need to think about the breadth and scope of your data and what it will take to answer your question appropriately.

Form and Function of Discourse Texts

The form and function of talk with friends was the focus of a study of adolescent members of various ethnic groups in London, England (Collier & Thompson, 1997). We found that discourse among friends served dual functions: (1) maintaining traditional and previous home cultural identity, language, and norms; and (2) developing a new national or ethnic identity. Using in-depth group interviews, we asked questions about three contexts: home, school, and socializing with friends, and the national and ethnic identities constructed in each. We asked respondents in each context to think of a situation in which they were aware of being from different cultural backgrounds. Then we asked about who was there, what was discussed, what activities took place, and the purpose and outcome of the contact.

The adolescents were most aware of their shared national identity as British citizens at school, and they were most aware of their different ethnic backgrounds at home because that was where home language was often spoken and where narrative rituals recalling history and people were most often seen. Several respondents pointed out that these family gatherings and storytelling episodes by grandparents served to bring the family together, remind them of their past and roots, and provide a way of reinforcing transcendent values and extended family ties.

Message Patterns and Themes

Another way to analyze communication texts is to look for message patterns and themes. For example, you may wish to see how often a particular phrase or idea such as feminism comes up, around what topics, and with which conversational partners. You may also want to analyze narratives or stories and look for themes that may emerge. For example, Hecht and Ribeau (1987) and Hecht, Ribeau, and Alberts (1989) analyzed recalled conversations of African Americans with European Americans and distinguished several improvement strategies such as asserting point of view and positive self-presentation.

Modes of Expression: Labels and Norms

Labels are a way of establishing identity. The same label may vary widely in its interpretation. The term *American* is perceived as acceptable and common by many residents of the United States, as ethnocentric and self-centered by residents of Central America and Canada, and as associated with a group that is privileged, wealthy, and powerful by some developing countries. Labels used in the discourse of people involved in the campus problem can potentially reveal a great deal about identities ascribed to outsiders.

For example, *Hispanic* is a general term that many social scientists use to describe "persons of Mexican, Puerto Rican, Cuban, Central or South American or other Spanish culture of origin, regardless of race" (Marin & Marin, 1991, p. 23). Persons may choose to describe their own ethnicity with a much more specific label such as Mexican American or Chicano or Chicana. The individuals may differ on their ideas about what it means to be a member of that culture. Whether the label was created by members of the group or members of another group (e.g., *Hispanic* is a term that was originally generated by the U.S. government) provides useful information about what the label means and how it is interpreted.

Norms are explicit or inferred prescriptions of modes of appropriate and effective communication. Norms are prescriptive or evaluative because they specify appropriate and acceptable behavior, moral standards, and expectations for conduct. Norms provide cultural group members with a criteria to decide to what degree another is behaving in a competent manner. Reviewing the historical, political, and ideological context of norms and expectations that group members may bring to the public forum on campus can be helpful when assigning interpretations to the chanting and loud interruptions by members of one group.

Cultural groups create and reinforce standards for "performing the culture" appropriately and effectively. An individual is successful at enacting identity when one is accepted as a competent member of the group. For example, all those who are registered as members of Native American Indian tribes in the United States are defined as "real Indians" only when they conduct themselves in ways that insiders judge to be appropriate and acceptable for Indians (Weider & Pratt, 1990). Norms and standards for acceptable conduct are general trends at best; they are constructed by group members and interpreted by individuals, and they change across contexts.

Affective, Cognitive, and Spiritual Components

Throughout history, many groups have felt strongly enough about the supremacy of their beliefs to conquer and convert outsiders. For instance, Jerusalem is a holy city to three of the world's largest religions, and Israeli control is contested by Muslim and Christian groups. Emotions and feelings are attached to identities, and these change across situation, historical context, political climate, and relationship with others. Sometimes, the avowal or featuring of a particular identity more strongly and more violently is a signal of the importance of that identity and the degree to which that identity is perceived to be threatened. When a colleague and I (Collier & Bowker, 1994) asked women friends who had different cultural identities what made a good intercultural ally, two of the African American women said that their European American friends needed to be able to hear their anger and rage about daily experiences with oppression, while their European American women friends said their feelings about the value of the friendship needed to be reciprocated.

The cognitive component of identity relates to the beliefs we have about that identity. Persons have a range of premises about each culture group to which they belong, but certain similarities become evident when you ask people to talk about what it means to be U.S. American or Thai or a member of the environmentalist group Earth First! Members of Earth First! share beliefs in the value of ancient forests, distrust executives who run the logging companies and politicians who support the lumber industry, and view spiking trees and sabotaging logging equipment as sometimes necessary forms of protest. Such beliefs can be summarized into a core symbol, here the name of the organization—Earth First!

STEP 7: WHAT IS THE CONTEXT OF THE INTERCULTURAL PROBLEM?

How we construct identities occurs in a broad context of history, power dynamics, social norms, and specific situations. Thus, it is important to ask questions such as: What factors outside of the messages can help me understand the intercultural communication? What is the physical environment? What histories and institutions (e.g., political, religious, educational) are relevant?

The site of one of my first exploratory studies of culture and communication was the Navajo reservation in Chinle, Arizona. I lived with a family and taught high school classes. I became interested in how Navajos developed and strengthened their cultural identities through family rituals and community events, and how their identities were threatened by institutions such as the Bureau of Indian Affairs schools in which students were forced to speak English.

Context includes the physical environment, for instance, where persons with different cultural identities have contact, or the location or place in which a media text, cultural product, or speech is produced, distributed, and interpreted by audiences or consumers, as well as a social and historical place in time. For example, in the campus problem, if someone argues that curriculum as well as programs of study should be based on the canons of traditional Greek knowledge as a foundation, it may be important to consider that Aristotle's ideas about rhetoric, for example, were created in a time in which women were excluded from political participation and in a place in which wealth and power were concentrated in the hands of a few of the elite.

In one of my studies, I wished to understand how young people from different cultural groups in South Africa in 1992 approached and experienced interpersonal, intercultural relationships. We (Collier & Bornman, in press) discovered, for instance, that interethnic and interracial friendships were more common among nonwhite group members and more common in private than in public contexts. We also found that blacks, Asian Indians, and coloureds (those of mixed race) emphasized the need to acknowledge history and the consequences of the apartheid system of government, while the Afrikaners and British we interviewed emphasized the need to be present- and future-oriented.

STEP 8: WHAT PERSPECTIVES AND PROCEDURES SHOULD I USE TO STUDY THE DATA?

Epistemological Perspectives

How can you best study the communication messages in which you're interested? Whether you are trying to understand an intercultural problem, an event, or asking a research question, you will need to decide if you should be as objective as possible, ask others how they make sense of their subjective experiences, be an engaged participant, or be a more distant but knowledgeable critic. Many perspectives to doing research are available to you as you approach inquiry about a particular intercultural communication situation or text. Becoming familiar with them will give you a better basis from which to choose one or more perspectives in answering your own question.

I describe three broad perspectives to epistemology, or what and how we know what we do, as follows.[3] We will talk about these types as epistemological perspectives because each is a way in which we can view knowledge building in intercultural communication. Although I emphasize research examples, you may also adapt these approaches to practical problems from your own experience.

Positivist and Objectivist Perspectives

Positivist approaches have the longest legacy in communication because of their origins in social science. Anderson (1996) notes that objectivist theories are based in principles of empiricism (observation), materialism, determinism (cause–effect relationships), and objectivity. Assumptions made by researchers taking this perspective are that a material reality "out there" can be discovered, observed, measured, and operationalized, and causal relationships proven. A common assumption is that psychological states such as beliefs, feelings, attitudes, and values can be discovered and quantified through behavioral assessments such as scaled questionnaires. Further, it is assumed that behaviors (actions that can be seen and categorized) are authentic representations of psychological states (what individuals are thinking or feeling).

Perhaps as you listen to people talk about the campus problem, you begin to hypothesize that students who have friends from other cultures or who have traveled in other countries are more likely to voice their support for keeping the cultural centers and various programs. You decide to test this relationship. You could develop a set of questions that measure the extent of previous intercultural contact (e.g., living in another country, number of friends who have a different nationality or ethnicity) and measure the likelihood that a person might make or agree with someone who makes such comments as, "Programs like ethnic studies are valuable for all students" or "Women's studies courses teach issues that can be useful for men and women to learn." You would be assuming that such questions would be interpreted and mean the same things to all students, and the extent to which they agreed or disagreed with each question would represent their overall attitude. You, like social science scholars who use positivism, would want to be able to predict, for example, particular kinds of communication behavior and partly explain that behavior by looking at the variable of previous intercultural contact.

Another example of positivist research is that of Gudykunst (1994), who proposed that because Japanese people are more collectivistic and group-oriented and emphasize contextual factors such as silence in interpretation more highly than do U.S. Americans, Japanese individuals communicating with strangers will experience a higher level of anxiety than will U.S. Americans. Assumptions made in anxiety and uncertainty management theory (Gudykunst, 1994) include that national culture is a predictor and explanatory variable for intergroup behavior and that relationships among such variables as uncertainty, anxiety, and mindfulness can predict and explain strangers' intergroup behavior.

Critical Deconstructionist Perspectives

As scholars in communication, the ways we come to know have changed dramatically over the last few centuries. One of the characteristic turns is the emergence of skepticism and questions about what we know, how we know, and who we are as scholars and people.

Certain overarching assumptions are shared by scholars aligned with a critical perspective. Scholars are primarily concerned with **exploitation, power, empowerment,** and the development of rhetorical tools to **deconstruct** and **critique** discourse and media texts and provide alternative interpretations. Prus (1996) characterizes the critical voice as "extreme skepticism in the viability of all forms of knowing" (p. 217).

One group of critical scholars describes the work it does as *postcolonialist.* These scholars not only criticize the use and misuse of power by particular groups, but they also point out that scholars may exert power and influence on the cultural identities and conduct of the masses by deciding what is important to study and how to describe groups and social issues.

An example of the *critical perspective* is the work of van Dijk (1993) on social cognition and racism. He examines the social, political, and cultural reproduction of racism by giving attention to what he calls *microlevel interactions* and *everyday conversational talk,* along with macrostructures, socially shared strategies and representations of power, dominance, and access. He has investigated forms of racism and sexism in television news reports as well as in newspaper articles and examined how institutions are represented, how political points of view are articulated, and how economic and social policies are challenged or reinforced. Similarly, you could take a critical perspective in analyzing the newspaper reports about the campus problem and

identify who is being interviewed, whose voices are featured most, what kind of examples are being quoted by members of particular groups, and the overall portrayal of particular groups.

Interpretive and Reconstructive Perspectives

A third type of epistemological perspective can be called *interpretive* because the goal is understanding. In most interpretive approaches, the goal of the researcher is to build an understanding of how respondents come to do, be, and know (Sachs, 1984) their cultural identities. Many scholars use interpretive approaches to build an understanding about the negotiation and enactment of cultural identities in particular interactional contexts.

One example of an *interpretive perspective* is CIT (Collier, 1998a, 1998b; Collier & Thomas, 1988; Hecht, Collier, & Ribeau, 1993), which I've featured throughout this article. To review, one of the major premises I make is the assumption that we align with various groups, and part of what we do when we communicate with others is define who we are and distinguish ourselves as members of groups. We also construct our cultural identities as a way of developing relationships, increasing or contesting our lack of power in various situations, and creating a history that can transcend situations, periods of time, and lifetimes.

In a CIT approach, cultural identities are historical, contextual, and relational constructions; we create to some degree through our communication, our pasts, and what we hand down to new members and teach in our institutions. The historical, social, political, economic, and relational context, as well as our physical surroundings, affect who we are and who we come to be with one another. Cultural identities are commonly intelligible and accessible to group members (Carbaugh, 1990). Cultural identities emerge in everyday discourse as well as in social practices, rituals, norms, and myths that are handed down to new members.

Each perspective is based on a set of assumptions about inquiry and knowledge building. Just as our social world is characterized by rapid and complex change, so our perspectives should be open to interrogation and modification.

Researcher Perspective

Identities are constructed by and can be studied as constructions of individuals, relational partners, or group members of a community. in addition to selecting an epistemological perspective, you'll also need to select a researcher perspective. You may wish to focus on the point of view of individuals. Each person has individual interpretations of what it means to be U.S. American or Austrian or Indian, for example, and each person enacts his or her cultural identities slightly differently. If we want to understand why an individual behaves in a particular way, then we can ask the individual to talk about his or her cultural identity and experiences as a group member.

You can also study culture from a relational point of view. You can observe interaction between people, friends, co-workers, or family members who identify themselves as members of a relationship and with different groups. Collier (1988) found that Mexican American friends emphasized the importance of their relationship in their descriptions of what is appropriate and effective (e.g., meeting frequently and spending a significant portion of time together). They also described the most important characteristics of friendship to be support, trust, intimacy, and commitment to the relationship.

You may also study culture in terms of its communal properties. This is giving attention to public communication contexts and activities in communities and neighborhoods. Rituals, rites of passage, and holiday celebrations are other sources of information about how people use cultural membership to establish community.

STEP 9: WHAT ARE MY PRELIMINARY AND ALTERNATIVE INTERPRETATIONS AND CONCLUSIONS?

The ninth set of questions has to do with your interpretations. What patterns are you observing? What are your preliminary answers to your research questions? What are your tentative conclusions?

After you formulate preliminary conclusions and answers to your questions, it will be useful to ask: What are alternative interpretations and conclusions? Who might disagree with these findings?

Would your respondents (people you interviewed) or the audience for the film or newspaper articles agree or disagree with your findings? Can you ask them for further information? Have any voices or views been heretofore silent and unspoken? It is also important to ask yourself: To what extent are my personal history, socialization, preferred norms of conduct, and cultural identities affecting my interpretations and conclusions? What are my personal biases that need to be identified? In the campus problem, would a student who had taken courses in women's studies, ethnic studies, or international studies have alternative interpretations of my data that might change my overall conclusions?

STEP 10: HOW CAN I APPLY MY INTERPRETATIONS?

Finally, the last set of questions asks you to pinpoint how you can apply what you learned from the intercultural problem to your own cultural identities and intercultural communication, as well as broader community, national, and international issues. Essentially, you should propose how your findings could be useful to improve your own intercultural relationships and ability to analyze critically what you read and hear, as well as how your findings may be useful for members of the cultural communities you studied or the wider community.

Sometimes what we learn has implications for similar cultural groups or intercultural interactions in a wide variety of contexts even from one country to another. How has what you learned changed how you be, do, know about intercultural communication? With whom should you share your findings? What are ethical or moral insights that you might have developed? How can you apply what you learned about the campus problem to comprehend better current political discourse about affirmative action? What do you still need to know or study?

CONCLUSIONS

The study of intercultural communication is complex and dynamic; occurs in broad historical, economic, political, and social contexts; and is characterized by distinctive social norms and practices in the particular situation. My goal is for the inventory to become a useful guide for you to build knowledge about how we co-create our cultural identities and relationships through our contact with one another. I hope the steps indicate some of the major issues that emerge in intercultural communication, such as cultural identities, power, quality of relationship, and context, as well as point you toward the many options you have to study and potentially manage intercultural problematics. Finally, I hope that the examples from the communication discourse of people in my classes and research studies encourage you to think about perspectives that are different from your own in a new way.

Learning about intercultural communication is a lifelong endeavor. It is a commitment to improving the quality of what exists now and transcends our lifetimes. Let the dialogue continue.

Endnotes

1. Melissa McCalla, Jennifer Thompson, and Charlene Belitz, doctoral students at the University of Denver, assigned a draft of this chapter in their undergraduate intercultural communication courses. The student feedback and recommendations were insightful and helpful.
2. I am grateful to Melissa McCalla for suggesting this term.
3. Please see Anderson (1996), Deetz (1994), and Mumby (1997) for additional reading about how these particular categories of knowing emerged.

References

Anderson, J. A. (1996). *Communication theory: Epistemological foundations*. New York: Guilford Press.

Banks, J. (1984). *Teaching strategies for ethnic studies* (3rd ed.). Boston: Allyn & Bacon.

Baxter, L., & Montgomery, B. (1996). *Relating: Dialogues and dialectics*. New York: Guilford Press.

Braithwaite, D. (1991). "Just how much did that wheelchair cost?" Management of privacy boundaries by persons with disabilities. *Western Journal of Speech Communication, 55,* 254–274.

Brislin, R. (1986). Prejudice and intergroup communication. In W. Gudykunst (Ed.), *Intergroup communication* (pp. 74–85). Baltimore: Edward Arnold.

Carbaugh, D. (1990). Intercultural communication. In D. Carbaugh (Ed.), *Cultural communication and intercultural contact* (pp. 151–176). Hillsdale, NJ: Lawrence Erlbaum.

Collier, M. J. (1998a). Researching cultural identity: Reconciling interpretive and post-colonial perspectives. In D. Tanno & A. Gonzalez (Eds.), *Communication and identity across cultures* (International and Intercultural Communication Annual, Vol. XXI, pp. 122–147). Thousand Oaks, CA: Sage.

Collier, M. J. (1998b). Intercultural friendships as interpersonal alliances. In J. Martin, T. Nakayama, & L. Flores (Eds.), *Readings in cultural contexts* (pp. 370–378). Mountain View, CA: Mayfield.

Collier, M. J. (1988). A comparison of conversations among and between domestic culture groups: How intra- and intercultural competencies vary. *Communication Quarterly, 36,* 122–144.

Collier, M. J., & Bornman, E. (In press). Core symbols in South African intercultural friendships. *International Journal of Intercultural Relations*.

Collier, M. J., & Bowker, J. (1994, November). *U.S. American women in intercultural friendships*. Paper presented at the annual Speech Communication Association conference, New Orleans.

Collier, M. J., & Thomas, M. (1988). Cultural identity: An interpretive perspective. In Y. Y. Kim & W. Gudykunst (Eds.), *Theories in intercultural communication* (pp. 99–122). Newbury Park, CA: Sage.

Collier, M. J., & Thompson, J. (1997, May). *Intercultural adaptation among friends: Managing identities across contexts and relationships*. Paper presented at the International Conference of Language and Social Psychology, Ottawa, Canada.

Deetz, S. (1994). The future of the discipline: The challenges, the research and the social contribution. In S. Deetz (Ed.), *Communication yearbook 17* (pp. 115–147). Thousand Oaks, CA: Sage.

Doi, T. (1989). *The anatomy of dependence*. Tokyo: Kodansha Publishers.

Foss, S. K. (1998). bell hooks. In S. K. Foss, K. A. Foss, & C. L. Griffin (Eds.), *Feminist rhetorical theories*. Thousand Oaks, CA: Sage.

Giles, H., Coupland, N., & Coupland, J. (1991). Accommodation theory: Communication, contexts and consequences. In J. Giles, N. Coupland, & J. Coupland (Eds.), *Contexts of accommodation: Developments in applied sociolinguistics*. Cambridge, England: Cambridge University Press.

Goffman, E. (1967). *Interaction ritual: Essays on face-to-face interaction*. Garden City, NY: Doubleday.

Goldman, A. (1992). *The centrality of "Ningensei" to Japanese negotiating and interpersonal relationships: Implications for U.S.–Japanese communication.* Paper presented at Speech Communication Association conference, Chicago.

Gudykunst, W. B. (1994). Anxiety/uncertainty management (AUM) theory: Current status. In R. Wiseman (Ed.), *International and Intercultural Communication Annual, Vol. XIX* (pp. 170–193). Thousand Oaks, CA: Sage.

Gudykunst, W. B., & Ting-Toomey, S. (1988). *Culture and interpersonal communication.* Newbury Park: Sage.

Halualani, R. T. (1998). Seeing through the screen: A struggle of "culture." In J. Martin, T. Nakayama, & L. Flores (Eds.), *Readings in cultural contexts* (pp. 264–274). Mountain View, CA: Mayfield.

Hecht, M., & Ribeau, S. (1987). Afro-American identity labels and communicative effectiveness. *Journal of Language and Social Psychology, 6,* 319–326.

Hecht, M., Collier, M. J., & Ribeau, S. (1993). *African American communication.* Newbury Park: Sage.

Hecht, M., Ribeau, S., & Alberts, J. K. (1989). An Afro-American perspective on interethnic communication. *Communication Monographs, 56,* 385–410.

Hofstede, G. (1980). *Culture's consequences.* Newbury Park, CA: Sage.

hooks, b. (1989). *Talking back: Thinking feminist, thinking black.* Boston: South End.

Katz, E. (1960). The functional approach to the study of attitudes. *Public Opinion Quarterly, 24,* 164–204.

Langer, E. (1989). *Mindfulness.* Reading, MA: Addison-Wesley.

Marin, G., & Marin, B. V. (1991). *Research with Hispanic populations.* Newbury Park, CA: Sage.

Martin, J. (1997). Understanding whiteness in the United States. In L. Samovar & R. Porter (Eds.), *Intercultural communication: A reader* (8th ed., pp. 54–62). Belmont, CA: Wadsworth.

Martin, J., Nakayama, T. K., & Flores, L. A. (1997). A dialectical approach to intercultural communication. In J. Martin, T. Nakayama, & L. Flores (Eds.), *Readings in cultural contexts* (pp. 5–14). Mountain View, CA: Mayfield.

McClintock, A. (1995). *Imperial leather.* New York: Routledge.

McPhail, M. (1997). (Re)constructing the color line: Complicity and black conservatism. *Communication Theory, 7,* 162–177.

Morgan, R. (1996). Introduction. *Sisterhood is global.* New York: The Feminist Press.

Mumby, D. (1997). Modernism, postmodernism, and communication studies: A rereading of an ongoing debate. *Communication Theory, 7,* 1–28.

Omi, M., & Winant, H. (1986). *Racial formation in the United States.* New York: Routledge & Kegan Paul.

Prus, R. (1996). *Symbolic interaction and ethnographic research.* Albany: State University of New York Press.

Sachs, H. (1984). On doing "being ordinary." In J. M. Atkinson & J. Heritage (Eds.), *Structures of social action: Studies in conversation analysis* (pp. 413–429). Cambridge, UK: Cambridge University Press.

Sturken, M. (1995). The television image and collective amnesia: Dis(re)membering the Persian Gulf war. In P. d'Agostino & D. Tafler (Eds.), *Transmission: Toward a post-television culture* (2nd ed., pp. 135–150). Thousand Oaks, CA: Sage.

Tajfel, H. (1978). Interindividual and intergroup behaviour. In H. Tajfel (Ed.), *Differentiation between social groups* (pp. 27–60). London: Academic Press.

van Dijk, T. (1993). *Discourse and elite racism.* London: Routledge.

Webster, Y. (1992). *The racialization of America.* New York: St. Martin's Press.

Weider, D. L., & Pratt, S. (1990). On being a recognizable Indian among Indians. In D. Carbaugh (Ed.), *Cultural communication and intercultural contact* (pp. 45–64). Hillsdale, NJ: Lawrence Erlbaum.

Concepts and Questions

1. What is the central purpose of the "series of steps" presented by Collier?

2. Which one of Collier's "approaches to culture" do you believe most directly relates to intercultural communication?

3. How would you answer the following question: What do I want to know about the communicative event, contact, discourse, text, and situation?

4. What does Collier mean by the phrase "multiple types of cultural identities"?

5. Why is power an important variable in intercultural communication?

6. How would you answer the following question: What kinds of communicative messages should I examine to study intercultural communication?

7. How is Collier using the word *context?* intercultural communication?

8. In what specific ways do you believe Collier's 10 steps can be applied to your personal study of intercultural communication?

chapter 8

Ethical Considerations: Prospects for the Future

The goal of this book is to help you understand intercultural communication and to assist you in appreciating the issues and problems inherent in interactions involving people from cultures that are different from your own—whether those cultures be across the street or across the ocean. To this end, we have presented a series of essays that examine some of the diverse variables operating during intercultural encounters. In previous chapters we have looked at what is already known about intercultural communication. We now shift our emphasis and focus onto issues that are much more speculative and harder to pin down. These are the ethical considerations that are part of every intercultural encounter. This chapter examines some of the questions we all must confront as we have contact with cultures that are different from our own. This contact raises both ethical and philosophical issues about the question of how people from diverse cultures can live together without destroying themselves and the planet. In short, what sort of interpersonal and intercultural ethic must we develop if we are to improve the art and science of intercultural communication?

To set the tone for this final chapter, we begin with an essay by Harlan Cleveland titled "The Limits to Cultural Diversity." Cleveland eloquently alerts us to some of the problems associated with cultural diversity while offering us guidance for the future. The basic problem brought about by increased cultural contact is clear for Cleveland: "Ethnic and religious diversity is creating painful conflicts around the world." Too often these clashes turn one culture against another in ideological disputes. When this happens, according to Cleveland, "culture is being used as an instrument of repression, exclusion, and extinction." Cleveland fears that when people see the chaos created by alien cultures, they "believe that their best haven of certainty and security is a group based on ethnic similarity, common faith, economic interest, or political like-mindedness." Cleveland rejects this "single culture" hypothesis. What he recommends is a counterforce of wider views, global perspectives, and more universal ideas. This universal view, according to Cleveland, rests in a philosophy that has civilization (universal values, ideas, and practices) as the basic core for all humanity. In this analysis, culture represents the "substance and symbols of the community," while civilization is rooted in compromise and built on "cooperation and compassion." With this orientation, people can deal with each other in ways that respect cultural differences while granting essential overarching values. Cleveland's optimism is clearly stated in his conclusion: "For the 21st century, the cheerful acknowledgment of differences is the alternative to a global spread of ethnic cleansing and religious rivalry."

Our next essay, "Intercultural Personhood: An Integration of Eastern and Western Perspectives" by Young Yun Kim, is based on one of the central themes of this book—the idea that today's interconnected and fast-changing world demands that you change your assumptions about culture and your individual places within that culture. Recognizing these changes, Kim advances a philosophical orientation that she calls "intercultural personhood." For Kim, intercultural personhood combines the key attributes of Eastern and Western cultural traditions. She presents a model that uses these attributes and considers the basic modes of consciousness, cognitive patterns, personal and social values, and communication behavior. The notion of intercultural personhood also leads us into the concept of the multicultural person, as set forth in the next two essays.

Communication in any form has the potential to affect others. An ethical dimension therefore must be present in communication to minimize the chance of causing harm to others. In intercultural settings where our ethnocentrism, prejudices, and lack of understanding about other cultures may influence our perceptions of others, the need for an ethical dimension in communicative interaction is paramount.

We begin our exploration of the ethical dimensions of intercultural communication with Robert Shuter's essay "Ethics, Culture, and Communication: An Intercultural Perspective." Shuter believes that previous works on ethics and communication have generally ignored the issue of culture. To help us gather insight into ethical intercultural communication, Shuter uses an intracultural communication perspective to examine worldviews, values, and communication patterns within a culture. He then explores Confucian and Hindu ethical systems in order to speculate about communication ethics within those systems. Lastly, Shuter discusses communication and demonstrates how communication ethicists have maintained an intracultural bias in their research by focusing on U.S. and Western communication ethics.

In the next essay by Martha C. Nussbaum we see yet another point of view toward establishing an intercultural ethic. In many ways the title of Nussbaum's essay, "Citizens of the World," might well serve as a summary of her hypothesis. Her thesis is a simple one: *people must operate as world citizens with sensitivity and understanding*. Nussbaum examines this notion historically by looking at the views of such philosophers as Diogenes, Cicero, Paine, and Tagore. Nussbaum makes it clear that being a citizen of the world does not mean you give up your local affiliations or cultural loyalties. In fact, world citizenship is viewed as an extension of these alliances. She suggests that being a citizen of the world can be viewed as living within a set of "concentric circles." The first circle is drawn around the self; the next takes in your immediate family; and the next encloses extended families, neighbors, local groups, community, and country. To these circles she adds groups formed on the basis of ethnic, religious, linguistic, historical, professional, and gender identities. According to Nussbaum, beyond all of these circles is found the largest—*humanity as a whole*. For Nussbaum, accepting this notion is the key to becoming an effective a citizen of the world.

We end this chapter and the book with a final essay by David W. Kale, entitled "Peace as an Ethic for Intercultural Communication," which offers several specific challenges. The future is made real by Kale as he presents you with current examples, ranging from your role in the rainforests of Brazil to events taking place in Eastern Europe. Kale begins by acknowledging that most people feel uncomfortable addressing cultural beliefs about what is right and wrong. He reminds you that most of these beliefs are at the foundation of your lives and your culture. Despite this uneasiness, increased contact with diverse cultures, combined with the problems that can occur when cultures clash, demand that you examine the issues associated with questions of right and wrong. To help you in that examination, Kale asks that you begin by looking at five interrelated issues directly associated with any evaluation of intercultural ethics: (1) a definition of communication ethics, (2) cultural relativity versus universal ethic, (3) the concept of spirit as a basis for intercultural ethics, (4) peace as the fundamental value in intercultural ethics, and (5) a universal code of ethics in intercultural communication. Kale amplifies the fifth issue by urging you to follow a specific code that is predicated on four principles that should guide the actions of ethical communicators: (1) address people of other cultures with the same respect that you would like to receive yourself; (2) seek to describe the world as you perceive it as accurately as possible; (3) encourage people of other cultures to express themselves in their uniqueness; and (4) strive for identification with people of other cultures.

As we end our readings in this chapter, it might serve us well to view Kale's as well as all the other selections included in this chapter as only a sampling of the many issues that confront those who are involved in intercultural communication. The field is relatively new, and the challenges are so varied that it is impossible to accurately predict future directions. Our intent in this chapter, therefore, is simply to introduce you to a few of the concepts that await further discussion as you move through the 21st century.

One final note: Much of what we offer in this chapter is subjective and may even appear naive to some of you. Neither the authors nor we apologize for maintaining that in intercultural contacts each person should aim for the ideal. What we introduce here are suggestions for developing new ways of perceiving yourself and others. In so doing, we can all help make this complex and shrinking planet a more habitable and peaceful place for its more than 6 billion residents.

The Limits to Cultural Diversity

HARLAND CLEVELAND

I'm engaged just now in an effort to think through the most intellectually interesting, and morally disturbing, issue in my long experience of trying to think hard about hard subjects. I call it The Limits of Cultural Diversity. If that seems obscure, wait a moment.

After the multiple revolutions of 1989, it began to look as if three ideas we have thought were Good Things would be getting in each other's way, which is not a Good Thing. What I have called the "triple dilemma," or "trilemma," is the mutually damaging collision of individual human rights, cultural human diversity, and global human opportunities. Today the damage from that collision is suddenly all around us.

In 1994, in the middle of Africa, ethnicity took over as an exclusive value, resulting in mass murder by machete. In ex-Yugoslavia (and too many other places), gunpowder and rape accomplish the same purpose: trampling on human rights and erasing human futures. Even on the Internet, where individuals can now join global groups that are not defined by place-names or cordoned off by gender or ethnicity, people are shouting at each other in flaming, capital-letters rhetoric.

Look hard at your hometown, at the nearest inner city; scan the world by radio, TV, or newspapers and magazines. What's happened is all too clear: Just when individual human rights have achieved superstar status in political philosophy, just when can-do information technologies promise what the U.N. Charter calls "better standards of life in larger freedom," culture and diversity have formed a big, ugly boulder in the road called Future.

"If we cannot end now our differences, at least we can help make the world safe for diversity." That was the key sentence in the most influential speech of

John F. Kennedy's presidency: his commencement address at American University on June 10, 1963. That speech led directly (among other things) to the first nuclear test ban treaty. For most of the years since then, we were mesmerized by the threat of strategic nuclear war, but now a big nuclear war has become the least likely eventuality among the major threats to human civilization. And that brings us face to face with the puzzle identified in Kennedy's speech: how to make diversity safe.

But is "cultural diversity" really the new Satan in our firmament? Or does it just seem so because "culture" is being used—as Culture has been used in other times and places—as an instrument of repression, exclusion, and extinction?

AN EXCESS OF CULTURAL IDENTITY

In today's disordered world, the collision of cultures with global trends is in evidence everywhere. Ethnic nations, fragmented faiths, transnational businesses, and professional groups find both their inward loyalties and their international contacts leading them to question the political structures by which the world is still, if tenuously, organized. The results are sometimes symbolic caricatures ("In Rome, can a Moslem minaret be built taller than St. Peter's dome?") and sometimes broken mosaics like the human tragedy in what used to be Yugoslavia.

More people moved in 1994 than ever before in world history, driven by fear of guns or desire for more butter and more freedom. (This was true even before a couple of million Rwandans left their homes in terror—and some were floated out of the country as cadavers.) This more-mobile world multiplies the incentives for individuals to develop "multiple personalities," to become "collages" of identities, with plural loyalties to overlapping groups. Many millions of people believe that their best haven of certainty and security is a group based on ethnic similarity, common faith, economic interest, or political like-mindedness.

Societies based on fear of outsiders tend toward "totalitarian" governance. Fear pushes the culture beyond normal limits on individuals' behavior. "To say that you're ready to *die* for cultural identity," said one of my colleagues at a workshop of the World

From *The Futurist*, March–April, 1995, pp. 23–26. Reprinted by permission of the World Future Society. Harlan Cleveland is president of the World Academy of Art and Science.

Academy of Art and Science in Romania last year, "means that you're also ready to kill for cultural identity." Said another: "The ultimate consequence of what's called 'cultural identity' is Hutus and Tutsis murdering each other."

The fear that drives people to cleave to their primordial loyalties makes it harder for them to learn to be tolerant of others who may be guided by different faiths and loyalties. But isolating oneself by clinging to one's tribe is far from a stable condition; these days, the tribe itself is highly unstable. Differences in birthrates and pressures to move will continue to mix populations together. So ethnic purity isn't going to happen, even by forcible "cleansing."

Besides, cultures keep redefining themselves by mixing with other cultures, getting to know people who look, act, and believe differently. In today's more-open electronic world, cultures also expose themselves to new faiths and fashions, new lifestyles, work ways, technologies, clothing, and cuisines.

The early stage of every realization of "cultural identity," every assertion of a newfound "right" of differences, does create a distinct group marked by ethnic aspect ("black is beautiful"), gender ("women's lib"), religion ("chosen people"), or status as a political minority. But when members of a group insisting on the group's uniqueness do succeed in establishing their own personal right to be different, something very important happens: They begin to be treated *individually* as equals and tend to integrate with more inclusive communities. Traditions of separateness and discrimination are often persistent, but they are never permanent and immutable. The recent history of South Africa bears witness.

Before the fighting in Yugoslavia, the most-tolerant people in that part of the world were seen by their close neighbors to be the Serbs, Croats, and Moslems living together in Bosnia and Herzegovina, with the city of Sarajevo as a special haven of mutual tolerance.

The problem does not seem to be culture itself, but cultural overenthusiasm. Cultural loyalties, says one European, have the makings of a runaway nuclear reaction. Without the moderating influence of civil society—acting like fuel rods in a nuclear reactor—the explosive potential gets out of hand. What's needed is the counterforce of wider views, global perspectives, and more-universal ideas.

Post-communist societies, says a resident of one of them, have experienced a loss of equilibrium, a culture shock from the clash of traditional cultures, nostalgia for the stability of Soviet culture, and many new influences from outside. What's needed, he thinks, is cultural richness without cultural dominance, but with the moderating effect of intercultural respect.

CULTURE AND CIVILIZATION

We have inherited a fuzzy vocabulary that sometimes treats *culture* as a synonym for *civilization*. At a World Academy workshop, my colleagues and I experimented with an alternative construct.

In this construct, *civilization* is what's universal—values, ideas, and practices that are in general currency everywhere, either because they are viewed as objectively "true" or because they are accepted pragmatically as useful in the existing circumstances. These accepted "truths" offer the promise of weaving together a civitas of universal laws and rules, becoming the basis for a global civil society.

What is sometimes called "management culture" appears to be achieving this kind of universal acceptance, hence becoming part of global "civilization." But nobody has to be in charge of practices that are generally accepted. For instance, the international exchange of money—a miracle of information technologies—is remarkably efficient, daily moving more than a trillion dollars' worth of money among countries. Yet, no one is in charge of the system that makes it happen. Recently, the puny efforts of governments to control monetary swings by buying and selling currencies have only demonstrated governments' incapacity to control them.

If civilization is what's universal, *culture* is the substance and symbols of the community. Culture meets the basic human need for a sense of belonging, for participating in the prides and fears that are shared with an in-group. Both culture and civilization are subject to continuous change. In our time, the most-pervasive changes seem to be brought about by the spread of knowledge, the fallout of information science and information technologies.

Civil society consists of many structures and networks, cutting across cultural fault lines, brought into being by their ability to help people communicate.

They are not very dependent on public authority for their charters or their funding, increasingly taking on functions that used to be considered the responsibility of national governments.

Many of these "nongovernments"—such as those concerned with business and finance, scientific inquiry, the status of women, population policy, and the global environmental commons—have become effective users of modern information technologies. In consequence, they are providing more and more of the policy initiative both inside countries and in world affairs.

Civilization is rooted in compromise—between the idea of a democratic state and a strong state, between a free-market economy and a caring economy, between "open" and "closed" processes, between horizontal and vertical relationships, between active and passive citizenship. The required solvent for civilization is *respect* for *differences*. Or, as one of my World Academy colleagues puts it, we need to learn *how to be different together*.

Civilization will be built by cooperation and compassion, in a social climate in which people in differing groups can deal with each other in ways that respect their cultural differences. "Wholeness incorporating diversity" is philosopher John W. Gardner's succinct formulation. The slogan on U.S. currency is even shorter, perhaps because it's in Latin: *E pluribus unum* ("from many, one").

LESSONS FROM AMERICAN EXPERIENCE

We Americans have learned, in our short but intensive 200-plus years of history as a nation, a first lesson about diversity: that it cannot be governed by drowning it in "integration."

I came face to face with this truth when, just a quarter century ago, I became president of the University of Hawaii. Everyone who lives in Hawaii, or even visits there, is impressed by its residents' comparative tolerance toward each other. On closer inspection, paradise seems based on paradox: Everybody's a minority. The tolerance is not despite the diversity but because of it.

It is not through the disappearance of ethnic distinctions that the people of Hawaii achieved a level of racial peace that has few parallels around our discriminatory globe. Quite the contrary. The glory is that Hawaii's main ethnic groups managed to establish the right to be separate. The group separateness in turn helped establish the rights of individuals in each group to equality with individuals of different racial aspect, different ethnic origin, and different cultural heritage.

Hawaii's experience is not so foreign to the transatlantic migrations of the various more-or-less-white Caucasians. On arrival in New York (passing that inscription on the Statue of Liberty, "Send these, the homeless, tempest-tost, to me"), the European immigrants did not melt into the open arms of the white Anglo-Saxon Protestants who preceded them. The reverse was true. The new arrivals stayed close to their own kind, shared religion and language and humor and discriminatory treatment with their soul brothers and sisters, and gravitated at first into occupations that did not too seriously threaten the earlier arrivals.

The waves of new Americans learned to tolerate each other—first as groups, only thereafter as individuals. Rubbing up against each other in an urbanizing America, they discovered not just the old Christian lesson that all men are brothers, but the hard, new, multicultural lesson that all brothers are different. Equality is not the product of similarity; it is the cheerful acknowledgment of difference.

What's so special about our experience is the assumption that people of many kinds and colors can together govern themselves without deciding in advance which kinds of people (male or female, black, brown, yellow, red, white, or any mix of these) may hold any particular public office in the pantheon of political power.

For the 21st century, this "cheerful acknowledgement of difference" is the alternative to a global spread of ethnic cleansing and religious rivalry. The challenge is great, for ethnic cleansing and religious rivalry are traditions as contemporary as Bosnia and Rwanda in the 1990s and as ancient as the Assyrians who, as Byron wrote, "came down like a wolf on the fold" but says the biblical Book of Kings, were prevented by sword-wielding angels from taking Jerusalem.

In too many countries there is still a basic if often unspoken assumption that one kind of people is anointed to be in general charge. Try to imagine a

Turkish chancellor of Germany, an Algerian president of France, a Pakistani prime minister of Britain, a Christian president of Egypt, an Arab prime minister of Israel, a Jewish president of Syria, a Tibetan ruler in Beijing, anyone but a Japanese in power in Tokyo.

Yet in the United States during the twentieth century, we have already elected an Irish Catholic as president, chosen several Jewish Supreme Court justices, and racially integrated the armed forces right up to chairman of the Joint Chiefs of Staff. We have not yet adjusted—as voters in India, Britain, and Turkey have done—to having a woman atop the American political heap. But early in the 21st century, that too will come. And during that same new century, which will begin with "minorities" as one in every three Americans, there is every prospect that an African American, a Latin American, and an Asian American will be elected president of the United States.

I wouldn't dream of arguing that we Americans have found the Holy Grail of cultural diversity when in fact we're still searching for it. We have to think hard about our growing pluralism. It's useful, I believe, to dissect in the open our thinking about it, to see whether the lessons we are trying to learn might stimulate some useful thinking elsewhere. We do not yet quite know how to create "wholeness incorporating diversity," but we owe it to the world, as well as to ourselves, to keep trying.

Concepts and Questions

1. What does Cleveland mean when he speaks of making diversity safe?
2. What does Cleveland imply when he refers to "an excess of cultural identity"?
3. How does loyalty to one's own cultural identity make it difficult to be tolerant of others?
4. What is meant by the term *cultural overenthusiasm*? How does it affect intercultural relations?
5. How does Cleveland differentiate between the concepts of *culture* and *civilization*?
6. What are the hallmarks of civilization? How can they be maintained?
7. What does Cleveland imply when he states that diversity cannot be governed by drowning it in integration?
8. What does Cleveland mean when he argues that there are limits to diversity?
9. What principles must be followed in order for diversity to flourish in American society?

Intercultural Personhood: An Integration of Eastern and Western Perspectives

Young Yun Kim

We live in a time of clashing identities. As the tightly knit communication web has brought all cultures closer than ever before, rigid adherence to the culture of our youth is no longer feasible. Cultural identity in its "pure" form has become more a nostalgic concept than a reality. As Toffler (1980) noted, we find ourselves "[facing] a quantum leap forward. [We face] the deepest social upheaval and creative restructuring of all time. Without clearly recognizing it, we are engaged in building a remarkable new civilization from the ground up" (p. 44). Yet the very idea of cultural identity, coupled with rising nationalism and xenophobic sentiments, looms over much of today's fractious world landscape. Can the desire for some form of collective uniqueness be satisfied without resulting in divisions and conflicts among groups? Can individuals who are committed to communal values and responsibilities transcend allegiance to their own people?

This essay addresses these issues by proposing the concept of *intercultural personhood*—a way of life in which an individual develops an identity and a definition of self that integrates, rather than separates, humanity. Intercultural personhood projects a kind of human development that is open to growth—a growth beyond the perimeters of one's own cultural upbringing.[1] In making a case for the viability of intercultural personhood, we will first survey some of the core elements in the two seemingly incompatible cultural traditions of the East and the West. We will focus on the cultural apriority, or "root ideas" that define these philosophical perspectives. An argument will be made that certain aspects of these two traditions, often considered unbridgeably incompatible, are profoundly complementary and that such complementary elements can be creatively integrated into a ground-level consideration of human conditions. We will then examine how the process of building an intercultural personhood is actually played out in the lives of people whose life experiences span both cultural worlds.

The current discussion of intercultural personhood owes much to the writings of several prominent thinkers of the 20th century who have explored ideologies larger than national and cultural interests and that embrace all humanity. One such work is Northrop's *The Meeting of East and West* (1966), in which an "international cultural ideal" was presented as a way to provide intellectual and emotional foundations for what he envisioned as "partial world sovereignty." Inspiration has also been drawn from the work of Thompson (1973), which explored the idea of "planetary culture," or how Eastern mysticism was integrated with Western science and rationalism. The primary sources for the current analysis of Eastern and Western cultural traditions also include Nakamura's *Ways of Thought of Eastern People* (1964), Campbell's *The Power of Myth* (1988), Gulick's *The East and the West* (1963), Oliver's *Communication and Culture in Ancient India and China* (1971), Capra's *The Tao of Physics* (1975), and Hall's *Beyond Culture* (1976) and *The Dance of Life* (1983).

EASTERN AND WESTERN CULTURAL TRADITIONS

Traditional cultures throughout Asia—including India, Tibet, Japan, China, Korea, and those in Southeast Asia—have been influenced by such religious and philosophical systems as Buddhism, Hinduism, Taoism, and Zen. On the other hand, Western Europe has mainly followed the Greek and Judeo-Christian traditions. Of course, any attempt to present the cultural assumptions of these two broadly categorized civilizations inevitably sacrifices specific details and the uniqueness of variations within each tradition. No

two individuals or groups hold identical beliefs and manifest uniform behaviors, and whatever characterizations we make about one culture or cultural group must be thought of as normative tendencies that vary rather than monolithic and uniform attributes. Nevertheless, several key elements distinguish each group from the other. To specify these elements is to indicate the general interconnectedness of different nations that constitute either the Eastern or the Western cultural world.

Universe and Nature

A fundamental way in which culture shapes human existence is through the explicit and implicit teachings about our relationships to the nature of the universe and the human and nonhuman realms of the world. Traditional Eastern and Western perspectives diverge significantly with respect to basic premises about these relationships. As Needham (1951) noted in his article "Human Laws and the Laws of Nature in China and the West," people in the West have conceived the universe as having been initially created and, since then, externally controlled by a Divine power. As such, the Western worldview is characteristically dualistic, materialistic, and lifeless. The Judeo-Christian tradition sets "God" apart from this reality; having created it and set it into motion, God is viewed as apart from "His" creation. The fundamental material of the universe is conceived to be essentially nonliving matter, or elementary particles of matter, that interact with one another in a predictable fashion. It is as though the universe is an inanimate machine wherein humankind occupies a unique and elevated position among the life-forms that exist. Assuming a relatively barren universe, it seems only rational that humans make use of the lifeless material universe (and the "lesser" life-forms of nature) on behalf of the most intensely living—humankind itself.

Comparatively, the Eastern worldview is more holistic, dynamic, and inwardly spiritual. From the Eastern perspective, the entirety of the universe is viewed as a vast, multidimensional, living organism consisting of many interdependent parts and forces. The universe is conscious and engaged in a continuous dance of creation: The cosmic pattern is viewed as self-contained and self-organizing. It unfolds itself because of its own inner necessity and not because it is "ordered" by any external volitional power. What exists in the universe are manifestations of a divine life force. Beneath the surface appearance of things, an "Ultimate Reality" is continuously creating, sustaining, and infusing our worldly experience. The all-sustaining life force that creates our manifest universe is not apart from humans and their worldly existence. Rather, it is viewed as dynamic and intimately involved in every aspect of the cosmos—from its most minute details to its grandest features.

The traditional Eastern worldview, then, reveres the common source out of which all things arise. As Campbell (1990) noted, "people in Eastern cultures—whether they are Indians, Japanese, or Tibetans—tend to think that the real mystery is in yourself. . . . Finding the divine not only within you, but within all things. . . . And what the Orient brings is a realization of the inward way. When you sit in meditation with your hands in your lap, with your head looking down, that means you've gone in and you're coming not just to a soul that is disengaged from God: you're coming to that divine mystery right there in yourself" (p. 89).

This perspective recognizes that everything in this world is fluid, ever-changing, and impermanent. In Hinduism, all static forms are called *maya*, that is, existing only as illusory concepts. This idea of the impermanence of all forms is the starting point of Buddhism. Buddhism teaches that "all compounded things are impermanent," and that all suffering in the world arises from our trying to cling to fixed forms—objects, people, or ideas—instead of accepting the world as it moves. This notion of impermanence of all forms and the appreciation of the aliveness of the universe in the Eastern worldview contrasts with the Western emphasis on the definitive forms of physical reality and their improvement through social and material progress.

Knowledge

Because the East and the West have different views of cosmic patterns, we can expect them to have different approaches to knowledge. In the East, because the universe is seen as a harmonious organism, there is a corresponding lack of dualism in epistemological patterns. The Eastern view emphasizes perceiving and knowing things synthetically, rather than analytically. The ultimate purpose of knowledge is to transcend the apparent contrasts and "see" the interconnectedness of all things. When the Eastern mystics tell us that they experience all things as manifestations of a basic oneness, they do not mean that they pronounce all things to be same or equal. Instead, they emphasize that all differences are relative within an all-encompassing phenomenon. Indeed, the awareness that all opposites are polar and, thus, a unity, is one of the highest aims of knowledge. As Suzuki (1968) noted: "The fundamental idea of Buddhism is to pass beyond the world of opposites, a world built up by intellectual distinctions and emotional defilements, and to realize the spiritual world of non-distinction, which involves achieving an absolute point of view" (p. 18).

Because all opposites are interdependent, their conflict can never result in the total victory of one side but will always be a manifestation of the interplay between the two sides. A virtuous person is not one who undertakes the impossible task of striving for the "good" and eliminating the "bad," but rather one who is able to maintain a dynamic balance between the two. Transcending the opposites, one becomes aware of the relativity and polar relationship of opposites. One realizes that good and bad, pleasure and pain, life and death, winning and losing, light and dark, are not absolute experiences belonging to different categories, but merely two sides of the same reality—extreme parts of a single continuum. The Chinese sages in their symbolism of the archetypal poles, yin and yang, have emphasized this point extensively. And the idea that opposites cease to be opposites is the very essence of *Tao*. To know the Tao, the illustrious way of the universe, is the highest aim of human learning.

This holistic approach to knowledge in the East is pursued by means of "concepts by intuition," a sense of the aesthetic components of things. A concept by intuition is something immediately experienced, apprehended, and contemplated. Northrop (1966) described it as the "differentiated aesthetic continuum" within which there is no distinction between subjective and objective. The aesthetic continuum is a single all-embracing continuity. The aesthetic part of the self is also an essential part of the aesthetic object, whether the object is a flower or a person. Taoism, for example, pursues an undifferentiated aesthetic continuum as it is manifested in the differentiated, sensed aesthetic qualities in nature. The Taoist claim is that only if we take the aesthetic continuity in its all-embracingness as ultimate and irreducible, will we properly understand the meaning of the universe and nature. Similarly, Confucianism stresses the all-embracing aesthetic continuum with respect to its manifestations in human nature and its moral implications for human society: Only if we recognize the all-embracing aesthetic manifold to be an irreducible part of human nature will we have compassion for human beings other than ourselves.

As such, the undifferentiated aesthetic continuum is the Eastern conception of the constituted world. The differentiations within it—such as particular scenes, events, or persons—are not irreducible atomic identities, but merely arise out of the undifferentiated ground-level reality of the aesthetic continuum. Sooner or later, they fade back into it again. They are transitory and impermanent. Thus, when Eastern sages insist that one must become *selfless*, they mean that the self consists of two components: one, a differentiated, unique element, distinguishing one person from any other person, and the other the all-embracing, aesthetically immediate, compassionate, and undifferentiated component. The former is temporary and transitory, and the cherishing of it, the desire for its immortality, is a source of suffering and selfishness. The part of the self that is not transitory is the aesthetic component of the self, which is identical not merely in all persons, but in all aesthetic objects throughout the universe.

While the Eastern knowledge tradition has concentrated its mental processes on the holistic, intuitive, aesthetic continuum, the Western pursuit of knowledge has been based on a doctrinally formulated dualistic worldview. In this view, because the world and its various components came into existence through the individual creative acts of a god, the fundamental question is, "How can I reach out to the external inanimated world or to other people?" In this question, there is a basic dichotomy between the knower and the things to be known. Accompanying this epistemological dualism is the emphasis on rationality in the pursuit of knowledge. Since the Greek philosopher Plato "discovered" reason, virtually all subsequent Western thought—its themes, questions, and terms—relies on an essential rational basis (Wei, 1980).

Even Aristotle, the great hero of all anti-Platonists, was not an exception. Although Aristotle did not propose, as Plato did, a realm of eternal essences ("really real") to justify the primacy of reason, he was by no means inclined to deny this primacy. This is an indication that, while the East has tended to emphasize the direct experience of oneness via intuitive concepts and contemplation, the West has viewed the faculty of the intellect as the primary instrument of worldly mastery. While Eastern thought tends to conclude in more or less vague, imprecise statements, consistent with its existential flexibility, Western thought emphasizes clear and distinct categorization and the linear, analytic logic of syllogism. While the Eastern cultural drive for human development is aimed at spiritual attainment of oneness with the universe, the Western cultural drive finds its expression in its drive for material and social progress.

Time

Closely parallel to differences between the two cultural traditions regarding the nature of knowledge are differences in the perception and experience of time. Along with the immediate, undifferentiated experiencing of here and now, the Eastern time orientation can be portrayed as a placid, silent pool within which ripples come and go. Historically, the East has tended to view worldly existence as cyclical and has often depicted it with metaphors of movement such as a wheel or an ocean: The "wheel of existence" or the "ocean of waves" appears to be in a continual movement but is "not really going anywhere." Although individuals living in the world may experience a rise or fall in their personal fortunes, the lot of the whole is felt to be fundamentally unchanging. As Northrop (1966) noted, "the aesthetic continuum is the greater mother of creation, giving birth to the ineffable beauty of the golden yellows on the mountain landscape as the sun drops low in the late afternoon, only a moment later to receive that differentiation back into itself and to put another in its place without any effort" (p. 343).

Because worldly time is not experienced as going anywhere and because in spiritual time there is nowhere to go but the eternity within the now, the future is expected to be virtually the same as the past. Recurrence in both cosmic and psychological realms is very much a part of the Eastern thought. Thus, the individual's aim is not to escape from the circular movement into linear time, but to become a part of the eternal through the aesthetic experience of the here and now and the conscious evolution of spirituality to "know" the all-embracing, undifferentiated wholeness. In contrast, the West has represented time either with an arrow or as a moving river that comes out of a distant place and past (which are not here and now) and that goes into an equally distant place and future (which also are not here and now). In this view of time, history is conceived of as goal-directed and gradually progressing in a certain direction (toward the universal salvation and second coming of Christ or, in secular terms, toward an ideal state such as boundless freedom or a classless society).

Closely corresponding to the above comparison is Hall's (1976, 1983) characterization of Asian cultures as "polychronic" and Western cultures as "monochronic" in their respective time orientations. Hall explained that individuals in a polychronic system are less inclined to adhere rigidly to time as a tangible, discrete, and linear entity; instead, they emphasize completion of transactions in the here and now, often carrying out more than one activity simultaneously. Comparatively, according to Hall, a monochronic system emphasizes schedules, segmentation, promptness, and standardization of activities. We may say that the Eastern polychronic time orientation is rooted in the synchronization of human behavior with the rhythms of nature, whereas the Western time orientation is driven by the synchronization of human behavior with the rhythms of the clock or machine.

Communication

The historical ideologies examined so far have shaped the empirical content of the East and the West. The respective Eastern and Western perspectives on the universe, nature, knowledge, and time are reflected in many of the specific activities of individuals as they relate themselves to fellow human beings—how individuals view self and the group, and how they use verbal and nonverbal symbols in communication.

First, the view of self and identity cultivated in the Eastern tradition is embedded within an immutable social order. People tend to acquire their sense of identity from an affiliation with, and participation in, a virtually unchanging social order. As has been pointed out in many of the contemporary anthropological studies, the self that emerges from this tradition is not the clearly differentiated existential ego of the West, but a less distinct and relatively unchanging *social ego*. Individual members of the family tend to be more willing to submit their own self-interest for the good of the family. Individuals and families are often expected to subordinate their views to those of the community or the state.

The Eastern tradition also accepts hierarchy in social order. In a hierarchical structure, individuals are viewed as differing in status, although all are considered to be equally essential for the total system and its processes. A natural result of this orientation is the emphasis on authority—the authority of the parents over the children; of the grandparents over their descendants; of the official head of the community, the clan, and the state over all its members. Authoritarianism is an outstanding feature of Eastern life, not only in government, business, and family, but also in education and in beliefs. The more ancient a tradition, the greater is its authority.

The Eastern view further asserts that who "we" are is not limited to our physical existence. Consciousness is viewed as the bridge between the finite and differentiated (one's sense of uniqueness) and the infinite and undifferentiated (the experience of wholeness and eternity). With sufficient training, each person can discover that who he or she is correlates with nature and the divine. All are one and the same in the sense that the divine, undifferentiated, aesthetic continuum of the universe is manifested in each person and in nature. Through this aesthetic connection, individuals and nature are none other than the Tao, the Ultimate Reality, the divine life force, Nirvana, God.

Comparatively, the Western view, in which God, nature, and humans are distinctly differentiated, fosters the development of autonomous individuals with strong ego identification. The dualistic worldview is manifested in an individual's view of his or her relationship to other persons and nature. Interpersonal relationships are essentially egalitarian—cooperative arrangements between two equal partners in which the personal needs and interests of each party are more or less equally respected, negotiated, or resolved by compromise. Whereas the East emphasizes submission (or conformity) of the individual to the group, the West encourages individuality and individual needs to drive the group. If the group no longer serves the individual needs, then it (not the individual) must be changed. The meaning of an interpersonal relationship is decided on primarily by the functions that each party performs in satisfying the needs of the other. A relationship is regarded as healthy to the extent that it serves the expected function for all parties involved. As extensively documented in anthropology and cross-cultural psychology (e.g., Hsu, 1981; Kluckhohn & Strodtbeck, 1960; Triandis, 1995), individualism is the central theme of the Western personality distinguishing the Western world from the collectivistic non-Western world.

This pragmatic interpersonal orientation of the West can be contrasted with the Eastern tradition, in which group membership is taken as given and therefore unchallenged, and in which individuals must conform to the group in case of conflicting interest. Members of the group are encouraged to maintain harmony and minimize competition. Individuality is discouraged, while moderation, modesty, and the bending of one's ego are praised. In some cases, both individual and group achievement (in a material sense) must be forsaken to maintain group harmony. In this context, the primary source of interpersonal understanding is the unwritten and often unspoken norms, values, and ritualized mannerisms pertinent to a particular situation. Rather than relying heavily on explicit and logical verbal expressions, the Eastern communicator grasps the aesthetic essence of the communication dynamic by observing subtleties in nonverbal and circumstantial cues. Intuition, rather than rational thinking, plays a central role in the understanding of how one talks, how one addresses the other, under what circumstances, on what topic, in which of various styles, with what intent, and with what effect.

These implicit communication patterns are reflected in the Eastern fondness for verbal hesitance and ambiguity—out of fear of disturbing or offending others (Cathcart & Cathcart, 1982; Doi, 1982; Kincaid, 1987). Even silence is sometimes preferred to eloquent verbalization in expressing strong compliments or affection. Easterners are often suspicious of the genuineness of excessive verbal praises or compliments because, to their view, truest feelings must be intuitively apparent and therefore do not need to be, and cannot be, articulated. As a result, the burden of communicating effectively is shared by both the speaker and the listener, who is expected to "hear" the implicit messages through empathic attentiveness. In contrast, the Western communicative mode is primarily direct, explicit, and verbal, relying on logic and rational thinking. Participants in communication are viewed as distinctly different individuals, and their individuality has to be expressed through accurate verbal articulation. Inner feelings are not to be intuitively understood but to be honestly and assertively verbalized and discussed. Here, the burden of communicating effectively lies primarily with the speaker.

The preceding characterization of Eastern and Western communication patterns is largely consistent with observations made by other scholars such as Kincaid (1987), Yum (1994), and Hall (1976, 1983). Hall, in particular, has depicted Asian cultures as *high-context* in comparison with the low-context cultures of the West. The focal point of Hall's cross-cultural comparison is "contexting," that is, the act of taking into account information that is either embedded in physical or social context (which includes nonverbal behaviors) or internalized in the communicator. In this scheme, low-context communication, which is more prevalent in the West, is observed when most interpersonal information is expressed by explicit, verbalized codes.

BEYOND CULTURAL DIFFERENCES

As has been pointed out, many of the specific differences that we observe between Eastern and Western societies hinge upon their respective worldviews. Based on an organic, holistic, and cyclic worldview, the East has followed an epistemology that emphasized direct, immediate, and aesthetic components in human experience of the world. The ultimate aim of human learning was to transcend the immediate, differentiated self and to develop an integrative perception of the undifferentiated universe. The goal is to be spiritually one with the universe and to find the eternal within the present moment, which is a reflection of the eternal. Alternatively, the eternal resides in the present moment. The Western tradition, in contrast, is rooted in the cosmology of dualism, determinism, and materialism. It engenders an outlook that is rational, analytic, and indirect. History is conceived as a linear progression from the past into the future. The pursuit of knowledge is not so much a pursuit of spiritual enhancement as a quest to improve the human condition.

These different worldviews, in turn, are reflected in the individual's conception of the self, the other, and the group. While the East has stressed the primacy of the group over the individual, the West has stressed the primacy of the individual over the group. Interpersonally, the East views the self as deeply merged in the group ego, while the West encourages distinct and autonomous individuality. Explicit, clear, and logical verbalization is a salient feature in the Western communication system, as compared to the emphasis on implicit, intuitive, and nonverbal messages in the Eastern tradition.

The cultural premises of the East and the West that we have examined suggest the areas of vitality, as well as areas of weakness, that are characteristic of each civilization. The Western mechanistic and dualistic worldview has helped to advance scientific efforts to describe systematically and explain physical phenomena, leading to extremely successful technological advancements. The West has learned, however, that the mechanistic worldview and the corresponding communication patterns are often inadequate for understanding the rich and complex phenomena of human relationships and that this lack of understanding can cause alienation from self and others. The West has seen that its dualistic distinction between humanity and nature brings about alienation from the natural world. The analytical mind of the West has led to modern science and technology, but it also has resulted in knowledge that is often compartmentalized, fragmented, and detached from the fuller totality of reality.

In comparison, the East has not experienced the level of alienation that the West has. At the same time, however, the East has not seen as much material

and social development. Its holistic and aesthetic worldview has not been conducive to the development of science or technology. Its hierarchical social order and binding social relationships have not fostered the civic-mindedness, worldly activism, humanitarianism, and volunteerism that flourish in the West. Many of the Asian societies continue to struggle to bring about democratic political systems that are based on the rights and responsibilities of individuals.

It should be stressed at this time that the Western emphasis on logical, theoretic, dualistic, and analytic thinking does not suggest that it has been devoid of intuitive, direct, purely empirical, aesthetic elements. Conversely, emphasizing the Western contributions of sociomaterial development is not meant to suggest that the East has been devoid of learning in these areas. The differences that have been pointed out do not represent diametric opposition, but rather differences in emphasis that are nonetheless significant and observable. Clearly, the range of sophistication of Western contributions to the sociomaterial domain far exceeds that of contributions from the East. However, the Eastern emphasis on aesthetic and holistic self-mastery has offered a system of life philosophy that touches on the depth of human experience vis-à-vis other humans, the natural world, and the universe.

Indeed, many have expressed increasing realization of limitations in the Western worldview. Using the term "extension transference," for instance, Hall (1976) pointed out the danger of the common intellectual maneuver in which technological "extensions"—including language, logic, technology, institutions, and scheduling—are confused with or take the place of the process extended. We observe the tendency in the West to assume that the remedy for problems arising from technology should be sought not in the attempt to rely on an ideal minimum of technology, but in the development of even more technology. Burke (1974) called this tendency "technologism": "[There] lie the developments whereby 'technologism' confronts its inner contradictions, a whole new realm in which the heights of human rationality, as expressed in industrialism, readily become 'solutions' that are but the source of new and aggravated problems" (p. 148).

Self-criticisms in the West have also been directed to the rigid scientific dogmatism that insists on the discovery of truth based on the mechanistic, linear causality, and objectivity. In this regard, Thayer (1983) commented:

> What the scientific mentality attempts to emulate, mainly, is the presumed method of laboratory science. But laboratory science predicts nothing that it does not control or that is not otherwise fully determined. . . . One cannot successfully study relatively open systems with methods that are appropriate only for closed systems. Is it possible that this is the kind of mentality that precludes its own success? (p. 88)

Similarly, Hall (1976) has pointed out that the Western emphasis on logic as synonymous with the "truth" denies that part of human self that integrates. Hall sees that logical thinking is only a small fraction of our mental capabilities and that there are many different and legitimate ways of thinking that have tended to be less emphasized in Western cultures (p. 9).

The criticisms raised by these and other critics of scientific epistemology do not deny the value of the rational, inferential knowledge. Rather, they are directed to the error of Western philosophy in regarding concepts that do not adhere to its mode as invalid. They refer to the arrogance or overconfidence in believing that scientific knowledge is the only way to discover truth, when, in reality, the very process of doing science requires an immediate, aesthetic experience of the phenomenon under investigation. Without the immediately apprehended component, the theoretical hypotheses proposed could not be tested empirically with respect to their truth or falsity and would lack the relevance to the corresponding reality. As Einstein once commented:

> Science is the attempt to make the chaotic diversity of our sense-experience correspond to a logically uniform system of thought. In this system single experiences must be correlated with the theoretic structure in such a way that the resulting coordination is complete and convincing. (Quoted in Northrop, 1966, p. 443)

In this description of science, Einstein is careful to indicate that the relation between the theoretically postulated component and the immediately experienced aesthetic component is one of correspondence. The wide spectrum of our everyday life activities demands both scientific and aesthetic modes of apprehension: critical analysis as well as perception of wholes; doubt and skepticism as well as unconditional appreciation; abstraction as well as concreteness; perception of the general and regular as well as the individual and unique; the literalism of technical terms as well as the power and richness of poetic language, silence, and art; relationships with casual acquaintances as well as intimate personal engagement. If we limit ourselves to the dominant scientific mode of apprehension and do not value the aesthetic mode, then we would be making an error of limiting the essential human to only a part of the full span of life activities.

As such, one potential benefit of incorporating the Eastern aesthetic orientation into Western cultural life is a heightened sense of freedom. The aesthetic component of human nature is in part indeterminate, and the ambiguity of indetermination is the basis of our freedom. We might also transcend the clockbound worldly time to the "Eternal Now," the "timeless moment" that is embedded within the center of each moment. By occasionally withdrawing into the indeterminate, aesthetic component of our nature, away from the determinate, transitory circumstances, we could overcome the pressures of everyday events into a basis for renewal of our human spirit. The traditional Eastern practice of meditation is designed primarily for the purpose of moving one's consciousness from the determinate to the indeterminate, freer state.

Second, incorporation of the Eastern view could bring the West to a greater awareness of the aliveness and wholeness of the universe we inhabit and the life we live. The universe is engaged in a continuous dance of creation at each instant of time. Everything is alive—brimming with a silent energy that creates, sustains, and infuses all that exists. With the expanded perspective on time, we would increase our sensitivity to the rhythms of nature—such as the seasons and the cycles of birth and decay. This integrative worldview is one that pacifies us. Because of its all-embracing oneness and unity, the indeterminate aesthetic continuum helps us to cultivate compassion and intuitive sensitivity—not only for other humans but also for all of nature's creatures. In this regard, Maslow (1971) referred to

Taoistic receptivity or "let-be" as an important attribute of self-actualizing persons:

> We may speak of this respectful attention to the matter-in-paradigm as a kind of courtesy or deference (without intrusion of the controlling will) which is akin to "taking it seriously." This amounts to treating it as an end, something per se, with its own right to be, rather than as a means to some end other than itself; i.e., as a tool for some extrinsic purpose. (p. 68)

Such aesthetic perception is an instrument of intimate human meeting, a way to bridge the gap between individuals and groups. In dealing with each other aesthetically, we do not subject ourselves to a rigid scheme, but do our best in each new situation, listening to the silence as well as the words, and experiencing the other person as a whole living entity with less infusion of our own egocentric and ethnocentric demands. A similar attitude can be developed toward the physical world, as is witnessed in the rising interest in the West in ecological integrity and holistic medicine (see Brody, 1997; Wallis, 1996).

What the preceding considerations suggest is that many Eastern and Western philosophical premises offer views of reality that are not competitive, but complementary. Of course, the entire values, norms, and institutions of the West cannot, and should not, be substituted for their Eastern counterparts, and vice versa. The West may no more adopt the worldview of the East than the East may adopt the worldviews of the West. Rather, we need to recognize that a combination of rational and intuitive modes of experiencing life leads to a life that is more real and more meaningful. With this understanding, we see the interrelatedness and reconciliation of the two seemingly incompatible perspectives.

Our task, then, is to reach for the unity in human experiences and simultaneously to express diversity. A general synthesis of East and West is neither possible nor desirable: The purpose of evolution is not to create a homogeneous mass, but to continuously unfold an ever diverse and yet organic whole. Yet knowledge of differing cultural traditions can help each society move toward greater collective self-understanding—especially by revealing blind spots that can be illuminated only by adopting a vastly different way of seeing. Each tradition can play a necessary and integral part in the continuing evolution of humanity, out of which another birth, a higher integration of human consciousness, may arise.

EMERGENCE OF INTERCULTURAL PERSONHOOD

The task of synthesizing elements of Eastern and Western cultural traditions is taken not merely to satisfy an esoteric academic curiosity but also out of keen relevance to the everyday realities of numerous individuals whose life experiences extend beyond their primary cultural world. Through extensive and prolonged experiences of interfacing with other cultures, they have embarked on a personal evolution, creating a new culture of their own, fusing diverse cultural elements into a single personality. As Toffler (1980) noted, they have created a new personal culture that is "oriented to change and growing diversity" that attempts "to integrate the new view of nature, of evolution and progress, the new, richer conceptions of time and space, and the fusion of reductionism and wholism, with a new causality" (p. 309).

Identity Transformation

The emergence of intercultural personhood is a direct function of dramatically increasing intercultural communication activities—from the personal experiences of diverse people and events through direct encounters to observations via various communication media such as books, magazines, television programs, movies, magazines, art museums, music tapes, and electronic mail. Communicating across cultural identity boundaries is often challenging because it provokes questions about our presumed cultural premises and habits, as well as our inevitable intergroup posturing and the us-and-them psychological orientation (Kim, 1991). Yet it is precisely such challenges that offer us openings for new cultural learning, self-awareness, and personal growth (Adler, 1982; Kim, 1988, 1995, 2001). The greater the severity of intercultural challenges, the greater the potential for reinvention of an inner self that goes beyond the boundaries of our original cultural conditioning. In this process, our identity is transformed gradually and imperceptibly from an ascribed or assigned identity to an achieved or adopted identity—an emergent intercultural personhood at a higher level of integration (Grotevant, 1993). Such an identity transformation takes place in a progression of stages. In each stage, new concepts, attitudes, and behaviors are incorporated into an individual's psychological makeup. As previously unknown life patterns are etched into our nervous systems, they become part of our new psyches.

The evolution of our identity from cultural to intercultural is far from smooth or easy. Moments of intense stress can reverse the process at any time because individuals may indeed regress toward re-identifying with their origins, having found the alienation and malaise involved in maintaining a new identity too much of a strain (De Vos & Suárez-Orozco, 1990). Such strain may take various forms of an identity crisis (Erickson, 1968) and cultural marginality (Stonequist, 1964; Taft, 1977). Yet the stress experience also challenges individuals to accommodate new cultural elements and become more capable of making deliberate and appropriate choices about action as situations demand.

The emerging intercultural personhood, then, is a special kind of mindset that promises greater fitness in our increasingly intercultural world (Kim, 1995, 2001; Kim & Ruben, 1988). It represents a continuous struggle of searching for the authenticity in self and others within and across cultural groups. It is a way of existence that transcends the perimeters of a particular culture and is capable of embracing and incorporating seemingly divergent cultural elements into one's own unique worldview. The process of becoming intercultural affirms the creative courage and resourcefulness of humans because it requires discovering new symbols and new patterns of life. This creative process of identity development speaks to a uniquely human plasticity, "our relative freedom from programmed reflexive patterns . . . the very capacity to use culture to construct our identities" (Slavin & Kriegman, 1992, p. 6). It is the expression of normal, ordinary people in the act of "stretching" themselves out of their habitual perceptual and social categories. In Adler's (1982) words, the development of an intercultural identity and personhood places strangers at a position of continually "negotiating ever new formations of reality" (p. 391).

This kind of human development echoes one of the highest aims of humans in the spiritual tradi-

tions of the Eastern cultures. Suzuki (1968) writes: "The fundamental idea of Buddhism is to pass beyond the world of opposites, a world built up by intellectual distinctions and emotional defilements, and to realize the spiritual world of non-distinction, which involves achieving an absolute point of view" (p. 18). A virtuous person in this tradition is not one who undertakes the impossible task of striving for the good and eliminating the bad, but rather one who is able to maintain a dynamic balance between good and bad. This Eastern notion of dynamic balance is reflected in the symbolic use by Chinese sages of the archetypal poles of *yin* and *yang*. These sages call the unity lying beyond *yin* and *yang* the *Tao* and see it as a process that brings about the interplay of the two poles. Yoshikawa (1988) described this development as a stage of "double-swing" or "transcendence of binary opposites" (p. 146). With this transcendental understanding, intercultural persons are better able to conciliate and reconcile seemingly contradictory elements and transform them into complementary, interacting parts of a single whole.

An Illustration

Indeed, many people have been able to incorporate experiential territories that have seldom been thought possible, attainable, or even desirable. In doing so, they have redrawn the lines of their original cultural identity boundary to accommodate new life patterns. They remind us of the fact that we humans are active, if not always successful, strategists of our own development in a world of competing and overlapping interests. Although few theories and empirical studies have systematically examined the phenomenon of identity development, many first-hand accounts are available that bear witness to the reality of intercultural personhood. Such accounts have appeared in case studies, memoirs, biographical stories, and essays of self-reflection and self-analysis (see, for instance, Ainslie, 1994; Copelman, 1993; Keene, 1994; O'Halloran, 1994). Many of these accounts present vivid insights into the emotional ebb and flow of the progress toward an eventual realization of intercultural transformation.

One example of a personal fusion of Eastern and Western cultural elements can be seen in the canvases of the artist C. Meng. Since leaving Shanghai in 1986, Meng has earned a Master of Fine Arts degree in the United States and has been teaching at a university in Texas. In response to Meng's recent exhibit in Dallas, art critic and reporter C. Mitchell characterized Meng's paintings as masterful expressions of "the contrast between Eastern and Western modes of thought." Mitchell (1992) noted the unique synthesis of the two sensibilities in Meng's method, which used both Chinese calligraphy and Western-style abstraction techniques.

An illustration of intercultural synthesis is also offered by Duane Elgin, who was born and raised in the United States as a Christian and studied Buddhism in Tibet and Japan for many years. In his book *Voluntary Simplicity* (1981), Elgin integrated the philosophical ideas of Eastern and Western worldviews into his concept of voluntary simplicity. He presented this idea as global common sense and as a practical lifestyle to reconcile the willful, rational approach to life of the West with the holistic, spiritual orientation of the East. Examining historical trends, cycles of civilizations, and related ecological concerns, Elgin proposed voluntary simplicity as a goal for all of humanity. The main issue Elgin addresses is how humans can find ways to remove, as much as possible, the nonessential clutter of life. He suggests, for example, that one owns or buys things based on real need and consider the impact of one's consumption patterns on other people and on the earth. Before purchasing nonessential items, one should ask oneself if these items promote or compromise the quality of one's nonmaterial life. One could also consciously simplify communications by making them clearer, more direct, and more honest, eliminating idle, wasteful, and manipulative speech. One should also respect the value of silence and nonverbal actions.

Perhaps one of the most succinct and eloquent testimonials to the present conception of intercultural personhood was offered by Muneo Yoshikawa (1978). As one who had lived in both Japan and the United States, Yoshikawa offered the following insight into his own psychic development—an insight that captures the essence of what it means to be an intercultural person:

> I am now able to look at both cultures with objectivity as well as subjectivity; I am able to move in both

cultures, back and forth without any apparent conflict. . . . I think that something beyond the sum of each [cultural] identification took place, and that it became something akin to the concept of "synergy"—when one adds 1 and 1, one gets [3], or a little more. This something extra is not culture-specific but something unique of its own, probably the emergence of a new attribute or a new self-awareness, born out of an awareness of the relative nature of values and of the universal aspect of human nature. . . . I really am not concerned whether others take me as a Japanese or an American; I can accept myself as I am. I feel I am much freer than ever before, not only in the cognitive domain (perception, thoughts, etc.), but also in the affective (feeling, attitudes, etc.) and behavioral domains. (p. 220)

Emerging from these and other personal stories are common patterns associated with the development of intercultural personhood. One such pattern is a mindset that is less parochial and more open to different perspectives. This outlook has been referred to as a "third-culture" orientation that enables us to transcend the "paradigmatic barrier" (Bennett, 1976) between divergent philosophical perspectives. Development of an intercultural personhood leads to a cultural relativistic insight (Roosens, 1989) or moral inclusiveness (Opotow, 1990) that is based on an understanding of the profound similarities in human conditions as well as recognition of important differences between and among human groups.

In becoming intercultural, then, we can rise above the hidden grips of our childhood culture and discover that there are many ways to be good, true, and beautiful. In this process, we attain a *wider circle of identification*, approaching the limits of many cultures and, ultimately, humanity itself. This process is not unlike climbing a mountain. As we reach the mountaintop, we see that all paths below lead to the same summit and that each path offers unique scenery. Likewise, the process of becoming intercultural leads to an awareness of ourselves as being part of a larger, more inclusive whole and gives us a greater empathic capacity to "step into and imaginatively participate in the other's world view" (Bennett, 1977, p. 49).

Such developments, in turn, endow us with a special kind of *freedom* and *creativity*, with which we can make deliberate choices about action in specific situations rather than to have these choices simply be dictated by habitual conventions of thought and action. This psychic evolution presents the potential for achieving what Harris (1979) defined as "optimal communication competence." An optimally competent communicator, according to Harris, has a sophisticated "meta system" for critiquing his or her own managing system and interpersonal system. The very existence of the meta system makes the difference between the optimal level and the other two levels of competence a qualitative one (p. 31).

In the end, people such as Meng, Elgin, and Yoshikawa constitute the sustaining core or cross-links of our intercultural world. They provide an infrastructure of moral cement that helps hold together the human and planetary community, and discourage excessive identity claims at the exclusion of other identities. They are the ones who can best meet the enormous challenge that confronts us all—that is, "to give not only yourself but your culture to the planetary view" (Campbell, 1990, p. 114).

Endnote

1. The term "intercultural personhood" represents other similar terms such as "multicultural man" (Adler, 1982), "universal man" (Tagore, 1961; Walsh, 1973), "international man" (Lutzker, 1960), and "species identity" (Boulding, 1990), as well as "meta-identity" and "transcultural identity."

References

Adler, P. (1982). Beyond cultural identity: Reflections on cultural and multicultural man. In L. Samovar & R. Porter (Eds.), *Intercultural communication: A reader*, 3rd ed. (pp. 389–408). Belmont, CA: Wadsworth.

Ainslie, R. (1994, May). Notes on the psychodynamics of acculturation: A Mexican-American experience. *Mind and Human Interaction, 5*(2), 60–67.

Bennett, J. (1976). *The ecological transition: Cultural anthropology and human adaptation.* New York: Pergamon.

Boulding, E. (1990). *Building a global civic culture.* Syracuse, NY: Syracuse University Press.

Brody, J. (1997, November 6). U.S. panel on acupuncture calls for wider acceptance. *The New York Times*, p. A10.

Burke, K. (1974). Communication and the human condition. *Communication, 1*, 135–152.

Campbell, J. (1988). *The power of myth* (with B. Moyers). New York: Doubleday.

Campbell, J. (1990). *An open life* (in conversation with M. Toms). New York: Harper & Row.

Capra, F. (1975). *The Tao of physics.* Boulder, CO: Shambhala.

Cathcart, D., & Cathcart, R. (1982). Japanese social experience and concept of groups. In L. Samovar & R. Porter (Eds.), *Intercultural communication: A reader*, 3rd ed. (pp. 120–127). Belmont, CA: Wadsworth.

Copelman, D. (1993, April). The immigrant experience: Margin notes. *Mind and Human Interaction, 4*(2), 76–82.

De Vos, G., & Suárez-Orozco, M. (1990). *Status inequality: The self in culture.* Newbury Park, CA: Sage.

Doi, T. (1982). The Japanese patterns of communication and the concept of amae. In L. Samovar & R. Porter (Eds.), *Intercultural communication: A reader*, 3rd ed. (pp. 218–222). Belmont, CA: Wadsworth.

Elgin, D. (1981). *Voluntary simplicity.* New York: Bantam Books.

Erickson, E. (1968). *Identity, youth, and crisis.* New York: Norton.

Grotevant, H. (1993). The integrative nature of identity: Bridging the soloists to sing in the choir. In J. Kroger (Ed.), *Discussions on ego identity* (pp. 121–146). Hillsdale, NJ: Lawrence Erlbaum.

Gulick, S. (1963). *The East and the West.* Rutland, VT: Charles E. Tuttle.

Hall, E. (1976). *Beyond culture.* Garden City, NY: Anchor Books.

Hall, E. (1983). *The dance of life: The other dimension of time.* Garden City, NY: Anchor Press.

Harris, L. (1979, May). *Communication competence: An argument for a systemic view.* Paper presented at the annual meeting of the International Communication Association, Philadelphia, PA.

Hsu, F. (1981). *The challenges of the American dream.* Belmont, CA: Wadsworth.

Keene, D. (1994). *On familiar terms: A journey across cultures.* New York: Kodansha International.

Kim, Y. (1988). *Communication and cross-cultural adaptation: An integrative theory.* Clevedon, UK: Multilingual Matters.

Kim, Y. (1991). Intercultural communication competence. In S. Ting-Toomey & F. Korzenny (Eds.), *Cross-cultural interpersonal communication* (pp. 259–275). Newbury Park, CA: Sage.

Kim, Y. (1995). Cross-cultural adaptation: An integrative theory. In R. Wiseman (Ed.), *Intercultural communication theory* (pp. 170–193). Thousand Oaks, CA: Sage.

Kim, Y. (2001). *Becoming intercultural: An integrative theory of communication and cross-cultural adaptation*. Thousand Oaks, CA: Sage.

Kim, Y., & Ruben, B. (1988). Intercultural transformation. In Y. Kim & W. Gudykunst (Eds.), *Theories in intercultural communication* (pp. 299–321). Newbury Park, CA: Sage.

Kincaid, L. (1987). Communication East and West: Points of departure. In L. Kincaid (Ed.), *Communication theory: Eastern and Western perspectives* (pp. 331–340). San Diego: Academic Press.

Kluckhohn, F., & Strodtbeck, F. (1960). *Variations in value orientations*. New York: Row, Peterson.

Lutzker, D. (1960). Internationalism as a predictor of cooperative behavior. *Journal of Conflict Resolution, 4*, 426–430.

Maslow, A. (1971). *The farther reaches of human nature*. New York: Viking.

Mitchell, C. (1992, June 15). Review. *The Dallas Morning News*, p. C6.

Nakamura, H. (1964). *Ways of thought of Eastern peoples*. Honolulu: University of Hawaii Press.

Needham, J. (1951). Human laws and the laws of nature in China and the West. *Journal of the History of Ideas, XII*.

Northrop, F. (1966/1946). *The meeting of the East and the West*. New York: Collier Books.

O'Halloran, M. (1994). *Pure heart, enlightened mind*. Boston: Charles E. Tuttle.

Oliver, R. (1971). *Communication and culture in ancient India and China*. Syracuse, NY: Syracuse University Press.

Opotow, S. (1990). Moral exclusion and inclusion. *Journal of Social Issues, 46*(1), 1–20.

Roosens, E. (1989). *Creating ethnicity: The process of ethnogenesis*. Newbury Park, CA: Sage.

Slavin, M., & Kriegman, D. (1992). *The adaptive design of the human psyche*. New York: Guilford.

Stonequist, E. (1964). The marginal man: A study in personality and culture conflict. In E. Burgess & D. Bogue (Eds.), *Contributions to urban sociology* (pp. 327–345). Chicago: University of Chicago Press.

Suzuki, D. (1968). *The essence of Buddhism*. Kyoto, Japan: Hozokan.

Taft, R. (1977). Coping with unfamiliar culture. In N. Warren (Ed.), *Studies in cross-cultural psychology*, Vol. 2 (pp. 121–153). London: Academic Press.

Tagore, R. (1961). *Toward universal man*. New York: Asia Publishing House.

Thayer, L. (1983). On "doing" research and "explaining" things. *Journal of Communication, 33*(3), 80–91.

Thompson, W. (1973). *Passages about earth: An exploration of the new planetary culture*. New York: Harper & Row.

Toffler, A. (1980). *The third wave*. New York: Bantam Books.

Triandis, H. (1995). *Individualism and collectivism*. Boulder, CO: Westview Press.

Wallis, C. (1996, June 24). Healing. *Time*, pp. 58–64.

Walsh, J. (1973). *Intercultural education in the community of man*. Honolulu: University of Hawaii Press.

Wei, A. (1980, March). *Cultural variations in perception*. Paper presented at the 6th Annual Third World Conference, Chicago, IL.

Yoshikawa, M. (1978). Some Japanese and American cultural characteristics. In M. Prossor, *The cultural dialogue: An introduction to intercultural communication* (pp. 220–239). Boston: Houghton Mifflin.

Yoshikawa, M. (1988). Cross-cultural adaptation and perceptual development. In Y. Kim & W. Gudykunst (Eds.), *Cross-cultural adaptation: Current approaches* (pp. 140–148). Newbury Park, CA: Sage.

Yum, J. (1994). The impact of Confucianism on interpersonal relationships and communication patterns in East Asia. In L. Samovar & R. Porter (Eds.), *Intercultural communication: A reader*, 7th ed. (pp. 75–86). Belmont, CA: Wadsworth.

Concepts and Questions

1. What is meant by the term "intercultural personhood"?
2. How do Eastern and Western teachings about humankind's relationship to the nature of the universe differ?
3. In what major ways do Eastern and Western approaches to knowledge differ?
4. How do Eastern time orientations differ from those found in the West?
5. How do differences in Eastern and Western views of self and identity affect intercultural communication?
6. What are the major differences between Eastern and Western modes of communication?
7. What strengths and weaknesses are found in Eastern and Western worldviews?
8. How could an integration of Eastern and Western perspectives benefit both Eastern and Western cultural life?
9. What conditions are required for the emergence of intercultural personhood?
10. What benefits accrue to both society and the individual from the development of an intercultural personhood perspective?

Ethics, Culture, and Communication: An Intercultural Perspective

ROBERT SHUTER

Ethics, culture, and communication are woven together in a cultural mosaic that makes them inseparable and yet distinct elements of each and every society. The inseparability has been alluded to in ethical and communication literature (Condon, 1977; Howell, 1986; Johannesen, 1990, 1994; Makau & Arnett, 1997), but the fusion has not been adequately articulated. In fact, books and articles on ethics and communication more often than not ignore the issue of culture or offer little more than clichés about culture and communication—values are different worldwide; ethical systems are not easily compared. As a result, leading books on ethics and human communication are essentially written from a Western perspective, with U.S. values and norms driving the ethical models and prescriptions provided in these texts (Jaska & Prichard, 1994; Johannesen, 1990; Nilsen, 1966). Even Makau and Arnet's (1997) edited text focuses almost exclusively on diversity and ethics in the United States. This is a major weakness in the literature because it provides little or no understanding of ethical systems that influence communication in social systems outside Western society or, more limited yet, the United States. It also can be argued that the literature on ethics and communication popularized in the field of communication studies have limited application to Europe and South America.

Using an intracultural communication perspective (Shuter, 1990, 1998), this essay examines the cultural myopia of current literature on communication ethics. Shuter's (1990, 1998) intracultural perspective uncov-ers worldviews, values, and communication patterns within a culture, and it should be quite revealing when used to examine communication ethics. Confucianist and Hindu ethical systems are also explored intraculturally, with the aim of speculating on communication ethics in these systems. Lastly, the essay discusses communication ethics from an intercultural perspective (Shuter, 1990, 1998).

ETHICS AND HUMAN COMMUNICATION: CURRENT PERSPECTIVES

Although literature abounds on ethics and communication, the authors and their works clearly reflect Western ethical premises with an implicit U.S. orientation. Evidence for this assertion can be found in analyzing communication ethics literature with the following framework: (1) communicator ethics, (2) message ethics, and (3) receiver or audience ethics. With respect to communicator ethics, Nilsen (1966) summarizes a common view advanced by communication ethical theorists on what constitutes morally right speech when he writes that ethics is "that which contributes to the well-being of others, to their happiness and fulfillment as human beings" (p. 13). Melvin Rader (1964) echoes Nilsen's perspective: "Only ethics that does justice to every essential side of human nature, as both individual and social, as mind and body, as thinking and feeling and desiring, is complete and complex enough to be the basis of valued ideals" (p. 435). Richard Johannesen (1990, 1994) adds to Nilsen and Rader's ethical criteria the concept of an "ethical contract" that requires "a fundamental implied and unspoken assumption that words can be trusted and people will be truthful" (p. 15). This is consistent with Jaska and Pritchard's (1994) notion that truthfulness is a significant ethical criterion for determining morally right communication.

Implicit in the ethical criteria offered by all of these communication theorists is the notion that the center of ethical decisions is the impact of behavior on human beings—their happiness, their feelings and thoughts, their personal and social relations. Similarly, the ethical criterion of truthfulness suggests that human beings can choose their course of action and be judged right or wrong on the basis of those choices. Robert Wargo (1990) argues that these implicit assumptions spring from a Judeo-Christian tradition that bifurcates the relationship between God, people, and nature. In the Judeo-Christian view, God is infinite, while people and nature are finite. As finite beings, humans have a soul while nature has no soul and is material. As a result, a hierarchy arises that places God at the apex, followed by human beings, and lastly material nature. It is the human soul—the spiritual side of being— that gives rise to ethics and ethical judgment (Wargo, 1990).

In the Judeo-Christian perspective, however, only human beings possess reason and can choose to make good or bad decisions. Free will—the possession of an intellect—separates humans from the rest of nature and makes ethical choices possible. A sin, then, is a human being's choice to commit an offense against God; however, culpability requires knowledge, volition, and capacity (Wargo, 1990).

Although communication ethicists do not generally ground their theories in Judeo-Christian doctrine, it is apparent they are linked. They place human beings at the center of their ethical constructs, and reason, free will, and the intellect are essential to making good ethical choices. As you will see later in this article, many Eastern ethical systems neither bifurcate human beings and nature nor reserve soul (spirit) for humans or make reason and free will an essential human capacity. In fact, Shintoism—a dominant ethical system in Japan— has no concept of good or evil, invests humans and the natural order with spirits, and removes reason and free will from ethical choices (Little, 1974).

A Western and U.S. cultural bias is also revealed in the ethical requirements of messages transmitted to others. Communicators are judged to be ethical depending on their truthfulness, as indicated earlier, and their willingness to provide significant choices to their audience.

Nilsen states: "It is choice making that is voluntary, free from physical or mental coercion. It is choice based on the best information available when the decision must be made. It includes awareness of the motivation of those who want to influence the values they serve, the goals they seek" (1966, p. 45). Information, then, is key to develop-

ing ethical messages, for it provides listeners with the ability to make voluntary choices based on the facts. Similarly, the willingness of communicators to disclose their intentions and goals helps expand listener choice. Johannesen (1990) cites Buber's dialogue as an example of an ethical interpersonal model because it emphasizes authenticity of the communicator and inclusion, exposing the listener to both sides of an argument.

For communication theorists, reason and logic are critical dimensions of ethical messages. The importance of reason and logic has developed from Aristotelian philosophy, which also has diminished the ethical value of emotional appeal. While Johannesen (1990, 1994) is among the only communication ethicists who suggests that cultures may have different logics, even his work fails to identify how culturally incompatible these communication caveats are in most regions of the world.

The preeminence of intellect and reason— hallmarks of Western civilization—are, for example, rejected in traditional Islamic ethical philosophy (Gibb, 1964; Hourani, 1971; Rahman, 1984). Intellectualism for its own sake in Islamic ethics is "a sin against human nature—maybe even a crime" (Hovannisian, 1985, p. 8). Similarly, openness, disclosure, and authenticity—important Western communicator ideals—are simply not valued in Islamic and Hindu ethical systems. Unlike Western cultures and particularly the United States, Hindu and Islamic societies do not revere the individual; hence, they are not grounded in an ethical communicative assumption that each person ought to have optimum information to choose logically between alternative positions.

Finally, communication ethics in Western culture and particularly the United States are grounded in an implicit assumption that listeners, regardless of their ethnicity, social class, race, or gender, ought to have equal access to information to make choices. Equal and universal access to information is an essential component of a participatory democracy according to Jaska and Pritchard (1994). As Nilsen (1966) writes: "The ethical touchstone is the degree of free, informal, rational, and critical choice—significant choice—that is fostered by our speaking" (p. 46). As a result, sexism, classism, ageism, or other forms of discriminatory language and messages are considered unethical. These messages, according to Johannesen (1990), "intentionally demean other people through embodying unfair negative value judgments concerning traits, capacities, and accomplishments" (p. 129).

Listener quality is not a fundamental value in many ethical systems outside the United States as detailed later in this essay. Suffice it to say that Confucianism, Hinduism, and Islamic philosophy implicitly give certain listeners and audiences more social value than others (Little & Sumner, 1978). These social hierarchies are often based on age, class, gender, and familial affiliation, and they regulate the frequency and content of listener and audience communication.

If communication ethics described in the literature is grounded in Western and U.S. ethical values, then what can be said about communication ethics in other societies? The next section of the article develops major principles of communication ethics associated with Confucianism and Hinduism. Because communication literature is devoid of published articles or texts that specifically analyze communication ethics in Confucianism and Hinduism, the communication ethical insights offered here are derived from general ethical theory associated with each of these major philosophies or religions.[1] Hence, this section is exploratory and integrative, offering communication ethical principles that influence world cultures beyond Western society and the United States.

AN INTRACULTURAL ETHICAL FRAMEWORK FOR COMMUNICATION: CONFUCIANISM AND HINDUISM

East Asia, Southeast Asia, and South Asia have been influenced quite dramatically by Confucianism and Hinduism (Little & Sumner, 1978). With respect to Confucianism, Taiwan, Korea, Japan, and the People's Republic of China have had significant involvement with Confucian thought and tradition that has influenced the ethical traditions of these societies to varying degrees. Hinduism has had enormous influence in South Asia, particularly India, and has affected the rest of the region as well—Sri Lanka, Nepal, Bangladesh, and Pakistan. Because Confucianism and Hinduism are so integral to Asia in

terms of its historical, cultural, and ethical development, it is logical that communication ethics in each of these world regions ought to reflect the dominant philosophy or religion (Chan, 1963; Chang, 1962). Confucianism and Hinduism—the latter being a religion and the former a philosophy of life—will be discussed in terms of communication ethics in the following areas: (1) communicator ethics, (2) message ethics, (3) receiver and audience ethics.

CONFUCIANISM

Communicator Ethics

Communicator ethics in Confucian philosophy is intimately tied to the concept of *Li*, a set of rituals and social practices, defined by Confucius. These rights and practices are derived from a central premise in Confucian thought: Obligation to parents and family is the *raison d'être* of human existence. The family, then, is at the center of Confucian thought and practice, and all rights and rituals spring from this value (Tu Wei-ming, 1976).

The ethical communicator is someone motivated by proper duty (*yi*) to one's parents and family first, and then the society at large. The Chinese concept of *Jen*—translated as benevolence—guides the ethical communicator to choose actions and attitudes that reveal a general concern for all people while reserving the greatest *Jen* for the family. The ethical communicator also displays *ksiao* (filial piety) and *ti* (respect for an elder brother). Reverence for parents and elders is central to Confucianism, and communicators are judged as moral or ethical based on this criterion.

In summary, communicator ethics in Confucian philosophy is based on exhibiting appropriate communicative behavior that reflects a keen family commitment to parents, elders, and the larger society. Confucian thought is so rooted in duty that the ethical communicator is obligated to display appropriate attitudes and actions in all settings.

Message Ethics

Reason, logic, evidence, and truthfulness are *not* the criteria for determining whether a message is ethical in Confucian philosophy (Ivanhoe, 1990). These standards would be considered morally insufficient because they don't focus on the nature of the message; that is, because Confucian philosophy is grounded in community or family obligations and duties, any message can be judged ethical only if it displays *Jen* (benevolence) for the community and family. Messages that focus on personal profit or benefit are too self-centered to be considered ethical. Hence, messages that are community- or family-centered are more ethical than arguments that focus on enlightened self-interest. Similarly, messages that communicate filial piety and respect for elder brothers are most compatible with Confucian philosophy. In fact, Confucianism obligates people to respect and follow elders, particularly male family members. As a result, all messages should demonstrate a reverence for aging and the aged to be considered ethical.

Confucian philosophy values a heart and mind (*hsin*) approach to evaluating ethical behavior (Ivanhoe, 1990). Confucian thought does not elevate reason and logic to the sublime; on the contrary, it places the heart—the essence of human nature—at the center of ethical behavior. It is the heart and mind—the total human being—that can judge ethical behavior, and by extension, ethical messages. Reason alone is insufficient because it fosters independent thinking and action rather than relying on a "sovereign"—a respected elder who guides one's behavior and messages.

Receiver and Audience Ethics

All listeners are not equal in Confucian philosophy; there is clearly a hierarchy of listener importance based on a listener's age, gender, family status, and authority role (Tu Wei-ming, 1976). Parents and elder brothers are the most revered. Males, older persons regardless of family status, and selected authority figures such as teachers are also highly regarded in Confucian philosophy. As a result, communication must be adapted to listeners in conformity with the ethical requirements of age, gender, family status, and authority role. This means that *who* the listener is ought to determine *what* is communicated, how much is revealed, the level of respect accorded to the receiver, and whether communication is a one-way or two-way process. For example, communicators are ethically required to communicate respectful messages bereft of challenges and disagreements to parents, elder broth-

ers, and teachers. And because women in Confucian philosophy are subordinate to men, there are gender implications for information access and receiver credibility and respect (Ivanhoe, 1990).

The preceding analysis of Confucianism serves as a foundation and catalyst for initiating further intercultural study of communication ethics in societies imbued in Confucian philosophy. Turning to Hinduism, this article speculates on communication ethics in this dominant Eastern religion.

HINDUISM

Communicator Ethics

Dharma is Hindu ethics, and it is the foundation of all Indian thought and action (Crawford, 1974; Sharma, 1965; Walker, 1986). It prescribes the ideals for human life in this world, people's relations with others, the duties of caste, and the stages of life. *Dharma* for Hindu scholars is the ethical glue that regulates human affairs, including bad habits to be broken (*yamas*) and good habits to be established (*niyamas*). As one studies *Vedas*—the inquiry into *dharma*—one learns Hindu ethical behavior that can purify individuals in this life and the lives to come.

The ethical communicator, then, ought to be influenced by *dharma* in thought and action. Although *dharma* does not directly focus on communicative action, it does comment implicitly on duties required of individuals in their different stages of life as students, family members, and retirees as well as the obligations attending to one's caste—social position within Indian society. For communicators, it is critical to understand one's own role in social institutions and the roles of others to formulate ethical messages and behave ethically (Dasgutta, 1961).

For example, the ethical communicator should construct messages that are appropriate for the caste one represents and the caste with which one is communicating. Similarly, family and gender duties required in *dharma* ought to affect the behavior of communicators when they encounter women and older persons who, according to Hindu ethics, must be treated in certain ways. Class, gender, age, and social position play important roles in *dharma* and, by extension, require communicators to be rhetorically sensitive.

Dharma also requires that communicators be a role model and live this code of conduct in all dimensions of life. *Karma*, an important Hindu concept that refers roughly to moral climate, is influenced by personal actions that are either compatible or incompatible with *dharma*. Like all human beings according to Hinduism, communicators ought to be conscious of their behavior to influence *karma* positively and achieve the ultimate end of human existence: extricating oneself from the baser instincts of human kind.

Message Ethics

Like Confucianism, reason is not celebrated in Hindu thought—it is not the touchstone for determining value or truth. In fact, emotion, subconscious connections through yoga, and deep spiritual reflection are the paths to truth and enlightenment. Reason is a temporal tool to be used in social relations but is limited in utility and scope (Coward, 1989).

As a result, messages that rely principally on reason to inform or persuade would not truly be ethical, particularly if they were not in concert with *dharma*. The normative requirements of *dharma* articulates in general terms what a person is obligated to do in each stage of life, and ethical messages ought to reflect this.

Central to Hinduism is reaching *moksha*, which is roughly translated as liberation or salvation. There are many possible yoga or paths to liberation, but each combines spiritual self-reflection with some degree of intellectual understanding. Hence, ethical messages within Hindu thought should in some way move people closer to *moksha*.

Finally, ethical messages in Hinduism differentiate between listeners and should be adapted to a receiver's position, class, caste, gender, and age. This is central to *dharma* and Hindu thought and is examined in the next section of the article.

Receiver and Audience Ethics

Like Confucianism, Hinduism is not based on the concept that all listeners are or ought to be equal. To the contrary, Varna *dharma* prescribes duties that are caste- and class-related, and it defines the relationship and communication between castes.

Similarly, Hinduism defines the roles of men and women quite clearly in *dharma* and *Yoga Sutras*, with women being considered more impure than men and thus "seen to be of a lower quality (lower class)" (Coward, 1989, p. 3).

Note that purity is a central concept in Hinduism and can be sought through right action (*dharma*); nevertheless, purity is influenced by past lives (reincarnation) and bodily functions. Because women are considered to have more bodily discharges than men, they are viewed as being more impure (Coward, 1989).

According to Hinduism, the social behaviors of caste and gender emerge from inborn qualities of these groups; that is, women and *Harigans* (the untouchable class), for example, are born with qualities that relegate them to subordinate positions in the culture. Even right conduct will not shield individuals from caste or gender distinctions (Crawford, 1974).

Communicators, then, are obligated to interact differently with castes and genders. For example, individuals from lower castes and women in general are neither supposed to receive the same type of information as men or people from higher castes nor be treated as equals. Coward (1989) details the clash between traditional Hinduism and the new Indian constitution, which guarantees rights to all regardless of caste or gender.

IS AN INTERCULTURAL COMMUNICATION ETHIC POSSIBLE?

While there are more dimensions to a Hindu communication ethic, clearly much of it is fundamentally incompatible with Western communication ethics. Confucian communication ethics is also on a collision course with Western ethical principles. The question remains: Can a communication ethic emerge that transcends culture and serves as a guideline when communicating interculturally?

Because an intracultural analysis uncovers deep structures in a society and its communication, it obviates easy cultural answers such as those traditionally offered about intercultural ethics: Be empathetic, understand that people are different, values vary from society to society, ad infinitum. In truth, one could attempt to follow all of these intercultural caveats and still reject the ethical premises that regulate a society's communication and relationships. At the base of rejection may be systemic cultural differences that are fundamentally at odds. In the case of Confucianism, Hinduism, and Western and U.S. communication ethics, such fundamental differences exist that it is difficult to conceive of a substantive and acceptable intercultural ethic that transcends banal intercultural caveats.

The intercultural ethical challenge, then, is to understand truly how deeply communication ethics are grounded in culture. With an intracultural perspective, people, society, and their communication can be approached and possibly understood from each culture's terms. As a result, an intracultural analysis probes the essence of communication ethics because it is so deeply rooted in culture. Contradictions, paradox, and social conflict are inevitably revealed when ethics and communication are examined within a society.

The intercultural goal is to develop an increasingly intimate understanding of the complexities of each society and its communication ethics. Communicators need to know and feel the ethical values and moral constraints of a society, the deeply held cultural beliefs and communication expectations that regulate human affairs. Authentic intracultural journeys challenge sojourners, exposing them to ethical and communication systems that may seem so different from their own. Only through multiple intracultural journeys can communicators achieve intercultural ethical enlightenment—a personal awareness of just how accepting one can be of ethical systems different from one's own. Intercultural prescriptions and caveats are nothing more than clichés unless communicators have a deep understanding of culture, ethics, and communication.

How do communicators journey intraculturally if the literature on communication ethics is so tied to Western and U.S. cultural ethics? First, communication ethicists need to admit that their research has an intracultural bias; that is, they are not writing about ethics per se but rather about U.S. and Western communication ethics. Next, the research focus must expand, with scholars studying communication ethics in societies outside the United States. Africa, Asia, Latin America, and Europe should be explored intraculturally with the aim of articulating

the ethical communication systems of countries within these global regions. With scores of intracultural insights, communicators may one day be able to predict, unravel, and maybe even resolve the ethical collisions that inevitably occur when cultures communicate cross-nationally.

Endnote

1. Although there are several articles and books on Confucianism and communication, no single article or text specifically examines communication ethics and Confucianism. Key articles on Confucianism and communication include:

Chao, Y. R. (1956). Chinese terms of address. *Language, 32,* 217–241.

Chang, C. Y. (1987). Chinese philosophy and contemporary communication theory. In D. L. Kincaid (Ed.), *Communication theory: Eastern and Western perspectives.* New York: Academic Press.

McBrian, C. (1978). Language and social stratification: The case of a Confucian society. *Anthropological Linguistics, 2,* 320–326.

Yum, J. O. (1997). The impact of Confucianism on interpersonal relationships and communication patterns in East Asia. In L. Samovar & R. Porter (Eds.), *Intercultural communication: A reader* (pp. 75–88). Belmont, CA: Wadsworth Publishing.

References

Chan, W. (1963). *Sourcebook in Chinese philosophy.* Princeton, NJ: Princeton University Press.

Chang, C. (1962). *The development of Neo-Confucian thought.* New York: Bookman Associates.

Condon, J. C. (1977). *Intercultural communication.* New York: MacMillan.

Coward, H. G. (1989). Purity in Hinduism. In H. Coward, J. Lipner, & K. Young (Eds.), *Hindu ethics* (pp. 9–40). Albany: State University of New York Press.

Crawford, S. C. (1974). *The evolution of Hindu ethical ideals.* Calcutta, India: Firma K.L. Mukhopadhyay.

Dasgutta, S. (1961). *Development of moral philosophy in India.* Calcutta, India: Orient Longmans.

Gibb, A. R. (1964). *Modern trends in Islam.* Chicago: University of Chicago Press.

Hourani, G. (1971). *Islamic rationalism.* New York: Oxford University Press.

Hovannisian, R. G. (1985). *Ethics in Islam.* Malibu, CA: Undena Publications.

Howell, W. S. (1986). "Foreword." In N. Asuncion-Lande (Ed.), *Ethical perspectives and critical issues in intercultural communication*. Falls Church, VA: Speech Communication Association.

Ivanhoe, P. J. (1990). *Ethics in the Confucian tradition*. Atlanta: Scholars Press.

Jaska, J. A., & Pritchard, M. S. (1994). *Communication ethics: Methods of analysis*. Belmont, CA: Wadsworth.

Johannesen, R. L. (1990). *Ethics and human communication*. Prospect Heights, IL: Waveland Press.

Johannesen, R. L. (1994). *Ethics and human communication*, 2nd ed. Prospect Heights, IL: Waveland Press.

Little, D. (1974). Max Weber and the comparative study of religious ethics. *Journal of Religious Ethics, 2*(2), 5–40.

Little, D., & Sumner, B. T. (1978). *Comparative religious ethics: A new method*. New York: Harper & Row.

Makau, J., & Arnett, R. (1997). *Communication ethics in an age of diversity*. Urbana: University of Illinois Press.

Nilsen, T. R. (1966). *Ethics of speech communication*. Indianapolis: Bobbs-Merrill.

Rader, M. (1964). *Ethics and the human community*. New York: Holt, Rinehart, & Winston.

Rahman, F. (1984). *Introduction to Islam and modernity*. Chicago: University of Chicago Press.

Sharma, I. C. (1965). *Ethical principles of India*. Lincoln, IL: Johnsen Publishing.

Shuter, R. (1990). The centrality of culture. *The Southern Communication Journal, L5*(3), 237–249.

Shuter, R. (1998). Revisiting the centrality of culture. In J. T. Nakayama & L. Flores (Eds.), *Readings in cultural context*. Mountain View, CA: Mayfield Publishing.

Tu Wei-ming (1976). *Neo-Confucian thought in action*. Berkeley: University of California Press.

Walker, B. (1986). *Hindu world: An encyclopedic survey of Hinduism*. London: George Allen & Unwin.

Wargo, R. J. (1990). Japanese ethics: Beyond good and evil. In D. Smith (Ed.), *Philosophy East and West* (pp. 129–138). Honolulu: University of Hawaii.

Concepts and Questions

1. What are some of the fundamental differences between Western Judeo-Christian–based ethical systems and Shinto-based ethical systems found in Japan?

2. In what ways are Western and U.S. ethical systems culturally biased?

3. What roles do reason and logic play in Western ethical systems? How does Islamic ethical philosophy treat reason and logic?

4. How is listener equality manifest in U.S. ethical systems?

5. What are the responsibilities of communicators in a Confucian-influenced ethical system? What forms of communicative behavior would you expect of communicators under such a system?

6. From a Confucian philosophic perspective, what criteria determine message ethics?

7. How does listener equality function in a Confucian-based ethical system?

8. From a Hindu perspective, what constitutes ethical communication?

9. In the Hindu tradition, what determines an ethical message?

10. Under Hindu ethics, what behaviors might you expect from an ethical receiver and audience?

Citizens of the World

MARTHA C. NUSSBAUM

When anyone asked him where he came from, he said,
'I am a citizen of the world.'

> **DIOGENES LAERTIUS**, *Life of Diogenes the Cynic*

Anna was a political science major at a large state university in the Midwest. Upon graduation she went into business, getting a promising job with a large firm. After 12 years she had risen to a middle-management position. One day, her firm assigned her to the newly opened Beijing office.[1] What did she need to know, and how well did her education prepare her for success in her new role? In a middle-management position, Anna is working with both Chinese and American employees, both male and female. She needs to know how Chinese people think about work (and not to assume there is just one way); she needs to know how cooperative networks are formed, and what misunderstandings might arise in interactions between Chinese and American workers.

Knowledge of recent Chinese history is important, since the disruptions of the Cultural Revolution still shape workers' attitudes. Anna also needs to consider her response to the recent policy of urging women to return to the home, and to associated practices of laying off women first. This means she should know something about Chinese gender relations, both in the Confucian tradition and more recently. She should probably know something about academic women's studies in the United States, which have influenced the women's studies movement in Chinese Universities. She certainly needs a more general view about human rights and about to what extent it is either legitimate or wise to criticize another nation's ways of life. In the future, Anna may find herself dealing with problems of anti-African racism, and with recent government at-

tempts to exclude immigrants who test positive for the human immunodeficiency virus (HIV). Doing this well will require her to know something about the history of Chinese attitudes about race and sexuality. It will also mean being able to keep her moral bearings even when she knows that the society around her will not accept her view.

The real-life Anna had only a small part of this preparation—some courses in world history, but none that dealt with the general issue of cultural variety and how to justify moral judgments in a context of diversity; none that dealt with the variety of understandings of gender roles or family structures; none that dealt with sexual diversity and its relationship to human rights. More important, she had no courses that prepared her for the shock of discovering that other places treated as natural what she found strange, and as strange what she found natural. Her imaginative capacity to enter into the lives of people of other nations had been blunted by lack of practice. The real-life Anna had a rough time getting settled in China, and the firm's dealings with its new context were not always successful. A persistent and curious person, however, she stayed on and has made herself a good interpreter of cultural difference. She now plans to spend her life in Beijing, and she feels she is making a valuable contribution to the firm.

Two years ago, after several years in China, already in her late thirties, Anna decided to adopt a baby. Through her by then extensive knowledge of the Chinese bureaucracy, she bypassed a number of obstacles and quickly found an infant girl in an orphanage in Beijing. She then faced challenges of a very different kind. Even in the most apparently universal activities of daily life, cultural difference colors her day. Her Chinese nurse follows the common Chinese practice of wrapping the baby's limbs in swaddling bands to immobilize it. As is customary, the nurse interacts little with the child, either facially or vocally, and brings the child immediately anything it appears to want, without encouraging its own efforts.

Anna's instincts are entirely different: she smiles at the baby, encourages her to wave her hands about, talks to her constantly, wants her to act for herself. The nurse thinks Anna is encouraging nervous tension by this hyperactive American behavior; Anna thinks the nurse is stunting the baby's cognitive development. Anna's mother, visiting, is appalled by the nurse and wants to move in, but Anna, by now a sensitive cross-cultural interpreter, is able to negotiate between mother and nurse and devise some plan for the baby's development that is agreeable to all. To do this she has had to think hard about the nonuniversality and nonnaturalness of such small matters as playing with a baby. But she has also had to think of the common needs and aims that link her with the nurse, and the nurse with her own mother. Her university education gave her no preparation at all for these challenges.

Had Anna been a student at today's St. Lawrence University, or at many other colleges and universities around the United States, she would have had a better basis for her international role, a role U.S. citizens must increasingly play (whether at home or abroad) if our efforts in business are to be successful, if international debates about human rights, medical and agricultural problems, ethnic and gender relations are to make progress as we enter the new century. As Connie Ellis, a 43-year-old waitress at Marion's Restaurant in Sycamore, Illinois, put it on July 4, 1996: "You can't narrow it down to just our country anymore—it's the whole planet."[2] We must educate people who can operate as world citizens with sensitivity and understanding.

Asked where he came from, the ancient Greek Cynic philosopher Diogenes replied, "I am a citizen of the world." He meant by this that he refused to be defined simply by his local origins and group memberships, associations central to the self-image of a conventional Greek male; he insisted on defining himself in terms of more universal aspirations and concerns.[3] The Stoics who followed his lead developed his image of the *kosmopolites*, or world citizen, more fully, arguing that each of us dwells, in effect, in two communities—the local community of our birth and the community of human argument and aspiration that "is truly great and truly common": It is the latter community that is, most fundamentally, the source of our moral and social obligations. With respect to fundamental moral values such as justice, "we should regard all human beings as our fellow citizens and local residents."[4] This attitude deeply

influenced the subsequent philosophical and political tradition, especially as mediated through the writings of Cicero, who reworked it to allow a special degree of loyalty to one's own local region or group. Stoic ideas influenced the American republic through the writings of Thomas Paine, and also through Adam Smith and Immanuel Kant, who themselves influenced the Founders.[5] Later on, Stoic thought was a major formative influence on both Emerson and Thoreau.

This form of cosmopolitanism is not peculiar to Western traditions. It is, for example, the view that animates the work of the influential Indian philosopher, poet, and educational leader Rabindranath Tagore. Tagore drew his own cosmopolitan views from older Bengali traditions, although he self-consciously melded them with Western cosmopolitanism.[6] It is also the view recommended by Ghanaian philosopher Kwame Anthony Appiah, when he writes, concerning African identity: "We will only solve our problems if we see them as human problems arising out of a special situation, and we shall not solve them if we see them as African problems generated by our being somehow unlike others."[7] But for people who have grown up in the Western tradition, it is useful to understand the roots of this cosmopolitanism in ancient Greek and Roman thought. These ideas are an essential resource for democratic citizenship. Like Socrates' ideal of critical inquiry, they should be at the core of today's higher education.

THE IDEA OF WORLD CITIZENSHIP IN GREEK AND ROMAN ANTIQUITY

Contemporary debates about the curriculum frequently imply that the idea of a "multicultural" education is a new fad, with no antecedents in long-standing educational traditions. In fact, Socrates grew up in an Athens already influenced by such ideas in the 5th century B.C. Ethnographic writers such as the historian Herodotus examined the customs of distant countries, both in order to understand their ways of life and to attain a critical perspective on their own society. Herodotus took seriously the possibility that Egypt and Persia might have something to teach Athens about social values. A cross-cultural inquiry, he realized, may reveal that what we take to be natural and normal is merely parochial and habitual. One cultural group thinks that corpses must be buried; another, that they must be burnt; another, that they must be left in the air to be plucked clean by the birds. Each is shocked by the practices of the other, and each, in the process, starts to realize that its habitual ways may not be the ways designed by nature for all times and persons.

Awareness of cultural difference gave rise to a rich and complex debate about whether our central moral and political values exist in the nature of things (by *phusis*) or merely by convention (*nomos*).[8] That Greek debate illustrates most of the positions now familiar in debates about cultural relativism and the source of moral norms. It also contains a crucial insight: if we should conclude that our norms are human and historical rather than immutable and eternal, it does not follow that the search for a rational justification of moral norms is futile.

In the conventional culture of 5th-century B.C. Athens, recognition that Athenian customs were not universal became a crucial precondition of Socratic searching. So long as young men were educated in the manner of Aristophanes' Old Education, an education stressing uncritical assimilation of traditional values, so long as they marched to school in rows and sang the old songs without discussion of alternatives, ethical questioning could not get going. Ethical inquiry requires a climate in which the young are encouraged to be critical of their habits and conventions; and such critical inquiry, in turn, requires awareness that life contains other possibilities.

Pursuing these comparisons, 5th-century Athenians were especially fascinated by the example of Sparta, Athens' primary rival, a hierarchical and nondemocratic culture that understood the goal of civic education in a very un-Athenian way. As the historian Thucydides depicts them, Spartan educators carried to an extreme the preference for uniformity and rule-following that characterized the Old Education of Athens in Aristophanes' nostalgic portrait. Conceiving the good citizen as an obedient follower of traditions, they preferred uncritical subservience to Athenian public argument and debate. Denying the importance of free speech and thought, they preferred authoritarian to democratic politics.

Athenians, looking at this example, saw new reasons to praise the freedom of inquiry and debate that by this time flourished in their political life. They saw Spartan citizens as people who did not choose to serve their city, and whose loyalty was therefore in a crucial way unreliable, since they had never really thought about what they were doing. They noted that once Spartans were abroad and free from the narrow constraint of law and rule, they often acted badly, since they had never learned to choose for themselves. The best education, they held, was one that equips a citizen for genuine choice of a way of life; this form of education requires active inquiry and the ability to contrast alternatives. Athenians denied the Spartan charge that their own concern with critical inquiry and free expression would give rise to decadence. "We cultivate the arts without extravagance," they proudly proclaimed, "and we devote ourselves to inquiry without becoming soft." Indeed, they insisted that Sparta's high reputation for courage was ill based: for citizens could not be truly courageous if they never chose from among alternatives. True courage, they held, requires freedom, and freedom is best cultivated by an education that awakens critical thinking. Cross-cultural inquiry thus proved not only illuminating but also self-reinforcing to Athenians: by showing them regimes that did not practice such inquiry and what those regimes lacked in consequence, it gave Athenians reasons why they should continue to criticize and to compare cultures.

Plato, writing in the early to mid-4th century B.C., alludes frequently to the study of other cultures, especially those of Sparta, Crete, and Egypt. In his *Republic*, which alludes often to Spartan practices, the plan for an ideal city is plainly influenced by reflection about customs elsewhere. One particularly fascinating example of the way in which reflection about history and other cultures awakens critical reflection occurs in the fifth book of that work, where Plato's character Socrates produces the first serious argument known to us in the Western tradition for the equal education of women. Here Socrates begins by acknowledging that the idea of women's receiving both physical and intellectual education equal to that of men will strike most Athenians as very weird and laughable. (Athenians who were interested in cultural comparison would know, however, that such ideas were not peculiar in Sparta, where women, less confined than at Athens, did receive extensive athletic training.[9])

But he then reminds Glaucon that many good things once seemed weird in just this way. For example, the unclothed public exercise that Athenians now prize as a norm of manliness once seemed foreign, and the heavy clothing that they think barbaric once seemed natural. However, he continues, when the practice of stripping for athletic contests had been in effect for some time, its advantages were clearly seen—and then "the appearance of absurdity ebbed away under the influence of reason's judgment about the best." So it is with women's education, Socrates argues. Right now it seems absurd, but once we realize that our conventions don't by themselves supply reasons for what we ought to do, we will be forced to ask ourselves whether we really do have good reasons for denying women the chance to develop their intellectual and physical capacities. Socrates argues that we find no such good reasons and many good reasons why those capacities should be developed. Therefore, a comparative cultural study, by removing the false air of naturalness and inevitability that surrounds our practices, can make our society a more truly reasonable one.

Cross-cultural inquiry up until this time had been relatively unsystematic, using examples that the philosopher or historian in question happened to know through personal travel or local familiarity. Later in the 4th century, however, the practice was rendered systematic and made a staple of the curriculum, as Aristotle apparently instructed his students to gather information about 153 forms of political organization, encompassing the entire known world, and to write up historical and constitutional descriptions of these regimes. The *Athenian Constitution*, which was written either by Aristotle or by one of his students, is our only surviving example of the project; it shows an intention to record everything relevant to critical reflection about that constitution and its suitability. When Aristotle himself writes political philosophy, his project is extensively cross-cultural. In his *Politics*, before describing his own views about the best form of government, he works through and criticizes many known historical examples, prominently including Crete and Sparta, and also a number of theoretical proposals, including those of Plato. As a result of this inquiry, Aristotle develops a model of good government that is in many respects critical of Athenian tradition, although he follows no single model.

By the beginning of the so-called Hellenistic era in Greek philosophy, then, cross-cultural inquiry was firmly established, both in Athenian public discourse and in the writings of the philosophers, as a necessary part of good deliberation about citizenship and political order.[10] But it was neither Plato nor Aristotle who coined the term "citizen of world." It was Diogenes the Cynic. Diogenes (404–323 B.C.) led a life stripped of the usual protections that habit and status supply. Choosing exile from his own native city, he defiantly refused protection from the rich and powerful for fear of losing his freedom, and lived in poverty, famously choosing a tub set up in the marketplace as his "home" in order to indicate his disdain for convention and comfort. He connected poverty with independence of mind and speech, calling freedom of speech "the finest thing in human life."[11] Once, they say, Plato saw him washing some lettuce and said, "If you had paid court to Dionysius, you would not be washing lettuce."[12] Diogenes replied, "If you had washed lettuce, you would not have paid court to Dionysius." This freedom from subservience, he held, was essential to a philosophical life. When someone reproached him for being an exile, he said that it was on that account that he came to be a philosopher.

Diogenes left no written work behind, and it is difficult to know how to classify him. "A Socrates gone mad" was allegedly Plato's description—and a good one, it seems. For Diogenes clearly followed the lead of Socrates in disdaining external markers of status and focusing on the inner life of virtue and thought. His search for a genuinely honest and virtuous person, and his use of philosophical arguments to promote that search, are recognizably Socratic. What was "mad" about him was the public assault on convention that accompanied his quest. Socrates provoked people only by his questions. He lived a conventional life. But Diogenes provoked people by his behavior as well, spitting in a rich man's face, even masturbating in public. What was the meaning of this shocking behavior?

It appears likely that the point of his unseemly behavior was itself Socratic—to get people to question their prejudices by making them consider how difficult it is to give good reasons for many of our deeply held feelings. Feelings about the respect given to status and rank and feelings of shame associated with sexual practices are assailed by this behavior—as Herodotus's feelings about burial were assailed by his contact with Persian and Egyptian customs. The question is whether one can then go on to find a good argument for one's own conventions and against the behavior of the Cynic.

As readers of the *Life of Diogenes*, we quickly become aware of the cultural relativity of what is thought shocking. For one of the most shocking things about Diogenes, to his Athenian contemporaries, was his habit of eating in the public marketplace. It was this habit that gave him the name "dog," *kuon*, from which our English label Cynic derives. Only dogs, in this culture, tore away at their food in the full view of all. Athenians evidently found this just about as outrageous as public masturbation; in fact his biographer joins the two offenses together, saying, "He used to do everything in public, both the deeds of Demeter and those of Aphrodite."

Crowds, they say, gathered around to taunt him as he munched on his breakfast of beets, behaving in what the American reader feels to be an unremarkable fashion. On the other hand, there is no mention in the *Life of Diogenes* of shock occasioned by public urination or even defecation. The reason for this, it may be conjectured, is that Athenians, like people in many parts of the world today, did not in fact find public excretion shocking. We are amazed by a culture that condemns public snacking while permitting such practices. Diogenes asks us to look hard at the conventional origins of these judgments and to ask which ones can be connected by a sound argument to important moral goals. (So far as we can tell, Cynics supplied no answers to this question.)

Set in this context, the invitation to consider ourselves citizens of the world is the invitation to become, to a certain extent, philosophical exiles from our own ways of life, seeing them from the vantage point of the outsider and asking the questions an outsider is likely to ask about their meaning and function. Only this critical distance, Diogenes argued, makes one a philosopher. In other words, a stance of detachment from uncritical loyalty to one's own ways promotes the kind of evaluation that is truly reason based. When we see in how many different ways people can organize their lives, we will recognize, he seems to think, what is deep and what is shallow in our own ways, and will consider that "the

only real community is one that embraces the entire world." In other words, the true basis for human association is not the arbitrary or the merely habitual; it is that which we can defend as good for human beings—and Diogenes believes that these evaluations know no national boundaries.

The confrontational tactics Diogenes chose unsettle and awaken. They do not contain good argument, however, and they can even get in the way of thought. Diogenes' disdain for more low-key and academic methods of scrutinizing customs, for example the study of literature and history, seems most unwise. It is hard to know whether to grant Diogenes the title "philosopher" at all, given his apparent preference for a kind of street theater over Socratic questioning. But his example, flawed as it was, had importance for the Greek philosophical tradition. Behind the theater lay an important idea: that the life of reason must take a hard look at local conventions and assumptions, in the light of more general human needs and aspirations.

The Stoic philosophers, over the next few centuries, made Diogenes' insight respectable and culturally fruitful.[13] They developed the idea of cross-cultural study and world citizenship much further in their own morally and philosophically rigorous way, making the concept of the "world citizen," *kosmou polites*, a centerpiece of their educational program.[14] A Seneca writes, summarizing older Greek Stoic views, education should make us aware that each of us is a member of "two communities: one that is truly great and truly common . . . in which we look neither to this corner nor that, but measure the boundaries of our nation by the sun; the other, the one to which we have been assigned by birth." The accident of where one is born is just that, an accident; any human being might have been born in any nation. Recognizing this, we should not allow differences of nationality or class or ethnic membership or even gender to erect barriers between us and our fellow human beings. We should recognize humanity—and its fundamental ingredients, reason and moral capacity—wherever it occurs, and give that community of humanity our first allegiance.

This does not mean that the Stoics proposed the abolition of local and national forms of political organization and the creation of a world state. The Greek Stoics did propose an ideal city, and the Roman Stoics did put ideas of world citizenship into practice in some ways in the governance of the empire. But the Stoics' basic point is more radical still: that we should give our first allegiance to *no* mere form of government, no temporal power, but to the moral community made up by the humanity of all human beings. The idea of the world citizen is in this way the ancestor and source of Kant's idea of the "kingdom of ends," and has a similar function in inspiring and regulating a certain mode of political and personal conduct. One should always behave so as to treat with respect the dignity of reason and moral choice in every human being, no matter where that person was born, no matter what that person's rank or gender or status may be. It is less a political idea than a moral idea that constrains and regulates political life.

The meaning of the idea for political life is made especially clear in Cicero's work *On Duties (De Officiis)*, written in 44 B.C. and based in part on the writings of the slightly earlier Greek Stoic thinker Panaetius. Cicero argues that the duty to treat humanity with respect requires us to treat aliens on our soil with honor and hospitality. It requires us never to engage in wars of aggression, and to view wars based on group hatred and wars of extermination as especially pernicious. It requires us to behave honorably in the conduct of war, shunning treachery even toward the enemy. In general, it requires us to place justice above political expediency, and to understand that we form part of a universal community of humanity whose ends are the moral ends of justice and human well-being. Cicero's book has been among the most influential in the entire Western philosophical tradition. In particular, it influenced the just-war doctrine of Grotius and the political thought of Immanuel Kant; their views about world understanding and the containment of global aggression are crucial for the formation of modern international law.

Stoics hold, then, that the good citizen is a "citizen of the world." They hold that thinking about humanity as it is realized in the whole world is valuable for self-knowledge: we see ourselves and our customs more clearly when we see our own ways in relation to those of other reasonable people. They insist, furthermore, that we really will be better able to solve our problems if we face them in this broader

context, our imaginations unconstrained by narrow partisanship. No theme is deeper in Stoicism than the damage done by faction and local allegiances to the political life of a group. Stoic texts show repeatedly how easy it is for local or national identities and their associated hatreds to be manipulated by self-seeking individuals for their own gain, whereas reason is hard to fake, and its language is open to the critical scrutiny of all. Roman political life in Seneca's day was dominated by divisions of many kinds, from those of class and rank and ethnic origin to the division between parties at the public games and gladiatorial shows. Part of the self-education of the Stoic Roman emperor Marcus Aurelius, as he tells the reader of his *Meditations*, was "not to be a Green or Blue partisan at the races, or a supporter of the lightly armed or heavily armed gladiators at the Circus."[15] Politics is sabotaged again and again by these partisan loyalties and by the search for honor and fame that accompanies them. Stoics argue that a style of citizenship that recognizes the moral/rational community as fundamental promises a more reasonable style of political deliberation and problem solving.

But Stoics do not recommend world citizenship only for reasons of expediency. They insist that the stance of the *kosmou polites* is intrinsically valuable: for it recognizes in people what is especially fundamental about them, most worthy of reverence and acknowledgment, namely their aspirations to justice and goodness and their capacities for reasoning in this connection. This essential aspect may be less colorful than local tradition and local identity, but it is, the Stoics argue, both lasting and deep.

To be a citizen of the world, one does not, the Stoics stress, need to give up local affiliations, which can frequently be a source of great richness in life. They suggest instead that we think of ourselves as surrounded by a series of concentric circles.[16] The first one is drawn around the self; the next takes in one's immediate family; then follows the extended family; then, in order, one's neighbors or local group, one's fellow city-dwellers, one's fellow countrymen—and we can easily add to this list groups formed on the basis of ethnic, religious, linguistic, historical, professional, and gender identities Beyond all these circles is the largest one, that of humanity as a whole. Our task as citizens of the world, and as educators who prepare people to be citizens of the world, will be to "draw the circles somehow toward the center," making all human beings like our fellow city-dwellers. In other words, we need not give up our special affections and identification whether national or ethnic or religious, but we should work to make all human beings part of our community of dialogue and concern, showing respect for the human wherever it occurs, and allowing that respect to constrain our national or local politics.

This Stoic attitude, then, does not require that we disregard the importance of local loves and loyalties or their salience in education. Adam Smith made a serious error when he objected to Stoicism on those grounds, and modern critics of related Kantian and Enlightenment conceptions make a similar error when they charge them with neglect of group differences. The Stoic, in fact, must be conversant with local differences, since knowledge of these is inextricably linked to our ability to discern and respect the dignity of humanity in each person. Stoics recognize love for what is near as a fundamental human trait, and a highly rational way to comport oneself as a citizen. If each parent has a special love for his or her own children, society will do better than if all parents try to have an equal love for all children. Much the same is true for citizenship of town or city or nation: each of us should take our stand where life has placed us, and devote to our immediate surroundings a special affection and attention. Stoics, then, do not want us to behave as if differences between male and female, or between African and Roman, are morally insignificant. These differences can and do enjoin special obligations that all of us should execute, since we should all do our duties in the life we happen to have, rather than imagining that we are beings without location or memory.

Stoics vary in the degree of concession they make to these special obligations. Cicero, for example, takes a wise course when he urges the Roman citizen to favor the near and dear on many occasions, although always in ways that manifest respect for human dignity. These special local obligations have educational consequences: the world citizen will legitimately spend a disproportionate amount of time learning about the history and problems of her or his own part of the world. But at the same time we recognize that there is something more fundamental

about us than the place where we happen to find ourselves, and that this more fundamental basis of citizenship is shared across all divisions.

This general point emerges clearly if we consider the relationship each of us has to a native language. We each have a language (in some cases more than one) in which we are at home, which we have usually known from infancy. We naturally feel a special affection for this language. It defines our possibilities of communication and expression. The works of literature that move us most deeply are those that exploit well the resources of that language. On the other hand, we should not suppose—and most of us do not suppose—that English is best just because it is our own, that works of literature written in English are superior to those written in other languages, and so forth. We know that it is more or less by chance that we are English speakers rather than speakers of Chinese or German or Bengali. We know that any infant might have learned any language because a fundamental language-learning capacity is shared by all humans. Nothing in our innate equipment disposes us to speak Hindi rather than Norwegian.

In school, then, it will be proper for us to spend a disproportionate amount of time mastering our native language and its literature. A human being who tried to learn all the world's languages would master none, and it seems reasonable for children to focus on one, or in some cases two, languages when they are small. On the other hand, it is also very important for students to understand what it is like to see the world through the perspective of another language, an experience that quickly shows that human complexity and rationality are not the monopoly of a single linguistic community.

This same point can be made about other aspects of culture that should figure in a higher education. In ethics, in historical knowledge, in knowledge of politics, in literary, artistic, and musical learning, we are all inclined to be parochial, taking our own habits for that which defines humanity. In these areas as in the case of language, it is reasonable to immerse oneself in a single tradition at an early age. But even then it is well to become acquainted with the facts of cultural variety, and this can be done very easily, for example through myths and stories that invite identification with people whose form of life is different from one's own. As education progresses, a more sophisticated grasp of human variety can show students that what is theirs is not better simply because it is familiar.

The education of the *kosmou polites* is thus closely connected to Socratic inquiry and the goal of an examined life. For attaining membership in the world community entails a willingness to doubt the goodness of one's own way and to enter into the give-and-take of critical argument about ethical and political choices. By an increasingly refined exchange of both experience and argument, participants in such arguments should gradually take on the ability to distinguish, within their own traditions, what is parochial from what may be commended as a norm for others, what is arbitrary and unjustified from that which may be justified by reasoned argument.

Since any living tradition is already a plurality and contains within itself aspects of resistance, criticism, and contestation, the appeal to reason frequently does not require us to take a stand outside the culture from which we begin. The Stoics are correct to find in all human beings the world over a capacity for critical searching and a love of truth. "Any soul is deprived of truth against its will," says Marcus Aurelius, quoting Plato. In this sense, any and every human tradition is a tradition of reason, and the transition from these more ordinary and intracultural exercises to a more global exercise of critical argument need not be an abrupt transition. Indeed, in the world today it is clear that internal critique often takes the form of invoking what is found to be fine and just in other traditions.

People from diverse backgrounds sometimes have difficulty recognizing one another as fellow citizens in the community of reason. This is so because actions and motives require, and do not always receive, a patient effort of interpretation. The task of world citizenship requires the would-be world citizen to become a sensitive and empathic interpreter. Education at all ages should cultivate the capacity for such interpreting. This aspect of the Stoic idea is developed most fully by Marcus Aurelius, who dealt with many different cultures in his role as emperor; he presents, in his *Meditations*, a poignantly personal account of his own efforts to be a good world citizen. "Accustom yourself not to be inattentive to what another person says, and as far as possible enter into

his mind," he writes (6.53); and again, "When things are being said, one should follow every word, when things are being done, every impulse; in the latter case, to see straightway to what object the impulse is directed, in the former, to watch what meaning is expressed" (7.4). Given that Marcus routinely associated with people from every part of the Roman Empire, this idea imposes a daunting task of learning and understanding, which he confronts by reading a great deal of history and literature, and by studying closely the individual characters of those around him in the manner of a literary narrator. "Generally," he concludes, "one must first learn many things before one can judge another's action with understanding" (11.18).

Above all, Marcus finds that he has to struggle not to allow his privileged station (an obstacle to real thought, as he continually points out) to sever him, in thought, from his fellow human beings. "See to it that you do not become Caesarized," he tells himself, "or dyed with that coloring" (6.30). A favorite exercise toward keeping such accidents of station in their proper place is to imagine that all human beings are limbs of a single body, cooperating for the sake of common purposes. Referring to the fact that it takes only the change of a single letter in Greek to convert the word "limb" (*melos*) into the word "(detached) part" (*meros*), he concludes: "if, changing the word, you call yourself merely a (detached) part instead of a limb, you do not yet love your fellow men from the heart, nor derive complete joy from doing good; you will do it merely as a duty, not as doing good to yourself" (7.13). The organic imagery underscores the Stoic ideal of cooperation.

Can anyone really think like a world citizen in a life so full of factionalism and political conflict? Marcus gives himself the following syllogism: "Wherever it is possible to live, it is also possible to live a virtuous life; it is possible to live in a palace; therefore it is also possible to live a virtuous life in a palace" (5.16). And, recognizing that he himself has sometimes failed in citizenship because of impatience and the desire for solitude: "Let no one, not even yourself, any longer hear you placing the blame on palace life" (8.9). In fact, his account of his own difficulties being a world citizen in the turmoil of Roman politics yields some important advice for anyone who attempts to reconcile this high ideal with the realities of political involvement:

> Say to yourself in the morning: I shall meet people who are interfering, ungracious, insolent, full of guile, deceitful and antisocial; they have all become like that because they have no understanding of good and evil. But I who have contemplated the essential beauty of good and the essential ugliness of evil, who know that the nature of the wrongdoer is of one kin with mine—not indeed of the same blood or seed but sharing the same kind, the same portion of the divine—I cannot be harmed by anyone of them, and no one can involve me in shame. I cannot feel anger against him who is of my kin, nor hate him. We were born to labor together, like the feet, the hands, the eyes, and the rows of upper and lower teeth. To work against one another is therefore contrary to nature, and to be angry against a man or turn one's back on him is to work against him. (2.1)

One who becomes involved in politics in our time might find this paragraph comforting. It shows a way in which the attitude of world citizenship gets to the root of one of the deepest political problems in all times and places—the problem of anger. Marcus is inclined to intense anger at his political adversaries. Sometimes the anger is personal, and sometimes it is directed against a group. His claim, however, is that such anger can be mitigated, or even removed, by the attitude of empathy that the ideal of the *kosmou polites* promotes. If one comes to see one's adversaries as not impossibly alien and other, but as sharing certain general human goals and purposes, if one understands that they are not monsters but people who share with us certain general goals and purposes, this understanding will lead toward a diminution of anger and the beginning of rational exchange.

World citizenship does not, and should not, require that we suspend criticism toward other individuals and cultures. Marcus continues to refer to his enemies as "deceitful and antisocial," expressing strong criticism of their conduct. The world citizen may be critical of unjust actions or policies and of the character of people who promote them. But at the same time, Marcus refuses to think of the opponents as simply alien, as members of a different and inferior species. He refuses to criticize until he respects and understands. He carefully chooses images that reflect

his desire to see in them as close to him and similarly human. This careful scrutiny of the imagery and speech one uses when speaking about people who are different is one of the Stoic's central recommendations for the undoing of political hatred.

Stoics write extensively on the nature of anger and hatred. It is their well-supported view that these destructive emotions are not innate, but learned by children from their society. In part, they hold, people directly absorb negative evaluations of individuals and groups from their culture, in part they absorb excessively high evaluations of their own honor and status. These high evaluations give rise to hostility when another person or group appears to threaten their honor or status. Anger and hatred are not unreasoning instincts; they have to do with the way we think and imagine, the images we use, the language we find it habitual to employ. They can therefore be opposed by the patient critical scrutiny of the imagery and speech we employ when we confront those our tradition has depicted as unequal.

It is fashionable by now to be skeptical of "political correctness," by which the critic usually means a careful attention to the speech we use in talking about minorities, or foreigners, or women. Such scrutiny might in some forms pose dangers to free speech, and of course these freedoms should be carefully defended. But the scrutiny of speech and imagery need not be inspired by totalitarian motives, and it need not lead to the creation of an antidemocratic "thought police." The Stoic demand for such scrutiny is based on the plausible view that hatred of individuals and groups is personally and politically pernicious, that it ought to be resisted by educators, and that the inner world of thought and speech is the place where, ultimately, hatred must be resisted. These ideas about the scrutiny of the inner world are familiar to Christians also, and the biblical injunction against sinning in one's heart has close historical links to Stoicism. All parents know that it is possible to shape a child's attitudes toward other races and nationalities by the selection of stories one tells and by the way one speaks about other people in the home. There are few parents who do not seek to influence their children's views in these ways. Stoics propose, however, that the process of coming to recognize the humanity of all people should be a lifelong process, encompassing all levels of education—especially since, in a culture suffused with group hatred, one cannot rely on parents to perform this task.

What this means in higher education is that an attitude of mutual respect should be nourished both in the classroom itself and in its reading material. Although in America we should have no sympathy with the outright censoring of reading material, we also make many selections as educators, both in assigning material and in presenting it for our students. Few of us, for example, would present anti-Semitic propaganda in a university classroom in a way that conveyed sympathy with the point of view expressed. The Stoic proposal is that we should seek out curricula that foster respect and mutual solidarity and correct the ignorance that is often an essential prop of hatred. This effort is perfectly compatible with maintaining freedom of speech and the openness of a genuinely critical and deliberative culture.

In our own time, few countries have been more rigidly divided, more corroded by group hatred, than South Africa. In spelling out its goals for society in its draft for the new Constitution, the African National Congress (ANC) recognized the need to address hatred through education, and specified the goal of education as the overcoming of these differences:

> Education shall be directed towards the development of the human personality and a sense of personal dignity, and shall aim at strengthening respect for human rights and fundamental freedoms and promoting understanding, tolerance and friendship amongst South Africans and between nations.[17]

Some of this language would have been new to Marcus Aurelius—and it would have been a good thing for Roman Stoics to have reflected more about the connections between the human dignity they prized and the political rights they frequently neglected. But the language of dignity, humanity, freedom, understanding, tolerance, and friendship would not have been strange to Marcus. (He speaks of his goal as "the idea of a Commonwealth with the same laws for all, governed on the basis of equality and free speech"; this goal is to be pursued with "beneficence, eager generosity, and optimism.") The ANC draft, like the Stoic norm of world citizenship, insists that understanding of various nations and groups is a goal for every citizen, not only for those who wish to affirm a minority identity. It insists that

the goal of education should not be separation of one group from another, but respect, tolerance, and friendship—both within a nation and among nations. It insists that this goal should be fostered in a way that respects the dignity of humanity in each person and citizen.

Above all, education for world citizenship requires transcending the inclination of both students and educators to define themselves primarily in terms of local group loyalties and identities. World citizens will therefore not argue for the inclusion of cross-cultural study in a curriculum, primarily on the grounds that it is a way in which members of minority groups can affirm such an identity. This approach, common though it is, is divisive and subversive of the aims of world community. This problem vexes many curricular debates. Groups who press for the recognition of their group often think of their struggle as connected with goals of human respect and social justice. And yet their way of focusing their demands, because it neglects commonalities and portrays people as above all members of identity groups, tends to subvert the demand for equal respect and love, and even the demand for attention to diversity itself. As David Glidden, philosopher at the University of California at Riverside, expressed the point, "the ability to admire and love the diversity of human beings gets lost" when one bases the demand for inclusion on notions of local group identity. Why should one love or attend to a Hispanic fellow citizen, on this view, if one is oneself most fundamentally an Irish-American? Why should one care about India, if one defines oneself as above all an American? Only a human identity that transcends these divisions shows us why we should look at one another with respect across them.

Endnotes

1. "Anna" is a woman I interviewed in China. Her name has been changed.
2. *New York Times*, July 4, 1996, p. 1.
3. All judgments about the Cynics are tentative, given the thinness of our information. The central source is Diogenes Laeritus's *Lives of the Philosophers*. See B. Branham and M.-O. Goulet-Gazé, eds., *The Cynics* (Berkeley: University of California Press, 1996).
4. Plutarch, *On the Fortunes of Alexander* 329AB = SVF 1.262; see also Senaca, *On Leisure* 4.1.

5. For Paine, see *The Rights of Man*, pt. 2; for Smith, see "Of Universal Benevolence," in *The Theory of Moral Sentiments* (Indianapolis: Liberty Classica, 1982), vol. 6, pt. 2, p. 3, with special reference to Marcus Aurelius; for Kant, see *Perpetual Peace*, in *Kant's Political Writings*, ed. H. Reiss, trans. H. Nisbet, 2nd ed. (Cambridge: Cambridge University Press, 1991). For a discussion of Stoic ideas in Kant's political thought, see Martha C. Nussbaum, "Kant and Stoic Cosmopolitanism," *Journal of Political Philosophy* 5 (1997): 1–25.

6. See Tagore, "Swadeshi Samaj," cited in Krishna Dutta and Andrew Robinson, *Rabindranath Tagore: The Myriad-Minded Man* (London: Bloomsbur, 1995).

7. Kawame Anthony Appiah, *In My Father's House: Africa in the Philosophy of Cultures* (New York: Oxford University Press, 1991).

8. See W. K. C. Guthrie, *History of Greek Philosophy*, vol. 3 (Cambridge: Cambridge University Press, 1969).

9. See Stephen Halliwell, *Plato: Republic V* (Warminster: Aris and Phillips, 1993).

10. The Hellenistic era is usually taken to begin at the death of Alexander the Great, 323 B.C.; Aristotle died in 322. Although Diogenes was a contemporary of Aristotle, his influence is felt in the later period. See A. A. Long, *Hellenistic Philosophy* (London: Duckworth, 1974).

11. The translation by R. D. Hicks in the Loeb Classical Library, volume 2, of Diogenes Laertius is inadequate but gives the general idea. All citations here are from that *Life*, but the translations are mine.

12. Dionysius was the one-man ruler of Syracuse in Sicily whom Plato attempted, without success, to turn into a "philosopher-king."

13. The Stoic school had an extraordinarily long life and a very broad influence, extending from the late 4th century B.C. to the 2nd century A.D. in both Athens and Rome.

14. Diogenes uses the single word *kosmopolites*, but Marcus Aurelius prfers the separated form.

15. See Marcus Aurelius, *Meditations*, trans. G.M.A. Grube (Indianapolis: Hackett, 1983).

16. The image is suggested in Cicero and is explicit in Hierocles, a Stoic of the 1st and 2nd centuries A.D. (quoted here); it is probably older.

17. This is material from a draft written by the ANC for the new constitution; it was presented by Albi Sachs to a meeting on human rights at Harvard University in October 1993.

Peace as an Ethic for Intercultural Communication

DAVID W. KALE

A Ford Foundation executive with more than 20 years of experience in overseas travel has been quoted as saying that "most problems in cross-cultural projects come from different ideas about right and wrong" (Howell, 1981, p. 3). This executive's statement refers to two problem areas that have caused a great deal of difficulty in intercultural communication. First, many people have been in the uncomfortable position of doing something completely acceptable in their own country, while unknowingly offending the people of the culture they were visiting. This problem arose when I took a group of university students to Guyana in South America. In that warm climate, our students wore the same shorts they would have worn at home, but the Guyanese were offended by what they considered to be skimpy clothing, particularly when worn by the women. A second problem that arises in intercultural situations results when we try to get the rest of the world to live according to our culture's ideas about right and wrong. Interestingly, we get rather upset when people of another culture tell us how to behave. We like to believe that the way our culture chooses to do things is the right way, and we do not appreciate people of other cultures telling us we are wrong.

Both of these problems have a bearing on ethics in intercultural communication. Discussing this topic causes stress to people of all cultures. Bonhoeffer suggests this is because we get the feeling that the basic issues of life are being addressed. When that happens, some of our most cherished beliefs may be challenged. When our cultural beliefs about right and wrong are

This original essay first appeared in the seventh edition. All rights reserved. Permission to reprint must be obtained from the author and the publisher. David W. Kale teaches at the Olivet Nazarene University, Kankakee, Illinois.

being threatened, we feel that the very foundation of our lives may be under attack (Bonhoeffer, 1965, pp. 267–268).

While such a discussion may be threatening, it must be undertaken nonetheless. With contact among people of various cultures rapidly on the rise, an increase in the number of conflicts over matters of right and wrong is inevitable. This essay addresses the ethics of intercultural communication by developing the following points: (1) a definition of communication ethics, (2) cultural relativity versus universal ethics, (3) the concept of spirit as a basis for intercultural ethics, (4) peace as the fundamental value in intercultural ethics, and (5) a code of ethics in intercultural communication.

A DEFINITION OF COMMUNICATION ETHICS

Richard Johannesen (1978, pp. 11–12) has said that we are dealing with an ethical issue in human communication when:

1. People voluntarily choose a communication strategy.
2. The communication strategy is based on a value judgment.
3. The value judgment is about right and wrong in human conduct.
4. The strategy chosen could positively or negatively affect someone else.

It is important to note in this definition that values are the basis for communication ethics. For example, we place a value on the truth, and therefore it is unethical to tell a lie to another person. Without this basis in values, we have no ethical system whatsoever.

We face a major problem in our society because some people think they can decide right and wrong for themselves with no regard for what others think. Such a mindset shows that these people really don't understand ethics at all. If they did they would know that ethics are based on values, and values are determined by culture. Thus, there can be no such thing as a totally individual system of ethics. Such an approach would eventually result in the total destruction of human society (Hauerwas, 1983, p. 3; Weaver, 1971, p. 2).

Within a culture there is a continual dialogue about the things that are the most meaningful and important to the people of that culture. As a result, cultures are continually in a state of change. When cultures change, so do the values that culture holds. Thus, we must acknowledge that there is no fixed order of values that exists within a culture (Brummett, 1981, p. 293). This does not mean, however, that we are free to determine right and wrong for ourselves. It is much more accurate to say that we are shaped by the values of our culture than to say that we shape the values of our culture (Hauerwas, 1983, p. 3).

CULTURAL RELATIVISM VERSUS UNIVERSAL ETHICS

Because the values on which our ethics are built are generated by dialogue within a culture, the question must then be asked whether a person of one culture can question the conduct of a person in another culture. The concept of cultural relativity would suggest that the answer to this question is generally "No." Cultural relativity suggests that a culture will develop the values it deems best for the people of that culture. These values depend on the context in which the people of that culture go to work, raise their children, and run their societies. As such, those who are from a different context will develop a different set of cultural values and therefore have no basis on which to judge the conduct of people in any culture other than their own.

Few people would be willing to strictly follow the concept of cultural relativity, however. To do so would suggest that it was all right for Hitler to murder 6 million innocent people because the German people did nothing to stop it (Jaska and Pritchard, 1988, p. 10). At the same time, few are willing to support the idea that people of all cultures must abide by the same code of ethics. We know that cultures develop different value systems and thus must have different ethical codes.

Both Brummett (1981, p. 294) and Hauerwas (1983, p. 9) have argued that because values are derived through dialogue, there is nothing wrong with attempting to persuade people of other cultures to accept our values. Before we do that, however, we must be convinced that our values are worthy and not based on limited self-interest. We must also be willing to work for genuine dialogue; too often these discussions tend to be monologues. We are generally far more willing to present the case for our own value system than we are to carefully consider the arguments for those of other cultures.

At the time of this writing, for example, people of many cultures are attempting to get the people of Brazil to stop cutting down their rainforests. As long as these persuasive efforts are based on a genuine concern for the negative effect cutting these trees is having on the global climate, there is nothing unethical about them. We must, however, also be willing to understand what is motivating the Brazilians' behavior and accept some responsibility in helping them to solve the serious economic problems their country is facing.

SPIRIT AS THE BASIS FOR ETHICAL UNIVERSALS

To develop the next point, how we are to make ethical decisions in intercultural communication, let me suggest that there is a concept on which we can base a universal code of ethics: the human spirit (Eubanks, 1980, p. 307). In the words of Eliseo Vivas:

> The person deserves unqualified respect because he (or she) is not merely psyche but also spirit, and spirit is, as far as we know, the highest form of being. It is through the human spirit that the world is able to achieve cognizance of its status as creature, to perceive its character as valuable, and through human efforts to fulfill a destiny, which it freely accepts. (p. 235)

It is this human spirit that people of all cultures have in common that serves as a basis of belief that there are some universal values on which we can build a universal code of ethics in intercultural communication.

We have watched dramatic changes take place in the world as people in Eastern Europe and the Commonwealth of Independent States (the former Soviet Union) have attempted to improve the quality of life for themselves and their offspring. We identify with their efforts because we share a human spirit that is the same regardless of cultural background. It is this spirit that makes us people who value in the first place. It is from this spirit that the human derives the ability to make decisions about right and wrong, to decide what makes life worth living, and then to make life the best it can possibly be. Therefore, the guiding principle of any universal code of intercultural communication should be to protect the worth and dignity of the human spirit.

PEACE AS THE FUNDAMENTAL HUMAN VALUE

There is a strong temptation for those of us in Western democracies to identify freedom of choice as the fundamental human value. Hauerwas (pp. 9–12) has convincingly argued that freedom of choice is an unachievable goal for human endeavor. He notes that it is not possible for everyone to have freedom of choice. At the time of this writing, some people in Czechoslovakia want to have the country stay together as a whole, while others want it to divide into two separate countries, with each being the home of a different ethnic group. It cannot be that both parties will have their choice.

A goal that is possible to achieve, however, is to direct our efforts toward creating a world where people of all cultures are living at peace with one another. This goal consists of three different levels: minimal peace, moderate peace, and optimal peace:

- *Minimal peace* is defined as merely the absence of conflict. Two parties in conflict with each other are at minimal peace when they would be involved in violent conflict if they felt free to act out their hostile feelings. Perhaps there are U.N. peacekeeping forces restraining the two sides from fighting. Perhaps both sides know that continual fighting will bring condemnation from the rest of the world community. Whatever the reason, the peace is only superficial.
- *Moderate peace* results when two conflicting parties are willing to compromise on the goals they want to achieve. In this case, each party has major concessions it is willing to make to

reach agreement, but considerable irritation still exists with the opposing party in the conflict. Each party considers its own goals as worthy and justifiable, and any of the other party's goals that conflict with its own are clearly unacceptable.

Moderate peace describes the situation that exists today between Israel and its Arab neighbors. Negotiations are proceeding in Washington between Israel and countries such as Syria, Jordan, and Egypt. The fact that these countries are at least willing to sit down at the same table and negotiate indicates that their relationship has developed beyond that of minimal peace. If those negotiations break off and hostile feelings intensify, they could be back to a relationship of minimal peace in a short period of time.

- *Optimal peace* exists when two parties consider each other's goals as seriously as they do their own. This does not mean that their goals do not ever conflict. The United States and Canada have a relationship that could be considered as optimal peace, yet there is considerable disagreement over the issue of whether acid rain from U.S. factories is destroying Canadian woodlands. Each side pursues its own goals in negotiations, but considers the other party's goals as worthy and deserving of serious consideration.

At the current time the Soviet republics of Armenia and Azerbaijan are locked in a bitter ethnic conflict over a territory within the republic of Azerbaijan that is populated mostly by Armenians. Because the territory is in their republic, the people of Azerbaijan say they should control it; because largely Armenians populate it, the Armenians say they should control it. Both groups cannot have freedom of choice in this situation, but they can live in peace if they are willing to submit to reasonable dialogue on their differences.

The concept of peace applies not only to relations between cultures and countries, but also to the right of all people to live at peace with themselves and their surroundings. As such it is unethical to communicate with people in a way that violates their concept of themselves or the dignity and worth of their human spirit.

A UNIVERSAL CODE OF ETHICS IN INTERCULTURAL COMMUNICATION

Before launching into the code itself, a "preamble" should first be presented based on William Howell's suggestion that the first step to being ethical in any culture is the intent to do what one knows is right (1982, p. 6). All societies set out rules of ethical conduct for people to follow based on cultural values. The foundation of ethical behavior is that people intend to do what they know is right. To choose to do something that you know to be wrong is unethical in any culture.

Principle #1—Ethical communicators address people of other cultures with the same respect that they would like to receive themselves.

It is based on this principle that I find ethnic jokes to be unethical. Some people may argue that ethnic jokes are harmless in that they are "just in fun," but no one wants to be on the receiving end of a joke in which their own culture is demeaned by people of another culture (LaFave and Mannell, 1978). Verbal and psychological abuse can damage the human spirit in the same way that physical abuse damages the body. Verbal and psychological violence against another person, or that person's culture, is just as unacceptable as physical violence. People of all cultures are entitled to live at peace with themselves and the cultural heritage that has had a part in shaping them. It is, therefore, unethical to use our verbal and/or nonverbal communication to demean or belittle the cultural identity of others.

Principle #2—Ethical communicators seek to describe the world as they perceive it as accurately as possible.

While in our culture we might call this telling the truth, what is perceived to be the truth can vary greatly from one culture to another. We know that reality is not something that is objectively the same for people of all cultures. Reality is socially constructed for us by our culture; we live in different perceptual worlds (Kale, 1983, pp. 31–32).

The point of this principle is that ethical communicators do not deliberately set out to deceive or mislead, especially since deception is damaging to the ability of people of various cultures to trust each other. It is only when people of the world are able to trust one another that we will be able to live in peace. That trust is only possible when the communication that occurs between those cultures is devoid of deliberate attempts to mislead and deceive (Bok, 1978, pp. 18–33; Hauerwas, 1983, p. 15).

Principle #3—Ethical communicators encourage people of other cultures to express themselves in their uniqueness.

This principle is reflected in Article 19 of the Universal Declaration of Human Rights as adopted by the United Nations. It states: "Everyone has the right to freedom of opinion and expression; this right includes the freedom to hold opinions without interferences and to seek, receive and impart information and ideas through any media and regardless of frontiers" (Babbili, p. 9).

In his book, *I and Thou*, Martin Buber (1965) cogently discusses the need for us to allow the uniqueness of the other to emerge if genuine dialogue is to take place. We often place demands on people of other cultures to adopt our beliefs or values before we accept them as full partners in our dialogue.

Is it the right of the U.S. government to demand that Nicaragua elect a non-communist government before that country is granted full partnership in the intercultural dialogue of this hemisphere? It is certainly possible that the people of that country will elect a communist government, and if they do, they are still entitled to equal status with the other governments of Central America. At the same time, we celebrate the fact that in central Europe people of several countries are finally being allowed to express themselves by throwing off the stranglehold of communist ideology imposed on them by forces outside their culture. Ethical communicators place a high value on the right of cultures to be full partners in the international dialogue, regardless of how popular or unpopular their political ideas may be. It is the height of ethnocentrism, and also unethical, to accord people of another culture equal status in the international arena only if they choose to express themselves in the same way we do.

Principle #4—Ethical communicators strive for identification with people of other cultures.

Identification is achieved when people share some principles in common, which they can do while still retaining the uniqueness of their cultural identities (Burke, 1969, p. 21). This principle suggests that ethical communicators encourage people of all cultures to understand each other, striving for unity of spirit. They do this by emphasizing the commonalities among cultural beliefs and values, rather than their differences.

At the present time we are, unfortunately, seeing an increasing number of racial incidents occurring on our college and university campuses. Many times these take the form of racist slogans appearing on the walls of campus buildings. The purpose of these actions is often to stir up racial animosity, creating wider divisions among ethnic groups. Such behavior is unethical according to this principle in that it is far more likely to lead to conflict than it is to peace.

Endnote

The author wishes to thank Angela Latham-Jones for her critical comments of an earlier version of this essay.

References

Babbili, A. S. (1983). *The problem of international discourse: Search for cultural, moral and ethical imperatives.* Paper presented at the convention of the Association for Education in Journalism and Mass Communication, Corvallis, Oregon.

Bok, S. (1978). *Lying: Moral choice in public and private life.* New York: Random House.

Bonhoeffer, D. (1965). *Ethics.* Eberhard Bethge, ed. New York: Macmillan.

Brummett, B. (1981). A defense of ethical relativism as rhetorically grounded. *Western Journal of Speech Communication, 45*(4), 286–298.

Buber, M. (1965). *I and thou.* New York: Peter Smith.

Burke, K. (1969). *A rhetoric of motives.* Berkeley: University of California Press.

Eubanks, R. (1980). Reflections on the moral dimension of communication. *Southern Speech Communication Journal, 45*(3), 240–248.

Hauerwas, S. (1983). *The peaceable kingdom.* South Bend, IN: University of Notre Dame.

Howell, W. (1981). *Ethics of intercultural communication.* Paper presented at the 67th convention of the Speech Communication Association, Anaheim, California.

Howell, W. (1982). *Carrying ethical concepts across cultural boundaries*. Paper presented at the 68th convention of the Speech Communication Association, Louisville, Kentucky.

Jaska, J., and Pritchard, M. (1988). *Communication ethics: Methods of analysis*. Belmont, CA: Wadsworth.

Johannesen, R. (1978). *Ethics in human communication*. Wayne, NJ: Avery.

Kale, D. (1983, September). In defense of two ethical universals in intercultural communication. *Religious Communication Today*, 6, 28–33.

LaFave, L., and Mannell, R. (1978). Does ethnic humor serve prejudice? *Journal of Communication*, Summer, 116–124.

Vivas, E. (1963). *The moral life and the ethical life*. Chicago: Henry Regnery.

Weaver, R. (1971). *Ideas have consequences*. Chicago: University of Chicago Press.

Concepts and Questions

1. How do culturally different concepts of right and wrong affect intercultural communication?

2. What conditions constitute an ethical issue in human communication?

3. Why does Kale suggest that there can be no such thing as a totally individual system of ethics?

4. Given the cultural relativity of ethics, under what conditions is it permissible for people of one culture to attempt to persuade people of other cultures to accept their values?

5. How may the human spirit serve as a basis for a universal ethic?

6. What is minimal peace? How does it differ from moderate peace?

7. Under what circumstances does optimal peace exist? Is optimal peace a realistic goal in international relations?

8. What is the first step to being ethical in any culture?

9. What is the main point associated with the ethical principle that communicators should seek to describe the world as they perceive it as accurately as possible?

10. How can individuals develop the capability to fulfill the ethical principle that ethical communicators strive for identification with people of other cultures?

Index